Organizational Behavior and Management

An Integrated Skills Approach

Ramon J. Aldag

University of Wisconsin-Madison

Loren W. Kuzuhara

University of Wisconsin-Madison

SOUTH-WESTERN ™

THOMSON LEARNING

Australia · Canada · Mexico · Singapore · Spain · United Kingdom · United States

To my wife, Holly, and my daughters, Lizzie and Kat.
—R. A.

To my wife, Lavina, my son, Daniel, my daughter, Carolyn, and Mom and Dad.
—L. K.

Organizational Behavior and Management: An Integrated Skills Approach
By Ramon J. Aldag and Loren W. Kuzuhara

Publisher: Jack Calhoun
Acquisitions Editor: John Szilagyi
Developmental Editor: Mary Draper, Draper Development
Production Editor: Tamborah E. Moore
Media Technology Editor: Vicky True
Media Development Editor: Kristen Meere
Media Production Editor: Mark Sears
Cover Design: Liz Harasymczuk, Liz Harasymczuk Design
Cover Illustration: ©Dean C. Kalmantis, The Stock Illustration Source, Inc.
Internal Design: Ann Small, A Small Design Studio
Design Coordinator: Rick Moore
Marketing Manager: Rob Bloom
Manufacturing Coordinator: Sandee Milewski
Production House: G&S Typesetters
Printer: Von Hoffman Press, Inc

Printed in the United States of America
1 2 3 4 5 04 03 02 01

For more information contact South-Western, 5101 Madison Road, Cincinnati, Ohio, 45227, or find us on the Internet at *http://www.swcollege.com*.

For permission to use material from this text or product, contact us by
• **telephone: 1-800-730-2214**
• **fax: 1-800-730-2215**
• **web: http://www.thomsonrights.com**

ISBN: 0-324-01330-2 (core text with InfoTrac)
        0-324-12560-7 (core text only)

Library Of Congress Cataloging-In-Publication Data

Aldag, Ramon J.
    Organizational behavior and management : an integrated skills approach / Ramon J. Aldag, Loren W. Kuzuhara.
        p.   cm.
    Includes index.
    ISBN 0-324-01330-2
    1. Organizational behavior.   2. Industrial management.   I. Kuzuhara, Loren W.
    II. Title.

HD58.7 .A428 2001
658.3—dc21   2001028147

Brief Contents

Table of Contents

Contents
Contents
Contents
Contents
Contents

v

Table of Contents

Table of Contents

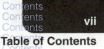

Contents
Contents
Contents
Contents
ix

Table of Contents
Contents

Table of Contents

The modern work environment—and life in general—demands a wide variety of behavioral skills—a skills portfolio. Traditional organizational behavior and management textbooks and courses in colleges and universities generally have continued to do a good job of surveying major concepts and theories and presenting examples of companies that apply them in some form. However, instructors, their students, and the employers who hire the students as they graduate from undergraduate and MBA programs increasingly want and need textbooks to do something more. They call for books that place a greater emphasis on "what to do to be an effective manager" and how to develop the right mix of skills that are needed to support the implementation of these behavioral strategies. In addition, students must learn how to apply these organizational behavior and management skills within complex, dynamic organizational and external environments while facing time, resource, political, and regulatory constraints. This vast array of challenges requires a new breed of textbook.

A BALANCE OF THEORY AND SKILLS APPLICATIONS

Organizational Behavior and Management: An Integrated Skills Approach is intended for those instructors hoping to combine solid content coverage with a rich, integrated skills emphasis. This book is appropriate for organizational behavior (OB) or management courses in which instructors prefer a very strong skills and real-world emphasis, or for a management/OB skills course.

We believe the text offers a richer mix of skills and provides significantly more opportunities for skill development and mastery than current offerings, as well as greater use of Internet resources. We have attempted to give the book an open, "clean," and integrated look and feel. Rather than provide a lengthy early discussion of theory in each chapter, we instead offer short presentations of theory as appropriate before each skill. We employ a broad variety of cases and examples, avoiding an overreliance on case studies in manufacturing settings. We place strong emphasis on "real-world" examples and applications and use a wide variety of unique approaches to bring important theories and tools to life.

VISION OF THE TEXT

We designed *Organizational Behavior and Management: An Integrated Skills Approach* to be unlike any other text on the market. It was developed to have the following distinctive "personality":

> **Skills-based.** Students appreciate, and increasingly expect, to learn concrete, practical, transferable skills. The primary focus of the text is on skill development through skill assessment, awareness, attainment, and application.

> **Social learning perspective.** As discussed in detail in Chapter 1 and illustrated on the inside front cover, the text applies a social learning perspective. The generalized steps of the social learning perspective include preassessment, conceptual learning and modeling, conceptual and behavioral practice, and life application. Our terms for these, to emphasize the skills focus and offer an organizing framework (4 A's), are skills assessment, skills awareness, skills attainment, and skills application. All text features are designed to aid with development of one or more of these steps.

> **Applications-oriented.** The text has an applied focus. Descriptive and theoretical content are presented only as needed to provide the foundation or rationale for applied materials.

> **Complete.** The text provides a comprehensive set of tools and techniques needed for effective management in real-world situations.

> **Rich.** We try to avoid the flavor of a technical manual in which students are pushed mechanically through a series of steps. Instead, our intention is to provide a rich learning environment in which students are pulled by interest in the material.

> **Engaging.** The text is designed to engage the student, but not by "dummying down." It attempts to use interesting examples, an open writing style, and humor where appropriate.

> **Real-world.** We avoid widgets and hypothetical firms. We choose tools and techniques that are applied in the real world. We regularly highlight the relevance of the text's content by explaining to students why it is important and how it is used in actual practice. We present interviews with practitioners in a variety of industries, organizations, and management levels to demonstrate the relevance of the content.

> **Current.** In today's environment, examples more than a few years old are stale, if not completely outdated and wrong. As such, our examples are drawn almost exclusively from the last few years.

> **Accessible.** The text is intended to be "friendly" in tone, layout, and content.

TEXT PHILOSOPHY

Every textbook has an underlying philosophy that guides its content and presentation. We feel it is important to make our philosophy clear so that you will better understand the flow and substance of the text. Here are some key elements of our philosophy:

> **Skills are the key to success in the modern environment.** More sophisticated technology and more dynamic and complex markets require more sophisticated workers.[1] This creates the need for a skills portfolio. In the modern workplace, it is skills, rather than firm-specific knowledge, that are most critical to career success.[2]

---

[1] L. J. Bassi, G. Benson, and S. Cheney, "The Top Ten Trends," *Training and Development,* November 1996, pp. 28–42.

[2] J. H. Sheridan, "Selling Skills, Not Experience," *Industry Week,* January 8, 1996, pp. 15–17.

> **Skills do not flow directly from knowledge.** The knowing–doing gap, discussed in Chapter 1, requires the actual application and practice of skills.

> **The most valuable skills are broadly applicable, durable, and transferable.** Students' career and personal growth will benefit from a portfolio filled with enduring and portable skills. Fortunately, unlike many technical skills, the managerial skills we will address will serve students well in many settings and over time.

> **Critical management skills can be learned.** While some people may seem more "gifted" than others at skills such as communicating, leading, or dealing with conflict, these and other skills we will address are primarily behavioral rather than trait-based.

> **Skill mastery requires a solid conceptual foundation.** Skills can't be applied blindly. To be effective, students need to know *why* and *when* the skill is needed and *how* it should be used. Just as knowing without doing is futile, doing without knowing is potentially misguided and dangerous.

> **Skills should be directed toward improving both personal and organizational outcomes.** We view organizational behavior and management as having many goals. While enhancing organizational performance and other outcomes of the firm are important goals, the lack of a clear, direct impact on organizational outcomes does not mean a skill is unimportant. Other goals, such as improving individual satisfaction and health or fostering positive workplace interactions, are important in themselves. Further, we view personal and organizational outcomes as generally congruent, or potentially congruent. That is, in some cases personal and organizational outcomes move together. In other cases, companies can use reward systems and other policies and practices to help align personal and organizational consequences.

> **Skill learning is a lifelong activity.** While many skills in students' portfolios will have enduring value, it will nevertheless be necessary to learn and apply new skills throughout one's career. Independent study, continuing education, on-the-job training, and professional associations may all help in this endeavor. This very important point is the primary theme of the final chapter of the text.

TEXT FEATURES

The text includes a variety of complementary features, consistent with our emphasis on skills assessment, skills awareness, skills attainment, and skills application.

> **Skills Objectives and Knowledge Objectives.** Each chapter begins with a set of specific skills (assessment, attainment, and application) objectives and related knowledge (that is, skills awareness) objectives.

> **Review of relevant content.** A solid overview of appropriate content is included in each chapter. This is presented in a logical flow and is interspersed with other features rather than presented as a block. While this material reflects current theory, research, and writing, there is very little emphasis on research per se. In addition, the intent is not to cata-

log theories; specific theories are discussed only if they are "major" and have unique value. Multiple theories are presented in a section only when they are complementary and/or cumulative. That is, the intent is not to provide a series of critiques.

> **Pre-Test Skills Assessment.** This activity consists of brief scenarios involving management challenges. All of the scenarios are based on actual dilemmas faced by real-world managers, and all focus on the "bottom-line" concern of what to do to handle a management problem or situation. The exercises are intended to provide students with a baseline measure of how much they know about understanding and applying chapter concepts, as well as to offer an appreciation of the difficulty of the particular challenge.

> **Self-Assessment materials.** Each chapter includes one or more self-assessments of things such as communication styles, personality, leadership, conflict styles, career goals, stress levels, and so on. The Instructor's Resource Manual contains additional information about scoring and interpretation of these materials and offers norm data from about 800 students. The associated website will regularly update the norm data.

> **Devil's Advocate.** This feature identifies and responds to some of the most common student concerns or questions about the content covered in the chapter. The major theme of the Devil's Advocate feature is addressing the issue of why chapter content is important.

> **Skills Assessment activities.** These activities—typically five to eight per chapter—provide intensive practice in the application of tools and techniques discussed in each chapter, facilitating personal, interpersonal, and managerial skills development. Many of these exercises are meant to be applied in a team context, or to offer that option. There are two levels of difficulty associated with these exercises—"basic" and "challenging." The exercises are intended to challenge students and prepare them for the work environment.

> **"Voice of Experience" practitioner interviews.** Interviews with a wide variety of managers, from recent graduates to seasoned professionals, are provided to capture the most difficult types of situations they have faced in the past, how they dealt with them, and what they learned from those experiences.

> **Focus on Management boxes.** Focus on Management boxes provide discussions of company applications of chapter materials as well as related Web addresses.

> **"Web Wise" materials.** Web Wise boxes discuss resources and suggest associated Internet links students can explore. Other Web links are also provided for organizations discussed elsewhere in the chapters.

> **Global Perspective boxes.** Global Perspective boxes highlight global examples of chapter material. Other global material is fully integrated into the body of chapters.

> **Real-World Management Challenges.** These exercises—one per chapter—put students in actual situations or challenges facing managers at well-known companies. Students develop skill in creating action plans for dealing with such situations. Supplementary materials permit students to compare their action plans with the actual decisions made by management at those companies to handle the situations.

Preface
Preface
Preface
Preface
Preface

xv

Preface

> **Lighten Up features.** We use humor as appropriate. As one example, we include Lighten Up boxes at the ends of chapters, focusing on the lighter side of topics. While humorous, each of these boxes is intended to reinforce key chapter content. More Lighten Up features are included at the textbook website.

> **"Bottom Line" figures.** Students often ask about the "bottom line" associated with various concepts covered in organizational behavior and management classes; that is, "How do I apply this?" The Bottom Line feature addresses this concern by translating discussions of key topics and skills into a set of steps for applying them effectively in an organizational context.

> **Real-world examples.** Real-world examples, drawn from a wide range of industries and situations, are used extensively throughout the text.

> **Top Ten List: Key Points to Remember.** Presented at the end of the body of the chapter, the Top Ten List provides key managerial guidelines that students should take away from the chapter. While students will not remember everything they learn from reading a textbook, these lists attempt to reinforce important points that students should remember—and act on—in the future.

> **Questions for Review and Reflection.** Each chapter contains Review Questions testing knowledge of chapter content. In addition, we provide thought–provoking questions to require students to critically assess issues and controversies relating to chapter material. These questions often require students to take and justify stands on chapter topics.

> **Chapter-end Web Exercises.** There are two chapter-end Web-based exercises per chapter. These require students to access and use chapter-related Web material.

> **Chapter-end Cases.** Chapter-end cases highlight recent events and challenges facing well-known companies and provide illustrations of chapter concepts. The student develops critical thinking and analytical skills by thoroughly analyzing the situation and applying appropriate tools or techniques to address the situation.

> **Chapter-end Video Cases.** Each chapter includes a video case showing an actual organization dealing with management challenges. The video cases include introductory material and questions for discussion geared to chapter content.

INSTRUCTOR RESOURCES

The following resources are designed to aid instructors and were developed entirely by the text authors.

> **Instructor's Resource Manual (ISBN: 0-324-01331-0).** The objective of the Instructor's Resource Manual is to provide a high-quality and comprehensive instructional resource designed to "make the instructor look great." This resource includes sample answers to Critical Thinking Questions, End-of-Chapter Cases, Real-World Management Challenges, and Video Cases. It provides chapter outlines, sample course syllabi, and lesson plans for each chapter. In addition, it provides further information about text Self-Assessment exercises, including norm data developed

specifically for the text, and it offers additional exercises, cases, activities, and Web links to enrich students' learning experiences. The Instructor's Resource Manual is designed to give instructors a confident grasp of all text material as well as to provide extra information, tips, anecdotes, and examples to allow the instructor to demonstrate mastery of the material and to give "value added" to students beyond the text material.

> **Test Bank (ISBN: 0-324-01333-7).** The Test Bank contains approximately 100–150 questions for each text chapter. These questions include all basic formats, including multiple choice, true and false, short answer, fill-in-the-blank, and essay, as well as a significant number of "scenario type" questions. The level of difficulty of each question is indicated next to the item. The objective of this resource is to make the design of a high-quality (relevant, challenging, and defensible) exam a simple and efficient process for the instructor, as well as to permit tailoring of the exam to the instructor's preferred testing style.

> **PowerPoint Slides (ISBN: 0-324-01332-9).** Approximately 40 PowerPoint slides are provided for each chapter, some drawn from text figures and others specifically designed for this resource. The PowerPoint slides include integrative figures, definitions of concepts, lists of important factors, practical implications, important conceptual frameworks, and other materials. Slides are attractively designed and fully animated to permit polished and professional presentations. Instructors may choose to use the presentations as they are provided, or to add their own content and enrichment features.

> **Videos (ISBN: 0-324-11659-4; 0-324-11660-8).** Designed to enrich and support chapter concepts, each of the videos presents real business issues faced by a variety of service and manufacturing organizations. The video cases challenge students to study management and OB issues and develop solutions to business problems.

> **ExamView Testing Software (ISBN: 0-324-01334-5).** You can create, deliver, and customize print and online tests in minutes with this easy-to-use testing and assessment system. ExamView offers both a Quick Test Wizard and an Online Test Wizard that guide you step by step through the process of creating tests, while its unique WYSIWYG capability allows you to see the test you are creating on the screen exactly as it will print or display online. With ExamView's complete word-processing capabilities, you can enter an unlimited number of new questions or edit existing questions.

> **Instructor's Website at** *http://aldag.swcollege.com.* The Instructor's Website, developed and maintained by the authors, contains the following features:

  • *Downloadable PowerPoint slides and the Instructors' Resource Manual.*
  • *Norm data for Self-Assessment exercises.* As noted earlier, the norm data to be provided in the Instructors' Resource Manual will be regularly updated on the Instructors' Website to provide a larger and more varied pool of comparison information.
  • *Additional Web links.* Links to hundreds of problem-solving resources on the Web are provided and are regularly updated.

- *Talk to the Authors.* This feature enables instructors to submit questions to the authors, request teaching tips regarding any aspect of the book, offer their own suggestions and examples, and so on. The authors will personally respond to e-mail queries.
- *"Management Skills in the Movies."* This unique feature offers a listing of movies (professional, training, and Hollywood-made) that illustrate skills discussed in the text. Many students enjoy watching videos that illustrate course concepts. This website feature will provide a listing of video clips that have been effectively used by instructors to illustrate important OB and management concepts and skills, as well as tips for their use.
- *Regular updates.* The website will be actively maintained to provide new information concerning management tools, the real-world examples used in the text, new examples, and new exercises relating to the Web links. Again, the text, Instructors' Resource Manual, and website will each incorporate a variety of exercises relating to these links.

STUDENT RESOURCES

> **InfoTrac College Edition (0-324-01330-2).** With InfoTrac College Edition, students get complete, 24-hour-a-day access to full-text articles from hundreds of scholarly journals and popular periodicals such as *Newsweek, Time,* and *USA Today.* Thousands of full-length, substantive articles spanning the past four years are updated daily, indexed, and linked. And because they're online, the articles are accessible from any computer with Internet access. InfoTrac College Edition is perfect for all students, from dorm-dwellers to commuters and distance learners.

> **Web Tutor**™ harnesses the power of the Internet to deliver innovative learning aids that actively engage students. Web Tutor was designed to help students grasp complex concepts and to provide several forms of interactive learning reinforcements. This rich collection of content, customized for *Organizational Behavior and Management: An Integrated Skills Approach,* is available to students online.

Thomson Learning has partnered with two of the leading course management systems available today—Blackboard and WebCT—to deliver WebTutor content cartridges to instructors around the world.

WebTutor on WebCT (ISBN: 0-324-11856-2)
Web Tutor on Blackboard (ISBN: 0-324-12764-2)
Personal WebTutor Access Certificate (ISBN: 0-324-13472-X)
Four-month Access (ISBN: 0-324-13473-8)
One-month Access (ISBN: 0-324-13474-6)

> **WizeUp Digital Edition (ISBN: 0-324-12865-7).** The WizeUp Digital Edition of this text contains the complete textbook, powered by WizeUp software. It features powerful study tools to help you study faster and easier. With the digital version, you can instantly find exactly what you need with powerful search tools, add notes anywhere in the textbook, search, sort, and print your notes to make a custom study guide, and much more.

> **Interactive Study Center at** *http://aldag.swcollege.com.* The Student Website, also developed and maintained by the authors, offers the following student resources:
>
> - *Interactive practice quizzes with feedback.* The best way to prepare for exams is to get as much practice as possible answering questions that test mastery of each chapter's content. The Interactive Study Center includes multiple choice and test questions for each chapter.
> - *Challenge topics.* This resource gives students easy-to-understand explanations of some of the most difficult concepts discussed in the book. Additional examples of each concept will be provided with the explanations.
> - *Cyber review sessions.* These offer concise overviews of the content covered in each chapter. Many students request review sessions from their instructors when it is exam time. This website feature provides students with a concise overview of the key topics covered in each chapter and helps students to see how all of the topics fit together into a coherent whole. This is an extremely valuable resource for students when they are preparing for an upcoming exam.

TEXT ORGANIZATION

The text begins with a chapter emphasizing the importance of skills in the modern workplace and presenting the book's management skills framework. There are then 11 "substantive" chapters and a "looking ahead" chapter. Each of the substantive chapters focuses on a particular skills cluster. While the text provides relatively comprehensive coverage of standard topics, those topics are clustered around common themes and skills. We believe this permits the use of richer, more integrated materials while minimizing redundancies.

Chapter 2, The Organizational Context, focuses on a variety of skills needed to get the "big picture" of the firm and to ensure that actions are consistent with overall organizational goals. Chapter 3, Understanding and Valuing Differences, stresses knowledge and skills required in increasingly diverse organizations, including personality, national culture, perceptions, and attitudes; together, these topics speak to the nature of diversity and the ways we may react to it. In Chapter 4, Solving Problems, we address skills needed for problem solving, creativity enhancement, and negotiating. Chapter 5, Communicating Effectively, offers approaches to improving such critical communication skills as written communication, effective speaking, active listening, attending to nonverbal communications and informal communications, and use of electronic communication tools. In Chapter 6, Motivating Effectively, we focus on skills related to understanding employee needs, applying learning theories, setting effective goals, linking effort to outcomes, assuring fairness, and designing jobs to be intrinsically motivating. Chapter 7, Leading Effectively, provides guidelines and exercises to develop your leadership knowledge and skills. In that chapter, we will consider how leaders gain power and exert social influence, and we will address key leader skills and behaviors.

Chapter 8, Organizational Culture, Empowerment, and Ethics, addresses

Preface
Preface
Preface
Preface
Preface
Preface

xix

Preface

topics which, taken together, are critical to the ongoing success and health of organizations. The chapter focuses on skills for assessing culture and managing cultural change, and it shows how cultures can be designed to empower employees and encourage ethical behavior. In Chapter 9, Fostering Personal Growth, we focus on skills you will need to proactively take charge of your life, effectively deal with stressors, and actively manage your career. Chapter 10, Managing Politics, Conflict, and Change, deals with three interrelated issues that are pervasive in organizations and create uncertainty, turmoil, and stress, and we will provide guidelines for dealing with each of them. Chapter 11, Attracting, Selecting, and Developing Employees, addresses key human resource skills. Chapter 12, Managing Teams, explores the management skills that you will need to effectively create and lead teams. Finally, Chapter 13 provides a summary of the skills addressed in the book and offers specific, detailed guidance for lifelong skills learning.

AN INVITATION

We have made every effort to offer in *Organizational Behavior and Management: An Integrated Skills Approach* and its supplements a unique, comprehensive, accessible set of resources for instructors who hope to employ a strong skills emphasis in an organizational behavior or management course. Through the text's website, we hope to work with you as you use these materials, not only to provide information but also to learn your perspectives, insights, concerns, examples, and approaches. We invite you to take full advantage and contact us via e-mail, phone, or in any other way, and we look forward to interacting with you as you help prepare students for the Brave New World of organizational behavior and management.

ACKNOWLEDGMENTS

Appreciation is extended to those colleagues who contributed to *Organizational Behavior and Management: An Integrated Skills Approach*. We have benefited from the detailed and constructive reviews provided by many individuals. In particular, we wish to thank the following educators who have served as reviewers: Susan Adams, Bentley College; David C. Baldridge, University of Connecticut; William Bommer, Georgia State University; Jean Bush-Bacelis, Eastern Michigan University; Arch Darrow, Bowling Green State University; William P. Ferris, Western New England College; Jacqueline N. Hood, University of New Mexico; Fred Hughes, Faulkner University; David M. Leuser, Plymouth State College; Ralph Mullin, Central Missouri State University; Marcella M. Norwood, University of Houston; Elizabeth C. Ravlin, University of South Carolina; Raymond T. Sparrowe, Cleveland State University; Gregory Stephens, Texas Christian University; and John Wagner, Michigan State University.

RAMON (RAY) J. ALDAG

Ray Aldag is the Glen A. Skillrud Family Chair in Business, co-director of the Weinert Center for Entrepreneurship, and past chair of the Department of Management and Human Resources at the University of Wisconsin-Madison. He received his B.S. in Mechanical Engineering, his M.B.A. in Production Management, and his Ph.D. in Management from Michigan State University. He has worked as a thermal engineer on various Apollo, Voyager, and other aerospace projects at the Bendix Aerospace Division in Ann Arbor, Michigan. At Wisconsin, he has served as Associate Director of the Industrial Relations Research Institute and was the 1993 recipient of the Jerrod Distinguished Service Award. He is a member of honorary societies in business, engineering, and decision sciences, is a Fellow of the Academy of Management, and is listed in Who's Who in America. He was the recipient of the 1995 Distinguished Service Award of the national Academy of Management.

Ray has 30 years of experience teaching management principles, organizational behavior, decision making, introduction to business, human resource management, business policy, and other courses. He has served on more than 50 Ph.D. thesis committees.

An active researcher on such topics as leadership, culture, group decision processes, task design, and motivation, Ray has published more than 70 journal articles and book chapters in *Administrative Science Quarterly, Academy of Management Journal, Academy of Management Review, Decision Sciences, Journal of Applied Psychology, Journal of Management, Psychological Bulletin,* and elsewhere. He is co-author of six books, including *Business in a Changing World* (fourth edition), *Management* (second edition), and *Leadership and Vision,* and has served as associate editor for organizational theory and behavior for the *Journal of Business Research,* essays co-editor of the *Journal of Management Inquiry,* and on the Board of Consulting Editors for the *Journal of Applied Psychology.* He currently serves on the Editorial Review Boards of *Organization and Environment* and the *Journal of Leadership Studies.* He has served as a proposal reviewer for the Office of Personnel Management and the National Science Foundation and has received NSF funding for his research.

Ray served as the 1991–1992 president of the National Academy of Management, a professional organization with 10,000 members in more than 80 countries, and as the 1992–1993 president of the Foundation for Administrative Research. He has also served on the Board of Governors of the Academy of Management and in other Academy of Management positions in the Research Methods, Public Sector, Organizational Behavior, and Social Issues Divisions and in the Organizations and the Natural Environment Interest Group. He also has served as President of the Midwest Academy of Management and in various roles in the Decision Sciences Institute and the Industrial Relations Research Association.

Ray has consulting experience with a wide variety of public and private sector organizations in such industries as information processing, publishing, financial services, staffing, utilities, health care, heavy machinery, insurance, law enforcement, and pharmaceuticals.

LOREN W. KUZUHARA

Loren Kuzuhara is a senior lecturer in the Department of Management and Human Resources at the University of Wisconsin-Madison School of Business. He teaches undergraduate courses in organizational behavior and human resource management. In addition, Loren works on an individual basis with many students who are pursuing a variety of independent research projects focusing on management consulting and training and development.

Loren is the faculty advisor for the UW-Madison student chapters of the Society for Human Resource Management (SHRM) and Sigma Iota Epsilon (SIE). He also is the Sam Walton Fellow for the UW-Madison Students in Free Enterprise (SIFE) team and the coach for the student team that competes in the annual HR Games competition.

Loren earned his bachelor's degree in psychology from the University of Illinois at Urbana-Champaign, and his Master of Business Administration and Ph.D. in management and human resources from the University of Wisconsin-Madison.

Loren has corporate experience working in the Strategic Research Department at American Family Insurance. He is an active management consultant as well.

Loren's research interests revolve around work motivation, leadership, team development, training and development, organizational effectiveness and human resource management.

THE MANAGEMENT CHALLENGE: CRITICAL SKILLS FOR THE NEW WORKPLACE

CHAPTER *One*

SKILLS OBJECTIVES

> To analyze the key duties and responsibilities of a manager.
> To analyze the critical skills that distinguish between effective managers and ineffective managers.
> To develop basic action plans for addressing organizational problems and challenges.
> To develop a personal learning plan for enhancing management skills.

KNOWLEDGE OBJECTIVES

> Identify characteristics of the modern workplace and the corresponding importance of management skills.
> Discuss reasons why you will need managerial skills during your career.
> Identify important differences between success in business and in school.
> Explain the knowing–doing gap.
> Discuss a management skills framework.
> Explain the stages of action planning and implementation.

The new world of work and organizations is complex, ambiguous, changing, diverse, and global. In today's organizations, hierarchies are flatter, deadlines are shorter, teams are pervasive, employees must manage themselves, and technology is transforming the nature, pace, and possibilities of work. The modern workplace demands speed, flexibility, creativity, cooperation, political savvy, proactivity, and attention to ethical behavior. It is a place where success requires the skills to react quickly and effectively at all times, often while working with others and with new technologies. These same skills also are increasingly needed for career and life success.

The job of a manager has become dramatically more complex over time. As such, we attempt in this text to do more than survey major concepts and theories. Rather, we will emphasize what to do to be an effective manager and how to develop the right mix of skills to support the implementation of these behavioral strategies. We also provide tools to help you apply these management skills within complex, dynamic organizational and external environments while facing time, resource, political, and regulatory constraints.

This chapter lays the foundation for the text's skills focus. We begin by providing a brief overview of the nature of the modern workplace and the need for management skills in this new work environment. We then discuss ways that organizations are seeking to develop their employees' skills, and we argue that those skills are important for you in both work and life in general. Next, we note important differences between school and business and we address the "knowing–doing gap"—the inability to translate knowledge into appropriate action. Following this, we present the social learning perspective underlying the text as well as our managerial skills framework. Finally, we discuss action planning and implementation and provide a brief overview of the text's organization. Today's (and tomorrow's) work environment will require you to develop a skills portfolio—a set of valuable and transferable skills that you can carry from job to job and from company to company. This chapter shows how the text will help you build a solid foundation for your management skills portfolio.

Before reading on, complete the following self-assessment to gain a greater understanding of your initial attitudes and beliefs about management. As you work through the various chapters of this book, some of your existing attitudes and beliefs about management may be reinforced. However, you likely will be surprised to learn about other management practices and principles and how they are implemented in real-world organizations.

Self-Assessment 1-1
Attitudes Toward Management

Answer each of the following questions regarding your attitudes toward managing others in organizations. Answer each question as honestly as possible using the response scale below.

1 = Disagree Strongly
2 = Disagree Somewhat
3 = Neither Agree Nor Disagree
4 = Agree Somewhat
5 = Agree Strongly

1. _____ I will only need management skills if I get a job as a manager or supervisor in an organization.

2. _____ Management skills will not be an important determinant of my long-term career success.

3. _____ Management skills are something that people either have or don't have—they cannot be trained.

4. _____ Once you become a manager, your job becomes easier because you are telling other people to do things rather than having to do them yourself.

5. _____ A person who demonstrates outstanding performance in an entry-level (nonmanagerial) job will almost always be an outstanding manager as well.

6. _____ Management is basically just a bunch of "common sense" ideas that I already know anyway.

7. _____ Managers need to develop a "big picture" perspective of their work units and organizations in order to be effective.

8. _____ The study of management is really only relevant to business students who are majoring in management.

9. _____ "Soft management skills," such as managing teams, communication skills, and leadership, are among the most important things needed for a person to be successful in real-world organizations.

10. _____ Poor management is responsible for a large percentage of company failures or bankruptcies.

Next, read the following management scenario and develop an "action plan"—that is, a set of things you would do—to address the key problems that you see in the situation.

Pre-Test Skills Assessment
Using Management Skills to Address Organizational Problems

You just graduated from college in May and after taking a fabulous trip around Europe and Asia you are now ready to start your new job in the "real world." You are excited about the prospects of being able to start doing more "hands-on work" in an actual organizational environment. Your new position is assistant store manager at a major department store located in Portland, Oregon. Your job is to coordinate the activities of all the department supervisors and sales associates, and to deal with customers. The pay and benefits you will be receiving are excellent, and you have been told that there are opportunities for advancement in the company if you do well.

A couple of weeks after starting the new job, your enthusiasm for the company is beginning to wear thin. This is due to a number of things you have noticed so far:

> Many of the departmental supervisors and sales associates do not see you as having any credibility as a store manager since you just graduated from college, have no relevant work experience (other than a summer internship), and are significantly younger than most of the employees in the organization.

> Managers and sales associates in different departments are highly competitive with each other in terms of sales performance.

> The local economy is faring poorly, resulting in consumers having less money to spend on shopping.

> New competitors have been emerging on an ongoing basis. Consequently, the retail market is saturated with department stores.

> The department store recently laid off 20 percent of its departmental supervisors and sales associates due to declining sales and poor financial performance.

> There are rumors floating around that the department store may be acquired by a much larger department store based in San Diego.
> Employee job satisfaction in the department store is at an all-time low of 33 percent and the overall employee turnover rate has increased to 50 percent per year.

As the new assistant store manager of this department store, develop an action plan for handling this situation. Be specific and focus on action.

DEVIL'S ADVOCATE

Management?! Why do I need a course on management while I'm still in school?

Actually, the first jobs that many students take immediately after graduation do involve management. For example, you may obtain a position as a production supervisor, team or project leader, management trainee, program coordinator, or customer service manager. A management skills course can help prepare you for these kinds of positions. Although you will still need to learn the organization and industry in which you will be a manager, a basic management skills course will help you to "hit the ground running" and to learn your management or supervisory position much more quickly.

Now, even if you do not get a management job immediately after graduation, there are still good reasons to take a management course while you are still in school. First, many of the skills discussed in this book (e.g., self-management, communication skills, and teamwork skills) will help you to become a more effective employee in the real world. Second, if you do well in your entry-level job, there is a good chance that you will be promoted to a management position within a couple of years.

I'm not a management major so I don't see the point in having to study this stuff. Can't I just take more classes in my major?

Employers tend to value a balance of "specialist" and "generalist" in their employees. While it is important to have specific knowledge and skills that enable you to perform a particular job, employers are attracted to students who also have a diversity of general knowledge and skills. They feel a balance enables a person to see the "big picture" and to deal more effectively with different types of people and situations. The courses you are taking in your major will help develop the specialization that you need. However, a management course, regardless of your major, gives you a complementary set of knowledge and skills that will develop the "generalist" side of your training.

Isn't management just a bunch of "common sense" ideas that we already know?

This is a fairly common sentiment among students who are taking their first management course. Due to this attitude, some students believe that management is easy and therefore does not require as much time and effort as other business courses. In reality, *some* of management boils down to using common sense and intuition. However, the fact is that *many* people do not translate com-

mon sense into common practice in performing their management jobs in the real world. This is due in part to a lack of a systematic approach to management and organizational constraints and barriers (e.g., time pressures).

The value of a formal course in management skills is that the focus is on understanding and applying the skills you will need to be a successful manager in the real world, using a systematic approach that recognizes how to achieve your objectives given the realities of organizational environments.

The bottom line is that common sense is simply not enough to make you an effective manager.

I'm an international student. Will the management knowledge and skills I acquire be applicable to my country as well?

Absolutely. While there are many differences in management practices and cultures in different countries, this text focuses on developing the key skills that are needed for managerial success. These key skills, for the most part, will apply across cultures. Where cross-cultural differences are known to be important, we highlight them. So there is definitely a lot you can learn here that you can take back and use in your home country in the future.

Assessment
Assessment
Assessment
Assessment
Assessment
5
Assessment

Chapter 1   The Management Challenge: Critical Skills for the New Workplace

MANAGEMENT SKILLS AND COMPANY SUCCESS

Web Wise

The Top 25 Managers of the Year

Business Week annually selects its "Top 25 Managers of the Year." In selecting its top managers for 1999, *Business Week* wrote, "Yet leaving the booming economy aside, there's a group of executives who deserve to raise their champagne flutes a bit higher than the rest. *Business Week*'s 25 Top Managers of 1999 pushed their companies—and often their stock prices—to new highs. Some stood out by making smart decisions at lightning speed. Others were more patient, relentlessly pursuing a crucial deal or taking the time to right a once-sinking ship. In a year marked by hype, these execs' accomplishments were legit."*

The Top 25 Managers of 1999 were a diverse group, including Minuru Arakawa of Nintendo America, Steve Case of America Online, Steve Jobs of Apple Computer and Pixar, Timothy Koogle of Yahoo!, Jenny Ming of Old Navy, Martha Stewart of Martha Stewart Omnimedia, Keiji Tachikawa of NTT DoCoMo, and Jack Welch of GE. Read about them and their accomplishments at

http://www.businessweek.com/2000/00_02/b3663001.htm

*"The Best Managers: What It Takes," *Business Week*, January 10, 2000, p. 158.

In an age of high technology and high finance, it is sometimes easy to forget the importance of management to company success. In fact, though, good management is critical to the prosperity, and even the survival, of firms. For example, one study of manufacturing firms over a five-year period considered a myriad of factors—such as firm size, market share, capital intensity, industry average return on sales, and the ability of managers to effectively manage their people—that might explain the firms' financial performance. The results were dramatic: Managers' ability was *three times* as powerful in explaining company profitability as all other factors combined.[1] Similarly, a study in the United Kingdom revealed management weaknesses to be the primary cause of most insolvencies, with poor management cited as at least a contributing factor in more than 80 percent of cases.[2] These and many other studies of large and small firms are consistent in pointing to management skills as critical to firm success.[3]

Recent examples of major companies facing difficulties because of poor management range from toy maker Mattel to underwear manufacturer Fruit of the Loom, from the conglomerate Procter & Gamble to the National Aeronautics and Space Administration (NASA) to computer software maker Baan.[4] Similarly, the rising mortality rate of "dot-com" firms is due in large part to management failures.[5]

Just as management has been implicated in company problems and failures, management success stories are abundant, cases in which management skills have created or transformed organizations in remarkable ways. Among the many we examine in future chapters, these cases include Herb Kelleher's development of a successful culture of fun at Southwest Airlines, Mary Kay Ash's inspirational leadership of Mary Kay Cosmetics, and Jack Welch's transformation of GE, all of which are widely known. Others, such as Aaron Feuerstein's humane management decisions at Malden Mills, are less visible but no less dramatic. We will examine all of these success stories and many more throughout the pages of this text. For now, visit the *Business Week* website, described in the accompanying Web Wise, and read about the Top 25 Managers of the Year. In considering the profiles of these outstanding managers, ask yourself what characteristics and behaviors they share, and which appear to be unique.

While successes and failures due to the quality of CEOs' management skills are often observed by outsiders, the same skills, such as the need to see the big picture, communicate effectively, interact well with others, and make good decisions, are becoming increasingly important at levels throughout the organization. The skills that help a CEO lead an organization can help a manager run a department or an employee deal with the demands of everyday work life.

The accompanying Voice of Experience presents an interview with Brad Pope and Jeff Millard, officers of the University of Wisconsin-Madison chapter of Sigma Iota Epsilon, the honorary and professional management fraternity. The interview explores how leaders of a student organization have learned valuable skills that help prepare them for the "real world."

Now complete Skills Practice 1-1. This exercise requires you to draw from your own experience to identify your best and worst bosses, and to analyze why you feel this way about them. This exercise will help you to see the role of skills in determining a manager's effectiveness.

Skills Practice 1-1
Best and Worst Managers

Skill Level: Basic

Skill Objective

To develop skill in evaluating how specific skills contribute to a manager's overall effectiveness.

Procedure

1. This exercise can be completed individually or in groups of 3–5 students.
2. Think about the part-time jobs and internships you have held (or currently hold) and the bosses you have had for each of these jobs.
3. Now identify the boss who you feel is or was the *best* manager you have had as a work-

---

VOICE OF EXPERIENCE

THE VALUE OF MANAGEMENT SKILLS

Brad Pope, President
Jeff Millard, President-Elect
Zeta Eta Chapter, University of Wisconsin-Madison
The Sigma Iota Epsilon (SIE) Honorary and Professional Management Fraternity

1. **Why are effective management and leadership important to the success of a student organization?**

    You have to remember that a student organization is a voluntary activity, so you need to work very hard to motivate members to join and to get involved in the organization's activities. Leadership is needed to provide a clear sense of direction for the organization. Members will not remain involved if they fail to see the purpose and objectives of the organi-

zation. Finally, the leadership in a student organization must provide an effective structure that provides opportunities for other student members to assume responsibility for fund-raising, finance, membership development, and social activities.

2. **What are some of the biggest management challenges you are experiencing in leading the SIE student organization?**

    The key challenges for our Sigma Iota Epsilon chapter have been the management of organizational growth (i.e., a significant increase in membership), member turnover due to graduation, leadership succession, establishing an appropriate strategic focus for the organization, and defining appropriate roles for members who want to contribute to the organization.

3. **How have you addressed these challenges?**

    One key change we have made in order to address the leadership succession issue was to create a Vice-President position in our Executive Team. The person who holds this position will serve one semester as a Vice-President and then become the President the next semester. This will provide the Vice-President with the time needed to learn the organization and to prepare for assuming the President position. The issue of strategic focus is a major challenge for the organization given that management is such a broad field. After extensive discussion, we decided that an appropriate focus for our chapter would be leadership development. We selected this focus because it is a key management competency and we know that many employers look for leader-ing individual. Write the name of this person on a separate sheet of paper and record your answers to the steps below under this person's name.

4. Think about the specific things *(management practices)* that your best boss did that made him or her so effective as a manager.

5. Given your answers in the previous step, identify the *skills* that your best boss possessed in order to do the things that made him or her a highly effective manager. Be specific.

6. Now, repeat steps 2–5 using the boss who you feel was the *worst* manager you have had as an employee. Use a separate piece of paper for recording your summary of this individual.

7. Finally, place the summaries of your best and worst managers next to each other.

8. Answer the following questions.

Discussion Questions

1. How do your best and worst managers differ from one another in terms of the things they did (i.e., management practices)?

2. How do your best and worst managers differ from one another in terms of the management skills they possessed?

ship skills when they interview students for full-time positions after graduation.

4. What kinds of management skills have you developed through your leadership roles in SIE?

(Brad) One key skill I have learned is how to delegate to others. At the beginning of the school year, I felt that I had to do everything myself. It didn't take long for me to realize that this was totally unrealistic so I had to delegate responsibility to others to handle certain issues and to trust them to get these things done. Fortunately, we have a *great* executive team that is very responsible and motivated.

(Jeff) Some of the skills I learned are problem solving, leadership, and teamwork. I was the head of the technology committee that was responsible for creating a website for our chapter. In the beginning, my committee members and I had no idea what we needed to do to accomplish this task. However, we studied the problem and learned how to create web pages by sitting around a computer together in the lab with a manual in front of us. Little by little, we saw the results of efforts as the website began to take shape. It has been a challenging, but rewarding, experience.

(Brad) One last thing I would add is that I learned the value of actively managing communication and following up with others so that we are all "on the same page." This takes a lot of time and effort, but it is absolutely critical to the success of any leader.

5. Have your management skills helped you to be more competitive in terms of obtaining in-ternships and looking for a job after graduation?

Definitely! Many employers use "behavioral interview" formats in which you must respond to questions by drawing from your personal experience. Our leadership experience with Sigma Iota Epsilon has greatly enhanced our ability to answer questions such as, "Tell me about a time when you added value to a team or organization." Based on our SIE experience, we can talk extensively about how we view our members as customers, try to understand what they want from their membership, and then look for ways to add value for them so that their SIE experience contributes to their professional development.

http://www.fsu.edu/~sie/

CRITICAL SKILLS ACROSS BUSINESS FUNCTIONS

Management skills are growing in importance for workers of all kinds. A study of financial staff identified as critical skills, in addition to financial leadership, these skills: strategic thinking, effective communication, and leadership.[6] Similarly, a survey of chief information officers found that more than three-fourths believe that more widespread use of technology will require IT workers to communicate more effectively and articulately.[7] With more frequent information exchange, skills such as communication, diplomacy, and problem solving will grow in importance. As another example, a study of "Sales Management Competencies for the 21st Century" identified eight competencies consistently demonstrated by top-performing sales managers. Among those competencies are providing strategic vision, assembling teams of skilled employees, sharing information with employees, coaching, diagnosing performance, negotiating, and selecting high-potential employees.[8] Similarly, the American Institute of Certified Public Accountants (AICPA) Core Competency Framework identifies the skills and competencies accounting professionals need to be competitive now and in the years ahead.[9] Along with functional competencies, key competencies that were identified include such personal skills as communicating, handling personal relationships, and facilitating learning and personal improvement, as well as such broad-business–perspective competencies as strategic thinking, critical thinking, and decision making. In short, success in jobs of all kinds—finance, information technology, marketing, accounting, and others—now depends on the sorts of skills we address in this text.

SKILLS TRAINING IN ORGANIZATIONS

As evidence of the importance placed on skills in the modern workplace—and of the conviction that skills can be learned—American corporations spend more than $64 billion annually for the training of their workforces, about 85 percent of it in the area of management skills.[10] The world's best companies recognize the value of continuing skills training.[11] Dana Corp. requires all of its employees to complete 40 hours of education each year. The company spent about $32.5 million on employee training programs in 1999, and it has three Dana University schools. IBM invests 6 percent of its profits on education. Merck & Co. spent 3.5 percent of its 1999 payroll, or about $100 million, on employee skills development programs. Abbott Laboratories offers one-week and three-week leadership development programs. Lucent Technologies is known for its dedication to learning. It knows that knowledge is all it has to sell, and it provides tuition reimbursement of up to $7,000 for undergraduate studies and $9,000 for graduate programs. Partly as a result, the company—with 120,000 employees—received 150,000 applications in 1999 and has a voluntary turnover rate of just 1 percent.

Similarly, General Electric spends about $1 billion annually on education and training programs. GE executives and managers also volunteer time to talk with students at many grade levels, and they brainstorm with college faculty to identify which skills should be part of school curricula. GE's paid college internships are among its strongest programs.[12] The company seeks to help

FOCUS ON MANAGEMENT

SKILLS TRAINING AT AT&T WIRELESS SERVICES*

AT&T Wireless Services, the nation's largest cellular service provider, is fighting to maintain its leadership in the face of intense competition and technological changes. AT&T Wireless Services is using a process called Managing Personal Growth (MPG) to help employees identify core competencies or critical skills, develop them with resources available through the company, and translate them into day-to-day decisions and actions that help the company meet its goals. Employees must take personal responsibility for developing those critical skills, not in company-mandated training sessions but on an ongoing basis. The MPG process forces employees to think about their personal values, what is important to them in life, what their current skills are, and what they hope to do in the future by acquiring new competencies. Employees then talk with their supervisors to develop an individual plan for their own development. A key function of the MPG process is to shift people to the idea of shared responsibility, making it clear that they are responsible for their own careers. Their job security is grounded not in the company but in what they know and the value they can create around themselves.

http://www.attws.com/

*G. Fleming and E. Emde, "Creating the Future: Developing the Critical Skills Is Everybody's Business," *Information Executive,* April 1998, p. 7.

the students build technical and business skills in a hands-on setting; students do real work that is measurable and deliverable, are given performance reviews, and are assigned mentors.

A survey conducted by the Conference Board showed that a full 98 percent of respondents reported that their skills training efforts reaped significant economic benefits for their firms.[13] Still, many companies are failing to develop key managerial skills.[14] For instance, in one study 72 percent of companies indicated that they were concerned about being able to predict which skills will be missing from their organizations in a year, but just 21 percent of companies were able to identify where employees want to be in terms of skill development in a year.[15] Another study showed that 58 percent of managers had received no leadership training, 68 percent had not been trained in delegation, 72 percent had received no training in giving feedback on performance, and 87 percent had no training in stress management.[16] As such, you cannot assume that every company will help you develop needed skills. Instead, you should seek out employers who are committed to helping you continuously develop and maintain those skills that will make you more valuable.[17] In addition, you must proactively identify and acquire key skills.

Kip Frautschi, an experienced marketing executive at the Webcrafters printing company, talks in the Voice of Experience about the importance of managerial skills in the business world.

Although most people are familiar with the term "management," many do not really understand what managers do and the knowledge and skills they need to be effective. By completing Skills Practice 1-2, you will develop a much better idea of what a manager's job entails and why it is important to the success of an organization.

Skills Practice 1-2

Skill Level: **Basic**

Profiling the Job of a Real-World Manager
(A Field Work Exercise)

Skill Objective

To develop skill in profiling the activities and skills associated with the job of a manager in an actual organizational setting.

Procedure

1. Identify a business professional you know who is currently in a managerial role in his or her organization and is willing to be interviewed for this exercise.
2. Schedule a meeting of between 30 and 60 minutes with the manager.

VOICE OF EXPERIENCE

THE VALUE OF MANAGEMENT IN ACHIEVING ORGANIZATIONAL EFFECTIVENESS

Christopher (Kip) Frautschi,
Director of Marketing
Webcrafters Corporation

1. Why is management important to the success of an organization?

The goal of an organization is to successfully create the product or service and do so while maintaining sufficient profitability to ensure a return of capital to investors, now and in the future. Most companies could, by firing all leaders and managers, improve their profit margin dramatically for about four months. Managers and leaders need to keep the firm focused on profitability and investment and ideas for the future. Also, competing demands for cash in different departments or areas need to be reconciled, along with what to invest in a product or service now, long before most nonmanagers see the need to change the operating and investing style and priorities of the

present. Similarly, most firms could save money and increase their profitability by cutting out a direct sales force. But, of course, nobody would really take such a short-sighted action.

2. How would you respond to people who say that the practice of management is nothing but common sense?

For the day-to-day operations of a company, perhaps it is only common sense; but that doesn't answer the question of why so few people have this common sense. To keep a team of people focused on the same goal at the same time seems easy when it is done well, but when it is, more commonly, done poorly, it is not difficult to observe the poor results and high costs that then occur.

3. What are the keys to being a good manager?

People are the key to any successful organization. Often, one finds two nearly identical companies, in the same industry, with similar market share, same found-

ing year, all the top executives in a given position went to school with their counterparts at the other company. But one firm is strongly profitable year in and year out, the other is barely profitable enough to stay in the business. Why? Because the strongly profitable firm has a successful culture—a can-do, on-time culture. Why? Because the managers have made the cumulative decisions that created over decades a better company. So successful management of people is the first point.

The second point blurs the line between manager and leader, but it is the willingness to lead. In the infantry the motto is "Follow Me!" The privates follow the second lieutenant up the hill into enemy fire because their second lieutenant is taking the risks too and leading and showing the way. Thus, a good manager must see the ways things can be improved and leads his team into that vision so they all share that vision.

http://www.webcrafters-inc.com

3.   In the interview, ask the manager the following questions.
   a.   What is your position title?
   b.   How long have you been in this position?
   c.   What is the name of the work unit that you manage?
   d.   How many employees report to you?
   e.   What are your primary duties and responsibilities in your position?
   f.   What do you like most about being a manager?
   g.   What do you like least about being a manager?
   h.   What are the key areas of knowledge that you need to be an effective manager?
   i.   What are the critical skills that you need to be an effective manager?
4.   Summarize the results of your interview.
5.   Answer the discussion questions below, based on the interview.

Discussion Questions
   a.   What did you learn about the job of a manager?
   b.   Which of the manager's responses, if any, surprised you? Why?
   c.   What do you see as being the most challenging aspects of being a manager?
   d.   What do you think a student can do to develop the knowledge and skills needed to prepare himself or herself for a management position in the real world?
6.   *(optional)* Present a brief summary of your interview to your class and discuss what you learned from the exercise.

DO *YOU* NEED MANAGEMENT SKILLS?

You may agree that firms need and want management skills in order to succeed, but may still question whether *you* personally need those skills. We believe there are at least three primary reasons why you will find management skills to be valuable: companies want them, they are becoming more crucial in the changing business environment, and they will serve you well in life.

MANAGERIAL SKILLS AND HIRING

Quite simply, companies are hiring for skills, including managerial skills. A report released in 2000 by the U.S. General Accounting Office provided succinct advice for organizations: "Hire, develop, and retain employees according to competencies. Identify the competencies—knowledge, skills, abilities, and behaviors—needed to achieve high performance of mission and goals, and build and sustain the organization's talent pool through recruiting, hiring, development, and retention policies and practices targeted at building and sustaining those competencies."[18] Many companies go further, by tracking skills acquisition of their workforce and tying pay to skills attained, even if they are not used.[19] This is a workforce where competencies rule. It is absolutely critical that you learn what skills employers value and then work to develop them.

Students are sometimes surprised to learn of the criteria that firms and their interviewers use when screening job candidates. A study by the U.S. Department of Labor and the American Society of Training and Development of "Skills Employers Want" revealed 16 critical skills, as shown in Figure 1-1. We will directly address almost all of these skills in subsequent chapters.

FIGURE 1-1
The 16 Basic Skills Employees Need

Knowing How to Learn	Self-Confidence
Reading	Motivational Goal Setting
Writing	Personal and Career Development
Mathematics	Interpersonal Skills
Listening	Negotiation
Oral Communication	Teamwork
Problem Solving	Organizational Effectiveness
Creative Thinking	Leadership

Source: American Society for Training and Development and U.S. Department of Labor, Workplace Basics: Skills Employers Want, 1988

Similarly, a survey of human resource managers' perceptions of the importance of various skills, knowledge, and experience as employment criteria (with an evaluation of "1" meaning "Not a Factor" and "5" meaning "Extremely Important") yielded the results presented in Figure 1-2. Perhaps the most striking finding is that factors such as GPA, references, and college attended, while important, are rather far down the list. Skills in communication, problem-solving, and human relations are all rated higher.

Now, stop for a moment and consider this fact: The Bureau of Labor Statistics predicts that the average 22-year-old college graduate in the year 2000 will have more than *eight* different employers before he or she reaches the age of 32; that's a change of employers every 15 months.[20] When you move to new employers, it will be your skills portfolio—not contacts in a past firm or firm-specific knowledge—that will be most important. As the information we've just presented indicates, "soft skills," such as communicating, problem solving, motivating, leading, negotiating, and working with others, will make up a large and critical part of that skills portfolio.

FIGURE 1-2
Ranking of Human Resource Managers' Perceptions of Criteria for Evaluating Business Graduates

Criterion	Mean	Criterion	Mean
Oral communication skills	4.6	Nonverbal communication skills	3.7
Listening skills	4.5	Work experience	3.7
Résumé	4.4	Cover letter	3.6
Interpersonal communication skills	4.4	References (at interview stage)	3.4
Written communication skills	4.3	GPA, in major	3.4
Problem-solving skills	4.2	GPA, overall	3.3
Poise	4.2	Software application skills	3.2
Human relations skills	4.2	Office information systems knowledge	3.2
Job-related technical skills	4.2	College attended	3.1
Neat appearance	4.1	References (at initial screening)	2.7
Appropriate attire	3.8	Contacts within the organization	2.2

FOCUS ON MANAGEMENT

HIRING FOR COMPETENCIES AT MERCK

When Merck and Company needed to fill a large number of field representative positions, it decided to focus specifically on competencies. Hiring managers were asked to identify the specific traits, skills, and behaviors most critical to job performance. A process was then developed to screen for those competencies at various steps of candidate assessment, including résumé screening, telephone evaluations, and the final interview. Each candidate then was scored on the criteria to give a rating of the candidate's potential. According to Merck chairman and CEO Raymond Gilmartin, the process was more efficient than previous approaches and yielded greater consistency across regions of the country. Gilmartin added, "There was another interesting effect: The people we hired were even more diverse than those we had hired as reps in the past. Diversity, in other words, was a welcome outcome of a process that was based entirely on business-directed criteria."*

http://www.merck.com/

*R. V. Gilmartin, "Diversity and Competitive Advantage at Merck," *Harvard Business Review,* January/February 1999, p. 146.

MANAGERIAL SKILLS IN THE NEW WORK ENVIRONMENT

Another reason to care about your managerial skills is that many developments in the new work environment are making such skills more important for career success. Here is a sampling of those developments, each of which we'll explore in depth in future chapters:

> **Entrepreneurship.** An increasing number of college graduates are becoming entrepreneurs, starting their own businesses.[21] A first-time entrepreneur faces many challenges, but perhaps the greatest is learning to become a boss. Recent evidence suggests that entrepreneurial success depends heavily on managerial skills, including social skills.[22] So, if you choose an entrepreneurial option, management skills are an absolute necessity.

> **Downsizing and Delayering.** By one estimate, more than 43 million jobs have been lost in the United States since 1979 due to organizational downsizing—deliberate reductions of personnel.[23] Job creation rates have been robust and unemployment is low, but this downsizing has served to make many organizations much leaner, often by eliminating many middle-level managers. One form of downsizing is delayering—the elimination of entire levels of the organizational hierarchy. For example, Champion International, a pulp and paper manufacturing firm, turned to delayering as part of its turnaround efforts, reducing management levels in its support functions from five to two.[24] Similarly, Dow Chemical embarked on a process of delayering in the mid-1990s that reduced its hierarchy from 10 layers to six.[25] One important effect of such delayering is to push managerial responsibilities down to lower levels in the organization.

> **Job Enrichment and Empowerment.** As companies seek to make workplaces more satisfying and motivating, they are adopting a variety of approaches to giving workers more personal responsibility for their

work. They are, for instance, giving employees "larger" jobs, with more autonomy and greater opportunities to use valued skills. While these job changes have many positive outcomes for employees and firms, they also place additional demands on employees. In essence, these job changes "make every employee a manager," weaving the need for managerial skills into the fabric of jobs.

> **Self-Managed Work Teams.** Companies are making sharply increasing use of self-managed work teams.[26] These teams have responsibility not only for allocating tasks among members, deciding how to do their jobs, and carrying them out, but also in many cases for disciplining team members, evaluating members' performance, and even selecting and terminating members from the team. As their name suggests, these teams have the responsibility and authority to manage themselves, and as such the teams' performance depends in large part on their members' managerial skills.

> **Hiring for the Second Job.** Many firms are now taking a forward-looking approach to hiring. Rather than focusing just on the job candidates' ability to perform well in an entry-level job, they are considering whether candidates have "the right stuff" for subsequent, higher-level positions. Thus, they are concerned relatively less with technical skills and more with the conceptual and interpersonal skills that will be needed in the future.

> **Growth in Management Positions.** Our earlier discussion of downsizing and delayering may give the impression that management ranks are shrinking. However, while specific firms have worked to trim their managerial numbers, economic growth and associated new firm formation have actually increased the overall number of managers in the United States. In fact, Bureau of Labor Statistics reports show that managers, administrators, and executives represent the *fastest growing* employment category.[27] As such, whether you expect it now or not, there is a good chance that you will end up in a management position.

MANAGERIAL SKILLS AND LIFE SUCCESS

Even a cursory look at the list of skills employers want and that we will address suggests a final reason to care about managerial skills: These are all skills that

FIGURE 1-3

Management Skills Needed for Success by Organizational Level

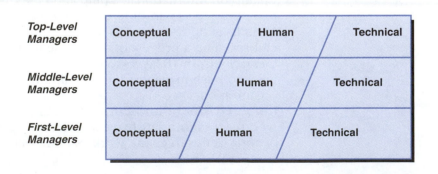

VOICE OF EXPERIENCE

MANAGEMENT SKILLS IN THE REAL WORLD

Tim Oswald,
Production Supervisor
General Motors Corporation

1. In what ways does working in the real world differ from life as a university student?

The decisions that I have to make now are much more important and can affect many more people. They are not just about getting a good grade anymore. Some decisions may now result in a profit or loss of thousands of dollars for the company. Many of these decisions have to be made quickly with relatively little information.

2. What were the major challenges you faced as a new supervisor? What did you do to handle them?

Dealing with the many different personalities and situations that I have to face on a daily basis. Everyone needs to be treated a bit differently, and every day a new situation comes up. I just have to look at every situation individually and learn from the past how to react in the future.

3. What advice would you give to recent college graduates who will assume supervisory/ managerial positions in the real world?

You really have to master your human relations skills. Dealing successfully with the employees that you are supervising is extremely important. The technical knowledge that you need will come with time, but you have to make an impact on your employees immediately.

http://www.gm.com/

will serve you well in life in general. The abilities to communicate, to interact effectively with others, to negotiate, to solve problems, to lead, to think critically, to motivate others, to listen well, to deal with conflict, and to continue learning are valuable in social relationships, making daily transactions, and leading a fulfilling life.

The lesson is that you will need an arsenal of managerial skills even before you formally enter a management position—or, indeed, even if you never enter one. As shown in Figure 1-3, those skills will remain important throughout your management career. In fact, the importance of conceptual skills increases at higher levels in the organization.

In the Voice of Experience feature, Tim Oswald, a recent college graduate who now works for General Motors, talks about his perspectives on real-world challenges, and what he has learned about critical management skills.

SUCCESS IN SCHOOL AND BUSINESS

It is sometimes tempting—and perhaps comforting—to assume that a successful college career will guarantee achievement in the business world. While some of the same things, such as intelligence, conscientiousness, and drive, may be helpful in both settings, you also should be aware of many important differences between school and businesses. As shown in Figure 1-4, success in school is based largely on individual performance. Your communication to professors is primarily written, test-taking is a critical ability, and performance criteria are generally well-specified and relatively objective. Further, you are in two enviable positions: You are a customer whose satisfaction is

FIGURE 1-4
Differences Between School and Business

	School	Business
Achieving Success	Individual	Teamwork
Critical Ability	Tests	Relationships
Structure	Quantified	Subjective
Graduate's Role	Customer	Employee
Performance	Objective	Judgments
Communication	Written	Verbal
Prestige	Senior	Trainee

Source: E. Taylor, *Graduates' Guide to Business Success: Solutions that Enable College Graduates to Excel in Business* (Hollywood, FL: Biography for Everyone, 1997), p. 13

important to your professors and school, and you are in a high-status position such as senior or graduate student. As you enter business, you will see that success depends much more on teamwork. You will have to rely more on verbal communication, and handling relationships will emerge as a critical skill. Your job will be less structured, and your performance ratings will be more judgmental. Finally, you will often initially be in the low-prestige position of trainee, and you will be an employee rather than a customer.

In view of all these differences, you may not be surprised to learn that a wide range of studies show that success in school does almost nothing to predict subsequent career success.[28] It is the growing evidence of this very weak link that has led many educators and managers to call for a greater emphasis on skills in the learning process. For example, the authors of a major study of management education sponsored by the American Assembly of Collegiate Schools of Business (AACSB) concluded that, "The challenge of how to develop stronger people skills needs to be faced by both business schools in their education of their degree program students and by corporations and firms in their management development activities."[29]

THE KNOWING–DOING GAP

A common reaction of students who are studying management for the first time is that management is little more than "common sense" ideas and principles that they already know. This sometimes leads to the perception of management in organizations as being "easy" or "unimportant" to the bottom line of an organization.

In reality, the study of management is deceptive in that much of it "makes sense" as you read it, but it becomes much more difficult once you try to apply these concepts and principles to actual case studies or work situations. This fundamental problem also occurs for many students when they take math classes. If they review for an exam by reading the textbook and their class notes, they can follow the logic of the sample problems that were solved.

However, once they get into an exam and are required to solve an actual problem for themselves, they don't have a clue how to solve the problem.

The bottom line here is that simply *knowing*—recognizing or understanding what to do to manage an organization—is not enough for an individual to become a successful manager. Jeffrey Pfeffer and Robert Sutton from Stanford University became intrigued by the large number of managers and executives that they worked with who knew what needed to be done to enhance the effectiveness of their organizations, but failed to implement it. Pfeffer and Sutton referred to this phenomenon as the "Knowing–Doing Gap." For example, most managers agree that it is important to reward employees for good performance and to link employee pay with job performance. However, in many organizations neither of these basic management principles is put into practice.

Many students wonder why the knowing–doing gap exists. Although there are many potential causes, Pfeffer and Sutton identified the following: [30]

> **Knowledge management efforts mostly emphasize technology and the transfer of codified information.** That is, the focus is on how to capture and distribute critical knowledge or information to management and employees. However, this does not address the issue of how the information can be used to make better decisions to enhance work-unit or organizational effectiveness.

> **Knowledge management tends to treat knowledge as a tangible thing, as a stock or a quantity, and therefore separates knowledge as a thing from the use of that thing.** The presumption is that simply possessing knowledge that can help make better decisions necessarily means that the knowledge will be used. In many cases, this is not the case.

> **Formal systems can't easily store or transfer tacit knowledge.** Tacit knowledge refers to information that is important for doing something effectively that cannot be captured, measured, or codified by formal knowledge systems in organizations. Tacit knowledge tends to be acquired through specific experiences, observations of others, trial and error, and stories. Due to these characteristics of tacit knowledge, it becomes more difficult to transmit this knowledge to others in an organization and to get them to use it.

> **The people responsible for transferring and implementing knowledge management frequently do not understand the actual work being documented.** This is a common problem in that the designers of formal knowledge management systems do not comprehend the key underlying business processes, and therefore do not have the capacity to design a system that facilitates the implementation of that knowledge by end users.

> **Knowledge management tends to focus on specific practices and ignore the importance of philosophy.** This refers to the tendency for people to want to know "what to do" to solve problems they face in their organizations. However, if the knowledge acquired by a manager or business professional is merely a collection of practices without a coherent, overarching philosophy, then it becomes difficult to implement these practices. One reason for this is that these individual practices are

not always consistent with one another (that is, they do not make sense when implemented together). It is the philosophy that provides a framework for thinking about and implementing a set of strategies geared toward achieving specific business objectives.

Overcoming the knowing–doing gap represents one of the greatest challenges to managers in real-world organizations. While meetings, planning sessions, mission statements, and strategic plans with conceptual frameworks help to develop the roadmap or blueprint for action in an organization, the ultimate success of the firm is determined by its ability to implement or execute its plans in order to achieve organizational objectives and business results.

Pfeffer and Sutton offer the following recommendations for bridging the knowing–doing gap that exists in so many organizations:[31]

> **Why before how: Philosophy is important.** Make sure that all members of an organization understand and are committed to the way of thinking about how to achieve given business objectives. This can be done through new employee orientations, formal training programs, and modifying the company's mission statement (formal statement of its purpose and values).

> **Knowing comes from doing and teaching others how.** Teaching through apprenticeships, coaching and mentoring helps organizational members see how to "do the right things." From this emphasis on action comes a deeper understanding of what needs to be done and why (i.e., knowing).

> **Action comes before elegant plans and concepts.** Too many organizations have wasted far too much time attempting to develop elaborate conceptual frameworks and elegant strategic plans only to fail when it came to their implementation. The key is to focus on the bottom line of taking action and to ensure that talking about what to do is always coupled with specific actions.

> **There is no doing without mistakes. What is the company's response?** Every organization, no matter how successful, makes mistakes. The key is, does an organization possess a philosophy, approach, and culture that enables it to learn from its mistakes to reduce the likelihood of committing the same error in the future? Organizations that bridge the knowing–doing gap are able to learn and become smarter based on their successes and failures in the marketplace.

> **Fear fosters knowing–doing gaps. So drive out fear.** Fear often prevents people from doing what they know they should do in organizations. Management must create a value system, organizational culture, and policies and procedures that do not punish individuals for doing the right thing even if the results are less than optimal.

> **Beware of false analogies: Fight the competition, not each other.** Many organizations have created organizational cultures and systems that promote internal competition such as forced distribution performance appraisal systems, and highly competitive reward and recognition systems. The presence of internal competition in an organization undermines cooperation and collaboration between individuals and work units. This results in a "we vs. they" mentality in which important knowledge or information that one individual or work unit possesses

may not be shared with others in the organization for the benefit of the overall firm. Clearly, management must promote a cooperative work environment where everyone is committed to working together in order to achieve the same business objectives.

> **Measure what matters and what can help turn knowledge into action.** The emphasis here is for management to identify a handful of critical measures of success for the organization and to track them on an ongoing basis. Focusing on these measures improves management's ability to identify and implement appropriate actions that will enhance the future performance of the company.

> **What leaders do, how they spend their time, and how they allocate resources, matters.** Ultimately, it is the responsibility of the leadership in organizations to create an organizational system and culture that values creating, managing, and sharing knowledge as well as taking appropriate action to ensure effective implementation.

Now complete Skills Practice 1-3. The purpose of this activity is for you to analyze why knowing–doing gaps may exist in a number of situations and then to develop specific strategies for eliminating these gaps. Remember, planning is important, but it is the implementation or execution of the plan that matters most in the end!

Skills Practice 1-3   **Skill Level: Challenging**
Bridging the Knowing–Doing Gap

Skill Objective
To identify sources of knowing–doing gaps and to develop strategies for eliminating them.

Procedure
1.   This activity may be done on an individual basis or in groups of 3–5 students.
2.   Read the list of common knowing–doing gaps that exist in many organizations in the "real world" that is displayed below.

Common "Knowing–Doing" Gaps in "Real World" Organizations
> (#1) Managers who say that they know that employees should be rewarded for doing a good job, but fail to put this into practice with their employees.
> (#2) Managers who say that they know that they should solicit the input of their employees when making decisions that affect the entire work unit, but fail to put this into practice with their employees.
> (#3) Managers who say that they know that the use of teams can improve work-unit and organizational performance, but fail to put this into practice with their employees.
> (#4) Managers who say that they know that a well-trained and highly skilled work force is critical for the long-term competitiveness of a firm, but fail to put this into practice with their employees.
> (#5) Managers who say that they know that employee pay increases should be based on their job performance, but fail to put this into practice with their employees.
> (#6) Managers who say that they know that a mission statement for an organization provides the overall direction and vision a company needs to be successful in the long term, but fail to put this into practice with their employees.
> (#7) Managers who say that employees need to receive effective and thorough annual performance appraisals so that they can develop professionally and improve their job performance, but fail to put this into practice with their employees.

3. Take a separate piece of paper and write the number associated with each of the knowing–doing gaps above on that paper. For each knowing–doing gap, identify some reasons why this gap may exist. Record your answers on your piece of paper.

4. Now identify at least one action that you could take to reduce or eliminate each knowing–doing gap above. Record your recommendations on your piece of paper.

5. Answer the discussion questions below. *(Optional)* You can also present a summary of your results to the rest of your class.

Discussion Questions

1. Based on this exercise, why do you feel that knowing–doing gaps in management practices are so prevalent in organizations?

2. What kinds of things do you think are most important in eliminating knowing–doing gaps in organizations?

3. Why isn't common sense enough for a person to be an effective manager in the real world?

THE SOCIAL LEARNING PERSPECTIVE

To enhance your learning experience, we apply a social learning perspective in this text.[32] The generalized steps of the social learning perspective are presented in Figure 1-5.

We apply the social learning perspective through a "4 A's" organizing framework, as shown in Figure 1-6.

Our steps, corresponding to the generalized steps of the social learning perspective, have the following content:

> **Skills Assessment.** This first step in skill learning is to get baseline measures on important skills and to foster interest in those skills. We encourage this in each chapter through Pre-Test Skills Assessment exercises and a variety of other Self-Assessment scales. In addition, some Skills Practice exercises contain skills assessment elements.

FIGURE 1-5
The Social Learning Perspective

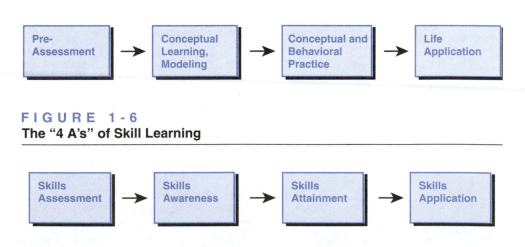

| Pre-Assessment | → | Conceptual Learning, Modeling | → | Conceptual and Behavioral Practice | → | Life Application |

FIGURE 1-6
The "4 A's" of Skill Learning

| Skills Assessment | → | Skills Awareness | → | Skills Attainment | → | Skills Application |

Futurework*

On Labor Day 1999 the U.S. Department of Labor issued a report titled *Futurework: Trends and Challenges for Work in the 21st Century.* The report sought to outline three major challenges for the 21st century workplace and workforce:

> "The challenge of being skilled, not stuck in the new economy— as technology and globalization open more opportunities for those who have access to the tools to build their skills, but reduce the supply of lower-end jobs.

> The challenge of flexibility and family as employers seek more flexibility to compete in the global marketplace and workers pursue more opportunities to spend time with their loved ones.

> The challenge of destiny and diversity as employers hire from a more diverse pool of workers in the future, creating new opportunities for economic growth but also raising the potential for persistent discrimination and inequality."

According to the Department of Labor report, "Skills are the ticket." The report notes, "In the information-based, skills-intensive economy of the twenty-first century, one thing is clear: knowing means growing."

Read the Futurework report at

http://www.dol.gov/dol/asp/public/futurework

*"Futurework: Trends and Challenges for Work in the 21st Century," *Occupational Outlook Quarterly,* Summer 2000, pp. 31–36.

> **Skills Awareness.** This step includes discussion of important background material, such as why the topic is important, key approaches to mastering the skill, and other relevant information. This text employs a wide range of tools to facilitate this step. Along with thorough coverage of key concepts in the body of the chapters, several other features are incorporated. These include a Devil's Advocate feature to respond to commonly raised questions, Voice of Experience interviews with practitioners, Web Wise features suggesting links to important Internet material, Focus on Management segments illustrating current management applications of concepts, Global Perspective features to highlight important international considerations, and Lighten Up boxes to showcase unique, creative, and sometimes humorous applications. In addition, Bottom Line figures provide visual summaries of important material, a Top Ten List summarizes some key lessons of the chapter, and chapter-end questions encourage review and critical thinking.

> **Skills Attainment.** Here, through a variety of experiential methods, you develop the skill. While several of the text features facilitate skill attainment, the several Skills Practice exercises in each chapter serve as the primary tools to help in this critical step. You will see that these take many forms, such as role-playing, fieldwork exercises, development of action plans, and practice with specific techniques.

> **Skills Application.** This final step involves life application. These include, for instance, using the skills in case analyses, life situations, field projects, and other applications. Text elements to support this step include Real-World Management Challenge exercises, many of the Skills Practice exercises, and chapter-end material such as two Web exercises, two cases, and a video case.

The following Bottom Line lays out the basic step-by-step procedure that will help you to master the key management skills needed for success in real-world organizations. You will see this process used throughout the book as the general framework for enhancing your skill-development process.

Read the scenario in the following Real-World Management Challenge and develop an action plan for handling the situation. This was an actual challenge that Toys "R" Us had to tackle. Later you will be able to compare your plan to the actions that management actually took to handle the situation.

Real-World Management Challenge

Fixing Toys "R" Us—Not Child's Play

The Situation

Toys "R" Us was started by Charles Lazarus in 1948 when he decided to sell baby furniture in his father's bike store. Lazarus then started opening toy supermarkets that provided customers with a wide selection of toys. In 1957, these stores were renamed as Toys "R" Us.

Over time, Toys "R" Us went on to become the world's largest toy retailer. The emergence of toys like Barbie and video game systems from Atari, Nintendo, and Sega enabled the company to generate $4.8 billion in sales in 1990.

The 1990s became a period of turmoil for the company. New competitors such as Wal-Mart, Target, and online retailer eToys exerted great pressure on Toys "R" Us. In fact, in

The Bottom Line: Mastering Management Skills

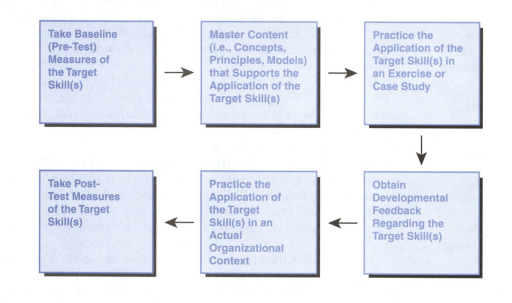

Take Baseline (Pre-Test) Measures of the Target Skill(s) → Master Content (i.e., Concepts, Principles, Models) that Supports the Application of the Target Skill(s) → Practice the Application of the Target Skill(s) in an Exercise or Case Study → Obtain Developmental Feedback Regarding the Target Skill(s) → Practice the Application of the Target Skill(s) in an Actual Organizational Context → Take Post-Test Measures of the Target Skill(s)

SKILLS IN THE GLOBAL LABOR MARKET

With lowered trade barriers, the growth of electronic communications, and the search for new markets and labor forces, firms and their management are becoming increasingly global. As just one illustration of this, a record number of foreign CEOs are now running major companies in the United States.* These include Fred Hassan, the Pakistani head of pharmaceutical giant Pharmacia & Upjohn; Alain Belda, a native of French Morocco and now a Brazilian citizen, who is CEO of Alcoa; and Samir (Sam) Gibara, the Egyptian head of Goodyear Tire & Rubber Co.

Surveys show that the number of international assignments of employees is expected to accelerate in the next five years. However, many people fail in international assignments, and almost half say they would not work abroad again. Between 20 percent and 40 percent return to their home country early, and many quit their firms within a year of returning.[†] This all suggests that employees often lack the skills needed to succeed in international positions. For example, such assignments require employees to be especially attuned to cultural differences and to subtle nuances of nonverbal communication, to adapt to change, to work in diverse teams, to be sensitive to others' perceptions, and to tailor their leadership and motivational behaviors to fit national differences.

*D. B. K. Lyons and S. Stuart, "International CEOs on the Rise," *Chief Executive,* February 2000, pp. 51–53.

†Ibid. See also M. Goldsmith, C. Walt, and K. Doucet, "New Competencies for Tomorrow's Global Leader," *CMA Management,* December 1999/January 2000, pp. 20–24; and J. P. Neelankavil, A. Mathur, and Y. Zhang, "Determinants of Managerial Performance: A Cross-Cultural Comparison of the Perceptions of Middle-Level Managers in Four Countries," *Journal of International Business Studies,* First Quarter 2000, pp. 121–140.

1998, Wal-Mart surpassed Toys "R" Us to become the #1 toy retailer in the United States. Toys "R" Us lost $132 million that same year.

Problems at Toys "R" Us peaked during the 1999 Christmas shopping season, in which it was unable to stock store shelves with popular toys. This problem was even more severe at its online store, ToysRUs.com, where it was unable to deliver many orders to customers before Christmas day.

The disastrous 1999 Christmas season resulted in badly damaged customer relations. Many customers were absolutely furious with the quality of service they received from Toys "R" Us sales associates. Stores were inundated with customer complaints about unfriendly and unknowledgeable sales associates. Moreover, customers found that the stores were also dirty and poorly maintained. Finally, a recent survey of customer attitudes toward major retailers put Toys "R" Us near the very bottom in areas of customer service and value.

The year 2001 is a critical year for the company as it attempts to turn itself around. However, ongoing tough competition from other toy retailers and the lack of a "must-have" toy like Furbie or Tickle Me Elmo will make it an uphill battle.

What Would You Do?

Suppose that you were the manager put in charge of implementing a turnaround at Toys "R" Us. What would you do? Be as specific as possible in developing the various elements of your program.

Source: "Toy Story," *Business Week*, December 4, 2000, p. 128.

THE MANAGEMENT SKILLS FRAMEWORK

Many practitioners and scholars have attempted to list and classify key managerial skills.[33] The lists, generated from observation of effective and ineffective managers, surveys of CEOs, managers, and interviewers, and other methodologies, show rather remarkable similarities. For example, most lists contain the skills of communicating, interpersonal relations, planning and goal setting, problem solving, managing conflict, motivating others, managing change, and teamwork. Some lists contain additional skills such as stress management, time management, strategic planning, delegating, group problem solving, and building power and influence. We will address each of these skills in this text.

Attempts to place managerial skills into categories generally yield three or four skills sets. For example, the skills may be classified as technical, interpersonal or human, and conceptual (as seen in Figure 1-3),[34] or as technical, human, political, and conceptual.[35] Technical skills include knowledge about methods, processes, and techniques designed to carry out some specialized activity as well as the ability to use tools and equipment related to the activity.[36] Interpersonal or human skills (sometimes split into human and political skills) deal with human behavior and interpersonal processes, communication, cooperation, and social sensitivity. Conceptual skills include analytical ability, creativity, efficiency in problem solving, and ability to recognize opportunities and potential problems. Thus, the typology distinguishes between abilities to deal with things, people, and ideas and concepts.

Our management skills framework, presented in Figure 1-7, focuses on human and conceptual skills. We classify the skills as primarily personal (such as self-management and critical thinking), interpersonal (such as communicating

FIGURE 1-7
Management Skills Framework

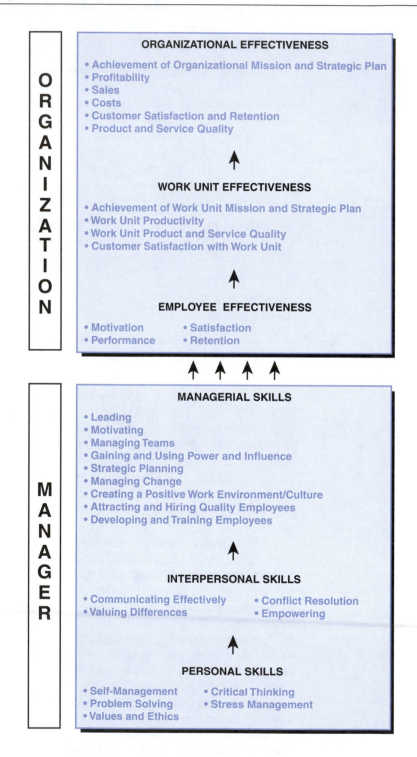

and resolving conflict), and managerial (such as leading, motivating, managing teams, strategic planning, and creating a positive work culture). Thus, each of these sets contains some skills that are conceptual and some that are human. We view the three sets as at least partly sequential. For instance, the ability to think critically may facilitate valuing of differences or conflict resolution, and the ability to communicate effectively or to empower others may assist in leading, motivating, and managing teams. The figure should not be taken to suggest that the categories are completely distinct, or that elements of one are not relevant to another. Instead, the intent is to provide a primary framework for classification of skills.

Further, our framework considers three levels of effectiveness—employee, work unit, and organizational. Employee effectiveness may be gauged by motivation, performance, participation behaviors (such as attendance and retention), and personal well-being and satisfaction. Work-unit effectiveness may relate to achievement of the work unit's mission and strategic plan, productivity, quality, and customer satisfaction. Finally, organizational effectiveness may take such forms as achievement of the organizational mission and strategic plan, profitability, customer satisfaction, and other criteria. As discussed in Chapter 2, we view organizational effectiveness broadly and do not consider it only in terms of profitability or shareholder returns. Again, we see these levels of effectiveness as sequential; employee effectiveness is an input to work-unit effectiveness that in turn fosters organizational effectiveness. We do not mean to imply that these relationships are simple or automatic, or that, for example, an effective work unit cannot facilitate employee effectiveness.

ACTION PLANNING AND IMPLEMENTATION

Recall that one of the things that you did in this chapter was to develop an action plan in the Pre-Test Skills Assessment activity. Similarly, you were asked to develop an action plan for the Real-World Management Challenge. You will be doing quite a bit of action plan development throughout this book as you work through the various exercises and learning activities in each chapter. Given this, let's talk a bit about what action planning is and what you need to do to apply it effectively.

Action planning is one of the most important activities that you will engage in as a manager. This refers to the process through which a manager formulates the specific steps that will be taken to address business problems and challenges. In the real world, the issue of what needs to be done is always a bottom-line concern. The action plan becomes the blueprint or road map for actual implementation. We will discuss action planning together with implementation, as they should be processes that are inextricably linked with one another. Unfortunately, many organizations fail to recognize this important link.

Here are some basic guidelines for developing and implementing effective action plans. First, the process *must* be systematic and actively managed. A manager needs to start with a clear understanding of his or her objectives and how to achieve them through the implementation of specific action steps.

In the real world, managers face complex and rapidly changing business environments, so a systematic process is needed. This is a challenge for many students who are more comfortable with an unstructured and spontaneous approach. Second, action planning requires a "layering" approach, in which action steps are translated into specific supporting actions in relation to each employee who will be involved with implementation. The basic question here is, "Who will be responsible for doing what in the implementation process?" Finally, there must be ongoing and systematic evaluation of the results achieved after the implementation of the action plan. This is absolutely critical in order to maintain a focus on achieving your bottom-line objectives as a manager. Again, this part of the process seems straightforward enough on the surface, but it requires ongoing effort on the part of the manager in order to evaluate the effectiveness of the action plan and to make appropriate modifications to ensure its long-term success.

A summary of the basic steps associated with developing and implementing an action plan is presented in the following Bottom Line.

Now complete the action planning exercise in Skills Practice 1-4. This will give you an opportunity to apply the basic steps of the action planning process to a specific management situation.

BOTTOM LINE

The Bottom Line: Action Planning and Implementation

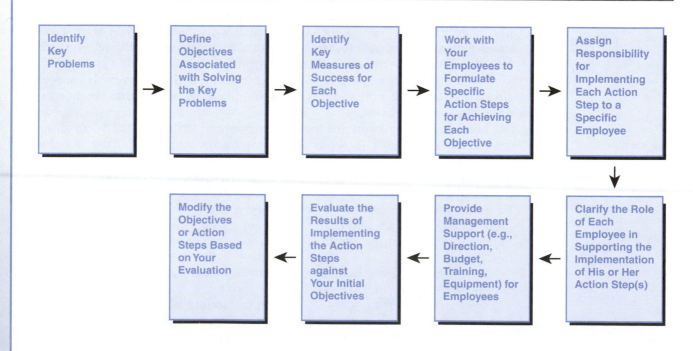

Identify Key Problems → Define Objectives Associated with Solving the Key Problems → Identify Key Measures of Success for Each Objective → Work with Your Employees to Formulate Specific Action Steps for Achieving Each Objective → Assign Responsibility for Implementing Each Action Step to a Specific Employee →

Clarify the Role of Each Employee in Supporting the Implementation of His or Her Action Step(s) → Provide Management Support (e.g., Direction, Budget, Training, Equipment) for Employees → Evaluate the Results of Implementing the Action Steps against Your Initial Objectives → Modify the Objectives or Action Steps Based on Your Evaluation

Skills Practice 1-4
Action Planning and Implementation

Skill Objective
To develop skill in creating action plans for addressing organizational problems and challenges.

Procedure
1.   This exercise can be completed on an individual basis or in groups of 3–5 students.
2.   Select and read one of the management scenarios below and develop an appropriate action plan using the action planning (Bottom Line) model described above. Record your plan on a piece of paper.

Management Scenario #1
You are the manager of an upscale continental restaurant located in downtown Chicago. Although the restaurant has a good reputation in general, you have been experiencing a variety of operational problems. First, food quality has been declining. Part of this is due to the fact that you have a new, less experienced head chef working in the kitchen. Second, you have been cutting some corners when ordering ingredients in order to reduce your costs. Third, customers have become increasingly frustrated with the 45–60 minute waits they have had to endure before being seated, even if they had reservations. The host who takes reservations has been overbooking reservations by 25 percent in order to ensure that the dining room is full at all times and to account for the fact that some people with reservations fail to show up. Fourth, you are concerned about the quality of service your servers are providing for guests. Some of them do not possess very customer service–oriented attitudes and it definitely shows in their interactions with guests. The servers also have been experiencing a high level of job stress as the number of servers scheduled to work each shift has declined. Consequently, each server has to handle an average of 25 tables each night as opposed to the 15 tables that was considered to be standard in the past.

Based on this situation, develop an action plan for addressing this situation and describe how you would manage the implementation process.

Management Scenario #2
You are the president of a business student organization that is suffering from a variety of problems. First, there are only 20 students who are considered to be members of the organization, but only about four (including yourself) that are involved to a significant degree. Second, the organization really lacks a clear sense of what it is supposed to be (i.e., what are its objectives?). Although it is a professional business student organization, most of the organization's activities have involved socializing and going out to the bars together. Third, the organization is virtually broke. The most recent bank statement you received showed an account balance of $10.

Based on this situation, develop an action plan for addressing this situation and describe how you would manage the implementation process.

3.   *(optional)* Present a summary of your action plan to the class and discuss it.
4.   Answer the following discussion questions.

Discussion Questions
1.   Evaluate the effectiveness of your action planning process. What were the most challenging aspects of the process? To what extent were you able to follow the steps in the action planning process model?

2. Identify and discuss the specific strengths and weaknesses of the action steps in your plan. Explain why you feel that the issues you identified are strengths and weaknesses.

3. What are the practical implications of this exercise for you as a future manager?

Skills Practice 1-5

Skill Level: **Challenging**

Developing My Management Skills Mastery Plan

Skill Objective

To evaluate your personal strengths and weaknesses and to identify specific management knowledge and skill objectives that you want to achieve after reading this book.

Procedure

1. Think about yourself in the context of how you have performed as a student and as an employee in your part-time jobs. Try to identify what you feel are your key personal strengths. These may include things such as the ability to get along with different types of people, teamwork skills, organizational skills, working well under pressure, analytical skills, and so on. Be as frank as possible in making this self-evaluation. List these key personal strengths on a piece of paper.

2. Again, think about yourself in the context of how you have performed as a student and as an employee in your part-time jobs. Try to identify what you feel are your key personal weaknesses. These may include things such as making decisions too quickly, not listening well to other people, failing to manage your time, not being open to different viewpoints, and so on. Although it is more difficult to do when examining your personal weaknesses (or "opportunities for improvement"), be as frank as possible in making this self-evaluation. List your key personal opportunities for improvement on a separate piece of paper.

3. Now, looking at the personal strengths and weaknesses you identified above, identify 3 to 7 key *knowledge objectives* (i.e., things that you want to know or understand) that you want to achieve by the time you have finished reading this book. These objectives should be things that you feel will be important for you once you become a manager in an actual organization after graduation. List these on a separate piece of paper.

4. Now, looking at the personal strengths and weaknesses you identified above, identify 3 to 7 key *skill objectives* (i.e., things that you want to be able to do) that you want to achieve by the time you have finished reading this book. These objectives should be things that you feel will be important for you once you become a manager in an actual organization after graduation. List these on a separate piece of paper.

5. Keep this plan for future reference, as you will use this as a basis for evaluating how much you have learned at the end of the book!

TOP TEN LIST: KEY POINTS TO REMEMBER

THE MANAGEMENT CHALLENGE: CRITICAL SKILLS FOR THE NEW WORKPLACE

10. Management effectiveness is a key determinant of organizational success or failure.

9. The skills needed for success in college and the skills needed for success in the business world are very different.

8. Managers must identify specific strategies for taking what they know about effective management and translating it into specific action.

7. The skills you learn from this book will be valuable to you even if you do not obtain a managerial or super-

visory job immediately after graduating from college.

6. Action planning is a systematic process for identifying appropriate steps to take to address a given problem or challenge.

5. It is the implementation or execution of business plans that is the key determinant of the ultimate success of an organization.

4. Learning is a lifelong process.

3. Use your Management Skills Mastery Plan to keep yourself focused on achieving specific learning objectives by the time you complete this book.

2. Developing management skills will greatly enhance your preparation for the real world of business organizations.

1. Effective management in the real world involves much more than just common sense.

QUESTIONS FOR REVIEW AND REFLECTION

REVIEW QUESTIONS

1. How are management skills related to company success?

2. What is some evidence that companies are concerned about employees' managerial skills and believe those skills can be learned?

3. What are 16 critical "skills employers want"?

4. Identify seven primary differences between determinants of success in school and business.

5. What are six developments in the modern workplace that are making managerial skills more important?

6. What is the knowing–doing gap? How might it be overcome?

7. Describe the steps in the social learning perspective and indicate which text features address each step.

8. Discuss the management skills framework on which the text is based.

9. Identify the stages of action planning and implementation.

CRITICAL THINKING QUESTIONS

1. As noted in the chapter, the Bureau of Labor Statistics predicts that the average 22-year-old college graduate in the year 2000 will have more than eight different employers before he or she reaches the age of 32. Consider the skills listed in Figure 1-1.
   a. Which of these skills might become more important because of frequent job changes?
   b. Which of these skills might be enhanced by frequent job changes?
   c. Which of these skills might be jeopardized by frequent job changes?
   For each answer, justify your choices.

2. The chapter discusses reasons for the knowing–doing gap. We indicated in our discussion of the text philosophy that it is also important to have a solid understanding of concepts in order to apply skills properly. The lack of that understanding might constitute a "doing–knowing gap." What characteristics of individuals and work environments might foster a doing–knowing gap?

3. Upon hearing that the Bureau of Labor Statistics projects that young college graduates will stay with an employer an average of just 15 months, a CEO says, "We need to rethink the value of skills training. Why should we be spending money to train someone who will probably only be here for a year or so?" How would you respond?

4. Consider the following characteristics of today's workplace: (a) globalization, (b) downsizing, (c) increasing diversity, and (d) increasing rates of change. For each of the trends, discuss how it might impact the importance of one of the skills listed in Figure 1-1.

5. When told that a company has a policy of "hiring for the second job"—that is, of considering skill requirements not just of the entry-level job but also of higher-level jobs in making a selection decision—a job applicant says, "That's not fair. I'm applying for an entry-level job, and I have good qualifications for that job. I'm not applying to be a manager." Do you agree with the applicant's argument? Why or why not?

6. We indicated that one philosophy of the text is that managerial skills should be directed toward enhancing both personal and organizational outcomes. Do you agree that managers should pay attention to things that may have no direct impact on organizational outcomes? Why or why not?

EXPERIENTIAL EXERCISES

WEB EXERCISE 1-1: *FORTUNE* SKILLS ARTICLES

Go to the *Fortune* magazine website at *http://www.fortune.com/fortune/*. In the "Search Fortune" box, type "skills." You will be given a listing of more than 1,000 *Fortune* articles dealing with skills, with titles such as "Are You Smart Enough to Keep Your Job?," "What Team Leaders Need to Know," "How Safe Is Your Job?," "Really Important Things You Need to Know," and "You Are Absolutely, Positively On Your Own." By clicking on a title, you will be given the full text of the article.

1. Select any two articles from the search.
2. Provide a one- to two-page summary of each article.
3. For each article, select one fact or idea that you think is especially important for your future career. Discuss the fact or idea and indicate why you think it is important.

WEB EXERCISE 1-2: HUMAN PRINCIPLES FROM NINE PRIVATE-SECTOR ORGANIZATIONS

The U.S. General Accounting Office (GAO) is the investigative arm of Congress. GAO exists to support Congress in meeting its constitutional responsibilities and help improve the performance and accountability of the federal government for the American people. In January 2000, the GAO released a report titled, "Human Capital: Key Principles from Nine Private Sector Organizations." The report calls for federal managers to turn to the private sector to find examples they "may wish to consider as they steer their agencies toward higher performance." The report also discusses 10 "Principles of Human Capital" based on the experience of such private-sector firms as Federal Express Corp., Marriott International, Merck & Co., Motor-

ola, and Southwest Airlines. Read the report at *http://frwebgate.access.gpo.gov/cgi-bin/useftp.cgi?IPaddress=162.140.64.21&filename=gg00028.txt&directory=/diskb/wais/data/gao* and then respond to the following questions:

1. What are the 10 principles identified in the report?
2. Select and discuss any one of the principles, based on information presented in the report and your own knowledge concerning the principle.
3. Summarize one of the case illustrations related to the selected principle.
4. Do you think federal agencies would be able to successfully implement the principle? Why or why not?

CASE 1-1
NOT YOUR DAD'S CAR ANYMORE—THE TRANSFORMATION OF CADILLAC

History of the Company

Cadillac is the luxury division of General Motors Corporation, the world's largest automaker. Cadillac has been around for almost 100 years now. Most Americans considered it to be the "Standard of the World" during the 1950s and 1960s. In those days, owning a Cadillac, with its signature tail fins and generous application of chrome, meant that "you had made it." Cadillac was the choice of vehicle among celebrities like Elvis Presley and Marilyn Monroe. At its peak in 1978, Cadillac sold 347,000 cars a year, making it the undisputed king of luxury cars in the United States.[39]

The Decline of an American Icon

However, in the late 1970s through the early 1990s, Cadillac began a gradual but dramatic slide in sales, profits, and prestige. The oil crisis in the 1970s resulted in customers seeking more fuel-efficient vehicles. Foreign competition from Japanese automakers such as Toyota and Honda flooded the U.S. market with high-quality, reliable, and fuel-efficient vehicles. Later, this led to the creation of luxury car lines, including Lexus, Infiniti, and Acura, that set new benchmarks for quality, performance, and luxury in the industry. Although European car makers (e.g., Mercedes-

Benz, BMW, Audi, and Jaguar) experienced some set-backs from Japanese competition as well, this led to large-scale transformations at these companies that produced a wide range of new luxury vehicles that were truly "world class." This has been especially true in the cases of Jaguar and Audi.

Meanwhile, Cadillac (and Lincoln, its domestic luxury car maker counterpart) clung to their traditional customer base by offering large sedans and coupes with powerful engines but "floaty" rides that some drivers described as being like "sailing on a yacht." Increasingly the traditional vehicles that Cadillac offered became less and less appealing to younger consumers.

Cadillac has often taken too many shortcuts in its product development. This has manifested itself in the form of "badge engineering," in which a vehicle from another General Motors division such as Chevrolet or Oldsmobile was taken, some cosmetic changes were made to the vehicle, and a Cadillac badge was attached to the vehicle. Savvy car drivers saw right through this strategy, though. This diluted and tarnished the Cadillac brand name. The most recent examples of this include the Catera entry-level luxury sedan, which is based on an Opel (a GM subsidiary in Germany) platform, and the Escalade, a luxury sport-utility vehicle that was rushed to market in less than a year based on the Chevrolet/GMC Tahoe and Yukon.[40]

The Current Situation

Today, when the name "Cadillac" is mentioned to consumers in their 20s and 30s, a common response is that these are cars for "older people in their 60s" or that a Cadillac is "their Dad's car." Cadillac has lost its position as the top-seller of luxury vehicles in the United States (Mercedes-Benz and Lexus were ahead of Cadillac in the 2000 calendar year). Cadillac sales have been stuck at around 180,000 vehicles per year.

In the area of quality and dependability, reviews from auto analysts and closely watched annual surveys of consumers such as JD Power and Associates and Consumer Reports have provided mixed results for the most part. For example, Cadillac rarely ranks among the top vehicles in JD Power and Associates initial quality surveys. None of its vehicles ranked among the top three in any category in the 2000 study.[41] Although Cadillac has traditionally scored well in the JD Power Five-Year Vehicle Dependability Study,

it fell to 11th place in the 2000 study from its more traditional ranking of 1st or 2nd (after Lexus).[42]

The greatest threat for Cadillac is that it is not even considered by many consumers when they are in the market for a luxury vehicle. Moreover, the average age of a Cadillac customer is about 67 years old. Cadillac's core customer base is literally dying off.

Management Actions

However, don't be so fast in counting out Cadillac in the global luxury vehicle race. Management at Cadillac has a plan that it hopes will revive Cadillac and once again make it the "Standard of the World." Although Cadillac has attempted to reinvent itself before, there is good reason to be cautiously optimistic this time. Michael O'Malley, the new head of the Cadillac division, is in the midst of implementing Cadillac's turnaround strategy. The cornerstones of the new Cadillac strategy revolve around a freshening of its corporate logo to give it a more contemporary look and new marketing concepts called "Art and Science" and the "Power of &." These new strategies have led to a new design philosophy that has produced futuristic-looking vehicles with sharp edges and creases. Some examples of vehicles designed with this approach are the 2002 Cadillac Escalade and the 2003 Cadillac Evoq roadster. Cadillac also participated in the 24-hour LeMans race in 2000 for the first time since 1950. This was done in order to enhance the visibility of Cadillac as a global brand name and to associate the name more with high-performance racing.

Cadillac management fully recognizes the stakes involved with their current turnaround strategy. In fact, some GM insiders have speculated that unless Cadillac can pull off its current turnaround, it could very well die. David Cole, the managing director of the University of Michigan's Office of Automotive Transportation, believes that Cadillac can come back, "if they execute well."[43]

Discussion Questions

1. What kinds of management problems contributed to Cadillac's current situation?
2. What kinds of management skills will be needed at Cadillac in order to successfully implement its turn-around strategy?
3. Evaluate Cadillac's turnaround strategy. Do you think it will work? Why or why not?
4. What are the implications of this case for you as a future manager?

CASE 1-2
MANAGING RISK AND UNCERTAINTY AT NAPSTER

The Company

Napster, the world's largest file sharing community, enables users to share a variety of media files with each other. The company was founded in May 1999 by Shawn Fanning, a Northeastern University student who dropped out to focus on developing the technology for Napster. Fanning created the original Napster application, which allows users to share music files with each other.[44] Napster's headquarters are based in Redwood City, California. Presently, Napster employs about 45 people.

On June 1, 1999, Napster officially began its operations and became an instant hit with approximately 4,000 people downloading its software program for sharing music files. By the fall of 1999, "Napster Fever" was spreading like wildfire through the campuses of U.S. colleges and universities. In some cases, schools decided to ban Napster because it had become so popular that it was using up a significant portion of the schools' bandwidth.

The Situation

Napster quickly encountered legal challenges from the RIAA (Recording Industry Association of America), which alleged that Napster was guilty of copyright infringement. RIAA filed a lawsuit against Napster demanding $100,000 for each "illegal" copy of a song that was made.

Napster's chief strategist, Jon Fanning (Shawn's uncle), studied legal cases that set relevant precedents regarding the "fair use" of material, and he strongly believed that Napster was in the right and would emerge victorious from its legal battles.

In September 1999, Napster hired Eileen Richardson as the company's first chief executive officer. It became apparent very quickly that Richardson did not possess the experience or the appropriate leadership style to handle the daunting challenges facing Napster at the time.[45] Richardson was arrogant and extremely abrasive in dealing with the record companies that were suing Napster. Employees and observers felt that Richardson's style destroyed any hope of negotiating any kind of a compromise with the RIAA. This was a huge missed opportunity because it may have been possible to reach an agreement if there had been more constructive dialogue between Richardson and the RIAA.

Over time, Napster grew to an operation employing 15 people, and with this came the need for skilled and experienced management that could help Napster to negotiate a settlement with the recording industry and to develop an actual "business model" that would enable Napster to make a profit. On May 21, 2000, Napster brought in a new CEO, Hank Berry, who it felt had the right mix of knowledge and skills to find some common ground among the "warring parties" and, it hoped, to reach a settlement.

New CEO Berry hired a couple of experienced executives from the music industry and held constructive discussions with companies from the record industry. Barry's focus was on selling record companies on the benefits of Napster to them. The only serious issue of contention was licensing issues (i.e., payments of royalties for downloading music).

On July 26, 2000, a U.S. District Judge ruled in favor of the recording industry and ordered Napster to stop allowing people to share copyrighted material (e.g., songs) with each other. Although this appeared to be a devastating blow to Napster, the Ninth U.S. Circuit Court of Appeals ruled just two days later that the company should be allowed to continue its operations.

Analysts feel that Napster and the recording industry should try to find a way to work together, possibly by having Napster charge a subscription fee to its users.

In November 2000, Bertelsmann, the world's third largest media company, struck a deal with Napster that would give Napster $50 million to develop software that would require users to pay a fee for downloading music. In return, Bertelsmann agreed to drop its lawsuit against Napster and to encourage other record companies to do the same.[46] The long-term objectives would be to develop a business model that would capitalize on Napster's technology in the future and would have Napster serve as a platform for offering other types of media as downloadable files (e.g., books, movies).

The Bertelsmann plan is filled with risks and uncertainties. How many of Napster's current users would be receptive to having to pay to download music files? Can Napster successfully modify its software to protect the copyright associated with various music files? Can Bertelsmann be successful in changing the positions of other recording companies in terms of getting them to withdraw their lawsuits and cooperate with Napster?

Discussion Questions

1. What are the key management challenges facing Napster?
2. What types of management skills are needed most given Napster's situation? Why?

3. What recommendations would you give to Napster management about what they should do to handle their current situation?
4. What are the practical implications of this case for you as a future manager?

VIDEO CASE
THE EVOLUTION OF MANAGEMENT:
A STUDY OF SUNSHINE CLEANING SYSTEMS, JIAN, AND ARCHWAY COOKIES

Running Time: 14:28

This video discusses three successful companies—Sunshine Cleaning Systems, JIAN, and Archway Cookies—that face very different environments and have chosen to rely on distinct philosophies in managing organizational behavior.

The video shows executives and other employees from each of the companies as they discuss the ways their companies have met the challenges of their competitive environments. After viewing the video, answer the following questions:

1. In what ways, such as markets, technologies, available labor pool, and other dimensions, do the environments of Sunshine, JIAN, and Archway differ?
2. According to the video, what are the respective philosophies adopted by Sunshine, JIAN, and Archway? Describe each of these philosophies.
3. Why is a loyal and dedicated workforce so important

to Sunshine? What steps has Sunshine taken to earn employee loyalty and dedication?
4. How has the competitive environment faced by JIAN shaped its management approaches? What sort of employees does JIAN need? What has JIAN done to create an organization that takes advantage of its strengths?
5. What are some signs that Archway has been successful in developing a satisfied and effective workforce?
6. What steps has Archway taken to ensure that it produces and delivers quality cookies?
7. Could the approaches taken by Sunshine, JIAN, and Archway be used together? Why or why not?

http://www.jian.com/
http://www.archwaycookies.com/

LIGHTEN UP[47]
PERFORMANCE!

Companies are seeking creative ways to develop their employees' skills, and many are turning to literature, music, and the arts. When management consulting firm McKinsey & Company wanted to develop its employees' abilities to inspire, it hired outsiders to help the firm's consultants and partners write and stage an opera in three days. At Sears, Lockheed Martin, and Bristol Myers Squibb, a conductor and symphony orchestra rehearse Brahms to bring alive issues of leadership and teamwork for aspiring top managers. Kodak, Arthur Anderson, and

Boeing have brought in poets to foster employees' creativity. Still other firms are using Shakespeare's *Henry V* as a case study on vision, strategy, and leadership skills, or are having employees act out playlets. Companies increasingly are coming to believe that, in an economy where firms such as Amazon.com have found ways to recombine resources to redefine whole industries, skills fostering vision, flair, and creativity are the new fuel. The arts are a natural reservoir for that fuel.

CHAPTER  *Two*

THE ORGANIZATIONAL CONTEXT: SEEING THE BIG PICTURE

SKILLS OBJECTIVES

> To develop appropriate measures of organizational effectiveness.
> To perform an environmental scan.
> To write an effective mission statement.
> To develop an overall strategic plan for an organization.

KNOWLEDGE OBJECTIVES

> Describe key environmental domains and characteristics.
> Discuss ways to assess organizational effectiveness.
> Identify steps in the strategic planning process.
> Understand the steps in strategic analysis.
> Discuss objective setting, including purpose, vision, and mission.
> Discuss corporate-level strategies, including grand strategies and portfolio strategies.
> Explain business-unit-level strategies, including use of the adaptation model and the competitive model.
> Discuss steps in implementing and evaluating strategies.

When IBM chose Louis V. Gerstner, Jr., then CEO of RJR Nabisco, as its Chairman and CEO, it handed him a monumental task. Critics of IBM argued that it was too bureaucratic, too slow in shifting its emphasis from the declining mainframe computer market to personal computers, had a labor force that should be cut by 80,000–100,000 employees, and was preoccupied with its own view of the world. As an outsider to the computer industry, Gerstner was seen as lacking technical knowledge, but a tough manager who could provide fresh perspectives and would not be constrained by the tradition and culture of IBM. The business world waited anxiously to see what strategies Gerstner would pursue. In taking over the reins of IBM, Gerstner faced many of the key issues considered in this chapter. He said, "What IBM needs right now is a series of very tough-minded, market-driven, highly effective strategies in each of its businesses." In this chapter, we consider the "big picture" facing firms, including how highly effective strategies are developed in the face of environmental demands.

Just as the coach of a basketball team must develop a "game plan" to guide her team during competition, leaders of organizations, such as Louis Gerstner, need a game plan that will enable the firm to meet its goals over the course of several years. In developing a strategic plan, leaders must consider the firm's past performance, current position, and goals and answer four strategic questions:

> How do we respond to new opportunities in the environment, lessen the impact of threats from the environment, and strengthen the mix of the organization's activities by doing more of some things and less of others?
> How do we assign resources among the various subunits, divisions, and activities of the organization?
> How do we compete with other organizations for customers through allocation of existing or new products and services?
> How do we effectively manage organizational activities at the departmental, divisional, and corporate levels of the organization?

We begin this chapter with a look at domains and characteristics of the organizational environment. We then consider approaches to determining organizational effectiveness and discuss the strategic planning process. Next, we offer guidelines for conducting a strategic analysis, for establishing a purpose, vision, and mission, and for defining strategic objectives. Following this, we discuss approaches for choosing corporate-level strategies and business-unit-level strategies. We conclude with suggestions for implementing and evaluating the strategic plan.

You will benefit more from this chapter—and those that follow—if you do some self-reflection in the process. The following two activities will help you do this. First, complete the brief self-assessment questionnaire (Self-Assessment 2-1) regarding your attitudes toward the material to be covered in this chapter. You'll be able to compare your answers to those of other college students and business professionals. Then do the Pre-Test Skills Assessment on strategic planning, relating to starting an Internet-based company. After reading the scenario, develop an outline that summarizes what you would do to handle the situation. The goal of the exercise is to help you better understand where you are starting out in terms of your understanding of this material.

DEVIL'S ADVOCATE

Some managers I have talked to in the "real world" told me that planning is a waste of time because it takes your focus off of the "real work" of getting the job done. How would you respond to this?
Well, if managers do not have a clear sense of their goals and how to achieve them, how would they know what to do? The kinds of problems managers face in the "real world" are oftentimes very complex. In addition, the environments in which managers operate tend to be quite dynamic. This makes the job of a manager even more difficult. These realities underscore the importance of having a good plan of action.

The benefits of a good strategic plan far outweigh the time needed to develop it, since it represents a framework or roadmap for the manager to achieve the goals of the work unit. So the bottom line is that a strategic plan is "real work" and very important work as well!

How can a mission statement possibly be of value when it is so broad and general?
A useful way of thinking about strategic plans is that they are made up of layers of goals and strategies for achieving them. Each layer has a different timeframe and degree of specificity. The starting point of the strategic plan is the mission statement. This represents a basic statement of the fundamental purpose of the organization. That is, why does the organization exist? What kind of organization does it want to be? What is important to the organization? These are basic but important questions that managers need to address in the beginning of the planning process. Although the mission statement itself is rather broad, it is critical to the success of an organization in that it also provides the foundation for developing more specific goals and action plans for the organization as a whole and for each of the divisions and work units within the firm.

Isn't strategic planning only something that the CEO and vice presidents would worry about? It's not really of concern to lower-level supervisors and managers, is it?
Actually, strategic planning occurs across many levels of management. Although the focus of senior managers will be the organization as a whole, lower-level managers and supervisors will often need to develop strategic plans for their work units that support the strategic plan of the organization.

I have a part-time job at a restaurant and the management throws around terms like "competitive advantage," "leveraging core competencies," and "pursuing continuous improvement" as part of their strategic plan for the company. To tell you the truth, though, nothing has changed around this place. Why is it that strategic plans don't translate into actual implementation?
If a company develops a strategic plan but doesn't implement it, then this undermines the purpose of having a strategic plan! There is a lot of variation among companies in terms of how strong the linkage is between strategic plans and implementation. In order for strategic planning to be effective, it is critical that managers take the time to develop appropriate plans they believe will work and that they use the strategic plan as a basis for evaluating the success of the work unit and organization. The point is, managers must use strategic plans as the drivers of their day-to-day management decisions, not just as a necessary evil that has to be done every year and then thrown into some file until the next year.

Self-Assessment 2-1
Attitudes Toward the Organizational Context and Strategic Planning

Answer each of the questions in this section using the following scale:

1 = Disagree Strongly
2 = Disagree Somewhat
3 = Neither Agree nor Disagree
4 = Agree Somewhat
5 = Agree Strongly

1. _____ Organizations need a broad plan of action in order to achieve their goals.

2. _____ Senior executives should be the only people involved in the process of determining an organization's overall goals and strategies.

3. _____ An organization's overall plan for achieving its goals does not need to be communicated to lower-level employees in the firm.

4. _____ Management should focus on taking action and not on thinking about what to do.

5. _____ Departmental managers do not need to concern themselves with developing work-unit goals and strategies.

6. _____ Mission statements that state the long-term purpose and goals of an organization in very general terms are not valuable to management since they are so broad.

7. _____ If a company identifies an appropriate set of goals and strategies in its plan of action, then the effective implementation of the plan is very easy.

8. _____ Most employees understand what they can do to help support the achievement of the organization's goals and strategies.

9. _____ Management should update the organization's plan containing its goals and strategies every one to two years.

10. _____ The identification of an organization's goals and strategies should be based on an analysis of key trends in the company's industry and general external environment.

11. _____ The identification of an organization's goals and strategies should be based on an analysis of the company's major strengths and weaknesses.

12. _____ The goals and strategies of work units and departments in an organization should all support the goals and strategies of the overall firm.

Pre-Test Skills Assessment
Strategic Planning

You and two buddies have decided to start an Internet-based company that sells college textbooks. You have sufficient funds to establish your company, but you need to develop a "plan of action" that will enable you make your firm a success in the long term. Describe the steps you would take to develop your plan, what the elements of the plan would be, and how you would handle the implementation of the plan. *Be specific.*

THE ORGANIZATIONAL ENVIRONMENT

While managers' decisions are often made at a "micro" level, dealing with individuals and small groups, it is important to recognize that organizations operate within environments that largely dictate what policies and practices are feasible, desirable, and even necessary. In this section we will consider key environmental domains and environmental characteristics.

ENVIRONMENTAL DOMAINS

As shown in Figure 2-1, organizations operate in the context of six key environmental domains—economic, political, social, technological, competitive, and physical. The natures of these domains help define appropriate organizational strategies and practices.

The Economic Domain Many economic factors, such as interest rates, trade deficits, inflation rates, gross domestic product indicators, and the money sup-

FIGURE 2-1
Environmental Domains of an Organization

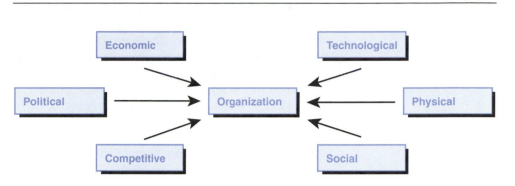

Web Wise

Political Risk Resources

This site offers links to resources on political risk-related information by country. The various resources include narratives, charts, and graphs on political risk, corruption ratings, U.S. government travel warnings, and other risk assessments for individual countries. Links are also provided to a variety of reports on the nature, components, and importance of political risk.

http://www.csupomona.edu/
~dhanne/polrisk.html

ply, may influence an organization's activities. Factors in the economic domain influence the ability of managers to get resources needed to produce goods and services and distribute those goods and services to a market. In addition, employees are likely to behave very differently depending on the nature of the economic environment. For instance, dissatisfied employees might stay with a company in a poor economy but may decide to leave the firm if the economy is good and other jobs are plentiful.

The Political Domain The political domain of the organization environment rests on laws and regulations passed by governmental agencies and legislative bodies. Legislation has been directed toward the elimination of discrimination based on gender, race, and age. Other legislation has been designed to bring about an end to sexual harassment in the workplace, prevent unfair pricing in markets, restrict pollution, protect consumers, discourage unethical behaviors, and regulate corporate taxation. However, the enforcement of these laws and regulations often varies because of differing beliefs by both political incumbents and the electorate about the need for such enforcement.

As companies are increasingly going global, a big consideration is the political risk associated with foreign governments. Political risk refers to the possibility that political decisions, conditions, or events in a country will affect the business climate in such a way that investors will lose money or will make less than they expected when the investment was made. For example, if there is a strong possibility that a country's government may suddenly change its policies, political risk is high. As such, examination of country political factors and associated risk is an important part of the decision process of multinational firms.[1]

The Social Domain The social domain of an organization's environment consists of societal values, attitudes, norms, customs, and demographics. Every society incorporates values and attitudes that may be uniform across a population or may vary by regional or ethnic groupings. Values are what people believe to be proper goals for members of the society to maintain or achieve. Attitudes reflect what individuals think about issues and behaviors that occur within a society.

In the United States, most citizens value freedom of speech as a necessary feature of their daily lives. They may, however, believe that other citizens are abusing that right. Citizens in other countries may feel that freedom of speech is unnecessary or is a value that only leads to disruption in their daily lives. Other values and attitudes that may differ by regions within a country or between countries concern the role of the family, the importance of clean air, and the role of religion in political institutions. Values and attitudes are often expressed in the legal codes of countries. The First Amendment of the United States Constitution, for example, guarantees the right of free speech to all citizens.

Values and attitudes, however, can change over time. Fifty years ago in the United States, many people viewed the role of "mother" as taking precedence over the mother's desire to work outside the home. This attitude has changed, despite some resistance, and over 50 percent of women with children under the age of six are now active in the workforce, up from just 12 percent in 1950. As another example, the idea of providing benefits to same-sex partners would have been considered radical until recently. However, as of mid-2000, 3,400 private and public employers in the United States, including about a fifth of the *Fortune* 500, provided domestic-partner benefits for lesbian and gay employees. Six of the top ten companies—General Motors, Ford, IBM, Citigroup Inc., AT&T, and Boeing—offer the benefits.[2]

The Technological Domain   The technological domain, or technology, refers to the application of knowledge to the production and distribution of goods and services. Technology is often viewed as a major source of environmental change for an organization. Technology is greatly affected by innovation. *Innovation* is the creation or modification of a process, product, or service. Innovation can occur at different rates, as can its transfer throughout the environment. *Technology transfer* involves the application of innovation to processes, products, or services either within or between industries. We will see many ways that technology and technological change are transforming organizations. Obvious examples are the growing use of personal computers and the explosion of the Internet. Coupled with these technological developments are fundamental changes in the way business is done, including the emergence of Web-based "dot com" companies such as Amazon.com.[3]

The Competitive Domain   Organizations can face a wide variety of competitive conditions in their environment. Some large organizations compete only with small organizations, often giving them an advantage in pricing of their products. Other competitive conditions arise from different mixes in the strategies that competitors pursue, as we will discuss later in this chapter.

Within a capitalistic system, organizations can compete in one of four competitive market structures: monopoly, oligopoly, monopolistic competition, or perfect competition. A *monopoly* exists when an organization has sole access to the market for its goods and services. In a monopoly situation, competitors either have been restricted from access to customers or have voluntarily chosen not to compete in the market. Restrictions to markets may occur when regulatory agencies or governments grant a single organization the right to provide a good or service to the market, such as in the case of utility agencies or police departments. An *oligopoly* exists when only a few firms are in competition to provide goods and services to a market. In this situation the number of firms producing a good or service is so small that actions by any single firm in the industry concerning price, output, product style, or terms of sale have a perceptible impact on the sales of the other firms. *Monopolistic competition* exists when many firms offer a similar good or service with only minor price differentials. For example, gasoline stations operate under conditions of monopolistic competition; customers may willingly spend a few cents more a gallon to avoid inconvenience, but will probably balk at a big price difference. *Perfect competition* exists when many organizations offer essentially the same good or service; price thus becomes the primary discriminator for the customer. Some agricultural commodities, such as wheat, operate in a market closely resembling perfect competition.

The competitive market structure is a major influence on a firm's strategies and practices. For example, a company in a monopoly position may have little need for flexibility and adaptability, and it may be able to offer its employees a stable and secure work environment. *Deregulation*—the relaxing of government controls on firms to permit greater competition—has transformed such industries as energy delivery, telecommunications, and financial services. Firms that were once in secure market positions now find themselves facing strong competition and pressured to be more responsive to market demands. This may require them to alter their structures, policies, and practices.

The Physical Domain All organizations must respond in some manner to factors in their physical domain. Weather conditions, for instance, may greatly influence the activities of a firm. Airlines must follow the location and movement of storm systems, construction companies in the upper Midwest must schedule their activities to avoid outside work during harsh winter months, and orange growers must make quick decisions about harvesting when frost warnings are issued.

The physical domain may also influence things such as availability of a large pool of qualified talent. For example, companies located in one of the "Best Places to Live," as identified, for instance, by *Money* magazine, may find themselves at an advantage.

http://www.money.com/money/bestplaces/fullranking.html

ENVIRONMENTAL DIMENSIONS

An organization's environment may vary on some important dimensions. Three such dimensions are *munificence, dynamism,* and *complexity.*

Munificence The *munificence* of an organization's environment refers to the level of resources available to the organization. The degree of munificence may range from rich to lean. Rich environments usually exist where resources are plentiful. However, a rich environment attracts other organizations, and, over time, environments will move from rich to lean. As such, rich environments usually exist in the early stages of industry development or under conditions of a monopoly market structure. When environments become lean, organizations may have to be more efficient in their use of resources or employ other tactics in order to survive.

Dynamism *Dynamism* refers to the rate of change in environmental factors. When environmental factors remain basically unchanged, the environment is stable. When those factors change rapidly, the environment is dynamic.

Complexity *Complexity* is the number of components in an organization's environment and the degree to which they are similar or different. An environment with few and similar components is less complex than one with many and varied components.

Together, dynamism and complexity influence the degree to which managers in an organization see the environment as unpredictable; this unpredictability is called *perceived environmental uncertainty.* In conditions where the environment is relatively uncertain, firms may have to emphasize flexibility and creativity over efficiency. Such an environment demands that managers and employees have sophisticated training and problem-solving skills. Conversely, a relatively certain environment may permit a firm to rely more heavily on standard routines and procedures. Since the environment holds few surprises, employees need fewer skills and ongoing training is less important. A recurring theme in future chapters is that organizational environments are increasingly dynamic and complex and thus that sophisticated skills and ongoing learning are crucial.

THE EFFECTIVE ORGANIZATION AND THE STRATEGIC PLANNING PROCESS

A key task of strategic planning is to make the organization more effective. But what *is* an effective organization? *Organizational effectiveness* can be defined as the degree to which the organization achieves its goals, maintains its health, secures resources needed for survival, and satisfies parties that have a stake in it.

This definition suggests that effectiveness has several dimensions. On one dimension, an organization is effective if it attains its goals. The approach to defining organizational effectiveness that focuses on this dimension is called the *goal assessment* approach. It is concerned with whether the organization reaches the growth, sales, profitability, or other goals management has set for it.

However, there are other ways to measure the effectiveness of an organization. For instance, is an organization effective if it is profitable but its workforce is unhappy? Is it effective if it has captured large markets this year but is faced with threats to its supplies of raw materials, labor, or capital? Is it effective if it boosts production capacity with new technology but in so doing upsets the local community or customers? These questions suggest three criteria, besides goal accomplishment, for measuring organizational effectiveness.

First, *internal process assessment* focuses on organizational health. According to this approach, an unhealthy organization cannot be called effective, regardless of profitability. This approach considers such measures of organizational health as employee satisfaction, levels of conflict, coordination of department activities, and production efficiency. Second, *systems resource assessment* considers whether an organization is able to acquire the resources it needs to survive and prosper. Social service agencies must acquire federal, state, or municipal funding to continue offering their services. Manufacturing firms must acquire labor and raw materials to continue operating. Biotechnology firms must have access to start-up capital and qualified scientists.

Finally, *strategic constituencies assessment* of effectiveness looks at groups inside or outside the organization that have a stake in it, such as cus-

VOICE OF EXPERIENCE

ORGANIZATIONAL EFFECTIVENESS

Manuel Perez,
Director of E-Commerce Strategy
Site Personnel Services, Inc.

1. What is the overall mission of your organization? What about its strategic objectives?

The mission of Site Personnel is "To provide high-quality staff personnel to clients in a manner that helps clients increase their revenue and helps us increase our own revenue." Our strategic objectives are: (1) to achieve 20 percent growth in market share this year, (2) to reduce overall operating costs by 12 percent this year, and (3) to transition the company fully to an Internet economy as a key driver of value.

2. What are the strategic objectives of your specific work unit? What kinds of strategies are you implementing to support the achievement of these objectives?

The mission of the E-Commerce Department, the area that I lead, is "To develop and maintain an e-commerce department that will support internal operations and marketing in order to increase revenue, decrease operating costs, and increase the valuation of the firm."

The strategic objectives of my unit for this year are: (1) to identify and increase the statistical contribution of information technology and e-commerce spending to the revenue and operations, (2) to decrease downtime on systems by 30 percent, and (3) to increase e-commerce systems usage by 25 percent.

There are many strategies I am implementing to support the mission and strategic objectives of my work unit and the organization. I have had to spend a lot of time building an effective e-commerce team. I also spend a lot of time analyzing and evaluating our current systems and educating internal users and senior management regarding e-commerce and information technology issues. I work very hard on developing rapport and credibility with my internal customers so that they feel that they can trust me and get their issues resolved on a timely basis. The issue of obtaining support from top management is critical for everything that I do. It's important that I view the role of information technology and e-commerce from a systems perspective, because it doesn't do any good if my area implements a new system and it is not aligned with the rest of the organization. Finally, I have developed critical measures of success for my unit based on my mission and objectives.

3. What are the biggest challenges you are facing in developing and implementing strategy in your work unit? How are you handling them?

I would say that the biggest challenges I have faced in implementing strategy are resistance to change from some employees and managers based on their concerns that change will threaten their established working relationships, fear of loss of control or power, and habit. Other challenges include being able to show that information technology spending impacts the overall valuation and operating costs of the firm.

4. What kind of advice would you give students regarding the development of overall organizational management skills?

Recognize the value of learning organizational behavior while you are still in school. Don't wait until you are in the corporate world to make mistakes in this area. They can be very costly. Develop a strong foundation in the major theories of organizational behavior, but recognize their limitations as well. Finally, make the practice of organizational behavior a priority every day you are at work. It really is critical to your success as a manager!

http://www.sitepersonnel.com/ site.htm

tomers, stockholders, the community, creditors, suppliers, and employees. According to this approach, an organization is effective when it has satisfied these important constituencies. The different approaches for assessing organizational effectiveness are shown in Figure 2-2. In determining whether an organization is effective, it is important to consider these various perspec-

FIGURE 2-2
Approaches to Assessing Organizational Effectiveness

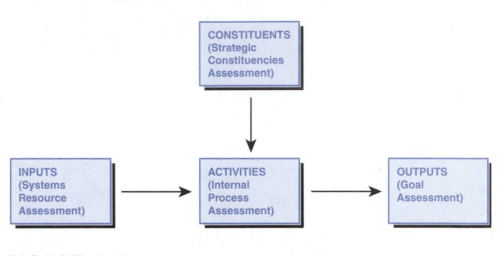

FIGURE 2-3
America's Most Admired and Least Admired Companies

The Top Ten	The Bottom Ten
1. General Electric	495. Humana
2. Microsoft	496. Revlon
3. Dell Computer	497. Trans World Airlines
4. Cisco Systems	498. CKE Restaurants
5. Wal-Mart Stores	499. CHS Electronics
6. Southwest Airlines	500. Rite Aid
7. Berkshire Hathaway	501. Trump Resorts
8. Intel	502. Fruit of the Loom
9. Home Depot	503. Amerco
10. Lucent Technologies	504. Caremark Rx

Source: E. Brown, "America's Most Admired Companies," *Fortune*, March 1, 1999, p. 68.

tives. Doing so highlights the fact that an organization, whatever its profits or losses this year or next, cannot be seen as truly effective if its workforce is dissatisfied and uncoordinated; if its sources of labor, materials, or finances are drying up; or if it is alienating important constituencies.

Every year *Fortune* magazine surveys more than 10,000 executives, directors, and securities analysts. They are told to choose the companies they admire most, regardless of industry. To create separate lists by industry, *Fortune* asked ballot recipients to rank companies in their own industry on eight criteria, ranging from long-term investment value to social responsibility. The result is an industry-by-industry guide to corporate America's best reputations. The results for 1999 are listed in Figure 2-3.

http://www.pathfinder.com/fortune/mostadmired/

Another way organizational effectiveness is assessed along multiple dimensions is with the Malcolm Baldrige National Quality Award. The award was established in 1987 to enhance U.S. competitiveness by promoting quality awareness, recognizing quality and business achievements of U.S. companies, and publicizing these companies' successful performance.[4] The award is based on rated performance on seven criteria: leadership, information and analysis, strategic planning, human resource development and measurement, process management, business results, and customer focus and satisfaction. Specific questions relating to each criterion are presented in Figure 2-4. Since 1988, 37 companies have received the award. The four 1999 winners of the award were STMicroelectronics—Region Americas, The Ritz-Carlton Hotel Company, Sunny Fresh Foods, and BI (a firm that designs and delivers performance improvement programs).

Now complete Skills Practice 2-1. The purpose of this exercise is to help you develop a useful way of thinking about what it means to be an "effective organization" and what types of things need to be done to actually create one.

Skills Practice 2-1
Visualizing the Effective Organization

Skill Level: Basic

Skill Objective
1. To develop skill in visualizing effective organizations in more concrete terms.
2. To identify the key elements of an effective organization and the types of policies and practices that are needed to support it.

Procedure
Note: This can be done as an individual activity or in small groups of three to five students.

1. It is often helpful to try to think about complex or abstract concepts in more concrete terms. Given this, answer the following question: If a highly effective or ideal organization were an *animal,* what would it be and why? Draw a picture of the animal (to the best of your ability) on a sheet of paper. Be sure to leave some room at the bottom of the page.
2. Now, using the picture of your animal as a guide, identify the characteristics or elements you feel are critical for a highly effective or ideal organization. List the top five to seven characteristics *in one row* under the picture of your animal. Again, make sure that you leave some room under this list of factors.
3. Ultimately, if you wanted to actually make this model of an effective organization a reality, you would need to get more specific. Given this, think about each of the characteristics you identified in the last step, and brainstorm a list of three to five specific organizational and management policies or practices that would support it.
4. Answer the following discussion questions.

Discussion Questions
1. Evaluate the results of the exercise you completed. Do the characteristics of a highly effective organization that you identified reflect characteristics of the animal you identified? Do the policies and practices you identified support the characteristics of your model of organizational effectiveness?
2. What is the value of this exercise? That is, how does it help you to be an effective manager?

In working to make their organizations effective, managers must develop strategic plans. *Strategies* are simply methods of competition. The *strategic*

Organizational Effectiveness Index—The Baldrige Award Criteria

Directions: This measure should be used to evaluate the extent to which a given organization is committed to quality management principles as outlined by the Malcolm Baldrige Quality Award criteria.

Leadership

1. Executives in the organization create and maintain a leadership system based on clear values and high expectations.
2. The values, expectations, and directions of the organization are effectively communicated and reinforced throughout the workforce.
3. Executives in the organization seek to identify future opportunities for the company and its stakeholders.
4. The organization takes action to promote legal and ethical conduct in all that it does.
5. The organization looks ahead to anticipate public concerns and to assess possible impacts on society of our products and services.

Information and Analysis

1. The organization's performance measurement system is designed to align operations with company objectives.
2. The organization's performance management system was developed based on customer needs and how these needs are met.
3. The organization uses competitive comparisons and benchmarking to set stretch targets that are consistent with the firm's competitive strategy.
4. The organization analyzes and integrates information and data from all relevant operations to support business decisions and planning.
5. The organization has a set of criteria that are used to identify appropriate information and data to be used for competitive comparisons and benchmarking.

Strategic Planning

1. Strategy development in the organization considers present and future customer requirements and expectations.
2. Strategy development in the organization assesses the relationship between the competitive environment and company capabilities.
3. The organization aligns work-unit and partner plans and targets.
4. Productivity, cycle time improvement, and waste reduction are included in the organization's plans and targets.
5. The organization generates two- to five-year projections regarding its operational performance compared with key competitors and benchmarks over this time period.

Human Resource Development and Management

1. The human resource planning and evaluation in the organization is aligned with the firm's strategic and business plans.
2. Reliable, valid, and complete HR information is available for company planning.
3. The design of jobs in the organization fosters flexibility and rapid response to changing requirements.
4. The compensation and recognition policies in our region reinforce the effectiveness of the design of jobs.
5. The company's training function helps to build company and employee capabilities.

Process Management

1. The organization translates service requirements into efficient and effective delivery processes.
2. The organization uses a measurement plan to maintain process performance.
3. The organization's key support service processes are designed and maintained so that current requirements are met and operational performance is continuously improved.
4. The organization works to improve its relationship with suppliers.
5. The organization uses feedback from suppliers to improve internal processes.

Business Results

1. The organization tracks current levels and trends in key measures of quality for products and services.
2. The organization uses current levels and trends in key measures of operational and financial performance to drive performance improvement efforts.
3. The organization tracks current levels and trends in key measures of employee well-being and satisfaction.
4. The organization tracks current levels and trends in key measures of supplier performance.

Customer Focus and Satisfaction

1. The organization employs an effective process for understanding which product and service features are most important to current and prospective customers.
2. The organization uses listening and learning strategies to address the future requirements and expectations of current and potential customers.
3. The organization has systems in place to resolve all customer complaints effectively and promptly.
4. The organization compares the satisfaction levels of customers with those at competing firms.
5. The organization analyzes current levels and trends in key measures of customer satisfaction and dissatisfaction segmented by customer groups and service types.

FOCUS ON MANAGEMENT

ALAGASCO PUTS CUSTOMERS SECOND

Alagasco, Alabama's largest utility—and the only utility on *Fortune* magazine's 100 Best Companies to Work for in America list—is proud of its philosophy of "putting customers second."* Alagasco believes that by putting employees first and treating

them well, good service to customers will naturally follow. As one sign of commitment to its employees, each year Alagasco employees at all levels meet to refine the corporate strategic plan for the coming year. Everyone then receives a copy of the final plan so at follow-up meetings they can ask questions about

the plan and learn more about their individual roles in helping Alagasco meet its objectives. Training in both work skills and corporate activities and philosophies is also a priority.

http://www.alagasco.com/

*S. Delenne, "Putting Customers Second," *American Gas,* March 1999, pp. 36–37.

F I G U R E   2 - 5
The Strategic Planning Process

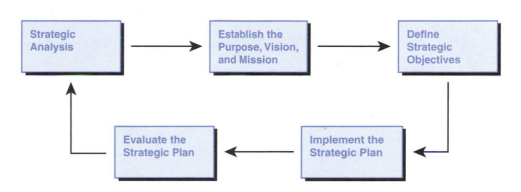

plan of an organization is a comprehensive plan that reflects the longer-term needs and directions of the organization or subunit. Strategic planning consists of several key components. Figure 2-5 shows those components and how they are linked together into the process of strategic planning.[5]

CONDUCT A STRATEGIC ANALYSIS

To formulate a strategic plan, managers must conduct a *strategic analysis* in order to understand the external environment and internal capabilities of the organization. One technique for doing this is the *SWOT analysis. SWOT* is an acronym for *s*trengths and *w*eaknesses of an organization's internal capabilities and *o*pportunities and *t*hreats in the organization's environment. SWOT analysis permits managers to develop a strategic profile of the organization. SWOT analysis assumes that an organization will achieve strategic success by increasing strengths and opportunities and lessening weaknesses and threats. Figure 2-6 lists key questions to guide managers in a SWOT analysis.

FIGURE 2-6

QUESTIONS TO GUIDE MANAGERS IN A SWOT ANALYSIS

INTERNAL

Strengths	Weaknesses
A distinctive competence?	No clear strategic direction?
Adequate financial resources?	A deteriorating competitive position?
Good competitive skills?	Obsolete factories?
Well thought of by buyers?	Subpar profitability?
An acknowledged market leader?	Lack of managerial depth and talent?
Well-conceived functional area strategies?	Missing any key skills or competencies?
Access to economies of scale?	Poor track record in implementing strategy?
Insulated from strong competitive pressures?	Plagued with internal operating problems?
Technology leader?	Vulnerable to competitive pressures?
Cost advantages?	Falling behind in research?
Competitive advantages?	Too narrow a product line?
Product innovation abilities?	Weak market image?
Proven management?	Competitive disadvantages?
Other?	Below-average marketing skills?
	Unable to finance needed changes in strategy?
	Other?

EXTERNAL

Opportunities	Threats
Serve additional customer groups?	Likely entry of new competitors?
Enter new markets or segments?	Rising sales of substitute products?
Expand product line to meet broader range of customer needs?	Slower market growth?
	Adverse government policies?
Diversify into related products?	Growing competitive pressures?
Vertical integration?	Vulnerability to recession and business cycle?
Ability to move to better strategic group?	Growing power of customers or suppliers?
Complacency among rival firms?	Changing buyer needs and tastes?
Faster market growth?	Adverse demographic changes?
Other?	Other?

Source: Adapted from A. A. Thompson, Jr., and A. J. Strickland, *Strategic Management: Concepts and Cases* (Plano, TX: Business Publications, Inc., 1990), 91.

SWOT analysis provides managers with a logical framework for assessing their organization's current and future positions. This assessment permits managers to identify a set of alternative strategies. SWOT analysis can be conducted periodically to keep managers informed about changes in important internal or external factors. It wasn't until Chrysler Corporation conducted a SWOT analysis after near-bankruptcy that managers fully understood what environmental threats and internal weaknesses they faced. The SWOT analysis enabled Chrysler's management to reassess its situation clearly and to successfully turn the company around. To develop your skill in performing an environmental scan, complete Skills Practice 2-2.

FOCUS ON MANAGEMENT

SWOT ANALYSIS AT RUBY TUESDAY

Ruby Tuesday operates and franchises more than 390 casual-dining restaurants in 32 states. As the first step in a thorough strategic management process, Ruby Tuesday conducted a SWOT analysis. Strengths identified included "growth rate of 20 percent," "strong technical skills," and "fast reaction time from management team." Among weaknesses were "lack of proactive approach (need outside help in developing)," "internal communications could be improved," and "need comprehensive review of compensation system." Some opportunities identified were "small markets are viable with smaller units," "delivery and takeout potential good," and "technology development in units and at headquarters." Finally, threats included "competition—direct: Chili's, T.G.I. Fridays, Bennigan's; indirect: Taco Bell, grocery stores, specialty markets," "difficulty in finding new sites (need population of 200,000 to support new site)," and "lack of differentiation in markets." The SWOT analysis results were then used throughout the remainder of the strategic planning process.*

http://www.ruby-tuesday.com

*This example is from R. H. Woods, "Strategic Planning: A Look at Ruby Tuesday," *Cornell Hotel and Restaurant Administration Quarterly,* June 1994, pp. 41–50.

Skills Practice 2-2   **Skill Level: Challenging**
Performing an Environmental Scan

Skill Objective

To develop skill in assessing the strengths and weaknesses of an organization in relation to opportunities and threats that exist in an organization's external environment.

Procedure

Step 1: Identify an organization to use as a basis for your environmental scan. This may be an organization you currently work for, you used to work for, or with which you are familiar. It may also be a student organization in which you are involved. Record the name of the organization on a piece of paper. Use this paper for recording your answers to Steps 2–6.

Step 2: Think about characteristics of the organization that help make it a more effective organization (e.g., skilled labor, technological expertise). List these strengths on your sheet of paper.

Step 3: Think about characteristics of the organization that make it less effective (e.g., resistance to change, poor product or service quality, low productivity, high costs). List these weaknesses on your sheet of paper.

Step 4: Identify threats to the organization from the external environment (e.g., new competition, changing customer preferences, costs of raw materials, technological change). List these threats on your sheet of paper.

Step 5: Identify opportunities for the organization from the external environment (e.g., unsatisfied customer needs, technological advances, rapidly growing economies). These are factors that can represent something an organization can take advantage of in order to enhance its effectiveness. List these opportunities on your sheet of paper.

Step 6: Based on your preceding analysis, brainstorm a list of actions the organization could take to use its strengths to take advantage of opportunities and to reduce the adverse effects of threats. List these potential action steps on your sheet of paper.

Discussion Questions
1. Why is it important to conduct environmental scans?
2. What are the most significant barriers to performing an effective environmental scan? What are some strategies for overcoming these barriers?
3. What are the practical implications of this exercise for you as a future manager or supervisor?

ESTABLISH THE PURPOSE, VISION, AND MISSION

Following strategic analysis, the next step in formulating a strategic plan is specifying the purpose, vision, and mission of the organization. The *purpose* of the organization is the reason for the organization's existence. For example, the purpose of an organization might be to earn a profit, preserve wetlands, or provide social services for citizens of a state. *Vision* is a vivid description of a preferred future. The vision can be simple or complex, concise or elaborate, but it must be clear, engaging, compelling, sincere, and stretching. In Martin Luther King's famous "I have a dream" speech, he was presenting his vision of a preferred future. Here are some vision statements:

> "A dynamic community, prosperous, environmentally committed, with boundless opportunity." Singleton Shire, New South Wales, Australia
> "The best people providing the best technologies for the world's best air force." U.S. Air Force Research Laboratory
> "To be recognized as the industry leader in total quality and customer service and to set the standard by which all others are judged in the aerospace industry." Superior Forge, Inc.
> "A healthier Nigeria in a healthier world." Association of Nigerian Physicians in the Americas (ANPA)

The organizational *mission* is the path managers choose to achieve the purpose and vision. The mission is often written down in the form of a *mission statement.* Selecting a mission is a critical decision.

FOCUS ON MANAGEMENT

BEN & JERRY'S MISSION STATEMENT

Ben & Jerry's mission statement notes that "Ben & Jerry's is dedicated to the creation and demonstration of a new corporate concept of linked prosperity. Our mission consists of three interrelated parts. Underlying the mission is the determination to seek new and creative ways of addressing all three parts while holding a deep respect for individuals inside and outside the company and for the communities of which they are a part." The three parts of the mission are:

Product: "To make, distribute and sell the finest-quality all-natural ice cream and related products in a wide variety of innovative flavors made from Vermont dairy products."
Economic: "To operate the company on a sound financial basis of profitable growth, increasing value for our shareholders, and creating career opportunities and financial rewards for our employees."
Social: "To operate the company in a way that actively recognizes the central role that business plays in the structure of society by initiating innovative ways to improve the quality of life of a broad community—local, national, and international."

http://www.benjerry.com/co-index.html

Stuckey's Inc., a restaurant chain, saw its mission as providing "convenient, moderately priced home cooking" to travelers along the interstates. The company enjoyed huge success until the late 1970s, when interstate travel decreased and consumer taste shifted toward gourmet cuisine. By defining its mission as servicing interstate customers rather than dine-out customers in general, Stuckey's was forced to close most of its interstate facilities. By 1998, the chain had only 51 facilities—down from 360 at its peak in the 1970s.[6] Thus, the choice of a mission can have a significant and long-lasting effect on an organization's ability to achieve its purpose.

Most large firms have developed mission statements, and some develop separate mission statements for their subunits. For instance, Marriott International Inc. developed separate mission statements for the corporation and for the hotel division and then asked each of its 250 hotels to craft mission statements of their own.[7]

http://www.marriott.com/

Now go to Skills Practice 2-3, Developing an Effective Mission Statement, to see the criteria for a good mission statement and to develop a mission statement for an organization.

Skills Practice 2-3
Developing an Effective Mission Statement

Skill Level: **Challenging**

Skill Objective

To foster skill in developing a mission statement for an organization that effectively describes its fundamental purpose and long-term objectives.

Note: This activity can be done individually or in groups of three to five students.

Foundation: Criteria for a Good Mission Statement

> Is the mission statement specific?
> Does the mission statement motivate or inspire others?
> Is the mission statement achievable?
> Does the mission statement have a long-term focus?
> Is the mission statement easy to understand?
> Does the mission statement give the fundamental purpose of the organization?
> Does the mission statement identify the key stakeholders of the organization?
> Does the mission statement identify the core values of the organization?

Procedure

1. Develop a mission statement for an organization via the following steps.

    Step 1: Identify an organization to use for developing a mission statement. This may be an organization you currently work for, an organization you used to work for, one you are familiar with, or a student organization in which you are involved.

    Step 2: Think more specifically about what this organization does. Try to summarize this in no more than four to five sentences on a separate piece of paper.

    Step 3: Now suppose that you needed to describe the organization you just summarized in Step 2 to someone who did not know anything about it. Keeping the criteria for a good mission statement in mind, construct a statement that describes who the organization is, what it does, and how it accomplishes what it does. In particular, make sure your mission statement is understandable and concise.

Step 4: *(optional)* Present your mission statement to the class, and evaluate it according to the criteria for a good mission statement.

Discussion Questions
1. In what ways is a mission statement valuable to an organization?
2. What are some key things that must be done in order to use a mission statement effectively?
3. What are the practical implications of this exercise for you as a future manager or supervisor?

The process model presented in the Bottom Line summarizes the basic steps associated with the development of an effective mission statement.

DEFINE STRATEGIC OBJECTIVES

Strategic objectives are needed to support the purpose, vision, and mission. Strategic objectives specify desired long-run and short-run results. Objective setting is an essential part of strategic planning, in that it specifies performance targets for managers at all levels of the organization. The setting of objectives is derived directly from the purpose, vision, and mission of the organization.

Existing objectives are often the result of prior strategic plans and are re-set when they have been achieved or have gone unmet or the context of the organization has changed substantially. For instance, events such as governmental deregulation of the industry, emergence of new competitors, unionization of workers, lowered demand for products or services, and the retire-

BOTTOM LINE

The Bottom Line: Developing a Mission Statement

| Identify the Basic Reasons Why the Organization Exists | → | List the Core Values of the Organization That Drive How It Will Do Business | → | Identify the Primary Business or Businesses of the Organization |

| Finalize the Mission Statement in a Way That Is Understandable and That Provides Inspiration and a Sense of Purpose to Employees | ← | Draft the Mission Statement in Writing, Evaluate It, and Modify It as Needed | ← | Identify the Primary Customers of the Organization |

FOCUS ON MANAGEMENT

ment of top executives can each necessitate such re-evaluation. When this occurs, managers must examine the organization's purpose, vision, and mission and determine whether strategic objectives need to be reset or the existing objectives are desirable and achievable.

Setting objectives provides managers with a base for formulating strategies. Objectives also provide managers with criteria for selecting and rejecting alternative strategies based on an evaluation of each strategy's potential for achieving goals at all levels of the organization. As we will discuss in the following sections, strategic objectives can be set at both the corporate and business-unit levels.

CHOOSE CORPORATE-LEVEL STRATEGIES

Web Wise

Corporate-level strategies provide direction for the total organization. Managers at the corporate level define a strategic direction that includes business units and departments within those business units. Managers often select either grand strategies or portfolio strategies for guiding their company.

GRAND STRATEGIES

A *grand strategy* is a broad plan to guide the organization toward reaching its goals. Depending on the size of the organization and the nature of the goals to be achieved, managers may choose to implement one of three grand strategies: growth, stability, or retrenchment.

A *growth strategy* is common in new, emerging industries or industries that are undergoing rapid growth and gaining new external opportunities. Growth strategies can be appealing and may lead to great success, but they can also be risky. By focusing on growth, firms may fail to pay proper attention to efficiency, the needs of current customers, or even safety.

A *stability strategy* is selected when managers want to protect the existing market share of the firm from external threats or have just completed a phase of rapid growth or divestment. A stability strategy allows managers to concentrate on increasing the internal strengths of the firm. After many years of growth, Holiday Inn chose to stabilize its operations by curtailing growth and focusing on upgrading its hotels to compete more effectively.

Finally, a *retrenchment strategy* is often selected when managers are faced with declining performance due to internal weaknesses and external threats. Many firms, including General Motors and IBM, have dramatically cut back on hiring, laid off workers, reduced salaries, and sold off units in recent years. In fact, almost 700,000 job cuts were announced in 1998—10 percent more than the previous record.[8] As another example of retrenchment, Procter & Gamble has lost market share in recent years to such rivals as Unilever, in part because of its large size and slow response to competitors' actions.[9] In June 1999, P&G announced a major cost cutting as part of its Organization 2005 restructuring program. The initiative will cut 15,000 staff, including 6,000 from Europe, the Mideast, and Africa. Designed to improve the speed of decision making and innovation, the initiative also includes a restructuring of operations to permit tailoring to the needs of local markets.

http://www.pg.com

For recent information and news about Organization 2005, click on "The 2005 Initiative" on the Web page.

Figure 2-7 shows how a SWOT analysis can help with the choice of a grand strategy. After conducting a SWOT analysis, managers can locate the cell that best describes their present position and choose a suitable strategy. For example, if there are many opportunities in the firm's environment and the firm has substantial internal strengths, a growth strategy is appropriate. On the other hand, if there are major threats in the environment and the firm has critical internal weaknesses, a retrenchment strategy may be needed.

PORTFOLIO STRATEGIES

A *portfolio strategy* considers the business mix of the firm—that is, the types of business units and product lines the firm controls. The BCG matrix

FOCUS ON MANAGEMENT

THE RISKS OF "GROWTH AT ANY COST"

The danger of "growth at any cost" was dramatically evident as ValuJet Flight 592 crashed shortly after take-off from Miami International Airport on May 11, 1996, disappearing beneath the Florida Everglades and killing all 110 people aboard. Remarkably, ValuJet—which had grown since its inception to serve 17 states—was only two years old. ValuJet had attempted to achieve growth through aggressive efforts to maintain low costs. To pursue this strategy, it paid low salaries, used planes averaging older than 26 years (versus the industry average of

10 years), turned planes around in 20 minutes from arrival to departure (in the process making it difficult for Federal Aviation Administration [FAA] inspectors to do their jobs), and relied heavily on maintenance.* ValuJet pictured itself as the Wal-Mart of airlines. However, as noted by one writer, "The problem: Wal-Mart does not conduct business 35,000 feet above the ground."† A National Transportation Safety Board report, issued in August 1997, cited ValuJet for failing to properly oversee its contract maintenance program and ensure that contractors complied with maintenance, training, and hazardous material require-

ments. One of those contractors—SabreTech Inc.—was charged in July 1999 with murder and manslaughter for its part in the disaster. The FAA grounded ValuJet after the crash. The airline later merged with discount carrier AirTran and now flies under the name AirTran.

http://www.airtran.com/

*See, for instance, D. Greising, "Growing Pains at ValuJet," *Business Week,* May 15, 1995, pp. 50–51; and J. T. McKenna, "FAA Inspection Cites ValuJet Oversight Lapses," *Aviation Week and Space Technology,* March 9, 1998, p. 59.

†M. Merzer and I. P. Cordle, "Seeds of ValuJet Disaster Found Fertile Soil," *Miami Herald,* May 4, 1997, p. A1.

GLOBAL PERSPECTIVES

RETRENCHMENT OF THE CHAEBOLS

Korea's largest family-owned conglomerates, or *chaebols,* have fallen on hard times. These conglomerates pursued growth at all costs. They sprawl across industries, have heavy debt loads, and are bloated, making little attempt to focus on core businesses. Korea's economic crisis has caused many companies to go bankrupt. Smaller chaebols have had to radically downsize to raise needed cash, selling off even their choicest assets.* For the larger chaebols, the crisis—and associated government and bank pressure—is forcing downsizing and streamlining. In late 1998, the five largest chaebols—Hyundai, Samsung, Daewoo, LG, and SK—reached a landmark agreement on corporate structuring reform. Under the plan, the chaebols will reduce the number of their subsidiaries from a total of 264 to 130 through the disposal of marginal and unprofitable units, while each chaebol will continue to specialize in a few core business lines.† For instance, in June of 1999, Hyundai announced that it would dissolve the current group configuration and concentrate on five core business segments—automobiles, electronics, heavy industries, construction, and financial services—for the 21st century.‡ Noncore businesses such as chemicals will be expunged.

http://www.hyundai-motor.com

*C. S. Lee, "Saving the Body," *Far Eastern Economic Review,* May 20, 1999, p. 42.

†"5 Companies in Korea Plan to Shed Units," *New York Times,* December 8, 1998, p. C2.

‡S. J. Yoo, "Chaebols Set Massive Downsizing Plans," *Business Korea,* June 1999, pp. 23–24.

and the GE matrix are two models used by many corporations in selecting a portfolio strategy.

BCG Matrix The *BCG matrix* model of strategy, developed by the Boston Consulting Group, emphasizes the nature of the internal mix of business units that are under the control of management. The BCG matrix views the overall investment a firm has made in various lines of business. Its objective is to help

FIGURE 2-7
Grand Strategy Selection Matrix

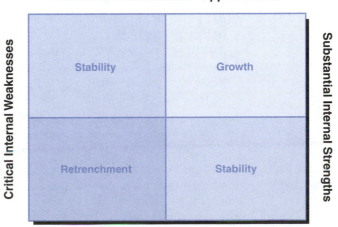

Numerous Environmental Opportunities

Critical Internal Weaknesses

Substantial Internal Strengths

| Stability | Growth |
| Retrenchment | Stability |

Major Environmental Threats

FIGURE 2-8
The BCG Portfolio Matrix

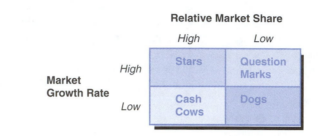

managers decide about the deployment of resources to each business unit or product line.[10]

In the BCG matrix, business units or product lines are classified according to two dimensions: overall market growth rate and market share held by the business unit. The classification of business units within the matrix leads to identification of the four strategic types shown in Figure 2-8: stars, cash cows, question marks, and dogs.

> A *star* is a business unit that has both a high market growth rate and a relatively large share of the market. Typically, this is a product line or business that has high potential for growth and needs large amounts of short-run cash to support rapid growth. Stars are attractive to organizations because they have the potential to increase sales and therefore to generate large amounts of profit in the future.

> A *cash cow* has a large share of the market, but there is little growth. Large amounts of surplus cash can be "milked" from a cash cow and channeled into stars.

> *Question marks* exist in a rapidly growing market but have a small market share. Managers must decide whether to invest more capital into the business unit or product to take advantage of the high growth opportunity (that is, to transform it into a star) or to divest it to emphasize other business units and products in the portfolio. Either way, managers are faced with some risk—in making a large investment that may result in failure or in passing up an opportunity that may later turn out to be highly profitable.

> A *dog* is a poor performer because of little growth in the market and a small market share. Usually, dogs are a cash drain on the organization because they are unable to support themselves with the small amount of revenue they can generate. Management must either try to sell the unit to another company or liquidate its assets.

GE Matrix The *GE matrix,* sometimes called the *GE nine-cell matrix,* provides upper managers with a way to evaluate existing business units and those they might like to acquire. Developed by General Electric with the help of the consulting firm McKinsey and Company, the GE matrix introduces multiple factors for evaluating business units. As shown in Figure 2-9, business units are plotted in the matrix on two dimensions: industry attractiveness and business strength. *Industry attractiveness* includes such factors as market size, market

FIGURE 2-9
The GE Matrix

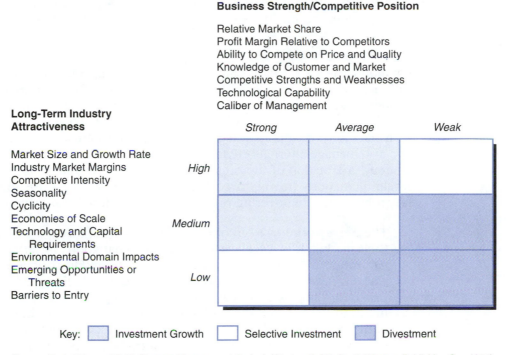

Business Strength/Competitive Position

Relative Market Share
Profit Margin Relative to Competitors
Ability to Compete on Price and Quality
Knowledge of Customer and Market
Competitive Strengths and Weaknesses
Technological Capability
Caliber of Management

Long-Term Industry Attractiveness

Market Size and Growth Rate
Industry Market Margins
Competitive Intensity
Seasonality
Cyclicity
Economies of Scale
Technology and Capital
    Requirements
Environmental Domain Impacts
Emerging Opportunities or
    Threats
Barriers to Entry

	Strong	Average	Weak
High			
Medium			
Low			

Key: Investment Growth   Selective Investment   Divestment

Source: R. J. Aldag and T. M. Stearns, *Management,* 2nd ed. (Cincinnati, OH: South-Western Publishing Co., 1991),
p. 200.

growth rate, seasonality, types of competitors, and technical complexity of products. *Business strength* is determined by such factors as profit margins, market share, quality of management, and manufacturing technology.

Based on where the business unit is located on the two dimensions, one of three basic strategies is recommended: investment growth, selective investment, or divestment. Business units falling in the lightly shaded cells of Figure 2-9 are candidates for investment and growth, because they rank high in both industry attractiveness and business strength. Business units falling in the white cells should only be invested in selectively. Investments should be cautious until a change in the unit's strength or degree of industry attractiveness occurs. Business units in the dark cells are candidates for divestment because they rank low in both industry attractiveness and business strength.

Grand strategies and portfolio strategies are useful for corporate strategists whether they seek to build the organization through internal growth or through acquisitions. Since the 1980s there has been extensive use of portfolio strategies as a means of evaluating business units as candidates for acquisition.

CHOOSE BUSINESS-UNIT-LEVEL STRATEGIES

Several models have been developed for describing and explaining different types of business-unit-level strategies. Two such models that are useful to managers in understanding how the strategy of their business units relates to their industry are the *adaptation model* and the *competitive model.* Each model makes different assumptions about the relationships between strategy, organization, and the environment. The following discussion of each strategic type will focus on its assumptions, alternative strategies that managers can consider, and the way the strategy can be implemented for success.

ADAPTATION MODEL

Raymond Miles and Charles Snow developed the adaptation model of organizational strategy.[11] The *adaptation model* contends that a major thrust of strategic management should be the alignment of organizational activities with key dimensions of the organization's environment. To accomplish this end, managers must set up a strategy that will adapt to environmental conditions and also manage internal activities of the organization to support the selected strategy. Adaptation of the organization to the environment is accomplished by simultaneously solving three critical strategic problems: the entrepreneurial problem, the engineering problem, and the administrative problem.

> The *entrepreneurial problem* considers what managers believe to be their market. It is solved by determining what goods or services the organization will produce for a defined product-market domain.

> The *engineering problem* is one of deciding which methods are appropriate for the production and distribution of goods and services. The solution to the engineering problem is determined by the solution of the entrepreneurial problem, or management's decision on what products or services will be provided to a market. The solution usually involves implementing systems for producing, controlling, and distributing the goods or services that support the organization's mission. Using robots on the production line, providing employees with authority to decide on the pace of work, and distributing goods or services to specific markets can be solutions to the engineering problem.

> The *administrative problem* addresses the need to develop an appropriate administrative system within the organization. It is solved by designing an organizational system that will enhance the coordination of activities to achieve the solutions to the entrepreneurial and engineering problems. Decisions about the degree of bureaucracy of the organization, number of employees supervised by each manager, and methods of hiring employees may be questions that must be answered to solve the administrative problem.

The adaptation model of organizational strategy contends that managers must interrelate the three solutions to the entrepreneurial, engineering, and administrative problems. Organizations that are most successful, according to this strategic model, will be those that have correctly matched the solutions to the conditions of the organization's environment. Four types of organizations, classified by the ways they solve these problems, are identified by Miles and Snow: defenders, prospectors, analyzers, and reactors.

Defenders   The *defender strategy* is carried out when management seeks or creates an environment that is stable. Managers will emphasize protecting the market share that they have gained. A defender solves the entrepreneurial problem by defining a narrow market segment and producing only a few products or services to provide to the market. It solves the engineering problem by emphasizing efficiency, thus lowering costs and permitting a price that competitors cannot match. It uses rigid bureaucratic controls to solve the administrative problem, thus reducing errors and increasing efficiency. The defender strategy is similar to the stability strategy we discussed previously. McDonald's exemplifies a defender organization by focusing on a narrow market segment (fast food consumers), maximizing efficiency in production (cooking methods that lead to product uniformity), and enforcing strict employee controls (dress and behavior codes for employees).

http://www.mcdonalds.com/

Prospectors The *prospector strategy* is the opposite of the defender strategy. The prospector seeks or creates an unstable environment in the form of rapid change and high growth in the market. Management tries to locate and exploit new product opportunities. It solves the entrepreneurial problem by defining the environment in broad terms to encourage innovation and diversity in activities. Since internal activities must be diverse and adaptable to new opportunities, managers solve the engineering problem by avoiding long-term commitments to any single method of production. Instead, large capital investments are avoided and multiple methods of production that can be changed as necessary are used. Administratively, managers encourage flexibility in member activities through loose controls to maximize growth and change.

Johnson & Johnson represents a prospector organization by broadly defining its market (home and personal products), employing multiple methods of production (more than 150 product divisions that are continually changing), and setting loose administrative controls (each division manager selects the administrative structure believed to be appropriate for his or her employees).

http://www.johnsonandjohnson.com/home.html

Analyzers An analyzer is an organization that exists between the two extremes of defender and prospector. The *analyzer strategy* involves adapting solutions from both the defender and prospector strategies to the three problems. Consistency is maintained by identifying two areas of activity for the organization. One is a stable market, where a defender strategy is pursued.

FOCUS ON MANAGEMENT

ANALYZER STRATEGY AT RJR NABISCO

Organizations such as RJR Nabisco represent the analyzer strategy. RJR Nabisco's original base of business is tobacco products, where profits are high but growth is slow. The management of RJR Nabisco chose to expand into more unstable markets by entering into food products (such as Life Savers, Chips Ahoy!, A.1, Grey Poupon, Snackwell's, Planters, and Oreos), which have high competition and rapid growth. Thus, original technologies and bureaucratic controls remain for the tobacco business while multiple technologies and loose controls have been set for the food-product lines of business.

http://www.rjrnabisco.com/annual97

The major concern of managers is to maintain a balance between organizational subunits that are defender oriented and subunits that are prospector oriented. The entrepreneurial problem is solved by identifying two market segments—one stable and the other changing. The engineering problem is solved by managers who emphasize methods of efficiency in production for the stable subunits and methods of flexibility for those subunits oriented to a changing market. The administrative problem is solved by setting up a structure with tight controls over stable subunit activities and loose controls for subunits engaged in developing new products.

Reactors   A reactor organization is basically one that has suffered strategic failure. This may be due to poor managerial decisions about the strategic plan. Miles and Snow note that use of the *reactor strategy* may be due to causes such as the following.

> Top management has not clearly articulated the organization's strategy.
> Management has not fully shaped the organization's structure and processes to fit a chosen strategy.
> Management has not changed the organization's strategy/structure relationship in the face of major environmental changes.

If an organization wants to end the reactor mode of strategy, management must develop either new solutions to the entrepreneurial, engineering, or administrative problem or solutions to all three, depending on what caused the failure.

COMPETITIVE MODEL

The competitive model of organizational strategy was developed by Michael Porter. The *competitive model* contends that the nature and degree of competition in an industry determine the strategy that is appropriate for managers to formulate and implement.

Industry Forces   Porter identified five industry forces that determine the degree of competition within an industry.

> *The threat of new entrants to compete in the industry.* New competitors entering an industry often bring with them large resources with the goal of gaining market share and profits. This may be achieved through the creation of a new company, as was the case with Kmart in the retail industry, or by diversification of a firm in one industry into another industry through acquisition, as Philip Morris did with the purchase of Miller Brewing. How serious the threat of entry is depends on barriers to entry that exist in the industry and on the reaction the new entrant can expect from existing competitors.
> *The bargaining power of suppliers in the industry.* In some industries, suppliers of materials to competing organizations can gain power by either raising prices for their materials or lowering quality. Thus, powerful suppliers can squeeze profitability out of an industry by dictating the price and quality of the materials that are bought by the competing firms.

Suppliers should not be thought of solely as firms that manufacture a product to provide to an industry. Labor unions can also be a supplier group. For instance, in the sports industry, players' unions can exert a strong influence over the profit of team owners, since the unions are more concentrated, there are few substitutes, the product is important to the buyer's business, products are differentiated (e.g., fan loyalties), and players could conceivably start their own league.

> *The bargaining power of customers in the industry.* The conditions that make customers powerful are similar to those that make suppliers powerful. Customers can force down prices, demand higher-quality goods and services, and play competitors against each other—all of which serve to lower profitability in the industry.

Customers, of course, include individual customers as well as organizations. Looking again at the sports industry, two types of customers for sports entertainment can be identified: fans who attend games, and television networks that provide games to viewers in their homes. It is easy to understand why television networks have more bargaining power over team owners than do fans attending the games.

> *The threat of substitute products or services from potential competitors.* Substitute products limit the potential prices of goods or services in an industry. If the price of a product is too high, buyers will seek substitutes. Producers of sugar have been faced with many substitutes that have greatly eroded profits and kept the price of sugar low. Saccharin, corn syrup, and aspartame have been introduced as substitutes for sugar and have been marketed at lower prices. As a result, sugar producers have been forced to accept a smaller share of the sweetener market.

> *Competitive rivalry among existing firms.* Rivalry among existing competitors takes the form of such tactics as price competition, advertising battles, new product introductions, and increased customer service or warranties. Rivalry occurs because managers of competing organizations believe they can improve their position in the industry by implementing one or more of these tactics.

The goal of a competitive strategy is to find a position in the industry where the organization can best defend itself against those forces or can influence them in its favor. Managers of organizations who best understand these forces, according to Porter, will have greater success at selecting a strategy that will be suited to conditions in the industry.

The competitive model provides a mapping of industry conditions that managers can examine to develop a strategy that will improve organizational performance. Once management has assessed the factors that influence competition within the industry, competitive opportunities and threats can be determined. Identification of organizational strengths and weaknesses will then enable management to identify a strategy that will help the organization compete effectively.

Competitive Strategies Porter identified three strategies that managers can implement to compete against other organizations in the industry: (1) overall cost leadership, (2) differentiation, and (3) focus. The degree of success of each competitive strategy depends on the amount of commitment members have to the strategy and the effectiveness of managers in implementing the strategy.

> **Overall cost leadership.** The *overall cost leadership strategy* requires management to formulate and implement a strategic plan that will lead to construction of efficient facilities; attainment of cost reductions; tight cost and overhead control; avoidance of marginal customer accounts; and minimal costs in areas such as research and development, service, sales, and advertising. By maintaining an efficient and low-cost organization, management can attain above-average returns in the industry and make it difficult for less efficient competitors to match the price of the product. If less efficient competitors are successful at matching the product price of the overall cost leader, their returns will be much lower because of their higher costs.

  The ability to achieve a position of overall cost leadership often requires a high market share, favorable access to raw materials, design of products for ease in manufacturing, maintenance of a wide line of related products, and service to all major customers to build volume. Organizations known for their success in implementing an overall cost leadership strategy are Briggs & Stratton, which holds a 50 percent worldwide market share in small-horsepower gasoline engines; Black & Decker, in the manufacture of power tools; and Du Pont, in the production of chemicals.

> **Differentiation.** The *differentiation strategy* recognizes that a firm's product is unique in relation to other products produced in the industry. Management cannot ignore costs in implementing the differentiation strategy; however, costs are a secondary rather than a primary consideration. A differentiation strategy is successful through emphasis on strong marketing abilities, creative product engineering, strong commitment to research and development, a reputation for quality or technological leadership, and a long tradition in the industry for having skilled employees.

  Often the adoption of a differentiation strategy means that a high market share must be sacrificed. When the product is perceived to be superior, margins can be raised. However, customers may recognize the superiority of the product but be unwilling to pay the high price. Organizations that have successfully implemented a differentiation strategy are Mercedes, in the auto industry; Macintosh, in stereo components; Coleman, in camping equipment; Hyster, in lift trucks; Fieldcrest, in towels and linens; and Bloomingdale's, in retail stores.

> **Focus.** The *focus strategy* pursues either an overall cost leadership strategy or a differentiation strategy by focusing on a narrow customer group, product line, or geographic market. The focus strategy provides products or services to a narrow segment, or niche, in the industry. Examples of successful focus strategies are Illinois Tool Works, which designs fasteners, and Fort Howard Paper, which provides industrial-grade paper.

The competitive model identifies five industry forces that managers must consider in formulating and implementing strategies that will lead to organizational effectiveness. Analysis of these five forces by management should enable it to devise a strategic plan that will lead to efficiency in operations (overall cost leadership), uniqueness of product (differentiation), or targeting a narrow market segment and developing efficiency or uniqueness (focus). Those organizations that develop the best methods for achieving these goals will be the most successful in the industry.

Take some time now to put on the hat of management consultant. Read the brief description of Hewlett-Packard presented in the accompanying Real-World Management Challenge. Based on your analysis of the case, develop a set of recommendations you would present to top management of Hewlett-Packard in order to effectively address the situation. Use material from the chapter to support your recommendations wherever possible.

Real-World Management Challenge

Hewlett-Packard

The Situation

Hewlett-Packard, based in Palo Alto, California, is a leading manufacturer of computers and computer peripherals such as printers and scanners. The company has 83,200 employees worldwide and does business in more than 120 countries.

The company's new President and Chief Executive Officer is Carleton (Carly) S. Fiorina. Although the company has had a long history of success in the computer industry, it has been experiencing a number of major strategic challenges, including:

> Challenge 1: HP remains the printer king and is growing fast in PCs, but it almost forgot the Internet.
> Challenge 2: Outgoing CEO Lewis Platt largely let HP run without setting a clear direction. Insiders say that he should have milked old-line businesses to invest more heavily in the Net and digital photography.
> Challenge 3: HP built its reputation by inventing groundbreaking products, but the inkjet printer in 1984 was the last one. Since then, most of HP's growth has been in PCs and printers, where cutting costs is as important as cutting-edge engineers. In addition, promising Net technologies wasted away in HP labs.
> Challenge 4: HP has struggled to strike a balance between decentralization and central control. Its history of giving 130-plus product groups autonomy worked beautifully in simpler times but proved an obstacle when it tried to pull together an overall Net strategy.
> Challenge 5: HP's balkanized approach of hawking stand-alone products does not fly in the Internet Age. Customers want a vision of the future and integrated suites of products to solve particular needs.
> HP's turnover is one-third that of the rest of Silicon Valley, but it may not be keeping the right people. Insiders worry that it is losing top talent because of its old pay practices and is dominated by "lifers" attracted by HP's safe, paternalistic ways.

What Would You Do?

What would you do to handle this situation? Be specific.

http://www.hp.com/

Source: P. E. Burrows and P. Elstrom, "The Boss," *Business Week,* August 2, 1999, p. 76.

IMPLEMENT THE STRATEGIC PLAN

Vince Lombardi, the famous coach of the Green Bay Packers football team, once said, "The best game plan in the world never blocked or tackled anybody." Like football coaches, managers must see that strategic plans are converted into action. To do this, they must effectively communicate the plan;

assign responsibility and authority for activities within the plan; motivate employees to achieve the plan; develop methods for measuring the results of activities; and develop procedures for taking any necessary corrective action. These are among the skills we will address in later chapters.

EVALUATE THE STRATEGIC PLAN

Web Wise

U.S. Department of Energy (DOE) Balanced Scorecard Resource Site

This site, developed by the Department of Energy to assist its employees and contractors, contains links to a great amount of information on the Balanced Scorecard (BSC). The site shows how the BSC can be used to translate an organization's vision into a set of performance indicators distributed among four perspectives: Financial, Customer, Internal Business Processes, and Learning and Growth. The site also discusses how those indicators are maintained to measure an organization's progress toward attaining its vision.

http://www.pr.doe.gov/bsc001.htm

We began this chapter with a discussion of ways to examine organizational effectiveness. That discussion suggested that there are many facets of effectiveness. If so, we must assess effectiveness of the strategic plan on those multiple facets. The *balanced scorecard* (BSC) is a conceptual framework for translating an organization's vision into a set of performance indicators distributed among four perspectives: financial, customer, internal business processes, and learning and growth.[12] Using the BSC, companies can monitor both their current performance (finances, customer satisfaction, and business process results) and their efforts to improve processes, motivate and educate employees, and enhance information systems—that is, its ability to learn and improve.

The accompanying Bottom Line presents a process model summarizing the basic steps associated with the implementation of the strategic planning process.

Now go to Skills Practice 2-4, The Balanced Scorecard, to learn the steps in developing and using a balanced scorecard. Then complete Skills Practice 2-5, Developing a Strategic Plan.

Skills Practice 2-4   Skill Level: **Challenging**
Applying the Balanced Scorecard

Skill Objective
To develop skill in applying the balanced scorecard concept.

Procedure
1.   Read the following scenario.

The Situation
You are a member of the Executive Management Team at Hospice Services, Inc., a hospice service firm based in Chicago, Illinois. The mission of Hospice Services is to provide high-quality, cost-effective, and humane home care services for individuals who are in the final stages of terminal illness. A primary objective of your organization is to provide services to terminally ill patients that preserve their dignity and allow them to die in their own homes surrounded by their loved ones.

Your organization employs more than 400 nurse practitioners and direct care providers. Employees work in teams of three to five to provide daily care for patients.

Hospice Services has been performing relatively well in the last few years, but increased competition and escalating costs have resulted in an urgent need for management to develop a formal measurement system to assess the extent to which the firm's mission is being realized.

2.   Apply the steps that follow to design the balanced scorecard and to identify appropriate actions to take when implementing the system. Use a separate piece of paper to record your answers.
     Step 1: Define the company's vision and strategy (see the situation just given)

Attainment
Attainment
Attainment
Attainment
Attainment

65

Chapter 2   The Organizational Context: Seeing the Big Picture

BOTTOM LINE

The Bottom Line: Managing the Strategic Planning Process

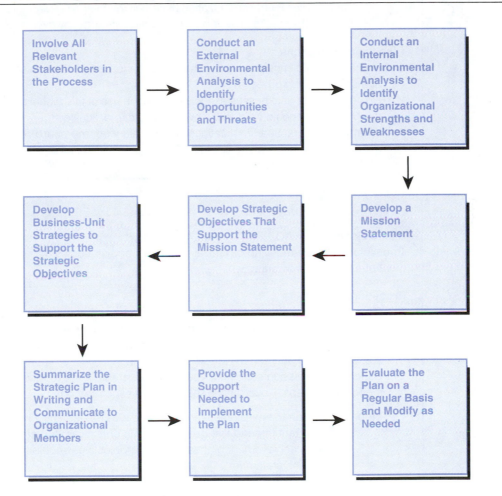

Involve All Relevant Stakeholders in the Process → Conduct an External Environmental Analysis to Identify Opportunities and Threats → Conduct an Internal Environmental Analysis to Identify Organizational Strengths and Weaknesses

Develop Business-Unit Strategies to Support the Strategic Objectives ← Develop Strategic Objectives That Support the Mission Statement ← Develop a Mission Statement

Summarize the Strategic Plan in Writing and Communicate to Organizational Members → Provide the Support Needed to Implement the Plan → Evaluate the Plan on a Regular Basis and Modify as Needed

Step 2: Clarify and translate the vision and strategy

a. *List financial-based measures of organizational performance.* Examples: return on investment, cost reduction, profits

b. *List customer-based measures of organizational performance.* Examples: satisfaction, retention, market share

c. *List internal business processes measures of organizational performance.* Examples: quality, response time, new product introductions

d. *List learning- and growth-based measures of organizational performance.* Examples: employee satisfaction, employee productivity, employee retention

Step 3: Communicating and linking. List the general action steps you would take to communicate and educate others in the organization about the plan. Set goals and link rewards to performance measures as well.

Step 4: Planning and target setting. List the basic things you would do to set targets, align strategic initiatives with the goals, allocate resources to support the strategic initiatives, and establish milestones (key points or achievements in a process).

Step 5: Strategic feedback and learning. List the things you would do to articulate a shared vision for the organization based on the foregoing plan and how you would evaluate the results of your plan (facilitating strategy review and learning).

Discussion Questions

1. How can the balanced scorecard help to enhance the effectiveness of the corporate strategic planning process?
2. Do you see any weaknesses associated with the use of this technique? If so, what are they? And what could be done to overcome these difficulties?
3. What are the practical implications of the balanced scorecard for you as a future manager?

Skills Practice 2-5
Developing a Strategic Plan

Skill Level: **Challenging**

Skill Objective

To develop skill in formulating organizational goals and strategies to support the achievement of a firm's mission statement.

Procedure

1. Obtain a mission statement to use for this exercise, perhaps from the corporate website of a company you are interested in, a current or previous job, a student organization you are involved in, or the one you developed when you completed Skills Practice 2-3: Developing an Effective Mission Statement.
2. Based on the mission statement you obtained, create a strategic plan by completing the following steps. Record your answers on a separate page.

Step 1: Based on the mission statement you are using, identify what you feel are the most important three to five goals (strategic objectives) to achieve as an organization. The achievement of these strategic objectives should reflect a realization of the mission statement.

Step 2: Identify what the organization does (i.e., the processes) that are critical to its success. This may include things such as billing, sales and distribution, and account maintenance. Identify the three to five key business processes of your organization.

Step 3: For each of the key business processes you just identified, give an action that could be taken to make that process "support" the achievement of the strategic objectives. Remember that everything needs to set up so that it helps the organization achieve its mission and its strategic objectives.

Step 4: For each key business process you just identified, name something (critical measures of success) that could be used to assess the effectiveness of that process. Some examples might include: customer satisfaction, costs related to project completion.

Discussion Questions

1. What are the strengths and weaknesses of creating a strategic plan? What action can be taken to overcome the weaknesses associated with the process?

Skills Application
Skills Application
Skills Application
Skills Application
Skills Application
67

Chapter 2 The Organizational Context: Seeing the Big Picture

2. What is the relationship between a corporate strategic plan and the goals and strategies of individual work units (e.g., departments, divisions)? How can the two be aligned with one another?

3. What are the practical implications of this exercise for you as future managers and supervisors?

TOP TEN LIST: KEY POINTS TO REMEMBER
THE ORGANIZATIONAL CONTEXT

10. Develop a mission statement that describes the fundamental business and long-term objectives of the organization.

9. Communicate the mission statement to all managers and employees in the organization to obtain their understanding of and commitment to the mission statement.

8. Perform an environmental scan on a regular basis in order to assess the strengths and weaknesses of the organization in relation to opportunities and threats that exist in the external environment.

7. Develop corporate strategic objectives to support the mission of the organization. Make sure that strategic objectives are in alignment with the mission.

6. Identify and track key measures of organizational effectiveness that reflect achievement of the corporate mission and strategic objectives.

5. Develop strategic plans based on the needs and interests of the key strategic constituencies of the organization.

4. At the work-unit level, develop strategic plans that are in alignment with the corporate strategic plan.

3. Follow up and systematically evaluate the strategic plan on an annual basis.

2. Modify the plan as needed based on changes in organizational goals and/or environmental factors.

1. Take action to maintain the visibility and meaningfulness of the strategic plan to managers and employees over time.

QUESTIONS FOR REVIEW AND REFLECTION
REVIEW QUESTIONS

1. What are the six primary environmental domains? What are three important environmental dimensions?

2. What is organizational effectiveness? Discuss four approaches to assessing organizational effectiveness.

3. Identify the five steps in the strategic planning process.

4. What is a strategic analysis? What is SWOT analysis?

5. Define purpose, vision, and mission and give an example of each.

6. Discuss three grand strategies as well as two models for selecting a portfolio strategy.

7. Discuss the Miles and Snow adaptation model, including the three critical strategic problems and four strategies in the model.

8. Explain the Porter competitive model, including the five industry forces that determine the degree of competition within an industry and the three primary competitive strategies.

9. Discuss issues involved in implementing and evaluating the strategic plan, including the balanced scorecard.

CRITICAL THINKING QUESTIONS

1. Identify and discuss three factors that might influence which of the six environmental domains would be most important for a particular firm.

2. A manager says in a meeting, "The bottom line is whether we make a good profit. If we do, we're effective. It's as simple as that." Do you agree? Why or why not?

3. Consider the Malcolm Baldrige National Quality Award

criteria shown in Figure 2-4. Which of those criteria do you think is *most* important in deciding whether an organization is "committed to quality management principles." Which do you think is *least* important? Defend your selections.

4. In an interview with a business magazine, a CEO says, "We don't have a strategic plan. In our industry, any strategic plan would be outdated after a few weeks." Do you think a strategic plan can be helpful in a very dynamic environment? Why or why not?

5. We indicated in the chapter that a retrenchment strategy is often selected when managers are faced with declining performance due to internal weaknesses and external threats. Do you think a retrenchment strategy is ever justified in other situations? Defend

your position. If you answered in the affirmative, what might be one or more such situation?

6. What do you think are the most important differences between the BCG matrix and the GE matrix? Can you think of a case where the two models would suggest different recommendations? Can the matrices be used together? Support your positions.

7. The Porter competitive model identifies five industry forces that determine the degree of competition within an industry. For each of the forces, identify an industry (other than one discussed in conjunction with the strategy in the chapter) where the force might be especially important as well as an industry where the force would likely have little influence.

EXPERIENTIAL EXERCISES

WEB EXERCISE 2-1

We began this chapter by noting the challenges faced by Lou Gerstner as he took over as head of IBM. Go to the IBM home page at:

http://www.ibm.com

Click on "About IBM." Then click on "Annual Reports." This will take you to IBM's most recent annual report (and will give you access to past annual reports). Based on

your reading of the most recent annual report, write a two-page analysis of IBM's competitive strategy. Be sure to read the "Letter to Shareholders," to learn about aspects of IBM's vision, and to read the "Company Mission." Also read the "Management Discussion" to learn about IBM's strategic acquisitions and divestitures and the various challenges faced by the firm.

WEB EXERCISE 2-2

Rank the most admired companies by your own criteria. Early in this chapter (Figure 2-3) we reported *Fortune* magazine's ranking of "America's Most Admired Companies." That ranking is based on assessments by more than 10,000 managers, directors, and analysts. You, though, may feel differently about which criteria—quality of management, quality of products/services, innovativeness, long-term investment value, financial soundness, employee talent, social responsibility, and use of corporate assets—are most important in making companies "admirable." Go to:

http://www.pathfinder.com/fortune/mostadmired/ search.html

When there, indicate the importance you place on each of the listed criteria and see how the companies are ranked on the basis of your importance ratings. How does your ranking differ from the original *Fortune* ranking of "America's Most Admired Companies"? What do you think accounts for the differences?

CASE 2-1
STRATEGIC MANAGEMENT AT PIXAR STUDIOS

The Company

Pixar Studios was founded in 1986 by current Chairman and CEO, Steve Jobs. Pixar has become an Academy

Award–winning animation studio by creating a new generation of animated films using computer technology. The company is based in Richmond, California, and employs approximately 450 employees. Pixar has had a string of three highly successful animated films in its history. Its first film was *Toy Story,* released in November 1995. This film went on to become the highest-grossing film in 1995. In 1998, the studio released *A Bug's Life,* its second animated film. This movie was also a hit at the box office and received critical acclaim. Finally, in 1999, the studio released *Toy Story 2,* which went on to become the second-highest domestic grossing film in history.

Pixar's Strategy

Steve Jobs' vision is for Pixar to become a movie studio for the 21st century that will rival Disney in the family entertainment movie industry. In fact, Pixar has established a close strategic partnership with Disney in the areas of marketing and distribution.

Jobs has relied on computer technology and innovation to provide the bases for realizing his vision. To support this, Jobs has created a free-wheeling and high-energy environment within which his employees might flourish. In addition, Jobs has focused on diversifying his workforce in terms of their backgrounds, including computer experts, landscape artists, puppeteers, and rock stars.

Creative genius John Lasseter has also played a key role in making Pixar films "heartwarming" and "charming" to moviegoers. Lasseter ensures that the story and characters in each movie are well developed and appealing. He works closely with his writers and artists in the development of a film and is willing to make last-minute changes in the story in order to enhance the overall quality of the film.

In order to establish Pixar as a recognized and respected "brand name" in Hollywood, Jobs has set an aggressive timeline of releasing one new animated film every year. However, some analysts are skeptical; they hold that

Pixar is too dependent on Disney for its future viability. In fact, Disney has been busy developing its own computer animation expertise. This could help Disney evolve into a major competitor with Pixar. Other competitors are looming on the horizon: Paramount Studios, 20th Century Fox, Dreamworks, and Universal Studios all have plans to increase their offerings in the family entertainment segment of the movie industry.

Pixar's future now rests on how its partnership with Disney evolves over time. As long as it maintains that partnership by continuing to develop films that appeal to Disney, Pixar will likely flourish. However, Pixar's agreement with Disney provides Disney the option of abandoning the partnership if it does not receive a proposal for a film within a specified period of time. If Disney were to walk away from Pixar, this could make Pixar vulnerable.

Discussion Questions

1. What is Steve Jobs' vision or mission for Pixar Studios?
2. What are the environmental threats facing Jobs and Pixar Studios?
3. What are the environmental opportunities for Jobs' and Pixar Studios?
4. What type(s) of strategies is Steve Jobs implementing in order to achieve his mission or vision for Pixar Studios?
5. What kinds of "employee factors" help Pixar Studios to achieve its mission and goals?
6. What would you do next at Pixar Studios, if you were Steve Jobs?

http://www.pixar.com/

Source: Based on P. Burrows and R. Grover, "Steve Jobs, Movie Mogul," *Business Week,* November 23, 1998, p. 140.

CASE 2-2
GROWTH STRATEGY AT AMAZON.COM

The Company

Amazon.com, based in Seattle, Washington, opened for business in July 1995 with a mission to make book buying faster, easier, and more enjoyable by using the Internet. The key foundation of this mission is customer satisfaction with the shopping experience. Since then, Amazon.com has developed a customer base in excess of 17 million people in more than 160 countries around the world.

Strategy at Amazon.com

Jeff Bezos, CEO of Amazon.com, has a vision that Amazon.com will become the center of the e-commerce universe, in which customers can eventually buy just about anything, including pet food, tennis shoes, musical instruments, and much more.

Presently, besides selling books over the Internet, Amazon.com has branched out into other product categories, including CDs, videos, DVDs, toys and games, and electronics. The company offers a variety of other websites, including an Internet movie database *(http://www.imdb.com)*, and a live-event Internet auction website *(http://www.livebid.com)*. Finally, Amazon.com has developed strategic partnerships with other Internet companies, such as drugstore.com, gear.com (selling sporting goods), and homegrocer.com.

Amazon.com is aggressively expanding its distribution network by building seven warehouses around the country that are specifically designed to process Internet-based customer orders in an efficient manner. Bezos once commented that the goal was "universal selection: earth's biggest river, earth's biggest selection."

The work environment at Amazon.com is highly energetic and charged with enthusiasm. The main instigator of this is Bezos himself. To further support the rallying of his troops around the Amazon.com vision, Bezos created "Radio Amazon," an internal radio station that plays tapes of Bezos talking about his plans.

On the negative side, most analysts feel that Amazon.com has a long way to go before it realizes its grand vision. The firm has been struggling in terms of all of the new product categories it has entered recently. In addition, manufacturers like Pioneer and Sony have refused to sell their products to Amazon.com in an attempt to protect traditional "brick-and-mortar" retailers.

Growing competition presents a huge challenge to Amazon.com, for the number of competitors has increased dramatically in the past two years (e.g., barnesandnoble.com, borders.com). In addition, the barriers to entry into Internet retailing are considered to be few, so anyone from a corporate giant to a one-person start-up could conceivably replicate what Amazon does.

Another challenge for Amazon.com is its recent Z-shops and All Products Search, which basically sends customers to competitors. Moreover, the Z-Shops venture will diminish Amazon's ability to control the provision of its famous and much-admired customer service. Bezos himself has stated that much of Amazon.com's repeat business is attributable to Amazon's "religious commitment to customer service."

Some analysts have also raised the issue of when Amazon.com will actually realize a profit (so far, there has been none).

While Amazon.com has had a lot of positive momentum since its inception in 1995, Bezos admits that there is no guaranteed success for his firm in the future.

Discussion Questions

1. What is Jeff Bezos' vision for Amazon.com? Do you think it is appropriate?
2. What are the opportunities and threats that Amazon faces? Which do you believe are most significant?
3. Evaluate Amazon's current strategies in relation to its external environment. To what extent are they appropriate?
4. What would you do next, if you were Jeff Bezos?
5. What are the practical implications of this case for you as a future manager?

For the official website of Amazon.com, visit:

http://www.amazon.com/

When there, click on "About Amazon.com" and "Press Releases" to learn more about the company.

VIDEO CASE
THE VERMONT TEDDY BEAR COMPANY:
A CASE STUDY IN STRATEGIC LEADERSHIP

Running Time: 10:55

John Sortino founded the Vermont Teddy Bear Company in 1981. Sortino first sold the handcrafted bears to his friends and then began to sell the bears from a peddler's cart at an open-air market in Burlington, Vermont. One day, a tourist to Burlington wanted a bear, but wanted it mailed to her home. Sortino got the idea to package a teddy bear and add delivery service and other extras to go with it. The Bear-Gram® concept was born. In 1990, the company began advertising the Bear-Grams® on radio in New York City by featuring well-known local radio celebrities endorsing Bear-Gram® gifts. Within two days, the company had reached its sales goal for the entire year. Today, the company handcrafts more than 350,000 bears for its Bear-Gram® gift delivery service, which employs 274 year-round staff.

The video shows President and CEO Liz Robert, Vice President of Operations Spence Putnam, and others as they discuss the strategic direction of the Vermont Teddy

Bear Company. After viewing the video, answer the following questions.

1. What factors caused the company to decide that it was "not in the Teddy Bear business"?

2. According to Liz Robert, why didn't the company need to think strategically in its early years? What subsequently caused the company to see the need for strategic thinking? What statements in the video lend support for the success of that strategic thinking?

3. How would you describe the way Liz Robert runs the company? According to Spence Putnam, how does Robert's style of leadership differ from his own?

4. According to Liz Robert, why did the management team rely on intuition in the past?

5. How would you describe the culture of the Vermont Teddy Bear Company? How does Robert's leadership style influence the culture?

6. How are human values and business principles linked at the Vermont Teddy Bear Company?

7. What does Spence Putnam mean when he says that people in the company have "constrained fun"?

http://www.vermontteddybear.com/

LIGHTEN UP

AMBUSHES AND GOLDEN PARACHUTES[13]

Here is some of the colorful language used by corporate strategists in discussing mergers and acquisitions.

Afterglow: Postmerger euphoria of acquirer and/or acquiree, usually soon lost.

Ambush: Swift and premeditated takeover attempt.

Big-game hunting: Planning and executing takeovers of large companies.

Big-hat boys: Texas moneymen interested in "big-game hunting."

Cyanide pill: Antitakeover finance strategy in which the potential target arranges for long-term debt to fall due immediately and in full if it is acquired.

Double Pac-Man strategy: Target firm makes tender offer for the stock of its would-be acquirer.

Golden parachutes: Provision in the employment contracts of top executives that ensures them a lucrative financial landing if the firm is acquired in a takeover.

Hired guns: Merger and acquisition specialists, other investment bankers, and lawyers employed by either side in any takeover.

Mushroom treatment: Postmerger problems from an acquired executive's standpoint: "First they buried us in manure, then they left us in the dark awhile; then they let us stew; and finally they canned us."

Pirates or raiders: Hostile acquirers.

Sharks: Takeover artists.

Shark repellent: Protective strategies for preventing or combating a hostile tender offer.

White knight: Acceptable acquirer sought by a potential acquiree to forestall an unfriendly takeover; the preferred suitor.

Wounded list: Executives of an acquired firm who develop health or career problems from the deal.

CHAPTER *Three*

SKILLS OBJECTIVES

> To develop organizational plans for enhancing workforce diversity.
> To assess individual differences in others and to develop strategies for dealing with those differences in a work group.
> To develop strategies for managing cross-cultural differences within a work group.
> To enhance perceptual accuracy in understanding situations and in making managerial decisions.
> To develop sensitivity to differences in others' perceptions of a situation.
> To assess employee job satisfaction and to identify strategies for enhancing it through managerial action and organizational policies and practices.

KNOWLEDGE OBJECTIVES

> Specify forms of diversity in organizations and why they are important.
> Describe approaches companies are taking to value and manage diversity.
> Identify and describe key personality dimensions on which employees may vary.
> Discuss why cross-cultural differences are relevant and identify important dimensions on which cultures may vary.
> Understand the perceptual process and describe potential perceptual errors.
> Discuss the components of attitudes and indicate why attitudes are important.

The modern workplace is much more than a melting pot in which contents are transformed into a uniform mass. It is more like a rich stew, with ingredients varying in origin and properties, providing differing flavors, nuances, and textures, and retaining their character while contributing to the whole. We will see in this and subsequent chapters that many characteristics of these ingredients are important, including race and ethnic origin, gender, age, abilities, sexual orientation, personality, attitudes, and much more. As the ingredients become more varied, they offer the potential for an expanded, more exotic and exciting menu. Still, it is a challenge to blend the ingredients in ways that bring out their best qualities. And, a stew that is a delight to one person may seem bland or bitter or simply unpalatable to another. In this chapter we will explore the challenge of recognizing and capturing the best qualities of available ingredients—valuing diversity—while creating a successful stew—managing that diversity. We will first explore company approaches to valuing and managing diversity, including efforts to bring more women and minorities successfully into the workplace. We will then consider two further important elements of diversity—personality and national culture. Next we will discuss perceptions and attitudes. We will see that perceptions as well as attitudes are important characteristics on which organization members may differ and that they are also key influences on reactions to diversity.

MANAGING DIVERSITY

The workforce is becoming dramatically more diverse. *Diversity* refers to the membership mix in organizations in terms of gender, race, ethnic origin, and other characteristics. The Pillsbury Company defines *diversity* as "all the ways in which we differ."[1] Before reading on, complete Self-Assessment 3-1, Attitudes Toward Diversity.

Self-Assessment 3-1
Attitudes Toward Diversity

Answer each of the questions in this section using the following scale:

1 = Disagree Strongly
2 = Disagree Somewhat
3 = Neither Agree nor Disagree
4 = Agree Somewhat
5 = Agree Strongly

1. _____ I enjoy working and interacting with people that have diverse racial/ethnic backgrounds.
2. _____ Older workers possess a lot of work and life experience that are of value to organizations.
3. _____ Men and women should receive the same treatment and opportunities in the workplace.
4. _____ A diverse workforce can help an organization to be more innovative.
5. _____ Organizations have a moral responsibility to make their workforces more diverse.
6. _____ I am annoyed that organizations need to make so many changes in policies in order to accommodate employees with different religious affiliations.

7. _____ Different ideas or ways of thinking should also be considered a form of diversity.

8. _____ The emphasis that many organizations have been placing on helping employees to better balance work and family life has gone too far.

9. _____ Gays and lesbians should have the right to work in an environment that is not hostile toward them.

10. _____ Diversity programs are often a form of "white male bashing" that results in reverse discrimination.

11. _____ In a hiring situation, the most qualified candidate should get the job even if it makes an organization less diverse in some way.

12. _____ Diversity in the workplace is just another management fad that will fade away in a couple years.

13. _____ I understand the meaning of the term *workforce diversity*.

14. _____ I understand how the effective management of workforce diversity can help a firm to enhance bottom-line results like profitability and customer satisfaction.

15. _____ Managers should emphasize what employees have in common rather than trying to accommodate so many differences between them.

Now, to get a basic idea of where you are starting in terms of some of the material covered in this chapter, try working through the following "Valuing Individual Differences" Pre-Test Skills Assessment. Don't worry if you don't know everything you'd like to complete the exercise; just do your best. Be as specific as possible in stating your recommendations.

Pre-Test Skills Assessment
Valuing Individual Differences

You are the team leader for a business team that has been charged with new product development for a company that designs and manufactures personal digital assistants (PDAs). These PDA devices have become extremely popular as a way to organize schedules, check and send e-mail, and surf the Web.

Your new team consists of people with very different backgrounds. Josh Kilzak, 23 years old, is a marketing specialist who will help your team to figure out how to sell the new PDAs you design. He is very outgoing and creative and believes that everything the team does must be based on what is best for the customer. Don Lee, 38 years old, is an electrical engineer at the company. His job is to provide technical expertise to the PDA development process. He is originally from Beijing, China. He is very bright, but rather shy and quiet. He does not like confrontation or conflict with people. To Don, meeting the technical specifications of the product design is the most important issue, regardless of how long it takes or whether it will dissatisfy a customer. Kristin Pellegrin, 49 years old, is a financial analyst at the company. She is a hard-core numbers person who is most concerned with calculating and controlling costs. She views the success of the project solely in terms of financial measures of performance (e.g., development costs, return on investment, profitability). Her personality is very aggressive and can at times be abrasive.

The first meeting of the team was a disaster, because nobody could agree on what to do or how to do it. Each person had a different set of priorities and objectives. At one point, the meeting deteriorated into a shouting match between Josh and Kristin regarding the issue of meeting customer needs vs. controlling product development costs. At the end of the meeting everyone left frustrated and pessimistic about the future chances of success for the team.

As the leader of this team, develop an action plan for handling this situation. Be specific, and focus on action.

DEVIL'S ADVOCATE

Why bother trying to understand people's perceptions? It's so subjective! Isn't it more important to focus on that which is objective?
Yes, you are correct in that perceptions are subjective (i.e., they depend on the person). That is, each individual has a unique way of viewing and interpreting the world. However, remember that a given individual's perceptions represent his/her "reality." It is this "reality" that a person reacts to in terms of his/her behavior on the job. This would include an employee's motivation, productivity, etc. So the bottom line is that perceptions, although potentially very different for different people, are exactly what a good manager needs to understand, manage, and influence.

Why should we be concerned with personality factors when the bottom line is really employee performance (behavior)?
From a managerial perspective, getting employees to attain high levels of performance is a critical goal. But when you start to think about how this can be done, then it becomes clear that the attitudes, values, and beliefs of your employees are important influences on how well someone performs his/her job, and thus must be managed. For example, have you

ever gone to a service establishment (e.g., restaurant, hotel, airline, bank) where you received really bad (unresponsive, rude, incompetent) service? Why does this happen?

Well, personality factors probably played a significant role in your getting lousy customer service. The service person may have had an unhelpful, unfriendly, or apathetic attitude. The key point is that personality traits clearly influence employee performance, so we need to be concerned with them as managers.

Isn't the idea of "workforce diversity" just another buzzword for quota systems and affirmative action?
There are a lot of different definitions of *diversity* floating around. *Workforce diversity* generally refers to a demographic trend in which the U.S. workforce is becoming increasingly diverse in terms of age, race/ethnicity, education, religious orientation, and sexual orientation. The changing composition of the U.S. workforce has been presenting challenges to employers in terms of how to reflect this diversity within their own workforces. Diversity is not the same thing as a quota system or affirmative action. A quota system or affirmative action program would

focus more on increasing the *representation* of different groups of people in a company's workforce (e.g., females, minorities). Diversity may focus on increasing representation to some degree, but it goes further in that it attempts to find ways to develop people who represent these different groups and to help utilize their talents in ways that will help an organization to be more successful.

Why is workforce diversity important to managers and organizations? Shouldn't they focus on things like profitability, cost reduction, and customer satisfaction?
Many employers have stated that it is their goal to make their workforce look like or reflect the characteristics of the general population. A company may value this diversity within its workforce because it can help the organization to better understand its customers in terms of their needs and desires. For example, a company based in Chicago may be interested in marketing its products to the Hispanic community in the Chicago area. If the company has some employees who are part of this target market, those employees can help the company to better understand how to position itself and its products.

Historically, many companies have focused on the potential problems created by a diverse workforce. It was felt, for instance, that there would be more misunderstandings and coordination problems as diversity increased. Further, very real prejudices against members of certain groups, such as blacks and women, could lead to conflict and mistrust.

Increasingly, though, organizations are learning to value diversity. Diversity can provide a powerful competitive advantage.[2] For one thing, a diverse workforce brings more perspectives and a wider range of knowledge to bear on problems, increasing creativity and decision-making effectiveness. Diversity also helps a firm understand and meet the needs of diverse markets. As noted by IBM CEO Lou Gerstner, "Our marketplace is made up of all races, religions, and sexual orientations, and therefore it is vital to our success that our workforce also be diverse."[3] Ted Childs, director of workforce diversity at IBM, adds, "We think it is important for our customers to look inside and see people like them. If they can't, it seems to me that the prospect of them becoming and staying our customer declines."[4]

Kraft Foods spells out its commitment to diversity in metaphors: "A stellar meal requires contrasting and complementing textures and tastes. A winning sports team depends on the different talents of its members. A first-class orchestra needs many varied instruments. And a successful business team requires a variety of thought, energy and insight to attain and maintain a competitive edge. Kraft Foods is comprised of people from different backgrounds, different ethnicities, different work styles, different values and different ways of thinking. We invite these differences. We seek them out. And we know that our business teams and the individuals thrive as a result."[5]

Companies that become successful at managing a diverse workforce also find their recruiting prospects enhanced. Firms such as Hallmark Cards, McDonald's Corporation, and Clorox, which appear in the book *The Best Companies for Minorities*[6] because of their commitment to diversity, are able to attract and retain women and minorities. As more females and minorities enter the workforce, this advantage will become even more important. *Fortune* magazine and the Council on Economic Priorities rate firms on their diversity efforts. Figure 3-1 presents the 1999 "Diversity Elite," the top 10 firms in those ratings.

As described in the accompanying Focus on Management, Celanese and a handful of other firms—including Xerox, Avon, AT&T, Burger King, and Levi

FOCUS ON MANAGEMENT

DIVERSITY AWARENESS AT CELANESE

Ernest H. Drew, the former CEO of Celanese (previously Hoechst Celanese), a large chemical company, became an advocate of a more diverse workforce while attending a 1990 conference for Celanese's top 125 officers, mostly white men, who were joined by approximately 50 lower-level women and minorities.* The group split into problem-solving teams, some mixed by race and sex and others all white and male. The teams addressed the question of how the corporate culture affected the business and what

changes might be made to improve results. When the teams presented their findings, one thing seemed clear to Drew. "It was so obvious that the diverse teams had the broader solutions," he says. "They had ideas I hadn't even thought of. For the first time, I realized that diversity is a strength as it relates to problem solving. Before, we just thought of diversity as the total number of minorities and women in the company, like affirmative action. Now we knew we needed diversity at every level of the company where decisions are made."† Drew also noticed that productivity was surging at the

Celanese plants where the workforce was becoming more diverse. As a result, Drew made Celanese a pioneer in attracting, retaining, and promoting women and minorities. It adopted a specific diversity target: at least 34 percent representation of females and minorities at all levels of the company by 2001, mirroring the company's prospective workforce.

http://www.celanese.com/en/ home.html

*This example is drawn from F. Rice, "How to Make Diversity Pay," *Fortune*, August 8, 1994, pp. 78–86.

†Rice, p. 79.

FIGURE 3-1
The Diversity Elite

Rank and Company	No. of Minorities on Board	% Minority Officials & Managers	Minorities as a % of New Hires	Comments
1. Union Bank of California	7 of 17	35.9%	56%	Managers at all levels participate in numerous social, business, and community groups affiliated with various minorities
2. Fannie Mae	4 of 16	27.3%	47%	Chairman and CEO Franklin Raines is the first black to head a Fortune 500 company
3. Public Service Company of N.M.	3 of 9	34.2%	48%	One of only five companies to win the Hispanic Association on Corporate Responsibility's top grade for board representation
4. Sempra Energy	5 of 16	28.0%	39%	Helps its minority vendors develop management skills, access capital, and obtain technical expertise
5. Toyota Motor Sales	13 of 18	19.3%	35%	Increased the number of women- and minority-owned dealerships by 22% between 1994 and 1998
6. Advantica	4 of 12	16.6%	Not Available	Aggressively pursues minority franchisees; nearly four in 10 Denny's franchises are minority owned, as are more than half of El Pollo Loco franchises
7. SBC Communications	4 of 21	28.7%	51%	Spends $1 billion with minority vendors; hiked its percentage of minorities in the workforce by 10% in 1998
8. Lucent Technologies	1 of 9	19.5%	30%	Has more people of color among its 25 highest-paid executives (nine) than any other firm in rankings; employees teach at colleges that produce African American engineers
9. Darden Restaurants	3 of 12	17.7%	35%	Richard Rivera, a Hispanic, is president of Red Lobster, the nation's largest seafood chain—making him the most powerful minority in the restaurant industry
10. Wal-Mart Stores	4 of 15	42.0%	31%	The largest corporate employer of blacks and Hispanics in the U.S.; highest percentage of minority officials and managers (42%) of any firm in the rankings

Source: Based on E. Robinson and J. Hickman, "The Diversity Elite," *Fortune,* July 19, 1999, pp. 62–70.

Strauss—have been at the vanguard of efforts to enhance workforce diversity, even in the face of downsizing and severe competition. These firms have learned that, if their efforts to increase diversity—or to achieve any other human resource goal—are to be successful, they must be reflected in all facets of human resources management.

VOICE OF EXPERIENCE

VALUING DIFFERENCES

*Karen O'Brien, Director
of Player Development
Las Vegas Bally's Hotel Casino*

1. What kinds of workforce diversity exist in your organization?

There is a lot of diversity in our employees. In terms of age, we hire a lot of younger and older workers for a variety of service and maintenance jobs. The younger and older workers tend to have different attitudes and personal values in many cases. In addition, our workforce is very diverse in race, ethnicity, and nationality. We have employees who come to us from all over the United States as well as from European, Latin American, and Asian countries. From a guest's perspective, this gives our hotel and casino operations a very international feel.

2. What kinds of strategies do you use to handle workforce diversity issues effectively?

I have a basic life philosophy that I try to put into practice. I believe that it is critical to learn how to get along with people. This requires flexibility in your approach to handling work issues. People should be treated like people. That is, everyone should be given respect and treated fairly. I always try to do things to make people feel comfortable in their jobs and with their work environment in general. Managers really need to be very people oriented in order to be successful with all of this.

3. What advice would you give students in terms of how to manage workforce diversity?

First, I think it is extremely important to "put yourself in another person's shoes." How would it feel if you were the one who was different in some way (e.g., being in a different country)? Wouldn't you feel out of place or maybe a bit awkward? It's really important to be sensitive to this issue. Try getting to know people before you make snap judgments about them based on stereotypes or a first impression. If you talk to them and get to know them, I'll bet that you will see that you have a lot more in common with them than you thought. Don't draw conclusions based on the fact that someone looks or talks differently than you do.

My managerial practice is to try and reach out to all employees by smiling, saying "hello," and offering assistance to them, if they need it. These practices have worked well for me over the course of my professional career.

http://www.ballys.com/

Web Wise

The SHRM Workplace Diversity Initiative

The Society of Human Resource Management (SHRM) maintains a Diversity Website. It contains information about diversity initiatives, sources of opposition to diversity, building a case for diversity, diversity recruitment and selection, and many other topics. In addition, it provides links to *Mosaics* (a bimonthly diversity publication from SHRM), a diversity reading room, diversity toolkits, and other resources.

http://www.shrm.org/diversity/

In the Voice of Experience box, Karen O'Brien discusses her views on workforce diversity and how those views drive her style for managing people at Bally's—Las Vegas.

Companies must do more than accept and tolerate diversity; they must take active steps to successfully foster diversity in the workplace. Some of those steps might include training for tolerance, rewarding diversity efforts, changing employee attitudes toward diversity, and developing personnel policies that support diversity.

TRAINING FOR TOLERANCE

Firms are adopting many approaches to training for tolerance. As one example, at Celanese the top 26 officers are each required to join two organizations in which they are a minority. Also, IBM's Systems Storage Division in San Jose, California (a city where 33 languages are spoken), launched an annual diversity day in 1993.[7] Employees dress in various ethnic costumes, perform traditional dances, and prepare authentic dishes for fellow workers. The festival has been so successful in defusing tensions that the plant's diversity council now prepares a monthly bulletin that lists diversity events in the city. The council will also produce a series of videos featuring a different culture monthly, to be played at gathering spots in the plant.

Firms are also providing training to integrate sexual orientation into ongoing diversity efforts. They explain that the reasons for valuing gay and lesbian employees are basically the same as for valuing women, religious minorities, and people of color: so that all employees can contribute to their fullest potential, unhampered by prejudice, stereotypes, and discrimination.[8] In addition, many firms are "gender training" to promote tolerance between the sexes.[9]

REWARDING DIVERSITY EFFORTS

Some firms are tying performance appraisal to their efforts to increase diversity. At Celanese, the giant chemical firm cited earlier, four sets of outcomes are equally weighted in performance appraisals: attainment of workforce diversity goals, financial success, customer satisfaction, and environmental and safety improvements.[10] As a result, managers at Celanese pay attention to diversity, knowing the success of their diversity efforts will be reflected in their salaries and bonuses.

As another example, Coca-Cola's new chairman and CEO, Douglas Daft, announced in March 2000 that he would tie his own compensation and that of others throughout the management ranks to diversity goals and would create an executive position for promoting minorities. Daft e-mailed employees worldwide, saying Coke would establish diversity goals and targets over the coming months and that "everyone in the corporation, including the CEO, will be accountable for meeting them." He added that "success and compensation" will be tied to meeting diversity goals. The reforms follow recommendations by Coke's Diversity Advisory Council, created in 1999 after current and former Coke African-American employees filed a lawsuit alleging discrimination in pay, promotions, and evaluations at Coke.[11]

CHANGING EMPLOYEE ATTITUDES TOWARD DIVERSITY[12]

Companies are using a variety of innovative approaches to develop more positive employee diversity-related attitudes and skills.

As an example, US WEST Dex, a division of US WEST that produces white pages and yellow pages phone directories, trains its employees via a three-day diversity awareness workshop. Further, the majority of its managers have completed another diversity workshop, called "Managing Inclusion," that teaches them that praising, critiquing, and otherwise communicating with employees requires a variety of approaches, depending on the personality and background of each employee. Senior managers who have gone through training talk in the training sessions about how the training makes good bottom-line business sense, and how they learned ideas they can use on their jobs. US WEST Dex also uses "resource groups," volunteer-driven meetings that address the concerns of particular employees, such as women, blacks, Hispanics, gays, and lesbians.[13] Attendance is not limited to employees matching a particular profile. Instead, all employees are encouraged to attend, to better understand the feelings and viewpoints of coworkers regarding specific issues

FOCUS ON MANAGEMENT

DIVERSITY SEMINARS AT ROHM & HAAS TEXAS INC.

Rohm & Haas Texas Inc., a Houston-based chemical company, began using cross-functional teams as part of its total quality efforts. About 40 percent of the firm's employees are minorities, and teams were selected to take advantage of the variety of experience and perspectives offered by diversity. However, employees had a hard time dealing with that diversity. As positions opened up on other teams, they began to migrate to teams composed of members with whom they felt they had more in common. African American employees, for example, would apply for teams with more African American members. Rohm & Haas recognized this as a sign of a deeper diversity problem. Working with an external diversity trainer, the company launched five-hour awareness seminars. The seminars stressed the benefits of diversity, and they focused on tension that any kind of difference—whether age, race, gender, religion, or even communication style—creates. While Rohm & Haas couldn't force unionized factory employees to attend, the union supported the effort, and 95 percent of employees participated. Employees were polled after the workshops and six weeks later, and responses were uniformly positive. The employees realized that two people can view the same situation and come to different conclusions and that neither conclusion is necessarily wrong. The programs helped employees see that many of their stereotypes were incorrect and that process improvements can be realized only if employees are comfortable working with, and perhaps challenging, one another. Rohm & Haas credits the seminars for getting its quality efforts back on track.

http://www.rohmhaas.com/

---

they are facing in the company and to offer suggestions. The company also does six-month follow-ups of programs, seeing if employees are applying their new skills to on-the-job situations. In addition, an annual companywide employee satisfaction survey incorporates questions on the state of diversity at US WEST Dex.

http://www.uswest.com/index.html

DEVELOPING PERSONNEL POLICIES THAT SUPPORT DIVERSITY

One unfortunate consequence of the massive layoffs now taking place is setbacks in efforts to increase diversity in the workforce. Many companies have found it difficult to achieve the dual goals of downsizing and diversity. One reason is that women and minorities hired to meet diversity goals often have little seniority, and thus are among the first to be cut during downsizing. Another is that firms sometimes downsize by closing facilities in areas with large numbers of minority workers. As a result, the percentages of African Americans laid off in recent years at firms such as Dial Corp. and Pet Inc. have dramatically exceeded those for the overall workforces at those companies.[14] Some firms, such as AT&T, Xerox, and Burger King, have been successful in pursuing both diversity and downsizing. For example, AT&T, which has announced major job cuts every year since 1990, monitors workforce reductions by department and finds creative ways to keep valued workers, regardless of their gender and color.[15] In some cases, large numbers of employees

Diversity Resources on the Web

The Web offers remarkably rich resources relating to diversity. Here is a sampling of sites. Each of these, in turn, will lead you to others:

Black Voices:

http://www.blackvoices.com.

This site provides a wealth of information about careers, business practices, an "Afro Mall," entertainment, and other topics. More than 2,500 job openings are posted, and there is a section to add your résumé to the database. While aimed at African Americans, this site provides many resources that are of general interest.

Latino Links:

http://www.hisp.com/links.html

Links are provided to sites dealing with Hispanic business and commerce, lifestyles and interests, news and politics, education, arts and entertainment, newspapers, and other topics.

AARP Webplace:

http://www.aarp.org

This is the site of the American Association of Retired Persons. It provides resources relating to money and work, health and wellness, legislative issues, leisure and fun, computers and the Internet, community/volunteer programs, life transitions, and other matters.

National Organization for Women:

http://www.now.org/

This site has many links to resources relating to women's issues as well as to racial and ethnic diversity.

The Glass Ceiling Commission:

http://www.ilr.cornell.edu/library/e_archive/gov_reports/glassceiling/default.html?page=documents

(continued on facing page)

are retrained for work elsewhere in the company. Other workers are assigned to the in-house temporary agency and are loaned out to various departments until permanent jobs can be found for them. Further, AT&T offers valued laid-off employees an "enhanced leave of absence" in which the employee takes two years off to go to school or travel, with full benefits and assurance of reemployment at the same level and pay if a job in the company is available upon return.

Now that we have examined some issues in managing diversity, consider the Real-World Management Challenge, Managing Diversity at Denny's. It presents a situation in which a firm was badly damaged by its failures to adequately deal with diversity and was challenged to improve. As one sign that attention to diversity can pay dividends, recall from Figure 3-1 that Advantica—the parent company of Denny's—was among the 1999 *Fortune* magazine "Diversity Elite."

Real-World Management Challenge

Managing Diversity at Denny's

The Situation

In December 1991, 18 African Americans at a Denny's restaurant in San Jose, California, were told they had to pay a $2 cover charge and prepay for their meals. This resulted in their leaving the Denny's and going to the *San Jose News* to tell their story. On March 24, 1993, a racial discrimination lawsuit was filed against Denny's by a law firm representing numerous plaintiffs, including the individuals from the 1991 incident.

On April 1, 1993, a federal judge approved a consent decree between Denny's and the Justice Department in which Denny's agreed to strengthen its policies related to equitable treatment of employees and customers and to communicate these policies to employees at all of its restaurants.

On May 24, 1993, six African American CIA agents filed a lawsuit against Denny's alleging that they were given unusually slow service at a Denny's restaurant because of their race (i.e., they were refused service).

On May 24, 1994, Denny's agreed to pay $46 million to African American customers who had made over 4,300 complaints of discriminatory treatment to the Justice Department. In addition, Denny's had no minority franchisees among its 1,500 restaurants, it purchased only 3.3 percent of its supplies from minority-owned vendors, and only 7 percent of its managers were minorities.

As a result of these events, Denny's image was severely damaged, and it had become known as a racist company.

If you were the CEO of Denny's, what would you do to handle this situation?

References

"Denny's does some of the right things," *Business Week,* June 6, 1994, pp. 25–26.

Faircloth, A. "Guess who's coming to Denny's," *Fortune,* August 3, 1998, pp. 108–110.

Harris, N. "A new Denny's—Diner by diner," *Business Week,* March 25, 1996, p. 166.

Hawkins, C. "Denny's: The stain that isn't coming out," *Business Week,* June 28, 1993, pp. 98–99.

"New image for Denny's: Rock around the clock," *South Florida Sun-Sentinel,* May 17, 1999 p. 3D.

To foster diversity in the workplace, managers need to design diversity programs that include training, reward programs, and policies that nurture diversity. Now try designing a diversity program that includes these elements by completing Skills Practice 3-1. This is a very challenging activity, so don't be surprised if you struggle with it a bit. You are likely to be involved in the design and implementation of a diversity program once you get out into the "real world," so this sort of practice—however difficult—is important.

Web Wise
(*continued*)

This page provides links to reports of the Glass Ceiling Commission. The *glass ceiling* refers to "invisible, artificial barriers that prevent qualified individuals from advancing within their organizations and reaching full potential." The report identifies the various barriers facing men and women of historically underrepresented groups and offers findings and recommendations.

ADA and Disability Information:

http://www.public.iastate.edu/~sbilling/ada.html

This site provides more than 100 links to resources relating to the Americans with Disabilities Act, general disability information, nonprofit organizations related to disabilities, and products and services related to disabilities.

Human Rights Campaign:

http://www.hrc.org/

This site provides many resources for gay, lesbian, bisexual, and transgendered employees.

U.S. Census Bureau:

http://www.census.gov/

The homepage of the U.S. Department of Commerce, Bureau of the Census. This is an excellent resource for social, demographic, and economic information. It includes a "Just for Fun" section that gives a "hands on" opportunity to use information available from the U.S. Bureau of the Census.

Skills Practice 3-1

Skill Level: Challenging

Developing an Effective Diversity Program

Skill Objective

To develop skill in designing and implementing an effective diversity program in an organization.

Characteristics of Effective Diversity Programs

1. A clear definition of diversity as the organization sees it
2. Integration of diversity into the organization's mission and strategic plan
3. Support of top management
4. Involvement of employees in the design of the program
5. A long-term perspective
6. Identification, tracking, and communication of critical measures of success for the program
7. Diversity training
8. A supportive organizational culture
9. A systems perspective that aligns HR systems (recruiting, selection, training and development, performance appraisal, and compensation) with the goals of the diversity program (e.g., attraction, development, and retention of underrepresented groups)

Procedure

1. Using the listed characteristics and material from the chapter, design a diversity program.
2. Discuss specifics in terms of how you would implement each of the elements of the program.
3. Identify and discuss what you feel are major challenges to the success of your diversity program. What could be done to overcome these barriers?

The process model presented in the following Bottom Line summarizes the basic steps associated with the development of a diversity program.

UNDERSTANDING PERSONALITY

While we tend to think of diversity in terms of things such as race, gender, and ethnic origin, the variety of personalities in the workplace is also critical. Personality determines how people respond to new situations, how they interact with others, whether they can work on their own, and much else. Personality also influences whether people behave ethically or unethically, are helpful or self-serving, are conscientious or try just to "get by," feel in control of their situations or at the mercy of fate. For all of these reasons and many others, we must understand and be sensitive to personality differences in the workplace.

Personality is the organized and distinctive pattern of behavior that characterizes an individual's adaptation to a situation and endures over time. The distinctive character of personality allows us to tell people apart—try to think of two people with identical personalities. The enduring character of personality permits us to recognize people and to anticipate their behaviors. Try to imagine a situation in which people had no enduring qualities. For instance, suppose your boss acted "like a different person" from day to day. While this could be interesting for a while, it would soon lead to chaos.

In this section, we will first consider emotional intelligence, a skill that includes the abilities to understand what motivates other people, how they work, and how to work cooperatively with them as well as to understand ourselves and to be able to use that understanding in our lives. We will then address theories of personality as well as specific personality characteristics that are important in the workplace.

EMOTIONAL INTELLIGENCE

In *The Nicomachean Ethics,* Aristotle wrote: "Anyone can become angry—that is easy. But to be angry with the right person, to the right degree, at the

BOTTOM LINE

The Bottom Line: Developing a Diversity Program

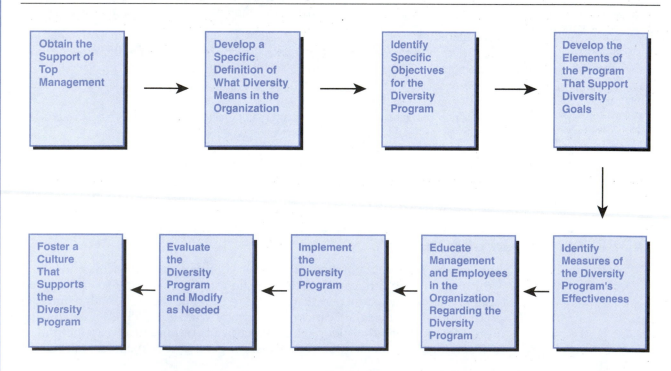

right time, for the right purpose, and in the right way—this is not easy."[16] Aristotle called on us to manage our emotional lives with intelligence. Our passions, when properly managed, can help us to act, prosper, and survive. Mismanaged, they can create havoc. The challenge, then, is to bring intelligence to our emotions.[17]

Most experts now agree that IQ scores are heavily influenced by a relatively narrow range of linguistic and math skills. So IQ taps only a small part of the full human intellect. Further, the skills assessed by IQ tests may be relevant to classroom performance, but IQ scores do little to predict performance in the "real world." This suggests the benefits of a broader view of intelligence. In one compelling demonstration of the need for this expanded view, children at age four were given an IQ test and the "Marshmallow Test." With the Marshmallow Test, the child is given a marshmallow and told that if she can put off eating it until later, she can have two. Twelve to 14 years later, this measure of ability to control impulse was twice as strong a predictor as IQ of how children did on the Scholastic Aptitude Test. It also predicted adjustment, popularity, confidence, and dependability.

When people—whether "experts" or not—are asked to describe an intelligent person, they use phrases such as "solves problems well," "displays interest in the world at large," "accepts others for what they are," "admits mistakes," "is goal oriented," and "converses well." Such phrases suggest that people focus on the worldly side of intelligence, as opposed to just "academic" intelligence.

Howard Gardner, in *Frames of Mind,* discusses several forms of intelligence, including logical-mathematical, linguistic, bodily-kinesthetic, visual-spatial, musical, interpersonal, and intrapersonal.[18] Gardner argues that these intelligences are intrinsically equal in value and that the degree to which people possess them helps explain how they learn and fare in the workplace. He further argues that it is possible to hone these intelligences and that they wither with lack of use.

Only the first two of these intelligences fit into "traditional" conceptions of IQ. Gardner's "personal intelligences"—interpersonal and intrapersonal—are defined as follows:

> **Interpersonal intelligence** is the ability to understand other people: what motivates them, how they work, and how to work cooperatively with them.
> **Intrapersonal intelligence** is the capacity to form an accurate model of oneself and to be able to use that model to operate effectively in life.

Together, interpersonal intelligence and intrapersonal intelligence comprise emotional intelligence.

Daniel Goleman, author of *Emotional Intelligence* and *Working with Emotional Intelligence,* describes *emotional intelligence* as a different way of being smart. Emotional intelligence is not IQ; it's how someone does in life, manages feelings, gets along with others, and is empathetic and motivated.[19]

While the sorts of intelligence gauged by IQ tests reside in the neocortex, or "rational" brain, EQ resides in the amygdala, in the deep recesses of the brain's limbic system. The amygdala's chemical surges produce everything from blind rage to fear to avoidance of pain to euphoria.

Emotional intelligence (EQ) is critical in answering questions such as:

> Should you trust a coworker with a confidence?
> Is a friend on the verge of a nervous breakdown?
> How should you behave in an escalating argument?
> How should you respond to a racist joke?

There are many reasons why EQ is important in organizations, and in life in general. For example:

> The emotional brain may "highjack" the rational brain. Fear, rage, and jealousy may prevent us from rationally addressing problems.
> EQ is especially important in higher-level jobs, including leadership roles. While technical skills may suffice in lower-level positions, the ability to deal with others becomes critical as we advance in the organization.
> EQ is critical for working in groups.
> EQ is needed to effectively manage diversity.
> EQ helps us adapt to new situations.

Emotional intelligence requires a rich set of abilities. These include self-awareness (recognizing an emotion as it engulfs us), emotion management (controlling reactions to emotion-laden events so that our response fits the situation), self-motivation (directing emotions in the service of a desirable goal), empathy (recognizing emotions in others), and relationship management (managing the emotions in others).

EQ is critical in the "real world." In business settings, EQ is related to leadership ability, group performance, individual performance, the quality of interpersonal exchange, change-management skills, and the ability to conduct effective performance appraisals.[20] Throughout this book we will address issues such as managing stress, self-motivation, coaching, and communicating, to help you develop your emotional intelligence.

Now, assess your emotional intelligence along six dimensions by using the scale in Self-Assessment 3-2, Emotional Intelligence.

Self-Assessment 3-2
Emotional Intelligence

Answer each of the questions in this section using the following scale:

1 = Disagree Strongly
2 = Disagree Somewhat
3 = Neither Agree nor Disagree
4 = Agree Somewhat
5 = Agree Strongly

1. _____ I try to manage my emotions and feelings in front of others.
2. _____ I am often able to resolve conflicts among others.
3. _____ My facial expression and conversational tone are important to me when I'm dealing with others.
4. _____ I have good people-handling skills.
5. _____ I am good at "reading" other people.

6. _____ I am sometimes paralyzed by my emotions; I get so angry or upset or depressed that I have trouble taking action.
7. _____ I think it's important to control my emotions.
8. _____ I "wear my heart on my sleeve"—I don't hide my emotions.
9. _____ I'm a good mediator in conflict situations.
10. _____ I sometimes don't realize how angry I am.
11. _____ When I get upset, I use the energy to help accomplish my goals.
12. _____ I am good at recognizing other people's emotions.
13. _____ I try to keep my emotions under control.
14. _____ I am generally able to get others to calm down when they're upset.
15. _____ I often don't recognize my emotions until someone else comments on them.
16. _____ I am able to use my emotions to motivate myself.
17. _____ I have a good "poker face"—people can't generally tell how I'm feeling.
18. _____ In general, I'm not even conscious of my emotions.
19. _____ I channel my emotions in productive ways.
20. _____ In group settings I am often the person who helps everyone work together smoothly.
21. _____ I can usually tell when people are trying to hide their true emotions.
22. _____ I sometimes lose my temper.

PERSONALITY THEORIES

Many theories of personality have been proposed. Some early personality theories saw behavior as being related to innate traits, such as independence, sociability, and humility. These traits were felt to be stable, enduring, and interrelated. The unique combination of these traits was seen as the clue to personality.

According to another early approach, Sigmund Freud's *psychoanalytic theory,* we are motivated by drives or instincts.[21] We may be unaware of these drives, and they are largely out of our control. In this theory, the unconscious mind plays an overwhelming role, sometimes revealed to us by "Freudian slips": inadvertent mistakes in speech or writing that suggest what is happening in a person's unconscious mind. The psychoanalytic model sees personality as a conflict between basic pleasure-seeking drives and a restrictive society. Unhappiness, neuroses, and psychoses are seen as the result of that conflict.

Humanistic-existential theories focus on the total personality of the individual instead of on the separate behaviors that make up the personality. They downplay the roles of the environment and biology and stress individual choice and personal responsibility. Instead of focusing on conflict, as in the Freudian model, they emphasize striving for awareness and fulfillment of the human potential. These strivings are seen as the basic force motivating human behavior. The work of Abraham Maslow, a key practitioner of this relatively optimistic approach, will be discussed in Chapter 6.

Finally, *learning theories*—which we will also discuss in Chapter 6— see personality as a set of patterns of learned behaviors. That is, personalities differ because people have different experiences in childhood and throughout life. According to this view, while personalities may be extremely complex, they are based upon simple learning principles.

Each of these theories of personality makes different assumptions about things such as the role of the environment versus the role of biology, the degree to which people are active or passive, and motivating forces. Together, the approaches provide a variety of potentially useful perspectives for examining and predicting human behavior.

IMPORTANT PERSONALITY DIMENSIONS

It is especially important to understand how people with particular personalities may behave. In this section we review some personality characteristics related to behavior or performance. Before we consider these characteristics, complete Self-Assessment 3-3, Personality Dimensions.

Self-Assessment 3-3
Personality Dimensions

Answer each of the questions in this section using the following scale:

1 = Disagree Strongly
2 = Disagree Somewhat
3 = Neither Agree nor Disagree
4 = Agree Somewhat
5 = Agree Strongly

1. _____ I can often be persuaded to change my mind.
2. _____ In an ideal world, I'd know in advance the exact consequences of each of my actions.
3. _____ I tend to behave very differently depending on who I'm with.
4. _____ I look forward to changes.
5. _____ I'm a "take charge" sort of person.
6. _____ I stick to my opinions pretty tenaciously.
7. _____ I generally like to "play it safe."
8. _____ I believe authority relationships should be clearly defined.
9. _____ I often have trouble persevering.
10. _____ I generally find that "what will be will be"—my actions often make little difference.
11. _____ I like to know what the rules are, and then I try to follow them.
12. _____ Before I say something, I usually want to get a good idea of what my "audience" wants to hear.
13. _____ It's really important to "look out for number 1"—if you're not careful, people will take advantage of you.
14. _____ I'm always trying to do several different things at the same time.
15. _____ I believe that life is what you make of it—"luck" and "fate" are less important than how we behave.
16. _____ I often find myself getting angry when I'm tied up in traffic.
17. _____ I am pretty much of a risk taker.
18. _____ I think of myself as a "go-getter."
19. _____ I generally show a lot of respect for people in positions of authority.
20. _____ If a goal is just and important, it may be OK to use some "unsavory" means to accomplish it.
21. _____ I generally see the bright side of the picture.
22. _____ I dislike ambiguous situations.

23. _____ I'm a pretty happy person.
24. _____ I generally say what I think, even in cases where the audience is likely to disagree.
25. _____ I take a lot of chances.
26. _____ I'm pretty "laid back"—I don't worry too much about time pressures.
27. _____ I believe that hard work and skill are the keys to success.
28. _____ It is never acceptable to tell a "white lie."
29. _____ I am generally satisfied with things.
30. _____ I am pretty stubborn at times.

Risk-Taking Propensity People—even those in the same position in the same organization—differ markedly in their *risk-taking propensity*.[22] Some are risk averse. They like to "play it safe," choosing alternatives that are likely to give a relatively low but certain return. Others—risk seekers—like to gamble. They prefer alternatives that may turn out very well or very poorly to those with little variance in outcomes. Risk takers tend to make fast decisions based on relatively little information. People with different levels of risk-taking propensity will make very different decisions in the same situation.

Proactive Personality *Proactivity* is the extent to which people take actions to influence their environments. Proactive individuals look for opportunities, show initiative, take action, and persevere until they are able to bring about change. People with proactive personalities have been shown to engage in high levels of entrepreneurial activities and to have relatively high levels of job performance.[23] This is consistent with the idea that the modern workplace rewards take-charge, self-motivated individuals. As a result, proactive personality is a trait that is highly valued by employers.

Authoritarianism *Authoritarian* individuals believe that power and status should be clearly defined and that there should be a hierarchy of authority. They feel that authority should be concentrated in the hands of a few leaders and that this authority should be obeyed. So authoritarian leaders expect unquestioning obedience to their commands; authoritarian subordinates willingly give it. If a leader is authoritarian and his or her subordinate is not, frustration or conflict may result. Authoritarian individuals are likely to be most comfortable in organizations that emphasize rules and following the chain of command.

Dogmatism *Dogmatic* individuals are closed-minded. They have rigid belief systems and "doggedly" stick to their opinions, refusing to revise them in the face of conflicting evidence. Dogmatic individuals make decisions quickly, based on relatively little information, and are confident in those decisions. They like to follow the rules and are unlikely to consider novel alternatives. They may perform acceptably in well-defined, routine situations, especially if there are time constraints. In other cases, especially those demanding creativity, they do poorly.

Locus of Control *Locus of control* refers to the degree to which individuals believe that the things that happen to them are the result of their own actions. Those who believe that such things are within their own control have an internal locus of control. Others have an external locus of control; they see their lives as being controlled by fate, circumstance, or chance. Externals are

Web Wise

Machiavelli's *The Prince*

The term *Machiavellian* comes from Niccolo Machiavelli, author of *The Prince*. Born in Florence, Italy, in 1469, Machiavelli wrote *The Prince* in 1513 as a practical guide for the ruling Medici family on how to deal with the problems a monarch faces in staying in power. The main theme of the book is that princes should retain absolute control of their territories and should use any means necessary to accomplish this end, including deceit. The book—controversial even at the time it was written—has caused Machiavelli's name to become synonymous with self-serving, manipulative, deceitful behavior.

http://www.sas.upenn.edu/~pgrose/mach/

To read *The Prince*, go to

http://www.geocities.com/SunsetStrip/Palms/4513/princetoc.html

unlikely to believe that they can do better if they try harder or that the rewards and punishments they receive depend upon how well they do. For each of these reasons, internals may be more highly motivated than externals. Internals have also been shown to be likely to respond in more positive ways to stress than externals, to behave in more ethical ways, to feel more empowered, and to be more entrepreneurial.[24]

Tolerance for Ambiguity Individuals with high *tolerance for ambiguity* welcome uncertainty and change. Those with low tolerance for ambiguity see such situations as threatening and uncomfortable. Since managers are increasingly facing dynamic, unstructured situations, tolerance for ambiguity is clearly an important characteristic.

Machiavellianism Individuals with a *Machiavellian* personality think that any behavior is acceptable if it achieves their goals. Machiavellians try to manipulate others. They are unemotional and detached. They "look out for Number One" and aren't likely to be good team players. Not surprisingly, they also are relatively likely to be unethical.[25]

Self-Monitoring *Self-monitoring* is the extent to which people vary their behavior to match the situation and make the best possible impression on others.[26] High self-monitors pay close attention to their "audience" and tailor their behaviors accordingly. For instance, a high self-monitor may act humble and respectful when dealing with the boss but be boastful and ill mannered with subordinates. Similarly, a high self-monitor may present very different opinions to different audiences. Low self-monitors, on the other hand, react to situations without looking to others for behavioral cues; they present the same face in different situations. Self-monitors are "chameleon-like," able to change their behaviors to fit the audience. While this may seem somewhat devious, it could also be seen as sensitive to the demands of the situation. Evidence seems clear that high self-monitors tend to do better. For example, a study that tracked business graduates showed that high self-monitors got more promotions, either cross-company or within their original firm, than low self-monitors.[27]

Type A and Type B The *Type A behavior pattern* is characterized by feelings of great time pressure and impatience. Type A's work aggressively, speak explosively, and find themselves constantly struggling. The opposite pattern—relaxed, steady-paced, and easygoing—is called the *Type B behavior pattern.* Individuals with Type A behavior patterns are much more likely than others to experience high stress levels and to show a variety of symptoms of stress, including coronary heart disease. Type A's have trouble delegating responsibility to others, don't work well in groups, and are impatient with tasks requiring prolonged problem solving. Because of these limitations and the health risks of being a Type A, relatively few Type A's rise to high levels in organizations. We'll explore Type A behavior in more detail in our discussion of managing stress in Chapter 9.

The "Big 5" Personality Dimensions Hundreds of personality characteristics have been identified, of which we have considered several of the most important. Evidence is accumulating that virtually all personality measures can be categorized into five consistent sets, now called the Big Five: extraversion, agreeableness, conscientiousness, emotional stability, and openness to experience. The Big Five categories hold up remarkably well across national cultures and over time.[28]

> **Extraversion:** Extraverts tend to be outgoing and gregarious, dominant and ambitious, and adventuresome. Extraverts tend to have positive emotions, to have a large number of close friends, and to take on leadership roles.
> **Agreeableness:** Agreeable persons are trusting, caring, good-natured, cheerful, and gentle. Agreeableness is especially significant in careers where teamwork or customer service is important.
> **Conscientiousness:** Conscientious individuals are hardworking and persistent, responsible and careful, and well organized. Conscientiousness is related to success at work. Conscientious individuals have higher levels of job performance, engage in fewer counterproductive work behaviors, are absent less often, and are less likely to leave the firm than those who are less conscientious.
> **Emotional stability:** Emotional stability is best recognized by its absence: anxiety, hostility, depression, self-consciousness, vulnerability, and impulsiveness.
> **Openness to experience:** Individuals who are open to experience tend to be intelligent, imaginative, and unconventional.

Take a few minutes now to rate yourself on the "Big 5" personality dimensions by completing Self-Assessment 3-4, The "Big 5" Personality Dimensions.

Self-Assessment 3-4
The "Big 5" Personality Dimensions

Answer each of the questions in this section using the following scale:

1 = Disagree Strongly
2 = Disagree Somewhat
3 = Neither Agree nor Disagree
4 = Agree Somewhat
5 = Agree Strongly

1. _____ I am quite outgoing.
2. _____ I can get along with just about anyone.
3. _____ I think of myself as intellectual.
4. _____ I can sometimes be rude.
5. _____ I am a very warm person.
6. _____ I am shy.
7. _____ I am quite energetic.
8. _____ I would describe myself as temperamental.
9. _____ I am often envious.
10. _____ I am philosophical.
11. _____ I am generally quite relaxed.
12. _____ I am sometimes careless.
13. _____ I am unimaginative.
14. _____ I am often sloppy.
15. _____ I am sometimes withdrawn.
16. _____ I would describe myself as creative.

17. _____ I am quite practical.
18. _____ I am a very kind person.
19. _____ I am rarely jealous.
20. _____ I am very organized.

Our discussion of personality should not be taken to suggest that people have no control over their actions. Instead, personality characteristics suggest tendencies to behave in certain ways. People's conscious decisions may help them overcome troublesome behavior patterns. For instance, employees may be able to take actions to alter Type A behavior patterns, to ensure that they consider more information before making a decision, and to modify their risk preferences.

Still, throughout your career you will be working with people who react very differently from one another with respect to risk, uncertainty, new ideas, rules and regulations, and much else. Some of your colleagues are likely to be more manipulative, self-serving, and unethical than others. Some will be self-starters and some will need a push. Some will be driven and some will be laid back. These diverse personalities will provide opportunities and challenges as you build teams, try out new practices, and simply get through the workday. By recognizing this variety and its implications, you will have made a good start toward successfully understanding, predicting, and influencing others in the workplace.

RECOGNIZING CROSS-CULTURAL DIFFERENCES

With *globalization,* the world's people are becoming more interconnected with respect to the cultural, political, technological, and environmental aspects of their lives. What does this mean for you?

> You are likely to spend at least part of your career in other countries—in fact, some companies now require international experience for their top managers.

> According to Andrew Grove, Chairman of Intel, with globalization "every employee will compete with every person in the world who is capable of doing the same job. There are a lot of them, and many of them are very hungry."[29]

> You may suddenly find yourself working for a foreign firm. International mergers and acquisitions reached an all-time high of $544.31 billion in 1998. While U.S. companies have historically been the world's biggest buyers, United Kingdom firms have now taken over the lead. Increasingly, you may be working for a firm headquartered in Germany, Sweden, Japan, or almost anywhere else in the world.

> Your firm—and your job—will increasingly depend on international trade. Directly or indirectly, international trade now accounts for about 20 percent of all jobs in the United States.

> You will be managing a culturally diverse workforce even if you never leave the United States. Consider the following: The Census Bureau estimates that by the year 2050, Asian Americans, Hispanics, African Americans, and other nonwhite groups will compose 47 percent of the U.S.

population. The Hispanic population is projected to grow from 24 million (9 percent of the population) to 81 million (21 percent); Hispanics will account for 33 percent of the nation's population growth. In addition, the number of Asian Americans is projected to jump from 7 million to 35 million by 2040. The diversity provided by these groups is even greater than a listing of categories such as "Asian American" and "Hispanic" might suggest. For example, Hispanics represent many nationalities and ethnicities, including Mexicans, Cubans, Puerto Ricans, Spanish, Dominican Republicans, and people from 15 other Central and South American countries, all with different histories, labor force characteristics, and growth rates.

Organizations of all kinds must learn to effectively manage cultural diversity. Consider the New York Yankees. During the 1998 season Yankees pitching coach Mel Stottlemeyer did a masterful job of overseeing one of the most international pitching staffs in major league baseball. The staff—which included Graeme Lloyd from Australia, Orlando "El Duque" Hernandez from Cuba, Hideki Irabu from Japan, and Ramiro Mendoza and Mariano Rivera from Panama—led the Yankees to 114 wins, the most in American League history.[30]

So whether you are living in Lima, Ohio, or Lima, Peru, you will be managing a culturally diverse workforce, dealing with global competitors, or even working for a foreign firm. What might we expect as we deal with people from other national cultures? Geert Hofstede, a Dutch researcher who worked as a psychologist for IBM, studied 116,000 people working in 64 countries and identified five important dimensions along which national cultures differ:[31]

> *Individualism versus collectivism.* In *individualistic* cultures, such as the United States and Australia, the cultural belief is that the individual comes first—social frameworks are loosely knit and people are chiefly expected to look after their own interests and those of their immediate family. There is an emphasis on individual achievement. Society offers individuals a great amount of freedom, and people are used to making independent decisions and taking independent action. In *collectivist* cultures, such as Colombia and Pakistan, there are tight social frameworks in which people expect the groups of which they are members to look after them and protect them in times of trouble. In exchange for security, loyalty is expected. A saying that reflects the collectivist view is: "The nail that sticks out will be pounded down."

> **Power distance** is the degree to which a society accepts the fact that power in institutions and organizations is distributed unequally. A high-power-distance society, such as the Philippines, Mexico, or India, accepts wide differences in power in organizations. Employees show great respect for authority, titles, status, and rank. Titles are important in bargaining. A low-power-distance society, such as Denmark, Israel, or Ireland, plays down inequalities as much as possible.

> **Uncertainty avoidance** refers to the way societies deal with risk and uncertainty. In low-uncertainty-avoidance countries, such as Switzerland and Denmark, people are relatively comfortable with risks and tolerate behaviors and opinions that differ from their own. In high-uncertainty-avoidance countries, such as Japan and Greece, there is a high level of

anxiety among the people. Formal rules and other mechanisms are used to provide security and reduce risk. There is less tolerance for deviant ideas and behaviors, and people strive to believe in absolute truths.

> Quality versus quantity of life. Some cultures, such as Japan and Austria, emphasize the *quantity of life* and value assertiveness and the acquisition of money and material things. Other cultures, such as the Scandinavian countries, emphasize the quality of life and the importance of relationships, and they show sensitivity and concern for the welfare of others. In quality-of-life cultures, people stop to smell the roses. In quantity-of-life cultures, people try to get as many roses as possible.

> Time orientation. Citizens of some countries, such as Japan and Hong Kong, have a *long-term orientation,* derived from values that include thrift (saving) and persistence in achieving goals. Those from other countries, such as France and Indonesia, have a *short-term orientation,* derived from values that express a concern for maintaining personal stability or happiness and living for the present.

Another key factor is whether cultures are high or low context. In a *high-context* culture, such as most Asian, Hispanic, African, and Arab countries, the context in which a communication occurs is just as important as the words that are actually spoken, and cultural clues are important in understanding what is being communicated. The context includes the social set-

GLOBAL PERSPECTIVES

DIVERSITY GOES GLOBAL AT IBM*

Since 1995 IBM has begun to develop a strategic approach to the concerns and experiences of female executives in the United States and abroad. In 1997, 81 women from 19 countries were brought together in the first Global Women Leaders Conference to begin to define common barriers to the advancement of women worldwide and to design remedies. The women returned to their work locations to develop regional strategies. The next year, the women were brought together again to share their successes and problems in developing and implementing strategies. In 1998 a second Global Women Leaders Conference was held, with 135 women in attendance from 29 countries. Top barriers identified were the "male-dominated culture" of the organization, difficulty with balancing work and personal responsibilities, lack of networking and mentors, access to key positions, and a "culture that doesn't take risks with women." These top five barriers emerged as the top five in every geographical region. Maria Ferris, manager of global workforce diversity initiatives at IBM, noted that these barriers are not the result of deep-seated norms in the external cultures. Instead, "They are things we can change in the IBM corporation." Since the 1998 conference, many new initiatives have been put in place. For instance, in the Asia/Pacific region a women's council was established for the entire region, and national women's councils were begun in Japan, China, Australia/New Zealand, and Korea. A policy statement was written, a mentor program established, and regular networking calls held. In the EMEA (Europe, Middle East, Africa) region, the first-ever work/life survey was conducted, a mentor program was established, and recruiting material was improved. The number of female executives grew from five in 1995 to 31 at the end of 1998, and there is an increased focus on women in leadership, development, and managerial roles.

*Based on M. B. White, "Women of the World: Diversity Goes Global at IBM," *Diversity Factor,* 1999, *7(4),* pp. 13–16.

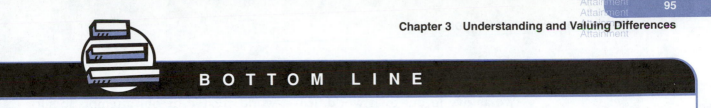

BOTTOM LINE

The Bottom Line: Managing Cross-Cultural Differences

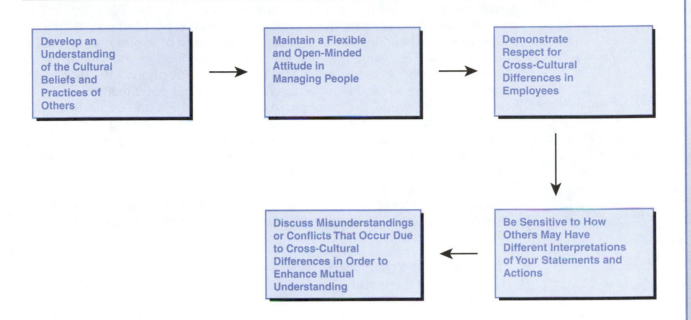

ting, use of phrasing, gestures, and tone of voice, and the person's history and status. In a *low-context* culture, such as Germany or the United States, the words used by the speaker explicitly convey the speaker's message to the listener.

This suggests that nonverbal communications (see Chapter 5), while important in all settings, are especially critical in high-context cultures. Most immigrants to the United States are now coming from high-context cultures. Nonverbal communications have dramatically different meanings across cultures.[32] For instance, nodding your head means "Yes" in most countries but "No" in Bulgaria and Greece. The classic "OK" sign of thumb and forefinger forming a circle can imply "money" in Japan, means "worthless" in France, and is considered an obscene gesture in Brazil, Germany, and Russia. In Saudi Arabia, to cross your legs in such a way that you display the sole of your foot to your host is a grievous affront. While North Americans often wave to signal "Hello" or "Goodbye," this action signals "No!" in much of Europe.

There are also cultural differences in the meaning of eye contact. While Americans generally expect eye contact in a conversation, many Asians and Hispanics consider eye contact, especially with a superior, to be utterly disrespectful. In countries such as Libya, looking a woman in the eye for more than a short time is considered a form of assault.

The accompanying Bottom Line presents a process model that summarizes the basic steps associated with managing cross-cultural differences.

MAINTAINING ACCURATE PERCEPTIONS

We all live in our own world. It is a world created by our attempts to sift through, to organize, and to interpret the tremendous number of things we see, hear, feel, and otherwise constantly sense. It is different from all other worlds—the unique product of a complex process.

Ms. Johnson, a fast-rising executive, exists in the world of one of her colleagues as hardworking and competent. In the world of another, she is driven and ruthless. The "same" job that in Sam's world is boring and routine exists in Carol's world as a source of challenge and opportunity. Mr. Bjornson's subtle messages to Mr. Peterson, carefully crafted and potentially powerful in Mr. Bjornson's world, are nowhere to be found in the world of Mr. Peterson.

The "truth" in our world depends on whether something is consistent with the rest of that world. Moreover, the nature of our unique world helps determine how we behave. How are these private worlds created? What makes each unique? How are we to deal with people living in other worlds?

In this section we will consider the nature of the perceptual process, noting key influences at each step and associated problems. We will then review the related process of causal attribution. Finally, we will discuss ways to reduce perceptual errors.

THE PERCEPTUAL PROCESS

Knowledge of the world is sent to our brains through our sensory systems—seeing, hearing, tasting, touching, and smelling. *Perception* is the complex process by which we select, organize, and interpret sensory stimuli into a meaningful and coherent picture of the world.[33] As shown in Figure 3-2, perception involves several steps. In the first step, sensation, many stimuli impact on our sensory filters, but only some are sensed. Others are filtered out, perhaps because they are at very low levels or are not within a particular range. In subsequent steps, stimuli which are sensed are selected, organized, and translated. Let's consider some things that occur at each of those steps.

Selecting Stimuli In this step, selection, some stimuli are selected for further processing. If our perceptions were not selective, we would be overwhelmed. For example, consider Figure 3-3. What do you see? An old man's face? A woman carrying a child? A woman's face? Another face? A gateway? A stooped old man? A hand? These and several other shapes can be found in the figure, but you would probably "see" only a few of them if you hadn't been prompted to search for more.

FIGURE 3-2

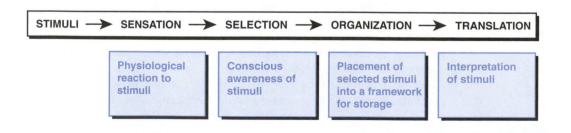

FIGURE 3-3
Nine Persons

Source: This is a black and white reprinting of a color painting by the Swiss artist Sandro Del Prete.

Ideally, we might select only the most important stimuli. However, many factors affect selection, some of which are potentially troublesome. For instance, we have all heard the saying "I'll believe it when I see it." The statement "I'll see it when I believe it" applies to perception. That is, we are more likely to see things we are expecting to see. This is called *perceptual readiness.* For example, executives in various departments of a manufacturing firm read a detailed case study from a business policy course. While they were told to analyze the case from a companywide perspective, they instead focused on their own areas—the areas where they were ready to see problems. Salespeople, for instance, saw marketing problems as needing attention, and production people identified organization and production problems as most pressing.[34] Thus, perceptual readiness may cause us to fail to "see the big picture."

Many other things influence the stimuli we select. For example, different people will select different stimuli based on their needs and personalities. A hungry person is likely to focus on the food in an advertisement for china. Insecure people may focus on cues that imply threat. Also, stimuli that contrast with the surrounding environment are more likely than others to be selected. That contrast could be in color, size, flavor, or some other factor. The only person talking in a theater or the only blue shirt in a sea of Wisconsin red on a football weekend almost demands attention. In addition, repetition of a stimulus has an additive effect, making it more likely to attract attention. Advertisers, of course, make use of this fact, regularly repeating a message. And you have probably had an experience similar to the following: You say "Hello" to a friend, Bob. Bob doesn't respond. You say "Hello" again. Bob replies, "Oh, hi. Sorry, I didn't hear you the first time." In fact, of course, Bob *had* to hear

FIGURE 3-4
The Hering Illusion

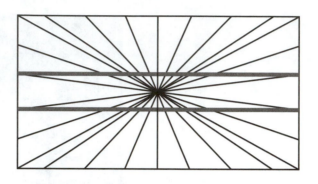

you the first time to make that statement. Further, stimuli that are intense, changing, or novel are more likely to be selected.

Organizing Stimuli Once stimuli have been selected, they must be organized in a useful framework. The way we organize stimuli is important. Things we group together tend to be recalled together, and their meanings tend to influence one another. In general, we are likely to group things that are somehow similar (for instance, in shape, size, or color) or that are close together in time or space (two accidents that occurred on the same day or two people seated together). Also, we tend to organize things so closure occurs. That is, we "close up" or "fill in" missing parts to create a meaningful whole.

Interpreting Stimuli Finally, we interpret stimuli at the translation step in the perceptual process. The way we translate the stimuli that we have selected and organized depends on the situation (for instance, whether it is friendly or hostile, relaxed or frantic), our characteristics, and characteristics of the thing being perceived. Many distortions of objective reality are possible at the translation stage. Some of these are simply due to quirks in the way our senses work. For instance, Figure 3-4 shows the "Hering Illusion," in which two parallel lines appear curved to us because of the nature of their background.

Other distortions are perhaps more subtle but certainly no less important. Some of the most important perceptual distortions are: stereotyping, Pygmalion effect, halo effect, projection, primacy/recency effects, and perceptual defense.

> *Stereotyping.* Walter Lippmann coined the term *stereotyping* in 1922, describing stereotypes as "pictures in people's heads" that distorted their perceptions of others.[35] The term is now often used to mean the forming of an opinion of people based on group membership. Stereotyping, if accurate, may be useful, since it efficiently places information into categories. When we face new situations, stereotypes provide guidelines to help classify people.

Unfortunately, stereotyping may lead to a distorted view of the situation if the stereotyping is based on false premises. For instance, one study found that labeling a photograph as that of a management representative led to a different impression than when the same photograph was labeled as that of a union leader.[36] In another study, hiring decisions were made on the basis of matched pairs of dossiers.[37] The dossiers differed only in one way: One in each set had a male name and the other had a female name. The dossier with the male name was more likely to be hired. Research suggests that stereotyping in work organizations may be harmful to minority group members, older workers, and females.

> *Pygmalion Effect.* We noted earlier that perceptual readiness influences the stimuli we select. It also influences how we interpret those stimuli. A prime example is the self-fulfilling prophecy, or *Pygmalion effect.* The term comes from mythology. As told by Ovid, a sculptor named Pygmalion created a sculpture of a young woman so beautiful that he fell hopelessly in love with it. Venus, the goddess of love and beauty, was fascinated by this new kind of lover and brought the sculpture to life. Pygmalion named the maiden Galatea, and they had a son, Paphos. The Pygmalion effect, then, refers to creating something in the image we have of it. For better or worse, teachers, managers, and others often demonstrate this effect.[38] For example, teachers who were told that certain students were especially intelligent (when, in fact, they were not) later perceived those students to show signs of greater intelligence and higher performance. As a result, they treated them differently. These "intelligent" students then showed gains in intellectual capacity, while others did not. Similar findings have occurred when leaders were told (again, incorrectly) that certain of their subordinates were high performers. The leaders apparently saw "high-performing" subordinates differently and gave them considerable decision-making authority. They closely supervised "low performers." Thus, perceptual readiness may cause us to color our perceptions based upon our expectations.

> *Halo Effect. Halo effect* refers to a process in which a judge uses a general impression that is favorable or unfavorable (a "horns effect") to evaluate specific traits. Because of this general halo, the judge doesn't evaluate each trait independently. Sometimes one trait, such as a subordinate's honesty or enthusiasm, forms the halo. So if the boss feels the subordinate is honest, the subordinate may also be seen as loyal, efficient, and courteous, and so on. That is, we have a tendency to perceive links between traits. If we make evaluations on the basis of a halo when the traits really aren't linked, halo error is the result. Of course, many traits are in fact related, so not all halo effect is really halo error.[39]

> *Projection.* The term *projection* has taken on a variety of related meanings in which individuals project their own characteristics onto others. For example, people may relieve their own guilt by projecting blame on others. Fearful people tend to see others as fearful. People with certain undesirable personality characteristics, such as stinginess or obstinacy, tend to rate others as relatively high on those traits.[40]

> *Primacy/Recency Effects.* The time at which we receive a stimulus influences the weight we give it. Quite often, the first information we receive has a very great influence on our final impressions. This is called a *primacy effect.* It has important consequences when a sequence of

alternatives is considered, such as in the case of job-choice decisions or of job interviews. Sometimes, information we have received recently has a great influence—a *recency effect.* The bottom line for communication is that it's important to start strong and finish strong.

> *Perceptual Defense.* When we face information we find to be threatening or unacceptable, our perceptions try to defend us. We may fail to perceive the troublesome stimuli, or we may distort our perceptions of the stimuli to make them less troublesome. Perceptual defense is especially evident when long-held beliefs or attitudes are challenged.

   To illustrate, in one study college students were given descriptions of factory workers.[41] These descriptions included the word *intelligent.* Since this description was contrary to the students' beliefs concerning factory workers, their perceptual defenses came to the rescue. Some students simply denied that the workers were intelligent. Most frequently, they modified or distorted the description. Students, for instance, might accept the term *intelligent* but would couple it with another characteristic, such as lack of initiative, to maintain their overall perception of the workers. Clearly, perceptual defense can result in a very distorted and potentially biased view. For example, RJR Nabisco spent more than $300 million on a "smokeless" cigarette, Premier, before abandoning the project after eight years of research and testing. Researchers had simply continued to shrug off negative feedback, including the facts that the company didn't know how to make the product in a factory and that the cigarette didn't taste right and caused a "hernia effect"—smokers had to inhale furiously to get much smoke. Rather than listen to the feedback, "Management would always say, 'We can fix this; we can fix that.'" A senior RJR executive said, "What happens is you get into a euphoria where you con yourself."[42]

   Before moving on, complete Skills Practice 3-2, Do You Know Me? This is a short but fun exercise that shows how we often possess at least some inaccurate impressions or perceptions of other people, especially those we don't know very well. Try it and you may surprise yourself with what you find out.

Skills Practice 3-2
Do You Know Me?

Skill Objectives

1. To develop skill in understanding one's biases in perceiving people, issues, etc.
2. To develop strategies for making perceptions more accurate.

Procedure

1. Find a partner in your class who you do not know. Take 2–3 minutes to get acquainted with one another.
2. Using the nine-point scale provided, do the following:
    a. respond to each statement in terms of the extent to which *you* agree or disagree with it (there are no right or wrong answers here, so please be honest!).
    b. respond to each statement in terms of how you think *your partner* answered it.

Web Wise

Perception Resources

There are excellent perception sites on the Web. For a vast array of perception links, see:

http://www.yorku.ca/eye/links.htm

Be sure to check out *The Joy of Visual Perception: A Web Book* (including the Fun Things links) at:

http://www.yorku.ca/eye

3. Once you and your partner have completed your ratings, share your responses with each other. Using the scoring summary, determine the total difference score between your predicted ratings of your partner and your partner's actual responses.

4. Now discuss with each other what information you used as a basis for making your predictions of your partner's ratings.

Scale to Be Used for Making Ratings

1	2	3	4	5	6	7	8	9
Strongly Disagree				Neutral				Strongly Agree

	Your Ratings	Your Prediction of Your Partner's Ratings	Difference
1. Money is the number 1 motivator of people.	_____	_____	_____
2. Downsizing and employee layoffs should be avoided at any cost.	_____	_____	_____
3. I do not like working in teams.	_____	_____	_____
4. The key to success in business is personal relationships.	_____	_____	_____
5. Managing people is just a matter of common sense.	_____	_____	_____
		Total Difference	_____

The process model shown in the accompanying Bottom Line summarizes the basic steps associated with increasing the accuracy of your perception of a situation.

IMPLICIT THEORIES

Implicit theories are theories in peoples' minds. For instance, we may believe that jobs offering more challenge also provide more authority. Or we may believe that leaders who let their subordinates participate in making decisions also care more about their subordinates. These implicit theories may be correct or incorrect. They may influence perceptions at the selection, organization, and translation stages. For instance, if we see evidence concerning one element of the theory, we will be likely to perceive other elements also. So if our boss lets us participate in decision making, we may also be more likely to see caring behaviors, to organize caring behaviors along with opportunities for participation, and to translate particular behaviors as more caring.[43]

Many working people—like many students—aren't big fans of formal academic theories that they see in textbooks. However, it is critical to recognize that we all have our own personal, implicit theories that represent our beliefs about how things work. Complete Skills Practice 3-3 to get a better understanding of your implicit theories and how they influence your behavior.

Skills Practice 3-3
Implicit Theories of Personality

Skill Level: **Challenging**

Skill Objective

To develop skill in understanding how individual differences affect work behavior.

Procedure

1. Brainstorm a list of the personality characteristics you feel are important for success in terms of one of the following:
   a. A good worker
   b. A good leader
   c. A good team player
   List all the characteristics you identified down the rows and across the columns of the table on the attached worksheet.
2. Discuss each personality trait you identified in terms of why you feel it is important.
3. Now think about how the various traits you identified are related to one another. Indicate the relationships between the various characteristics in your "implicit theory" by putting a "+" if you feel that the trait in a given row has a positive effect on the trait in

BOTTOM LINE

The Bottom Line: Increasing Perceptual Accuracy

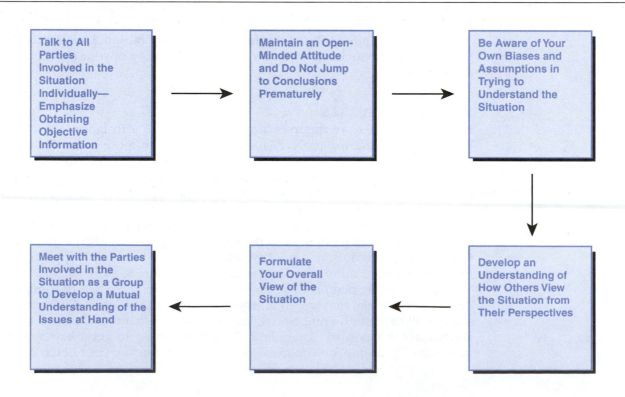

Talk to All Parties Involved in the Situation Individually— Emphasize Obtaining Objective Information → Maintain an Open-Minded Attitude and Do Not Jump to Conclusions Prematurely → Be Aware of Your Own Biases and Assumptions in Trying to Understand the Situation ↓

Meet with the Parties Involved in the Situation as a Group to Develop a Mutual Understanding of the Issues at Hand ← Formulate Your Overall View of the Situation ← Develop an Understanding of How Others View the Situation from Their Perspectives

a given column. If you feel that the trait in a row has a negative effect on the trait in a column, indicate this with a "−." Finally, if you feel that there is no relationship between a trait in a given row and another trait in a column, indicate this with a "0."

4. Based on the personality type you just developed, discuss specific strategies employers could use to find and/or develop these kinds of individuals. Be as specific as possible.

Worksheet: Implicit Theories of Personality Exercise

I.   Personality Type to Be Developed (e.g., a good worker): _____

II. Personality Summary Table

Key: + = Trait in row has a positive effect on trait in column
        − = Trait in row has a negative effect on trait in column
        0 = Trait in row has no effect on trait in column

	Trait 1	Trait 2	Trait 3	Trait 4
Trait 1	X			
Trait 2		X		
Trait 3			X	
Trait 4				X

CAUSAL ATTRIBUTION

We must often form perceptions of the causes underlying others' behaviors. This process is called *causal attribution.* As an example, a district sales manager may want to determine what caused a salesperson's poor performance in the fall quarter. It may be especially important to determine whether the behavior was the result of internal factors, such as the person's motives or traits or of external factors, such as luck or the situation. For example, if the sales manager feels that her subordinate's poor performance is due to lack of effort (an internal factor), she may want to consider disciplinary actions. If she feels the poor performance is due to an economic downturn, such actions would seem unfair.

According to Harold Kelley's *attribution theory,* we try to sort out the causes of an individual's behavior by considering three factors.[44] For instance, in the case of our poor-performing salesperson, the boss might ask three questions. First, did others act the same way in this situation? That is, did others also have a poor period in the downturn? Second, does this salesperson always act this way in this situation? That is, does he always do poorly in economic downturns? Third, does this salesperson act differently in other situations? That is, does he do better in the absence of an economic downturn? If the boss answered yes to each of these questions, she would probably not blame her subordinate. On the other hand, if other people had done well in the downturn and this subordinate always does poorly, it would be hard to blame the situation.

Unfortunately, causal attribution is a process that is prone to error. For instance, we tend to attribute the behavior of others to internal factors, even when this is not appropriate. That is, we often blame or commend people for

FOCUS ON MANAGEMENT

ATTRIBUTION THEORY AT BOOTS THE CHEMIST

Boots the Chemist, a British pharmaceutical firm, wanted a test to select potential sales assistants. Dissatisfied with available tests, it developed a new questionnaire for its own use based on attribution theory (which, as noted in the text, looks at the ways in which people explain why events occurred). It was predicted—and shown in subsequent research—that the most successful sales performers and those rated most highly for their customer care would be more likely to attribute outcomes to internally controllable factors, such as their own effort or choice of sales strategy. The questionnaire is now used in the selection process for sales assistants and to help identify developmental needs.

http://www.the-times.co.uk/news/ pages/changing-times.html?999

things that are really outside their control. Also, the *self-serving bias*—the tendency to take credit for successes and deny personal responsibility for failures—is often seen.

REDUCING PERCEPTUAL ERRORS

Perception is so important and plays such a major role in determining our behavior that we must make every effort to do it right. For instance, people who are aware of their own characteristics make fewer errors in perceiving others and are less likely to see the world in black-and-white terms. Also, people who are able to accept themselves as they are can see a wider range of characteristics in others. They may also be less prone to projection. Further, simple knowledge of such tendencies as halo error, stereotyping, and self-serving bias may help to avoid them. Finally, it is important to make a conscious effort to attend to relevant information and to test reality. Actively seek evidence of whether or not your perceptions are accurate. Compare your perceptions with those of others and try to account for any differences. Look for objective measures relating to the perceptions. If you think Mr. Tanaka is a poor performer, check his output levels.

You will encounter many "real-world" management situations in which the people involved have very different perceptions of an issue. Complete Skills Practice 3-4 to get some practice in dealing with such situations.

Skills Practice 3-4   **Skill Level: Challenging**
He Said, She Said

Skill Objective
To develop skill in managing different perceptions of a situation.

Procedure
1. Read the following scenarios.
2. Using the general guidelines for reducing perceptual errors discussed in the chapter, identify specific strategies for managing the perceptual differences in each scenario.

Scenario 1—The Team Slacker

You are the manager of a team of sales associates at a large department store. One day, Lisa, one of your high-performing employees, comes to talk to you about a problem she is experiencing. She states that Phil, one of the other sales associates, is not being a "team player." Specifically, he never does his fair share when it comes to performing the nonsales responsibilities and duties of his job (e.g., stocking the shelves with new products, doing inventory, putting tags on products). Lisa perceives this to be grossly unfair since she feels that it negatively affects her ability to perform her job effectively. What would you do?

Scenario 2—The New Process

You are the manager of a team of production workers at a manufacturing facility. In order to enhance overall work unit efficiency and effectiveness, you have decided to adopt some new technology that will automate certain aspects of the production process. You believe that this will enhance quality and productivity while reducing costs. However, at a recent departmental meeting, many of your employees expressed negative views of the new technology as a "management trick" to get them to worker harder for the same pay and then to eliminate their jobs altogether. What would you do?

Scenario 3—Obtaining the Commitment of a Senior Executive

You are the Director of Marketing at a medium-sized financial services firm. Six months ago, the vice president of your division requested that you conduct a study to identify strategies for enhancing customer retention. The results of your study have clearly revealed that your customers view the company as being stale and outdated and the quality of customer service provided as low. Based on this, you need to recommend some fundamental changes in the firm's marketing strategy. The major barrier is that you must make a presentation of your findings and recommendations to your vice president at the next Marketing Division meeting. In particular, the vice president is a strong advocate of maintaining the status quo. She also does not like hearing bad news and has been known to "shoot the messenger" when bad news is presented to her. Given this, how should you approach the situation?

Scenario 4—Butting Heads on the Cross-Functional Team

You are the manager of a product development team at a computer corporation. The goal of the team is to develop highly innovative products that exceed consumer expectations in terms of cost, quality, and features. You are experiencing some serious clashes of personalities and perspectives on your team. Specifically, marketing and engineering team members have very different perceptions of what the team's goals should be and how it should work toward achieving its goals. Marketing team members place great emphasis on understanding the needs and wants of customers and capitalizing on market opportunities in an aggressive manner. Engineering team members are more concerned with technical issues of new products (e.g., making sure the design is right) and are not willing to compromise their technical standards in order to meet short-term customer needs. How would you handle this situation?

Next, complete Skills Practice 3-5, designed to help you develop a greater sensitivity toward others' perceptions of a situation or problem that may differ from your own.

Skills Practice 3-5
Walking a Mile in the Shoes of Another

Skill Objective

To demonstrate the importance of testing your understanding of how others perceive a given situation.

Procedure

1. Select an employed individual to follow ("shadow") for at least half a day. Ideally, this should be a person whose job you are only familiar with at a general level.
2. In a couple of paragraphs, write a description of what you think this person's job entails. Make sure you do this *before* you meet with the person. Be sure to address the following questions.
    a. What are the tasks and responsibilities associated with this job?
    b. Why is this job important to the organization?
    c. What kinds of knowledge and skills are important in order to be successful at this job?
    d. What are the most difficult aspects of this job?
3. Spend half a day observing the person you selected performing his/her job. Ask the person the questions you listed in item 2.
4. Compare the description of the job you wrote in item 2 (before observing the job) vs. item 3 (what you actually learned about the job). How similar or different were they? What are the practical implications of this exercise for you as a future manager?

ATTITUDES

Attitudes are the beliefs, feelings, and behavioral tendencies held by a person about an object, event, or person (called the *attitude object*). In this section we'll consider the nature of attitudes and look at some specific work attitudes. We will also discuss how attitudes are formed and see how work attitudes are related to work behaviors.

THE COMPONENTS OF ATTITUDES

Our definition of *attitudes* indicates that they have three components, as shown in Figure 3-5: cognitive, affective, and behavioral tendency.

> The *cognitive component* of attitudes is our cognitions, or beliefs about the facts pertaining to the attitude object. This is descriptive information rather than liking or intentions. We may, for example, believe that salespersons in our firm receive high pay or that our firm is the oldest in the industry. These beliefs may, of course, be correct or incorrect.

> The second component of attitudes, the *affective component,* is made up of our feelings toward the attitude object. The affective component (which shares the same root as *affection*) involves evaluation and emotion. For instance, we may think favorably or unfavorably about another employee or think a particular rule is good or bad.

> The third component, the *behavioral tendency component,* is the way we intend to behave toward the attitude object. We may, for example, intend to tell off the boss or ask for a raise or outperform a coworker.

Sometimes, our cognitions may influence our feelings, which may, in turn, influence our behavioral tendencies. For example, our belief that pay is $7 an hour (cognitive component) may lead us to be dissatisfied with pay (affective component), which may lead us to decide to look for another job (behavioral tendency). However, people with the same beliefs may develop different feelings (for example, some people may be satisfied with pay of $7 an hour), and

FIGURE 3-5
Components of Attitudes

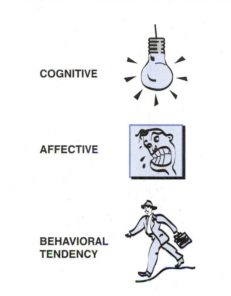

COGNITIVE

AFFECTIVE

BEHAVIORAL
TENDENCY

different people with the same feelings may develop different behavioral intentions (some people, even though dissatisfied with pay, may never decide to seek work elsewhere). Also, there may even be cases in which our beliefs will be influenced by our feelings (as in the saying "Love is blind") or by our behavioral tendencies (as when, after learning we'll be required to move to another town, we begin to find things wrong with our current location). Further, as we'll discuss later, the components of our attitudes may even be influenced by our actual behaviors. The point, then, is that the various components of attitudes are rather intimately and intricately linked and may continually influence one another.

WHY CARE ABOUT ATTITUDES?

It might seem that managers should be concerned about employee behaviors, not their attitudes. After all, it's behavior, such as performance or absenteeism, that shows up on the "bottom line." It could even be argued that there is something sinister about trying to influence people's attitudes—what right do managers have to try to change (or even know) what people think?

In fact, though, there are many reasons why managers should care about employee attitudes. First, as we suggested earlier, attitudes may influence work behaviors. As shown in Figure 3-6, attitudes may influence such work outcomes as performance, turnover, and absenteeism (we'll see whether or not they actually do influence those behaviors later in the chapter). If so, managers may try to improve behaviors by bringing about changes in attitudes. Statements such as "A satisfied employee is a productive employee" show that many people do believe that attitudes (in this case, satisfaction) are related to work behaviors (here, productivity). So it is important to see what links, if any, really do exist between employee attitudes and their behaviors.

FIGURE 3-6
Some Potential Relationships of Attitudes to Behaviors

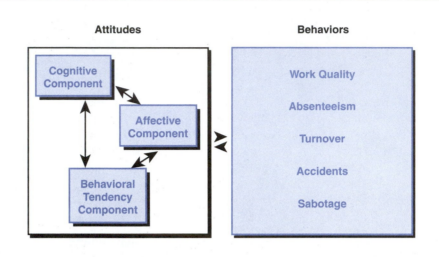

Second, work attitudes may influence things of direct concern to the employee, such as stress levels, ability to sleep, and attitudes toward other aspects of life. As we learn more about behavior in organizations, one thing becomes increasingly clear: there is no magic door separating work and nonwork life. Things that happen at work have important consequences off the job, and vice versa. As one example, research shows that fathers who have autonomy and supportive bosses at work tend to have higher self-esteem, to treat their children with greater acceptance and warmth, and to use less harsh discipline than do fathers with less autonomy and support at work.[45] When one father in the study, a trucker who had been working overtime, complained that he hadn't seen his family for three days, his supervisor announced in front of 11 other drivers, "You can always get another family but you can't get another job like this one."[46]

Finally, attitudes are important for their own sake, independent of their consequences. Employees spend half their waking lives at work. Caring managers may want to learn how to make the working hours of employees more pleasant or how to make employees' jobs more involving. Further, managers may feel it is appropriate to reduce certain undesirable attitudes among their subordinates, such as prejudice.

JOB SATISFACTION

Job satisfaction is the best-known and most commonly measured and studied work attitude. *Job satisfaction* is the affective component of work-related attitudes. Quite simply, it is how employees feel about their jobs.

Managers are often concerned about employees' satisfaction with specific facets of the job, as well as about overall job satisfaction. They may, for instance, want to know how employees feel about their pay and whether satisfaction with pay is higher in some departments than in others. Or they may simply ask, "Taking everything into consideration, how do our employees feel about their jobs?" Figure 3-7 shows the relationship of job-facet satisfaction to overall job satisfaction.

FIGURE 3-7
Job Facet Satisfaction and Overall Satisfaction

MEASURING JOB SATISFACTION

It is very important to measure levels of employee satisfaction. This provides important information concerning what is, and is not, being done correctly in the workplace. For example, if it is found that satisfaction with supervision is low, supervisory practices might be carefully assessed. Similarly, if satisfaction is found to sharply increase or decrease in a department, the sources of that change should be explored. Further, of course, we would like satisfaction levels to be high in general. If they are not, some serious diagnosis is in order.

The most popular approach to measuring satisfaction is to use standardized scales. These scales have generally been widely used and tested, so the user can be confident that they provide accurate measures. In addition, norm data are often available for standardized scales. Norm data tell us how other people have scored on the scales. The data may, for instance, tell us the average score and distribution of scores of all past users of the scale, or they may provide such information for specific groups or industries. This provides useful comparative information.

The best-known scale to assess facets of job satisfaction, the Job Descriptive Index (JDI), measures satisfaction with the work itself, pay, coworkers, supervision, and promotions.[47] Figure 3-8 presents sample items from the supervision subscale of the JDI. By tapping satisfaction with particular job facets, a scale such as the JDI helps managers to pinpoint sources of dissatisfaction and to take appropriate actions. For example, if it is clear that employees are satisfied with all aspects of their jobs except promotions, attention can be devoted to that area.

Overall job satisfaction, or general job satisfaction, is concerned with the overall feelings of an employee regarding the job. While examining facet satisfaction is very useful, it may fail to see the forest for the trees. That is, measures of facet satisfaction can't give us the complete picture because employees may give differing weights to various job facets and may combine information about facets in different ways. For example, if an employee reports low satisfaction with promotional opportunities but doesn't really care about

FIGURE 3-8

Job Descriptive Index: Supervision Subscale Sample Items

The following adjectives and phrases describe five aspects of a job: the work itself, supervision, pay, promotions, and coworkers. Carefully consider each adjective or phrase and indicate whether or not it is true of your job by circling:

Y   for YES, this is true of my job.

?   for I cannot decide if this is true of my job.

N   for NO, this is not true of my job.

The Supervision on My Job

> Asks my advice	Y	?	N
> Hard to please	Y	?	N
> Impolite	Y	?	N
> Influential	Y	?	N
> Stubborn	Y	?	N
> Knows job well	Y	?	N

Source: P. C. Smith, L. M. Kendall, and C. L. Hulin, *The Measurement of Satisfaction in Work and Retirement.* Chicago: Rand McNally, 1969.

promotions, there will be little impact on overall job satisfaction. Also, there are probably many aspects of overall job satisfaction besides the specific facets measured in the JDI (this is suggested in Figure 3-7 by the fact that the satisfaction facets do not completely fill the job satisfaction circle). Thus, overall satisfaction measures provide useful additional information. In addition, it may be overall satisfaction with a job that most directly influences some behaviors, such as quitting. Many measures of overall job satisfaction are short and easy to use. One, the Faces Scale, asks employees to indicate how satisfied they are with their jobs by circling an appropriate face, ranging from one with a big smile to one with a big frown. Another, the Brayfield–Rothe scale, asks employees simply to indicate their degree of agreement with each of 18 statements about the job, such as "I find real enjoyment in my work" and "My job is like a hobby to me."[48]

In addition to paper-and-pencil tests, satisfaction may be assessed by use of the critical incidents method, interviews, or confrontation meetings. The *critical incidents method* as applied to the measurement of job satisfaction asks employees to recall incidents that were particularly satisfying or dissatisfying to them. Thus, rather than simply assessing levels of satisfaction, the specific determinants of satisfaction and dissatisfaction may be isolated. *Interviews* are useful since they allow in-depth questioning. That is, if signs are seen of satisfaction or of dissatisfaction, further probes can seek to better understand their nature and causes. Finally, *confrontation meetings* bring together groups of employees who are encouraged to openly express their feelings about their jobs. In such a group setting, employees may feel free to say things they might hold back if interviewed alone.

DETERMINANTS OF JOB SATISFACTION

There are two primary views concerning the determinants of job satisfaction—situational and dispositional. The *situational perspective* sees satis-

FIGURE 3-9
Work-Related Influences on Satisfaction

Work Factors	Effects
❑ Work Itself	
> Challenge	Mentally challenging work that the individual can successfully accomplish is satisfying.
> Physical Demands	Tiring work is dissatisfying.
> Personal Interest	Personally interesting work is satisfying.
❑ Reward Structure	Rewards that are equitable and that provide accurate feedback on performance are satisfying.
❑ Working Conditions	
> Physical	Satisfaction depends on the match between working conditions and physical needs.
> Goal Attainment	Working conditions that promote goal attainment are satisfying.
❑ Others in the Organization	Individuals will be satisfied with supervisors, coworkers, or subordinates who help them attain rewards. Also, individuals will be more satisfied with colleagues who see things the same way they do.
❑ Organization and Management	Individuals will be satisfied with organizations that have policies and procedures designed to help them attain rewards. Individuals will be dissatisfied with conflicting roles and/or ambiguous roles imposed by the organization.
❑ Fringe Benefits	Fringe benefits do not have a strong influence on job satisfaction for most workers.

Source: Adapted from F. J. Landy, *Psychology at Work,* 4th Ed. Pacific Grove, CA: Brooks/Cole, 1989, p. 470.

faction as largely due to things in the environment of the employee, such as the nature of the job, reward system, and supervision. If this view is correct, it may be possible to influence satisfaction levels by changing such things. The *dispositional perspective,* to the contrary, sees satisfaction as due to individual factors—some people are simply more satisfied in general than are others—and thus as relatively stable and more difficult to change. If this view is valid, varying the situation may have little impact on satisfaction.

Situational Determinants of Satisfaction Many work-related factors influence job satisfaction. These are summarized in Figure 3-9. Among these, equitable rewards, work itself, and others in the organization (such as the supervisor) are often quite important. We examine the specific roles of many of these factors in detail in later chapters.

Dispositional Determinants of Satisfaction As noted earlier, dispositional views see some people as generally satisfied and others as generally dissatisfied. A direct approach to examining the dispositional perspective is simply to measure the degree to which people seem to be generally positive or negative in their outlooks; these are called *positive affectivity* and *negative affectivity.*[49] Research consistently shows these measures to predict levels of job satisfaction.

The dispositional view is also supported by studies that follow people as they move across jobs through their lives. For example, one study tracked subjects from early adolescence to adulthood. It found that a measure of affective disposition—including items such as "cheerful," "warm," and "irritable (reversed)"—predicted overall attitudes from early adolescence through late adolescence and through two stages of adult life, a span of nearly 50 years.[50]

Another interesting approach to examining the dispositional view looks at identical twins who were reared apart. Such research—some of which considers more than 2,000 twins born in the state of Minnesota between 1936 and 1955—finds considerable similarity in the satisfaction levels of the twins, despite different jobs.[51] The authors of a review of information on these twins concluded: "It may be that trying to be happy is as futile as trying to be taller, and therefore is counterproductive."[52] Such research, which suggests that people may have a satisfaction "set point" from which they may diverge but to which they quickly return, clearly supports a dispositional perspective.

Taken together, these research approaches provide some support for a dispositional view. So we must recognize that, even in an identical situation, people may have very different attitudes. The results certainly do not, though, argue that the situation is irrelevant. Instead, they suggest that some people may have generally higher or lower levels of satisfaction than others. Situational factors are still very important.[53]

The accompanying Bottom Line presents a process model that summarizes the basic steps associated with enhancing employee job satisfaction.

BOTTOM LINE

The Bottom Line: Enhancing Employee Job Satisfaction

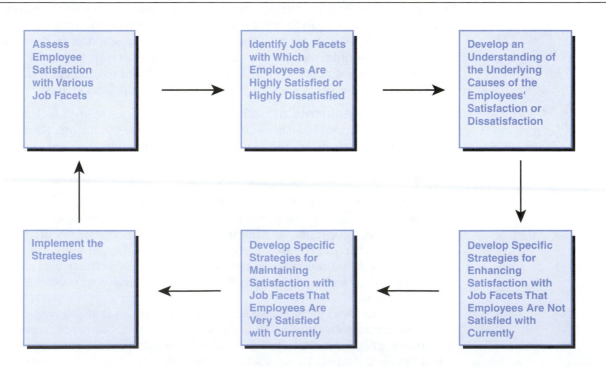

Now, complete Skills Practice 3-6, Field Work—Analyzing Employee Job Satisfaction. The purpose of the activity is for you to get out into "the field" in order to assess the job satisfaction of an actual employee or manager and to propose specific actions that could be taken to enhance that individual's job satisfaction.

Skills Practice 3-6
Field Work—Analyzing Employee Job Satisfaction

Skill Level: **Basic**

Skill Objectives
1. To develop skill in analyzing employee job satisfaction data.
2. To develop skill in formulating action plans for enhancing job satisfaction.

Procedure
1. Identify an employee or manager currently working in an organizational setting who is willing to be interviewed for this activity.
2. Ask the following questions in the interview.
   a. What is your job title? What are your primary tasks, duties, and responsibilities?
   b. How satisfied are you with the *work you perform* as part of your job? Why do you feel this way?
   c. How satisfied are you with the *supervision* you receive in your job? Why do you feel this way?
   d. How satisfied are you with your *coworkers* in your job? Why do you feel this way?
   e. How satisfied are you with the *compensation and benefits* you receive as part of your job? Why do you feel this way?
   f. How satisfied are you with the *opportunities for advancement* in your organization? Why do you feel this way?
   g. How satisfied are you with the *organization* you work for? Why do you feel this way?
   h. How satisfied are you with your *overall job?* Why do you feel this way?
3. Discuss the results of the job satisfaction assessment you just performed.
4. Develop an action plan to enhance the job satisfaction of the person you interviewed for this activity. Be specific.
5. Optional: Present a brief summary of your analysis and action plan to your class for discussion purposes.

JOB INVOLVEMENT

Job involvement is the degree to which employees really are involved with— that is, "get into"—their jobs. Job involvement is high when the job is very important to the person's life or central to the person's self-concept. A person with a high degree of job involvement would agree with statements such as: [54]

> The most important things that happen to me involve my job.
> The major satisfaction of my life comes from my job.
> I live, eat, and breathe my job.

While companies want their workers to be involved in their jobs, overly high levels of job involvement may be undesirable. At the extreme, employees who are "workaholics" may neglect their families and outside activities and may even suffer health problems.[55]

A related attitude, *work involvement,* is the degree to which an employee is involved with work in general rather than with a specific job.

GLOBAL PERSPECTIVES

WORK INVOLVEMENT ACROSS CULTURES

There appear to be some major differences in work involvement across cultures. For instance, Japanese employees tend to be highly involved with their jobs and work. Relatively few Japanese work just a 40-hour week or even take the vacation time they are entitled to. In the Japanese scale of values, the worker often rates the economic welfare of the company higher than his or her own good. Workers also see to it that

their children attend school 5½ days per week, including 8:30 a.m. to 1 p.m. on Saturdays. Several years ago the Japanese Department of Statistics and Information of the Ministry of Health and Welfare asked workers a question of priorities that went something like this: If you were heading to your job and an earthquake broke out, and you were limited to a single phone call, who would you phone—your wife, your physician, your children, your employer, or your parents? The over-

whelming majority selected their employer.* On the other hand, German workers have a generally different view of work, as reflected in the chapter-end case. They put in substantially shorter workweeks than Americans and place greater emphasis on leisure.†

*"Priorities of Life," *Parade Magazine,* September 4, 1988, p. 21.

†D. Benjamin and T. Horwitz, "German View: 'You Americans Work Too Hard—and for What?'" *Wall Street Journal,* July 14, 1994, pp. B1, B5.

ORGANIZATIONAL COMMITMENT

Organizational commitment reflects the degree to which the employee shows (1) a strong desire to remain as a member of the organization; (2) a willingness to exert high levels of effort on behalf of the organization; and (3) a belief in, and acceptance of, the values and goals of the organization.[56]

There are several ways to classify commitment. One important distinction is between affective commitment and continuance commitment.[57] *Affective commitment* is an emotional attachment characterized by strong affective ties to the organization and psychological identification with the organization. In other words, affective commitment flows from liking the organization, sharing its values, and caring about its fate. People with strong affective commitment *want* to stay with the firm. *Continuance commitment* results from consideration of the benefits of organizational membership and the perceived costs of leaving. It involves asking the questions "Can I afford to quit? What would I gain and lose?" As such, continuance commitment flows from the belief that one *needs* to stay with the firm since equal or better alternatives are not available elsewhere.

It might seem that a company would like to see very high levels of organizational commitment in its workforce. For instance, as might be expected, employees with high levels of organizational commitment have low levels of turnover. This relationship is strongest for younger employees, perhaps because they have less vested in the job than do older employees.[58] There is also evidence that commitment causes job satisfaction: Employees who are committed to their organizations apparently develop levels of satisfaction consistent with that commitment.[59]

Nevertheless, there are cases where higher levels of commitment may not be desirable. For one thing, if low-performing employees are very committed to the organization, they may be reluctant to leave. If management is constrained from terminating low-performing employees, such commitment could be costly to the firm. Also, we have all heard of cases in which employees have been so committed to an organization or to a cause that they have been afraid to "rock the boat" or to criticize others in the firm. In extreme cases, commitment has led to the commission of illegal or unethical acts. As such, more commitment, like more of most things in life, is not necessarily better.

A subject of great current interest is how the massive downsizing of firms affects commitment. One stream of reasoning is that workers, recognizing that their firms treat them as expendable, will become disillusioned and stop caring about the organization, reducing commitment. Another is that in a climate of dramatic downsizing, workers will feel grateful for their jobs and cling to them fiercely. Perhaps it is the case that downsizing has counterbalancing effects, decreasing affective commitment but increasing continuance commitment.

REAL AND EXPRESSED ATTITUDES

We should pause here and make an important, if obvious, point—people's expressed attitudes may differ dramatically from their true attitudes. People may hide or falsely report their true attitudes because they feel the attitudes will be unpopular or somehow lead to retribution. Further, they may attempt to disguise their emotions, since emotions reflect attitudes. In many cases, in fact, employees are required to express certain emotions as part of their work roles.[60] For example, employees at one chain of supermarkets are told to be friendly and courteous with customers and that "a friendly smile is a must." As such, these employees' smiles say nothing about their true feelings.[61]

FORMING ATTITUDES

We can form attitudes in a variety of ways—through direct personal experience, association, or social learning. Let's consider these in turn.

> **Direct Experience.** For one, we may have direct personal experience with the attitude object. We may, for instance, have met a candidate for public office and liked what she had to say.
> **Association.** We may also form attitudes through association. That is, we may transfer an attitude about a particular attitude object to a new attitude object that is somehow similar. For example, if we like all of our current acquaintances who are runners, we may like a new acquaintance after learning that she runs.
> **Social Learning.** Finally, we may form attitudes indirectly through social learning. Here, attitudes are influenced by information provided by others. We may read about the latest CD of the Indigo Girls, for instance, or may hear it discussed on MTV or listen to friends debating its merits.

Attitudes formed in any of these ways may be intensely held. However, those attitudes formed through direct personal experience are more clearly defined, held with greater certainty, more stable over time, and more resistant to counterinfluence than attitudes that are formed indirectly.

THE RELATIONSHIPS OF ATTITUDES TO BEHAVIORS

We said earlier that one reason that managers may care about attitudes is that attitudes may be associated with important behaviors. If so, knowledge of the relationships of work attitudes to work behaviors could be valuable. Here we explore three possible ways they may be related—attitudes may cause behaviors, behaviors may cause attitudes, or they may cause each other. Think carefully about the following issues—they are absolutely critical to understanding many issues in organizational life (and life in general).

Do Attitudes Cause Behaviors? Are you enjoying reading this chapter? Is there anything you'd rather be doing? If so, why don't you do it? Think about it for a minute and make a list of some of the reasons.

We said earlier that one reason why managers care about employee attitudes is that those attitudes may influence behaviors. This seems to make sense. If we have negative attitudes concerning the consumption of horsemeat, we might refuse to eat it. Similarly, if we don't like our jobs, it seems reasonable that we might not put our full effort into them. This general view, you'll recall, was suggested by Figure 3-6.

In fact, though, many researchers have found that the link between attitudes and behaviors is sometimes surprisingly weak. In the first major study of attitude–behavior relationships, R. T. LaPiere reported on his travels through the United States with a Chinese couple.[62] During those travels, the couple was almost always treated hospitably at hotels and restaurants. However, a survey of owners of the same establishments found their attitudes toward Orientals to be very negative. In fact, 90 percent said that as a matter of policy Orientals would not be served. Clearly, attitudes were not being translated into behaviors, at least in any simple and direct way.[63]

More recent attempts to sort out this puzzle have suggested reasons why the attitude–behavior linkage may be weak. For instance, even though people have certain attitudes, they may have no choice but to behave in certain ways. They may, for instance, have to keep a job they hate because no other job is available. It is important to recognize that a person's behavior is the result of many things beyond attitude, including pressures exerted by others, the nature of the job market, and personality characteristics. For example, in the LaPiere research, the hotel and restaurant owners may simply have needed the money, they may have reported attitudes that they didn't really hold, or they may have felt uncomfortable refusing service to actual people as opposed to hypothetical abstractions.

On the other hand, research may underestimate attitude–behavior relationships if, as we've suggested may sometimes be the case, reported attitudes or behaviors are false. For example, if employees falsely report how satisfied they are (perhaps from fear of retribution) or how they have behaved (perhaps because they were supposed to engage in the behavior but didn't), research on the link of satisfaction to that behavior will probably understate the strength of the relationship. Also, the strength of relationships will be understated if the instruments used to measure attitudes or behaviors lack validity or reliability.

In general, attitudes will probably best predict behavior when four conditions are present:[64]

> **The attitude is specific to the behavior.** An attitude such as intention to quit is probably a better predictor of turnover than a more general attitude, such as general job satisfaction.

FIGURE 3-10
Some Potential Consequences of Dissatisfaction

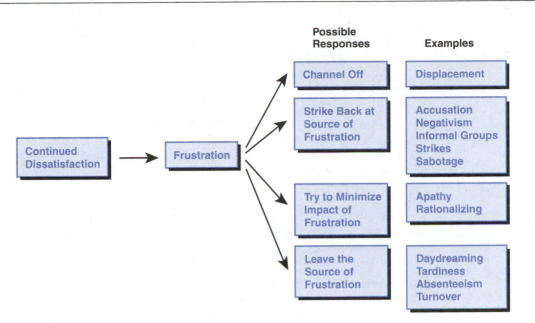

> **The attitude is potent.** The stronger the attitude in one's thinking, the more it will influence subsequent behavior. In general, attitudes from personal experience are more potent than attitudes based on second-hand information or less direct sources.

> **The attitude is salient.** Attitudes are more salient when they are more noticeable or prominent in our attention. Salient attitudes are more likely to be recalled and acted upon. Attitudes may be made more salient by *priming,* using cues or reminders to bring them forward in one's memory. For instance, a poster about workplace safety may prime or retrieve a worker's earlier opinions concerning safety. Once recalled, the attitudes are more likely to be acted upon.

> **The behavior is not constrained or subject to other influences.** Attitudes will have little impact on behavior if the behavior cannot be varied or if there are many other things affecting the behavior.

These factors suggest that attitudes will have the greatest impact on behavior if they are specific, formed through direct experience, made salient, and unconstrained. Clearly, these conditions don't always hold.

Now, let's briefly consider evidence concerning the relationships between satisfaction and work behaviors. We focus here specifically on satisfaction, since it has certainly been the subject of more interest and research than other work-related attitudes. Before turning to research findings, let's consider Figure 3-10. According to that figure, continued dissatisfaction will lead to frustration. Since frustration is painful, we seek ways to reduce that pain. We can do this in a variety of ways:

> One way would be to *channel off the frustration.* For instance, after a bad day at work we might go home and yell at our children or spouse;

this process of venting our frustration somewhere other than where it was caused is called *displacement.*

> A second possibility is that we might *strike back at the source of frustration* by making accusations about people who are upsetting us, making negative statements about the company, joining informal groups that resist organizational rules and pressures, going out on strike, or even engaging in small acts of sabotage, such as intentionally denting a fender.

> Further, we might try to *minimize the psychological impact of the frustration* by becoming apathetic about the job—and thereby perhaps paying little attention to the quality of our work—or by convincing ourselves that things aren't so bad.

> Finally, we might choose simply to *leave the source of frustration.* We can leave psychologically by daydreaming or physically through tardiness, absenteeism, or turnover.

Now, let's look at some of these relationships in more detail. In particular, let's consider how satisfaction is related to turnover, absenteeism, performance, and work violence.

Satisfaction and Turnover Retention simply means remaining with an organization. Its opposite—turnover—has many costs to firms, including disruption of the work process, the expenses of recruiting and training new employees, the loss of employees with valuable skills, knowledge, and experience, and low productivity of new employees during the training period. In some industries, turnover rates may exceed 100 percent annually. Overall, rates in the United States were 14.4 percent in 1999, the highest level in two decades.[65]

Research clearly shows that more satisfied workers are less likely to leave the firm.[66] These studies find a little over 15 percent of the variance in turnover to be related to variance in satisfaction. While that percentage may not seem like a lot, a decrease—or an increase—in turnover of even a few percentage points may determine the success, or even survival, of many firms.

Figure 3-11 presents a model of the relationship of satisfaction to turnover.[67] That model shows that the link of satisfaction to turnover is indirect. That is, job satisfaction doesn't influence turnover directly. Instead, it influences things that may affect turnover, such as thoughts of quitting, intention to search for a new job, and intention to quit or stay.[68] In addition, the intention to quit or stay is also influenced by whether or not the employee thinks another acceptable job is available. Also, while not explicitly shown in the model, many sorts of pressures and factors, such as the wishes of one's family members and friends, feelings about the community, and aversion to change, may play roles.

In addition, economic conditions are important, since we're less likely to quit our jobs, even when we're unhappy with them, if times are hard and no other jobs are available. It is probably the case that satisfaction is a better predictor of turnover in good economic times than in bad.[69] In good times, a dissatisfied employee may feel confident that other jobs will be available and therefore quit. In bad times, an employee may simply put up with dissatisfaction rather than take a chance on being out of work.

F I G U R E   3 - 1 1
A Model of the Relationship of Satisfaction to Turnover

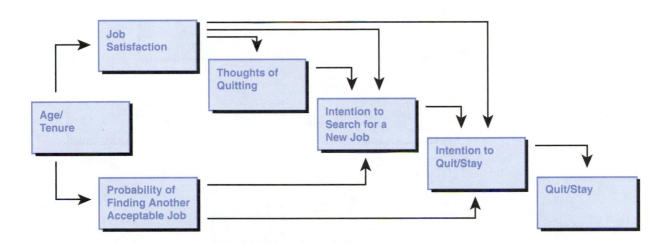

Satisfaction and Absenteeism Attendance relates to whether an employee reports for work on a given day. Failure to attend—absenteeism—can be quite costly for companies. Typically, companies continue to pay absent employees. Further, absenteeism causes costly disruptions, such as the need to reschedule work and reassign employees. One estimate is that such disruptions cause productivity to drop by as much as 2.5 percent for every 1 percent increase in absenteeism.[70] Those disruptions may also result in products of decreased quality, since regular employees are replaced by "swing" employees who move from one job to another. The defect-plagued "Monday car"—largely assembled by "swing" employees because of high absenteeism in auto assembly plants on Mondays—is an example.

An estimated 400 million person-days are lost annually through absenteeism—about four times the number lost in strikes. Total annual costs of absenteeism have been put in excess of $25 billion, and are on the rise. In 1998, absenteeism cost U.S. firms an average of $757 per employee, up from $593 in 1994.[71] Of course, it's hard to tell how much of this absenteeism is avoidable (that is, due simply to the employee's desire not to go to work that day) or unavoidable (due to factors such as illness or transportation problems). The reason for this is that, even if companies tried to keep track of such distinctions, there is one fairly safe bet in organizations: Nobody calls in bored. Instead, absent employees often invent more acceptable reasons for their failure to come to work. It is probably the case, though, that avoidable absenteeism makes up a large share of the total.

Research shows that satisfaction and absenteeism are negatively related but that the association is not as strong as we might expect. In fact, an analysis examining many past studies that examined the relationship between job satisfaction and absenteeism found that little more than 2 percent of the variance in satisfaction is somehow associated with variance in absenteeism.[72]

However, satisfaction may play a larger role in determining absenteeism than such figures indicate. This is because, as we just indicated, much absen-

FIGURE 3-12
A Model of the Relationship of Satisfaction to Attendance

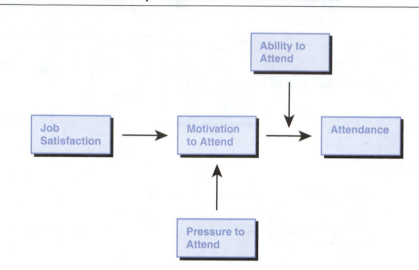

teeism is unavoidable due to things such as illness and family emergencies. If the relationship of satisfaction to avoidable absenteeism could be assessed, it would probably be considerable. In addition, some facets of satisfaction may predict absenteeism better than do others.

Figure 3-12 presents a model of the relationship of satisfaction to attendance. The model indicates that job satisfaction may influence motivation to attend but that motivation to attend also depends on other pressures to attend, such as a spouse or peer who tells us to get our lazy self to work. Further, whether or not motivation to attend results in attendance depends on the ability to attend. For example, we may want to go to work but be unable to do so because we are ill or our car breaks down. Perhaps the relatively low overall negative relationship between satisfaction and absenteeism is a reflection of the many pressures faced by employees and the many constraints on their behavior.

Satisfaction and Performance There is a strong, and understandable, tendency to assume that satisfied employees will also be motivated and productive. As noted earlier in the chapter, this tendency is seen in statements such as "A satisfied worker is a productive worker." However, things are more complex than such statements would suggest.

Findings concerning the relationship of satisfaction to performance show us why research is often needed to augment common sense. While it seems reasonable to expect that satisfied workers would be more productive, many studies show that this is really not the case, at least to any appreciable degree. Early reviews of the satisfaction–performance relationship concluded that the relationship of satisfaction to performance is so low as to be negligible and that satisfaction does not imply motivation for strong performance.[73] Further, a major statistical summary of previous research (including 74 studies with more than 12,000 subjects) revealed that only about 3 percent of variance in performance was associated with variance in satisfaction.[74]

FIGURE 3-13
Two Views of the Satisfaction–Performance Relationship

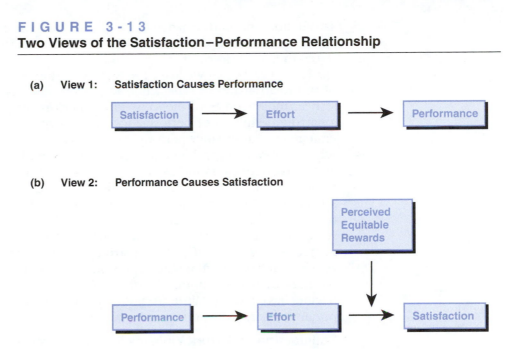

(a)   View 1:   **Satisfaction Causes Performance**

Satisfaction → Effort → Performance

(b)   View 2:   **Performance Causes Satisfaction**

Perceived Equitable Rewards

Performance → Effort → Satisfaction

To help make sense of these findings, consider Figures 3-13a and 3-13b. Figure 3-13a presents the traditional view of the satisfaction–performance relationship: Satisfied employees exert more effort to perform and subsequently perform at higher levels. If this were an accurate picture of how satisfaction and performance are related, we would certainly expect to see a stronger relationship than is the case. Figure 3-13b suggests a different possibility: Performance may indirectly influence satisfaction. That is, performance levels affect the rewards employees receive. If employees feel their rewards are fair, they will be satisfied. If, on the other hand, they see the rewards as unfair, they will be dissatisfied. This model, then, turns the traditional wisdom on its head, viewing satisfaction as a consequence of performance rather than a cause.

If this model is correct—and research suggests that it is—why aren't satisfaction–performance relationships stronger? Quite simply, some companies don't properly reward their employees. For example, as we'll discuss in more detail in Chapter 6, if a company pays all of its employees the same amount, or if low performers get more than high performers, high performers will feel unfairly treated and low performers may be pleased. As such, high performers will be dissatisfied and low performers will be satisfied, resulting in a negative relationship between satisfaction and performance. Other companies may tie pay and other rewards directly to performance and may thus have very satisfied high performers, and vice versa, resulting in a positive satisfaction–performance relationship. This all says that the relationship between satisfaction and performance among a firm's employees is important; if it is negative, the company should carefully examine whether it is properly rewarding employees. There is still another reason why firms would like the relationship of satisfaction to performance to be positive. Since absenteeism and turnover are negatively related to satisfaction, a positive relationship between satisfaction and performance helps ensure that a firm's high performers will continue to participate and that absenteeism and turnover will be concentrated in low performers.

However, before we leave this topic we should point out that the question of the relationship of satisfaction to performance is still not settled. For instance, most studies of the satisfaction–performance relationship have used a narrow definition of performance, such as quantity of output or quality of craftsmanship. Broader performance behaviors—such as helping coworkers with a job-related problem, accepting orders without a fuss, making timely and constructive comments about the work unit or its head to outsiders, and protecting and conserving organizational resources—may in fact result from satisfaction.[75] Research shows that relationships between job satisfaction and these *organizational citizenship behaviors* are much stronger than is typical of studies of the satisfaction–performance relationship where performance is narrowly defined. The stronger relationships may be because citizenship behaviors generally represent actions more under the control of workers than conventional performance measures.[76] These citizenship behaviors have received little attention, but in many cases they may be just as important as narrower performance measures.

Satisfaction and Work Violence Figure 3-10 suggested that dissatisfied employees may strike back at the source of their frustration. Unfortunately, we've seen what happens when this reaction to frustration becomes extreme.[77] Workplace violence, including homicides, is increasing. More than 1,000 workers are murdered on the job each year.[78] Homicide is now the number-3 work-related cause of death, behind car crashes and other machinery accidents, and it is the *leading* cause of death for women in the workplace. Certainly, not all of these murders are due to job dissatisfaction, but it appears that dissatisfaction does play a role. Violence is especially great in regimented settings, such as post offices, where employees feel they have no control over their work. In the face of dozens of killings in post offices, attention was focused on employees' jobs, described as treadmills of angry monotony, with labor–management hostility heightening tension.[79] The Centers for Disease Control and Prevention have formally declared workplace homicide an epidemic. To deal with threats of violence, some firms are training managers to recognize aggressive behavior and effectively deal with it through communication and conflict management.[80] Some, such as IBM, have threat-assessment teams that meet to evaluate any threats that are made and to decide what action to take, including notification of law enforcement authorities. Firms must also recognize the danger of violence in the wake of downsizings and must be especially sensitive to the needs of those affected. Further, some organizations, such as the post office, now screen applicants in the hope of keeping out potentially aggressive individuals.[81]

Satisfaction and Nonwork Life An intriguing, and important, question is how job satisfaction relates to satisfaction with nonwork life. For instance, perhaps job satisfaction somehow carries over to life satisfaction. Or perhaps employees who are satisfied at work devote so much time and energy to work that they ignore other aspects of their lives, resulting in low satisfaction with nonwork life. Still another possibility is that employees compensate for dissatisfaction at work by focusing more on home life and finding satisfaction there.

If increasing employee job satisfaction were found to reduce nonwork satisfaction, such increases would be a mixed blessing. Happily, most research supports the spillover view—satisfaction in one sphere of life, such as the job, seems to increase satisfaction in other spheres.

The Financial Impact of Attitudes   The failure to find that satisfaction causes better performance, at least in terms of traditional performance measures, shouldn't lead us to conclude that attitudes don't influence financial performance. Instead, as we've tried to show, absenteeism, turnover, and many other employee behaviors also have substantial costs. The area of *behavioral accounting* is now trying to assess the financial impact of attitudes. It does this by examining the costs of such behaviors as turnover and absenteeism and the strength of their links to attitudes. While this is still a relatively new field, and fraught with measurement problems, some of its conclusions are remarkable.

For instance, one study used behavioral accounting to estimate the costs of absenteeism, turnover, and balancing shortages of 160 bank tellers.[82] The study concluded that moderate improvements in attitudes averaging perhaps 0.7 on a seven-point scale would yield the bank total savings of $781,892, or $4,886.83 per employee. Another study has estimated that, on a national basis, a very modest improvement in employee attitudes of perhaps 0.15 on a seven-point scale would result in a total financial benefit of over $1 billion.[83]

THE ROLE OF MOOD

Our discussion to this point has focused on a number of work-related attitudes, such as satisfaction, organizational commitment, and job involvement, which we would expect to be rather heavily influenced by aspects of the job and to be at least somewhat enduring. However, some mental states are more ephemeral. *Mood* is a transient mental state or attitude, perhaps caused by something as fleeting as a sunny sky, convenient parking spot, pleasant odor, or good meal. Mood can affect job satisfaction as well as behaviors.[84] One of the most consistent findings in the literature of psychology is that happy people are helpful people. People who are in a good mood—whether because of finding change in a public phone coin slot, receiving a gift of free stationery, having access to sunshine, falling in love, or getting a cookie—do helpful things. Interestingly, bad mood *also* often leads to helping behaviors. Helping others seems to be a way we can feel better about ourselves. Thus, helping softens a bad mood and sustains a good mood.[85] As such, important work behaviors such as prosocial behaviors may be heavily influenced by mood.

DO BEHAVIORS CAUSE ATTITUDES?

The evidence we've reviewed shows that work attitudes often do influence work and nonwork behaviors, though sometimes in rather complex ways. Now we turn ourselves to the flip side of the question: Do behaviors cause attitudes? The answer is a clear "yes." Here, we'll consider a few ways that behaviors may influence attitudes.

Dissonance Reduction   Leon Festinger proposed a theory of cognitive dissonance that suggests how behaviors may cause attitudes.[86] *Cognitions* are thoughts and *dissonance* refers to lack of harmony. So *cognitive dissonance* is a situation in which we have conflicting thoughts. For example, if we don't like a coworker, Janet, but must treat her nicely because of job demands, we may experience such conflict.

As detailed by Festinger, cognitive dissonance is a tense, uncomfortable state.[87] People will do something to reduce that tension. One way to do so is to change one or both of the cognitions to make them consistent.

Furthermore, Festinger proposed, some cognitions are more resistant to change than others. For instance, cognitions based on physical reality, such as the fact that we just treated Janet nicely, are more resistant to change than are cognitions based on opinions and attitudes, such as our negative feelings toward Janet. The bottom line, then, is that we may change our attitudes to make them consistent with our behaviors. We may actually begin to like Janet.

We said earlier that the high levels of reported job satisfaction may be artificially high. Dissonance theory suggests another reason why that may be the case. A set of thoughts such as "I continue to work on this job, yet it is dissatisfying" reflects dissonance. To reduce that dissonance, employees may convince themselves that they are in fact satisfied with their jobs.

Consequences of Behavior There are other important routes by which behaviors may influence attitudes. For one thing, as suggested by our discussion of the relationship of satisfaction to performance, behaviors may lead to consequences that affect attitudes. For instance, a high-performing employee may get a big raise, which may in turn increase satisfaction with pay. Or simply eating a food we've always shunned may lead us to like it.

Self-Attribution There is evidence that behaving in a certain way can lead us to make corresponding attributions about ourselves. For example, smiling (for no good reason) can apparently induce a good mood and increase willingness to laugh at humorous material. Even though we are playing a role, we seem to internalize the attitudes and moods that maintain the role.[88]

Indoctrination Brainwashing and cult recruitment are two forms of indoctrination that have proven to be effective. With brainwashing, torture or threat may be used to cause victims to yield to their oppressors' cause. Further, there is evidence that brainwashing is most effective when pressures are withheld and the victim is induced, step by step, to behave more and more in agreement with the captors.[89] As the victim begins to engage in the behavior with pressure withheld, he or she comes to infer that the behavior was voluntary, and attitudes change accordingly.

Cults tend to bring about attitude change by isolating their members, shielding them from outside perspectives and influences and controlling their interpretations of events. Cults tend first to invite prospective members to inquiry meetings and then to ask them to make gradually stronger commitments by attending education sessions, doing favors for other members, or tithing larger amounts for cult support.[90] Over time, a "momentum of compliance" is established and the member's commitment to the cult grows.

While indoctrination does not take these blatant forms in work organizations, these same actions may be seen there in weaker forms. Indoctrination tactics provide additional evidence that behaviors may cause attitudes.

Skills Application
Skills Application
Skills Application
Skills Application

125

Chapter 3   Understanding and Valuing Differences

TOP TEN LIST: KEY POINTS TO REMEMBER
UNDERSTANDING AND VALUING DIFFERENCES

10. Understand and adapt to personalities and working styles of others in your organization.

9. When making hiring decisions, assess the quality of fit or compatibility of an individual's personality with his or her job as well as with the culture of the work unit and the organization.

8. Remember that perception is the "reality" to which other people respond in organizations.

7. Perceptions of a given issue or situation can vary widely across people in an organization. Encourage others to share their perspectives with one another to develop a greater understanding of the issue and to move toward establishing a common ground.

6. Be aware of the biases you possess and the assumptions you make about others in your organization. Make a conscious effort to minimize the influence of these factors on how you perceive a situation or issue.

5. When dealing with perceptual differences between employees, be sure to get all sides of the story before making a decision.

4. When managing diversity, make sure that you have a clear definition or vision of diversity for your organization that includes specific objectives and measures for assessing the effectiveness of your diversity program.

3. Take a systems view of organizations when implementing a diversity program. Implement diversity strategies that will enable your organization to attract, motivate, develop, and retain your target employees.

2. Maintain an open and flexible attitude in dealing with cross-cultural differences among your employees.

1. Assess employee job satisfaction on a regular basis, and develop specific strategies for either maintaining or improving job satisfaction through managerial and organizational policies and practices.

QUESTIONS FOR REVIEW AND REFLECTION
REVIEW QUESTIONS

1. What is diversity? What are specific steps (e.g., training, rewarding) that companies are taking to manage diversity successfully?

2. What is emotional intelligence? Why is it important in organizations?

3. Describe each of the following personality characteristics: risk-taking propensity, proactive personality, authoritarianism, dogmatism, locus of control, tolerance for ambiguity, Machiavellianism, self-monitoring, and Type A and Type B behavior patterns.

4. Discuss the "Big 5" personality dimensions, including how they may be relevant at work.

5. Give five ways that globalization is likely to affect you.

6. List six dimensions on which national cultures differ.

7. Describe the stages of the perceptual process.

8. Discuss each of the following perceptual distortions: stereotyping, Pygmalion effect, halo effect, projection, primacy/recency effects, and perceptual defense.

9. What is causal attribution? What are the three factors we consider when trying to sort out causes of an individual's behavior?

10. What are attitudes? What are the three components of attitudes? How are those components interrelated? Why are attitudes important?

11. What is job satisfaction? How is it measured? What are six work-related influences on satisfaction?

12. Define *job involvement* and *organizational commitment*. What is the difference between affective commitment and continuance commitment?

13. Discuss how job satisfaction levels are related to turnover, absenteeism, performance (including organizational citizenship behaviors), and work violence.

14. Identify four ways that behaviors may influence attitudes.

CRITICAL THINKING QUESTIONS

1. A colleague makes the following argument: "I can accept the fact that I shouldn't discriminate against minorities. What I can't accept is that I have to change my attitudes toward minorities. The company can define unacceptable behavior at work, but it has no right telling me what to think." Take and defend a position for or against this argument.

2. Consider the dimensions on which national cultures differ (that is, individualism versus collectivism, power distance, uncertainty avoidance, and so on). Select one of those dimensions. Discuss consequences in the workplace if someone from another culture differing on the dimension from the United States were to take a job in a U.S. company. Then indicate what steps (policies, practices, training, or whatever) you believe the U.S. company should take to help accommodate the differences.

3. Emotional intelligence is currently a very popular concept. However, as with many popular concepts, some people have dismissed it as a fad, seeing it as "just another call to get in touch with your feelings." Do you agree? Why or why not?

4. Take a position for or against the following statement: "Companies should have the right to refuse to hire people who have high levels of negative affectivity. Those people are going to be dissatisfied no matter what the company does, and they're likely to turn off customers and colleagues."

5. Consider the specific personality dimensions that were considered in this chapter (that is, risk-taking propensity, proactive personality, authoritarianism, etc.). Use those personality dimensions to describe each of the following: (1) a successful CEO of a large computer equipment retailer; (2) a successful entrepreneur; (3) someone you'd like for your boss;

   (4) someone you'd like for your subordinate. What are the reasons for any differences in the personality profiles across the four individuals?

6. After you tell a colleague about the "Pygmalion effect," he replies, "It sounds to me like when we assign new subordinates to bosses, we should overstate their qualifications. That way, the bosses will treat them better, they'll perform better, and everyone will be happy." Do you agree? Why or why not?

7. One of your friends says, "I was torn about whether or not to quit my job here. Now that I've made the decision to quit, though, I've really started to see a lot of the problems here more clearly. This place really stinks." How might you want to counsel your friend about her changing perceptions of her current job?

8. The well-known saying "Nobody on her deathbed ever said, 'I should have spent more time at the office'" would seem to suggest that people tend to be too involved in their work, at the expense of their personal lives. Do you agree? Why or why not?

9. A colleague says, "I guess I just don't get it with these organizational citizenship behaviors. As I understand it, they're behaviors that are good and useful but that aren't included in the job description. I have two concerns. First, if they're really desirable, why aren't they in the job description? Second, should people be rewarded for engaging in organizational citizenship behaviors? On the one hand, they're doing something that helps the company, which is good. On the other hand, I've always believed that people should be rewarded for doing their defined jobs as well as possible. Is it fair to reward people for things that are really outside the scope of their jobs? Won't that lead to favoritism?" How would you respond?

EXPERIENTIAL EXERCISES
WEB EXERCISE 3-1

Go to the following Web page, titled "Valuing Diversity: An Ongoing Commitment," which describes IBM's current diversity efforts:

http://www-3.ibm.com/employment/us/diverse/diverse.htm

Write a three-page typewritten report on the material on this site. In your report, be sure to include a discussion of:

> Why IBM has an ongoing commitment to diversity
> IBM's policy on equal opportunity
> The ideals on which IBM's workforce diversity "bridge" is built
> The challenges identified by IBM's Global Workforce Diversity Council

WEB EXERCISE 3-2

Select any *three* of the "Diversity Resources on the Web" sites included in the Web Wise feature at the end of the "Managing Diversity" section. Explore those sites and write a report discussing one interesting feature from each site.

CASE 3-1
PERSONALITY FACTORS AT MARTHA STEWART LIVING OMNIMEDIA INC.

The Company

Martha Stewart, generally regarded as "America's Lifestyle Queen," has built up her empire since just 1997, when she gained control over *Martha Stewart's Living Magazine* from Time-Warner for an estimated $75 million. Since then, her company has achieved some remarkable increases in sales and profits. For example, in 1999 Kmart Corporation sold over $1 billion worth of Martha Stewart Everyday products. Her website had record sales for both the 1998 and 1999 Christmas seasons. Finally, on October 19, 1999, her company made an initial public offering that was very well received by investors.

Personality Factors: Martha Stewart

Martha Stewart maintains an intense work schedule that requires her to juggle many different things simultaneously. In fact, a typical workday for Martha Stewart begins at 5:30 a.m. with a vigorous workout. Stewart is a workaholic who is driven to "show people how to create the good life" and then provide them with all the goods they would need to actually do it. Stewart has demonstrated a willingness to go against convention by viewing herself as being "a purveyor of information" rather than a publisher or merchandiser. In addition, she has a strong need for control of operations in her company. Many stories exist about her extraordinary obsession regarding details. For example, Stewart flew into a rage when she discovered that some maintenance workers had not followed her specifications for her TV kitchen set. Finally, Stewart's perceived lack of a sense of humor has resulted in her being ridiculed by celebrities such as David Letterman.

Personality Factors: Support Staff and Management

Stewart's management team is composed of a group of "Mini-Marthas" working as editors in the areas of food, travel, garden, crafts, style, and weddings. These individuals tend to emulate the style of their boss. Sharon Patrick, the president of the company, was hired because she possesses skills that complement those of Stewart. Specifically, "Martha chases the deals," while Sharon checks the details and actually does the deals.

Business Challenges

The key challenge facing the company is the issue of how to establish the Martha Stewart name in a way that the brand will outlive Martha Stewart herself. The organization has always been highly dependent on Martha Stewart herself in the development and marketing of new products and services.

http://www.marthastewart.com/

Discussion Questions

1. What personality factors are relevant in this case? How?
2. How can the organization become less dependent on Martha Stewart for its future success?
3. What are the practical implications of this exercise for you as a future manager?

Source: Based on D. Brady, "Martha Inc—Inside the Growing Empire of America's Lifestyle Queen," *Business Week,* January 17, 2000, p. 62–72.

CASE 3-2
CASE STUDY: CROSS-CULTURAL CLASHES AT DAIMLERCHRYSLER

The Companies

On November 12, 1998, Daimler-Benz of Germany and Chrysler Corporation of the United States completed a "merger of equals" that created the world's fourth largest automobile manufacturer, with a market capitalization of $95 billion and 440,000 employees. The rationale for the merger was brilliant in the eyes of many analysts. Daimler-Benz wanted to grow its presence in the U.S. auto market by expanding its range of product offerings beyond traditional luxury vehicles. Chrysler, on the other hand, was a mass production auto maker that wanted to grow in European markets where it had a small presence. Daimler-Benz's and Chrysler's product lines and key competencies overlapped very little as well. Daimler-Benz had a world-class reputation for excelling in engineering; Chrysler's key strengths were in product design and development, and cost containment. Ultimately, the goal was to create and leverage a variety of synergies between the two companies.

The new company that emerged from the merger, "DaimlerChrysler," had two CEOs (Jurggen Schrempp from Daimler-Benz and Robert Eaton from Chrysler). The new corporation also maintained two headquarters, one in Stuttgart, Germany, and one in Auburn Hills, Michigan.

This was a match made in heaven for the two companies . . . Or was it?

Cultural Differences

As the "honeymoon phase" of the new corporate marriage began to fade, major cultural differences between German and American managers began to surface and strain working relationships. As time went on, it became apparent that Jurggen Schrempp and the Germans as a whole were really "running the show." Robert Eaton, the former Chrysler CEO, surprised many when he announced that he would be retiring in the near future. Eaton's announcement of his upcoming retirement made him a "lame duck" and severely weakened the position of the Chrysler unit of the new corporation.

Jurggen Schrempp's leadership style was also a source of concern for many of the Chrysler executives. He created a work environment in which direct confrontation between managers was encouraged and "survival of the fittest" was the rule. Schrempp pushed his people very hard so that the postmerger transition process could be completed within one year. This process resulted in conflict, decreased morale, and the departure of quite a few Chrysler and Daimler-Benz executives. Many of the American managers, on the other hand, preferred a more consensus-based approach to implementing the merger.

The American and German managers could not even agree on the size of business cards they would use. European business cards were slightly larger than the typical American business card. In the end, everyone used the European-style business cards.

Some of the basic rituals, such as the use of titles and the degree of formality in working, were also quite different for the Germans versus the Americans. For example, German custom involved the use of the title of "Dr." when addressing each other. This was in sharp contrast to the more informal style of the former Chrysler executives.

One of the most fundamental differences between the Germans and the Americans was that the Germans placed a tremendous emphasis on extensive and detailed planning, research, and analysis in managing all aspects of the company. This approach ran counter to Chrysler management's style, which was more free-wheeling, risk-seeking, and willing to make fundamental changes in plans at almost any moment. The approach of the Americans focused more on setting stretch goals and then allowing the plan to evolve over time based on the situation.

In September of 1999, Thomas Stallkamp, President of Daimler-Benz's North American Unit, announced that he was leaving the company's management board. Many felt that Stallkamp was leaving DaimlerChrysler because he had questioned or challenged too many of Schrempp's strategies or initiatives. This event, combined with the retirement of Robert Eaton, continued to shift the balance of power in the direction of Schrempp and other Germans.

Given all the problems associated with cultural differences between Daimler-Benz and Chrysler managers, the two units are functioning independent of one another for the time being. However, if any of the desired synergies are to be realized, a greater degree of cooperation will be required in the future.

Finally, DaimlerChrysler recently agreed to purchase a controlling stake in Mitsubishi Motors of Japan. Although this strategic partnership will increase DaimlerChrysler's presence in fast-growing Asian markets, some analysts have expressed concern about the new challenges associated with cultural differences between the companies.

Discussion Questions

1. How do the cultures of the two organizations differ from each other?

2. What can be done to overcome the cultural differences in this case?

3. What are the practical implications of this case for you as a future manager?

http://www.daimlerchrysler.com/

Sources: "Worldwide Fender Bender," *Time*, May 24, 1999, pp. 58–62; J. Ballard and S. Miller, "Full Speed Ahead—Stuttgart's Control Grows with Shakeup at DaimlerChrysler," *Wall Street Journal*, September 24, 1999, p. A1.

VIDEO CASE
DIVERSITY AND COMMUNICATION IN BUSINESS: A STUDY OF HUDSON'S

Running Time: 12:00

Hudson's, with 22 stores, is part of Target Corporation. The fourth largest retailer in the United States, with more than 1,200 stores in 44 states, Target Corporation (formerly Dayton-Hudson Corporation) is a Minneapolis-based firm that also includes Dayton's, Target, Mervyn's, and Marshall Fields.

Founded in 1881, Hudson's has shown a strong commitment to the well-being of the communities where its stores are located. Today, Hudson's continues its tradition of more than half a century of contributing 5 percent of federally taxable income to support the communities in which it operates. Over the last 15 years, Hudson's has awarded over $20 million to nonprofit organizations for programs designed to enrich the quality of life.

The video shows President and CEO Dennis Toffolo and other Hudson's executives as they discuss diversity issues at Hudson's. After viewing the video, answer each of the following questions.

1. According to Dennis Toffolo and other Hudson's executives, why is Hudson's committed to diversity?

2. How does Northland Store Manager Larry Williams describe the meaning of diversity at Hudson's?

3. What is the role of each Hudson's store's Diversity Committee?

4. What are some specific ways Hudson's shows its commitment to diversity?

5. How has Hudson's modified its stores to facilitate diversity?

6. How does Hudson's address stereotyping in its diversity training?

http://www.hudsons.com/

LIGHTEN UP
THE LIPSTICK TEST

There are many personality and other tests on the Web. For a broad selection, go to:

http://www.queendom.com/test_frm.html

This site includes personality tests, general health and lifestyle assessment, career choice and preparation, mental and emotional health assessment, and other tests. Check out the "Funny Personality Tests" for the Lipstick Test, Kingdomality, and other not-so-serious assessments.

CHAPTER *Four*

SKILLS OBJECTIVES

> To apply the general problem-solving process to systematically analyze and resolve organizational challenges.
> To use problem-solving tools to enhance the effectiveness of business decision making.
> To take appropriate actions to overcome common constraints on the problem-solving process.
> To use creativity-enhancement techniques to generate innovative ideas and solutions to business problems.
> To apply the basic principles of bargaining and negotiation in order to achieve desired agreements between two or more parties.

KNOWLEDGE OBJECTIVES

> Understand why decision making is important in organizations.
> Discuss the five stages of the problem-solving process.
> Identify influences on problem solving and ways that people make decisions in the face of those influences.
> Discuss the many faces of intuition.
> Explain the stages of the creative process.
> Discuss techniques for enhancing creativity.
> Identify characteristics of creative organizations.
> Discuss five strategies for negotiating.
> Discuss guidelines for attaining win-win solutions.

Decisions are constantly being made at all levels of organizations. Corporate strategists plot mergers, devise financial and market gambits, and determine plant locations. Middle managers consider motivational tools, planning and control techniques, and ways to reduce subordinates' resistance to change. Lower-level employees decide whether to go to work, to produce at a certain level, to join informal groups, and to follow company procedures. Decisions are the fabric of organizations.

Can you think of some examples of companies where management is faced with tough decisions about how to solve organizational problems? Well, what if you were Richard Wagoner, the president of General Motors? What decisions would you make to help the world's largest automaker regain market share in the United States as well as in markets where GM's presence is still small, such as Japan and Southeast Asia? The management ranks at GM are filled with bright and hard-working people, but the problems the company faces are complex and dynamic. What about Levi Strauss, the American icon that has seen its sales plummet in the last 10 years? And what about Toys "R" Us, the toy retailer that has struggled to the point that Wal-Mart overtook it as the #1 toy retailer in the United States? How can it get back on track?

There are many reasons why you should care about solving problems. For example:[1]

> Organizational members are increasingly being evaluated on their problem-solving ability. So decisions may affect your career, rewards, and satisfaction.
> The quality and acceptability of your decisions will affect how well you perform and the degree of your satisfaction with work.
> Solving problems takes considerable time and effort and is often uncomfortable. It makes sense to try to do well on something on which you will spend so much time and psychic energy.
> Activities in organizations are generally the results of decisions. By examining how decisions are made, you may better understand how organizations work.

In this chapter we will examine the problem-solving process and offer guidelines for each step of the process. We will then discuss the PDCA cycle. Next we will consider a variety of factors that influence our problem solving and will then consider how we solve problems in the face of those factors. We will next consider the nature of creativity and address techniques for enhancing creativity and for developing creative organizations. Finally, we will discuss negotiating and bargaining, including strategies for negotiating and guidelines for attaining win-win solutions. Together, the chapter material offers a framework and tools for understanding and improving problem solving.

Before reading further, complete Self-Assessment Exercise 4-1 regarding attitudes toward problem solving. This self-assessment will give you some insights into your attitudes and beliefs about problem solving in general as well as into your problem-solving style. Then complete the Pre-Test Skills Assessment on solving problems. This will help you to assess your current level of skill development in the area of problem solving.

DEVIL'S ADVOCATE

Why do I need to worry so much about *how* I solve problems? Don't I just do it?

The quality of the process you use to solve problems (the *how*) is a critical determinant of how likely you are to be successful in solving the problem. Too often, managers are so focused on achieving results that they don't use a good approach to analyzing the problem and identifying solutions to it. In addition, many organizations also value decisiveness, or resolving problems in a timely manner. This makes it even more difficult to think in terms of process. The bottom line, though, is that you need to balance your focus on achieving results and process (what you want to achieve and how you get there).

The basic problem-solving model seems to be logical to me. Doesn't everybody solve problems like this?

On paper, some management techniques create the illusion of being "logical" and easy to use. However, in actual practice many managers default to using the "path of least resistance." "This can result in managers' not defining the problem cor-

rectly, not identifying a comprehensive set of alternatives, or not evaluating alternatives very carefully. While this has the advantages of being convenient and comfortable, it can significantly reduce the quality of the outcome of the problem-solving process.

The creativity-enhancement tools you discuss are too much work for me to use. They require me to follow such a rigid and structured approach. How do you respond to this?

One of the most important characteristics of effective management is being systematic. The creativity techniques discussed in the chapter are simply valuable tools for ensuring that all of the key components of a process that enhances creativity are addressed. Rather than viewing these techniques as things that constrain or limit your behavior, view them as tools that provide you with a roadmap or blueprint for solving the problems you will face as a manager.

Suppose that I "buy in" to this idea of the importance of problem-solving and creativity-enhance-

ment techniques. How can I actually use these techniques in the future?

A lot of this depends on the particular situation you are dealing with as a manager. However, there are a few guidelines we can provide for you. First, if you want to involve your staff in the problem-solving process, you need to take the time to educate them regarding how the tools covered in this chapter work and why they will help enhance the quality of the outcome. It is absolutely critical to obtain the commitment and support of your staff in order for these techniques to be effective. Second, make the use of these kinds of techniques part of your department's basic approach. If your work unit develops annual strategic and operational plans, you can state in them that "the systematic use of management tools to support decision making and implementation" will be a key component of the process for getting things done. Finally, maintain a positive attitude regarding the use of problem-solving and creativity-enhancement techniques by focusing on the value they can add for you as a manager.

Self-Assessment 4-1
Attitudes Toward Problem Solving

Please answer the questions that follow about your attitudes toward solving problems in the business world. You will learn more from this chapter if you become more aware of your beliefs and feelings about problem solving. Answer each question as honestly as possible using the following response scale:

1 = Disagree Strongly
2 = Disagree Somewhat

3 = Neither Agree nor Disagree
4 = Agree Somewhat
5 = Agree Strongly

1. _____ Solving business problems is mostly a matter of just using your common sense.
2. _____ Problem solving should involve the use of a systematic procedure.
3. _____ People spend too much time analyzing problems, which takes away from doing what is needed to solve them.
4. _____ Identifying problems in a given situation is usually the simplest part of the problem-solving process.
5. _____ Problem-solving tools should be used only when other methods for solving a problem have failed.
6. _____ The key measure of problem-solving effectiveness is efficiency in resolving the problem.
7. _____ An ideal or perfect solution to a problem can be implemented in most situations.
8. _____ In most cases, determining a solution to a problem is easier than implementing it.

Pre-Test Skills Assessment
Solving Problems

As a way to introduce the material in this chapter and for you to assess your general problem-solving skills, read the following case and develop a plan for how you would handle the situation.

You are the manager of a 200-room hotel that provides lodging for business travelers who need high-quality but affordable accommodations. Your unit is part of a national chain of over 200 hotels, with the main headquarters in Minneapolis, Minnesota.

Recently, the corporate office has announced a new performance measurement system that will be used to assess the performance of each hotel in the chain. The primary measure in the system is the Guest Satisfaction Index (GSI). This measure will be obtained by asking each customer to complete a survey at the time of checkout to assess his/her overall satisfaction with the hotel. Overall scores will be sent to each hotel manager on a quarterly basis (for each three-month period).

You receive the first GSI score for your hotel, and it indicates that only 30 percent of customers in the past quarter stated that they were satisfied or highly satisfied with their overall stay at your hotel. You are obviously alarmed about these disappointing results. What is the problem, and how do you fix it?

Develop an action plan for solving the problem(s) facing your hotel.

THE PROBLEM-SOLVING PROCESS

Successful problem solvers recognize there is more to a good decision than just choosing one option over another. Instead, they follow the five steps in the problem-solving process shown in Figure 4-1.

DEFINE THE PROBLEM

Careful problem definition is crucial. Unless proper time and care are taken at this stage, we may solve the wrong problem. A problem occurs when there

FIGURE 4-1
The Problem-Solving Process

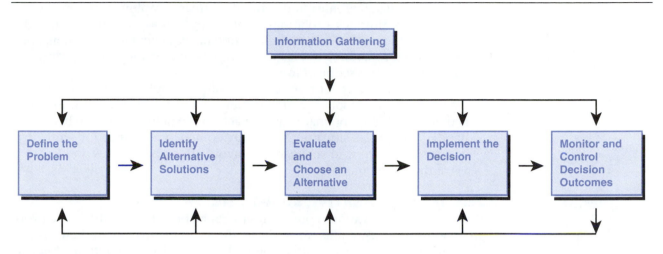

is a gap between the desired and the actual situation. Declining profits, high scrap rates, or inability to increase market share are all possible problems. Too often, the problem is defined in terms of symptoms. For instance, management may define the problem as employee apathy instead of seeing that apathy as a symptom of a deeper problem, such as low wages. Or the problem may be defined in terms of a preferred solution. A problem statement such as "Gloria is a poor manager" focuses on proposed solutions relating to Gloria rather than directly addressing the criterion of interest, such as declining performance in Gloria's department.[2] Here are some guidelines for writing a good problem statement:

> **State the problem explicitly.** We have a tendency to assume that the problem is too obvious to require an explicit statement. However, even "obvious" problems are seen differently by different people or not seen at all.

> **Specify the standard(s) violated.** There are many different types of standards that may be violated. These could be personal (such as violation of privacy or trust), group (such as violation of equal treatment or lack of opportunity to participate), organizational (such as poor quality or high scrap rates), or even societal (such as socially irresponsible behavior).

> **State the problem in specific behavioral terms.** Don't use broad generalizations such as lack of communications, personality conflicts, or the like. What specific behavioral standards are being violated? What specific behavioral change is desired? What behavior would constitute a solution to the problem?

> **Specify whose problem it is.** This helps to narrow down who must be involved in problem resolution. That is, who "owns" the problem? The problem statement should make clear the perspective being taken. For instance, is the problem statement from the perspective of a particular manager? Of a team?

> **Avoid stating the problem merely as an implied solution.** For instance, suppose productivity has declined. A problem statement such as "The plant manager must find ways to motivate employees to improve productivity" implies a solution—motivating employees. In fact, though, the problem may lie in equipment problems, management decisions, or much else. Prematurely focusing on employee motivation inappropriately narrows the scope of inquiry.

> **Avoid stating the problem as a dilemma.** People sometimes state a problem as an unsolvable predicament. They may say, "The problem is that we will lose no matter which action we take" or "We've been handed a hopeless situation." This may come from a desire for sympathy or attention or to gain vengeance or avoid effort, but it does nothing to solve the problem.

IDENTIFY ALTERNATIVE SOLUTIONS

Alternatives are the various approaches that may be taken to solving the problem. Good solutions require good alternatives. Unfortunately, in their rush to judgment, problem solvers often slight the alternative-generation stage. At this stage *divergent thinking* is needed. That is, problem solvers must stretch their minds, seeking new possibilities. Creativity—which we will discuss shortly—is especially important at the alternative-generation stage. In the business world, divergent thinking is sometimes referred to as "thinking outside the box," where the "box" is the conventional approach to thinking and acting.

EVALUATE AND CHOOSE AN ALTERNATIVE

Once alternatives are thoroughly generated, they can be evaluated and a choice can be made. This stage requires *convergent thinking,* a narrowing in on a solution. There are two general approaches to evaluation and choice. With *screening approaches,* each alternative is identified as satisfactory or unsatisfactory. Unsatisfactory alternatives are screened out, leaving only those that can clear all hurdles. *Scoring approaches* assign a total score to each alternative. Then the alternative with the best score can be chosen.

The Screening Table in Figure 4-2 is an example of a screening approach. Alternative solutions (in this case, digital cameras) are listed in the left-most column. Important attributes of the alternatives are listed along the top row, from most important to least important. Entries in the matrix are the scores of the alternatives on the attributes. Finally, constraints are presented for each attribute. These constraints represent the hurdles, or cutoff scores for acceptable levels, of each attribute. The nature of the constraints will depend on the attributes. For some attributes, such as price and delay between shots, lower levels are better, so the constraints specify maximum acceptable levels. For others, such as resolution and image capacity, higher levels are better, so the constraints specify minimum levels. For some decisions it is even possible that constraints will specify acceptable ranges (such as a comfortable temperature range).

Once this table is developed, it can easily be used to make a choice. One approach (called *elimination by aspects*) would be first to screen out those alternatives not satisfying the constraint for the most important attribute, then to screen out those remaining that don't satisfy the constraint for the next

FIGURE 4-2
Screening Table

| | | ATTRIBUTES | | |
| | | | | |
Alternatives	Price ($)	Width Resolution (Pixels)	Image Capacity	Delay Between Shots (Seconds)
Polaroid				
PhotoMAX PDC-640	249.00	640	36	10
Sony				
Mavica MVC-FD85	799.95	1280	40	3
Canon				
PowerShot S10	699.00	1668	61	2
Constraints	<800.00	>1000	>32	<5

most important attribute, and so on. This can be continued until only one alternative remains or until we run out of attributes. If more than one alternative remains after all constraints are considered, we could add further attributes and corresponding constraints, could make constraints more stringent and recheck, or could choose from among the acceptable alternatives on some other basis (such as looking at the degree to which each exceeds the constraints or even flipping a coin). In the example given in Figure 4-2, we would start with the most important attribute, price, and screen out no alternatives, because all cost less than $800. We would then see whether the alternatives satisfy the second constraint, width resolution, and so on. In this case, the Polaroid camera fails the resolution constraint, so it is eliminated. This leaves the Sony and Canon cameras. These cameras satisfy both the image capacity constraint and the delay between shots constraint, so either would be acceptable. In looking at attribute levels and the constraints, though, it is evident that the Canon is better than the Sony 2 for *every* attribute. It has lower scores on attributes for which low levels are desirable (those with "less than" constraints—price and delay time) and higher scores on those for which high levels are desirable (those with "greater than" constraints—width resolution and image capacity). Because of this, the Canon is said to *dominate* the Sony for the attributes considered, and should always be chosen.[3]

Another screening approach is to check the alternatives against the constraints, one alternative (rather than one attribute) at a time. That is, we would first check to see if the Polaroid satisfies all the constraints. Since it doesn't (it has low resolution and a long delay time between shots), we would then see if the Sony satisfies all the constraints. It does, so we would choose it. This approach, which selects the first acceptable alternative, is called *satisficing*. Satisficing simplifies and speeds the decision process, since we can collect information on alternatives one at a time; if we find an acceptable alternative, we don't have to gather information on others. Unfortunately, satisficing makes us slaves to the order in which alternatives are considered. In this case, we would choose the Sony camera even though the Canon camera (which we wouldn't consider if using satisficing) is better for *every* attribute considered. Thus, satisficing represents a common trade-off in decision making between ease of decision making and decision quality.

Now complete Skills Practice 4-1 to help develop your skill in using a screening table to make choices.

Skills Practice 4-1   **Skill Level: Challenging**
Developing and Using a Screening Table

Skill Objective
To develop skill in applying a screening table to make choices.

Procedure
1. Select a choice-making exercise that is relevant to you. This could be, for instance, a job-choice decision, a choice among alternative products or services, a choice about daily activities, or so on. Specify the choice.
2. Identify alternatives. For instance, if you are considering alternative jobs, list those jobs. If you are thinking of purchasing a new bicycle, go to a source (such as *Consumer Reports*) that provides information on bicycles and identify four or five from among which you'd like to choose.
3. Identify at least four attributes of the alternatives (but as many attributes as you'd like). For example, for a job choice this could include starting salary, job type, location, benefits, or whatever attributes you think are most important.
3. Rank the attributes from most important to you to least important to you.
4. For each attribute, select a cutoff level. Recall that this is the level that must be satisfied if the alternative *is not to be rejected.* As such, this is more than just a "want" level; it is a level that, if not satisfied, would cause you to reject the alternative. Recall too that the nature of the cutoff will vary with the attribute. For instance, for price you would typically want a "less than" constraint, causing you to reject alternatives that have prices above the constraint. For quality or durability or warranty, you would typically want a "greater than" constraint. You may even have constraints saying that only certain ranges, or even only certain levels, are acceptable (for instance, you might say that location is acceptable only if the job is in the southwest).
5. For each alternative, determine a score on each attribute. These may be "hard" data, such as prices, salt content, or calories, drawn from a source such as *Consumer Reports,* or your own subjective evaluation (for instance, for appearance of a car you might use your own taste to classify the appearance as "very attractive," "somewhat attractive," "somewhat unattractive," or "very unattractive").
6. Use a screening table like the one shown in Figure 4-2. On the left-hand (vertical) axis, list the alternatives you are considering. Along the top (horizontal) axis, list the attributes you are considering, arraying them from most important to least important.
7. On the last row of the table, fill in the constraints you have specified for each attribute. Be sure to indicate the nature of the constraint (e.g., less than, less than or equal to, equal to, greater than or equal to, greater than).
8. Fill in the table using the scores you have developed for each alternative on each attribute.

Discussion Questions
1. How did you select the alternatives that you considered?
2. How did you select and rank the attributes that you considered?
3. How did you select the cutoff score for each attribute?

4. What choice would you make using the elimination-by-aspects screening approach (that is, eliminating on an attribute-by-attribute basis)?
5. What choice would you make using the satisficing screening approach (that is, considering one alternative at a time and selecting the first acceptable alternative)?
6. Are your choices the same using elimination-by-aspects and satisficing? Would your satisficing choice have been different if the alternatives had been ordered differently?
7. Are you comfortable with the choices you made using these methods? Why or why not? If not, what might you do to make yourself more comfortable with your choices?
8. What are three practical implications of these screening approaches for you as a future manager?

Scoring approaches add levels of complexity to choice making. First, instead of having cutoff levels for each attribute, the attributes are given weights according to their relative importance. Second, the attribute levels are assigned utilities according to their relative levels of satisfactoriness. For example, the best level of an attribute could be assigned a utility of 100 and the worst attribute level a utility of 0. Other attribute levels are then assigned utilities corresponding to their respective satisfactoriness relative to the best level. Once these weights and utilities are assigned, the utility of each alternative can be determined by multiplying the alternative's utility for each attribute times the weight of that attribute and summing across all attributes. That is, the utility for alternative i is calculated across the n attributes as:

$$U_i = \sum_{j=1}^{n} (W_j \times U_{ij})$$

where

U_I is the overall utility, or satisfactoriness, of alternative i
W_j is the relative weight given to attribute j
U_{ij} is the utility, or satisfactoriness, of alternative i on attribute j

Then the alternative with the highest overall utility (that is, the highest level of satisfactoriness) can be chosen. As you can see, this is a more complex process than a screening approach. It does, though, give the opportunity of finding a "best" solution, as opposed to just a satisfactory one.

Some decision situations are even more complicated because they contain elements of risk, uncertainty, or conflict. With decision making under risk, the quality of alternatives depends upon which of multiple events (such as levels of rainfall, changes in the Dow Jones Average, or levels of student enrollments) occurs, *and* we are somehow able to attach probabilities to those events. In the case of decision making under uncertainty, the quality of alternatives depends on which of multiple events occurs, but we are unable to attach probabilities to the events. In the case of decision making under conflict, the quality of alternatives (sometimes called *strategies*) depends on the actions taken by a competitor. These situations require additional tools, such as decision trees, decision matrices, and game theory.[4]

IMPLEMENT THE DECISION

Together, the first three stages of the problem-solving process are called *decision making*. Some people make the mistake of assuming the problem-solving process is over once they have completed these stages. Unfortunately,

Web Wise

Netscape Decision Guides

Netscape offers "Decision Guides" to help you make choices regarding cars, electronics, travel options, careers, personal finance, and other decisions. The guides vary somewhat in format depending upon the particular decision type. You are asked a series of questions that create a list of, for instance, "ideal cars for you," and you are then given further information to help make side-by-side comparisons among the alternatives that best fit your criteria. The guides generally use screening approaches, to eliminate alternatives from the "ideal" list, and scoring approaches, to choose a preferred alternative from that list.

home.netscape.com/decisionguides/index.html

decisions do not implement themselves. Necessary resources must be available for implementation. Also, those who will be involved in implementation must fully understand and accept the solution. For that reason, implementers are often encouraged to participate in the earlier stages of the process.

A fundamental question at this stage is how long to persist in trying to successfully implement the decision. It is easy to err in either direction. The many difficulties that typically arise when trying to implement a major decision can lead to frustration, discontent, and the temptation to throw in the towel. As noted by Rosabeth Moss Kanter, "Everything looks like a failure in the middle."[5]

At the same time, decision makers are also prone to *escalation of commitment.* This is the tendency to "throw good money after bad," continuing to pour more time and resources into a failing project. Some powerful forces lead to escalation of commitment.[6] For instance, we find it hard to ignore "sunk costs," the resources that are already "down the drain." Also, as long as we are putting more resources into a project, we don't have to admit we've failed. Further, there are many social rewards for persistence; people tend to praise managers who "stick to their guns" in the face of opposition and bleak odds. For these and other reasons, escalation of commitment is a tempting, and dangerous, tendency. Here are some guidelines for minimizing the dangers of inappropriate escalation of commitment:[7]

> Create "stopping rules" prior to launching a project. These stopping rules specify the conditions under which the project should be abandoned.
> Specify objective criteria for evaluating the status of a project.
> Actively gather information on project performance, and accept warning signals when they occur.
> Make it clear that "pulling the plug" is a viable option, and don't be afraid to follow through when needed.
> Be wary of penalizing managers if their projects fail. If managers feel their careers will be damaged by failure, they may escalate commitment rather than admit failure.
> Seek objective views on project status, such as from external auditors.

FOCUS ON MANAGEMENT

ESCALATION OF COMMITMENT IN THE NATIONAL BASKETBALL ASSOCIATION

Examples of escalation of commitment can be found everywhere. In one interesting study, new players in the NBA were examined. The researchers found that players for whom the initial investment was greater, as measured by their higher draft position, had more playing time and longer NBA careers, independent of their performance. The NBA draft is highly visible, and team managers may have expected criticism if they failed to field their expensive players. As such, they gave their higher draft choices more opportunities to play, even when their performance didn't justify it.*

*B. M. Staw and H. Hoang, "Sunk Costs in the NBA: Why Draft Order Affects Playing Time and Survival in Professional Basketball," *Administrative Science Quarterly,* 1995, *40,* pp. 474–494. See also C. F. Camerer and R. A. Weber, "The Econometrics and Behavioral Economics of Escalation of Commitment: A Re-Examination of Staw and Hoang's NBA Data," *Journal of Economic Behavior and Organization,* May 1999, pp. 59–82.

FOCUS ON MANAGEMENT

THE ROAR OF THE CROWD

Bill Walsh, formerly the offensive coordinator of the Cincinnati Bengals football team, recalls a close game where the Bengals trailed the Oakland Raiders 31–28 with three minutes left in a playoff game at Oakland. The Bengals had the ball but the noise of the home crowd was deafening. In addition, the phone system Walsh used to communicate with his spotter in the press box began to malfunction. Between the roar of the crowd, the mechanical difficulties, and the excitement of the players, coordination broke down and the Bengals lost. Walsh says this experience taught him the importance of contingency planning. He wrote, "We lost the game, and I decided that I would never again be confronted by circumstances I hadn't prepared for, no matter how unlikely they might seem."

http://www.nfl.com/bengals/index.html

*For instance, see B. Walsh, "When Things Go Bad," *Forbes*, March 29, 1993, pp. 13–14.

MONITOR AND CONTROL DECISION OUTCOMES

The final step in the problem-solving process is to monitor decision outcomes and take necessary corrective action. If decision control is to be effective, steps must be taken to ensure that necessary information is gathered. And contingency plans must be developed to permit changes if the decision does not turn out well. *Contingency planning* is the process of developing alternative courses of action that can be followed if a decision, perhaps because of unexpected events, does not work out as planned. Contingency plans ensure that backups are available, and they help remove the panic element in unforeseen situations. The book and movie *The Perfect Storm* describe a situation in which a series of freakish weather conditions came together in the worst possible way to create a horrendous storm. Contingency plans are sometimes developed to deal with a "worst-case" scenario, the situation in which events fall together in the worst possible way to create the organizational equivalent of the "perfect storm."

Thus, contingency planning requires preparing for the worst even while hoping for the best. The need for contingency planning was seen in the bombing of the World Trade Center. Some firms in the building continued business with few problems since they had developed elaborate backup plans in the event that operations in the Trade Center were disrupted. Others, without such plans, were devastated.[8]

Now that we have examined each of the steps in the general problem-solving process, complete Skills Practice 4-2 to develop skill in applying the process to business problems.

Skill Level: Basic

Skills Practice 4-2
Applying the General Problem-Solving Process

Skill Objective

To develop skill in applying the general problem-solving process to business problems.

Directions

1. Identify a problem you are dealing with in your organization or school or something you have heard about in the news. Then write a one-paragraph statement of the problem you select. Some example problems follow.

a. The Cadillac Division of General Motors Corporation is experiencing difficulty in making its vehicles more appealing to younger consumers.
b. The U.S. Armed Forces cannot recruit enough new people to meet its demand for labor.
c. A student organization has a low level of member involvement in the organization's activities.
d. A business school is struggling to identify what it needs to teach students in preparing them for the "real world."
e. Traditional retailers are losing market share to Internet-based retailers.

2. Carefully define the problem.
3. Identify alternative solutions to the problem.
4. Identify the criteria you will use to evaluate your alternative solutions and evaluate your alternative solutions on the basis of those criteria.
5. Select the best alternative solution to your problem.
6. Identify the action steps you would take to implement your decision and to monitor and control the outcomes associated with the decision.
7. Evaluate your process. What were its strengths and weaknesses? What are the practical implications of this exercise for you as a future manager?

THE PDCA CYCLE

Many teams involved in decisions relating to quality improvement or other issues involving large, complex processes have found it useful to apply the PDCA (plan, do, check, act) cycle, sometimes called the Deming cycle, shown in Figure 4-3.[9] The PDCA cycle can be applied to any recurring activity, such

FIGURE 4-3
The PDCA Cycle

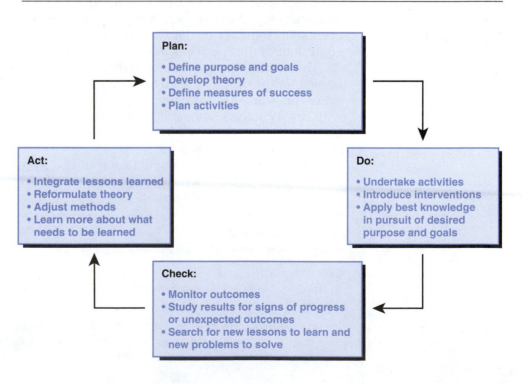

Plan:
- Define purpose and goals
- Develop theory
- Define measures of success
- Plan activities

Do:
- Undertake activities
- Introduce interventions
- Apply best knowledge in pursuit of desired purpose and goals

Check:
- Monitor outcomes
- Study results for signs of progress or unexpected outcomes
- Search for new lessons to learn and new problems to solve

Act:
- Integrate lessons learned
- Reformulate theory
- Adjust methods
- Learn more about what needs to be learned

as annual planning processes or everyday work such as materials handling, billing, and order taking.

The PDCA cycle permits learning, thus helping make sense of problems that may at first seem overwhelming. As suggested by the name, there are four steps: a plan is developed (plan), the plan is tested on a trial basis (do), the effects of the plan are evaluated and monitored (check), and appropriate corrective actions are taken (act). In the Plan stage, the team's purpose and goals are identified, a theory is developed, measures of success are defined, and activities are planned. In the Do stage, the plan is executed by undertaking activities, introducing interventions, and applying best knowledge to the pursuit of the desired purpose and goals. In the Check (or Study) stage, outcomes are monitored by testing the validity of the theory and plan. Results are studied for signs of progress or success or unexpected outcomes. The team searches for new lessons to learn and new problems to solve. Finally, in the Act stage the lessons learned are integrated, the theory reformulated, and methods adjusted. The team learns what more it needs to learn. And the cycle continues, providing a constant dialogue of theory and application.

Now, complete Skills Practice 4-3 to practice applying the PDCA cycle to a specific problem.

Skills Practice 4-3
Applying the Plan-Do-Check-Act Model

Skill Level: Basic

Skill Objective
To develop skill in applying the PDCA model in order to solve problems.

Procedure
1. Form teams of 3–5 people each.
2. The teams are to develop a process that will enable them to build the tallest house of cards. Each team will need to demonstrate its process from start to finish at the end of the exercise as a basis for evaluating the team's process and for awarding the 1st-place prize (if one is to be awarded). You must apply the PDCA model to your developmental process. That is, think of a possible approach, try it, evaluate it, modify your approach, and then try that.

Materials You Will Need to Provide
  > One standard deck of cards for each team
  > A ruler
  > A reward for the winning team (optional)
4. Teams have about 20 minutes to work on their process.
5. At the end of the 20-minute trial period, each team should demonstrate its process for building a house of cards. The prize will be awarded to the team with the tallest house of cards.

Discussion Questions
1. How did your team apply the PDCA model to its process? To what extent was this model helpful in accomplishing your task?
2. What kinds of "real-world" tasks or processes could benefit from the application of the PDCA model?
3. What are the practical implications of the PDCA model for you as a future manager?

INFLUENCES ON PROBLEM SOLVING

Figure 4-4 provides a rough outline of the steps information goes through as it is used for problem solving. That is, the individual must perceive and cognitively process available information. A decision is then made and implemented. Finally, the consequences of the decision are evaluated and stored for use in future problem solving.

Ideally, the decision maker would have all the information needed—and no more—when it was needed and in the desired form. The perceptual processes would select and process the information in an unbiased way. The cognitive processes would quickly, accurately, and objectively evaluate the information and arrive at an optimal choice. Subsequent evaluation of consequences would be unbiased and storage would be efficient. The "real-world" situation is far from this idyllic scenario. Many factors may impede a successful decision-making process, as described in this section.

INFORMATION INPUTS

People must often act on the basis of less-than-perfect information. It may be incomplete, late, or in the wrong form. There may be too much of it, and it may simply be wrong.

There are many reasons why information may be imperfect. For one, there simply may be too little time to carry out a full information search. And rapidly changing, complex situations make it especially difficult to get good information. Some sorts of problem solvers—including those who are young, risk takers, or dogmatic—act on the basis of relatively little information. Those with opposite characteristics feel especially uncomfortable if information is not abundant.

FIGURE 4-4
Factors Influencing Decision Making

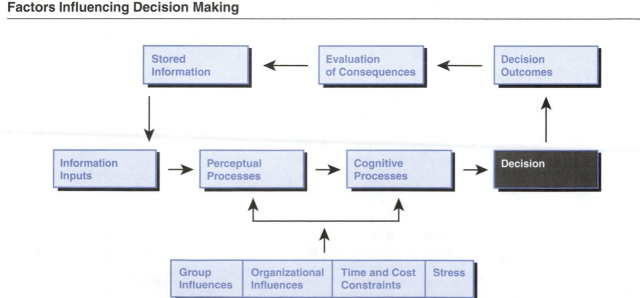

It is important to recognize that "perfect information" may simply not be attainable. In reality, information is often badly flawed, but decisions must still be made.

PERCEPTUAL PROCESSES

As we saw in Chapter 3, our perceptual processes can result in distortions. Recall, for instance, that we tend to perceive what we're expecting to perceive. Our perceptual selection is influenced by needs and personality factors and many things other than the nature of the object being perceived. When we interpret information, we are subject to stereotyping, halo error, projection, perceptual defense, and a host of other troublesome influences.

COGNITIVE PROCESSES [10]

Human problem solvers also face a variety of cognitive constraints. These include the following.

> We have very limited short-term memories, with a capacity for only a few pieces of information.

> We are basically serial- (rather than parallel-) information processors. That is, we find it difficult to deal with multiple problems simultaneously. As a result, we process information relatively slowly.

> We have limited computational ability. The sorts of calculations implied by theories of maximization, such as the rational economic man so popular in microeconomics, cannot be handled without assistance.

> Unlike a computer, we care about the outcomes of our decisions. This causes us to have doubts about whether our decision is correct.

> We evaluate information differently depending on how it is presented to us. Consider the following example to illustrate these framing effects.

One group of people was asked the following question:

Imagine that you have decided to see a play and paid the admission price of $10 per ticket. As you enter the theater you discover that you have lost the ticket. The seat was not marked and the ticket cannot be recovered. Would you pay $10 for another ticket?

Another group was asked this question:

Imagine that you have decided to see a play where admission is $10 per ticket. As you enter the theater you discover that you have lost a $10 bill. Would you still pay $10 for a ticket to see the play? [11]

The outcomes for both situations are identical: a $10 cost with no ticket or a $20 cost with a ticket. But of those faced with the first question, most (54 percent) said they would not buy another ticket. Of those asked the second question, only 12 percent indicated they wouldn't buy the ticket.

To explain this apparent paradox, decision theorists Tversky and Kahneman proposed a psychological account in which people keep track of transactions. The loss registers in the "ticket account" in the first case but not in the second. [12]

Awareness
Awareness
Awareness
Awareness
Awareness
Awareness

FOCUS ON MANAGEMENT

DEEP BLUE

There is ongoing debate and controversy over whether computers can "think" and whether computers can really outperform humans at challenging mental tasks. One battleground in the human–computer skirmishes is the chessboard. In 1997, a much-watched match between world chess champion Gary Kasparov and IBM's Deep Blue supercomputer ended with Kasparov's resignation in the sixth and final game and his losing the competition to Big Blue by a score of $3\frac{1}{2}$ to $2\frac{1}{2}$. This was the first time any chess champion had been beaten by a machine in a traditional match and the first time Kasparov had lost a multigame match against an individual opponent. A dispirited Kasparov said, "I'm a human being. When I see something that is beyond my understanding, I'm afraid."

http://www.research.ibm.com/ deepblue/home/html/b.html

GROUP INFLUENCES

Groups influence problem solvers in several ways. For one thing, they exert pressure for conformity to group norms. For another, they influence the individual's risk preferences, generally in the risky direction for most business-related decisions. We consider group influences in more depth in Chapter 12, Managing Teams.

ORGANIZATIONAL INFLUENCES

Problem solvers act within the context of the organization and are continually influenced by it. For instance, the organizational reward system influences the way decisions are made. If it rewards cautious decisions, employees will learn to play it safe. If it rewards taking chances, employees will learn to take risks. Rewards for creativity will reinforce the making of creative decisions.

TIME AND COST CONSTRAINTS

Obviously, time and cost constraints restrict our ability to get good, thorough information. Less obviously, time constraints also may cause us to change the nature of our decision processes. When pressed to make a quick decision, for instance, we may seek negative information about alternatives to screen them out quickly instead of carefully balancing positive and negative aspects.[13] Many managers face strong pressure from their organization to "be decisive" and to take action as quickly as possible (to be "a doer") rather than to analyze an issue at length (to be "a thinker").

STRESS

Decision makers often act under great psychological stress. Especially when the stakes are high, we may find it difficult to react with cool rationality. Chemical disasters, nuclear incidents, plane crashes, and product tamperings are notable examples, but executives face less visible hot decision situations regularly. We will see that such situations may lead to inadequate decision making.[14]

PROBLEM SOLVING IN THE FACE OF CONSTRAINTS

The many barriers faced by decision makers have a variety of consequences, some obvious and others not. In view of all the difficulties people face in problem solving, we do remarkably well. For instance, studies show that humans do a very good job of making statistical inferences.[15] Further, we may do even better in the "real world" than lab experiments suggest.[16] Nevertheless, the various barriers we have discussed do hinder problem solving in some important ways. Figure 4-5 presents some of the consequences of decision barriers.

Before reading further, complete the problem-solving quiz in Self-Assessment Exercise 4-2. It illustrates several issues we will consider in the following section.

Self-Assessment 4-2
Problem-Solving Quiz

The following questions present a variety of types of problem-solving situations. Respond to each question.

1. Which of the following sequences of outcomes of 10 flips of a fair coin is more likely?

    SEQUENCE A: HHHHHHHHHH
    SEQUENCE B: HTTHTHHTTT
    _____ Sequence A is more likely
    _____ Sequence B is more likely
    _____ The two sequences are equally likely.

FIGURE 4-5
Consequences of Decision Barriers

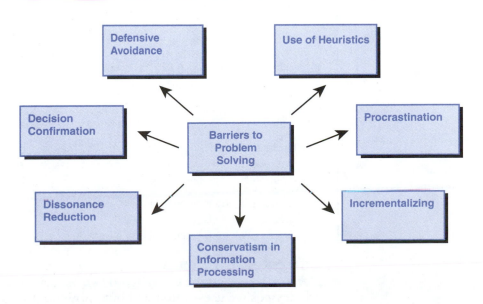

2. A number of pairs of causes of death in the United States are listed. For each pair, indicate which cause is responsible for more deaths annually in the United States.

PAIR A: _____ Motor vehicle accidents
_____ Lung cancer

PAIR B: _____ Strokes
_____ All accidents

PAIR C: _____ Tuberculosis
_____ Fire and flames

PAIR D: _____ Emphysema
_____ Homicide

3. Would days with over 60 percent male births be more common in a maternity ward with 15 births per day, or in a larger ward with 45 births per day, or about the same in the two wards?

_____ More common in the smaller ward
_____ More common in the larger ward
_____ Equally likely in the two wards

4. A gas station charges $1.50 for a gallon of gas if the customer pays with a credit card, but gives a five cent discount for a cash payment (that is, the price is $1.45 a gallon if the customer pays cash). Do you think it is fair that the gas station has these different prices?

_____ Yes, it is fair.
_____ No, it isn't fair.

Now, suppose the gas station charges $1.45 for a gallon of gas if the customer pays with cash, but adds a five cent surcharge for a credit card payment (that is, the price is $1.50 a gallon if the customer pays with a credit card). Do you think it is fair that the gas station has these different prices?

_____ Yes, it is fair.
_____ No, it isn't fair.

5. Athletes who are at their peak are frequently shown on the cover of *Sports Illustrated* magazine. After appearing on the cover, they often do less well. This has been referred to as the "*Sports Illustrated* jinx." Assuming that athletes do in fact perform less well after appearing on the *SI* cover, do you think this is evidence of a jinx?

_____ Yes
_____ No

6. Linda is a bright 31-year-old woman who majored in philosophy in college, where she was actively involved in issues of social justice. Rank the following statements from most likely (1) to least likely (3).

_____ Linda is a feminist
_____ Linda is a bank teller
_____ Linda is a feminist and a bank teller

USE OF HEURISTICS [17]

Heuristics (from the Greek word *heuriskein,* meaning "to find or discover") are devices we use—often without knowing it—to simplify decision making.

They are simplifying rules of thumb. While they typically do make things easier for the decision maker, they generally result in less than optimal solutions. Here are some important heuristics.

> *Satisficing* (as noted earlier in the chapter) means choosing the first acceptable alternative rather than looking for the best. So instead of trying to find the sharpest needle in a haystack, we may stop searching once we have located the first needle.[18] Satisficing is certainly a timesaver, since we don't have to gather information about all alternatives, only those we consider before making a choice. A problem with satisficing, of course, is that a far better candidate may be one or two or three alternatives down the list. That alternative will never even be considered.

> Often when we face a great amount of information, such as the full résumés of many job candidates, we may simply ignore most of the information and focus on only one or two attributes, such as previous experience and physical appearance.

> *Representativeness* is the tendency to place something in a class if it seems representative of the class. So if someone looks like an astronaut to us, we might classify that person as an astronaut, although there are very few astronauts. Representativeness can have serious consequences since it is closely related to stereotyping. For instance, if we think that men "look like" executives and women "look like" administrative assistants, we may behave accordingly. This could result in hiring or promotion biases against women.

> *Availability* is the tendency to estimate a probability of an event on the basis of how easy it is to recall examples of the event. To illustrate: Is it more likely that a word in the English language starts with the letter r or that it has r as the third letter?[19] Most people incorrectly guess that r is more common as the first letter. The reason for this is that we store information by the first rather than the third letter (witness the phone directory) and can thus retrieve it more easily on that basis. As another example, because certain causes of death are more likely than others to receive publicity in the newspapers and elsewhere, they are more available in our memories than are others. As a result, we tend to overestimate their probabilities.[20]

> When we face a sequence of information, it is often difficult to combine it all properly to come up with a solution. For instance, in one study two groups of high school students had five seconds to estimate a numerical expression on the blackboard. One group was told to estimate the following product:

$$8 \times 7 \times 6 \times 5 \times 4 \times 3 \times 2 \times 1$$

The other group estimated the following product:

$$1 \times 2 \times 3 \times 4 \times 5 \times 6 \times 7 \times 8$$

The median estimate for the first group, with the descending sequence, was 2,250. For the second group, with the ascending sequence, it was 512. The correct answer is 40,320.[21]

> *Anchoring and adjustment* is the tendency to use an early bit of information as an anchor and then use new information to adjust that initial anchor. If we weighted all that new information properly this would be

fine. However, we tend to give too little weight to new information. So in the example, insufficient revision resulted in both estimates being too low for both groups. The first group started with a higher initial anchor and thus came up with a higher, but still insufficient, estimate.

Heuristics, while potentially harmful, may not be all bad. For one thing, the problems that heuristics cause in laboratory experiments may be less severe in actual job settings. As an example, we often receive continuous feedback concerning our performance; for instance, as we trim a hedge, we can see what remains to be trimmed, whether we need to trim a section further, and so on. So if a heuristic "points us in the right direction," we can often then use feedback later to make adjustments. For this and other reasons, heuristics may actually be helpful in some cases. A weakness is that, even though we often use heuristics, we may not know it. For instance, one study found that job interviewers were unaware that they used simplifying procedures in making their judgments.[22] This inadvertent use of heuristics, especially in one-time decision situations, may be dangerous.

PROCRASTINATION

Because we find decision making to be uncomfortable, we may put off making and announcing a decision as long as possible. This procrastination delays the time at which we commit ourselves to the decision and thus makes it more difficult for us to reverse that decision. We may justify our delay on the grounds that we are using the time to gather additional information. Secretly, we may be wishing that the problem would simply go away. Procrastination can cost time, money, reputation, and opportunity. Careers have been ruined—and companies destroyed—by chronic procrastination.[23] When Blimpie International submarine shops teetered on the brink of insolvency in 1988, founder Anthony Conza identified procrastination in decision making as a major cause. In response, he set specific goals for improvements and provided firm dates for task completion. Within five years, Blimpie's had rebounded; it more than tripled in size, to more than 700 restaurants, and its share price rose from $0.125 to $11.50.[24] Procrastination can also lead to scrambling to meet deadlines and even to cheating or other unethical behaviors.[25]

http://www.blimpie.com/

INCREMENTALIZING

Suppose you wanted to design a perfect mousetrap. How would you begin? Most people would think of the best currently available mousetrap and then begin to revise it bit by bit, adding a better spring or disposal mechanism. This procedure of changing one attribute a little and then another is called *incrementalizing.*[26] While incrementalizing may be appropriate if only a "somewhat better" product is needed, it can seriously stifle truly creative alternatives. To learn more about creative mousetraps, see Web Exercise 4-2.

CONSERVATISM IN INFORMATION PROCESSING

We tend to show *conservatism in information processing,* characterized by underrevision of our estimates when presented with new information. For instance, if we initially believe the probability of an event is .5 and are presented with new information that should increase the probability to .8, we are more likely to revise our estimate to only .6 or .7. Conservatism can have serious consequences for decision making since we don't fully respond to changing situations.[27]

DISSONANCE REDUCTION

Most decisions require us to make difficult choices. Even though we make the choice that seems best overall, we may still like some things about the alternatives we reject and may not care for some things about the chosen alternative. This creates a condition of conflicting thoughts, called *cognitive dissonance* ("I've rejected something, yet it has some good characteristics; I've accepted something, yet it has some undesirable characteristics"). Cognitive dissonance is uncomfortable. We take a variety of actions, including a search for confirming information, a distortion of attitudes, and an avoidance of disconfirming information, to justify our decisions. As a result, we are likely to overestimate the quality of our past decisions (and thus to underestimate the need to improve our decisions).

DECISION CONFIRMATION

Dissonance reduction that occurs before the announcement of a decision has been called *decision confirmation.* Peer Soelberg showed, for instance, that by studying students' decision processes, he could identify their job choices weeks before they announced them. According to Soelberg, the students actually made a decision fairly early in the process. The remainder of the process was spent building a case for the preferred alternative. Then when they finally announced a decision, they could present a strong argument in its favor.[28]

DEFENSIVE AVOIDANCE

Psychological stress in hot decision situations may result in errors in scanning of alternatives.[29] When a hot situation—such as a major decision, an impending attack, or major surgery—occurs and it looks like important goals cannot be met, stress increases. This stress is especially great if someone—such as a confirmed smoker hearing the Surgeon General's warnings—is committed to a course of action that is challenged by new information. As stress grows, there is a tendency to lose hope of finding a better solution to the decision conflict, and *defensive avoidance* occurs. This is a condition in which the individual avoids information about risks of the chosen alternative or opportunities associated with an unchosen alternative.

A state of defensive avoidance is characterized by:

> Lack of vigilant search
> Distortion of the meanings of warning messages
> Selective inattention and forgetting
> Rationalizing

Because of defensive avoidance and other undesirable reactions to hot decision situations, many large industrial companies have formal crisis planning and management teams. These teams are trained to ask hard questions before they occur. George Greer, vice president and coordinator of the crisis management team at H. J. Heinz Co., says, "We try to say, 'What would we do if the president of the company were kidnapped, if a plant burned down, if somebody allegedly tampered with a product?'"[30] The apparently chaotic response of Exxon to its huge Alaskan oil spill demonstrates the dangers of failure to carefully consider such questions.

THE MANY FACES OF INTUITION

The many difficulties we face when trying to make good decisions leads to a question: Why not just rely on intuition? After all, we don't want to make "sterile" decisions, based just on numbers and formulas and computer programs. And we can all think of cases when a "gut" decision worked well. Unfortunately, the term *intuition* is used in so many ways, with so many different—and often opposing—implications and varying levels of empirical support, that it has become almost meaningless. Nevertheless, you will repeatedly encounter calls to "use your intuition," so you need to think through this issue. Here are some ways "intuition" is used.[31]

> **Intuition as paranormal power or sixth sense.** Authors using intuition in this sense believe that intuitive managers succeed because they use extrasensory powers that their nonintuitive counterparts lack or haven't fully developed.

> **Intuition as a personality trait.** Some authors treat intuition as a personality characteristic that a person is born with or acquires in early childhood and that is then essentially fixed for life. This personality type is seen as preferring to rely on hunches, inspiration, and insight to solve problems.

> **Intuition as an unconscious process.** According to this view, intuition is a set of processes that occur at the unconscious level at the same time that analysis is proceeding at the conscious level. Those taking this view of intuition generally believe that we can learn to attend to our unconscious (that is, to decide intuitively) and that this will lead to better decisions.

> **Intuition as a set of actions.** Sometimes intuition is seen as a set of observable methods or actions used by decision makers. These are evident in the ways decision makers gather, process, and use information. For instance, successful intuitive decision makers are said to often skip levels and seek information directly from key individuals, to meet face to face with those individuals and to subtly probe for information in a way that is unlikely to trigger defensive reactions.[32]

> **Intuition as distilled experience.** Here, intuition is seen as "analyses frozen into habit and into the capacity for rapid response through recognition."[33] That is, a manager who makes the same sorts of decisions many times over the years can identify an appropriate course of action without conscious information processing.

> **Intuition as a residual category.** This perspective says essentially that any choice that isn't a product of systematic, conscious data gathering and analysis must be intuition.

It seems obvious that statements such as "Managers should rely on intuition" are meaningless unless we know how the term is being used. Here are some guidelines regarding the various uses of the term.

> If someone refers to *intuition,* be sure to ask what he or she means by the term.

> There is simply no support for the "intuition as paranormal power" perspective and no reason to believe that such abilities could be developed if they did exist.

> There is no value in treating intuition as a residual category (that is, as anything that doesn't look like systematic problem solving). Such a perspective—telling us what intuition is not—gives absolutely no guidance on how better "intuitive" decisions could be made.

> If intuition is seen as a personality trait, it may be possible to select managers based on their intuitive ability, but training will have little impact. There is, though, relatively little evidence to suggest that certain personality traits are associated with more *effective* "intuitive" decisions (though it is possible to identify people who prefer to make decisions in nonsystematic ways).

> If intuition is seen as distilled experience, it is learnable but not teachable; developing intuition will require years of practice. There is evidence to support the contention that some decision makers (such as chess masters) are able over time to learn patterns and otherwise make what appear to be good "intuitive" decisions.

> If intuition is conceptualized as an unconscious process it may not be possible to develop the unconscious, but it may be feasible to train decision makers to rely more on "its often-faint whisper."[34] Unfortunately, there is little solid guidance for how this might be done.

> If intuition is viewed as a set of actions taken by certain types of decision makers, it may be possible to study those decision makers and learn from them. To a great extent, this chapter deals with actions that successful decision makers take to get information, behave creatively, make good choices, properly implement decisions, and so on. Much of what some people call intuition is simply use of good, learnable decision techniques.

In general, though, it seems clear that intuition is a complicated—if not confused—concept. Much more must be learned about the nature of intuition, its impacts, and the ways it may be learned before it will be possible to make confident claims for its ability to improve decision making.

IMPROVING PROBLEM SOLVING

Despite the obstacles that managers face in solving problems, there are techniques that can enhance the problem-solving process, summarized in Figure 4-6. We have already examined some of these techniques and will address others in subsequent sections and chapters.

The Voice of Experience box presents an interview with Kenji Yamanouchi, a sales specialist at IBM. It offers one practitioner's views on problems faced in a corporate environment and how he has learned to respond to those problems over time.

FIGURE 4-6
Guidelines for Improving Problem Solving

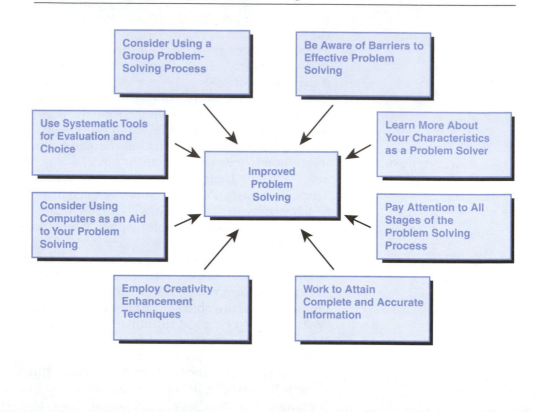

VOICE OF EXPERIENCE

PROBLEM SOLVING IN ORGANIZATIONS

Kenji Yamanouchi, RS6000
Sales Specialist
IBM Corporation

1. What are some of the most difficult problems you have experienced on your job?

The two most difficult problems have been getting things done while dealing with internal bureaucracy in a large corporation and operating in the competitive and ever-changing UNIX market. The internal bureaucracy affects how quickly orders get processed, how to get special terms and conditions approved to be able to offer a customer to close a sale, and the expected level of updat-

ing tools for mid-manager reports beyond just forecasting.

2. What specific actions have you taken to solve these problems?

For bureaucracy, I have had to learn when to do things as they are outlined by the company and when I can circumvent the system to get the same task accomplished. Networking within IBM is very key to understanding when you might have an opportunity to circumvent normal procedures.

For the competitive nature of the UNIX market, I have had to ensure that I keep up with IBM's product line but also learn through reading, education, and asking fellow coworkers about competitive offerings.

3. What advice would you give to students regarding how to analyze and solve business problems effectively in the real world?

To solve business problems effectively, I suggest the following.

> Use common sense.
> Look out for your customers' interests first. This really builds credibility with your customers.
> Listen to your customers. Don't assume you already know the answer to their business issues.
> Don't be afraid to say "I don't know" to your customer. I feel it is extremely important to ask others who have more expertise on a particular business issue.

FOSTERING CREATIVITY

Web Wise

Creativity Sites

The Web offers a wide array of creativity resources. The following sites offer a variety of information, techniques, tests, and links relating to creativity.

The Creativity Web:

http://www.ozemail.com/ ~caveman/Creative/

Provides resources for creativity and innovation, including discussions of creativity basics and techniques, "creativity kick-starts," quotations, problems and games, humor, and a creativity "hall of fame."

The Creativity Site:

http://www.mindbloom.com/

Offers creativity exercises and tests, suggestions for corporate creativity, examples of applications of creativity-enhancement techniques, and other creativity information.

Creativity and Innovation:

http://www.thebesemer.com/ currentmarketplace.html

Focuses on creativity in the workplace, including examples of creative approaches to hiring, culture transformation, and enhancement of innovation.

Good problem solving occurs when managers have many viable, creative alternatives to consider. To inspire employees to approach problems creatively and to nurture a creative environment, organizations follow three general approaches. These include hiring creative individuals, applying specific creativity-enhancement techniques, and developing a creative organization. After discussions of the nature of creativity, the creative process, and views of creativity, we will consider these approaches in turn.

THE NATURE OF CREATIVITY

Creative behavior is defined as production of ideas that are both new and useful. *Creative ability* is the ability to produce ideas that are both new and useful. These definitions may seem constraining, since the usefulness of some truly creative alternatives might not be immediately evident. One scholar has addressed this dilemma by differentiating between originality and creativity. He wrote, ". . . 7,363,474 is quite an original answer to the problem 'How much is 12 + 12?' However, it is only when conditions are such that the answer is useful that we can also call it creative."[35] Thus, the answer 7,363,474 is original but not creative. As we will discuss in Chapter 6 and elsewhere, ability may not translate into behavior. Both motivation and a proper setting may be necessary if innate creative ability is to blossom into creative output.[36]

THE CREATIVE PROCESS

Creativity involves more than the sudden moment of inspiration in which a cartoon light bulb flashes in the brain. Instead, as shown in Figure 4-7, there are four stages to the creative process: preparation, incubation, insight, and verification.[37]

> *Preparation* involves gathering, sorting, and integrating information and other materials to provide a solid base for a later breakthrough. The discoveries of penicillin, the benzene ring, or gravity, while each involved a moment of insight, would have been impossible without a firm grasp of related information.

> During the *incubation* stage, the mind is not consciously focused on the problem. The individual may be relaxed, asleep, reflective, or otherwise involved. A. E. Housman wrote that "As I went along, thinking nothing in particular . . . there would flow into my mind, with sudden and unaccountable emotion, sometimes a line or two of verse, sometimes a whole stanza at once."[38]

> The *insight* ("Eureka!") stage is the familiar, sudden moment of inspiration. While this is what we often think of as creativity, it is only one step in the creative process.

FIGURE 4 - 7
The Creative Process

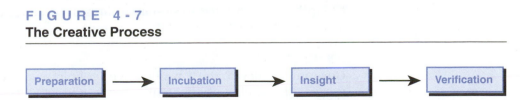

> Finally, *verification* is necessary. Here, the individual carries out the chores involved in carefully checking facts to support the insight, carrying out research to determine that the DNA molecule is in fact a double helix or that a meteorite did really create a dust cloud that led to the extinction of the dinosaurs. This process further supports the contention that creativity does not just happen. It is a thorough and often-painstaking activity.

CHARACTERISTICS OF CREATIVE INDIVIDUALS

Creative persons seem to be sensitive and to prefer complexity.[39] They typically value independence, enjoy esthetic expressions, have high aspiration levels, are open minded, and have a wide range of interests.[40] They were generally given the opportunity to act responsibly early in life.[41]

Studies across a wide range of occupations show creative behavior to peak in the 30s or early 40s.[42] This may be because motivation to be creative declines later in life. Creativity has only a weak relationship to IQ. Females outperform males on some figural and all verbal creativity tests after about age 10 in our society, though different patterns appear in other societies.[43] This suggests that these gender differences may be due to socialization processes.

Creative individuals resist conformity pressures if they see those pressures as interfering with their creative accomplishments, but otherwise they are willing to conform.[44] They tend to have high turnover rates, leaving schools and jobs more frequently than those who are less creative.[45]

TECHNIQUES FOR ENHANCING CREATIVITY

A wide variety of popular techniques have been developed to enhance creativity, as described in this section. We will address additional techniques in Chapter 12, Managing Teams.

GORDON TECHNIQUE [46]

William J. J. Gordon worked with creative-thinking groups and had a creative variety of other pursuits, among them salvage diver, horse handler, ambulance driver, college lecturer, and pig breeder (". . . a lot of bone and not much bacon, but they were the fastest pigs in the East.")[47] He was concerned that people, when asked to come up with a creative new idea, would instead incrementalize. That is, they would take an available alternative and improve it bit by bit. While this might lead to marginally better alternatives, the alternatives probably would not be real breakthroughs.

Gordon decided that one way to avoid this problem would be simply not to tell people what they were inventing. Thus, the *Gordon technique* uses an initial focus on function. Rather than being told to build a better mousetrap, the group might first be told that the focus was capturing. Instead of the group being instructed to design an improved knife, the function could be given as severing.[48]

SYNECTICS

Gordon also developed a well-known technique called *synectics. Synectics* means "the joining of apparently unrelated elements." It means this in two senses. First, very different sorts of people are put together in synectics groups in order to get a great diversity of perspectives. Second, synectics relies heavily on the use of analogies. Synectics techniques have been widely adopted by both businesses and educational institutions.[49] Three synectics tools, according to Gordon, are direct analogy, personal analogy, and fantasy analogy.

> **Direct analogy.** This involves looking for parallel facts, knowledge, or technology in a different domain from the one being worked on. For instance, can we think of anything similar that occurs in nature? Alexander Graham Bell's words, recalled by Gordon, illustrate this approach:

It struck me that the bones of the human ear were very massive, indeed, as compared with the delicate thin membrane that operated them, and the thought occurred that if a membrane so delicate could move bones relatively so massive, why should not a thicker and stouter piece of membrane move my piece of steel? And the telephone was conceived.[50]

> **Personal analogy.** With this approach, synectics group members try to identify psychologically with key parts of the problem. In one case, for example, the group was asked to design a mechanism that would run a shaft turning at 400 to 4,000 rpm so that the power-takeoff end of the shaft would turn at a constant 400 rpm. To address this question, members of the group metaphorically entered the box and tried to use their bodies to attain the required speed without undue friction.

> **Fantasy analogy.** Sigmund Freud saw creativity as the fulfillment of a wish or fantasy. Fantasy analogy asks, How in my wildest dreams can I make this happen? Gordon gives the example of a synectics group with the task of inventing a vapor-proof closure for space suits. Their solution was a spring mechanism based on the fantasy analogy of rows of trained insects clasping claws to hold shut the closure.

There is more to synectics than just the use of analogy. The technique follows a structured problem-solving sequence in which a client and other participants interact to develop a workable solution to the client's problem. For instance, after the problem has been introduced and discussed, there is a "springboards" stage in which the problem is opened up by asking the client to convert concerns, opinions, and desires into statements such as "I wish . . ." or "How to . . ." Later, after an initial idea has been developed and refined, an "itemized response" stage requires the client to think of three useful aspects or advantages of the idea and to generate key concerns. Still later, after the group works to modify the suggestion to overcome these concerns, the "possible solution" is checked for elements of newness and feasibility and whether there is sufficient commitment to the solution to take additional steps. Finally, the client lists actions to be taken to implement the solution, including timing and the personnel to be used.

Betsy Means, vice president and director of product management for the values product group of Citibank, regularly uses analogies to name a new product.[51] She first brainstorms with a group to come up with a new fraction of an idea and then builds on it by bringing together ideas from unrelated disciplines. Through her efforts at Citibank, Means in a single year signed up more than 2 million new customers for Citibank's Visa and MasterCard.[52]

158 Chapter 4 Solving Problems

Awareness
Awareness
Awareness
Awareness
Awareness

Now complete Skills Practice 4-4 to develop your skill in using the synectics technique for generating creative solutions to problems.

Skills Practice 4-4
Applying Synectics Analogies

Skill Level: Basic

Skill Objective
To develop skill in using the synectics technique for generating creative solutions to business problems.

Directions
1. Read the following scenario:

The Case of the Christmas Crunch
You are the product designer for a major toy manufacturer based in the United States. One of the keys to success in the toy business is the ability to design and develop innovative products that capture the interest and imagination of children. Your boss has given you the task of developing a "big smash" toy for the next holiday season. In the past, these kinds of big hit toys have included the Nintendo 64 video game system, Tickle Me Elmo, Furby, and Pokemon.

Note: If you prefer, you can use your own problem for completing this exercise.

2. Apply the various synectics techniques to address the problem in this case. For example:
    a. Use direct analogies by completing the following sentence stem: The problem I am working on is like _____.
    b. Use personal analogies by completing the sentence following stem: One thing I can do to identify with this problem is _____.
    c. Use fantasy analogies by completing the following sentence stem: In my wildest dreams I could solve this problem by _____.

Discussion Questions
1. To what extent do you think the synectics analogies were effective?
2. Discuss some examples of "real-world" problems that could be solved through the use of synectics.
3. What are the keys to the successful implementation of synectics in "real-world" organizations?

IDEA CHECKLISTS

Several *idea checklists* have been developed to enhance creativity.[53] These involve asking a series of questions about how we might use something that we already have. For example, one checklist of idea-spurring questions is called SCAMPER (for Substitute? Combine? Adapt? Modify or magnify? Put to other uses? Eliminate or reduce? Reverse or rearrange?). Here's an example of adapting: Clarence Birdseye worked as a fur trader in Labrador before World War I. He noted that Inuit preserved fish by quick-freezing and that the fish, when thawed, were flaky and moist. Birdseye adapted this process to make quick-frozen food available to the general public. This replaced the old slow-freeze process that left food dry and tasteless. The huge success of quick-frozen food led to the creation of General Foods.

And here's an example of eliminating: Kiichiro Toyoda, the founder of Toyota, sought ways to eliminate large inventories and the need for warehouses. American supermarkets fascinated him, and he noted that they require vast amounts of food that can't be stored on site because of spoilage and space considerations. When supplies run low, the staff contacts the appropriate supplier and items arrive "just in time." Toyota adopted this concept and streamlined its operation, eliminating waste and warehouses and reducing costs dramatically. Toyota's "just-in-time" approach gave it a huge competitive edge. Just-in-time is now being adopted worldwide.

George Washington Carver asked the question "How can peanuts be put to other uses?" and came up with over 300 applications. Many creative ideas have resulted from asking how waste products could be put to other uses. Rubber bands are made from surgical tubing; garbage is compressed into construction blocks; petrochemical waste is sold as Silly Putty; the Goodyear Tire Company has a pollution-free heating plant in Michigan that uses discarded tires as its only fuel.

Perhaps the best-known listing technique is the "73 idea-spurring questions" devised by Osborn.[54] This checklist can be applied to any alternative. Here are some of the questions.

> Put to other uses? New ways to use as is? Other uses if modified?
> Adapt? What else is like it? What other ideas does this suggest? Does past offer parallel? What could I copy? Whom could I emulate?
> Minify? What to subtract? Smaller? Condensed? Miniature? Lower? Shorter? Lighter? Omit? Streamline? Split up? Understate?
> Substitute? Who else instead? What else instead? Other ingredient? Other material? Other process? Other power? Other place? Other approach? Other tone of voice?
> Rearrange? Interchange components? Other pattern? Other layout? Other sequence? Transpose cause and effect? Change pace? Change schedule?
> Combine? How about a blend, an alloy, an assortment, an ensemble? Combine units? Combine purposes? Combine appeals? Combine ideas?

ATTRIBUTE LISTING

According to the developer of *attribute listing,* Robert Crawford, "Each time we take a step we do it by changing an attribute or a quality of something, or else by applying that same quality or attribute to some other thing."[55] There are two forms of attribute listing: attribute modifying and attribute transferring.[56]

With attribute modifying, the main attributes of the problem object are listed. Then ways to improve each attribute are listed. For instance, the technique might be used to concentrate on ways to improve the running shoe attributes of weight, stability, cushioning, and durability. Attribute transferring is similar to direct analogy in synectics. Attributes from one thing are transferred to another.

CHECKERBOARD METHOD

The *checkerboard method,* also called *morphological analysis,* is an extension of attribute modifying. Specific ideas for one attribute or problem dimension are listed along one axis of a matrix. Ideas for a second attribute are listed along the other axis. If desired, a third axis (and attribute) can be added.

FIGURE 4-8

The Checkerboard Method

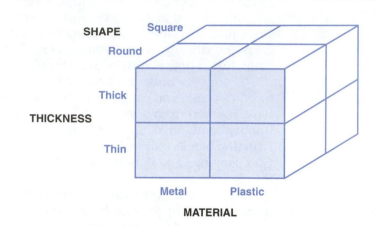

The cells of the matrix then provide idea combinations. For instance, the axes for a vehicle might be *type of energy source* (e.g., steam, magnetic fields, compressed air, nuclear), *medium of travel* (e.g., rollers, air, water, rails), and *type of vehicle* (e.g., cart, chair, sling, bed).[57] Figure 4-8 shows a simple application of the checkerboard method to the design of paper clips.

The benefit of the checkerboard method of analysis is that it makes us aware of all possible combinations of the attributes. Many, of course, will prove to be of little value, but others may be worthwhile. Like other creativity-enhancement techniques, the checkerboard method makes us view the world from a different perspective. It is very useful for producing large numbers of new ideas.[58]

Skills Practice 4-5 will help you develop skill in applying the checkerboard method to specific business scenarios.

Skills Practice 4-5   **Skill Level: Challenging**
Applying the Checkerboard Technique

Skill Objective
To develop skill in applying the checkerboard technique for enhancing creativity.

Procedure
1. Select one of the following scenarios. Based on the scenario you select, identify two relevant product or service attributes and brainstorm levels/types for each attribute. *Note:* Use more than two attributes if appropriate.

Problem Scenario 1
The McDonald's Corporation has been faced with the challenge of expanding its traditional burger-and-fries menu in order to support the continued growth of the company. Use the checkerboard technique to address this issue.

Problem Scenario 2
General Motors Corporation has been trying to identify new types of cars and trucks that consumers will find appealing. It is critical for GM to do this in order to strengthen its mar-

ket share in North America as well as in global markets. Use the checkerboard technique to address this issue.

Problem Scenario 3

Amazon.com is interested in identifying new opportunities for growth beyond its core Internet bookstore business. This is critical for Amazon.com, given growing competition in Internet-based bookstore retailers.

2. List your two attributes along with the list of attribute levels/types you brainstormed.
3. Develop a checkerboard matrix with levels/types for attribute 1 on the horizontal axis and levels/types for attribute 2 on the vertical axis.
4. Evaluate the various ideas identified by the checkerboard. Circle the ideas that appear to have merit.

Discussion Questions

1. How effective was the checkerboard as a tool for enhancing creativity?
2. If you were really using the checkerboard to address the issue you analyzed for this exercise, what would be the next step?
3. What would be the key strategies for using this technique effectively as a manager in a "real-world" situation?

RETRODUCTION

We are the slaves of our assumptions; they dictate the way we behave. *Retroduction* involves changing an assumption. This may serve two purposes. First, our assumptions may be wrong. Second, even if our assumptions are correct, we may gain valuable new perspectives from looking at things from a different angle. Albert Einstein, for instance, revised Isaac Newton's assumption that space is flat to the assumption that space is curved and developed a new perspective on time and space.

As a simple example of the power of assumptions, consider paper clips, the subject of Figure 4-7. The standard Gem paper clip, invented in 1899, accounts for most of the 20 billion paper clips sold every year. More than 100 alternative designs have been patented, varying in size, material, and shape. "Ring" clips, "owl" clips, "arrowhead" clips, "butterfly" clips, and many others have been offered, and their inventors present compelling cases for their superiority. Nevertheless, they haven't made a noticeable dent in Gem's market superiority. Why? It would seem that the inventors share a common—and incorrect—assumption, that paper clips are used to clip sheets of paper together. In fact, though, research shows that only 20 percent of paper clips are used to hold papers. The rest are twisted or broken by people during phone conversations, unwound to clean pipes, nails, or ears, used to reinforce eyeglasses, or put to other creative uses. The Gem, unlike its competitors, can easily be taken apart and reshaped.[59]

One retroduction technique says, "Suppose *X* were *Y*." For instance, "Suppose custodians were chief executives." Another technique pairs apparently distinct concepts, such as *power* and *satisfaction* or *perception* and *structure,* and sees what new alternatives might be suggested. Yet another asks "What if?" For example, what if employees could design their own jobs? What if we viewed customers as owners of the firm?[60] One individual who applied these retroduction techniques generated such questions as "What are the structural irregularities of semiconductors?" and "Can arteries have rashes?" Each of these questions is now the subject of study and debate, the first among physicists and the second among researchers on disease processes.[61] Henry Ford questioned the practice of moving workers to material, asking "What if we moved the work to the people?" This questioning led to the birth of the assembly line. Retroduction offers new perspectives and helps free people from mental ruts.

Here's a final example: For years, bankers assumed that customers preferred human tellers. In the early 1980s Citibank felt that installing automatic tellers would help it cut costs. However, since Citibank executives assumed people would prefer not to use machines, they reserved human tellers for people with large accounts and relegated smaller depositors to the machines. The machines proved unpopular and Citibank stopped using them, taking the failure as proof that its assumption was correct. Later, another banker challenged this assumption. He asked, in effect, "What if people really like to use automatic tellers? What if the Citibank customers who used the machines simply resented being treated as second-class citizens?" He brought back the automatic tellers with no "class distinctions" and they were an immediate success.[62]

Skills Practice 4-6 is designed to develop your skill in applying the questioning of assumptions and "what if" approaches to retroduction.

Skills Practice 4-6
Applying Retroduction Techniques

Skill Level: Challenging

Skill Objective
To develop skill in using the questioning of assumptions and "what if" approaches to retroduction in order to identify creative solutions to business problems.

Directions
1. Read the following scenario:

The Relentless Pursuit of Academic Excellence
Suppose that the department chair of the field in which you are majoring at your college or university has asked you to help her to develop a list of creative ways to enhance the quality and effectiveness of the academic program in which you are enrolled. This is a critical strategic issue for the department chair because it has long-term implications for the future of your academic program. Use the retroduction techniques of challenging assumptions and asking "what if" to generate a list of ideas. Remember, the chair is counting on you to deliver, so don't disappoint her!

Note: You may also use your own problem for this exercise, if you wish.

2. Carefully consider the scenario and identify at least four assumptions you would typically make when developing creative alternatives for your department chair. Now see what new alternatives you can generate if you change each of those assumptions.

3. In addition, try to generate alternative solutions to the problem by responding to each of the following "what if" questions (or to any other "what if" questions you can devise): What if unlimited funding were available to enhance the program? What if you could use *any* resources you want—people, techniques, technologies, programs, or whatever—to develop an "ideal" program? What if students could design their own courses? What if it were no longer possible to use books, lectures, or classrooms?

Discussion Questions

1. To what degree were the retroduction techniques helpful in generating creative solutions to your problem? Why?
2. Discuss some specific ways in which retroduction techniques could be applied to "real-world" managerial problems.
3. What are the keys to the successful implementation of retroduction techniques?

The accompanying Bottom Line shows the key steps of each of the creativity-enhancement techniques we have considered. It also shows how alternatives generated by the techniques can serve as inputs to later steps in the problem-solving process.

BOTTOM LINE

The Bottom Line: Problem Solving and Creativity Enhancement Tools

Gordon Technique

- Identify the function of the problem solution, but do not specify the exact nature of the problem
- Generate alternatives that satisfy the function

Checkerboard Method

- State the problem
- Identify the attributes or problem dimensions
- Generate ideas for improving each attribute or problem dimension
- Insert ideas for each attribute or problem dimension in a matrix
- Combine ideas across attributes or problem dimensions

Synectics Technique

- Create a diverse group of people
- State the problem
- Use "springboarding" to clarify the problem
- Use analogies to develop potential solutions

Attribute Modifying

- State the problem
- List primary attributes on which solutions to the problem may vary
- Find ways to improve each attribute

Attribute Transferring

- State the problem
- List primary attributes on which solutions to the problem may vary
- For each attribute, find some thing (object, idea, etc.) that has desirable properties for the attribute
- Transfer those attribute properties to the current problem situation

Evaluate Alternatives

↓

Select Alternatives

↓

Implement Decision

↓

Evaluate Outcomes

Retroduction Technique

- State the problem
- Identify assumptions held in viewing the problem
- Change each of the assumptions
- Identify alternative solutions

THE CREATIVE ORGANIZATION

Along with use of specific creativity-enhancement techniques, an organization may try to choose appropriate structure and processes to foster creative behavior. Some writers have studied creative individuals and their desires and have drawn a picture of an organization that would seem to suit them best. One such picture is shown in Figure 4-9. The loose, free-flowing, adaptive nature of this organization is quite similar to the organic organization structure discussed in other chapters. Such a structure seems appropriate in dynamic, complex, uncertain situations—exactly those most requiring creativity. We'll see later in this section what companies are doing to create such structures.

The importance of these dimensions is perhaps best seen in their absence. For instance, Japan has in recent years been losing its best and brightest young pure scientists to the United States and other countries. The reason: the scientists are unwilling to accept a system that relies on bureaucratic constraints and seniority and that stifles individualism, job mobility and open debate. In the Japanese system, young scientists are expected to plug away patiently under the close supervision of older scientists. If they are unhappy, they can't easily move because the notion of lifelong employment is powerful in Japan and job-hoppers are seen as pariahs. Open debate is so rare that when one speaker was challenged at a conference, he froze, unable to answer. In another case a young scientist held back from questioning the data of an elderly,

F I G U R E   4 - 9
Characteristics of a Creative Organization

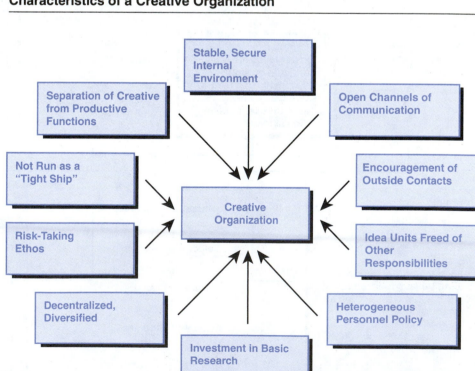

influential author because the elder "would have lost face and . . . I would have been indirectly punished some day when I filed an application" for a grant. Bureaucratic rules regularly crimp freedom; for instance, scientists must apply months ahead for government consent to leave the country. Rather than taking risks and exploring new areas, scholars search Western journals to find research topics. One consequence of this lack of a creative environment is that only five Japanese scientists have ever won Nobel prizes, compared to more than a score of French scientists and well over 140 Americans.[63]

If it is not possible to change the organization markedly to make it more conducive to creativity, another option is to free some units from bureaucratic entanglements by setting up relatively autonomous units. For instance, when General Motors launched its Saturn project, the first new nameplate in the GM line since 1918, it wanted a clean-slate approach without unnecessary ties to past ways of designing, engineering, manufacturing, or selling the product. As a result, it set up a new organization in order to free Saturn from the inefficiencies and overstaffing of the then-current GM bureaucracy.[64]

Now complete Skills Practice 4-7 to develop an action plan for promoting a creative organization.

Skills Practice 4-7
Developing Creative Organizations

Skill Level: **Basic**

Skill Objective
To develop skill in formulating an action plan for fostering a creative organization.

Directions
For each of the following characteristics of a creative organization, brainstorm a list of actions that could be taken by management to incorporate it into a firm.

Characteristics of Creative Organizations
> Open channels of communication
> Outside contacts
> Freeing idea units of other responsibilities
> Heterogeneous personnel policies
> Investment in basic research
> Decentralized and diversified organization
> Risk-taking ethos
> Not running the organization as a "tight ship"
> Separating the creative and productive functions
> Promoting a stable and secure internal environment

Discussion Questions
1. How would your proposed strategies help an organization to be more creative?
2. What kinds of challenges might you encounter in actually implementing the strategies you identified?
3. How does this exercise demonstrate the value of theoretical frameworks?
4. What are the practical implications of this exercise for you as a future manager?

VENTURE TEAMS

A *venture team* is a temporary grouping of organization members for generating new ideas.[65] So that creative thinking is not stifled, team members are freed of the organization's bureaucracy and in many cases have a separate location and facilities—these separate entities are known as *skunk works.*[66] Major corporations such as IBM, 3M Company, Dow Chemical, and Texas Instruments have used venture teams to solve technical problems and promote change. Ford Motor Company used a skunk works to keep the new Mustang alive.[67] Faced with tight budgets, tough time constraints, and an uncertain vision of the new Mustang, Ford formed the 400-member "Team Mustang." Team members thought of themselves as independent stockholders of the "Mustang Car Co.," which happened to be financed by Ford. They set up Mustang Car Co. in a converted furniture warehouse, got approval to move Ford engineers from various locations to the warehouse, and grouped employees into "chunk teams," with responsibility for every "chunk" of the car. Mustang Car Co. did away with many elements of the traditional hierarchy and many restrictive rules and procedures. The result: the fundamentally redesigned new Mustang was completed in three years and for about $700 million— 25 percent less time and 30 percent less money than for any comparable new car program in Ford's recent history.

IDEA CHAMPIONS

An *idea champion* is a member of the organization who is assigned responsibility for the successful implementation of a change. The idea champion may be a senior manager or a nonmanager, such as the inventor of the idea that has prompted the change. An idea champion is devoted to the change and is willing to spend time and energy to see that the change takes place. Idea champions will fight resistance to change and will actively pursue resources necessary to carry out the change. Idea champions may be critical to the success or failure of change. For example, Texas Instruments reviewed 50 successful and 50 unsuccessful technical projects. One consistent finding was that every failure also lacked an idea champion. As a result, Texas Instruments set up as its number-one criterion for project approval the presence of an idea champion.[68]

FOCUS ON MANAGEMENT

METROJET

Two dozen mechanics, flight attendants, dispatchers, and reservation agents of US Air, selected by senior managers and union leaders, were offered an unusual assignment: Help start a low-fare airline for US Air.* US Air had decided that it needed the low-fare airline to help counter the expansion of Southwest Airlines into the east, and it put the project into the hands of its front-line employees. In the unusual experiment in worker empowerment, the employees—each of whom knew his or her job well, but none with experience starting a business, much less an airline—worked under the code name US2. They priced peanuts, conducted focus groups, and argued over everything from how fast to fly the planes to whether to keep pillows and blankets aboard. Taking just one day off (to watch the Super Bowl) the team completed its assignment in only four months. Named MetroJet, based on 4,200 entries in an employee contest, the airline has been a great success.

http://www.flymetrojet.com/

*S. Carey, "US Air 'Peon' Team Pilots Start-Up of Low-Fare Airline," *Wall Street Journal,* pp. B1, B8. See also A. L. Velocci, Jr., "MetroJet's Expansion Tests Rivals' Mettle," *Aviation Week and Space Technology,* April 12, 1999, p. 57.

INTRAPRENEURSHIP

Many people have praised the flexibility, creativity, risk taking, and energy that are often associated with small firms and entrepreneurship and have asked how these elements might be instilled in larger organizations. *Intrapreneurship* is the name given to entrepreneurial activities within a larger organization, and *intrapreneurs* are essentially internal entrepreneurs.[69]

Intrapreneurs and entrepreneurs have many things in common.[70] For instance, they value creativity and autonomy and have a strong desire to achieve. On the other hand, since intrapreneurs work within a corporate system, they face the benefits and constraints of that system. Unlike entrepreneurs, they operate under a corporate accounting system and must report to hierarchical superiors. They do not personally face the financial risks that entrepreneurs do, nor do they enjoy the same rewards. They can draw on the rich financial resources of the corporation.

Intrapreneurs may need different competencies to succeed than do entrepreneurs. For instance, intrapreneurs must be somewhat skilled at organizational politics, something that entrepreneurs may find reprehensible and that may, in fact, motivate them to work for themselves. Further, while entrepreneurs must provide their own goals and rewards, intrapreneurs are within the reward system of the formal organization.

A number of "freedom factors" serve as scissors to cut away excessive paperwork controls and to create a nurturing environment for intrapreneurship. These "freedom factors" include the following.[71]

> **Self-selection.** Intrapreneurs appoint themselves to their role and receive the corporation's blessing for their self-appointed task. Management cannot appoint someone an intrapreneur, tell him or her to become passionately committed to an idea, and then expect success. The self-selection process often begins with bootlegging: The intrapreneur works nights or weekends or on time borrowed from approved projects to build the case for official sanction of self-appointed tasks.

> **No handoffs.** Innovation is not a relay race in which an idea can be handed off from runner to runner. When a developing business or product is "handed off" from a committed intrapreneur to whoever is next in line, commitment to the project may suffer.

> **The doer decides.** The intrapreneur's job is to create a vision of a new business reality and then make it happen. The primary problem in big organizations is not blocking the vision, but blocking the action. The solution lies in letting the doer decide; the intrapreneur must be allowed to act.

> **Corporate slack.** When all corporate resources are committed to what is planned, nothing is left for trying the unplannable. Yet innovation is inherently unplannable. Intrapreneurs need discretionary resources to explore and develop new ideas. Employees should be given the freedom to use a percentage of their time on projects of their own choosing and to set aside funds to explore new ideas when they occur.

> **Ending the home-run philosophy.** Today's corporate culture favors a few well-studied, well-planned attempts to hit a home run. But nobody bats a thousand, and it is better to try more times with less careful and expensive preparation for each. Companies that demand projection

of the huge payoff before entering a market rarely get in on the ground floor of new industries, and even if they do they rarely find the high-profit segments.

> **Tolerance of risk, failure, and mistakes.** Innovation cannot be achieved without risk and mistakes. Even successful innovation generally begins with blunders and false starts.

> **Patient money.** Innovation takes time, even decades, but the rhythm of corporations is annual planning. Sophisticated investors in innovation have the courage and patience to let their investments prove themselves or go bust.

> **Freedom from "turfiness."** Executives' emphasis on beating their peers in the race to the top leads to an obsession with turf. Because new ideas almost always cross the boundaries of existing patterns of organizations, a jealous tendency to turfiness blocks innovation. An effective organization must focus competition on performance and contribution, not politics.

> **Cross-functional teams.** Small teams with full responsibility for developing an intraprise solve many of the basic problems of bigness in innovation. Since whenever a new idea begins, it encounters resistance from other functional areas, each idea needs the support of all functions before it can be a success. But some companies resist the formation of cross-functional teams.

> **Multiple options.** Entrepreneurs live in a multioption universe. If one venture capitalist or supplier can't or won't meet their needs, there are many more to choose from. Intrapreneurs, however, often face single-option situations that may be called *internal monopolies.* They must have their product made by a certain factory or sold by a certain sales force. Too often these groups lack motivation or are simply wrong for the job, and a good idea dies an unnecessary death. Intrapreneurs should have the freedom to select from all possible ways to get the job done—internal or external.

In addition to these "freedom factors," two other factors foster intrapreneurial success. First, sponsorship of intrapreneurs is important. Sponsors ensure that the "intraprise" gets the required resources, and they can help temper the grievances of those who feel threatened by the innovation. Many intrapreneurs have several sponsors: lower-level sponsors to take care of day-to-day support needs, and higher-level sponsors to fend off threatening strategic attacks. Second, there must be suitable rewards for intrapreneurship. Traditional rewards for success don't match the risks of innovating or intrapreneuring. Also, the basic reward in most companies is promotion, which doesn't work well for most intrapreneurs; they seek freedom to use their intuition, take risks, and invest the company's money in building new businesses and launching new products and services. For this reason, a key reward for intrapreneurs is intracapital. *Intracapital* is a discretionary budget earned by the intrapreneur and used to fund the creation of new intraprises and innovation for the corporation.

Hoping to grow and compete in a fast-paced market, Bell Atlantic turned to intrapreneurship, with great success. Within a few years, more than 130 intrapreneurs had championed more than 100 projects, at least 15 products were on or near the market, and 15 patents had been awarded. Potential revenues estimated from the projects total a minimum of $100 million within five years.[72] Similarly, at Xerox, many creative ideas were lost before being turned into marketable products. As a result, Xerox recognized the need to nurture entrepreneurs within the corporation. The company formed Xerox Technology Ventures (XTV), a venture-capital group that allows Xerox to bring creative products to the market through intrapreneurship. XTV has become so successful that it is now a role model for other firms.[73]

CREATIVITY AND DIVERSITY

People differing in gender, age, race, disability status, and sexual orientation bring to organizations a variety of attitudes, values, and perspectives as well as a broad and rich base of experience to address a problem.[74] As a result, as the group becomes more diverse, the potential for creativity is enhanced. Innovative organizations have generally done a better job than others in eradicating racism and sexism, and they tend to employ more women and nonwhite men than do less innovative firms.[75] In addition, brainstorming groups made up of diverse ethnic and racial groups produce higher-quality ideas than do homogeneous groups.[76] Further, the presence in groups of individuals holding minority views leads to critical analysis of decision issues and alternatives, resulting in consideration of a larger number of alternatives and more thorough examination of underlying assumptions.[77] And because homogeneous groups tend to value conformity and agreement and their members are sometimes afraid to "rock the boat," such groups often discourage critical thinking. Because of this, diversity may foster more open, honest, and effective decision making.[78] Taken together, this all suggests that diversity can yield many benefits for decision making and creativity. However, diversity may also increase the potential for misunderstandings and increase conflict and anxiety among members.[79] The challenge is to manage cultural diversity in such a way as to capture its benefits while minimizing potential problems.[80]

COMPANY PROGRAMS TO ENHANCE CREATIVITY

Firms are using special programs to foster their employees' creativity. Many send their employees on retreats and outings to jolt them out of routine ways of thinking.[81] Quaker Oats Co. executives go horseback riding when they need fresh approaches to budget and marketing problems. American Greeting Co.'s licensing unit, Those Characters From Cleveland, which created Strawberry Shortcake and the Care Bears, has a half dozen weekend retreats in the woods each year, where its creative personnel brainstorm, play games, and sketch to come up with creative ideas.

At Omron Corp., a maker of electronic controls, midlevel employees attend a monthly *juku,* or cram school, where they try to think and plan as if they were 19th century warlords, private detectives, or Formula One racecar drivers. Fuji Film asks its senior managers to study topics such as the history of Venice and the sociology of apes. While such exercises may sometimes appear bizarre or even humorous, they encourage the employees to break out of their corporate shells and think in different ways.

Management at the Polaroid Corporation faced a situation in which it needed to find a way to develop new photographic products that would enable the company to grow and regain profitability. Read the background in-

GLOBAL PERSPECTIVES

CREATIVITY PROGRAMS WORLDWIDE

The growing emphasis on creativity is evident worldwide. For example, independent thinking and improvisation have historically been stifled in many Japanese firms. As a result, Japanese companies have excelled at improving on existing products but have rarely been pioneers. Now, though, competitive pressures and rapid change are demanding greater creativity to invent new products, find new markets, and start new businesses, and Japanese firms are trying to respond.* For instance, Shiseido, Japan's largest cosmetics maker, has implemented a series of four seminars to enhance the creativity of its managers. The four-day seminars, held at resorts on Mount Fuji, cover such topics as "Time and Space," "Expression and Language," "Beauty and Truth," and "Body and Soul." In one session, managers are told that the company needs to become a "living system" that adapts to its surroundings much as an organism does. Then they are asked to ponder a goldfish and a crab, answering a series of questions about each and deciding which of the animals' characteristics would be desirable for Shiseido. In another session, participants are told to try to change their mannerisms in order to act and speak like Americans; they walk around the room with exaggerated movements, talking loudly and flailing their arms. In yet another, which focuses on the importance of equilibrium and patience, the managers watch the leader of a renowned dance troupe slowly contort his body.

http://www.shiseido.co.jp/e/index5.htm

*This section is based on E. Thornton, "Japan's Struggle to be Creative," *Fortune,* April 19, 1993, pp. 129–134.

formation on Polaroid in the Real-World Management Challenge and then indicate what you would have done to handle the situation if you were the CEO of Polaroid. Later you can compare your recommendations with what management actually did in this situation.

Real-World Management Challenge

Problem Solving at Polaroid

The Company

The Polaroid Corporation designs, manufactures, and markets imaging products such as digital imaging systems, light polarizing filters, secure identification systems, and sunglasses, on a worldwide basis. Polaroid has always emphasized technological innovation as its competitive advantage. It is probably most famous for its instant photographic cameras that enable users to snap pictures and to watch them develop before their eyes in a matter of a couple minutes. Polaroid is the worldwide leader in instant imaging products.

The company's headquarters is in Cambridge, Massachusetts. Polaroid has annual sales of approximately $2 billion.

The Situation

Although Polaroid was a high-flying company in the 1970s, the 1990s were for the most part a period of struggle for the firm. The company lost hundreds of millions of dollars in the late 1990s, laid off about a third of its workforce, and saw its stock price plummet.

The growing popularity and declining cost of digital cameras has been a tremendous threat to Polaroid's traditional instant photography technology and product line. As a result,

Polaroid's corporate image and instant photographic cameras lost much of their appeal in the eyes of investors and consumers.

What Would You Do?

If you were the CEO of Polaroid, what would you do to solve the problem of turning around the company in the 21st century?

http://www.polaroid.com/

Source: P. Patton, "Style Team Reinvents Polaroid as a Toy," *New York Times,* May 18, 2000, p. F4.

NEGOTIATING AND BARGAINING

Decision making is difficult enough when we must "simply" choose alternatives. When our decision making is in the face of another party who may have opposing interests, things become even more complicated.

STRATEGIES FOR NEGOTIATING

Parties to negotiation (or, in general, to a conflict situation) tend to adopt one of five negotiation strategies, each with its own objectives, behaviors, rationale, and probable outcomes. These strategies reflect differing levels of emphasis on assertiveness (attempting to satisfy one's own interests) and cooperativeness (attempting to satisfy the other party's concerns), as shown in Figure 4-10.

> **Forcing.** With forcing, the negotiator is assertive and uncooperative, attempting to satisfy his or her own needs at the expense of those of the other party. If the negotiator is successful, this results in a form of "win-lose" outcome, with a clear winner and loser.

FIGURE 4-10
Negotiating Styles

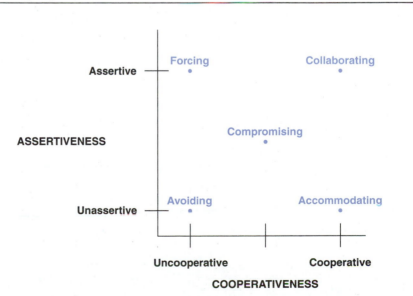

> **Avoiding.** A negotiator adopting an avoiding strategy is neither assertive nor cooperative, neglecting the interests of both parties by trying to sidestep the conflict or put off making a decision. Regular use of this strategy may lead to frustration, uncertainties, and stalemates, yielding a "lose-lose" outcome, with neither party's needs being satisfied.

> **Compromising.** A compromising negotiator shows moderate levels of both assertiveness and cooperation. The compromise doesn't fully satisfy the needs of either party, but the pain is shared.

> **Accommodating.** Some negotiators are cooperative without being assertive, thus satisfying the other party's needs while neglecting their own. The accommodating party may thus become a "sucker," being taken advantage of and losing stature and self-esteem. Thus, this creates another "win-lose" situation, with the accommodating party being the loser.

> **Collaborating.** A negotiator adopting the collaborating style is both cooperative and assertive, focusing on satisfying the needs of both parties. This style—sometimes called a problem-solving style—has the potential for yielding "win-win" outcomes, satisfying the needs of both parties.

Another way to view these styles is in terms of their emphasis on distribution—dividing a fixed-size pie among the parties—or integration—with the parties finding ways to enlarge the pie. As shown in Figure 4-11, distributive styles are zero-sum, with any gain to one party coming at the expense of the other. Conversely, integrative styles are non-zero-sum, with the joint decisions of the parties dictating the ultimate size of the resources to be shared. Of the styles considered earlier, only the collaborating style is integrative, or "win-win." All others involve suboptimal outcomes for one or both parties.

FIGURE 4-11
Distributive and Integrative Approaches

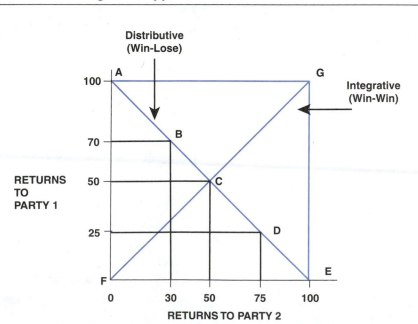

While it may not always be possible to find an integrative solution, we won't find one if we don't try.

Note in Figure 4-11 that with a distributive approach the sum of the two parties' outcomes is 100. If Party 1 gets 70, Party 2 gets 30 (Point B); if Party 1 gets 50, Party 2 gets 50 (Point C); and so on. That is, any gain to one party is a corresponding loss to the other. With an integrative approach, on the other hand, the sum of the two parties' outcomes depends on their mutual choices. At Point F, neither party gets anything; at Point C, each gets 50; at Point G, each gets 100.

GUIDELINES FOR ATTAINING WIN-WIN SOLUTIONS[82]

Here are some specific guidelines for reaching win-win, integrative agreements.

> **Think win-win.** In the heat and emotion of negotiations, it's often difficult to focus on mutual gain. Instead, we begin to think about out-maneuvering the other party, coming out ahead, or simply venting our feelings. As such, it is critical to keep focused on the goal of a mutually acceptable, integrative solution.

> **Plan for the negotiations.**[83] Invest the time to determine the who, what, when, and why of negotiations. That is, *who* will you be negotiating with, and what can you learn about them, their personalities, motivations, and interests? *What* is the subject matter of the negotiations, and what strengths and weaknesses do you and the other party bring to bear in addressing that subject matter? *When* must the negotiations commence and be completed? If the parties have different deadlines, the party with the longer deadline has an advantage. If there are no specific deadlines, it may be useful to develop a time line to keep negotiations on track. *Why* are we negotiating? What are the desired results? By focusing on these desired results, rational negotiations and integrative outcomes are more likely.

> **Know your BATNA.**[84] BATNA stands for "the **B**est **A**lternative **T**o a **N**egotiated **A**greement." This gives the minimum outcome we require of a negotiated settlement. Any negotiated alternative that gives us a better outcome than our BATNA is better than an impasse; any negotiated alternative that is less than the BATNA should be declined. Thus, the BATNA determines our *reservation point,* the point at which we are indifferent, between a negotiated agreement and an impasse. If you don't have a clear BATNA, work to develop one. If you don't have the ability to walk away from a deal, you'll have the least power and leverage in bargaining.

> **Work to understand the other party.** While you hope to be objective in the negotiating process, you will be dealing with other humans, who bring their own emotions, values, motivations, beliefs, backgrounds, and perceptions. Win-win solutions demand a relationship of trust and respect. Such relationships are based on mutual understanding and sensitivity.

> **Focus on a common objective and depersonalize the problem.** Throughout the negotiations, remain focused on a central question: How can we mutually achieve our common objectives? The problem—not the other party—becomes the adversary. If negotiators act as ad-

versaries in personal confrontation, it will be impossible to separate substantive issues from personal relationships. Comments may be interpreted as personal attacks, and each side may become defensive and stubborn. Consider the following analogy.

Like two shipwrecked sailors in a lifeboat at sea quarreling over limited rations and supplies, negotiators may begin by viewing each other as adversaries. Each may view the other as a hindrance. To survive, however, those two sailors will want to disentangle the objective problems from the people. They will want to identify the needs of each, whether for shade, medicine, water, or food. They will want to go further and treat the meeting of those needs as a shared problem, along with other shared problems like keeping watch, catching rainwater, and getting the lifeboat to shore. Seeing themselves engaged in side-by-side efforts to solve a mutual problem, the sailors will become better able to reconcile their conflicting interests as well as to advance their shared interests.[85]

> **Negotiate from interests, not positions.** Negotiations may stall if each side pushes for its position and fights the other party's position. When negotiators bargain over positions, they tend to start with an extreme position, hold fiercely to it, hide true motivations, and yield ground only grudgingly. Try to focus instead on underlying interests. If positions are stated, what are the interests that explain the positions? Ask "why" questions, such as "Why do you need to have a one-year limit on the contract?" or "Why do you need the parts to meet that specific standard?" And ask, "Why not?" What stands in the way of the other party accepting what you're asking for?

> **Build on differences.** It might seem that negotiations would be easiest when all parties to the negotiations had common interests, perspectives, and so on. In fact, though, successful negotiations may flow from differences. For instance, if I need money now and you don't need it until later, we have the potential for a deal. If I think one of my ballplayers is past his prime and you think he has the potential for further years of productivity if he joins your team, we both have incentive to make a trade. If you think one of your investments is too risky to keep and I'm trying to build additional risk into my portfolio, we might both benefit if I were to acquire the investment. As such, differences in time preferences, estimates of the probabilities of future outcomes, and risk preferences may each provide the impetus for a successful transaction.

> **Work to control emotions.** As noted in our discussion of emotional intelligence, emotions may short-circuit rational thinking. Negotiations can be frustrating, and may even invoke anger. Avoid the temptation to lash out. Try to understand your emotions and those of the other party, and treat them as legitimate. If your side feels anger about an issue or the negotiating process, let the other party know, and treat this as a topic for discussion. Similarly, give the other party the opportunity to identify and release feelings of frustration.

> **Use active listening.** Active listening gives you what the other person really wants and is willing to concede, and it ensures that you recognize the flow of the negotiations. Careful listening also conveys to the other

party that you are serious about working together toward a solution. And sometimes a period of silence induces the other party to "open up," giving away information to fill the void.

> **Be creative.** For instance, challenge your assumptions about available resources, the other party's motivation, and the scope of the bargaining. The next section provides some specific guidelines for creatively achieving integrative, win-win agreements.

TECHNIQUES FOR REACHING INTEGRATIVE AGREEMENTS[86]

Here are five techniques to help reach an integrative agreement. Each somehow encourages us to think creatively about the negotiations process, by challenging our assumptions, broadening our perspectives, or encouraging the development of innovative new options.

> **Obtaining added resources.** Earlier in this chapter we said we are slaves to our assumptions. If we're faced with the challenge of negotiating for resources, such as personnel or funds, we may simply assume that additional resources aren't available. Since this assumption may not be true, we should ask whether additional resources might in fact be available. So if two departments are negotiating to get authorization to purchase a new computer system this year, and it appears that only one system will be authorized, they might first try to make the case that two systems should be approved. While obtaining added resources may not always be feasible, we should at least consider the possibility.

> **Providing nonspecific compensation.** With nonspecific compensation, one party gets what it wants and the other is paid on some unrelated issue. For instance, if only one computer system is approved, the department that gets the system might agree to purchase a database needed by both departments.

> **Trading issues.** Trading issues means each party concedes on low-priority issues in exchange for concessions on higher-priority issues. Thus, each party gets the part of the agreement that it considers most important. Perhaps Department A feels it is critical to have physical control of the computer system and Department B, while it would like to have physical control, is concerned primarily with having access to the system at certain peak times. The system could thus be located in Department A, but with guaranteed access for Department B as negotiated.

> **Cost cutting.** With cost cutting, one party gets what it wants and the other gets the costs associated with the concession reduced or eliminated. For instance, if one department gets a computer system, the department that doesn't get the system might nevertheless get restricted access to the system.

> **Bridging.** With bridging, neither party gets its initial demands, but a new option that satisfies the major interests of both parties is developed. This might involve, for instance, using the funds that would be applied to a single computer system to find two lower-cost systems, or jointly controlling the system and agreeing on a time-sharing arrangement.

TACTICS TO ENCOURAGE SHARING OF INFORMATION[87]

Productive negotiation and problem solving require the sharing of information. However, people are often reluctant to provide information, since they

Web Wise

Guide to Negotiations and Resolving Conflict

Professor Edward Wertheim of Northeastern University has assembled an excellent Web guide to negotiations and resolving conflict. Visit this guide for information about causes of conflict, modes of conflict resolution, rational and emotional aspects of negotiation, planning for negotiations, and more.

http://www.cba.neu.edu/
~ewertheim/interper/
negot3.htm

may fear it will be used against them or will put them at a competitive disadvantage. Here are some tactics to encourage sharing of information.

> **Decide on a distribution rule in advance.** Often, full and open sharing of information would help the parties to negotiation to find a good solution. However, each party may be afraid to share information, since this might permit the other party somehow to "win" or to get more than a fair share. In such cases, it may be useful to agree on a distribution rule in advance. For instance, both sides might agree that if an agreement following information sharing results in some "surplus" over the best solution that could be found prior to sharing of information, each party will get half of the surplus. This clearly demonstrates the benefit of sharing while minimizing vulnerability.

> **Ask questions.** People often use negotiating situations primarily to try to influence others. As a result, they spend a lot of time talking and relatively little time asking questions and listening. Even when the other party is talking, we may be thinking about what we're going to say next rather than really trying to understand what is being said. In communication situations, we should consider what information we need from the other party, and then ask the questions necessary to get that information. While we may not get answers to all our questions, we're more likely to get answers if we ask than if we don't.

> **Strategically disclose information.** To develop trust, it is often important to create a climate of openness. One way to do this is to provide some useful—but probably not critical—information to the other party. In communication, behaviors are often reciprocated. If we scream, others may scream; if we apologize, others may apologize. Similarly, if we give information, the other party is likely to share information in turn. Continued reciprocity can result in full sharing of important information.

> **Make multiple offers simultaneously.** When dealing with someone in a bargaining situation, we tend to make a single offer or proposition and then wait for a response. If the offer is rejected, we may "go back to the drawing board," fashion another, and hope for a better result. However, an option is to put together a set of offers. Ideally, the offers would be equally desirable to us but may differ in their attractiveness to the other party. This gives the appearance that we are flexible, and it also lets us collect useful information. If one of the multiple offers is accepted, we have an agreement. If not, we can at least ask which of the offers was most desirable and use that information to craft further offers.

> **Search for postsettlement settlements.** People are often reluctant to "put all their cards on the table" until they have an agreement. Prior to that agreement, they may feel that full disclosure could be harmful. A very useful approach is to search for postsettlement settlements. That is, once the parties have found a mutually acceptable agreement, they can employ a third party who is given full information and is told to search for another agreement that is better for both parties. Either party to the initial agreement can veto any new such postsettlement settlement proposed by the third party. The initial settlement is essentially insurance in hand, and it leads to an increased willingness to seek a carefully crafted, preferable alternative.

Skills Practice 4-8 will help develop your skill in negotiating in a business context by applying negotiating techniques to one of two specific negotiating situations.

Skills Practice 4-8
Applying Negotiating Techniques

Skill Objective
To develop skill in negotiating in a business context.

Procedure
1. Work with one other student in this exercise.
2. Select one of the following negotiating scenarios. Apply the tactics for sharing of information and attaining a win-win solution that are discussed in the chapter.
3. Role-play the scenario, with the goal of negotiating an acceptable agreement.
4. Discuss the questions that follow the scenarios.

Scenario 1—Negotiating an Employment Contract
This scenario involves a negotiation process between a job candidate and an employer regarding the terms of a job offer for a management trainee position.

Role 1—The Job Candidate
Your goal is to maximize your salary and benefits (bonuses, flexible work schedules, stock options, a private office, holidays and days off, etc.). Overall, you feel that an appropriate starting salary would be somewhere around $40,000–50,000. You are very interested in the job and you like the company. Although you have no prior work experience, you have graduated from a top-notch university where you did very well academically (GPA of 3.5/4.0). You know there is intense competition among employers for the best workers.

Role 2—The Employer
Your goal is to get the job candidate to accept the job offer while minimizing costs. You are very interested in this job candidate, and you are willing to add some reasonable "perks" in order to entice the job candidate to accept your offer. The salary range for the management trainee position is $30,000–45,000.

Given the job candidate's lack of work experience, you feel it is appropriate to provide a starting salary near the bottom of the salary range. This is consistent with your previous practice with new hires.

Scenario 2—Negotiating a Merger Deal
This scenario involves the heads of two companies who are attempting to merge their companies.

Role 1—CEO from Company 1
You are the CEO of a major auto company based in the United States. Your company designs and manufactures a full line of cars, trucks, minivans, and sport-utility vehicles. The corporate headquarters of your firm is in Detroit, Michigan, but you have international operations (research and development, assembly, dealerships) in Europe, Asia, and Latin America.

The company has a strong market position in the United States but is still trying to establish itself abroad. The company is currently implementing an aggressive plan to increase its presence in other countries around the world.

Due to weakness in global demand for autos and the tremendous long-term investments needed to design and manufacture vehicles, many firms in the industry are scrambling to develop strategic alliances, to merge, or to acquire other firms.

Due to a string of extremely profitable years, your firm has deep pockets and is anxious to acquire another firm. You will base the amount you are willing to spend on the prices of recent acquisitions in the industry (checking these prices should be part of your preparation).

Role 2—CEO from Company 2

You are the CEO of a major auto company based in Asia. You design and manufacture a full line of cars, trucks, minivans, and sport-utility vehicles. You have a reasonably strong position in international markets but have been losing ground to other competitors in your home markets.

You are interested in exploring a possible merger with another firm, but due to cultural differences and national pride you are hesitant. Ideally, you would like to form a strategic alliance with an appropriate firm that would enable you to reduce costs and to strengthen the market position of the company in international markets.

Discussion Questions

1. How would you describe the negotiating style you used in your negotiating scenario (that is, which tactics discussed in the chapter did you apply)? To what extent was your negotiating style effective? Why?
2. How would you describe the negotiating style of the other person in this scenario (that is, which tactics discussed in the chapter did that person apply)? To what extent was that person's negotiating style effective? Why?
3. In retrospect, what actions could each individual have taken to enhance the effectiveness of the negotiating process (for example, to come to a better agreement)?
4. What are the practical implications of this exercise for you as a future manager?

TOP TEN LIST: KEY POINTS TO REMEMBER

EFFECTIVE PROBLEM SOLVING

10. Be aware of the problem-solving process and take care to properly address each of its stages.
9. Use data to drive the problem-solving process.
8. Identify the root cause of a problem as a basis for developing appropriate solutions.
7. Use problem-solving tools to ensure that a systematic approach to problem solving is being used.
6. Follow up on decisions to evaluate outcomes and to take corrective action if needed.
5. Implement a Plan-Do-Check-Act approach to problem solving that incorporates an emphasis on the use of data, experimentation, evaluation, and modification.

4. Be aware of your use of inappropriate heuristics that may diminish the quality of your problem-solving process.
3. Foster a work environment and work culture that support creative thinking and exploration of ideas.
2. Create and leverage workforce diversity as a means for promoting creativity and innovation.
1. Be aware of alternative negotiating styles and work to achieve integrative solutions.

QUESTIONS FOR REVIEW AND REFLECTION

REVIEW QUESTIONS

1. Discuss the five steps in the problem-solving process.
2. Identify six guidelines for problem definition.
3. Differentiate between screening approaches and scoring approaches.

4. Discuss the four steps in the PDCA cycle.
5. Identify seven influences on problem solving.
6. What are seven consequences of barriers to problem solving?

7. Identify eight guidelines for improving problem solving.
8. What are the four stages of the creative process?
9. Discuss six techniques for enhancing creativity.
10. Identify 10 characteristics of the creative organization.

11. Discuss venture teams, idea champions, and intra-preneurship.
12. Describe five strategies for negotiating and 10 guidelines for attaining win-win solutions.

CRITICAL THINKING QUESTIONS

1. In view of the various problems we, as humans, face in making decisions, some people have suggested that we should use computers to help us. For instance, the computer can calculate its choice of an optimal decision based on the best available data and specified criteria. We can then decide to use, somehow to revise, or to reject that decision. This use of computers as inputs to our decision making is called *clinical synthesis*. What do you see as potential benefits and difficulties associated with clinical synthesis?

2. You mention to your boss that you have learned what you think are very useful guidelines for defining a problem. She answers, "Defining a problem! I *know* what my problems are. I need solutions!" How would you defend the need for careful problem definition?

3. We have seen that creativity is especially important in situations that are complex and dynamic. Do you think it is worthwhile to devote resources to enhancing creativity in firms in more stable, traditional industries? Why or why not?

4. We have examined some characteristics of creative individuals. Suppose someone said to you, "We really need creativity in our company. Let's put together a checklist of characteristics of creative individuals and use that in our hiring." What do you see as some potential benefits and costs of a policy of hiring "creative types"?

5. One difficulty with introducing creativity-enhancement techniques is that some people just don't feel comfortable using them. The techniques seem "different," and most people haven't given much thought to increasing their creativity. Sometimes they are afraid that using the techniques will make them look foolish. What are some things you might do to encourage your team members to try some of the creativity-enhancement techniques discussed in this chapter?

6. Told about the benefits of "win-win" solutions, your colleague says, "That's fine if the other guy is willing to go along. But if I'm trying for integrative solutions and he isn't, I'll get killed." How would you respond?

EXPERIENTIAL EXERCISES

WEB EXERCISE 4-1

Go to the Mind Tools home page at

http://www.mindtools.com/index.html

Select one tool from the "Techniques to Help You Think Excellently" section. This section includes tools in the categories of "Problem-Solving Techniques and Analytical Methods," "Information Skills," "Improving Your Memory," and "Increasing Creativity." Write a one-page executive summary describing the tool and indicating how it might be useful in a managerial career.

WEB EXERCISE 4-2

Feeling creative? Think you have a patentable idea? Go to the IBM Intellectual Property Network at:

http://www.delphion.com/

This wonderful source permits you to search and view patent documents from the United States, Europe, and Japan as well as patent applications published by the World Intellectual Property Organization (WIPO). Remember our discussions of paper clips? Type *paper clip* in the search engine and you'll find more than 190 patent documents relating to paper clips. Or you could search for *toothpick* and find more than 180 patent documents, including patents for a "combination writing implement and toothpick dispenser," a "therapeutic toothpick for treating oral and systemic diseases," a "prismatic light transparent toothpick," a "tobacco-impregnated toothpick," and a "nicotine-containing toothpick." Have an idea for a better mousetrap? You'd better check out the mousetrap patents first—you'll find a "magnetic computerized mouse trap," a "low oxygen scented mouse trap," a "marbles counter weighted repeating mouse trap," and many more. Or check out the 4,500 robot-related patent documents or the 60+ harmonica-related documents.

Before answering the following questions, go to the "Gallery of Obscure Patents" (at the link given earlier). Visit both the current gallery and the previous selections from the gallery. You'll find such inventions as a combined earthquake sensor and nightlight, an unforgettable umbrella, a flushable vehicle spittoon, and a combination bird trap and cat feeder.

1. Select three of these patents and indicate why you chose them.

2. Which of the patents do you think is most creative? Least creative? Why?

3. Try to identify a creativity-enhancement technique that may have inspired each of the patents. For instance, could the patent have been inspired by a form of analogy, by a listing technique, or by retroduction?

4. Go to the patent search engine and find one patent that you would nominate for the Gallery of Obscure Patents (note that you can actually make a nomination if you like). What was the basis for your choice?

CASE 4-1
FIXING CUSTOMER SERVICE PROBLEMS AT NORTHWEST AIRLINES

The Company

Northwest Airlines is the world's fourth-largest airline. It operates more than 2,600 flights to nearly 250 destinations worldwide on a daily basis. The company's world headquarters are in Minneapolis/St. Paul, Minnesota. It employs more than 53,000 pilots, flight attendants, maintenance workers, and support staff worldwide.

The vision of Northwest Airlines is "To build together the world's most preferred airline with the best people, each committed to exceeding our customers' expectations every day."

The supporting mission statement of Northwest Airlines is as follows:

The people of Northwest Airlines will provide reliable, convenient, and consistent air transportation that meets or exceeds customer expectations and earns a sustainable profit.

Northwest Airlines' guiding principles include: Never compromise safety, always emphasize cleanliness, always put customers first, always support and inspire each other, and always strive to improve.

Key Challenges

During the 1990s, Northwest Airlines' image was badly damaged due to a range of labor problems with its pilots, flight attendants, and mechanics. In one case in 1998, a labor dispute with its pilots led to a costly 15-day strike that forced the cancellation of flights and sent travelers scrambling to find alternate service providers for air travel.

As if these events were not bad enough, Northwest Airlines was widely criticized for its handling of passengers on a flight that sat on a runway for eight hours in Detroit due to a snowstorm. Passengers on the plane were furious that they were not allowed to leave the plane, not allowed to eat anything, and not even allowed to go to the bathroom while they were stranded on the runway.

Management's Response

Although the airline had been focusing its strategy on upgrading its hubs around the world, fixing up and adding new planes, and integrating new ground operations technology, it discovered that its biggest challenges were customer and employee relations.

In an attempt to repair Northwest Airlines' battered image and poor customer relations, management decided to take a number of actions. First, they set up an advisory council composed of 13 of the best customers from the airline's WorldPerks Elite frequent flier program. These were individuals who spent hundreds of hours on Northwest Airlines flights each year. Through the council, management hoped to better understand the needs of its customers and how to satisfy them and exceed their expectations.

Skills Application
Skills Application
Skills Application
Skills Application

181

Chapter 4 Solving Problems

Skills Application

At one meeting of the advisory council, these customers told management that poor employee relations and a lack of support from top management were the primary causes of the airline's poor image among customers. They suggested that management create training programs to enhance employee understanding of various programs, services, and promotions and to implement new technologies that would make a customer's air travel experience "hassle-free."

Outcomes

Northwest Airlines management went on to create additional training programs to help employees better understand customer needs and how to satisfy them as well as to create a formal customer service department. Employees would then receive approximately 65 hours of customer service training per year. In addition, management played a videotape of comments from the advisory council at a management meeting a few months later. These comments were used as a springboard for discussion and brainstorming ideas for improving employee morale and customer service. Management also met with various ground operations workers to hear what they had to say about how to improve customer service.

Northwest introduced new software to better support its employees in identifying the airline's best customers and then customizing its services based on those identi-fied preferences. And soon, Northwest customers should be able to print out their boarding passes from a personal computer at home and use self-service machines at airports for expediting the check-in process.

So far, members of the advisory council and some analysts are impressed with Northwest Airlines' initiative to improve customer service. However, the real test will be how the rest of Northwest Airlines' customer base responds to these changes.

Discussion Questions

1. How effectively did management at Northwest Airlines implement the basic steps in the problem-solving process?
2. Which problem-solving or creativity tools could have been used in this case to help management? How could these tools have been implemented?
3. Northwest Airlines has experienced some initial success with its attempt to improve employee and customer relations. What needs to be done to ensure that this program or initiative is successful in the long term?
4. What are the practical implications of this case for you as a future manager?

http://www.nwa.com/

Source: "People Power," *Chicago Tribune,* May 28, 2000, Transportation sec., p. 1.

CASE 4-2
CREATIVITY AT NOKIA

The Company

Nokia Corporation is a world leader in the design, development, and manufacture of digital wireless phones. The company is based in Espoo, Finland, and employs more than 56,000 people worldwide. Nokia maintains research and development centers in 14 countries and manufacturing operations in 10 countries. It's mobile phones are sold in 130 countries.

In 1998, Nokia passed Motorola to become the world's number-1 maker of mobile phones. In 1999, its market share stood at 27 percent; this is expected to grow in the future.

The Nokia Approach

Given the tremendous success of the 135-year-old corporation, Nokia has been subjected to a great deal of scrutiny and analysis, with the focus being on trying to explain how Nokia has survived and prospered (that is, its secret code).

A major element of Nokia's approach has been to cooperate with competitors by signing deals that would provide for the sharing of common technologies and standards used in mobile phones. Consequently, the strategic challenge for Nokia is to be more innovative than its competitors in terms of coming out with more stylish and technologically advanced mobile phones.

In the 1990s, Nokia was generally very successful in offering more innovative products than its competitors. Its phones had logical user interfaces and stylish designs with desirable features, and it was able to get the right products to market on time and in sufficient quantities.

Nokia CEO Jorma Ollila attributes a major part of the company's success to the way in which the organization creates a "meeting of the minds." Specifically, he tries to create an environment that rewards merit, is fun to work in, encourages unconventional thinking, and does not punish failure.

Moreover, just about every important project is assigned to a team. And Ollila and his senior management team do not play "political games" with each other.

Another key player in Nokia's success in the mobile phone business was a young marketing executive named Anssi Vanjoki. His major contribution was that he studied successful brands such as Nike and Phillip Morris and concluded that the critical factor in explaining the success of those brands was that they shared a "holistic approach," in that everything from design, production, distribution, and advertising needed to be driven by a deep understanding of the function and overall vision of the product. What made Vanjoki's insight especially important for Nokia was that he was the first to apply this holistic approach to mobile phones.

Pertti Korhonen, the vice president of R&D, was put in charge of the project to develop a digital phone for the three major standards around the world (GSM, TDMA, and PDS). He coordinated a global, cross-functional team composed of designers, marketers, manufacturing specialists, and suppliers in pursuing the team's objectives. One of the team's major breakthroughs resulted from its struggle to design a user interface for the Japanese market. Based on extensive brainstorming, this led to the development of a large screen with a text menu.

Other dominant characteristics of the work environment at Nokia are the degree to which people are given the freedom to make their own decisions about how to perform their jobs and the lack of formalization of many systems in the organization. Sometimes this approach makes it difficult to figure out who is in charge. To balance the lack of formal controls, there are certain individuals whose role is to impose some degree of structure in the company.

Finally, Nokia holds annual meetings called the "Nokia Way" that use global brainstorming sessions, involving all employees at all levels in the organization, about what Nokia's strategic priorities should be in the future. These meetings have produced strategic priority statements such as "Bring the Internet to everybody's pocket" that serve to inspire and focus the activities of Nokia workers around the world.

A Major Challenge

Despite its success, a major challenge that Nokia will need to respond to is the that the company is becoming less "Finnish" as over 50 percent of its employees come from other countries. This could pose a threat to the unique "Nokia Way" that has helped the company prosper. How will Nokia be able to sustain its momentum in the mobile phone business given its innovation strategy?

Discussion Questions

1. What kinds of creativity tools does Nokia use to support its product innovation strategy?
2. Which characteristics of a creative organization are illustrated by Nokia?
3. If you were the CEO, what would you do to sustain Nokia's success?
4. What are the practical implications of this case for you as a future manager?

http://www.nokia.com/main.html

Source: J. Fox, "Nokia's Secret Code," *Fortune*, May 1, 2000, pp. 160–168.

VIDEO CASE
NEXT DOOR FOOD STORE:
A STUDY IN DECISION MAKING

Running Time: 11:21

Headquartered in Mount Pleasant, Michigan, Next Door Food Store is a family-run business with more than 30 outlets in Michigan and Indiana. The stores sell gasoline and a wide variety of grocery and general merchandise items. Along with many other challenges, Next Door must deal with a diverse customer base as well as the convenience store industry's remarkable 100 percent average annual turnover rate.

The video shows Next Door Food Store's President and CEO, Dave Johnson, other Next Door executives, and representatives of Next Door's channels of distribution as they discuss key decisions faced by the company. After viewing the video, answer the following questions.

1. What are the two fundamental decisions faced by the Next Door Food Store?

2. How does the nature of the convenience industry influence Next Door's goals and constraints? What has Next Door identified as its goals? As its constraints?

3. What were the alternatives considered by Next Door in regard to distribution channels? Which of those alternatives did Next Door choose? Why?

4. Do the decisions made by Next Door seem to be based more on use of screening approaches or more on scoring approaches? Why do you conclude that?

5. Why does Next Door consider the product mix to be risky? How does the Coca-Cola example illustrate that risk?

6. What were factors that led Next Door to decide to allocate cold vaults to such products as bottled waters, teas, and sports drinks?

7. How might you determine whether Next Door's problem solving has been effective?

http://www.nextdoor1.com/

LIGHTEN UP

THE WORLD'S EASIEST QUIZ

Was our discussion of difficulties in decision making getting discouraging? Take a few minutes to complete "The World's Easiest Quiz." The answers follow.

1. How long did the Hundred Years War last?
2. Which country makes Panama hats?
3. From which animal do we get catgut?
4. In which month do Russians celebrate the October Revolution?
5. What is a camel's hair brush made of?
6. The Canary Islands in the Pacific are named after what animal?
7. What was King George VI's first name?
8. What color is a purple finch?
9. Where are Chinese gooseberries from?
10. How long did the Thirty Years War last?

Answers:

1. 116 years, from 1337 to 1453.
2. Ecuador.
3. From sheep and horses.
4. November. The Russian calendar was 13 days behind ours.
5. Squirrel fur.
6. The Latin name was Insularia Canaria—Island of the Dogs.
7. Albert. When he came to the throne in 1936 he respected the wish of Queen Victoria that no future king should ever be called Albert.
8. Distinctively crimson.
9. New Zealand.
10. Thirty years, from 1618 to 1648.

THE IG® NOBEL PRIZE

Each year 10 individuals whose achievements "cannot or should not be reproduced" are honored with Ig® Nobel Prizes. At the ceremony (held in 1999 at Harvard University), 1,200 spectators watch the winners step forward to accept their prizes, handed out by bemused genuine Nobel laureates. Some recent winners:

Peace: Charl Fourie and Michelle Wong of Johannesburg, South Africa, for inventing an automobile burglar alarm consisting of a detection circuit and a flamethrower.

Managed health care: The late George and Charlotte Blonsky, for inventing a device (U.S. Patent #3,216,423) to aid women in giving birth—the woman is strapped onto a circular table, and the table is then rotated at high speed.

Chemistry: Takeshi Makino, president of the Safety Detective Agency in Osaka, Japan, for his involvement with S-Check, an infidelity detection spray that wives can apply to their husbands' underwear.

Environmental protection: Hyuk-ho Kwon of Kolon Company of Seoul, Korea, for inventing the self-perfuming business suit.

Medicine: To Patient Y and to his doctors, Caroline Mills, Meirion Llewelyn, David Kelly, and Peter Holt, of Royal Gwent Hospital, in Newport, Wales, for the cautionary medical report "A Man Who Pricked His Finger and Smelled Putrid for 5 Years" (*The Lancet,* November 9, 1996, p. 1282.)

Nutrition: John Martinez of J. Martinez & Company, Atlanta, for Luak Coffee, the world's most expensive coffee, which is made from coffee beans ingested and excreted by the luak, a bobcat-like animal native to Indonesia.

http://www.improbable.com/ig/ig-top.html

CHAPTER *Five*

SKILLS OBJECTIVES

> To enhance the accuracy of communications with others through the effective management of the basic communication process.
> To overcome barriers to effective communication.
> To enhance the effectiveness of speaking within a management context.
> To use active listening in order to enhance understanding of communication with others within organizations.
> To effectively use nonverbals to support and understand communications with others.
> To encourage and manage informal communication with others.
> To enhance communication with others in a cross-cultural context.

KNOWLEDGE OBJECTIVES

> Identify the functions of communication.
> Explain the steps in the communication process.
> Discuss communication channels, including key channel dimensions.
> Identify communication networks differing in centralization and relative centrality and discuss the relative merits of each.
> Discuss principles of supportive communication.
> Explain guidelines for understanding and overcoming communication barriers.
> Present guidelines for effective speaking and active listening.
> Understand guidelines for effective use of e-mail.
> Identify approaches to e-commerce.
> Discuss ways to read and use nonverbal communication.
> Discuss the importance of informal communication, including the grapevine.
> Identify tips for effective cross-cultural communication.

Tom Peters and Robert Waterman sought in their book *In Search of Excellence: Lessons from America's Best-Run Companies* to discover the secrets of America's truly excellent companies.[1] Their findings led them to argue that the amount, nature, and uses of communication in the excellent companies were remarkably different from those of their nonexcellent peers. Peters and Waterman found that the excellent companies they examined use a variety of philosophies, practices, and structures to encourage communication. At IBM and Delta Airlines, open-door policies were pervasive. At Hewlett-Packard and United Airlines, versions of "management by wandering about" were practiced, in which managers were encouraged to get out of their offices and informally communicate. Corning Glass installed escalators rather than elevators in its new engineering building to increase the chance of face-to-face contact. At Citibank, the desks of operations officers and lending officers were moved to the same floor and intermingled to encourage communication. Intel's new buildings in Silicon Valley were designed to have an excess of small conference rooms, filled with blackboards to facilitate communication, where people can eat lunch or solve problems. What these examples have in common, according to Peters and Waterman, are "lots of communication" (p. 122).

This emphasis on communication is not surprising. Communication affects virtually every area of work. Communication with employees about plant closings, performance appraisals, organizational goals, probable salary increases and job changes, and even the date of the company picnic are essential to the proper functioning of the firm. If communication is inaccurate or inadequate, the likely results are uncertainty, apprehension, errors, and dissatisfaction.

Organizations also must communicate effectively with parties outside their boundaries. Lee Iacocca's televised messages concerning Chrysler's resurgence and Sanford Sigoloff's television commercials declaring the Wickes Cos. to have come back strong were credited with a significant part of the success of those firms. And, as we discuss later in the chapter, companies regularly find themselves communicating with the public to quell rumors.

Further, much of a manager's time is spent communicating. In a classic study, Henry Mintzberg observed chief executive officers on a daily basis to see how they actually spent their time. He found CEOs to spend 78 percent of their time on communication-related activities involving direct contact with others, including scheduled and unscheduled meetings, telephone calls, and tours of facilities. Even the 22 percent of time spent on what was called "deskwork" included answering mail and was thus related to communication. Also, the CEOs said activities involving direct communication with others were more interesting and valuable than more routine activities. The chief executives regularly communicated with peers, clients, suppliers, associates, subordinates, members of the board of directors, and others. And face-to-face communication appears to demand large amounts of time at all managerial levels. Mintzberg estimated such communication to take 59 percent of the time of supervisors and 89 percent of the time of middle managers.[2]

In this chapter we will examine a variety of important issues relating to communication. We will first consider functions of communication and the nature of the communication process. We will then address communication channels, including important dimensions on which channels may vary, fol-

DEVIL'S ADVOCATE

I don't get it. Why is effective communication so hard to manage in organizations? Don't you just tell people what to do and then they do it?

Well, it would certainly be nice if all a manager had to do was to simply tell people what to do, and they would understand what they were supposed to do and then do it. There are a variety of reasons why communication is so difficult to manage and maintain. First, it requires a lot of attention to detail and a lot of time on the part of the manager in order to make sure that everyone understands what is going on and what each person needs to do. Second, the types of tasks, issues, problems, and challenges facing "real-world" managers are so complex and multifaceted (e.g., how to design a new product) that it is very difficult to get others to understand your view of the situation and what they are supposed to do to address it. Third, some managers don't have the verbal skills needed to make themselves clear to others. Fourth, some employees are just not very motivated to listen carefully to what their managers are telling them. Finally, in many cases, the situation and the task are "moving targets" that require managers to update employees as to changes that affect them on a regular basis.

I don't have time to worry about communicating and listening effectively. I have real work to do, and that is to get the job done.

How do you define "real work," anyway? Is "real work" the accomplishment of "bottom-line" outcomes such as increasing sales, reducing costs, and enhancing profitability?

Whatever the case may be, there are always processes that underlie the achievement of any business outcomes. A major component of the management of these processes is effective communication that monitors, guides, and influences employee behaviors. So an appropriate way to think about communication is that it is "real work" too, in that it is a means to achieving desired ends.

Look, I listen to people by focusing on the *exact* words they use in communicating with me. By doing this, I can be totally objective in understanding what they are telling me.

You are dealing with people here, so just focusing on the words they use to understand what they are trying to tell you will probably lead to a lot of misunderstandings. Why? Well, people don't always say exactly what they mean. The most important thing is that others comprehend the meaning of your message. Obviously, the words a person uses to communicate something to you are very important, but you should consider other factors that may actually tell you a lot more about what the person is saying. For example, look at the facial expressions of the person, the tone of voice, body posture, eye contact, and hand gestures.

Note also that in some cultures being direct in communication (saying exactly what you mean) is rarely practiced, especially when it comes to giving others bad news or criticism.

Hey, if I am the boss, it's the responsibility of my employees to figure out what I'm telling them. I shouldn't have to do all the work so that they understand what I'm telling them.

Not exactly. If it is your responsibility as the manager to ensure the success of your work unit, then it is mainly *your* responsibility to make sure that others understand their objectives and what they are supposed to do to support them. Yes, your employees have a responsibility to ask for clarification, if they don't understand something. But it is the manager's job to create and maintain good communications among all staff in the work unit.

lowed by a review of communication network types. Next we will examine communication barriers and ways they can be overcome. We will then present guidelines for effective written communication, effective speaking, and mastering active listening. Following this, we will address forms and functions of nonverbal communication. Next, we will consider important issues in electronic communication, including e-mail, the Internet and the World Wide Web, teleconferencing and videoconferencing, and e-commerce. We will close with discussions of informal communication, coaching and counseling, and cross-cultural communication.

Before continuing, complete Self-Assessment Exercise 5-1 to evaluate your personal communication style. Then complete the Pre-Test Skills Assessment.

Self-Assessment 5-1
Your Personal Communication Style

Answer each of the following questions using the following scale:

1 = Disagree Strongly
2 = Disagree Somewhat
3 = Neither Agree nor Disagree
4 = Agree Somewhat
5 = Agree Strongly

In discussions with others:

1. _____ I tend to speak my mind in a direct and straightforward way.
2. _____ I argue my points fully and thoroughly.
3. _____ I would rather say nothing than hurt someone's feelings.
4. _____ I believe in carefully discussing things before making decisions.
5. _____ I quickly "cut to the bottom line" in getting my point across.
6. _____ I really enjoy the process of conversing.
7. _____ I am a good listener.
8. _____ I am sometimes accused of being long-winded.
9. _____ I am very concerned with others' feelings.
10. _____ I rarely interrupt others.
11. _____ I value brevity and frankness.
12. _____ I hesitate to offer advice or criticism.
13. _____ I expect others to appreciate my input and to deal with it in a constructive way.
14. _____ I feel it is best to say what I think and to avoid emotion.
15. _____ I offer a lot of detail in support of my position.
16. _____ I am soft-spoken.
17. _____ I enjoy debating others.
18. _____ I think it is better to say what I really believe than to "pretty up" my views to try to make people feel comfortable.
19. _____ I give very complete, precise directions to others.
20. _____ I use as few words as possible.
21. _____ I try to keep things warm and supportive.

Pre-Test Skills Assessment
Communicating

You are the Vice President of the Organizational Development Division at a major manufacturing firm. Your division is composed of two departments—total quality management and organizational research. Each department is headed by a manager. The function of the total quality management department is to work with management throughout the company to embrace total quality management principles and to implement them in their work units. A major objective of the department is to get managers to use data to drive their decision making regarding the operation of their work units.

The organizational research department has the goal of working with management to identify research projects that will enhance the long-term competitiveness of the firm. These projects cover issues ranging from strategic analysis, to quality, human resources, marketing, and administration.

One of the most significant challenges facing your division is that there is no communication between the total quality and organizational research departments. Part of the problem is that your two departmental managers have very different styles and do not get along at all. Although the two departments are physically located next to each other, the staff from both units (10–15 employees in each department) are not communicating with each other about opportunities for mutually beneficial projects. This problem has resulted in a significant reduction in the overall effectiveness of the division.

Develop an action plan for handling the key issues in the foregoing situation. Be specific.

FUNCTIONS OF COMMUNICATION AND THE COMMUNICATION PROCESS

Communication is the transfer of information from one person to another. It may serve several important functions.[3]

> **Information function.** Communication provides information to be used for decision making. Managers require information concerning alternatives, future events, and potential outcomes of their decisions to make reasoned choices.

> **Motivational function.** Communication encourages commitment to organizational objectives, thus enhancing motivation. Lee Iacocca's visible role as the spokesperson for the Chrysler Corporation was credited as being motivational both for Chrysler employees and for Americans in general.[4]

> **Control function.** Communication clarifies duties, authority, and responsibilities, thereby permitting control. If there is ambiguity concerning such things, it is impossible to isolate sources of problems and to take corrective actions.

> **Emotive function.** Communication permits the expression of feelings and the satisfaction of social needs. It may also help vent frustrations. After the breakup of AT&T, there was a marked increase in the number of customers who yelled at operators, a convenient target for anger.

Communication is a process involving several steps, as shown in Figure 5-1.[5] The first step is the development of an idea that the sender wishes to transmit. Step 2 is to encode the idea into words, charts, or other symbols for transmission. Step 3 is to transmit the message by the method chosen, such as memo, phone call, e-mail, or personal visit. Step 4 is the receipt of the message by another person. The receiver of the message must play an active role at this stage. If the message is oral, the receiver must be a good listener. Step 5 is to decode the message so that it can be understood. Such understanding occurs only in the mind of the receiver, and no guarantee exists that the message as intended by the sender will be the same as the message understood by the receiver. That is, the message must successfully cross the "bridge of mean-

FOCUS ON MANAGEMENT

COMMUNICATING AFTER THE OKLAHOMA CITY BOMBING*

Kerr-McGee Corp. is an Oklahoma City–based oil and gas exploration and production company with assets of approximately $7 billion. The Kerr-McGee Corp. building complex is located just two blocks from the site of the April 1995 bombing of the Murrah Federal Building in downtown Oklahoma City. While Kerr-McGee has extensive crisis communication plans for all its facilities, nothing like the bombing had ever been anticipated. After the initial bomb, it was thought that a second bomb was about to explode. The Kerr-McGee buildings were designated as part of the "crime scene," complete with yellow tape. That designation brought many questions from employees, such as: Were any of our people hurt or killed? Can we help? When can we move our cars? When can we go back to work? How can we get our paychecks if we can't get back to work? With the buildings evacuated, how can we know what's going on? The problem Kerr-McGee faced was how to communicate with 900 scattered, confused, concerned employees in the face of chaos. Within minutes after the bombing, Kerr-McGee's executive management group was transformed into a corporate communications team. About a dozen top executives combined with three members of the corporate communications staff to develop and implement strategic plans to let employees know what was going on. Among the many steps taken were the following.

> One hour and 17 minutes after the bombing, a brief employee bulletin was sent by e-mail to all downtown employees. The e-mail said there had been some minor injuries in the McGee Tower as well as some office and window damage and that a doctor was standing by.

> At about the same time, rumors of a second bomb caused evacuation within a two-block radius of the Murrah building, including the Kerr-McGee complex. A public address announcement asked employees to clear the building in an orderly manner and to gather at a nearby convention center. There they were told to return home to await further information.

> A "calling tree" was formed, whereby top executives would contact their direct reports, who would contact their direct reports, and so on, until all employees were contacted. The message said in effect, "We don't know when we can get back in the building, but we'll try to keep you posted."

> A "command center," complete with 15 phone lines, was set up in another Kerr-McGee facility in Oklahoma City. The executive/communications team staffed the phones round the clock for four days in order to respond to employees' questions.

> On the Monday employees returned to work, Kerr-McGee's top executives stationed themselves at all entrances to the building. They handed out "memorial ribbons" to returning employees and gave them each a hug.

> Kerr-McGee's management hired Crisis Management International (CMI), a firm composed of psychologists and psychiatrists who specialize in personal counseling following tragic events. Their first order of business was to have mass meetings with all employees. These were followed by "Let's talk about it" sessions with groups of 20 employees. Finally, the CMI people were made available to employees and their family members on a one-to-one basis for several weeks.

http://www.kerr-mcgee.com/

*D. Dozier, "Case Study: Employee Communications at Kerr-McGee in the Aftermath of the Oklahoma City Bombing," *Public Relations Quarterly,* Summer 1998, pp. 13–18.

ing." Once receivers have obtained and decoded a message, they may accept or reject it, which is Step 6. Whether or not the message will be accepted depends on things such as perceptions of the message's accuracy, the authority and perceived expertise of the sender, and the implications of the message for the receiver. Finally, in Step 7, the receiver uses the message. This may involve discarding it, storing it for future use, or taking action consistent with the message.

FIGURE 5-1
The Communication Process

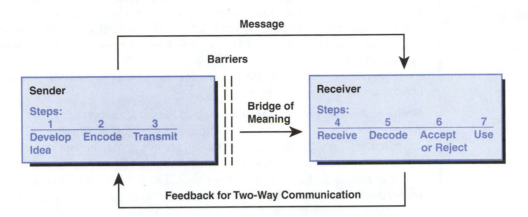

While Figure 5-1 shows feedback, not all communication includes such feedback. As we'll discuss in the next section, communication may be one-way or two-way; there are relative benefits and costs to each, depending on the situation.

Skills Practice 5-1 will provide an opportunity for you to develop skill in effectively implementing the various elements of the basic communication process in order to enhance the likelihood that others will properly receive your message.

Skill Level: Basic

Skills Practice 5-1
Managing the Communication Process

Skill Objective
To develop skill in effectively applying and managing various aspects of the communication process.

Procedure
Read each of the brief scenarios that follow and identify how you would address the communication issues in each by going through the steps in this communication process model:

    a.   What is your idea?
    b.   What is your message?
    c.   Which channel of communication will you use?
    d.   How will you ensure that the receiver receives the message and decodes it properly?

Scenario 1—Informing Employees of a Layoff
Your company has just announced a round of employee layoffs that will have a significant impact on your work unit. Specifically, your boss has told you that you need to reduce your staff by 50 percent. After a very difficult process, you have decided which employees will be laid off.

Using the communication process model, how would you communicate your decision to the employees who are going to be laid off?

Scenario 2—Explaining a New Policy or Procedure to Your Staff

Your company has just adopted a new performance appraisal system that requires employees to evaluate the performance of their bosses. You believe that many of your employees will resist any required participation in this process because they are concerned about confidentiality and potential repercussions associated with any critical remarks they may make about you. You would like to obtain their commitment to this new performance appraisal system.

Using the communication process model, how would you deal with potential employee concerns about the new system?

Scenario 3—Making Recommendations to Senior Management

You are the Director of Marketing Research at a large consumer products corporation based in New York City. Your job is to manage teams of researchers who work on identifying market opportunities for new or existing products and to assess customer satisfaction with your products. Recent research has indicated that the majority of customers are dissatisfied with your products and view them as being of low quality relative to comparable products from competing firms.

Senior management has asked you to present the findings of your department's research at the quarterly cabinet meeting. Your challenge is how to break the bad news to them given the tendency at your company for management to "shoot the messenger" when bad news is being delivered.

Using the communication process model, how would you communicate the news about customer dissatisfaction?

Discussion Questions

1. Evaluate your plan for dealing with each of the scenarios. Which aspects would be the most challenging to handle and why?
2. In the "real world," these issues would most likely be far more complex to handle. Why?
3. What are the implications of this exercise for you as a future supervisor or manager?

As Self-Assessment 5-1 demonstrated, people tend to use different styles when communicating. For instance, some are careful to explain their views, while others are not. Some are more assertive than others. Some are very concerned about the other person's feelings, while others say we should keep emotions out of our discussions. Some rely more on nonverbal communications than others, and so on.

COMMUNICATION CHANNELS

As noted earlier, a communication channel is the medium through which a message is sent. This would include both human channels, such as speech and body movements, and mechanical channels, such as computer networks, the mail, and the telephone. In choosing appropriate channels, you may want to consider several channel dimensions.[6]

CHANNEL DIMENSIONS

Important dimensions on which channels may differ include capacity, modifiability, duplication, immediacy, one-way vs. two-way flow, number of linkages, appropriateness, and richness.

> **Capacity.** Channel capacity is the amount of information that can be sent through a channel over a given period of time without significant

distortion. A telephone, for instance, has greater capacity than a memo, since the memo is constrained by reading speed.

> **Modifiability.** Modifiability is the degree to which the rate of transmission can be varied. Modifiability of a memo or other written message is high; the recipient can read at a chosen speed and even set the memo aside for a while. A televised message is typically less modifiable (though VCRs are changing this).

> **Duplication.** It is sometimes useful to use subchannels to reiterate or elaborate on a message, especially when it is complex or novel. A television commercial, for instance, may use both visual and auditory subchannels to sell a product.

> **Immediacy.** Immediacy is the speed at which a message can be transmitted. E-mail now transmits reports and other information almost instantly. The U.S. Postal Service may take a few days, or more, to deliver the same message.

> **One-way vs. two-way flow.** Some channels, such as a memo and a videotaped lecture, are essentially one-way. *One-way communication* gives a message without opportunity for immediate feedback, such as when a plant manager sends a memo to all employees in the plant. In contrast, *two-way communication,* such as a telephone conversation or a face-to-face chat, allows the message recipient to ask questions and provide feedback. Research shows that:[7]

  - One-way communication is faster than two-way.
  - Two-way communication is more accurate than one-way.
  - Receivers are more sure of themselves and make more correct judgments of how right or wrong they are with two-way communication.
  - The sender may feel less secure in two-way communication. The message recipients can point out errors, interrupt a stream of thought, disagree, or otherwise challenge the sender.
  - Two-way communication is relatively noisy and disorderly. One-way communication appears neat and efficient to an outside observer, but the communication is often less accurate.

> **Number of linkages.** Some channels provide direct contact between a sender and the ultimate recipient, while others involve intermediate linkages. Longer channels invite omission and distortion. Use as few linkages as possible.

> **Appropriateness.** Some channels are "made for" certain types of messages and may be completely inappropriate for others. A billboard may be fine for an advertising message, but it is probably not the place to reprimand an employee.

> **Richness.** Richness is the potential information-carrying capacity of data. If the communication of an item of data, such as a wink, conveys substantial new information, it is considered rich. If it provides little new understanding, it is low in richness. Face-to-face communication is the richest form of communication. It provides immediate feedback; with that feedback, understanding can be checked and interpretations corrected. Face-to-face communications also permit the observation of multiple cues, including body language, facial expression, and tone of voice, as we'll discuss later in the chapter. Face-to-face communications are followed, in declining order of information richness, by the tele-

phone, written personal communications, written formal communications, and computer output.[8]

SELECTING CHANNELS

When sending messages, consider the characteristics we have just presented. How much information must be transmitted? How fast? Does the message require elaboration? Is speed of the essence? Is feedback necessary? Are certain channels unsuited to the nature of the message? You may decide after weighing these factors that available channels somehow must be modified or that multiple channels are needed. Whatever the result, the choice of channels should be carefully weighed.

COMMUNICATION NETWORKS

Communication channels may be linked in a variety of ways to form *communication networks.*[9] These networks are used to structure the information flows among network members. Whether you realize it or not, you will be making decisions about communication networks on a regular basis. You will need to decide, for instance, who should be "in the loop" to receive certain types of messages and to whom they should be instructed to respond. In making such decisions, you will determine who has direct and speedy access to information, who is most central in communication networks, who will be able to get information only after others have received it, and so on. Communication networks influence decision quality, member satisfaction, message quality, and other variables. Figure 5-2 shows six common networks.

The chain network links members sequentially. The Y network modifies the chain to have one member communicating to three others. With the wheel network, all communication must flow through a central individual. The circle network permits each member to communicate with two others. With the star network, any member can communicate directly with any other. A variant of the star, called the com-con network, permits all members to communicate directly but also has a central member who is considered to be the leader.

These networks clearly differ on a number of dimensions. For instance, with networks such as the chain and the circle, it may be necessary for a mes-

F I G U R E 5 - 2
Communication Networks

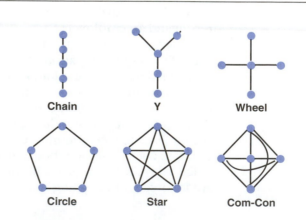

Chain   Y   Wheel

Circle   Star   Com-Con

sage to pass through multiple links to reach its destination. With the star and com-con networks, one link is sufficient. The networks also vary in degree of centralization. The circle and star networks are decentralized—everyone is as central as everyone else. On the other hand, the wheel and the com-con networks clearly have central members.

Relative centrality is the degree of centrality of an individual in a network. In the wheel network, there is clearly a central member. Since information more often flows through central members, they are likely to be perceived as leaders and to have high status. They are also likely to be more satisfied than their less central counterparts. Again, in the circle and star networks, all members are equally central.

Along with the degree of relative centrality of members within a network, the overall centralization of the network is also of interest. *Centralization* is a measure of the variability in member relative centralities. So the wheel, with one relatively central member and all others much less central, is highly centralized. The star, with equal member relative centralities, is completely decentralized.

Centralized networks tend to permit rapid decision making, but average member satisfaction is low. Centralized networks may be efficient for simple problems. But as complexity increases, more decentralization (and thus more participation in decision making) is needed, so the wheel network might be appropriate for routine, well-structured tasks, especially if there are time constraints. However, a network such as the circle or star would probably be better for tasks requiring creativity and a wide range of member inputs.

UNDERSTANDING AND OVERCOMING COMMUNICATION BARRIERS

Unfortunately, many things can interfere with effective communication. Some of the more common include semantics, distraction, misrepresentation, information retention, and perceptual factors.

SEMANTICS

Semantics, or *code noise,* occurs when the meaning of a message to the sender differs from its meaning to the recipient. Too often, this may be the result of "jargon," involving pretentious terminology or language specific to a particular profession or group. Here's an example of pretentious terminology: The *Wall Street Journal* reported on a federal tax case in which a fire alarm was described as a "combustion enunciator," a door as a "removable partition," a manhole as "equipment access," and windows as "decorative fixtures." [10]

Here is a sampling of jargon relating to computers and the modern workplace:

> *Salmon day:* Fighting uphill; swimming against the current.
> *Blamestorming:* Discussing a project failure with coworkers.
> *PEBCAK:* "Problem exists between chair and keyboard." That is, an operator error. [11]
> *Easter eggs:* Undocumented bits of code hidden in computer applications and operating systems that, once accessed, provide a bit of information or entertainment, such as a game, a joke, or the names of people who developed the program. [12]

> *Sticky eyeballs:* People who spend a lot of time at a website.
> *Cube farm:* Rows of cubicles instead of private offices.
> *RTM:* Read the manual.

For an extensive dictionary of management jargon, go to:

http://members.xoom.com/wieker/mj/index.htm

DISTRACTION

Distraction, or *psychological noise,* occurs when a recipient does not understand the sender's message because he or she is simply thinking about something else. For instance, the recipient may be distracted by financial worries or upcoming deadlines. Often, of course, recipients don't understand senders' messages, because they are thinking about their own replies rather than concentrating on the message to which they are going to reply. Thus, active listening is an important communication skill, as explained later in this chapter.

MISREPRESENTATION

Misrepresentation may also cause the failure of communication and may take various forms. Deliberate lies are an extreme example. People sometimes lie on their résumés (sometimes called *padding*), in their advertising messages (sometimes called *puffery*), and in their campaign promises (sometimes called *politics*). More often, information may be subtly distorted to the sender's benefit. A memo that focuses on sales increases but downplays drops in profit, an annual report that tries to hide changes in accounting format, and a brochure from a drug manufacturer that ignores hazardous side effects would be examples of this kind of misrepresentation.

Indeed, some forms of misrepresentation are so common that examples to the contrary are newsworthy. For instance, it is almost "common practice" for company annual reports to present the year's events in a favorable light. The "Dear Stockholder" letter in an annual report of poultry producer Holly Farms Corp. broke that mold. It began, "You already know the Bad News about our past fiscal year. We were wrong about chickens. The chicken market did not recover from salmonella publicity and we entered a sharp chicken depression. We lost money in chickens—our worst year in history. And the poor performance was mostly our fault." [13]

INFORMATION RETENTION

Information is a valuable resource. Those who control it are in positions of power. Some employees may retain specific sorts of information, such as a formula or a filing system, and thereby make themselves more necessary. Others are in positions that give them the ability to channel—or not to channel—information to various individuals inside and outside the organization. Still others are in positions in which they process information, sending only some of it along. Each of these sorts of individuals has the potential to create barriers to proper communication.

PERCEPTUAL FACTORS

Most perceptual errors are directly relevant to communication. Stereotyping, as discussed in Chapter 3, may cause us to ignore or distort the messages of people we have classified in certain ways. A manager may, for instance, feel that union representatives are not trustworthy. As a result, the manager may misinterpret conciliatory gestures from the union. Selective perception may cause us to ignore communication that conflicts with our beliefs and expectations. Halo error may lead us to bias our evaluation of a message because of some unrelated characteristic of the message sender, such as physical appearance. Projection may lead us to infer information in a message we receive based upon our own feelings. If we are angry, for instance, we may see anger in the message. Primacy and recency effects may cause us to give differing weights to various communications, depending on when we receive them.

The following Voice of Experience is an interview with Peter Fox, Secretary of the Wisconsin Department of Employment Relations. The interview provides valuable insights regarding common communication problems in organizations and recommendations for becoming a good communicator.

VOICE OF EXPERIENCE

COMMUNICATING EFFECTIVELY

Peter D. Fox, Secretary of the Wisconsin Department of Employment Relations

1. Based on your experience, what are the most difficult challenges you have faced in terms of managing communication in organizations effectively?

The most difficult challenges have been the communication needs involved in the process of conflict resolution and creating beneficial change within an organization and the degree of precision and amount of time and resources needed in clearly and thoroughly communicating intricate/involved/strategic messages within an organization in a timely manner.

2. What kinds of specific strategies have you used to handle these communication challenges?

Make the message as direct (simplified) as possible. Look for or create opportunities for multiple repetitions of key messages. Test the accuracy of the delivery of key messages by consulting with those to whom it is directed: What do you understand I have communicated? Look for opportunities to have other, significant messages originate from other key leaders or even in a "bottoms-up" manner. Never assume a constituency has heard the message unless you are certain it has been delivered. In short: "Tell them what you're going to tell them; tell them what you're telling them; tell them what you told them." Also, a communications component should be included in virtually any type of training conducted by the organization, from the lowest to the highest levels of control.

3. What kind of general advice would you give students regarding what they will need to do to become effective communicators once they enter the "real world?"

Most important: Acquire a broad-based education, and work hard to know your "clients" and how they receive—and process—their information. Don't assume that others receive and process the same way you do. Be comfortable in your style, but also ask people to critique you so that you might consider ways to improve your communication style. Select an appropriate medium for the message that has to be delivered, particularly in today's electronic age (don't send a harsh personnel message via impersonal e-mail is one example). Understand that individuals vary in how they receive information—some people are visual learners, some prefer a thorough written explanation, some need charts, graphs, and illustrations to combine with words. Finally, for very important messages, look for ways to "test" what you intend to send, before you send it, for appropriate tone and clarity to optimize chances your message will be received in the manner you intended and with the degree of clarity desired.

http://der.state.wi.us/static/der.htm

OVERCOMING COMMUNICATION BARRIERS

There are many approaches to overcoming the causes of communication failures. For instance, feedback, repetitions of the messages, use of multiple channels, and simplified language may reduce problems due to semantics, selective perception, and distraction. Simplified language includes use of simple words and phrases, short and familiar words, personal pronouns (such as *you* and *them*), short sentences and paragraphs, active verbs, and illustrations, examples, and charts.

Communication overload may be reduced by careful review of the material needed by the recipient and by use of the exception principle. The *exception principle* states that only exceptions should be reported—there is no need for messages stating that the production line didn't break down or that absenteeism or competitive conditions are unchanged. Short-circuiting may be reduced through careful consideration of who has a "need to know" the material. Electronic data-processing techniques that automatically route messages to certain people may also help.

Information retention and misrepresentation are more difficult problems and have led to some very different prescriptions. Some call for tightened formal controls and even organizational audit groups. An *organizational audit group* is designed to ferret out the points at which omissions or distortions are taking place. Others have argued just the opposite, saying that fewer formal controls and a more open, trusting organizational climate are needed.

These suggestions make it clear that there is no free lunch when dealing with communication. Things that lessen one problem are likely to worsen another. For instance, feedback, redundancy, and multiple channels may make communication overload worse. The exception principle makes misrepresentation and information retention easier. This does not mean that the situation is hopeless, only that we must pay serious attention to these problems and carefully weigh the resultant trade-offs.

In Korea and Japan, some companies are taking a novel approach to reducing communication overload. They specify one hour in the morning when no one—including the chief executive—is to be interrupted by phone calls, coworkers, or meetings. Some corporations, including Samsung and Hyundai, say the system has enhanced creativity and produced major administrative productivity gains.[14]

GUIDELINES FOR EFFECTIVE WRITTEN COMMUNICATION

Written communication is required when the action called for is complex and must be done in a precise way. Written communication also provides a permanent form of record keeping and can reach a large number of people easily. Here, we briefly discuss six forms of written communication in organizations—three for communicating downward and three for communicating upward.

FORMS OF DOWNWARD COMMUNICATION

Downward communication involves messages from senders relatively high in the organizational structure to receivers in lower-level positions, such as from a supervisor to a subordinate. It is used for such purposes as giving instructions, providing information about policies and procedures, giving feedback about performance, and indoctrinating or motivating. In addition to letters and memos, three written forms of downward communications are manuals, handbooks, and newsletters.

A company manual is an integrated system of long-term instructions, brought together between covers, classified, coded, indexed, and otherwise prepared to maximize its reference value. Manuals have a high degree of authority. They deal primarily with policy, procedure, or organization. Since manuals are technical and complex, employees should be trained to use them.

Handbooks are usually less authoritative, formal, and lengthy than manuals and generally apply at lower organizational levels. The employee handbook, for example, outlines the duties and privileges of the individual worker. Handbooks generally have a low-key, friendly, personal approach.[15]

Company newsletters are usually issued biweekly or monthly. Informal in tone, they are used to disseminate information to many employees. Newsletters might announce company social functions, contain stories about employees cited for superior performance or attendance, or provide answers about employment issues. Unlike a manual, a newsletter has a mix of personal, social, and work-related information. Japanese firms sometimes send out newsletters in the form of comic books. Comic books, or *mangas,* are widely read in Japan, and dozens of Japanese companies now use this form to convey information to employees.[16]

FORMS OF UPWARD COMMUNICATION

Upward communication involves communication from sources in lower-level positions to receivers in relatively higher positions. It is often used to

Web Wise

Manuals and Handbooks Online

For excellent information about handbooks and manuals, including many examples, go to the following sites:

HR Guide to the Internet: Employee Handbook:

http://www.hr-guide.com/data/023.htm

HRM Manuals and Handbooks Online:

http://www.nbs.ntu.ac.uk/depts/hrm/list/hrmh.htm

FOCUS ON MANAGEMENT

PATHFINDERS AT LLOYDS TSB*

The merger of Lloyds and TSB created a single British bank with 77,000 members and 15 million customers. The "new" bank won a Marketing Society Award for the care it took to launch and explain the merged organization to its employees. Lloyds TSB realized that it needed to win the hearts and minds of its personnel if they were to be motivated to "deliver the brand" to customers. It ran a comprehensive and sustained internal program, highlighted by a live event called "Your Life. Your Bank." Staff nominated colleagues to act as brand ambassadors, called "pathfinders," whose role was to attend the event, absorb the key messages, and pass them on to 15 of their colleagues. A total of 5,000 staff acted as pathfinders. The event comprised a 28-stand exhibition, representing each of the bank's departments, with interactive elements to show how Lloyds TSB is aligning itself with the customer. A morning session explored how Lloyds and TSB are coming together, while in the afternoon the focus was on brand understanding. Following the event, pathfinders passed on what they had learned to their colleagues in prearranged, structured cascade sessions. They were supplied with a pack containing bullet-point summaries, visual support on overhead transparencies, a computer disk, and a video summary. On customer launch day, the bank's chief executive addressed the staff live on business TV. All staff received a letter welcoming them to their new bank. Subsequent research revealed very positive employee responses to the process.

http://www.lloydstsb.co.uk/

*"Internal Communications," *Marketing,* June 6, 2000, p. 19.

give information on achievement or progress, to point out problems that are being encountered, to pass on ideas for improvement of activities, and to provide information about feelings on work and nonwork activities. Three techniques that are especially useful in upward communication are suggestion systems, grievances, and attitude surveys.

A *suggestion system* permits employees to submit ideas or suggestions for improving company effectiveness. The suggestions are then evaluated, generally by a panel of managers, and the valuable ones are acted on. The initiator of the idea may get a cash award, a letter of commendation, or an insignia. The idea behind a suggestion system is that employees are in the best position to contribute ideas to make their jobs more effective.[17]

Grievances are formal, written complaints submitted by employees regarding alleged unfair treatment on the job.[18] They may cover such topics as working conditions, promotions, pay, disciplinary action, supervision, and work assignments. Grievance procedures often involve several steps. In the first step, the employee's immediate supervisor reviews the grievance. Failure to resolve the grievance at that step might lead to appeals at higher levels, perhaps including the company's industrial relations office or an outside mediator. Grievances allow employees to channel their frustrations and feelings of injustice in productive ways.

Attitude surveys are often conducted annually or biannually. The surveys provide information about employees' feelings and attitudes on many employment issues, such as satisfaction with pay and supervision. Responses are usually anonymous so that employees can feel free to speak their minds. Results of the surveys are tabulated and a report is prepared. The company then acts on the information provided.[19] About half of large firms use surveys, often for a wide range of purposes. For instance, at Wells Fargo & Co. in San Francisco, employees have been asked about such things as the effectiveness

FIGURE 5-3
Guides for Readable Writing

- Use simple words and phrases, such as *improve* instead of *ameliorate* and *like* instead of *in a manner similar to that of.*
- Use short and familiar words, such as *darken* instead of *obfuscate.*
- Use personal pronouns, such as *you* and *them,* if the style permits.
- Use illustrations, examples, and charts. These techniques are even better when they are tied to the reader's experiences.
- Use short sentences and paragraphs. Big words and thick reports may look impressive, but the communicator's job is to inform people, not impress them.
- Use active verb forms, such as "The manager said . . . ," rather than passive verb forms, such as "It was said by the manager that . . ."
- Don't use unnecessary words. For example, in the sentence "Bad weather conditions prevented my trip," the word *conditions* is unnecessary. Instead, write, "Bad weather prevented my trip."

Source: From *Human Behavior at Work: Organizational Behavior,* 7th ed., by K. Davis and J. W. Newstrom. Copyright 1985 by McGraw-Hill Book Company.

of the bank's advertising, the quality and innovation of its products, and its responsibility to the community.

Skills Practice 5-2 provides an opportunity for you to develop skill in designing and implementing employee attitude surveys in organizations. Be careful: Some students initially think that this is an easy activity. In reality, this is a very complex and challenging process, if you want to do it right.

Skills Practice 5-2   **Skill Level: Challenging**
Designing and Implementing Employee Attitude Surveys

Learning Objectives
1. To develop skill in designing an employee attitude survey.
2. To develop skill in administering an employee attitude survey.

Procedure
1. Break up into teams of 3 to 5 students.
2. Select an organization that you are familiar with based on general knowledge or past or present work experience. If you can't think of a "real-world" organization to use, then select a student organization that someone is involved with.
3. Suppose that the president of the organization you selected has asked you to design and administer a survey to assess employees' perceptions and attitudes toward their jobs and the general work environment. The purpose of the survey is to identify specific strategies for enhancing the quality of the work environment for employees.
4. As a team, design your survey by brainstorming a list of appropriate questions.
5. Identify the steps you would take in administering the survey once it is designed.
6. Present your list of survey questions and your plan for administering the survey to the class.
7. Answer the following discussion questions as a class.

Discussion Questions
1. What are the keys to effectively designing employee attitude surveys?
2. What are the keys to effectively implementing employee attitude surveys?
3. What are the practical implications of this exercise for you as a future manager?

Whatever form written communications take, it is critical that they be easy to understand. Figure 5-3 presents some guides for readable writing.

GUIDELINES FOR EFFECTIVE SPEAKING

Effective speakers communicate logically, clearly, and confidently.[20] Effective speaking requires thorough preparation. Knowing your purpose and your audience are critical; 2,800 years ago Aristotle said that outstanding communicators must first understand their audiences and gear their language and persuasive appeals to them. Physical delivery, including presence, voice control, eye contact, and other nonverbal cues to be discussed in the next section, may make the difference between success and failure. The way you speak reflects your intelligence, ability to think, and ability to organize. These abilities are highly valued in business and in society in general and can be crucial in social relationships and job opportunities.

What follows are guidelines for effective speaking. Since speaking involves both verbal and nonverbal aspects, some of these guidelines touch on issues we'll explore in more detail in the next section.

> **Determine the purpose of your communication.** Is it to explain ideas to others? To recognize outstanding efforts? To entertain? To induce an emotion? To instill a belief? Your speech should be tailored to facilitate the desired purpose of your communication.

> **Consider issues of time and space.** Determine the best time and location for delivering your message. Consider how much time you will have and how your message might relate to other messages delivered before and after it. Think about what recent events might be in the minds of your listeners and whether you should refer to those events.

> **Adapt to your listeners.** Consider the size of the audience as well as factors such as audience age, gender, interests, level of knowledge about the subject, and values. You'll need to prepare very differently for a one-to-one talk, a small-group presentation, and a lecture to a large audience. Also consider audience expectations. For example, is the audience expecting an entertaining after-dinner talk, a stirring inspirational message, or how-to tips? Consider as well if there may be hearing-impaired audience members or an international audience that cannot speak fluent English.

> **Use appropriate vocabulary.** Speak at the proper level for the particular audience. Seek clarity. Avoid use of words that may have different meanings to various members of the audience, and avoid unnecessary jargon.

> **Practice voice control.** Consider proper speech volume, pitch, and speaking rate. Avoid mumbling and awkward pauses. It is helpful to listen to yourself on an audiotape and to observe your mannerisms on videotape. Ask others to critique your presentations.

> **Use appropriate gestures.** Properly used, gestures can make a presentation more engaging, and they may help disguise anxiety. Avoid short, jerky movements that may appear as nervousness, and use a variety of gestures so you don't seem to be in a rut. Use gestures to reinforce spoken points or even as substitutes.

> **Organize your presentation.** Any oral presentation can be divided into three parts: gaining attention, presenting the information, and closing effectively. The amount of time devoted to gaining attention will depend on the audience members' familiarity with, and interest in, the subject. A personal greeting, a stunning statement or opinion, a suspenseful question, or humor may help gain attention. To effectively share information, ask how you can give the subject high priority in the minds of listeners, how you can bring the subject more clearly into focus, and how you can develop it in a form that satisfies your listeners. Finally, an effective closing gives a sense of completion and reinforces key points.

The step-by-step process model shown in the nearby Bottom Line identifies the basic actions that a manager would take in order to use speaking skills to make effective speeches or business presentations in an organizational setting.

The Bottom Line: Developing Effective Speaking Skills

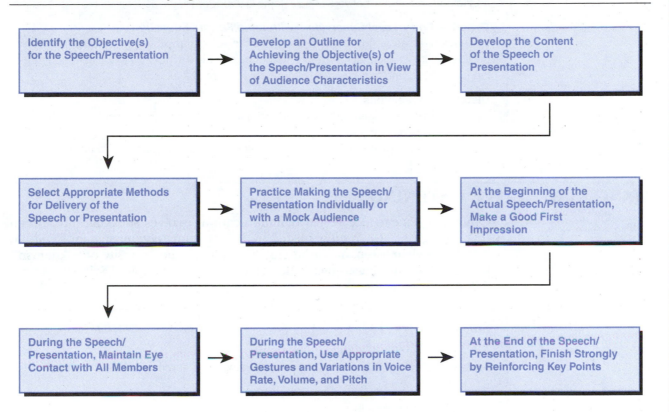

Skills Practice 5-3 will increase your skill in tailoring your business presentations to characteristics of your audience. This is a critical skill that you will need to possess in the workplace.

Skills Practice 5-3
Effective Speaking

Skill Level: Basic

Skill Objective

To develop skill in making effective presentations to different types of audiences.

Procedure

1. Select a topic (e.g., a theory or concept) to use as a basis for your speeches from any content area in this book.
2. Read the following case scenarios.
3. Select one scenario, and prepare a 3–5 minute speech to present to your class.
4. Present the speech, and obtain feedback from your classmates regarding the effectiveness of your speech.
5. Talk about the discussion questions that follow.

Skill Practice Scenarios

Case 1—Senior Executives

You have been asked to make a brief presentation of your topic to a group of senior executives at your company. Your goal is to explain your topic to them in an appropriate manner and to convince them that your chosen topic is important to the success of the organization.

Case 2—Entry-Level Supervisors with Little Formal Education

You have been asked to make a brief presentation of your topic to a group of entry-level supervisors with little formal education. Your goal is to provide them with a clear understanding of the topic and to see why it is important to them in their jobs.

Discussion Questions

1. What kinds of adjustments did you make in order to take into consideration the characteristics of your audience?
2. What are the managerial implications of this exercise for you in the future?

MASTERING ACTIVE LISTENING

Obviously, face-to-face verbal communication involves speaking. More than that though, it also requires listening.[21] Unfortunately, most people would rather talk than listen. According to one old joke, the opposite of talking isn't listening, it's waiting to talk.[22] Before reading on, complete Self-Assessment 5-2, Active Listening.

Self-Assessment 5-2
Active Listening

Answer each of the questions in this section using the following scale:

1 = Disagree Strongly
2 = Disagree Somewhat
3 = Neither Agree nor Disagree
4 = Agree Somewhat
5 = Agree Strongly

When listening to someone:
1. _____ I ask questions to be confident that I understand.
2. _____ I am able to keep quiet.
3. _____ I pay attention to the other person's nonverbal cues.
4. _____ I often find my mind wandering.
5. _____ I often paraphrase what was said to make sure I've understood.
6. _____ I often find myself interrupting.
7. _____ I tend to think about what I'm going to say next.
8. _____ I tend to get emotionally involved.
9. _____ I generally try to make eye contact.
10. _____ I am often impatient.
11. _____ I tend to lean forward, toward the speaker.
12. _____ I often doodle, tap my pen, or shuffle papers.
13. _____ I am able to stay focused.
14. _____ I try to understand the speaker's feelings as well as the intellectual content.
15. _____ I often sit with my arms crossed.

16. _____ I often make comments to show that I understand.
17. _____ I am generally looking for an opening to get the floor.
18. _____ I tend to evaluate and make judgments about the speaker.
19. _____ I sometimes look at my watch.
20. _____ I use gestures of understanding, such as nods of the head.
21. _____ I often succumb to distractions, such as ringing telephones or activity in the hallway.
22. _____ I sometimes express irritation at the speaker's speech patterns or hesitancy.
23. _____ I pay attention to signs of emotion in the speaker's voice.
24. _____ I maintain a relaxed posture.
25. _____ I periodically ask the speaker if I'm understanding his or her message correctly.

Listening can take many forms. Casual or marginal listening, such as when colleagues chat about sports over lunch, requires only a passive effort, since there is little pressure to learn or remember the message. With attentive listening, as when a manager is delivering a performance appraisal, the listener is motivated to hear, understand, and remember. With active listening, such as counseling situations and conflict interviews, it is important to listen to more than just the content of the message. Attention to nonverbal cues will also be important. Active listening requires that you convey to the speaker a sense of trust, identify with his or her feelings and thoughts, and encourage him or her to be as specific as possible about feelings and concerns.

Here are some guidelines for active listening.[23]

> **Control the physical environment.** Try to minimize noise and other distractions, such as an uncomfortable room temperature or improper lighting. Don't sit near doorways or under air-conditioning vents. If the location is noisy or uncomfortable, move to a quieter setting. Take steps to minimize unnecessary distractions.

> **Be alert.** Give your full attention, and allot the necessary time to listen.

> **Be mentally prepared.** Do your homework in advance of the conversation. Anticipate the encounter by learning new terminology and background information about the persons, organization, or issues.

> **Be emotionally prepared.** Keep an open mind about what is being said, even if it is unpleasant. Give the speaker the opportunity to complete his or her message before raising questions.

> **Be attentive.** Continually review the speaker's message, and tie the various ideas or segments of the message together. Think of each idea as a link in a chain. Take notes if necessary, but record only main points. Develop an effective system of note taking.

> **Read nonverbal cues.** Pay attention to the speaker's tone of voice, expressions, gestures, and other nonverbal cues. We'll discuss nonverbal cues in more detail in the next section.

> **Distinguish among facts, inferences, and value judgments.** Try to sort out whether what is being said is a fact that can be verified, an inference (that is, a conclusion reached after consideration of a set of facts), or a personal judgment based on the speaker's value system. These may all be important, but you should do your best to determine which is which.

BOTTOM LINE

The Bottom Line: Developing Active Listening Skills

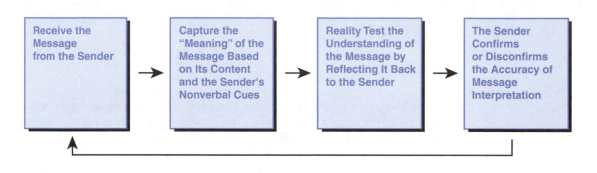

| Receive the Message from the Sender | → | Capture the "Meaning" of the Message Based on Its Content and the Sender's Nonverbal Cues | → | Reality Test the Understanding of the Message by Reflecting It Back to the Sender | → | The Sender Confirms or Disconfirms the Accuracy of Message Interpretation |

> **Offer and solicit feedback.** The best form of feedback in a listening situation is to paraphrase the speaker's message. This allows the speaker to verify the accuracy and completeness of what was transmitted and to make necessary changes or additions.

The step-by-step process model shown in the nearby Bottom Line identifies the basic actions that a manager would take in order to use active listening skills to enhance communication with others in an organizational setting.

Skills Practice 5-4 focuses on helping you to develop the ability to listen to others more effectively. This is a skill managers need all the time but that many do not put into practice very well.

Skills Practice 5-4
Active Listening Skills

Skill Level: Challenging

Skill Objective

To use active learning to develop skill in capturing the meaning of messages communicated by others in order to enhance one's understanding of a work situation or issue.

Procedure

1. Find a partner in your class. Try to work with someone you do not know, if possible.
2. Work through the following exercise.
3. Identify and discuss the practical implications of this case for you as a future manager or supervisor. Why is active listening a valuable skill for a good manager? What are the key considerations in using it effectively in the "real world?"

Active Listening Exercise

Step 1: One person should assume the role of the "speaker" (storyteller) and the other person should play the role of the "listener." After one round of the exercise is completed, the roles should be switched.

Step 2: (The Speaker) Think about the best (or worst) job you have ever held. Tell your partner why you liked (or disliked) this job so much (e.g., coworkers, type of work, pay). Try to provide as much detail as possible by using specific examples.

Step 3: (The Listener) Try to use active listening in listening to your partner's description of his/her favorite/worst job. You can do this by trying to capture the *meaning* of what your partner is saying rather than just the words spoken. This means that you should consider nonverbal cues (e.g., facial expressions, posture) as well as the emotions you observe in the other person as he/she is speaking (e.g., enthusiasm, frustration).

Occasionally, you should try to "reality test" your understanding of what the other person is saying by making a statement such as "So what I hear you saying is . . ." or "So what you mean is . . ." This is to ensure that your understanding of what the speaker is trying to communicate to you is accurate. Sometimes this is called "being on the same page." When the other person has completed his/her story, try to summarize, in your own words, the main ideas or points he/she made. This is an excellent test of whether you actually understand the main ideas contained in his/her message.

Step 4: Switch roles and repeat Steps 1 and 2.

USING AND READING NONVERBAL COMMUNICATION

Nonverbal communication is communication that uses no words or uses words in a way that conveys meaning beyond their strict definition. It may take place through such channels as the body, the face, the tone of voice, and interpersonal distance. A wink, a touch, or a change of body position can all convey worlds of meaning. Further, that meaning may vary markedly depending upon the situation, the gender of the parties, and the culture. Studies generally suggest that a substantial amount of information transmitted during a conversation—perhaps 80 or 90 percent—is nonverbal.[24] It was clear from our discussion of speaking and listening that it's impossible to talk about face-to-face verbal communication without also introducing issues of nonverbal communication.

FUNCTIONS OF NONVERBAL COMMUNICATION

Nonverbal communication provides five functions: accenting, contradicting, substituting, complementing, and regulating.[25]

> **Accenting** is adding emphasis to a verbal message. For instance, an angry boss who pounds on the desk and slams a door while reprimanding a subordinate is using nonverbal communication to reinforce the verbal scolding.

> **Contradicting** is signaling the opposite of the verbal message. Sometimes, an interviewee, salesperson, or boss will say one thing but, through eye movements, hand gestures, smiles, posture, or some other means of nonverbal communication, relay a very different message. For instance, a police chief noted that "Eyes move in patterns. They move differently when you're remembering and when you're creating. And if you're creating when you're talking to me about a crime, you're lying."[26] Nonverbal cues are typically more spontaneous and less consciously controlled than verbal cues, and they are viewed as more accurate. So when verbal and nonverbal communications are contradictory, the nonverbal communications tend to be given most weight.

> **Substituting** is replacing the verbal message with a nonverbal message. Some nonverbal cues have distinct and widely recognized meanings, so they may appropriately substitute for their verbal counterparts. For example, a nod may replace a spoken "yes."

> **Complementing** involves sending the same message nonverbally that is sent verbally. A hug accompanying a statement of "I love you," a pat on the back accompanying "Good job!" and a "high five" accompanying "Congratulations!" are all examples of complementing.

> **Regulating** is using nonverbal communication to control the flow of the verbal message. For instance, a boss who is becoming impatient with an overly long presentation by a subordinate and wants him to speed up may begin to conspicuously look at her watch or may start tapping a pencil on the desktop.

FORMS OF NONVERBAL COMMUNICATION

Nonverbal communication can take many forms, as shown in Figure 5-4, including paralanguage, hand movements, facial expressions, eye contact, posture, touch, dress, and proxemics.[27]

Paralanguage concerns *how* something is said rather than what is said. It includes all vocal aspects of speech other than words.[28] For example, voice qualities—such as pitch, rhythm, tempo, and volume—influence interpretation of a verbal message. A soft, low-pitched voice and a slow rate indicate liking, while a high-pitched voice indicates anger. Moderate rate, pitch, and volume indicate boredom.[29] Similarly, *vocal characterizers,* such as coughing, yawning, clearing the throat, and grunting, may be important. While they can sometimes be used effectively, they generally are distracting and annoying, and they should be avoided. *Vocal qualifiers* are variations in

FIGURE 5-4
Forms of Nonverbal Communication

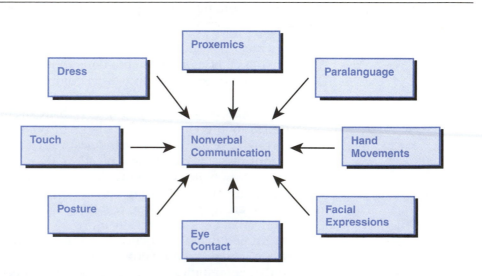

GLOBAL PERSPECTIVES

THE SMILE TRAINERS

The Japanese are too serious, says Yoshiko Kadokawa, author of the book *Power of a Laughing Face* and president of the Smile Amenity Institute. At a seminar for managers, his students bite on a chopstick or pen. Kadokawa then instructs them to "lift the edge of your mouth higher than the edge of the chopstick. Hold your cheeks and count: *idi, ni, san.* This is how you form your mouth shape." Smiling trainers in Japan use techniques such as "underwater training," in which students put their faces in water and then exhale when laughing. Some firms in Japan look for smiling faces in the hiring process. Yurchiro Koiso, dean of McDonald's Japanese training programs, explains that job applicants are asked to describe their most pleasant experience, and then managers evaluate whether their faces reflect the pleasure they are discussing. Applicants who don't have genuine smiles are banished to making burgers rather than greeting customers. "Service is smile and hustle," says Koiso.

tone or intensity of speech. For example, increases in rate or volume may indicate impatience or anger, respectively. The power of verbal qualifiers can be seen by repeating the sentence "I didn't say he stole your car" seven times, stressing a different word each time. Finally, *vocal segregates* are pauses between utterances, and may include "ahs" and "ums." In situations such as interviews, prolonged pauses suggest a lack of confidence and organization.[30]

There are several types of hand movements. Some have a specific meaning that is understood in a particular culture or occupation, such as a thumbs-up gesture. Others, such as touching oneself or others, may be associated with anxiety, guilt, hostility, or suspicion. For example, interviewers are sometimes taught that a hand-to-face movement is a sign of deception.[31]

By one estimate, the human face can make 250,000 different expressions.[32] The Roman scholar Pliny the Elder wrote more than 2,000 years ago that "The face of man is the index to joy and mirth, to severity and sadness." Facial expressions are generally understood to have a particular meaning. For example, facial expressions communicating six emotions—happiness, sadness, anger, fear, surprise, and disgust—are recognized worldwide. Even when people try to suppress facial expressions, they may make very short expressions lasting a fraction of a second that will reveal true meaning.

Eye contact is a major regulator of conversation. Generally, eye contact suggests understanding and interest.[33] Seeking eye contact connotes the desire to open a conversation. Conversely, someone hoping to avoid communication—such as an unprepared student in class—will avoid eye contact. Also, some characteristic eye-contact patterns have specific meanings. For instance, the slow blink—a pattern in which an individual closes his or her eyes for two to four seconds and then slowly opens them—indicates doubt or suspicion. When combined with a condescending or impatient tone of voice, it communicates superiority or disinterest.

Posture is the way people position their bodies with respect to others. For example, if a customer's arms are relaxed and open and she leans forward as she talks to a salesperson, her posture reflects approval and acceptance of the salesperson's message. If she leans back with arms tightly crossed, her posture suggests rejection or disagreement.

Touch can convey warmth, understanding, and intimacy. Touch may also enhance positive feelings about the touching person and the situation. For example, studies show that when a store assistant, server in a restaurant, or product demonstrator lightly touched a customer on the arm, the customer saw the touching person more positively, had a more positive attitude toward the situation, and was more likely to comply with the toucher's suggestions.[34] Note, though, that this research involved casual touching of the arm. To the contrary, many other forms of touching may be resented, and unwanted touching can be a form of sexual harassment.[35]

When we encounter others, one of the first things we notice is the way they are dressed. Dress can convey characteristics such as image, mood, identity, power, wealth, and authority.[36] People who are dressed formally are better able to command respect. For instance, research has shown that pedestrians are more likely to cross against traffic lights when led by a well-dressed person than when led by a poorly dressed individual.[37] People in positions of authority, such as doctors and police officers, often wear distinctive uniforms to reinforce their status. In addition, we all wear our own uniforms, that is, the particular way we choose to dress to communicate something about ourselves to others. Because of the importance of dress, many companies have a dress code to ensure that appropriate signals are conveyed to customers and others, and violation of a dress code may even be a cause for dismissal.[38] Increasingly, though, companies are relaxing dress codes in order to create a more relaxed and egalitarian climate. Others are instituting "dress-down days," often Fridays, when employees can wear more casual clothes.[39] These dress-down days are very stressful for many people. Deciding what to wear— once not a real option—has become complex, controversial, and perplexing. Many companies are, in fact, quite formal about what is considered to be acceptable casual dress. For example, Southland Corp. put on a "fashion show," with employees modeling what is—and isn't—acceptable to wear for casual day, compiled a two-inch-thick binder of catalog clippings, with sections marked "appropriate" and "inappropriate," and formed an eight-member "Employee Dress Code Committee" to resolve disputes over questionable dress.[40] Casual dress day at American General Corp. got the ax after employees arrived dressed as—among other things—Santa Claus, the Easter Bunny, and a duck.

Proxemics is the use of interpersonal space (that is, proximity) to convey status or degree of intimacy. Sitting at the head of a table conveys status, standing close to another conveys intimacy, and sitting behind a desk (as opposed to alongside it) indicates a superior–subordinate relationship. Two elements of proxemics—personal space and seating arrangements—are especially relevant in organizational settings.[41] We'll discuss proxemics in more detail in Chapter 12.

Skills Practice 5-5 is designed to help you see the role of nonverbal sources of information in the overall communication process. Remember, nonverbal communication can provide large amounts of information to the receiver, so it must be actively managed along with verbal forms of communication.

Skills Practice 5-5
Understanding and Managing Nonverbal Communication

Skill Level: **Basic**

Skill Objective
To develop skill in managing nonverbal forms of communication.

Procedure
1. Get into groups of 3–5 people.
2. As a group, brainstorm a list of general guidelines or "rules of thumb" for effectively managing each of the following forms of nonverbal communication:
   > Dress
   > Touch
   > Posture
   > Eye Contact
   > Facial Expressions
   > Hand Movements
   > Paralanguage
   > Proxemics

Focus on trying to represent your guidelines in the form of "action steps" or specific things that can be done.

Discussion Questions
1. What kinds of things could be done to translate the "rules of thumb" you developed into actual practice? That is, how could you use the ideas you came up with in order to be more effective as a manager or supervisor?
2. What should be the relationship between your use of verbal and nonverbal communication? What can you do to establish this relationship?
3. What would be some general guidelines for managing nonverbal communication when you deal with many different types of people, that is, different genders, races, ethnicities, or functional backgrounds (e.g., marketing, engineering)?
4. What would be some general guidelines for managing nonverbal communication when you are a manager in a cross-cultural context?

Web Wise

Nonverbal Communications Exercises

The following "Exploring Nonverbal Communication" site provides a variety of very interesting nonverbal communications exercises that ask you to make choices about meanings of gestures, the sincerity of a smile, and other issues in nonverbal communications.

http://zzyx.ucsc.edu/~archer/

ELECTRONIC COMMUNICATION

Computers are transforming communication. In this section we will consider e-mail, the Internet and the World Wide Web, teleconferencing and video-conferencing, and e-commerce.

E-MAIL

The exploding technology of *electronic mail,* or *e-mail,* the electronic transmission of written information, provides a very fast, inexpensive, and efficient means of communicating. Nestle SA, a Swiss-based multinational food corporation, installed an electronic mail system to connect its 60,000 employees in 80 countries. Nestle's European units can use the system to share information about production schedules and inventory levels in order to ship excess products from one country to another.[42] About 70 million employees in the United States now use e-mail, and they send billions of e-mails daily.[43] E-mail can help speed up communications, build and maintain business relationships, cut mailing costs, and create a sense of community.[44] Programs can now translate e-mail messages into a variety of languages, and wearable PCs let users read e-mail while on the move.[45] Soon, the vast majority of mobile phones will offer Internet access.[46] Here are some simple guidelines for using e-mail.

> **Be careful.** Both sending and receiving e-mail demand caution. Don't send sloppy or hastily reasoned messages simply because e-mail seems informal. Also, a simple "slip of the finger" can be devastating. For example, a corporate chief executive hit the wrong key while on a public e-mail network and misaddressed a note intended for the firm's head of product development. As a result, he sent a total stranger the company's product plans for the next year and a half.[47] As yet another reason for caution, opening e-mail attachments can introduce harmful viruses to a computer, sometimes causing irreparable damage.

> **Recognize privacy issues.** "Privacy in the digital age is dead."[48] While people often treat e-mail as private and impermanent, it actually may remain on servers for years, and it can later be made available for public inspection, criticism, or ridicule. Many companies routinely monitor employees' e-mail, and the e-mail administrator of most systems has the ability to read all e-mail messages. In fact, someone has called using e-mail the digital equivalent of shouting out the window. As such, don't write anything in e-mail messages that you would not want to be widely read.[49]

> **Keep messages clear, simple, and short.** Use a subject line that clearly conveys the content of the message. Be concise. Some experts suggest that e-mails should not exceed 25 lines. Avoid lengthy attachments; they may take many minutes to download, and some readers' computer systems can't handle attachments at all. Also, resist the temptation to use fancy formatting, such as multiple fonts and colors—messages that look beautiful on your computer screen may be a jumbled mess when received.

> **Reply only to appropriate persons.** Resist the temptation to "reply to all" or to copy your message to everyone you can think of. Ask yourself who really needs the message.

> **Personalize your e-mail as appropriate.** E-mail doesn't give the opportunity for personal social interaction, including nonverbal communication. To help compensate for this, people sometimes use forms of emotional punctuation, called *smileys,* to convey their feelings. Smileys can add a personal touch to e-mails. However, they shouldn't be overused, and they may be inappropriate in some formal e-mails.[50]

> **Be considerate.** Avoid using e-mail to vent frustration and anger through hostile messages. This practice, known as *flaming,* can create a climate of distrust, fear, and anger.[51] Unfortunately, flaming is common, and e-mail is also sometimes used to harass others, including for sexual harassment and to make threats of violence or blackmail.[52] E-mail is more likely to be irresponsible and to contain profanity and negative sentiment than face-to-face communication. This is probably because e-mail is conveyed in the form of text by a person who is physically removed from the recipient and because e-mail messages are erroneously seen as fleeting in nature and thus as permitting greater freedom of expression and self-disclosure.[53] Because of these factors, "Netiquette"

(that is, *Net etiquette*) is especially important. Netiquette is addressed in Web Exercise 5-2.[54]

> **Check e-mail at least once a day.** Respond as quickly as possible to messages. If your response will be delayed, let the sender know you have received the message and when you will respond.

> **Manage your e-mail with folders and filters.** E-mail can lead to the equivalent of electronic junk mail, with employees receiving dozens of unwanted messages daily. Also, e-mail users often join lists to share information with people with common interests, such as project management, labor law, or communications. Remarkably, surveys reveal that an average office worker gets 190 messages daily.[55] Set up folders to organize e-mails. Use filters to eliminate junk e-mail and to transfer low-priority messages to designated folders.[56]

THE INTERNET AND THE WORLD WIDE WEB

In an IBM ad, a group of nuns is walking through a Prague convent; subtitles tell us that they are discussing their computers' operating system. One nun's face lights up as she says, "I'm dying to surf the net."[57] The "Net" referred to by the nun is the *Internet*—a worldwide collection of computer networks permitting access to libraries, news sources, and groups with special interests. Dubbed the "Information Superhighway" by the popular press, the Internet was born in 1969 when the ARPANET (Advanced Research Projects Agency Network) was developed under contract with ARPA, the Advanced Research Projects Agency of the U.S. Department of Defense. The ARPANET was constructed so researchers could share information with university, military, and defense contractors and to study how communications could be maintained in the event of nuclear attack.[58] When, after a series of developments, the National Science Foundation took over management of the Internet in the mid-1980s and subsequently increased the capacity of its circuits, the number of users exploded. The Internet is growing faster than any other telecommunications system ever built, including the telephone network.[59]

Perhaps the most exciting part of the Internet is the World Wide Web. The *World Wide Web,* or Web as it is sometimes called, is a collection of standards used to access the information available on the Internet.[60] A key feature is that Web documents include links to other Web documents. With the Web, users can leap from one computer database to another at the click of a mouse, following ideas, color photographs, interactive diagrams, sound, and video clips, all linked by a technology known as *hypertext.*[61] The Web was conceived in 1989 at the European Laboratory for Particle Physics (known as CERN, from an earlier French name), in Geneva, Switzerland. The creators saw it as a way to distribute and evaluate document-based information among high-energy physicists around the world. Since the development a few years later of Mosaic, software to navigate the Internet using the Web's coding system, and then of Netscape and other "browsers," growth of the Web has been dramatic.[62]

Companies are now taking advantage of the Web by developing corporate portals. *Corporate portals* provide access to internal company information via a Web browser. They take one of two forms.[63] Most common is a workplace community portal. This displays many types of information that may be interesting or important to employees, such as notices of employee gatherings

W e b   W i s e

Enquire Within Upon Everything

The World Wide Web was invented by Tim Berners-Lee in 1989. Berners-Lee's idea for the Web came from a Victorian book entitled *Enquire Within Upon Anything,* a volume full of all sorts of useful advice about a wide range of topics. To read Berners-Lee's views on the World Wide Web and the Internet, and to learn more about their histories, visit:

http://www.w3.org/People/ Berners-Lee-Bio.html/FAQ.html

The New Marketplace of Ideas

The Internet has become an electronic global village. Connected computer networks now permit individuals and businesses to communicate easily and inexpensively with others around the world. When the U.S. Supreme Court struck down the so-called Communications Decency Act, which would have regulated the content of material on the Internet, Justice John Paul Stevens wrote: "Through the use of chat rooms, any person with a phone line can become a town crier with a voice that resonates farther than it could from any soapbox. Through the use of Web pages, mail exploders, and newsgroups, the same individual can become a pamphleteer."* To read the full Supreme Court decision, go to:

http://www.ciec.org/SC_appeal/opinion.shtml

*For a discussion of the Supreme Court ruling, see J. Quittner, "Unshackling Net Speech," *Time*, July 7, 1997, pp. 28–29.

and information about job postings and benefits packages. The second form, taken by the new generation of portals, displays information from virtually all of the company's most important databases, including financials, sales and marketing, inventory, supply-and-demand tracking, human resources, procurement, and research and development. A Merrill Lynch report called portals "The Yahoo of company information." Data can easily be accessed, integrated, and entered into various applications. A wide range of companies, such as Staples, Inc., and General Electric Appliances, are installing portals to better access and manage information, cut costs, free up time for managers, and add to the bottom line. Du Pont estimates that it will save up to $66 million from the first phase of its portal.

TELECONFERENCING AND VIDEOCONFERENCING

As another example of electronic communication, *teleconferencing* permits a group of people to "confer" simultaneously via telephone or electronic mail. Teleconferencing that also has the capability to let participants see each other over video screens is called *videoconferencing.* Such technologies offer businesses tremendous savings in time, energy, and money. Many firms conduct sales meetings, editorial conferences, and job interviews via teleconference.[64] In addition, these systems enable companies to form work teams able to overcome the barriers of time and space. Dan Denardo, manager of global videoconferencing for Dow Chemical Company, says videoconferencing improves customer service, helps deliver products faster, and slashes travel costs. Denardo, who supervises more than 160 video cameras at Dow's headquarters, estimates the company saves more than $7 million annually on travel costs alone.[65] Further, videoconferencing permits meetings on the spur of the moment.

The price on videoconferencing is plummeting, with group videoconference rooms costing about $10,000 as of 1999.[66] In addition, monitor-top video systems were available as of 1999 in the range of $100.[67] It is estimated that there will be 2.1 million videoconferencing points in use by the year 2003.[68]

According to AT&T Bell Laboratories President John Mayo, videoconferencing components based on light waves should start to augment slower electronic parts by early in this century. This will permit seamless networks of data, voice, and moving pictures. In AT&T's vision, videoconferencing with built-in language translation across national borders will be as common as today's word processing programs.[69]

E-COMMERCE

E-commerce is defined as ". . . the sharing of business information, maintaining business relationships, and conducting business transactions by means of telecommunications networks."[70] As this definition suggests, e-commerce is more than buying and selling over the Web, though that aspect has certainly exploded in recent years. Instead, e-commerce involves using network communications technology to engage in a wide range of activities up and down the value-added chain, both within and outside the organization.[71] That is, it might include use of electronic communication technologies for such things as purchasing of materials, hiring employees, collaborative planning and scheduling of production with suppliers and customers, and much more.

FOCUS ON MANAGEMENT

LERNOUT AND HAUSPIE HAS THE WORLD TALKING*

Lerner and Hauspie, a fast-growing Belgian company, is the world's leading provider of speech and language technology products, solutions, and services to businesses and individuals. It is the firm's mission to break down language barriers through advanced translation technology and to enable people to interact by voice—in any language—with the machines that empower them. Through such enhanced communication, L&H believes people will lead richer, more fulfilling lives. Jo Lerner, cofounder and managing director of the firm, is one of the visionaries for Europe's information economy. In early 2000 he presented some of his views concerning developments in voice technology:

> By 2005, there will be 500 million devices in use containing speech-enabled systems to permit e-commerce by telephone.
> By the end of 2000, devices will be available to plug into the telephone to permit some forms of real-time language translation. Within 3–5 years you will be able to carry on a conversation with someone in Japan with real-time translation.
> In 2002, you will be able to talk to mobile devices as well as use touch screen options, and you will be one button away from intelligent Internet agents that will help you to shop, work, and play. These agents will have the same look and feel on your phone, in your car, or on your television screen.
> By 2005, your television will be Web enabled and your fridge will have a screen to call up your virtual assistant in the kitchen. You will be able to talk with anyone anywhere in the world by telephone with the help of real-time and highly accurate machine translation tools.

http://www.lhsl.com

*R. Evans, "The Value of Voice," *Communications International,* June 2000, pp. 43–48.

E-commerce can be initiated by business and aimed at business (business to business, or B2B), consumers (business to consumer, or B2C), or government (business to government, or B2G). It can be initiated by the consumer and aimed at business (consumer to business, or C2B), consumers (consumer to consumer, or C2C), or government (consumer to government, or C2G). It can be initiated by government and aimed at business (government to business, or G2B), consumers (government to consumers, or G2C), or government (government to government, or G2G). B2B transactions account for the majority of e-commerce sales volume and are projected to reach $4 trillion by 2003, while B2C transactions could reach $400 billion by that date. Figure 5-5 presents examples of each of these combinations.

FIGURE 5-5
Types of E-Commerce Sites

	To Business	To Consumer	To Government
Initiated by Business	Free Markets http://www.freemarkets.com	Buy.com http://www.buy.com	FedCenter.com http://www.fedcenter.com
Initiated by Consumer	Mob Shop http://www.mobshop.com	eBay http://www.ebay.com	GovWorks http://www.ezgov.com
Initiated by Government	Small Business Administration http://www.sba.gov	Washington, D.C., Site http://www.washingtondc.gov	Fed Services Site http://www.fedworld.gov/ fedservices/fedworld

Here are a few examples of the impact and promise of e-commerce.

> **Online retail sales.** Internet retailers (called *e-tailers*) are among the more visible players in the Internet economy. According to the U.S. Department of Commerce, U.S. consumers spent more than $7 billion on goods, services, and travel purchases online in just the first quarter of 1999. It is predicted that the number of households shopping online will reach 38 million by 2002.[72] The Web has revolutionized retailing in many ways, including by blurring the boundaries between types of companies. For instance, Amazon.com began as a bookseller and is now expanding far into other markets. Some e-tailers, such as Amazon.com, are Internet based (and known as "*dotcoms*"). Others are traditional firms, such as Dell and Barnes & Noble, that have developed a Web presence (these firms are sometimes referred to as "click-and-mortar" retailers). In the latter case, an emerging question is how to coordinate the efforts of the Web business and of the traditional retail element (known as the *legacy business*).[73] In addition, collections of retailers sometimes operate out of a common website in electronic malls, or "cybermalls."[74]

> **Online recruiting.** There are now dozens of major job sites on the Web; in 1999 about 10 percent of newly hired employees found their jobs on the Internet.[75] A 30-day classified ad in a major newspaper costs an average of $3,295, while a 30-day posting on a major job board averages just $167. Further, businesses can place job ads on the Web and start receiving résumés within minutes. Those résumés can then be forwarded to managers, screened out, or otherwise processed. In addition, companies can use the Web to offer job prospects a wealth of information about the job and company culture.

> **Collaborative planning.** An *extranet* is a Web-based platform that controls the exchange of data with outside parties. Companies are using extranets to share internal company information with outside parties, such as a manufacturer with its suppliers, distributors, and other collabo-

GLOBAL PERSPECTIVES

DOCOMO*

E-commerce in Japan is growing less rapidly than that in the United States and Europe, because many fewer people own computers. However, NTT DoCoMo may be Japan's last, best hope in the global Internet race. The company's name is based on the Japanese word for "anywhere." The firm's "I-mode" cell phones provide cheap and continuous wireless access to the Internet as well as voice-recognition technology. Users don't have to make new dial-up connections to get on the Internet; they are always connected as long as they have a signal and a charged battery. Subscribers can swap e-mail and pictures and access more than 4,000 specially formatted websites. It is said that there are three things a Japanese teenage girl won't leave home without: her six-inch platform shoes, touch-up toner for her hair color of the day, and her colorful I-mode phone (which is worn like jewelry). In part as a result, DoCoMo is now the world's most valuable cell phone company, with 6 million users, $5 billion in annual profits, and a market cap of more than $300 billion, as well as Japan's hottest stock.

http://www.nttdocomo.com/

*"Multinational Monitor," *Business Europe,* May 17, 2000, p. 3; D. Young and R. L. Wickham, "The Movers and Shakers of 2000," *Wireless Review,* June 1, 2000, pp. 18–26; "A High-Tech Surprise from Japan," *Business Week,* January 17, 2000, p. 118; and I. M. Kunii and S. Baker, "Amazing DoMoCo," *Business Week,* January 17, 2000, p. 24.

rators.[76] Extranets determine who has access to data and the nature of their access (for instance, whether they can edit data or only have viewing privileges). Heineken, with its headquarters in Europe, faced delays between order placement in the United States and delivery of 10–12 weeks.[77] To reduce that time, Heineken recently implemented an extranet to connect with its customers and suppliers. Called HOPS (Heineken Operational Planning System), the system allows for real-time forecasting and ordering interaction with distributors. Distributors log onto customized Web pages, enter identification and a password, and then can view sales forecasts and modify and submit orders by pressing a button. Order submissions are immediately available at the Heineken brewery in Europe, which can then adjust brewing and shipment schedules. HOPS has helped Heineken cut delivery times to distributors in half while reducing inventories and cutting costs. It also provides a calendar permitting Heineken to notify distributors of events and e-mail to broadcast new products, newsletters, or problems.

INFORMAL COMMUNICATION

Web Wise

Rumors of Satanism

Procter & Gamble Co. has struggled for 20 years to fight rumors that its moon-and-stars trademark is linked to Satanism. Lawsuits, changes in the P&G trademark, and responses to up to 200 concerned callers a day have not halted the persistent rumors.* Now P&G has gone to the Web to fight back. It has set up a website specifically to combat the rumors. The site contains a discussion of the history of the P&G moon-and-stars logo, claims that Amway distributors were spreading the rumors, and letters from the Billy Graham Evangelistic Association, Jerry Falwell, and the archbishop of Cincinnati (P&G's home town) refuting the rumors.†

http://www.pg.com/rumor/

*Z. Schiller, "P&G Is Still Having a Devil of a Time," *Business Week,* September 11, 1995, p. 46.

†N. Kulish, "Still Bedeviled by Satan Rumors, P&G Battles Back on the Web," *Wall Street Journal,* September 21, 1999, p. B1.

While formal communication channels are important, much information flows in other, officially unrecognized ways. *Informal communication* is information shared without formally imposed obligations or restrictions.[78]

The following Real-World Management Challenge focuses on the issue of how management should respond when negative misinformation about the organization is being distributed over the Internet. Read the material and think about what you would do if you encountered this type of situation.

Real-World Management Challenge

Responding to Misinformation About Your Company on the Internet

Many well-known companies have had to deal with false information and rumors about them that have been spread by disgruntled customers or former employees. For example, a Kmart employee who designed the company's original website was terminated for linking another website, with inappropriate material, to the corporate site. This employee subsequently created a Web page called "Kmart Sucks," which received thousands of hits from Web surfers. Tommy Hilfiger, the apparel designer, was the victim of a nasty Internet rumor that he had appeared on *The Oprah Winfrey Show* and made racist comments about Asians, Blacks, and Hispanics. Other companies, including McDonald's, Neiman Marcus, and Samsung Electronics, have experienced similar problems.

Suppose that you work for a company that has become the target of a smear campaign on the Internet that is designed to damage your company's image and to convince consumers not to do business with your firm. How would you respond to this situation? In addition, how could you prevent this kind of problem from recurring in the future?

In organizational settings, information that is communicated informally among employees is referred to as the *grapevine.* Over three-fourths of the information sent over the grapevine is accurate. However, because even one error can change the whole meaning of a message, such a figure may be misleading. Further, grapevine information is often incomplete, giving a partial picture. As a result, many people view the grapevine negatively. Studies show

G L O B A L   P E R S P E C T I V E S

THE ROLE OF THE GRAPEVINE

The importance of the grapevine varies with national culture. For example, the grapevine and associated rumors are especially important in Mexico. In the office, the grapevine is often the most important source for employees to find out about new changes, especially those affecting personnel. There are probably several reasons for this. For one thing, rumors tend to be formed when uncertainty is high and formal channels of communication fail to provide good information; these conditions prevail in Mexico. In addition, Mexico has a strong oral tradition, and Mexicans have developed a suspicious attitude toward "official" information.*

*I. Adler, "Inside the Rumor Mill," *Business Mexico,* November 1997, pp. 14–15.

that people see the grapevine as a primary source of information, but rank it very low as a preferred source.

Despite their problems, grapevines do fill needs. They often carry messages that formal systems do not. They are fast and flexible, and they provide messages that are understandable to employees. Further, the tendrils of the grapevine wind their way around often-formidable barriers, seeking out information from people in the know. Whatever the accuracy of information carried over the grapevine, employees tend to view it as accurate. Because of this, grapevine information is often powerful.

Whatever managers think of the grapevine, they must accept the fact that it exists. Smart managers try to learn who is on the grapevine and how it works. They act to reduce misunderstandings and other negative effects of the grapevine. They may, for instance, provide accurate information to squelch unfounded rumors. They may also harvest the grapevine, using it to get feedback about employee attitudes and ideas. Managers may also use the grapevine as a message channel to carry information that is somehow inappropriate for formal channels.

Skills Practice 5-6 will help you to recognize the value of informal communication in organizations and to develop some strategies for managing it more effectively.

Skills Practice 5-6
Managing Informal Communication

Skill Level: **Basic**

Skill Objective
To develop skill in managing informal communication in organizations more effectively.

Procedure
Go through the following steps to develop some general strategies for managing informal communication:

1. Identify the work unit(s) you will use as a focus for this exercise.
2. Brainstorm some specific strategies for enhancing informal communication with respect to the work units you just identified. Try to be as creative as possible.

3. Evaluate your ideas and decide on three to five specific strategies you would like to implement within your work unit.
4. Develop a list of the steps you would take to support the implementation of your strategies.
5. Finalize your plan into a concise summary of your strategies for enhancing informal communication.

Discussion Questions

1. In what ways can informal communication contribute to the success of a work unit beyond the use of formal methods of communication? That is, why should we care about managing informal communication?
2. What might be some barriers in a "real-world" organization to the successful implementation of the strategies you identified?
3. What are the managerial implications of this exercise for you as a future manager?

COACHING AND COUNSELING

One key function of communication is that of coaching employees to improve their performance and career development. Here are some guidelines for effective coaching.[79]

> **Create a situation where you are prepared to coach and the employee is open to coaching.** Develop a climate of trust and mutual respect where employees feel open to share their views, needs, and concerns and to try new ideas.
> **Use reflective listening—focus both on words and their emotional content.** Facilitate self-discovery by letting employees think for themselves and present their opinions. Ask, "What do you think?"
> **Talk to your employees, not at them.** Avoid phrases like "You should . . ." and "I want . . ." and instead ask questions such as "What can we do about this?" and "How can we get this done?"
> **Value different perspectives.** Try to understand the differing motivations, work values, goals, and capabilities of individual employees. Learn what tasks interest them, what they find difficult, and to what they aspire.
> **Mutually identify goals.** Focus on behaviors rather than attitudes; behaviors can be changed, while attitudes tend to be inflexible. If you feel an employee has a "bad attitude," give feedback on behaviors that might be changed rather than criticizing the attitude.
> **Ask questions.** Use questions to open new possibilities, explore perceptions and assumptions, and provide new ways of examining the same information.
> **Give useful feedback.** Focus both on outcome feedback and on how behavior change can lead to improved outcomes. Ask the employee what he or she thinks should be worked on. Then suggest one of more of those areas on which the employee might concentrate.
> **Track, follow through on your promises, and reward improved behavior.** Recognize and reinforce changed behavior.

B O T T O M   L I N E

The Bottom Line: Developing Coaching Skills

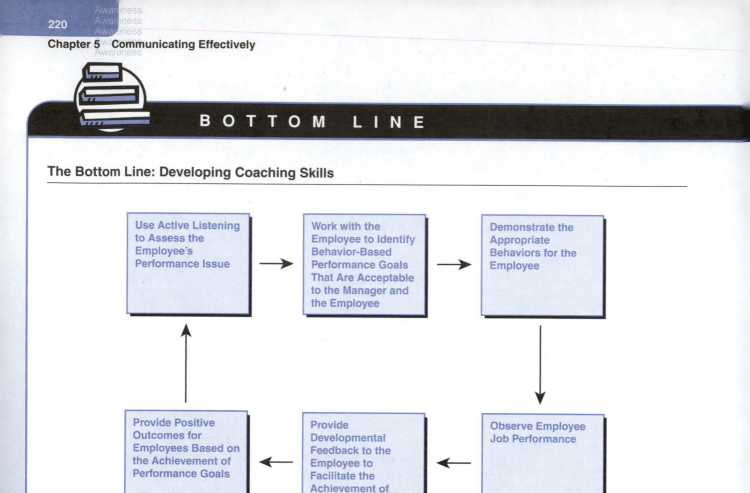

The step-by-step process model shown in the nearby Bottom Line identifies the basic actions that a manager would take in order to use coaching skills to handle job performance issues in an organizational setting.

GUIDELINES FOR CROSS-CULTURAL COMMUNICATION

Interdisciplinary teams bring together individuals with different training, expectations, experience, and attitudes. These differences in background are one reason for communication problems in teams. But if teams made up of individuals from the same company (or at least the same country) have difficulty communicating, you can imagine how much greater the differences and problems that occur when representatives of different cultures must work together. Here are some guidelines for more effective cross-cultural communication.

> **Learn all you can about the other party's culture.** Sometimes a person thinks he or she is communicating well but is too ignorant of the message receiver's culture to know that he or she is not. For example, communications professors in the United States tend to emphasize the need for *writer-responsible* written work. This means the writer takes

responsibility for making the message so simple and transparent that the receiver could not possibly read in anything other than the direct message. But in Chinese society, communication, including business communication, is much more indirect.[80] Chinese communications are intended to have more than one level of meaning and interpretation. Unlike countries such as the United States and Canada, which are considered to be relatively low-context cultures, countries of the Pacific Rim are high-context cultures. In a *high-context culture,* the real meaning of the message is immersed in the context of the communication.[81] In such a culture, the burden is placed on the receiver to uncover the full meaning of the message from the context in which it was sent; the sender provides pieces of a puzzle, and the receiver must provide the missing links. In a *low-context culture,* the fundamental meaning of the message is in the explicit statement made. Therefore, translating from one language to another or writing a business letter in one culture versus the other involves much more than substituting Chinese for English words.

> **Try to speak the language.** We learn much about a culture, and certainly facilitate communication, by speaking its language. By speaking the language—even if haltingly—we are more likely to recognize subtle nuances of meaning, to avoid gaffes, and to show a sense of caring and commitment. Lack of adequate knowledge of another language can lead to many problems. Horror stories even of "simple" translation are common. Coca-Cola had to change the name of its soft drink in China after discovering that in Chinese the words mean "Bite the wax tadpole." The new name translates to "May the mouth rejoice." Microsoft Corp. had to issue apologies after it released a Spanish-language version of its Word 6.0 program. The thesaurus accompanying the program suggested that "vicious" and "perverse" could substitute for *lesbian* and that "bastard" is a synonym for *people of mixed race.*[82]

Children in many European and Asian countries begin learning English in elementary school. In the last three decades more than 40 million Japanese have taken the Society for Testing English Proficiency (STEP) exam to demonstrate their competence in the English language. In addition, many thousands annually take proficiency exams in Korean, Indonesian, and—increasingly—Chinese.[83] American business students have only recently been realizing the benefits of learning a second, and perhaps a third, language. The more progressive colleges of business have developed language classes to meet the special needs of international commerce. For example, some students can now take a course in Italian for Business.[84] Instead of reading classics of Italian literature, they read Italian advertisements and learn in class how to open a bank account or apply for a credit card in Italy.

> **Challenge your stereotypes and assumptions.** Even when a person speaks the language, stereotypes and assumptions can get in the way of good communication. To avoid this, constantly challenge your own stereotypes about the culture when dealing with another society.[85] The goal is to replace your original assumptions and beliefs about the society in question (often acquired from watching movies or television) with information received from actual members of that society. If you do not

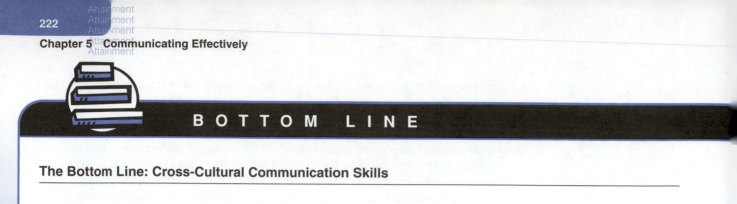

BOTTOM LINE

The Bottom Line: Cross-Cultural Communication Skills

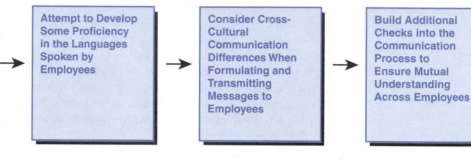

Study the Communication Style, Customs, Norms, and Taboos of Employees' Cultures → Attempt to Develop Some Proficiency in the Languages Spoken by Employees → Consider Cross-Cultural Communication Differences When Formulating and Transmitting Messages to Employees → Build Additional Checks into the Communication Process to Ensure Mutual Understanding Across Employees

challenge your stereotypes, you may find that you have unknowingly offended an international business representative.

> **Withhold evaluation.** In your interactions with people of other cultures, try to gather facts while avoiding evaluation. Too often, we interpret words or behaviors from the perspective of our own culture. Put on the other party's hat (or beret, fez, conch hat, bowler, sombrero, or whatever) and try to understand the situation from his or her position.

The step-by-step procedure presented in the nearby Bottom Line shows the basic actions a manager should take to handle cross-cultural communication issues effectively when working with people from other cultures in multinational teams and/or organizations.

Skills Practice 5-7 will give you a number of opportunities to analyze cross-cultural differences in communication within a variety of business settings.

Skills Practice 5-7
Managing Cross-Cultural Communication

Skill Level: Challenging

Skill Objective
To develop skill in managing communication in a cross-cultural context.

Procedure
1. Form groups of three to five people.
2. Assign one scenario to each group.
3. The task of each group is to develop a set of steps it would take to handle the issue of cross-cultural communication in relation to its particular scenario. Be as specific as possible in developing your guidelines.
4. Make a brief 3–5-minute presentation of your plan to the class for discussion purposes.

Mini-Case 1—"Up a Creek Without a Paddle"
You are the marketing manager at a U.S. computer corporation that designs and manufactures personal computers, software applications, mainframe computers, and computer

peripherals. You have been asked by your boss to pick up a group of five Chinese businessmen at the local airport. Your company is attempting to negotiate a deal with this Chinese company to become one of their major suppliers of computer peripherals (e.g., disk drives, modems). If the deal can be made, this would provide your firm with a tremendous opportunity for long-term growth.

The major obstacle you face is that although the Chinese businessmen you are meeting speak some English, they are not fluent in English. On the other hand, you don't know a word of Chinese.

What would be your plan for overcoming the communication problems you are sure to encounter in this situation?

Mini-Case 2—"Leading a Global Team"

You are a manager of a U.S. multinational corporation based in Chicago, Illinois. Your firm specializes in offering management consulting services (e.g., information technology solutions, change management, total quality) to clients all over the world.

You have just been assigned to lead a newly formed consulting team that will work with a client in France on managing a merger or acquisition. The composition of your team is multinational, consisting of consultants from France, India, Brazil, Japan, and the United States. Although everyone on the team is fluent in English, there are many "stylistic differences" in communication.

Although the multinational diversity on your team is a strength in many ways, you know that you will need to work hard to maintain effective communication with the various team members.

What would be your plan for dealing with the communication issues in this situation?

Mini-Case 3—"The Yankee in Jakarta"

You are a U.S. expatriate from a San Francisco–based consumer food and beverage company. You have been assigned to assume the manager position at a new marketing office in Jakarta, Indonesia. The objective of this new office is to capitalize on the emerging food products market in Indonesia and Southeast Asia. There are 20 local Indonesians (mostly professionals with college degrees) who report to you.

Fortunately, you are semifluent in the Indonesian language. In addition, your staff understands a fair amount of English. The key challenge is that your communication style is very direct and explicit (characteristic of a low-context culture), whereas your staff's communication style is very indirect and implicit (characteristic of a high-context culture). You realize that the differences in communication styles will create some significant challenges for you and your staff.

What would be your plan for dealing with the communication issues in this situation?

TOP TEN LIST: KEY POINTS TO REMEMBER

HOW TO COMMUNICATE EFFECTIVELY

10. Stay focused on communicating a very specific idea to your receiver(s).

9. Make sure that your message captures the key meaning of your idea.

8. Consider the type of message and the communication style of your receiver(s) when sending your message.

7. Analyze verbal and nonverbal cues from the sender when receiving a message.

6. Establish and maintain communication networks to create formal communication linkages and to institutionalize key patterns of interaction.

5. When making presentations, be especially concerned with adapting your message to characteristics of your audience.

4. Use active listening to test your understanding of what others are communicating to you.

3. Take steps to encourage more informal interaction among your employees and between your work unit and other key players in your organization.

2. Be sensitive to differences in communication styles across cultures.

1. Actively manage communication with your employees to keep them up to date on issues that affect them.

QUESTIONS FOR REVIEW AND REFLECTION

REVIEW QUESTIONS

1. What are the four primary functions of communication?
2. Describe each of the steps in the communication process.
3. Describe eight key dimensions of communication channels.
4. Draw three communications networks (e.g., wheel, circle, star), and indicate how they are likely to differ in terms of the satisfaction of each of the members, the speed of decision making, and the ability to deal with complex tasks.
5. Identify and briefly discuss five major barriers to communication.

6. Identify three forms of upward communication in organizations and three forms of downward communication.
7. Provide seven guidelines for effective speaking.
8. Provide seven guidelines for active listening.
9. Give five functions of nonverbal communications and eight forms of nonverbal communication.
10. Discuss eight guidelines for effective use of e-mail.
11. Identify nine guidelines for coaching and counseling.
12. Discuss four steps to effective cross-cultural communication.

CRITICAL THINKING QUESTIONS

1. In anticipation of a pending merger between their firm and another, employees have been showing signs of growing stress and concern. Many are worried about whether they will lose their jobs, face cuts in pay and benefits, or otherwise be hurt by the merger. Management has communicated nothing to employees about likely consequences of the merger, saying, "We don't know everything ourselves yet about how things will play out." How might you advise management regarding its response?

2. A human resources manager refuses to use e-mail, saying it doesn't offer an opportunity for nonverbal communication. Take a position either in support of or in opposition to her view. In defending your position, be sure to indicate arguments in support of the position and your anticipated reactions to criticisms of the position.

3. You are the founder of a small computer software company that derives most of its revenue from a video-editing program. The program has been commercially successful, but you have learned that a few users have experienced problems and have apparently suf-

fered damage to many of their video files as a result. You are concerned that if you notify other adopters of the problems and provide either a "patch" to fix the bug or a replacement program, the publicity could cripple sales. How would you proceed? What might be some dangers associated with your proposed course of action?

4. Your company is concerned about anecdotal evidence that employees are abusing their Internet access, "surfing" the Web for sports and entertainment sites during work hours. A number of alternatives have been proposed, including:
   > Prohibit Internet access during work hours.
   > Monitor employees' Internet use with surveillance software.
   > Place "blocking" software on the company's computer network to severely restrict access to certain types of sites.
   > Develop a policy on appropriate Internet use, and put employees on an honor system to follow the policy.
   > Do nothing.

Select one of these options—or develop an alternative of your own. Justify your choice, and indicate how you would notify employees of your selected option.

5. Management is aware that informal communication—the grapevine—is rampant in the organization. Rumors about pending events, "leaks" of management plans, gossip about office romances, and torrents of other information are swelling the grapevine and extending its tendrils. During a recent meeting of the top management team, one manager recounted a story he had overheard two employees discussing. He expressed concern that the story, which contained sexual innuendoes, could be viewed as contributing to a hostile work environment and could potentially lead to charges of sexual harassment against the firm. "We need to stamp out these sorts of stories," he argued. Another manager responded with caution, saying there was no way to stop informal communications and that any management action could lead to a backlash. Yet another said management should somehow "tap" the grapevine, asking a trusted employee to pass on to management any informal communications that might be viewed as inappropriate or harmful. What would be your inputs to this discussion?

6. As Director of Training you are committed to making employees aware of cross-cultural issues and have implemented related training and education programs. However, several employees have vocally complained that this sort of "touchy-feely stuff" is a waste of time. "I'm planning to work right here in Dubuque for the rest of my career," one said. How might you respond to such concerns from employees who anticipate no international assignments?

EXPERIENTIAL EXERCISES

WEB EXERCISE 5-1

Go to the following site, titled "A Beginner's Guide to Japan":

http://www.shinnova.com/part/99-japa/abj17-e.htm

On this page, you will be able to access a wide variety of information about Japan and its language and culture and about traveling and doing business in Japan. In the "Culture" section, click on "Nonverbal Communication." Write a two-page memo to your boss, who will soon be traveling to Japan. In your memo, discuss the roles in Japan of silence and the meaning of specific facial expressions, touching, and gestures. Also, indicate how objects are shown respect in Japan.

WEB EXERCISE 5-2

Etiquette is important any time we communicate. As we have seen in this chapter, electronic mail offers wonderful opportunities for communication as well as unique challenges. Etiquette—in this case, Net etiquette, or "Netiquette"—is especially critical with e-mail. Conduct a Web search on "Netiquette," and prepare a one-page memorandum giving 10 guidelines for Netiquette. One excellent Netiquette resource can be found at:

http://www.dtcc.edu/cs/rfc1855.html

CASE 5-1
PROFILE OF LAWRENCE WEINBACH, MASTER COMMUNICATOR

Background
Lawrence Weinbach is the president and chief executive officer of Unisys Corporation, a leading computer software and hardware services firm. Previously, Mr. Weinbach was a managing partner and chief executive of Andersen Worldwide. He is a graduate of the Wharton School of Business at the University of Pennsylvania.

Weinbach received the 1999 Excellence in Communication Leadership Award for the effectiveness of his communication strategy in achieving a turnaround in employee morale and productivity and corporate financial performance.

Strategies for Effective Communication

Weinbach has always maintained that effective communication skills are absolutely critical for the success of any executive or manager in an organization. At the time that he assumed his leadership role at Unisys in 1997, the company was not performing well and employee morale was low. In response to this situation, Weinbach set out to revive the company based on a comprehensive communication strategy. He hit the road to talk to employees about their concerns and ideas for improving Unisys. He also used this opportunity to explain his plans for Unisys to employees. In the end, he spoke to approximately 12,000 employees.

Weinbach encouraged all Unisys employees to send their ideas to him. He was a strong believer that the best ideas for improvement came from "the field." The response from employees was tremendous—he received 4,500 e-mail messages in six weeks. Weinbach personally responded to a large percentage of these messages.

Weinbach implemented an "Ask Larry" feature on the company's intranet so that he could respond to general questions from employees. In addition, he created a company newsletter that was sent out on a regular basis in order to keep employees "in the loop" on issues that pertained to them.

This approach to communication has also been extended to dealing with Unisys's shareholders. Weinbach has always maintained open lines of communication with shareholders. For example, when he first became president and CEO, he sent a letter to shareholders introducing himself and encouraging them to write to him if they had any comments, concerns, or suggestions. Weinbach personally responded to these messages.

At the corporate level, Weinbach coordinated communication issues by hiring a vice president of corporate communications who reported directly to him. This corporate communications executive worked closely with Weinbach to ensure that Weinbach was effectively addressing internal and external communications with employees, customers, shareholders, etc.

Weinbach's Advice for Improving Communication Skills

Weinbach offers the following tips for future managers and executives in terms of improving communication skills.

> Be consistent in your message when communicating with people.
> Be direct when communicating both good news and bad news.
> Always answer questions presented to you—"No comment" responses are unacceptable.
> Be caring and available for your employees. This will build the trust, rapport, and loyalty among employees that are needed for modern organizations that emphasize empowerment and decentralization.
> Always keep your vision of the company in mind in managing internal and external communications.

Discussion Questions

1. Why is Weinbach an effective communicator?
2. Which principles of communication discussed in this chapter does Weinbach effectively implement at Unisys?
3. What are the practical implications of Weinbach's communication strategy for you as a future manager?

Read about Lawrence Weinbach at:

http://www.unisys.com/news/releases/1997/sep/weinbach_bio.html

Source: G. Gordon, "Wow! This Guy Can Communicate!" *Communication World*, August/September 1999, pp. 17–20.

CASE 5-2
CRISIS MANAGEMENT COMMUNICATIONS AT THE COCA-COLA COMPANY

Background

The Coca-Cola Company is the largest manufacturer, marketer, and distributor of nonalcoholic beverages in the world. It is generally considered to be the most recognized global brand among consumers as well. Its numerous brand names are sold in nearly 200 countries around the world. Coke's corporate headquarters is in Atlanta, Georgia. The company employs over 31,000 employees.

The Situation

In June 1999, 120 people in Belgium became ill (i.e., vomiting, headaches) after drinking Coca-Cola. More than 50 of these people, many of them children, needed to be hospitalized.

The Belgian health ministry immediately launched an investigation of the incident and demanded that Coke remove its other brands, such as Nestea and Minute Maid.

The governments in France, Spain, and the Netherlands also imposed bans on products produced by Coca-Cola.

Coke Management's Handling of the Crisis

Two days after the first reports that people were becoming ill from drinking Coke emerged, Coke withdrew 2.5 million bottles of Coca-Cola, Coca-Cola Light, Fanta, and Sprite. However, Coke still did not provide a formal explanation to the general public as to why drinking Coke had made the individuals sick. It also refused to establish and maintain an open dialogue with the Belgian Health Ministry immediately after the incident. Rather, it elected to launch its own independent, internal investigation of the issue.

About a week after the beginning of the crisis, Douglas Ivester, Coca-Cola's Chairman, issued an explanation and an apology. Specifically, he stated:

> I want to reassure our consumers, customers, and governments in Europe that the Coca-Cola company is taking all necessary steps.

Coke published its formal apology in Belgian newspapers, set up a consumer hotline to answer questions from customers, and offered to pay all medical bills for the individuals made sick by drinking Coke.

The two explanations Coca-Cola offered for the crisis were that a small number of bottles from its Antwerp plant contained defective carbon dioxide and that some cans from its French factory had been contaminated by a fungicide.

Coke indicated that a small number of the contaminated cans might still be on sale at small, independent retailers in the United Kingdom. The company stated that it had no plans to inform the general public of this issue because it believed that media coverage had already taken care of this.

The Aftermath

Coke management has received mixed reviews from analysts and customers in Europe for its handling of the Belgian crisis. Some analysts feel that Coke has done irreparable damage to its brand image and has lost the confidence of customers. Coke management, however, believes strongly that the company will rebound in Europe with no long-term negative impact on sales and profits resulting from the incident.

Discussion Questions

1. Evaluate Coke management's handling of the crisis in Belgium and other European countries. What did they do well? Where could they have improved?
2. Which specific principles of effective communication discussed in the chapter were either implemented or not implemented?
3. If you were the CEO of Coke at the time of this crisis, what would you have done to handle the crisis?
4. What are the practical implications of this case for you as a future manager?

http://www.thecoca-colacompany.com/

Source: S. Bell, "Coke Pays the Price of a Mishandled Crisis," *Marketing,* June 24, 1999, p. 15. "Coke's Hard Lesson in Crisis Management," *Business Week,* July 5, 1999, p. 102.

VIDEO CASE
BANK OF ALMA: A STUDY IN LISTENING AND COMMUNICATING

Running Time: 10:02

The Bank of Alma is a small community bank emphasizing customer service and individual attention. The video presents John McCormack, the bank's President and CEO, and other officers as they describe the importance of listening and communicating at the Bank of Alma and as they interact with customers. After viewing the video, answer the following questions.

1. Why are communications so important at the Bank of Alma?
2. What communications techniques are used at the Bank of Alma to provide personalized customer service?
3. What are some specific obstacles to effective communication in a bank setting?
4. What are some guidelines for good listening as practiced at the Bank of Alma?
5. How are nonverbal communications important at the Bank of Alma? What nonverbal communications do bank employees use in their interactions with customers?

LIGHTEN UP

BAD MICKEY

A hipo, a Wallenda, and an imagineer order drinks at a bar. They do a little work—edit a violin, nonconcur with a wild duck, take care of some bad Mickey—and then ask for the bill. "This is on the mouse," says one of the three. Who picks up the tab?

It's not uncommon to hear chatter like this from the mouths of corporate employees. Sometimes, translating it requires knowing the jargon, not of MBAs, industries, or regions, but of particular companies.

For instance, an employee at IBM who is fluent in IBM-speak knows that a "hipo" is an employee on the fast track to success—someone with "high potential." (According to one IBMer, an employee with low potential is known as an "alpo.") IBM-speakers don't disagree with their bosses—they nonconcur. And anyone who nonconcurs often and abrasively, but constructively, is a "wild duck" in IBM-speak. Former Chairman Thomas Watson, Jr., borrowed that tag from Kierkegaard.

Like other tribal entities, corporations develop their own dialects as a way of linking members of the tribe and delineating their ranks. "It has the double purpose of bonding the user to the group and separating the user from general society," says Robert Chapman, editor of the *New Dictionary of American Slang*. "It makes us feel warm and wanted. This works in any society—a company, a school, a family, a saloon."

Slang often occurs in offices where words are the company's business, such as newspapers and magazines. *Newsweek*'s top editors are known as *Wallendas*, after the famous family of aerialists—a reference to the precarious nature of their jobs. *Newsweek* writers also call each week's top story the "violin." A spokesman says that's because the story is supposed to "reflect the tone" of the news.

Walt Disney Co., one of the world's shrewdest manufacturers of cultural imagery, is a rare example of a company that has consciously invented its own jargon. It calls the division that plans its theme parks "Walt Disney Imagineering." At orientation sessions (at Disney University), new theme-park employees are carefully told to say they are "on stage" while at work and "backstage" while taking a break. They are also told to consider each other not as employees but as "cast members."

Jack Herrman, a former Disney World publicist, recalls that his colleagues would brand anything positive "good Mickey" and anything negative—like a cigarette butt on the sidewalk—"bad Mickey." He also remembers putting lunch on the Disney World expense account and calling it "on the mouse." "You're immersed in the jargon they impose upon you as a way of life," he says.[86]

SMILEYS

E-mail takes away much of the opportunity for nonverbal communication. You can't raise your voice, gesture, pound on the desk, or wink. You can, though, use *emoticons*—series of symbols that, when read sideways, resemble little faces and convey emotions. These emoticons are better known as *smileys*. There are thousands of smileys. Here is a sampling:

:-)	I'm just kidding
:8)	I'm a pig
:-(	I'm sad
:-o	I'm bored (yawn)
B-)	I'm cool

:-*	Kiss
:-#	My lips are sealed
:=8)	I'm a baboon
:-&	I'm tongue-tied
':-)	I accidentally shaved off one eyebrow
;-)	Wink
C=>:*'))	I'm a drunk demonic chef with a cold and a double chin[87]

To check out hundreds of smileys, go to:

http://members.aol.com/bearpage/smileys.htm

HAVE YOU HEARD?

Have you heard:

About the African consumers who were horrified by an American baby food company's packaging? When they saw a picture of a baby on the jar's label, they assumed the jar contained babies!

About the customer who picked up some fried chicken from a fast food outlet and discovered that an unusual-tasting piece was actually a batter-fried rat? The victim sued the restaurant and won a six-figure award.

That the Chevrolet Nova sold poorly in Spanish-speaking countries because its name translates as "doesn't go" in Spanish.

That colleges and universities have regulations specifying that a student whose roommate commits suicide will automatically receive a 4.0 grade point average for the current school term? The institutions believe that the stress caused by the suicide would make it impossible for the roommate to perform well in class, unfairly resulting in poor grades.

About the schoolchildren who were given cartoon character tattoos laced with LSD?

That an early experiment in subliminal advertising at a movie theater resulted in tremendously increased sales of popcorn and Coke?

That Finland once banned Donald Duck because he wears no pants?

About the thriving colony of large alligators that lives deep in the bowels of the New York City sewer system? Apparently, baby alligators brought back as pets from Florida by tourists were dumped into the sewers.

That colleges and universities have regulations specifying how long students must wait in the classroom before leaving if the instructor fails to appear and that these wait times vary depending upon the academic rank of the instructor?

That designer Tommy Hilfiger shocked the world when he appeared on *Oprah* and said, "If I knew that Blacks and Asians were going to wear my clothes, I would have never designed them"?

That rice thrown to wish newlywed couples well can kill birds? The rice expands explosively in the birds' stomachs.

If you've heard any of these things, you've heard an **urban legend.** Urban legends are compelling stories that appear mysteriously and spread spontaneously in varying forms. They often contain elements of humor or horror. And—like *all* of the preceding stories—they are often false (but persist nonetheless). To learn more about these urban legends and many others (and about some wild stories that actually *are* true), go to the Urban Legends Reference Pages at:

http://www.snopes2.com/

CHAPTER *Six*

MOTIVATING EFFECTIVELY

SKILLS OBJECTIVES

> To assess employee needs and develop strategies for increasing work motivation.

> To use operant learning techniques to facilitate the acquisition of desired employee behaviors.

> To use operant learning techniques to eliminate undesired employee behaviors.

> To set appropriate goals for employees that will increase work motivation.

> To use expectancy theory principles to increase work motivation, job performance, and job satisfaction.

> To use fairness theories to create a positive work environment and to increase work motivation.

> To design jobs that satisfy the active needs of employees and increase work motivation.

KNOWLEDGE OBJECTIVES

> Identify special challenges of motivating in the modern workplace.

> Understand the nature of motivation, including need theories and process theories of motivation.

> Be able to apply learning theory, including forms of learning, contingencies of reinforcement, and schedules of reinforcement.

> Understand key characteristics of effective goals.

> Understand how jobs can be designed to foster intrinsic motivation.

In Chapter 1 we discussed how the modern workplace is complex, ambiguous, changing, diverse, and global. In this new world of work, hierarchies are flatter, deadlines are shorter, teams are pervasive, employees must manage themselves, and technology is transforming the nature, pace, and possibilities of work. The new world of work demands speed, flexibility, creativity, cooperation, self-management, and political savvy. Facilitating effective behaviors has probably never been more difficult, and never more important. In this chapter we will cover a variety of topics and associated skills that can help you with these challenges. We will address issues relating to motivation, including understanding employee needs, applying learning theories, setting effective goals, linking effort to outcomes, and ensuring fairness.

Before reading on, complete Self-Assessment 6-1. It gauges your attitudes toward a variety of motivation-related issues we will address in this chapter. Then complete the Pre-Test Skills Assessment to get an indication of your initial level of skill in managing motivation.

Self-Assessment 6-1
Attitudes Toward Motivation

Answer the questions that follow regarding your attitudes toward motivating others in organizations. You will learn more from this chapter if you develop a greater awareness of your beliefs and feelings about work motivation. Answer each question as honestly as possible using the following response scale:

1 = Disagree Strongly
2 = Disagree Somewhat
3 = Neither Agree nor Disagree
4 = Agree Somewhat
5 = Agree Strongly

1. _____ For all practical purposes, managers cannot influence employee motivation.

2. _____ Employee motivation has surprisingly little impact on the company's bottom line.

3. _____ Money is the key motivator for the vast majority of workers.

4. _____ Most managers have a good understanding of what motivates their employees.

5. _____ Managers shouldn't have to worry about how to motivate their workers because workers should be motivated on their own.

6. _____ The most effective goal for employees is a "do your best" goal.

7. _____ Using rewards and incentives to motivate employees is morally wrong because it represents a form of bribery.

8. _____ Even highly motivated employees often aren't able to perform at a high level.

9. _____ While employees may be upset if they feel they are getting less than they deserve, they will be happy if they think they are getting more than they deserve.

Assessment
Assessment
Assessment
Assessment
233
Chapter 6   Motivating Effectively
Assessment

10. _____ The sole objective of job design is to maximize worker efficiency.

11. _____ Fairness in the treatment of employees has a significant impact on the level of worker motivation.

12. _____ Giving workers rewards and incentives for doing a good job is not generally feasible because it is too costly and time consuming to implement.

Pre-Test Skills Assessment
Motivation

As a way to assess your initial level of skill in managing motivation issues, please read the following scenario and develop an action plan for how you would handle this situation.

You are the Director of Operations at a major amusement park located in Orlando, Florida. You are experiencing some major problems with the employees you hired for the busy summer season. These are typically college students looking for summer employment, but others are local residents looking for part-time work and extra income to supplement the income from other jobs they hold. The jobs these seasonal employees perform include working in concessions, park maintenance, and ride operations. The hourly wages offered for these jobs are at or above the pay levels for other seasonal jobs in the area.

Your experience with the seasonal employees has revealed that many of these employees have an "I don't care" attitude, they want to do as little work as possible, they routinely come to work late or not at all, and they even leave their work areas during their shifts if they think there is nothing to do. Clearly, all of this is incompatible with the park's goal to create a fun-filled experience for its customers.

What would you do about this situation?

FUNDAMENTALS OF MOTIVATION

Motivation comes from the Latin *movere,* "to move." Motivation is about moving ourselves and others to some goal. Motivation requires arousal to initiate behavior toward a goal, direction to properly focus that behavior, and persistence to ultimately attain the goal. In the following sections we will examine a variety of approaches to motivation. Think of these as a toolkit. Some of the approaches (called *content theories* or *need theories*) help us understand what people want. Others—called *process theories*—focus on the motivation process. The questions asked and the corresponding theories we will address are:

> How can valued outcomes be tied to behaviors in order to reinforce desired behaviors and eliminate undesired behaviors? This is the domain of *learning theory.*

> How can goals be set to properly motivate behavior? This is the question addressed by *goal-setting theory.*

> What elements must be present in a situation if a person is to be motivated? *Expectancy theory* addresses this issue.

> What causes a person to see a situation as fair or unfair, and to be motivated accordingly? *Equity theory* and related theories of fairness examine this question.

> How can jobs be designed to make them intrinsically motivating? *Job characteristics theory* provides one useful approach to the design of jobs that are motivating.

It is important to recognize that these are not really competing theories. Instead, they provide an arsenal of tools to address the many aspects of motivation.

UNDERSTANDING EMPLOYEE NEEDS

All people have needs. A *need* is something that people require. *Satisfaction* is the condition of need fulfillment, such as when a hungry person eats or when a person driven by the desire for success finally achieves that goal. *Motivation* is the attempt to satisfy a need. The need satisfaction process is shown in Figure 6-1. The practice of management is largely concerned with motivating employees to work harder, more efficiently, and more intelligently. We will look at five theories of motivation and at how each relates to motivating people in the workplace. We will see that these theories have some similar implications for rewarding employees.

MASLOW'S NEED HIERARCHY

Psychologist Abraham Maslow did much of the classic work on motivation theory. He believed that the key to motivating people is understanding that they are motivated by needs, which are arranged in a hierarchy of importance. This hierarchy is known as *Maslow's need hierarchy* (see Figure 6-2).[1] Maslow theorized that people seek to satisfy needs at the lowest level of the hierarchy before trying to satisfy needs on the next-higher level. What needs

FIGURE 6-1

The Need Satisfaction Process

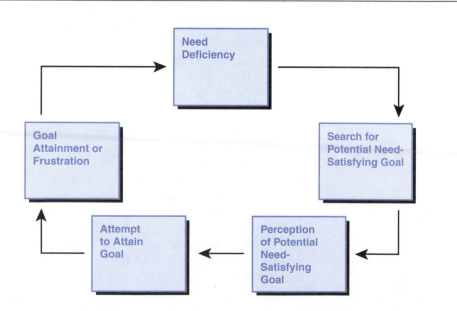

F I G U R E   6 - 2
Maslow's Need Hierarchy

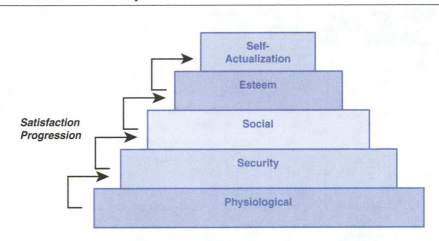

motivate a person depends on where that person is on the hierarchy at that time. In particular, Maslow believed that motivation should be examined in terms of five sets of needs:

1. *Physiological:* the need for food, sleep, water, air, and sex
2. *Security:* the need for safety, family stability, and economic security
3. *Social* or *affiliation:* the need to belong, to interact with others, to have friends, and to love and be loved
4. *Esteem:* the need for respect and recognition from others
5. *Self-actualization:* the need to realize one's potential, to grow, to be creative, and to accomplish

Maslow argued that as we satisfy any one of these five sets of needs, that set becomes less important to us and motivates us less. Eating, for example, satisfies the physiological need of hunger and leaves us less interested in food. In the same way, the need for affiliation and friendship is strongest for someone who feels excluded. Once this person makes friends, the need to belong becomes less important.

Climbing the Hierarchy   Maslow believed that these needs were arranged in a hierarchy from "lowest" to "highest," as shown in Figure 6-2. Maslow suggested that we "climb" the hierarchy. That is, we first satisfy our basic physiological needs. Only when we have done so are we motivated by the needs at the next-higher level of the hierarchy: the need for safety and security. When this group of needs is met, we move on to the next level, and so on. This move up the hierarchy as needs are satisfied is called *satisfaction progression.*

Lessons from Maslow's Hierarchy   Maslow's view of motivation shows that people have a variety of needs. People work for many reasons besides the paycheck that buys them food and shelter. They work so that they can be with others, gain respect, and realize their potential. Management must consider these needs when it designs reward systems for employees. Also, Maslow's hierarchy emphasizes that people differ in the needs that are currently most important to them. For example, a worker faced with heavy mortgage payments

Web Wise

The Official Abraham Maslow Publications Site

Maslow's writing has gained new interest thanks to the Internet. His book *Eupsychian Management* was published in 1965 but didn't sell well and soon went out of print. In the early 1990s, the book was posted on a popular website, and its views on enlightened management and self-actualization struck a responsive cord. It was republished in 1998 as *Maslow on Management.**

http://www.maslow.com/index.html

**For excerpts from* Maslow on Management, *see "The Enlightened Manager's Guidebook,"* Inc., *1998, 20, pp. 44–45+.*

may focus primarily on security needs. Another, with the mortgage paid off, may be more concerned about social needs. While the former employee might be strongly motivated by money, the latter may be more motivated by being included in a group. Finally, the hierarchy also makes it clear that need importance and need satisfaction are very different things—need importance (which drives motivation) often flows from dissatisfaction.

Maslow's need hierarchy provides useful perspectives for understanding motivation, and it has been widely accepted. However, more recent research suggests that it is only partially correct. For instance, satisfying needs at the top of the hierarchy generally does not lead to a decrease in motivation. Instead, people who are able to self-actualize become *more* motivated to take on self-actualizing activities. Further, instead of five sets of needs, people's needs seem to cluster in just two or three sets, as discussed later. Also, the climb up the hierarchy is rather unpredictable; once we've satisfied needs at the lowest levels, needs at any of the other levels may become more important to us.

ALDERFER'S ERG THEORY

Maslow's need hierarchy provided an important starting point for an improved theory of human needs. Clayton Alderfer developed the *existence– relatedness–growth (ERG) theory,* which revised Maslow's theory to make it consistent with research findings concerning human needs.

There are three key differences between Alderfer's ERG theory and Maslow's need hierarchy. First, since studies have shown that people have two or three sets of needs rather than the five Maslow hypothesized, Alderfer collapsed his needs into three sets:

> **Existence needs.** These include all forms of material and physical desires.
> **Relatedness needs.** These include all needs that involve relationships with others. Relatedness needs include anger and hostility as well as friendship. For instance, we may feel the need to yell at one person and befriend another. Isolation from others would cause deprivation of relatedness needs in either case.
> **Growth needs.** These include all needs involving creative efforts that people make toward themselves and their environment.

Alderfer revised Maslow's theory in other ways as well. First, he argued that the three need sets form a hierarchy only in the sense of increasing abstractness, or decreasing concreteness. As we move from existence to relatedness to growth needs, the ways to satisfy the needs become less and less concrete.

Second, Alderfer recognized that, while satisfying our existence and relatedness needs may make them less important to us, such is not the case for growth needs. Instead, our growth needs become increasingly important as we satisfy them. As we are able to be creative and productive, we raise our growth goals and are again dissatisfied until we satisfy these new goals. Recall that this is consistent with the evidence we reviewed concerning Maslow's need hierarchy.

FIGURE 6-3
Alderfer's ERG Theory

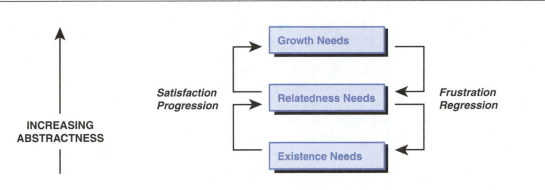

Finally, Alderfer reasoned that we are likely to focus first on needs that can be satisfied in concrete ways. We then attend to those with more abstract means of satisfaction. This is similar to Maslow's idea of satisfaction progression. However, Alderfer added the idea of frustration regression. *Frustration regression* occurs when our inability to satisfy needs at a particular level in the hierarchy causes us to regress and focus on more concrete needs. If we are unable to satisfy our growth needs, we will "drop back" and focus on relatedness needs. If we are unable to satisfy our relatedness needs, we will focus on existence needs. Alderfer's needs, as well as satisfaction progression and frustration regression, are illustrated in Figure 6-3. The combination of satisfaction progression and frustration regression can result in cycling as we focus on one need, then another, then back again.

MCCLELLAND'S MANIFEST NEEDS
Another way to look at motivation was offered by management theorist David McClelland. Whereas Maslow argued that people were born with a particular set of needs, which become more or less important over time depending on their satisfaction, McClelland believed that needs were acquired through the interaction of the individual with his or her environment.[2] Because these needs are not innate but rather become apparent over time, they are referred to as *manifest needs.* McClelland focused primarily on three manifest needs: the need for achievement, the need for affiliation, and the need for power over others.

> **Need for achievement.** People with a strong *need for achievement* want to do well no matter what goal they pursue. They also desire personal responsibility and want quick feedback about how well they have done at a given task. Some jobs, such as those in sales, are best for people with a strong need for achievement because of the responsibility and feedback they provide. Strong need for achievement, however, is not necessary in all work situations. For example, McClelland tested a large number of scientists, including several Nobel Prize winners, and found them to be only about average in need for achievement.[3] He rea-

soned that people with high need for achievement would not be drawn to such jobs, since research is conducted over many years and feedback may be very slow.

McClelland argued that the need for achievement can be developed in people by getting them to believe that they can change and by helping them to set personal goals. This process also includes learning to "speak the language of achievement." By this we mean that people can be taught to think, talk, and act as if they were achievement oriented.

In practice, McClelland was successful in developing the need for achievement. For example, after he conducted training sessions for 52 businesspersons in Kakinada, India, the achievement activity of the trainees nearly doubled while that of people who couldn't participate in the programs because of space constraints remained about the same.[4] Achievement activity meant starting a new business or sharply increasing company profits. One trainee raised enough money to put up the tallest building in Bombay—the Everest Apartments.

> **Need for affiliation.** The *need for affiliation* is the desire to establish and maintain friendly and warm relations with other people, much like Maslow's social need. People with a strong need for affiliation welcome tasks requiring interaction with others, while those having less of this need may prefer to work alone.

> **Need for power.** The *need for power* is the desire to control other people, to influence their behavior, and to be responsible for them.[5] McClelland saw the need for achievement as most important for entrepreneurs and the need for power as most important for managers of large organizations. Those who have a strong need for power can try to dominate others for the sake of dominating, deriving satisfaction from conquering others. Or they can satisfy their need for power through means that help the organization, such as leading a group to develop and achieve goals. McClelland felt that the need for power, when exhibited in ways that help the organization, was the most important factor in managerial success. People who have a strong need for achievement might be overly concerned with personal achievement, and those with a strong need for affiliation might not take necessary actions if they could offend the group.

Lessons from McClelland's Perspective McClelland's work gives us an expanded view of workers' needs. It also suggests that appropriate training might actually develop employees' needs in ways that could benefit both their careers and the organization. While Maslow essentially viewed needs as buckets to be filled, McClelland saw them as seeds to be grown. This is an important difference from Maslow's theory. Also, McClelland's perspective helps identify the characteristics of people who may be most suitable for particular kinds of jobs in organizations.

IMPLICATIONS OF NEED THEORIES

Taken together, the three need theories we have considered have a number of important implications for managing.

> **Different people have varying need structures as well as differing needs that may be salient at a given time.** Some people generally

care more about a particular need or set of needs, such as relatedness needs, than others. In addition, people at a given point in time will vary in the level to which the needs they care about are satisfied.

> **While satisfaction occurs when needs are met, motivation flows from lack of need satisfaction.** We must be careful not to fall in the trap of equating satisfaction with motivation. Some things that are very satisfying may be *demotivating.* For example, an employee whose pay is so high that she can afford anything she wants may not be motivated to gain an incentive for reaching a particular performance goal.

> **A reward may satisfy multiple needs.** It is sometimes tempting to assume that a particular reward, such as pay, will satisfy only certain needs, such as lower-order needs. However, such a viewpoint is simplistic. For example, employees may use money to buy food, pay the mortgage, go on a date, purchase a prestigious automobile, or finance a hobby or self-improvement class.

> **Needs appear to form two clusters (lower-order and higher-order) or three (existence, relatedness, and growth).** It is useful to understand how needs cluster in order to find ways to satisfy needs in a particular set. For example, recognizing that employees tend to have a cluster of needs called growth needs permits us to explore ways to satisfy that cluster. Conversely, if employees had a very large set of clusters of needs—say, 10 or 20—we would need to look more narrowly at ways to satisfy each salient need set.

> **While most people focus first on existence needs when those needs are not satisfied, it is not possible to say which needs will next become most important.** Again, there is no lockstep climb up a fixed need hierarchy. We should not expect that we can easily predict which needs an employee will focus on next.

> **Both satisfaction progression and frustration regression are important.** Not only do employees move from a focus on one need to a focus on another, but they somehow move back again. This is a continuous, dynamic process in which multiple needs are likely to be somehow salient at the same point in time.

> **The "top" cluster of needs, sometimes called *growth needs,* behaves differently from others.** While most needs become less motivating as they are satisfied, growth needs become more motivating. Thus, designing jobs or otherwise rewarding employees in ways that satisfy growth needs may cause people to place more emphasis on those needs rather than less. This is encouraging, since it suggests there is no "cap" on growth needs.

> **It may be possible to develop people's needs.** The structure of needs may not be fixed. For example, some employees who never placed much emphasis on growth needs may develop those needs when given the opportunity to satisfy them. Thus, employees may "grow into" jobs offering challenge and responsibility, giving greater importance to growth needs in the face of enriched job demands.

The accompanying Bottom Line presents a process model showing how need theories can be applied to manage employee motivation.

BOTTOM LINE

The Bottom Line: Need Theories

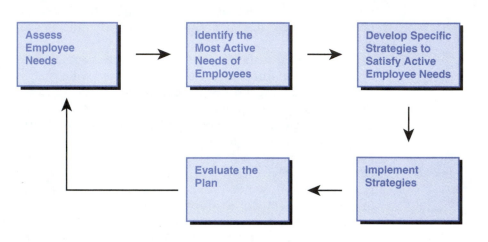

Skills Practice 6-1 will help you to develop skill in analyzing employee needs and to use creative motivational strategies to satisfy those needs.

Skills Practice 6-1   Skill Level: **Basic**
Developing Motivational Strategies Using 1001 Ways
to Reward Employees *and Content Theories*

Skill Objective

To develop skill in analyzing employee needs and linking them to appropriate motivational strategies from the best-selling book *1001 Ways to Reward Employees*.

Procedure

1. Form groups of 3–5 students each.
2. Read the employee profiles that follow and identify what kinds of motivational strategies you might use to satisfy each employee's active needs, based on the sampling of innovative motivational strategies identified by *1001 Ways to Reward Employees* as well as on your understanding of the need or content theories of motivation.
3. When your team is done, have one person from the team present to the class a summary of your motivational plan for each employee.
4. The class should evaluate each team's motivational plan and offer suggestions for improving it.

Employee 1

Mike recently received his bachelor's degree in finance from the University of Michigan. He has accepted a position as a financial analyst at a major commercial bank in New York. Mike's starting salary is $35,000 per year.

Mike possesses a high need for achievement; he wants the opportunity to work on the "high-impact" projects at the firm. Mike excelled in his coursework at Michigan, so he knows that he is good. He will work hard for the company, but he expects to be rewarded handsomely for his work. On the negative side, Mike tends to be high on introversion and low on agreeableness.

What is your assessment of Mike's active needs? As a manager, what kinds of strategies would you use to satisfy those needs?

Employee 2

Susan is a single mother of two children. She has been employed as a financial analyst with the same bank as Mike for 10 years. She possesses a bachelor's degree from the University of Wisconsin—Madison. Susan's work has always been very good. She is responsible, a good team player, and high on conscientiousness and extraversion. Given that Susan has two children, she is especially concerned about maintaining her employment with the company in order to meet her family's financial needs. In addition, Susan has been struggling to balance her work and family schedules (e.g., picking kids up from school, doctor's appointments). Susan's current salary is $47,000 per year.

What is your assessment of Susan's active needs? As a manager, what kinds of strategies would you use to satisfy those needs?

Examples of Motivational Strategies from *1001 Ways to Reward Employees*

✓ Call an employee into your office just to thank him/her	✓ Send an e-mail message expressing your appreciation of an employee's efforts	✓ Assign an employee to an important company task force or committee	✓ Order a pizza for a communal lunch
✓ Put a thank you note on an employee's cubicle or office	✓ Send an employee to a professional conference or training program of his/her choice	✓ Give an employee a round of golf	✓ Give an employee more autonomy
✓ Acknowledge individual achievements by using employee names when preparing status reports for top management	✓ Give an employee a weekend trip	✓ Grant an employee an extra day off	✓ Give an employee a special project to work on
✓ Create a Hall of Fame wall with photos of outstanding employees	✓ Arrange for the employee to have lunch with an executive	✓ Grant an employee an extra break or a two-hour lunch	✓ Make a donation to an employee's favorite charity
✓ Award dinners for two to employees when they do something special	✓ Give employees tickets to a sports or cultural event	✓ Give an employee a gift certificate for something he/she likes	✓ Give an employee a computer/laptop to use at home
✓ Take an employee out to lunch	✓ Give an employee his/her choice of assignments or projects	✓ Give an employee $50 in cash with a thank you note	✓ Pay for an employee to get a free manicure or massage
✓ Buy an employee something to use in his/her hobby	✓ Give an employee responsibility for a key project	✓ Schedule a staff meeting off-site in a more relaxed atmosphere	✓ Feature an employee in a company publication

Source: B. Nelson, *1001 Ways to Reward Employees*. New York: Workman, 1994, pp. 4–75.

APPLYING LEARNING THEORIES

Learning is any relatively permanent change in behavior produced by experience. Changes in behavior due to physical variations, such as growth, deterioration, fatigue, and sleep, are not learning. Similarly, temporary changes are not true learning. Also, the changes may not be desirable; we have probably all learned some behaviors that have caused us to be less effective or less adaptive than before. Here, we will briefly review three types of learning: classical conditioning, operant conditioning, and social learning. Together, these learning theories help explain how our behaviors are determined through our own experiences as well as the experiences of others.

CLASSICAL CONDITIONING

To many people, mention of learning theory brings to mind thoughts of Pavlov's dog. In Pavlov's experiments, a dog was taught to salivate in response to any of a variety of stimuli, such as a touch on the paw or the sound of a bell.[6] This was done by continually pairing the bell or other stimulus, which originally produced no increase in saliva, with food. Salivation was a normal physiological response to food in the mouth. The repeated pairing of the bell with the food caused the dog to salivate simply upon hearing the bell. Figure 6-4 shows this process.

The learning that took place in these experiments is called *classical* or *Pavlovian conditioning.* It occurs when, through pairing of stimuli, a new stimulus is responded to in the same way as the original stimulus. The thought of dangling rewards in front of salivating employees is a bit unseemly. Happily, this is *not* the sort of learning that is most relevant in organizational settings. There are at least three reasons for this:

> It is often difficult to use classical conditioning.
> There are ethical concerns about its use.
> It can't be used to teach a new behavior—it is useful only for transferring an existing behavior from one stimulus to another. Since the point of applying learning theory is often to teach and change the strength of current behaviors, other approaches are needed.

Web Wise

Ivan Petrovich Pavlov
Visit a site devoted to Pavlov at the following address:

http://arbl.cvmbs.colostate
.edu/hbooks/pathphys/
digestion/misc/pavlov.html

FIGURE 6-4
Classical Conditioning

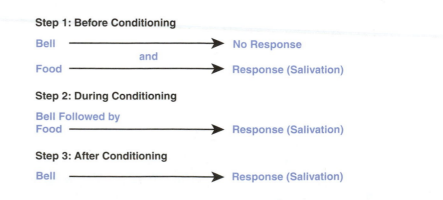

Step 1: Before Conditioning

Bell ⟶ No Response

and

Food ⟶ Response (Salivation)

Step 2: During Conditioning

Bell Followed by
Food ⟶ Response (Salivation)

Step 3: After Conditioning

Bell ⟶ Response (Salivation)

Awareness
Awareness
Awareness
Awareness
243
Awareness
Chapter 6   Motivating Effectively

F I G U R E   6 - 5
Operant Conditioning

OPERANT CONDITIONING

Most learning in organizations relies on the law of effect. The *law of effect* states that behavior that is rewarded will tend to be repeated; behavior that is not rewarded will tend not to be repeated. So if we want someone to continue acting in a certain way, we should see that they are somehow rewarded for acting in that way. If we want them to stop particular undesirable behaviors, we should make sure we are not rewarding them for those behaviors. The sort of conditioning that relies on the law of effect is called *operant conditioning* or, after its best-known researcher and theorist, *Skinnerian conditioning.*[7] Figure 6-5 illustrates operant conditioning.

Individuals enter organizations, and particular situations within organizations, with very different histories of reinforcement. That is, they have learned different things. Some have learned that working hard is the way to get ahead. Others have learned to be stubborn in the face of challenge. Still others have learned to avoid troublesome situations. Thus, many differences in behaviors among employees may be due to the different ways their behaviors have been rewarded or punished in the past.

SOCIAL LEARNING

Both classical conditioning and operant conditioning focus on learning as something that develops out of our own experiences. However, much of what we have learned comes from the experience of others. Because others have been burned by a hot stove or have failed in their attempts to start a new company or have found that certain leader behaviors are ineffective, we don't have to get burned ourselves to learn what they learned. Instead, we can benefit from social learning. *Social learning* is learning that occurs through any of a variety of social channels—newspapers, books, television, conversations with family members, friends, and coworkers, and so on. Social learning accounts for much of our knowledge. Coaching and mentoring are important organizational examples of social learning.

USING CONTINGENCIES OF REINFORCEMENT

We said earlier that operant conditioning uses rewards or unpleasant consequences to strengthen desired behaviors or to weaken undesired behaviors. The various ways we can tie consequences to behaviors are called *contingencies of reinforcement.* As shown in Figure 6-6, three contingencies of reinforcement—positive reinforcement, escape learning, and avoidance learning—are used to strengthen desired behaviors.

Positive reinforcement involves giving a reward when desired behavior occurs, in order to increase the likelihood that the behavior will be repeated. A bonus for a job well done or a pat on the back for a good effort are ex-

FIGURE 6-6
Arranging Contingencies to Increase Desired Behaviors

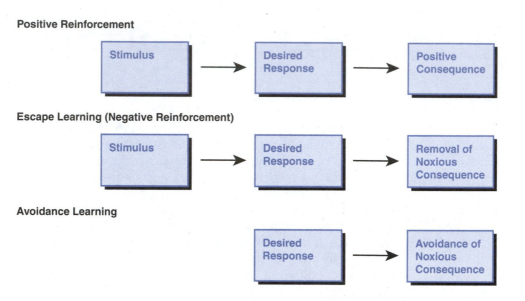

Positive Reinforcement

Stimulus → Desired Response → Positive Consequence

Escape Learning (Negative Reinforcement)

Stimulus → Desired Response → Removal of Noxious Consequence

Avoidance Learning

Desired Response → Avoidance of Noxious Consequence

amples. In many jobs, bonuses and other forms of merit-based compensation are very important, often exceeding base salaries.

Another way to increase the likelihood of desired behavior is to remove some unpleasant consequence when that behavior occurs. For example, suppose a rat is subjected to a loud, irritating noise until it presses a lever. Once it presses the lever, the noise stops. The rat would soon learn to press the lever to escape the grating noise. This is called *escape conditioning.* If pressing the lever would actually prevent the onset of the noise, this would be called *avoidance conditioning.* In some companies, there are certain jobs that employees feel are very good, and others that are clearly "the pits." If employees feel that they will be transferred from the bad jobs if they perform well, we have an example of escape conditioning. If employees in good jobs feel they can avoid being transferred to bad jobs if they continue to perform well, we have an example of avoidance conditioning.

Skills Practice 6-2 will give you the chance to develop skill in thinking strategically about identifying employee behaviors you want to promote in your work unit and in linking appropriate consequences to the behaviors so that employees will continue to engage in them.

Skills Practice 6-2   Skill Level: Challenging
Reinforcing Desired Work Behaviors

Skill Objective

To develop skill in identifying target behaviors and linking appropriate consequences to them in order to reinforce appropriate work behavior.

Procedure

1. Select one of the following work scenarios to use for this exercise. If you prefer to substitute a situation from your current or past work experience, that will be fine as well. You may work in groups of 3–5 individuals for this exercise if you wish.

Scenario 1—Rotten Airline Customer Service

Customers of a major airline are very dissatisfied with the quality of service they have been receiving from flight attendants. Specifically, they feel that many of the flight attendants are rude, unresponsive, and uncaring. Using the procedure just presented, describe how you would handle this situation.

Scenario 2—Botched Orders at the Fast Food Drive-Thru

The manager of a fast food (burger and fries) restaurant is experiencing major problems, with the wrong orders being given to drive-thru customers. Customers have been absolutely furious when they discover after they have driven away that they received the wrong order. Using the process presented earlier, describe how you would handle this situation.

2. Using the following steps, apply the basic process for reinforcing desired behaviors. Document your plan in writing, on a separate piece of paper.
    a. Identify the target behavior. Be as specific as possible.

    Examples of general types of work behaviors:
    Attendance
    Quality of work
    Safety practices
    Thinking creatively ("out of the box")
    Timeliness
    Customer service
    Sales calls
    Attention to detail
    Productivity
    Teamwork
    Risk-taking behavior

    Examples of specific target behaviors:
    > To achieve an attendance rate of 95 percent over the next three months
    > To achieve a rate of timeliness (i.e., getting to work on time) of 100 percent over the next six months
    > To achieve an average productivity rate of 50 units/hour over the next 12 months
    > To achieve a defect rate of 1 percent over the next quarter
    > To return all phone calls from customers within 24 hours
    b. Identify appropriate consequences to link to the desired behavior.
    > If you want to use *positive reinforcement,* then identify positively valued consequences that could be linked with engaging in the desired behavior.
    > If you want to use *avoidance learning,* then identify specific negative consequences that would be avoided (not experienced) as a result of engaging in the desired behavior.
    > If you want to use *escape learning,* then identify the specific negative stimulus that would be removed or eliminated as a result of engaging in the desired behavior.
    c. State how you will link the consequences you identified to the target behavior.
3. Present your plan to the class and explain why it will work.

As seen in Figure 6-7, undesired behaviors may be reduced by nonreinforcement or by punishment. *Nonreinforcement* causes extinction of an undesired behavior by removing the reinforcing consequence that previously followed the behavior. Consider the case of Sam. We have (unintentionally)

FIGURE 6-7
Arranging Contingencies to Reduce Undesired Behaviors

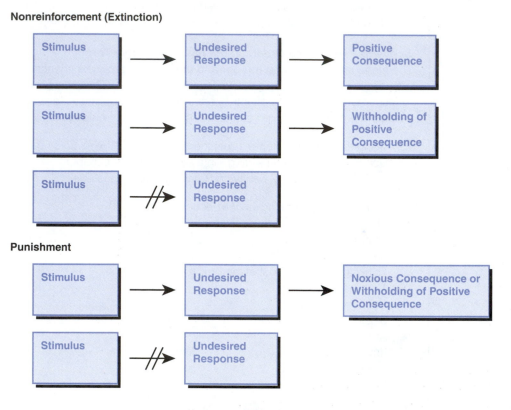

been teaching Sam to make unwarranted demands by regularly giving in to those demands. How can we get him to stop? One answer is simply to stop rewarding him for that undesired behavior. That is, don't give in to the demands. He will learn that unwarranted demands aren't rewarded, and he will eventually stop making them.

A second way to reduce undesired behavior, *punishment,* is defined as presenting an unpleasant consequence, or removing a desired consequence, whenever an undesired behavior occurs. So when Sam makes his demands, we could put a letter of reprimand in his file (an unpleasant consequence), or we could stop interacting with him socially (removal of a desired consequence). Note that both nonreinforcement and punishment can involve removal of a desired consequence. With nonreinforcement, the reward we would withhold (agreeing to demands) was the one previously tied to the behavior. With punishment, the reward withheld (social interaction) was not previously a reinforcer of that behavior.

It is often tempting to apply punishment, and there are certainly situations in which punishment can't be avoided. However, punishment should be used only as a last resort. Problems with punishment include the following.

> Managers don't like to punish others.
> Managers may feel constrained from using punishment because of company policy or threat of reprisal.

> Punishment may engender resentment.
> Punishment may lead to revenge and retaliation.
> Punishment leads to adherence only when the person administering the punishment is present or monitoring.
> Others may misinterpret the reasons for punishment.
> Punishment may reduce an undesired behavior, but it doesn't directly teach a desired behavior.

APPLYING REINFORCEMENT SCHEDULES

One learning theory issue, which we've just addressed, is *how* outcomes should be tied to behaviors to motivate desired behaviors and minimize undesired behaviors. However, suppose we decide that we are going to use money to reward employees for high performance. How do we decide *when* we should give the money? Should we give it immediately after the desired behavior? After the desired behaviors have continued for a week? Every 10 times the desired behavior occurs? That is, what should be our *schedule of reinforcement?*

In choosing a schedule of reinforcement, there are several things we might seek:

> **Rapid learning.** Ideally, we would use a schedule of reinforcement that very quickly teaches desired behaviors.
> **High response rate.** We would like a high "bang for the buck." That is, we would like to choose a schedule of reinforcement that yields high levels of motivation at relatively little cost.
> **High response stability.** We would like to encourage employees to engage in desired behaviors on a regular basis. We wouldn't, for instance, want an employee to work hard only the day before he or she will be paid or to take safety precautions only before a scheduled inspection.
> **Low extinction rate.** Once a desired behavior is learned, we would like it to be maintained even if we might have to stop rewarding for a while.

There are many ways to arrange schedules of reinforcement, and we will see that they vary in terms of the degree to which they might satisfy the conditions we've just discussed. One basic distinction is whether or not behavior is reinforced every time it occurs (such as for every unit produced). *Continuous reinforcement* occurs if every behavior is reinforced. Continuous reinforcement leads to rapid learning. However, if for some reason it is necessary to stop reinforcing (for instance, if the supervisor must leave the room), rapid extinction occurs. Most of the time, it is simply impractical to reinforce on a continuous basis, so a partial-reinforcement schedule is used.

Partial-reinforcement schedules can be time based or behavior based. Also, they can be administered on a fixed, unchanging basis, or they can be varied around some mean. There are four basic partial-reinforcement schedules.

With a *fixed-interval schedule,* a reinforcer is given at fixed time intervals, such as once a week. Weekly paychecks and monthly inspections are common examples. Fixed-interval schedules, while easy to use, result in slow learning and a moderately fast extinction rate. They also have a low response rate (that is, frequency of response per reinforcement) and very low response stability (people speed up just before the time of reinforcement and then slow down).

A *variable-interval schedule* is also time based. However, a reinforcer is administered randomly around some average interval. For instance, an instructor might announce that there will be four pop quizzes during the semester, but will not say when they will occur. Learning rate, extinction rate, response rate, and response stability are all better for the variable-interval than for the fixed-interval schedule. However, they are generally not as good as for ratio-based schedules.

A *fixed-ratio schedule* provides a reinforcer after a given number of acceptable behaviors. Commissions given on the basis of sales levels (such as for every 10 sales) and bonuses given for every three meritorious behaviors are examples. Fixed-ratio schedules have very high response rates and response stability. They have high learning rates but, unfortunately, rapid extinction rates as well. Fixed-ratio schedules can be "stretched" to foster learning and increase response rate. For instance, we might want to teach a new behavior by first reinforcing every instance of that behavior (that is, by using a continuous-reinforcement schedule), then stretch the schedule so a reward is given for only two instances of the behavior (called a 2:1 schedule), then for three instances (a 3:1 schedule), and so on. By stretching schedules in this way, Skinner trained pigeons to peck at rates faster than machine-gun fire.

While a fixed-ratio schedule reinforces after every *n* response, a *variable-ratio schedule* reinforces *on average* every *n* responses. For instance, a "one-armed bandit" might have a payoff an average of once in every 10 pulls of the handle. However, precisely when the payoff will occur is unknown. Response rates and response stability are similar to those for fixed-ratio schedules, but learning is slower. However, extinction is very slow. Companies have made some very creative attempts to use variable-ratio schedules. For instance,

FOCUS ON MANAGEMENT

INCENTIVES AT LINCOLN ELECTRIC

Founded in 1895, Lincoln Electric is the global leader in the arc welding industry, with 1999 revenues of more than $41 billion and more than 6,000 employees at manufacturing sites in 17 countries. Lincoln Electric attributes much of its success to its dedicated, highly talented workforce. On its website Lincoln notes that "people are Lincoln's fundamental advantage—the source of all our other strengths. Our people are highly trained and motivated. They are productive and team oriented."

To foster that motivation, Lincoln has developed a unique incentive Performance System. In 1923 Lincoln Electric was among the first companies in the United States to offer workers paid vacations, and in 1925 it was one of the first to provide an employee stock ownership plan. Lincoln has one of the oldest "pay-for-performance" systems in the country. Lincoln provides piecework incentives for all production work—that is, pay is tied directly to output levels. In addition, Lincoln has an annual profit-sharing bonus plan and offers guaranteed employment after

three years of service—it has not laid off an employee in U.S. operations since 1948. Lincoln's website states: "Through this well-defined group of incentives, Lincoln encourages and compensates individual initiative and responsibility. Employees work together to reduce costs and improve quality. These individual and cooperative efforts create a more profitable company, the success of which each person shares according to his or her own contribution."

http://www.lincolnelectric.com/ corporate/career/default.asp

FIGURE 6-8
Comparing the Schedules of Reinforcement

	SCHEDULE OF REINFORCEMENT				
Measure	Continuous	Fixed Ratio	Variable Ratio	Fixed Interval	Variable Interval
Learning Rate	Very fast	Fast	Slow	Very slow	Moderate
Response Rate	Very low	Very high	Very high	Low	Moderate
Response Stability	Very high	High	High	Very low	Low to moderate
Extinction Rate	Very fast	Fast	Very slow	Moderately fast	Slow

in one firm, names of employees who didn't use their sick leave were placed in a lottery for a large prize. Sick-leave costs fell by 62 percent.[8]

Figure 6-8 compares the various schedules of reinforcement.

It is clear in looking at Figure 6-8 that there are some trade-offs when using the various schedules of reinforcement. For example, a variable-ratio schedule is very powerful in most ways, but results in slow learning. As such, it may be desirable to combine schedules. For example, as noted earlier, a behavior might be taught by initially using continuous reinforcement, followed by stretching of the schedule to yield a fixed-ratio schedule, and then adding a variable element.

Of course, there are other practical considerations in choosing schedules. For instance, employees need to pay their bills on a regular basis and may count on a weekly paycheck (a fixed-interval schedule). Also, it is easy to administer a fixed-interval schedule. Nevertheless, the relatively greater power of other schedules suggests that we should seek creative ways to employ other schedules of reinforcement whenever possible.

ORGANIZATIONAL BEHAVIOR MODIFICATION

Organizational behavior modification (OBM) is the use of the principles of learning theory to manage behavior in organizations. Organizational behavior modification practitioners and theorists typically use some combination of operant conditioning techniques and social learning to achieve their goals.

Here are some guidelines for effectively using learning techniques in organizations.[9]

1. **Don't give the same reward to all.** Reward those who exhibit desired behaviors (such as high performance) more than those who don't.
2. **Recognize that failure to respond to behavior has reinforcing consequences.** Managers must remember that inaction, as well as action, has reinforcing consequences. They should ask, "What behavior will I reinforce if I do nothing?"
3. **Tell a person what behavior gets reinforced.** Make the contingencies of reinforcement clear to employees. Don't make them guess which behaviors will be rewarded or punished.
4. **Tell a person what he or she is doing wrong.** If the manager does not make clear to an employee why, for instance, a reward is being with-

held, the employee may attribute the action to a past desired behavior rather than the behavior the manager wants to extinguish.

5. **Don't punish in front of others.** When employees are punished in front of others, they "lose face" and are doubly punished. This can cause resentment and a variety of problems.

6. **Make the consequences equal to the behavior.** Overrewarding desired behavior makes an employee feel guilty. Underrewarding desired behavior or overpunishing undesired behavior causes anger. Underpunishing undesired behavior seems like a "slap on the wrist" and may have little impact.

7. **Reinforce behaviors as soon as possible.** As suggested in the nearby Focus on Management, immediate rewards can be very powerful.

Note that some of the rules we've listed rely heavily on cognitions. This recognizes that employees can learn through observation and advice as well as from their own experiences.

Organizational behavior modification often uses behavioral shaping. *Behavioral shaping* is the learning of a complex behavior through successive approximations of the desired behavior. Initially, the employee gets a reward for any behavior that is in any way positively related to the desired behavior. Subsequently, responses are not reinforced unless they are more and more similar to the desired behavior. Responses are "shaped" until the desired complex behavior is achieved.

Properly applied, learning theory works very well. Many firms, including Emory Air Freight, General Electric, and Weyerhaeuser, have implemented very successful programs. In fact, some critics worry that learning theory works *too* well, possibly pushing the employee to exhaustion or to other undesirable outcomes. They see this as especially troublesome, since this behavior—particularly when noncognitive, operant conditioning is used—is to some extent outside the control of the employee, overriding free will. From this perspective, learning theory has Orwellian overtones.

We feel that, when used with intelligence and caution, learning theory can be extremely useful. After all, managers are reinforcing behavior all the time;

FOCUS ON MANAGEMENT

HACIENDA BUCKS

Rewarding a person in June for a job well done in January does little to reinforce the behavior. Recognizing this, Hacienda Mexican Restaurants hires "mystery shoppers" to pose as customers and report back on employees who have gone out of their way to serve a customer or help one another. When either these "mystery shoppers" or supervisors in the firm see such behaviors, employees are immediately rewarded with "Hacienda Bucks" that can be redeemed for food or beverages in any of the restaurant's locations.* In general, the more immediately a reward is given, the more powerful is its motivating effect. For another example of the power of immediate rewards, see this chapter's Video Case, Motivating for Performance: A Study of Valassis Communications, Inc.

http://www.haciendafiesta.com/

*S. Nelton, "Saying 'Gracias' On The Spot," *Nation's Business,* May 1993, p. 12. See also "Hacienda Mexican Restaurants Award Winner," *Foodservice Equipment and Supplies,* October 1999, pp. 47–48.

Awareness
Awareness
Awareness
Awareness
Awareness
251

Chapter 6   Motivating Effectively

The Bottom Line: Organizational Behavior Modification (OBM)

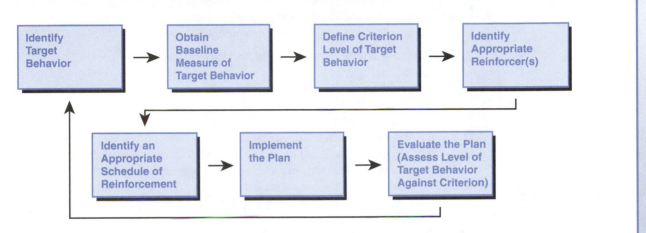

the trick is to do it right. Cognitive approaches, in which employees know why they are being rewarded or punished and are aware of the contingencies of reinforcement, overcome some of the concerns that employees are being ruthlessly manipulated. In addition, proponents of learning theory are essentially unanimous in advocating positive reinforcement (the carrot) over punishment (the stick). As such, proper application of learning theory helps guarantee that employees get the rewards they want while fostering desired organizational outcomes.

The nearby Bottom Line shows how organizational behavior modification can be systematically implemented to encourage the learning of desired behaviors as well as the unlearning of undesired behaviors.

Skills Practice 6-3 gives you another opportunity to develop skill in applying learning theory principles. In this case, you are asked to apply the principles to reduce levels of undesired work behaviors.

Skills Practice 6-3
Managing Undesired Employee Behaviors

Skill Level: Challenging

Skill Objective

To develop skill in identifying undesired employee behaviors and linking appropriate consequences to them in order to eliminate inappropriate work behavior.

Procedure

1.   Select one of the following work scenarios to use as a basis for applying the process.

Scenario 1—The Problem Team Member

You are the project leader of a product development team at a computer firm. The team itself is composed of 10 employees representing various functional areas in the firm, including marketing, engineering, finance, and human resources. The objective of the team is to develop new and innovative computer hardware in a cost-effective and efficient manner.

The team has been meeting on a weekly basis for a number of months. While the overall product development process has been fairly smooth so far, you are experiencing a problem with one team member who consistently shows up for meetings 15–20 minutes late or fails to attend meetings at all. This employee's behavior is slowing the progress of the team since some key decisions have been delayed.

What would you do to handle this employee?

Scenario 2—The Rotten Customer Service Provider

You are the manager of a high-end restaurant located in a luxury hotel in Seattle. Although the restaurant has long held a reputation for its outstanding international cuisine, satisfaction with customer service has been declining.

Your wait staff is very professional and service oriented as a whole, but the tight labor market has made it increasingly difficult to find qualified employees. You have received a number of complaints from customers about one employee in particular. This employee has made a number of mistakes: serving the wrong orders, overcharging customers, and even making some rude comments to customers. You believe that this employee has the potential to be a good server, but you need to address some of her behavioral issues immediately.

What would you do to handle this situation?

Scenario 3—The Hypercompetitive Sales Associates

You are the supervisor of the housewares department at a major department store in Atlanta. You manage a staff of 25 sales associates who work on a commission system based on sales volume. Your sales associates are given sales goals they are expected to meet each day they work. Employees who meet or exceed their sales targets receive a variety of rewards, including higher commissions, recognition, and a more attractive work schedule.

One problem that has emerged from the commission system used at your company is that sales associates are highly competitive with each other, sometimes even stealing sales from one another. Moreover, there is no cooperation or teamwork among the sales associates, because they feel that the work environment is one of "survival of the fittest."

You are not happy with the work environment that has evolved in your department. You believe that competition between sales associates will ultimately damage the quality of service they provide to customers.

What would you do to eliminate the competitive behavior in this situation?

2. Apply the following steps to develop a systematic plan for addressing the problem behavior in the scenario you have selected.

    a. Identify the undesired employee behavior (e.g., unsafe work practices, poor customer service). Be as specific as possible.

    b. Decide whether you want to use punishment or nonreinforcement to address the problem behavior.

        > *If you decide to use nonreinforcement,* then identify the specific actions you would take to ensure that the employee's behavior is not reinforced in any way, Your action plan would stop here, and there is no need to go through the remaining steps.

        > *If you decide that the use of punishment is appropriate,* identify negatively valued consequences (e.g., verbal reprimands, less desirable work assignments). Make sure these outcomes are negatively valued by the employee.

    c. Identify the schedule of reinforcement you think would be most appropriate for the situation.

Web Wise

The Society of Industrial/ Organizational Psychology

The Society of Industrial/ Organizational Psychology (SIOP) is a division of the American Psychological Association. The society publishes *TIP, The Industrial/Organizational Psychologist,* a quarterly journal of issues relating to learning and other issues. The SIOP website offers links to TIP, including its online version, and to other information relating to industrial and organizational psychology. Visit the SIOP site at:

http://www.siop.org/

   d.   Link the negatively valued consequences to the target behavior.
   e.   Identify the new (desired) employee behavior that you want to replace the unde-
        sired behavior. Reinforce this behavior. Such reinforcement is important so that
        employees understand what they should do instead of the undesired behavior.
3.   Answer the discussion questions as a class.

Discussion Questions
1.   Describe your action plan for dealing with the problem employee behavior in the sce-
     nario you selected. Why do you think it will work?
2.   What steps would you take if the plan you just described did not work?
3.   What are the practical implications of this exercise for you as a future manager?

EFFECTIVE GOAL SETTING

A *goal* is simply a desired end state, that is, something we want. Certainly, employee behavior often seems to be goal directed. Employees may strive to
reach quotas, to win contests, to make it through the workday, or to outperform their coworkers. Sometimes their goals are difficult, sometimes easy.
Sometimes they are very specific and sometimes vague. As we will see, the nature of employee goals, and how they are set, can be very important. Goal setting is also simple and inexpensive.

FUNCTIONS OF GOALS
Goals serve a variety of important functions. For instance:[10]

>   Goals let employees know what they are expected to do.
>   Goals relieve boredom. Consider how boring most games would be
    if you didn't keep score and try to reach goals.
>   Reaching goals and getting positive feedback leads to increased liking
    for the task and satisfaction with job performance.
>   Attaining goals leads to recognition by peers, supervisors, and others.
>   Attaining goals leads to feelings of increased self-confidence, pride in
    achievement, and willingness to accept future challenges.

EFFECTIVE GOAL SETTING
Research on goal setting has yielded some clear and useful findings. Here are
some guidelines for effective goal setting (see Figure 6-9).

>   **Set specific goals.** Quite simply, specific goals lead to higher perfor-
    mance than just "do your best" goals. In fact, "do your best" goals have
    about the same effect as no goal at all. Imagine a runner circling a track,
    shouting to her coach, "How much farther do I have to go?" A reply
    from the coach of "Just do your best" won't help much.
        Specific goals are so powerful as to overwhelm other things. In one
    study, subjects were assigned to either a "low-motivation" or a "high-
    motivation" group based on performance, ability, and attitude ratings.[11]
    The low-motivation group received specific task goals, while the high-
    motivation group was told to "do your best." Performance of the low-
    motivation group quickly caught up to that of the high-motivation group.
        Of course, goals must be appropriate. If some goals are specific and
    others are not, the nonspecific goals will not receive much emphasis.

FIGURE 6-9
Important Goal Characteristics

Also, there is a danger that a manager may really care about X but, because Y is easier to quantify, will set goals for Y instead.

> **Set difficult goals.** There is a positive, linear relationship between goal difficulty and task performance. This relationship holds for various kinds of tasks, time horizons, and ages of subjects. However, employees must believe the goal is attainable. If not, they will not accept it. Also, people pursue many goals at the same time. If they believe one is too difficult, they will focus on other, more attainable goals. Interestingly, when people face difficult goals, they engage in more problem analysis and creative behavior than when faced with simple goals. So they both work harder and work smarter.

> **Give feedback on goal progress.** Feedback keeps behavior on track. Feedback may also stimulate greater effort (we will see later in this chapter that feedback from the job itself is a major determinant of the motivating potential of a job). A video game without a score would soon be abandoned. And when people get feedback concerning their performance, they tend to set personal improvement goals. The nature of the feedback makes a difference. As we will discuss later in the chapter, feedback from the job itself is generally better than that provided by others. Finally, feedback is clearly more important for some people than for others. We've seen elsewhere, for instance, that people with a high need for achievement have especially strong desires for feedback.

> **Consider peer competition for goal attainment.** If employees are working toward individual goals, such as salespersons pursuing independent sales goals, competition for goal attainment may be useful. Its impact is especially great in zero-sum situations, that is, where there is a fixed pie to divide. However, competition can hurt if tasks are interdependent. In such a case, an employee's attempts to excel may harm the

performance of another. Also, if competition focuses on the quantity of output, quality may suffer.

> **Use participation in goal setting.** Participation isn't a panacea. Some people simply don't like to participate, and in some situations (such as under severe time constraints) participation may be inappropriate. In general, though, participation increases understanding and acceptance of the goal. Participation often leads to setting of more difficult goals, which may in turn lead to higher performance.[12]

> **Encourage goal acceptance.** Goal acceptance is the degree to which individuals accept particular goals as their own. If a goal is not accepted, the other goal attributes don't matter. Goal acceptance is likely to be lacking if the individual sees goals as unreachable or sees no benefit from reaching the goal.

> **Encourage goal commitment.** Goal commitment is the degree to which individuals are dedicated to trying to reach the goals they have adopted. Like goal acceptance, it is a necessary condition for goal-directed effort. Goal commitment is affected by the same factors as goal acceptance. Those factors influence goal acceptance before the goal is set and goal commitment once the individual is pursuing the goal.

Of course, most goal setting involves changes in a number of goal attributes. As one example, consider a field experiment in the logging industry. Trucks carrying logs from the woods to the mill varied in the number of trees they hauled from one time to the next since the trees varied in size. As a result, considerable judgment entered into the decision of what was a full load. However, analyses showed that trucks were carrying an average of only about 60 percent of their legal net weight. Eventually the researchers, management, and the union decided that a goal of 94 percent of legal net weight was difficult but reachable. The drivers, who were responsible for loading the trucks, were assigned this 94 percent goal. After about a month, performance increased from the initial 60 percent to about 80 percent of capacity. It then dipped to 70 percent for another month before rising to 90 percent, where it remained for the next six months. Company accountants estimated the results translated into a savings to the company of a quarter of a million dollars worth of new trucks alone. Several goal attributes had been changed—goals were difficult, were more specific than in the past, and had apparently been accepted.[13]

MANAGEMENT BY OBJECTIVES

Management by objectives (MBO) is a motivational technique in which the manager and employee work together to set employee goals. The employee's performance is later measured against these goals. *Management by objectives* combines many of the goal-setting principles we have just described. The MBO process begins by identifying general areas of responsibility that are important to the firm. Once this has been done, the employee and manager get together and agree on specific objectives that the employee will meet during some future period of time. For example, one key responsibility area in sales management might be sales volume, and the objective might be to increase sales by 35 percent over the next six months. Once the manager and the employee have agreed on specific objectives, they develop a strategy together for meeting these objectives. The manager and the employee then meet periodically to review how the employee has done relative to the agreed-upon objectives. If there is a problem, they discuss why objectives have not been met. The final step in the MBO process is either to set new goals for the next time period or to develop new strategies to meet the previously agreed-upon goals. The entire procedure then begins anew.

Management by objectives was one of the most popular motivational tools in the 1960s and 1970s, and it is still widely used in various forms. However, MBO is not perfect. For example, it may be difficult and time consuming to implement. Sometimes the agreed-upon goals are not specific enough, resulting in employee frustration. Also, MBO has been faulted for encouraging people to focus only on goals that can be easily expressed in numbers (such as the number of units produced in a week or the average number of sales calls made per day), ignoring goals that are hard to measure (such as quality of products or creativity).

On the other hand, MBO does encourage planning and goal setting, and it lets employees know how they are doing on the job. Also, it allows employees to participate in setting goals, which is good for morale and motivation. It helps spot deviations from performance goals before it is too late to do anything about them. Since MBO combines three elements that have been found to improve productivity—goal setting, feedback, and participation—it might be expected that MBO would also be successful. In fact, one review found that 68 of 70 major studies on the issue showed MBO to result in productivity gains.[14] These studies also demonstrate that top-management commitment to MBO is critical for success. When top-management commitment was high,

BOTTOM LINE

The Bottom Line: Goal-Setting Theory

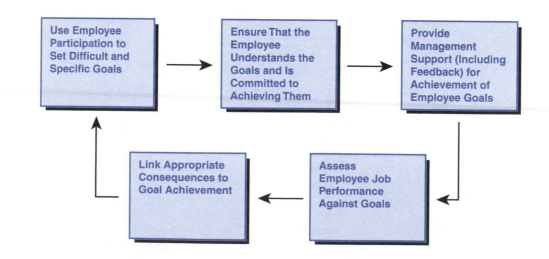

MBO resulted in an average productivity gain of 56 percent. When top-management commitment was low, the average gain in productivity was only 6 percent.

The process model presented in the nearby Bottom Line illustrates how goal-setting principles can be applied in order to enhance employees' motivation and job performance.

Skills Practice 6-4 will encourage you to think more systematically about the process of identifying specific goals you want to achieve and the processes needed to achieve them.

Skills Practice 6-4
Applying Goal-Setting Theory to Motivate Employees

Skill Level: Basic

Skill Objective
To develop skill in setting goals that provide appropriate direction and enhance goal-directed effort.

When to Use It
When identifying desired ends to be achieved at the organizational, work unit, team, and/or individual level.

Steps in Using It
Step 1: Identify your ultimate goal in terms of:

    a.   What you want to accomplish in specific, measurable terms
    b.   When you want to accomplish it

Make sure that your goal is something you believe will be challenging but not impossible to accomplish (e.g., one of General Motors' 1999 goals was to capture 32 percent of the automobile market in the United States). If you are setting work unit or organizational goals, involve relevant managers and employees in the process.

Examples:

> To complete our group project assignment by the due date
> To accomplish a 20 percent reduction in operating costs by the end of the 2003 fiscal year
> To increase worker productivity by 10 percent within the next quarter
> To increase customer retention by 30 percent within the next three years

Step 2: Given your overall goal, identify what you will need to do to achieve it (e.g., subgoals). These subgoals deal with the process you will use to accomplish your goals.

Example:

Overall goal: To increase worker productivity 10 percent by December 31, 2003.

Subgoal	Completion Date
Analyze our current work process and develop a flowchart to describe it.	June 15, 2003
Develop a list of 3–5 key action steps for eliminating inefficiencies in the process.	July 1, 2003
Pilot-test action steps and perform evaluation in terms of impact on productivity.	August 15, 2003

Subgoal	Completion Date
Identify modifications to action steps or additional action steps that may support the overall goal.	September 15, 2003
Implement modified or new action steps.	October 1, 2003
Monitor results and evaluate in terms of impact on productivity trends for the year.	November 30, 2003
Conduct final evaluation of work process and communicate results to senior management.	December 31, 2003

Key Tips for Effective Goal Setting

1. Always keep the ultimate (long-term) goal in mind.
2. Keep your subgoals (process) in alignment with your ultimate goal.
3. Summarize your goals in a formal document. Make sure that everyone involved in implementing the plan understands it and is committed to it.
4. Monitor your progress toward achieving your goals on a regular basis. Make adjustments to your goals as needed.

Now it's your turn. Using the principles of goal setting discussed in this exercise and in the chapter, do the following.

1. Identify a class project you are or will be working on this semester. This can be an individual or group project. An especially complex or challenging project would be ideal for this exercise.
2. Develop an appropriate goal-setting plan for the project you identified in Step 1. Document your plan on a piece of paper. As shown in the earlier example, this plan should contain your overall goal, subgoals, and dates for completion.
3. Identify and discuss any barriers to the implementation of the plan and how you will address these issues.

Read the Real-World Management Challenge, Motivating Excellence at Hilton Hotels Corporation, and develop an action plan that outlines what you would do to address the motivational issues at the company. Make sure that your recommendations are as specific as possible and that they focus on action.

Real-World Management Challenge

Motivating Excellence at Hilton Hotels Corporation

The Company

The Hilton Hotels Corporation, based in Beverly Hills, California, is an upscale player in the hospitality industry. It operates approximately 1,800 hotels under brand names that include Hilton, Hampton Inns, Doubletree, Embassy Suites, Homewood Suites, Conrad International, and Red Lion Hotels and Inns. The strategic focus of the company is on providing customers with the highest-quality accommodations, service, amenities, and value for both business and leisure guests. The company employs approximately 78,000 people worldwide.

The Situation

Senior management at Hilton recently decided that it wanted to develop a corporate initiative that would achieve the following objectives:

> To promote teamwork among Hilton employees at all its locations
> To motivate and empower Hilton employees to take greater pride in their jobs
> To recognize exceptional performance among Hilton hotels and their employees
> To increase shareholder value

What Would You Do?

If you were the CEO of Hilton Hotels, what corporate initiatives would you implement to achieve these objectives?

Source: "In the Zone, The Hilton Pride Program," *Incentive,* October 1998.

LINKING EFFORT TO OUTCOMES: EXPECTANCY THEORY

If someone is going to try to engage in some behavior, three conditions have to be satisfied. First, the person must believe that his or her efforts are somehow tied to the behavior. If not, why try? Second, the behavior must somehow be tied to outcomes. If not, why attempt the behavior? Third, those outcomes must be *valent* (that is, valued). If the outcomes aren't valued, why try to attain them? If any of these three conditions isn't satisfied, the individual has no reason to try. This simple idea is the essence of expectancy theory. *Expectancy theory* is an approach to the understanding of motivation that examines the links in the process from effort to ultimate rewards.[15]

EXPECTANCY THEORY CONCEPTS

The key elements of expectancy theory are as follows (see Figure 6-10).

> **First-order outcome.** A *first-order outcome* is the direct result of effort. The first-order outcome may be performance, creativity, low absenteeism, low turnover, or any other desired behavior. There may be more than one first-order outcome.

> **Second-order outcome.** A *second-order outcome* is anything, good or bad, that may result from attainment of the first-order outcome. Typically, there are many second-order outcomes, such as pay, esteem of coworkers, and approval of the supervisor.

> **Expectancy.** *Expectancy* is the perceived linkage between effort and the first-order outcome. There is an expectancy for each first-order outcome. If a worker feels that trying harder won't improve his or her performance, the expectancy of effort for the attainment of performance would be low. If a worker feels that more effort will translate directly into higher performance, expectancy would be high. Expectancies are often expressed as probabilities.

Figure 6-11 shows some of the things that may affect the actual linkage between effort and the first-order outcome of performance. One of these, of course, is ability. If ability is completely lacking, effort won't help much. Another is the situation. In some situations, such as the assembly line, the employee is constrained. Greater effort simply won't

FIGURE 6-10
The Components of Expectancy Theory

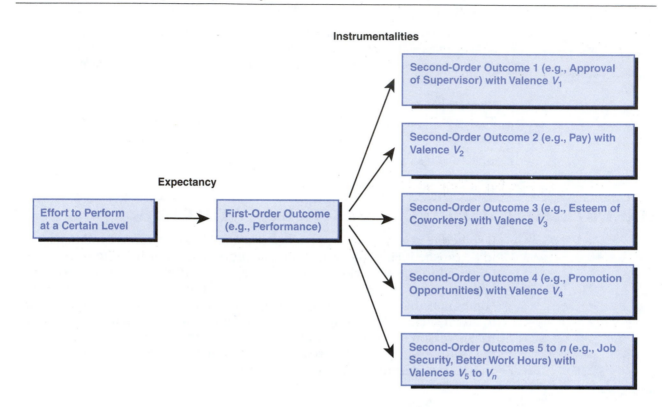

Instrumentalities

Effort to Perform at a Certain Level → Expectancy → First-Order Outcome (e.g., Performance)

Second-Order Outcome 1 (e.g., Approval of Supervisor) with Valence V_1

Second-Order Outcome 2 (e.g., Pay) with Valence V_2

Second-Order Outcome 3 (e.g., Esteem of Coworkers) with Valence V_3

Second-Order Outcome 4 (e.g., Promotion Opportunities) with Valence V_4

Second-Order Outcomes 5 to n (e.g., Job Security, Better Work Hours) with Valences V_5 to V_n

FIGURE 6-11
The Linkage of Effort to a First-Order Outcome

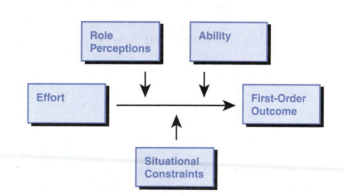

Role Perceptions   Ability

Effort → First-Order Outcome

Situational Constraints

speed up the line. A final factor is role perceptions. If employees don't know what their roles are (that is, what management expects of them), they will probably misdirect their efforts. Each of these factors is likely to influence expectancies.

> **Instrumentality.** *Instrumentality* is the perceived linkage between a first-order outcome and a second-order outcome. There is an instrumentality for each combination of first- and second-order outcomes. Like

expectancy, instrumentalities are often expressed as probabilities.[16] If an employee feels that higher performance will lead to pay increases, the instrumentality of performance for the attainment of pay increases would be high. If an employee feels that performance and pay are unrelated, that instrumentality would be zero.

> **Valence.** *Valence* is simply the value an individual attaches to an outcome. The valences of second-order outcomes are the values of such things as pay increases, supervisory approval, security, and esteem of coworkers. The valence of a first-order outcome, such as performance, depends upon the valences of second-order outcomes and on the instrumentalities of the first-order outcome for the attainment of those second-order outcomes. In particular, it is the sum of the products of the valence of the first-order outcomes and the instrumentality of the first-order outcome for the attainment of the second-order outcomes. That is:

$$\begin{pmatrix} \text{Valence of} \\ \text{first-order} \\ \text{outcome} \end{pmatrix} = \sum_{i=1}^{n} \begin{pmatrix} \text{Valence of} \\ \text{second-order} \\ \text{outcome } i \end{pmatrix} \times \begin{pmatrix} \text{Instrumentality of first-order} \\ \text{outcome for the attainment of} \\ \text{second-order outcome } i \end{pmatrix}$$

> **Force to perform, or effort.** As Figure 6-12 shows, the degree to which an employee exerts *force to perform,* or *effort,* to attain a first-order outcome depends on both the expectancy that effort will lead to an increase in that first-order outcome and the valence of the first-order outcome.

For instance, expectancy theory would predict that an employee would exert no effort to perform at a higher level if he or she either saw no possibility that effort would lead to higher performance or did not value higher performance. Formally:

$$\begin{pmatrix} \text{Effort to attain the} \\ \text{first-order outcome} \end{pmatrix} = \text{Expectancy} \times \begin{pmatrix} \text{Valence of the} \\ \text{first-order outcome} \end{pmatrix}$$

Expectancy theory is at base, then, a theory that focuses on values and perceived (or subjective) probabilities. People may place different values on outcomes, and they may have very different perceptions about probabilities. Expectancy theory suggests that managers should not assume they know what employees want or think. Instead, valences, expectancy perceptions, and instrumentality perceptions should be directly assessed. Questionnaires can be used to make these assessments. In those questionnaires, valence is usually

F I G U R E 6 - 1 2
Determinants of Effort to Perform

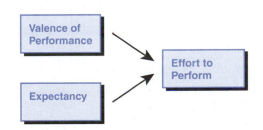

rated on a scale of −10 to +10. Expectancies and instrumentalities are usually rated on scales of 0 (no chance the outcome will occur) to 1 (it will definitely occur).

IMPLICATIONS OF EXPECTANCY THEORY

Expectancy theory provides a variety of important implications for managers. For example:

> **Recognize that three conditions are necessary for motivation to perform.** These are valued rewards, a perceived link of effort to performance (expectancy), and perceived links of performance to valent outcomes (instrumentalities). If *any* of those elements is missing, motivation will be low.

> **Assess perceptions of each of those conditions.** This can provide extremely useful information. For example, you may find that employees don't really value some of the rewards you have been using or that they don't believe their efforts will translate into performance or their performance into rewards. Conversely, you may be surprised to find that employees place great value on rewards that could be easily and inexpensively provided or that employees have surprisingly strong expectancy or instrumentality perceptions.

> **Identify gaps between employee and management perceptions.** For example, a common response of management upon learning that employees don't believe their rewards are tied to their performance levels is "They're wrong! We tightly link pay and other rewards to performance." From an expectancy theory perspective, whether or not the employees' perceptions are wrong is irrelevant; perceptions drive behavior. If rewards actually are tied to behaviors in ways that employees don't recognize, management's job is to convince employees of that fact.

> **As suggested earlier, and consistent with our discussion of need theories, make sure that you are giving employees rewards that they value.** One option is to employ *cafeteria-style benefit plans.* In these plans, employees can choose from a range of alternative benefits. For instance, employees of differing ages or marital status may desire different benefits. One employee may choose all salary with no other

DILBERT reprinted by permission of United Feature Syndicate, Inc.

benefits; another may choose the total allowance for pension and insurance contributions. As an example, Du Pont's U.S. employees can choose from a menu of medical, dental, and life insurance options as well as financial planning.

> **Ask what factors may be weakening expectancy perceptions.** Do employees know what they are supposed to do? Have they been properly trained? Are there characteristics of the situation—resource constraints, poor tools, or whatever—that make it difficult for employees to perform well regardless of their efforts?

> **Ask what factors may be weakening instrumentality perceptions.** Is it the case that rewards really aren't tied to performance? Is management simply not communicating well with employees about the nature of the reward system?

> **If employees appear to be poorly motivated, work backwards.** Try to determine which of the expectancy theory conditions may be lacking.

Which of the expectancy theory components appears to be especially weak in the company depicted in the nearby Dilbert cartoon?

The process diagram in the nearby Bottom Line shows how expectancy theory can be applied to effectively manage employee motivation and performance.

BOTTOM LINE

The Bottom Line: Expectancy Theory

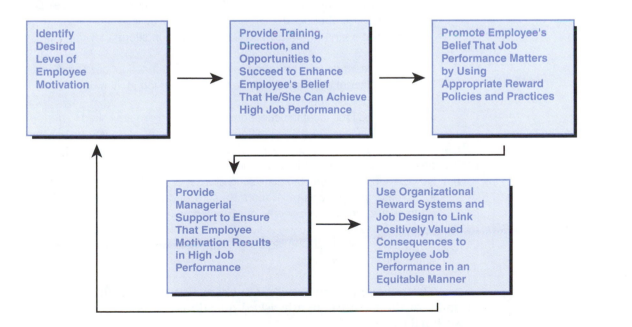

| Identify Desired Level of Employee Motivation | → | Provide Training, Direction, and Opportunities to Succeed to Enhance Employee's Belief That He/She Can Achieve High Job Performance | → | Promote Employee's Belief That Job Performance Matters by Using Appropriate Reward Policies and Practices |

| Provide Managerial Support to Ensure That Employee Motivation Results in High Job Performance | → | Use Organizational Reward Systems and Job Design to Link Positively Valued Consequences to Employee Job Performance in an Equitable Manner |

Skills Practice 6-5 will help you develop skill in conducting a comprehensive analysis of worker motivation and performance using expectancy theory. This exercise is a bit more work than some others, for you need to actually go "into the field" to interview a working person in order to conduct your analysis. We believe the insights you will gain will justify the effort.

Skills Practice 6-5
Applying Expectancy Theory

Skill Objective
To develop skill in applying expectancy theory to the effective management of employee motivation.

Procedure
1. Form groups of 3–5 students (optional).
2. Identify an individual who is currently employed on a full-time basis. This person can be an employee or a manager and can work for any type of organization. Ask if you can interview him/her for about 15 minutes.
3. Based on expectancy theory, ask the person you are interviewing the following questions.

Expectancy Theory Assessment Interview Questions
> What is your position title?
> What is the name of your company?
> What business(es) is your company involved in?
> What are the key tasks and responsibilities that your job entails?
> Overall, to what extent are you motivated to perform your job at a high level?
> To what extent do you believe that you can perform your job at a high level, if you make an effort? Why is this the case? Be specific.
> To what extent do you think there are positive consequences (e.g., rewards) associated with performing your job at a high level? Why is this the case? Be specific.
> How do you feel about the consequences you believe are linked to performing your job at a high level? Do you like them, feel indifferent toward them, or dislike them? Why?
> To what extent do you think there are negative consequences (e.g., verbal or written reprimands) associated with performing your job at a low level? Why is this the case? Please be specific.
> How do you feel about the consequences you believe are linked to performing your job at a low level? Are you indifferent toward them, or do you dislike them? Why?

5. Once you have completed the interview, assess the person's level of work motivation based on his/her expectancy, instrumentality, and valence perceptions.
6. Now develop an action plan consisting of a set of specific actions that could be taken to increase this person's motivation. Be sure to discuss how your recommendations address the various components of expectancy theory.
7. Present your assessment and action plan to the class. Be sure to present your recommendations in terms of specific things you would do to enhance the motivation of the employee in the scenario.

The accompanying Devil's Advocate feature identifies and responds to some of the most frequently asked questions that students have about motivational issues.

DEVIL'S ADVOCATE

MOTIVATION

Why do we need to be concerned with how to manage employee motivation? Doesn't this take a manager's focus away from the "real work" of getting the job done and helping the organization to be more profitable?

First of all, if you are a manager, then motivating your employees is central to your job and therefore it constitutes "real work." As a manager, you are obviously concerned with supporting the achievement of specific "bottom-line" outcomes such as increased sales and profitability. However, you must also be concerned with how you go about achieving those outcomes as well (i.e., the process). In terms of process concerns, the effective motivation of your employees will increase the likelihood that they will perform their jobs well. Wouldn't this in turn help you achieve your work unit's goals? And if you are doing this, then wouldn't you also be contributing to the success of your organization? So the bottom line here is that motivation is one of the key managerial processes you have to attend to in order to help your employees, your work unit, and your organization to be ultimately successful.

I'm a bit skeptical. I've had Maslow's hierarchy of needs theory in about four classes during my college career. Does this theory have anything to say about specific things that can be done to motivate employees in organizations?

You're correct in observing that Maslow's hierarchy of needs is presented in a lot of college classes in different fields, such as psychology, advertising, and marketing. You know, you could argue that this means that Maslow's theory has had an influence on a lot of fields and this is a good thing. Anyway, if you understand the theory, you can see that it does have some valuable things to say about how to motivate employees. Basically, it says that you need to take the time as a manager to figure out which of your employee's needs are unsatisfied (active) and therefore have the ability to motivate the worker. Once you know which needs are most active, you can try to develop a plan that contains things you can provide for an employee that will help to satisfy his/her active needs (e.g., challenging work, opportunities for development, a safe work environment).

There are too many theories of work motivation! How am I supposed to keep them straight? Which one is the best one?

There *are* quite a few theories of motivation, aren't there? Well, the best way to keep them straight is to remember the general types of motivation theories and how they each view motivation. First, you have your content or need theories of motivation, like Maslow's hierarchy of needs. These are sometimes called the "why" theories, because they help explain why people are motivated: because they are seeking to satisfy their active needs. Another basic type of motivation theory is the reinforcement theories. These theories, like Pavlov's classical conditioning and operant learning, look at motivation in terms of people learning to be motivated to engage in certain behaviors due to the consequences that are associated with those behaviors. Finally, there are the process theories, such as goal-setting theory and expectancy theory. These theories are sometimes called the "how" theories, because they provide a more detailed explanation for the process by which a person becomes motivated.

In the end, there really isn't one best motivation theory. A good way to appreciate the value of these theories is to recognize that each theory captures a piece of reality and gives you one perspective for analyzing work motivation. This will help you to better analyze a wider range of motivational problems and decide what to do about them in your role as a manager.

I have a bit of an issue with goal-setting theory. Do we really need a formal theory to explain something that is so straightforward and basic?

Although goal setting may seem simple at a conceptual level, it is infinitely more difficult to do in practice. Goal-setting theory is valuable because it identifies the important things managers must do to ensure that employees have clear directions regarding what they are supposed to work toward and the proper commitment needed to actually get there. You would be surprised or even shocked to see how many employees say that their managers fail to give them a clear sense of what they are trying to achieve and how to get there! If you remember the basic principles underlying goal setting, you will be less likely to be one of those managers.

ASSURING FAIRNESS

It goes without saying that we should treat people fairly. What, though, do we mean by fair? Certainly, fairness has something to do with not cheating others or blatantly playing favorites. But fairness is more complex than that. There are at least two important types of fairness: distributive fairness and procedural fairness. These deal, in turn, with fairness in regard to the sorts of things we get and the processes used to allocate rewards.

Equity theory, which focuses on distributive fairness, is one of a family of theories based on the idea that people want to maintain balance. By focusing on the balance of the inputs, or contributions, people make to the outcomes they receive, equity theory helps us understand how employees determine whether they are being treated fairly.

WHY BE FAIR?

According to equity theorists, people want to maintain distributive fairness. *Distributive fairness* exists when someone thinks people are getting what they deserve—not less, certainly, but *not more either.* According to equity theory, people feel uncomfortable when they get less than they deserve (because they feel cheated) or more than they deserve (because they feel guilty). Research evidence supports this contention.[17] There are several reasons why people want distributive fairness.[18] For instance:

> When people experience a situation they feel is not fair, they experience an unpleasant state of tension. Restoration of distributive fairness reduces that tension.
> Some people try to be fair because they think others will reward them for being fair.
> Behaving fairly may bolster a person's self-esteem.
> Most people find it comforting to believe that life is fair. By giving others what we think they deserve, we strengthen that belief.

Employers may have other, more specific reasons for wanting to treat their employees fairly.[19] They may, for instance, want to do the following:

> **Conform to business norms.** For example, people in business generally agree that employees who do better work should get more rewards.
> **Attract superior workers to their company and weed out inferior workers.** If rewards are fairly tied to performance, a positive relationship between satisfaction and performance should result. Thus, high performers should be satisfied and disposed to stay with the firm, while low performers should be dissatisfied and leave the firm.
> **Motivate employees to produce.** As expectancy theory indicates, tying rewards to performance should enhance instrumentality perceptions and thus increase motivation to perform well.
> **Develop trust.** A trusting environment is extremely important to workers, especially in turbulent job environments. Managers who don't treat their employees fairly will not be trusted.

DETERMINING EQUITY

How do people determine whether outcomes are equitable? J. Stacey Adams proposed the following equation for an equitable relationship.[20] It is based on the writings of an earlier student of behavior, Aristotle:[21]

$$\frac{O_p}{I_p} = \frac{O_o}{I_o}$$

Where:

O_p is the person's perception of the outcomes he or she is receiving.

I_p is the person's perception of his or her inputs.

O_o is the person's perception of the outcomes some comparison person (called a comparison other) is receiving.

I_o is the person's perception of the inputs of the comparison other.

This equation says that equity exists when a person feels the ratio of his or her outcomes to his or her inputs is *equal to* that ratio for some comparison other. Neither is seen as getting less or more than his or her inputs justify. Note that *each* of the elements in the equation is a perception. While actual conditions may (or may not) influence those perceptions, they do not directly enter the equity calculations.

The comparison other may be another individual (such as a coworker or friend), a group of other people (such as workers on another job), or some abstract combination of people. It may even be the perceiving person at an earlier point in time.

INPUTS AND OUTCOMES

At base, inputs are anything employees believe they are contributing to the job. Outcomes are anything they believe they are getting from the job. So inputs might include such things as seniority, time, performance, appearance, dedication to the organization, effort, intelligence, and provision of needed tools. Outcomes might include pay, promotional opportunities, job status, job interest, esteem of coworkers, monotony, praise, fatigue, and dangerous working conditions. Note that employees may view some outcomes of the job negatively, such as fatigue and dangerous working conditions. Obviously, different people care about different inputs and outcomes. An input for one person may even be an outcome for another. For instance, one worker may value increased responsibility, viewing it as an outcome. Another may see that same increased responsibility as a burdensome input.

In the nearby Dilbert cartoon, it is clear that Alice and her boss have very different perceptions about what factors should weigh into the equity equation.

DILBERT reprinted by permission of United Feature Syndicate, Inc.

RESTORING EQUITY

If an individual perceives a situation to be inequitable, there are many ways to restore equity. For instance, suppose that Frank feels underpaid relative to his coworker Karen. He could try to restore equity in each of the following ways.

> **He can raise his actual outcomes.** For instance, Frank might demand and get a raise.

> **He can lower his inputs.** Frank might slow down on the job, withhold important information, or stop doing unpaid overtime work.

> **He can perceptually distort his inputs and/or outcomes.** Frank could reason that he was actually getting things out of the job he hadn't been considering, or he could downgrade the values of his inputs.

> **He can perceptually distort Karen's inputs and/or outcomes.** Frank could devalue the nonpay outcomes Karen is receiving, or he could increase his estimates of Karen's inputs.

> **He can leave the situation.** With a big enough feeling of inequity, Frank might psychologically withdraw from the situation or might actually apply for a transfer or quit.

> **He can act to change Karen's inputs and/or outcomes.** Frank could try to convince Karen to raise her inputs, could talk to the boss about lowering Karen's pay, or could take steps to try to make Karen leave her job.

> **He can change his comparison other.** Frank could begin to compare his situation to that of Paul rather than to that of Karen.

People do use these mechanisms to restore equity. For instance, field studies and laboratory experiments have shown that individuals withdraw from tasks when they are inequitably treated—even, in some cases, when they are overpaid.[22] There is also considerable evidence that people change their perceptions to restore equity.[23] Underpaid workers often perceive that they have made relatively low inputs and begin to see themselves as less qualified than others.[24] Some also exaggerate their outcomes, rating their jobs as far more interesting than others do.

FOCUS ON MANAGEMENT

INEQUITY AT IBM

Employees are sensitive to perceived inequities. For instance, in May 1993 IBM confronted the worst crisis in its history. In the previous eight years, it had cut more than 180,000 of its 405,000 jobs, and by the end of the year it would report an annual loss of more than $8 billion. In the face of these cutbacks and the threat of further belt tightening, employees were dismayed by the perks the company maintained for managers and top salespeople—country clubs with golf courses and skeet-shooting; a large fleet of private jets; a Rose Bowl Parade float; and elaborate sales meetings featuring a five-act circus, Bob Newhart, Larry King, Liza Minelli, and others. Whatever the merits of such expenses, they created a sense of great inequity and led to many angry complaints.*

http://www.ibm.com/

*M. W. Miller, "As IBM Losses Mount, So Do the Complaints About Company Perks," *The Wall Street Journal,* October 27, 1993, p. A1.

GLOBAL PERSPECTIVES

THE GLOBAL DEBATE OVER CEO PAY

CEO pay increases in large U.S. companies averaged 24 percent in 1999, bringing the average compensation package to $9.4 million.* These dramatic increases—and the growing disparity between CEO pay and that of other employees—has led to charges of greed and concerns about the impact of perceived inequities.† Pay in the United States for CEOs is now about 420 times more than that of the average blue-collar worker, much higher than in the past. By one estimate, if current pay growth rates continue over the next 50 years, the average CEO will be paid more than 150,000 American factory workers.‡ In contrast to the U.S. ratio of 400+ to 1, the norm in Europe and Japan is for CEOs to receive about 15–20 times the compensation of the average factory worker.§ Further, many U.S. CEOs are earning huge bonuses even as they lay off workers in cost-cutting moves. While some supporters of high CEO pay levels note that much of the compensation is in the form of stock options and argue that these extreme levels have fueled U.S. economic growth, others argue that there is little evidence that higher CEO pay results in higher company performance.‖ Further, U.S. employees aren't the only ones complaining about inequities—CEO compensation packages are beginning to rise worldwide as foreign executives are eyeing the staggering sums received by their U.S. counterparts.#

*R. Poe and C. L. Courter, "Fast Forward," *Across the Board,* March 2000, p. 5.

†R. W. Thompson, "Report on CEO Pay May Fuel Congressional Debate," *HRMagazine,* November 1999, p. 12; and, C. R. Weinberg, "CEO Compensation: Greed or Glory?" *Chief Executive,* September 1999, pp. 44–59.

‡"Rocketing Pay," *Strategic Finance,* June 1999, p. 96.

§C. G. Wagner, "Soaring CEO Salaries," *The Futurist,* November 1999, pp. 9–10.

‖J. Reingold and R. Grover, "Executive Pay: The Numbers Are Staggering, but So Is the Performance of American Business. So How Closely Are They Linked?" *Business Week,* April 19, 1999, p. 72.

#T. Leander, "The Global Shakeup in Executive Comp," *Global Finance,* August 1998, pp. 12–14.

As an example of the ways employees may take action to restore equity, consider the case of a manufacturing plant that made small mechanical parts for the aerospace and automotive industries. When important contracts were canceled, the company announced a 15 percent pay cut for all employees in the plant. Compared to employees in another plant, whose pay was not cut, the affected employees reacted by doubling their normal theft rate of tools and supplies from the company, and turnover jumped to 23 percent (compared to a normal 5 percent). When the pay cut ended after 10 weeks, theft returned to normal levels.[25] Apparently, employees in the plant experienced underpayment inequity, and some reacted by stealing. Others apparently decided simply to leave the inequitable situation.

While equity theory would permit any of a wide range of adjustments to restore equity, it would be useful to know specifically which change is most likely to occur. Adams has provided the following set of propositions concerning how people choose from among the alternatives available to reduce inequity.[26]

> They will first try to maximize valued outcomes.
> They will be reluctant to increase inputs that are difficult or costly to change.
> They will resist actual or perceived changes in inputs or outcomes that are central to their self-concept and self-esteem.

> They will be more resistant to changing perceptions about their own inputs and outcomes than to changing perceptions about their comparison others' inputs and outcomes.
> They will leave the situation only when inequity is great and other means of reducing it are not available. Partial withdrawal, such as absenteeism, will occur more frequently and under lower conditions of inequity.
> They will be reluctant to change their comparison others.

The process model presented in the nearby Bottom Line shows how equity theory can be systematically implemented to establish and maintain an employee's sense of perceived equity in his or her work situation.

OTHER RULES FOR DETERMINING DISTRIBUTIVE FAIRNESS

Equity theory is based on the contributions rule. The *contributions rule* says that distributive fairness is determined by equating contributions (inputs) with outcomes. However, people may use other rules when determining distributive fairness. They may, for example, employ the *needs rule,* feeling it is fair to give people what they need rather than what they contribute. Or they may employ the *equality rule,* arguing that it is fair for everyone to get the same amount.

BOTTOM LINE

The Bottom Line: Equity Theory

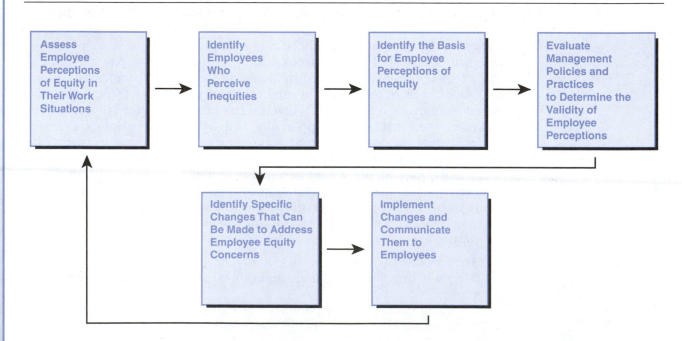

Assess Employee Perceptions of Equity in Their Work Situations → Identify Employees Who Perceive Inequities → Identify the Basis for Employee Perceptions of Inequity → Evaluate Management Policies and Practices to Determine the Validity of Employee Perceptions → Identify Specific Changes That Can Be Made to Address Employee Equity Concerns → Implement Changes and Communicate Them to Employees → (loop back to Assess Employee Perceptions)

A variety of things determine the weights we give to these various rules, including the following.

> **Self-interest.** People tend to assign higher weights to rules that favor them. A high performer will likely favor the contributions rule, while a needy person will favor the needs rule.
> **Conformity.** People tend to conform to the beliefs and behaviors of others with whom they regularly interact. So if all of a manager's coworkers favor the equality rule, the manager may also apply that rule.
> **Availability of relevant information.** People are reluctant to use a rule for which they don't have sufficient information. For instance, if a manager doesn't know what subordinates need, the needs rule probably won't be applied.

In addition, some things affect the weights given to specific rules. For instance, if it is important that high performers maintain their output levels, the contributions rule will be weighted heavily. When someone feels responsible for the receivers' welfare, the needs rule is likely to be applied. And the equality rule is easy to apply. People may also turn to the equality rule when needs and contributions are hard to assess.

PROCEDURAL FAIRNESS

Distributive fairness depends on whether receivers get what they deserve. People may also be concerned with procedural fairness. *Procedural fairness* is whether the process used to allocate outcomes is fair. If procedures seem unfair, people may also question the distribution of rewards. On the other hand, even if people don't get what they want, they may be satisfied as long as they believe the allocation process was fair.

Not surprisingly, people tend to think procedures are fair when those procedures favor their interests. They also believe procedures to be fairer when they have some control over the allocation process. Further, they are likely to consider a procedure to be unfair when it uses questionable means to get information about the receivers' behavior (such as the use of hidden cameras) or if the evaluations of receivers seem to be based on unreliable or irrelevant information (such as faulty performance appraisals).

IMPLICATIONS OF FAIRNESS THEORIES

Equity theory and related theories of fairness have important implications for managing behavior in organizations, including the following.

> **Fairness is absolutely critical to employees.** Fairness influences both employee attitudes and their behaviors.
> **Perceptions play a central role in determinations of fairness.** Whether or not management thinks something is fair, employees will react negatively if they perceive it to be unfair.
> **Fairness involves a comparison process.** Employees don't decide whether something is fair by looking only at their own paychecks and other rewards. Instead, they compare their rewards and contributions to those of relevant others. As such, it is critical to make sure that rewards are equitably distributed across employees.

> **Both distributive fairness and procedural fairness are important.**
While employees obviously care about whether they're getting what they think they deserve, they also are very concerned about whether the process used to determine rewards was fair. Even if employees are pleased with what they received, they may have qualms if they think the allocation process was unfair. They may, for instance, feel guilt, or they may question whether the process will give them what they deserve next time. If employees get less than they feel they deserve, a clear explanation of exactly how rewards were determined may temper their reactions. This, of course, puts the onus appropriately on management to actually use a fair allocation process.

> **Both overreward and underreward may cause problems.** While underreward may cause anger, overreward may cause guilt.

> **Employees may consider inputs and outcomes that are different from those we may expect.** Indeed, what some employees consider inputs, others may see as outcomes.

> **We need to find what people really value and what they think they are contributing.** We cannot assume that people value what we expect them to value or that they see their contributions as we do. Perhaps the best way to find what people see as inputs and outcomes is to ask them.

> **Employees may find many ways to reduce perceived inequity.** In the case of underreward inequity, these might include producing less, producing lower-quality work, quitting, or even sabotage or theft.

> **While the exact means employees will use to reduce inequity may be difficult to predict, almost all are harmful to organizations and perhaps to the individuals themselves.** Not only may inequity lead to bad outcomes for the organization, it may also generate stress in employees and perhaps even cause them to question their self-worth.

Skills Practice 6-6 will help you develop skill in translating the concept of equity into managerial practice through a systematic process of analysis, evaluation, and action planning.

Skills Practice 6-6
Applying Equity Theory

Skill Level: **Challenging**

Skill Objective
To develop skill in applying equity theory to "real-world" work situations.

Procedure
1. Select one of the following scenarios.

Scenario 1—The Unbalanced Workloads
You are the supervisor of the bill-processing department at a large utility company based in Boca Raton, Florida. You have 16 clerical workers who are responsible for processing the payment of incoming bills from the company's customers. Everyone in your work unit has a cubicle in an open work environment where employees can see each other pretty easily. As the supervisor of the department, you have an office located adjacent to the area where your clerical employees perform their jobs.

All of the clerical workers in your department are relatively new, so their job tenure and compensation all fall within a narrow range. Merit pay increases are supposed to be given each year, but management has decided just to give everyone a standard 3 percent pay increase each year rather than differentiate pay increases based on performance.

A recent job satisfaction survey that was administered to your employees revealed that many of them perceive tremendous inequities in the amount of work they have to do relative to their coworkers in the department. On the survey, many employees commented that some employees always get a lot of work to do, while others sit around having personal conversations on their phones, surfing the Internet, or playing electronic blackjack on their computers.

This has resulted in a high level of frustration for many of the clerical employees. Some employees have been talking about transferring to other departments or finding employment with another company altogether.

Based on equity theory, what would you do to handle this situation?

Scenario 2—The Compensation "Outlier"

You are the Director of Software Applications at a medium-size business software firm based in California. You have a team of 10 software programmers that work to develop new software for the firm. Your current staff members have an average of seven years of programming experience and make an average of $50,000 per year.

Recently, the company has experienced a dramatic increase in the need for new, talented programmers for entry-level positions. Given a tremendous shortage of qualified computer programmers graduating from the top universities, the starting salaries for new, entry-level programmers has risen to $45,000–$50,000 per year. While this is generally accepted as the norm among employers hiring computer programmers in today's job market, it has created significant frustration and dissatisfaction among your existing staff. Specifically, your experienced staff does not feel it is fair for new programmers straight out of college to be making almost as much money (or in some cases the same amount) as they do. In addition, they know that the new programmers are not capable of handling the kinds of advanced projects they are working on at the present time.

While nobody has quit over this issue yet, you are concerned about the adverse effect it has had on some current employees' morale and motivation.

Using equity theory, how would you handle this situation?

2. Develop an action plan (i.e., a list of steps you would take) for establishing and maintaining payment equity in the scenario you selected.
3. Answer the following discussion questions as a class.

Discussion Questions

1. Why are perceptions important in equity theory? Why are perceptions important in the "real world?"
2. What was the problem in the scenario you selected? What were the relevant perceptions of the employees in your scenario?
3. What kinds of actions did you recommend in order to establish and maintain payment equity in your scenario?
4. What are the practical implications of this exercise for you as a future manager?

DESIGNING MOTIVATING JOBS

Jobs are central to the lives of most people. They consume a large part of our days and often our nights. To a great extent, many of us rate our success in life on the basis of the status, pay, and other characteristics of our jobs. And others often size us up by our response to "Tell me, what do you do?" Indeed, it is hard to imagine not working. Albert Camus has written, "Without work, all life goes rotten. But when work is soulless, life stifles and dies." What is it about jobs that makes them important to people? What makes them exciting? Why are some soulless? What makes jobs "good" or "bad"? Does everyone want the same things from jobs? And what can management do to improve jobs and increase their motivating potential?

THE CASE FOR SPECIALIZATION

Frederick Taylor introduced scientific management.[27]. According to scientific management, the "one best way" to perform a job should be found. That "one best way" usually results in job simplification, with each worker performing the same few activities over and over. Advantages cited for specialization include the following.

> The worker should be better able to perform the task and should find it to be easier.
> Time is not lost moving from one piece of machinery to another.
> The use of specialized machinery is encouraged.
> Replacement of employees who are absent or who leave the organization is easier, since the job is simpler and easier to learn.
> Especially where assembly lines are used, the worker will adjust to the required pace and be drawn along by "traction."

Scientific management was credited with some notable successes. For instance, application of its principles in one case increased the number of bricks laid per worker-hour from 120 to 350. Further, scientific management permitted the worker to maximize performance by focusing on a narrow range of activities. If the worker was paid on a piece-rate basis, this would result in higher pay. As a result, scientific management was widely adopted in the United States and elsewhere.

However, Taylor is now often criticized for his emphasis on efficiency at the possible expense of employee satisfaction. He did consider the human element, but many of his views today seem inhumane. He wrote, for instance, that the kind of person who made a good pig-iron handler was "of the type of the ox." Whether or not criticisms of Taylor are correct, it does seem that the simplified, routine jobs he proposed may have some unforeseen results. For instance, they may lead to boredom, dissatisfaction, or other negative outcomes, as shown in Figure 6-13.

FIGURE 6-13
Potential Reactions to Specialized Jobs

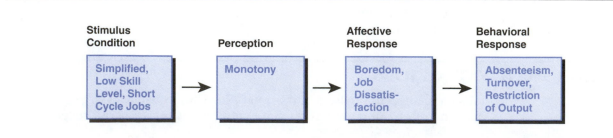

JOB SIZE

If we believe "small" jobs are demeaning and dissatisfying for workers, a logical question to ask is how we can make jobs larger. There are at least two major dimensions to job size. They are job depth and job scope, or range.

Job depth refers to the degree to which employees can influence their work environments and carry out planning and control functions. *Job scope* is the number of different activities the worker performs, regardless of their content. Increases in job depth are usually called *job enrichment,* while increases in job scope are referred to as *job enlargement.* Most job changes are likely to influence both depth and scope, but these are separate dimensions and they can be independently changed.

The following are among the suggested advantages of increases in scope.

> There should be less fatigue of particular muscles, since a greater variety of muscles may be used.
> Since the employee will complete a larger part of the task, there may be more of a feeling of accomplishment.
> The employee may exercise a greater variety of skills.
> Large increases in scope may enhance managerial flexibility. For instance, if a company uses assembly teams rather than assembly lines, it can shut down a small number of the benches used by assembly teams rather than the entire line.

The presumed benefits for increased depth are primarily psychological. For instance, Chris Argyris has suggested that since small, routine jobs are frustrating to the drives of "mature" individuals, they may result in use of a variety of defense mechanisms.[28] Those *defense mechanisms* are ways in which the employee may try to reduce the tensions caused by frustration. They might involve physically leaving the source of frustration (such as through absenteeism or turnover), mentally leaving (through apathy or daydreaming), or striking back (perhaps by slowing down on the job or by making negative comments about the company). As shown in Figure 6-14, Argyris has argued that the typical firm's response to such defense mechanisms is to make jobs even more specialized, tighten up on rules, and emphasize authority relationships. These actions further frustrate maturity drives, and a self-reinforcing cycle occurs. Argyris reasons that to break out of that cycle, it is necessary to treat employees as mature individuals. Giving them more opportunity for planning and control is one step in that direction.

Others made similar arguments.[29] For instance, M. Scott Myers said the assumption underlying work simplification is that there are two groups of employees. One group, responsible and highly motivated, is known as *managers.* The other, irresponsible and in need of close supervision, is called *workers.* Because of those assumed differences, companies call on managers to plan, direct, and control. They expect workers simply to carry out orders. Myers argued that companies must break down this artificial dichotomy and "make every employee a manager." This would involve turning many planning and control functions over to workers. That is, it would require enriching their jobs.

Companies in many industries are using job enrichment. In the hotel industry, for instance, front-desk clerks, housekeepers, bellhops, and other employees are being given more authority to make decisions on their own and to

FIGURE 6-14
The Argyris Maturity Drive Frustration Cycle

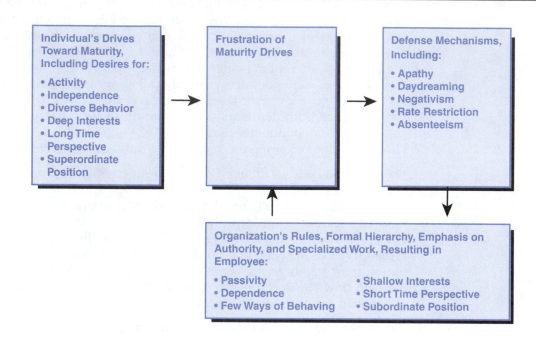

handle disputes with customers. At the Ritz-Carlton Hotel Company, for instance, front-desk clerks can now take off up to $2,000 from a guest's bill if the guest feels service was not up to par.[30] At John Deere & Co., workers who assembled parts for machines are now, after six months of training, traveling around the Midwest speaking to groups of farmers as part of the Deere marketing team. Other hourly workers routinely give advice on cost cutting and improving product quality. Job enrichment is part of Deere's plan to use its workers as a source of competitive advantage.[31] And truck drivers for Ryder System Inc., which has a contract with Xerox to deliver and install that firm's copying machines, now are fluent with computers and fax machines. Sporting the title of "service associates" and carrying business cards, they fax invoices, train office workers in how to use the latest office technology, and generally help customers solve problems.[32]

THE JOB CHARACTERISTICS MODEL

If we want to change jobs, we need to know which job dimensions are important to employees. In particular, before we can enrich jobs, we need to know what makes a job enriched. The examples we have just cited provide some clues. The jobs might, for instance, involve more responsibility, freedom, and challenge and a richer set of job duties. But are these necessary conditions for enrichment? Are there additional elements to enrichment?

The *job characteristics model,* shown in Figure 6-15, describes jobs as having five core task dimensions and two interpersonal dimensions.[33]

FIGURE 6-15
The Job Characteristics Model

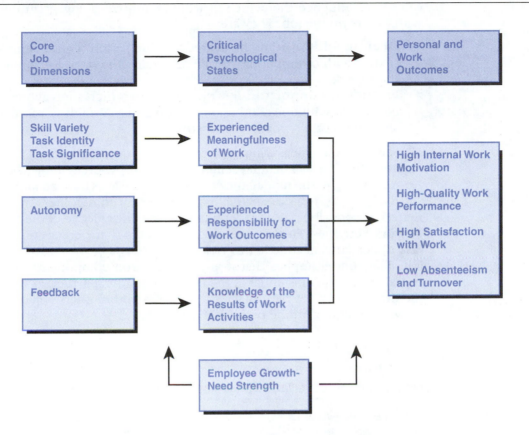

CORE TASK DIMENSIONS

The *core task dimensions* are characteristics of the job itself that are believed to be key influences on employee motivation. They include the following.

> **Skill variety.** The degree to which the job requires employees to perform a wide range of operations in their work and/or the degree to which employees must use a variety of equipment and procedures in their work.
> **Autonomy.** The extent to which employees have a major say in scheduling their work, selecting the equipment they will use, and deciding on procedures they will follow.
> **Task identity.** The extent to which employees do an entire piece of work and can clearly identify the result of their efforts.
> **Task significance.** The extent to which the job has a strong impact on the lives and work of other people.
> **Feedback.** The degree to which employees receive information while they are working that reveals how well they are performing on the job.

INTERPERSONAL DIMENSIONS

The *interpersonal dimensions* (not shown in the figure) are job characteristics that influence the degree to which employees engage in relationships with others on the job. They are:

> **Dealing with others:** the degree to which a job requires employees to deal with other people (inside or outside the firm) to complete their work

> **Friendship opportunities:** the degree to which a job allows employees to talk with one another on the job and to establish informal relationships with other employees at work

Sample items measuring each of the core task dimensions are shown in Figure 6-16. Can you match each item to the appropriate dimension?

According to the model, the core task dimensions have an impact on three *critical psychological states:* experienced meaningfulness of work, experienced responsibility for work outcomes, and knowledge of the actual results of work activities. Further, the model indicates that perceptions of the core task dimensions fit together to yield the *motivating potential score* of the job. This model implies that if any of the three components are very low, overall motivating potential of the task will be low. Further, as long as any of the three remain at very low levels, increases in the others will do little to improve overall motivating potential.

FIGURE 6-16

Measuring the Core Task Dimensions

Listed here are five statements that may (or may not) describe your job. You are to indicate the degree to which each statement is an accurate description of the job on which you work. Do this by writing the appropriate number in the left-hand margin, based on the following scale:

1	2	3	4	5	6	7
Very untrue of the job	Mostly untrue of the job	Slightly untrue of the job	Uncertain	Slightly true of the job	Moderately true of the job	Very true of the job

Please make your descriptions as objective and factually accurate as possible, without regard for whether you like or dislike your job.

1. The job requires me to use a variety of complex or high-level skills.
2. The job gives me considerable opportunity for independence and freedom in how I do the work.
3. The job provides me with the chance to finish completely the pieces of work I begin.
4. Just doing the work required by the job provides many chances for me to figure out how well I'm doing.
5. The job is one where a lot of other people can be affected by how well the work gets done.

Source: Adapted from J. R. Hackman and G. Oldham, *Work Redesign.* Reading, MA: Addison, Wesley, 1980, pp. 300–301.

EVIDENCE REGARDING THE JOB CHARACTERISTICS MODEL

The job characteristics approach has dominated recent job design efforts. Questions have been raised concerning whether all employees actually view their jobs on these specific dimensions.[34] It does seem, however, that the dimensions may serve as useful guides for understanding reactions to jobs and for planning redesign strategies.

Studies show that perceptions of the core task dimensions are related to job satisfaction, job involvement, organizational commitment, and other favorable attitudes. However, those perceptions are usually not related in any consistent way to quantity of performance.[35] Employees on enriched jobs typically get the benefits of enrichment simply by carrying out the task, regardless of their performance levels. So we would expect the core task dimension perceptions to translate into increased performance only when persistence on the task is important.[36]

Research shows that the combinatory model proposed by the job characteristics model (in which a very low level on one dimension would neutralize the impact of changes in other dimensions) is probably not valid. That is, task dimension perceptions somehow seem to "add up" to influence reactions rather than representing a series of hurdles.[37] This is a welcome finding since it suggests that improvements on any of the dimensions may help.[38]

THE FOCUS ON PERCEPTIONS

Remember that the job characteristics approach focuses on employee perceptions of task characteristics. This is appropriate since we act on the basis of our perceptions. However, many things may affect perceptions. For instance, in one study students were asked to perform a simple assembly task.[39] The task was the same for all students, but the way they perceived the task depended on their ages and personalities. As an example, older students felt the task offered more skill variety and feedback but less task identity than did younger students. In general, we might expect that an employee with considerable experience and training on a task would see it very differently than would a "rookie."[40]

This makes the job of job design more difficult. It is not enough to make objective changes in feedback, skill variety, or the other task dimensions. We must also discover how those objective changes translate into perceptions.

IMPLEMENTING JOB ENRICHMENT

Implementing principles for job redesign are job changes that might influence the core task dimensions.[41] Figure 6-17 presents those implementing principles. As our previous examples suggest, implementing principles include such actions as giving workers tasks to perform that require a larger variety of skills, letting workers do a larger part of the job in order to increase task identity and task significance, permitting employees to have increased contact with clients in order to increase skill variety, autonomy, and feedback, vertically loading the job (that is, giving more "management" responsibility) to enhance autonomy, and opening new feedback channels. Another, related, way to enhance the core task dimensions is through job rotation. With *job rotation,* employees systematically move from one job to another, getting a

FIGURE 6-17

Implementing Principles for Job Redesign

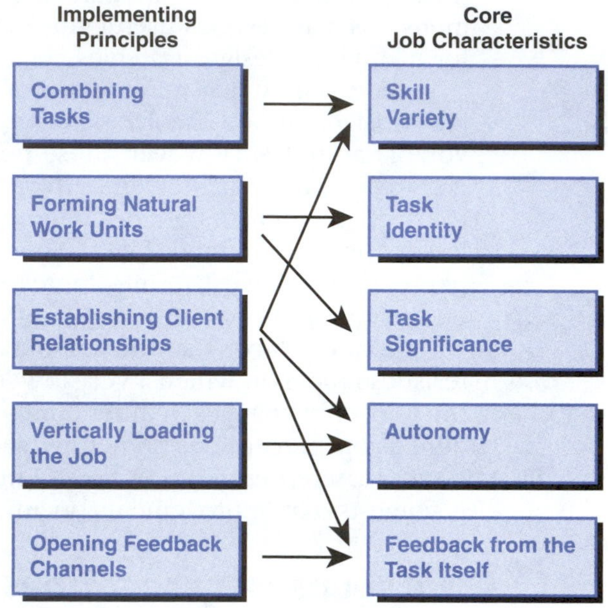

change of pace and duties, learning more about the company, and often developing a broad foundation for future advancement.[42]

These principles may be useful in providing suggestions for how companies can change jobs to increase levels of the core task dimensions. However, their use must take place as part of a systematic assessment of the particular situation. For instance, if job enrichment is to be successful, it must fit with the organization's employees, practices, structure, and technology.

THE CONDITIONS FOR SUCCESSFUL REDESIGN

A family of jobs should be considered for redesign if:[43]

> The employees perceive their jobs to be deficient in the core task dimensions. It is important to stress here that worker perceptions, not just the assumptions of management or consultants, are crucial.

> Employees are fairly well satisfied with pay, fringe benefits, and working conditions. If workers are unhappy with these factors, they are likely to resent and resist job redesign.

> The current structure and technology of the unit where the jobs are housed are hospitable to enriched jobs. If the overall organization has a mechanistic structure or technology such as assembly lines, redesign attempts may be expensive and hard to implement. They are also likely to ultimately fail.

> Employees want the sorts of things—variety, autonomy, feedback, and so on—that enriched jobs provide.

These conditions suggest that job redesign should be undertaken carefully and selectively. It may be appropriate only in a limited set of situations and, as we discuss in the next section, it must be carefully and systematically implemented.

STEPS IN IMPLEMENTATION

If conditions seem appropriate for redesign, a job redesign task force made up of management and labor representatives should proceed through the steps summarized in Figure 6-18.

WHO WANTS JOB ENRICHMENT?

You probably know some people who would like more challenge, variety, and responsibility from their jobs and others who might be indifferent to them. Still others might say, "If you're going to give me all the decision-making responsibility of my boss, give me my boss's pay." The direct measure of the degree to which an employee wants an enriched job is called *growth-need strength (GNS).* This is basically the degree to which an individual wants such things as challenge and responsibility. While most employees respond positively to high levels of the core task dimensions, those with strong GNS react most favorably. This suggests a simple and reasonable way to determine who wants job redesign: If we don't know whether employees are likely to react favorably to job enrichment, we can ask them.

The process model presented in the nearby Bottom Line illustrates how job characteristics theory can be applied in order to enhance employees' intrinsic motivation and yield desirable personal and organizational outcomes.

FIGURE 6-18
Stages in Job Redesign

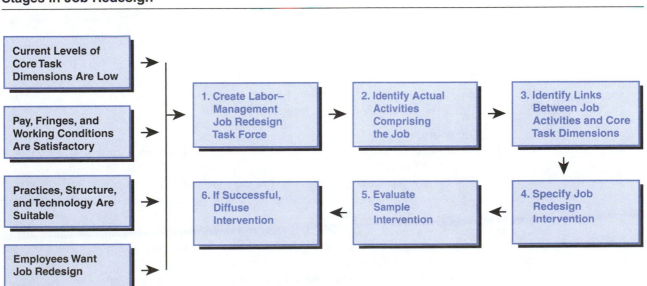

The Bottom Line: Job Characteristics Theory

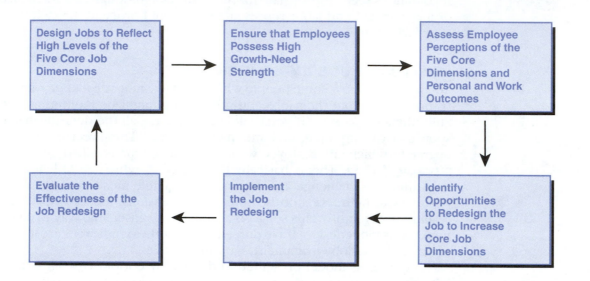

Skills Practice 6-7 will show you how to apply job characteristics theory in order to enrich a job and achieve higher levels of satisfaction, motivation, and performance from employees.

Skills Practice 6-7
Applying Job Characteristics Theory to Increase Employee Motivation

Skill Level: Challenging

Skill Objective
To develop skill in using job characteristics theory to enrich jobs and enhance employee motivation, performance, and satisfaction.

Procedure
1. Select one job that you are familiar with. Ideally, this will be a current job or one you held in the past.
2. Now take a piece of paper and list the major tasks and responsibilities associated with the job you selected. This does not need to be exhaustive; just try to identify the most important aspects of the job.
3. Below your list of job tasks and responsibilities, rate the job in terms of the following:
   > Perceived levels of each of the five core job dimensions (i.e., low, moderate, or high)
   > Your satisfaction with the job
   > Your motivation to perform the job
   > Your actual performance on the job

4. Now take another piece of paper and write the name of each core job dimension on it with some space underneath each one. Brainstorm a list of things (2–3 strategies) that could be implemented in order to increase your perceived level of each core job dimension. Remember that you want to perceive that the job possesses a high level of all five of the core job dimensions. Be as specific and action oriented as possible.

5. Present to the class your job redesign plan from the preceding step. Explain why each of your strategies would help to increase the perceived level of each core job dimension and the personal and work outcomes identified by the theory.

6. Answer the following discussion questions.

Discussion Questions

1. Why should a manager be concerned about job design?

2. How is job characteristics theory useful in designing good jobs?

3. What are the keys to the successful implementation of job design and job redesign in organizations? What are the major barriers to making job design work?

4. What are the practical implications of this exercise for you as a future manager?

The accompanying Voice of Experience interview with Annette Mondry of American Family Insurance explores the issue of motivating employees effectively through the use of appropriate job design and leadership strategies.

VOICE OF EXPERIENCE

MOTIVATING

Annette Mondry,
Director of Field Training
American Family Insurance

1. What do you do to motivate your employees?

Determine what they enjoy doing, the environment they work best in, and try to create a world where they can operate most comfortably. Understand that people are self-motivated and you can only help facilitate their motivation—you can't actually motivate them. Give room for individuals to experiment. Praise risk taking, even if it fails.

2. What advice would you give to a new manager regarding what needs to be done to be an effective leader and motivator?

Listen to many differing points of view so that you learn to understand people. Then follow your instinct. Leaders must be learners, so it's a good idea to get exposed to as many disciplines as possible. Study psychology, sociology, accounting, strategic planning, international relations, etc. Don't think of yourself as an "accountant" or a "trainer." The world changes rapidly. Become proficient in many areas so that you will be flexible enough to switch careers. Be ready to shift to a whole new environment—the world changes fast.

3. What strategies do you use to establish an effective power base (capacity to influence others) in your job?

Communicate even if you don't know all of the answers. People appreciate knowing what's going on. Learn, read, and become an expert in many areas. Become interested in areas that are out of your "normal" job—take on projects just to learn new skills. Influence through your own actions. Maintain a positive but real attitude. Be honest with people whenever possible.

Always talk with a variety of people—network inside and outside your industry. Pilot-test ideas whenever possible, and implement the winners full scale. Combine data-based decision making with intuition.

http://www.amfam.com/

284

Chapter 6 / Motivating Effectively

Skills Application
Skills Application
Skills Application
Skills Application
Skills Application

TOP TEN LIST: KEY POINTS TO REMEMBER

HOW TO MOTIVATE EFFECTIVELY

10. Assess employee needs and identify those that are most active (unsatisfied). Take specific actions to satisfy these needs through an employee's job and overall work experience in your organization.

9. Align the satisfaction of employee needs with the achievement of organizational goals through your managerial policies and practices.

8. Demonstrate to employees that good job performance "makes a difference" by linking positive outcomes or rewards to performance.

7. Demonstrate to employees that poor performance will not be tolerated by linking negative outcomes with poor performance or by eliminating positive outcomes that inadvertently led to the poor performance.

6. Develop and implement managerial policies and practices that enable workers to learn through the experience and wisdom of others.

5. Set specific and challenging goals and objectives for your employees and ensure that they are aligned with the goals of the overall work unit. Monitor progress toward goal achievement and take appropriate corrective action as needed.

4. Develop and maintain employee motivation by ensuring that they feel that they have the ability to be successful on their job, that consequences are linked to performance, and that these consequences are appropriately valued by employees.

3. Provide managerial support for employee motivation so that it results in high levels of job performance.

2. Monitor employee perceptions of their treatment by you and the organization. Take action to ensure that employees feel that they are treated fairly.

1. Design jobs so that the characteristics of the job provide a good fit with the knowledge, skills, abilities, goals, and values of each employee.

QUESTIONS FOR REVIEW AND REFLECTION

REVIEW QUESTIONS

1. Define *need, satisfaction,* and *motivation* and describe the need satisfaction process.

2. Identify the five needs in Maslow's need hierarchy, the three needs in Alderfer's ERG theory, and the three manifest needs considered by McClelland.

3. Discuss eight implications of need theories.

4. What is learning? Discuss classical conditioning, operant conditioning, and social learning.

5. Describe three contingencies of reinforcement to increase desired behaviors and two contingencies of reinforcement to reduce undesired behaviors.

6. Compare continuous reinforcement and four partial-reinforcement schedules in terms of learning rate, response rate, response stability, and extinction rate.

7. Provide seven guidelines for the effective use of organizational behavior modification.

8. Give five reasons why goals are important, and provide seven guidelines for effective goal setting.

9. Discuss the elements of expectancy theory as well as seven implications of the theory.

10. Discuss reasons why people seek fairness in general as well as why employers may want to treat their employees fairly.

11. According to equity theory, how do employees determine if they have been treated fairly? What are seven ways an employee may attempt to restore equity when underrewarded?

12. Present nine implications of fairness theories.

13. Discuss the job characteristics model, including the five core task dimensions and two interpersonal dimensions.

14. Identify approaches to implementing job enrichment and the conditions for successful job redesign.

CRITICAL THINKING QUESTIONS

1. A manager says, "We pay our employees to do their jobs, and we pay them well. That should be motivation enough." How would you respond?

2. When you say you have been reading about learning theory and are hoping to apply it in the workplace, a colleague expresses alarm. She says, "There's enough stress in this place without having people playing mind games to jack up performance." Do you agree with this position? Why or why not?

3. Larry Bird upon retiring as coach of the Indianapolis Pacers commented on the difficulty of motivating professional basketball players. A common reaction to his comments was: "These players make tens of millions of dollars. How can they *not* be motivated?" Use the theories discussed in this chapter to give some reasons why it might be difficult to motivate such players.

4. A production worker says, "They say they're going to enrich my job. From what I've heard, it looks to me like I'm being asked to learn more things and take more responsibility. If that's enrichment, I don't want it." Discuss this response in view of the theories presented in this chapter. Do you believe it is right to require employees to accept enriched jobs? Why or why not?

5. When you suggest using a lottery in your plant in order to reduce absenteeism, your boss replies, "No way. We're not going to have any gambling here while I'm in charge." How would you respond?

6. Describe a situation in which avoidance learning might be effectively and ethically used in an organizational setting.

7. Perceptions are central to expectancy theory, equity theory, and job characteristics theory. Do you think it is the responsibility of managers to try to influence employees' perceptions? Can you envision situations in which it would be inappropriate or unethical for them to attempt to alter employees' perceptions?

8. We discussed concerns about potential inequity raised by the extremely high ratio of U.S. CEOs' pay relative to that of blue-collar workers (and to that of most others in organizations). Ben & Jerry's was one company that tried to keep CEO pay quite low relative to that of operative-level employees (initially the ratio was capped at 5 to 1, then it was raised to 7 to 1). From the perspective of Ben & Jerry's, what might be some of the benefits and some of the problems associated with this low ratio?

EXPERIENTIAL EXERCISES

WEB EXERCISE 6-1

Go to the Funderstanding "About Learning" page at:

http://www.funderstanding.com/about_learning.html

This section of the Funderstanding site provides links to resources exploring how learning can be enhanced. Click on the "Theories" link to access 10 theories of how people learn. Select any four of the theories and provide a one-page summary of each.

WEB EXERCISE 6-2

Go to the website of the Psychology Centre of Athabasca University, "Canada's Open University," and access the page on "Demonstrations and Tutorials" at:

http://server.bmod.athabascau.ca/html/aupr/demos.shtml

You will find links to many resources at Athabasca University and elsewhere relating to learning theory and other topics in psychology. Click on the "Positive Reinforcement Tutorial" to get a self-instructional exercise. The exercise discusses positive reinforcement and gives several specific examples of positive reinforcement and counter-examples that do not represent positive reinforcement. It then presents a 14-item exercise to give you practice in correctly identifying examples of positive reinforcement. Read the materials and complete the exercise. Then write a one-page report indicating five lessons regarding positive reinforcement that you derived from the materials.

CASE 6-1
MOTIVATION AT MICROSOFT CORPORATION

The Company

Microsoft Corporation is the world's leading producer of operating systems for personal computers, server applications for client/server environments, business and productivity applications, interactive media programs, and Internet platform and development tools. Its products and services have been dominant in their respective markets, with products such as Windows, Word, and Excel established as household names. In 2001, Microsoft is even jumping into the highly competitive video game market, not just with video games but with a new video game system called X-Box. Microsoft products are sold in more than 30 languages and in more than 50 countries.

The CEO of Microsoft is Bill Gates, the Harvard University dropout who went on to become one of the most respected and wealthiest business executives in the world today.

The company's world headquarters are in Redmond, Washington. They employ over 31,500 people worldwide and had net revenue of $19.75 billion for the 1999 fiscal year.

The basic mission of Microsoft Corporation is as follows:

To create software that empowers and enriches people in the workplace, at school, and at home.

Today a major focus in relation to this mission is how to develop products that will provide greater value to customers by leveraging the power of the Internet.

The Motivational Challenge

Microsoft has certainly had its hands full with a variety of issues related to allegations of antitrust violations and unfair business practices. However, Bill Gates recently sent a memo to his staff stating that the most significant problem facing Microsoft today is how to motivate many Microsoft employees who have become "stock option millionaires." Specifically, Bill Gates' concern is that many Microsoft employees who have been with the company during its rise to greatness and dominance in the software industry have become extremely wealthy due to their participation in the company's employee stock ownership program. These well-off individuals, he fears, may not possess the drive needed to sustain the company's success. If this is the case, what types of rewards could Bill Gates use to keep his "stock option millionaires" fired up and motivated to keep Microsoft on the cutting edge of innovation in the future?

Discussion Questions

1. Apply content theories of motivation to explain the motivational challenge facing Bill Gates.
2. Apply process theories of motivation to explain the motivational challenge facing Bill Gates.
3. If you were Bill Gates, what would you do to handle this situation? Be specific and action oriented in your recommendations.
4. What are the practical implications of this case for you as a future manager?

http://www.microsoft.com

Source: J. M. Steiner, "First Person: What Advice Would You Give Bill Gates?" *Incentive*, February 1999, p. 68.

CASE 6-2
MOTIVATING THE "CELEBRATION OF CHILDHOOD" AT GYMBOREE CORPORATION

The Company

The Gymboree Corporation, started in 1976 by Joan Barnes, designs, contract manufactures, and retails a line of unique and high-quality apparel and accessories for children to seven years of age. The company operates over 550 retail stores in the United States and a number of other countries, including Canada and the United Kingdom.

Gymboree's retail stores are known for being "child and parent friendly." Each store possesses features such as full-length mirrors, stroller-sized aisles, and various children's videos that make it easier for parents to shop.

The vision statement at Gymboree reads as follows:

The Gymboree Corporation provides children, parents, and communities around the world with products and services that enrich, support, and celebrate childhood.

We succeed by knowing our customers and exceeding their expectations for quality and customer service. We grow by drawing on the strengths and abilities of every member of the Gymboree team. We build our brand through creativity and innovation in developing and delivering a unique array of products and services.

We at Gymboree, are committed to stakeholder value. We are inspired by children, and dedicated to growing the most respected children's company in the world.

The key corporate values at Gymboree include: celebration of childhood, customers, teamwork, creativity, talent, learning, and innovation.

The Challenge

One of the corporate values that has been central to the "Gymboree Way" is the "celebration of childhood." Given that the company is in the business of creating innovative and high-quality children's apparel, this is quite appropriate. In a nutshell, Gymboree management wanted to create a work environment that supported "playfulness," "creativity," and "spontaneity." The challenge was how to do it. What kinds of specific company policies, practices, procedures, etc., would motivate employees to fulfill Gymboree's vision?

Management Action

Gymboree management implemented a wide range of innovative employee policies and practices to motivate employees to "celebrate childhood" each and every day of work. Every Thursday at 3 p.m., the company rings a bell over the intercom system indicating that it is time for employee's to go to "recess." Recess?! During recess, employees play with rubber balls, skip rope, play hopscotch, and draw on the sidewalk with chalk.

On Wednesday afternoons, employees take a "snack time" break by munching on root beer floats, chips and dips, and pretzels.

The company also implements special benefits for employees who are pregnant or who have spouses that are expecting. The company has a "Pager Program" that provides all moms- or dads-to-be with pagers to maintain an emergency communications link with their spouses or doctors during the last three months of a pregnancy. Other benefits include on-site diaper-changing rooms and paternity or adoption leave for employees.

Finally, the company created a "GymCares" program that links employee volunteers from Gymboree with specific community service opportunities involving children.

Discussion Questions

1. How does Gymboree Corporation use an understanding of need theories of motivation to effectively motivate its employees? To what extent do you feel that these strategies are appropriate? Justify your response.

2. How does Gymboree Corporation use an understanding of process theories of motivation to effectively motivate its employees? To what extent do you think that these strategies are appropriate? Justify your response.

3. To what extent do you believe that the Gymboree Corporation would be a motivating place for you to work? Justify your response.

4. What are the practical implications of this case for you as a future manager?

http://www.gymboree.com

Source: K. Hein, "Gymboree," *Incentive,* January 1999, pp. 42–44.

VIDEO CASE
MOTIVATING FOR PERFORMANCE:
A STUDY OF VALASSIS COMMUNICATIONS, INC.

Running Time: 13:17

Based in Livonia, Michigan, Valassis Communications, Inc. (VCI), is a leading publisher of freestanding, four-color coupon booklets distributed in Sunday newspapers. It also offers consumer samples bundled with newspapers, creates single-advertiser promotional materials, and puts clients' ads directly on the pages of newspapers. VCI is expanding onto the Internet through 50 percent-owned

save.com to provide online coupons and a stake in Independent Delivery Services, which offers e-commerce software to grocery stores. In 1999, Valassis had 1,679 employees and a net income of $114.2 million on $794.6 million in sales.

Valassis Communications is rated by *Fortune* magazine as one of the 100 Best Companies to Work for in

America. *Fortune* notes that "Celebrations are big at this newspaper-insert printer. When the stock hit a target price, employees partied at an airport hangar and were given flights on a vintage B-17 bomber. The company has an on-site hairstylist, manicurist, and doctor, and new parents are given an infant car seat."

The video shows Chairman and CEO David Brandon and other Valassis officers as they discuss motivating strategies at Valassis and as they interact with employees. After viewing the video, answer the following questions.

1. Why is employee motivation important in the creation of a corporate culture where people are performing at a high level?

2. What sort of people does Valassis try to hire to achieve its goals?

3. To what does Valassis attribute its extremely low turnover?

4. What sorts of monetary rewards does Valassis use to motivate employees? To what does it tie those rewards?

5. What is Champion Pay? According to learning theory, what aspect of Champion Pay should make it a very powerful motivator?

6. Other than monetary rewards, what approaches does Valassis use to motivate its employees?

http://http://www.valassis.com/

LIGHTEN UP
RUNNING THE RATS

Many experiments on operant conditioning use laboratory rats, often teaching them to navigate through mazes. Now you can run virtual rats through mazes to demonstrate and test learning theory principles. Two simulations, *AlleyRat* and *MazeRat,* allow students to do such things as design mazes, vary amount and schedules of reinforcement, and set criteria for learning mazes. Another simulation,

MazePerson, puts you in the role of the rat as you attempt to negotiate the famous maze of Hampton Court, built in the late 1600s. Demonstration versions are available for free downloading.

http://www.thecroft.com/psy/alley.rat.html

CHAPTER *Seven*

SKILLS OBJECTIVES

> To develop and implement strategies for enhancing leader power and influence.
> To match appropriate leadership styles to the needs of the situation.
> To develop and implement leadership practices that support the implementation of organizational strategy.
> To develop and implement leadership practices that support the transformation of organizations.
> To systematically evaluate the performance of a leader and to develop recommendations to enhance a leader's effectiveness.

KNOWLEDGE OBJECTIVES

> Understand emerging perspectives on leadership.
> Discuss traits that are related to success as a leader.
> Identify bases of interpersonal power and subunit power.
> Discuss social influence tactics.
> Explain key leader behaviors, including consideration and initiating structure.
> Understand the path–goal theory of leadership.
> Identify substitutes for, and neutralizers of, leadership.
> Discuss leader–member exchange theory.
> Understand transformational leadership, including specific transformational leader behaviors.
> Identify key elements of the language of leadership.

Steve Jobs has been called "a classic comeback kid" and "the Lazarus of the PC world." [1] With his friend Steve Wozniak, Jobs founded Apple Computer in his father's garage in the 1970s and gave birth to the microcomputer revolution. Jobs had a passionate vision that many described as a near-religion, challenging engineers to build, not good, but "insanely great" products that would "make a dent in the universe." But Jobs had no management training and no business skills, and his style wasn't suited to building a stable corporation. He was ousted from Apple in 1985, his reputation apparently forever tarnished. Jobs resigned himself to smaller ponds, founding NeXT, which made an elegant black computer for the university market, and buying Pixar Animation Studios. Under his leadership, Pixar became a powerhouse, with blockbusters including *Toy Story, A Bug's Life,* and *Toy Story 2.* In 1995, just after *Toy Story*'s release, Jobs took Pixar public and became a billionaire.

Meanwhile, for a decade after Jobs' departure, Apple floundered, with its market share falling to single digits and its prospects dim. In 1997, Jobs was invited back to Apple as interim CEO. Since then, he has helped to restore Apple's pride, quadruple its market share, and bring it back to solid profitability. He has introduced new products such as the iMac, iBook, and G3 Cube, launched a "Think Different" ad campaign, signed a pact with Microsoft, unveiled an ambitious Internet strategy, and helped dispel feelings of anxiety and helplessness. While he appears to have mellowed somewhat, Jobs is still described as temperamental, driven, dashing, charismatic, erratic, eccentric, brilliant, pompous, and given to wild bouts of infectious enthusiasm. With the "interim" now removed from his Apple title, he continues his quest, viewing both Apple and Pixar as embodying his vision of the computer as an empowering cultural force. Still, some wonder if the mercurial Jobs is what Apple needs now that it has emerged from the edge of crisis.

Men and women have sought since the beginning of recorded history to become leaders and to succeed in leadership roles. The fact that some leaders have been remarkably successful while others—although often intelligent, well meaning, and conscientious—have failed dismally suggests that becoming an effective leader may not be easy and that the ways to do so are far from obvious. The realization that some leaders—like Steve Jobs—have bounced back and forth between success and failure makes the task seem even more daunting.

In this chapter we will provide guidelines and exercises to develop your leadership knowledge and skills. We will first define leadership and distinguish between *leading* and *managing.* We will then examine emerging perspectives on leadership to see how views of leadership have evolved to meet the demands of the modern workplace. Next, we will consider whether it is possible to identify traits of successful leaders—that is, whether there are "born leaders." Then we will explore how leaders can develop power bases and employ social influence tactics. We will then turn our attention to leader behaviors, including theories to help explain when those behaviors are needed. Following this, we will examine transformational leadership, including both transformational leader behaviors and how leaders can employ the "language of leadership" to inspire followers. We will conclude the chapter with some suggestions for choosing a leadership style.

Take a moment now to complete Self-Assessment 7-1. You will learn more from this chapter if you start off with a greater awareness of your beliefs and feelings about leadership.

Self-Assessment 7-1
Attitudes Toward Leadership

Please answer the questions that follow regarding your attitudes toward leading others in organizations. Answer each question as honestly as possible using the following response scale:

1 = Disagree Strongly
2 = Disagree Somewhat
3 = Neither Agree nor Disagree
4 = Agree Somewhat
5 = Agree Strongly

1. _____ A person needs to be feared by his/her employees in order to be an effective leader.
2. _____ There is one best way to lead people in organizations.
3. _____ A major part of leadership is providing direction for employees.
4. _____ A person needs to consider the characteristics of the situation in order to become an effective leader.
5. _____ Leaders should rely on the use of their formal authority or position in the organization as the best way to influence their employees.
6. _____ Leadership ability is something that cannot be developed, since you either have it at birth or you don't.
7. _____ Leadership effectiveness should be measured solely in terms of the financial performance of the organization.
8. _____ Effective leaders must be trusted and respected by their employees.
9. _____ Workers in today's modern business environment don't value or need leadership from management.
10. _____ The knowledge and skills needed to perform well in a nonmanagerial position are pretty much the same as those needed to be an effective leader in an organization.

Now, as a way to assess your initial level of skill in leading others, read the scenario in the following Pre-Test Skills Assessment and develop an action plan for how you would handle this situation. Be as specific as possible in stating your recommendations.

Pre-Test Skills Assessment
Leading

You are the new production supervisor at a global computer corporation based in San Antonio, Texas. You have a team of 500 employees who assemble different models of laptop computers using a variety of components. The work requires a high level of worker knowledge and skill, for they must custom-build these computers based on specifications from customers.

Your employees are a mix of young, inexperienced individuals who possess marginal work skills and limited formal education, part-time college students who want to "get their feet wet" and are anxious to move up in the organization and develop careers for themselves, and very experienced people who have worked on the company's assembly line for more than 20 years but are not comfortable with all the new technology they are required to learn for their jobs.

DEVIL'S ADVOCATE

What's the point in trying to learn how to be a better leader? Either you're born a leader or you're not, right?
Leadership is a critical skill that is badly needed by many employers. In fact, a growing number of companies are reporting problems finding enough employees with leadership abilities. Numerous research studies have also identified leadership skills as being one of the most critical skills needed for success in the business world.

While some research seems to show that there is some truth to the idea of a "born leader," it even more strongly suggests that most people can significantly increase their innate leadership ability through training and relevant experience.

There are so many leadership theories! Which one are we supposed to use? Do we focus on traits, behaviors, the situation, or what? I'm confused.
Remember that each theory gives you a unique perspective on the leadership process. Each theory is like a different camera lens that you can use to analyze leadership issues. Leadership just isn't simple enough to boil down to a single theory that tells you everything you need to know and do in order to be an effective leader. Different leadership theories will provide valuable guidance to you in different types of situations. The bottom line is that traits, behaviors, and the situation may all be important elements of the leadership process.

I'm not a management major. Why do I need to be concerned with leadership?
Leadership should be a concern not just to management majors. If you are majoring in a technical field like accounting, finance, or engineering, your technical skills will be helpful to you in an entry-level position. However, if you have any aspiration to move up in your organization, then technical skills will not be enough. Rather, you will need things such as leadership and teamwork skills in order to succeed in your transition into a management position.

I don't feel comfortable with the idea of doing things that will make me more powerful. It all sounds so manipulative!
You are not alone if you don't feel entirely comfortable with the idea of power. The bottom line is that a manager *must* be able to influence the behavior of his/her employees and others outside the work unit in order to be effective. In today's modern organizations, just holding the title of "manager" does not mean that you will necessarily have much power and influence over your employees. In addition, using threats and punishment to gain power over others is generally not the best way to obtain employee commitment in your work unit. So, while the idea of developing and using power makes many people a bit uneasy, it really is essential for the success of any manager.

Your work unit has been experiencing problems with quality (i.e., high defect and customer return rates), high costs, and low productivity. In addition, the previous supervisor of this unit had to be terminated because his leadership style was so abrasive that many employees threatened to quit if the company did not get rid of him.

As the new supervisor of this work unit, develop an action plan for handling this situation. Be specific, and focus on action.

WHAT IS LEADERSHIP?

We define *leadership* as the ability to influence others toward the achievement of goals. Leadership, then, relates to the ability to influence others. This suggests that leaders may not always be influencing but can do so when needed. It suggests, too, that leadership is about dealing with others and, as such, that a variety of interpersonal skills may be needed by effective leaders. Finally, leadership is related to goal achievement; the leader exerts influence not for its own sake but to yield desired outcomes.

Leadership may sound like another name for *management,* but the terms and related functions are generally viewed as distinct. While management aims at providing consistency and order to organizations, leadership seeks to produce constructive and adaptive change. While management is focused on accomplishing activities and mastering routines, leadership involves influencing others and creating visions for change. While management is directed toward coordinating activities in order to get a job done, leadership is concerned with the process of developing mutual purposes. Both management and leadership somehow involve influencing others toward goal attainment, but management relies more on a one-way authority relationship, while leadership relies more on a multidirectional influence relationship. In the words of leadership experts Warren Bennis and Burt Nanus, "Managers are people who do things right and leaders are people who do the right things."[2]

Now complete Skills Practice 7-1: Field Work—Interview with a Leader. The purpose of the exercise is to give you the opportunity to get out into the "real world" and learn about leadership issues by interviewing an individual who is a leader in an organization. This exercise will literally "bring to life" many of the issues discussed in this chapter.

Skills Practice 7-1   **Skill Level: Basic**
Field Work—Interview with a Leader

Learning Objective
To understand the types of challenges faced by leaders of organizations and the tactics they use to handle those issues effectively.

Procedure
1. Identify someone who is in a leadership position in an organization and is willing to be interviewed for this assignment. The organization may be of any type; the main issue here is to select a firm that interests you in some way.
2. In the interview with your leader, ask the following questions.
   > What is your position title? What are the primary tasks and responsibilities associated with your job?
   > Describe your organization in terms of its products and services, mission, structure, and any other characteristics you think are important.
   > How would you define *effective leadership* as it relates to your job?
   > What have been the most difficult leadership challenges you have experienced in your job? How did you handle them?
   > What kind of advice would you give students regarding the best ways to develop their own leadership skills for the future?
3. Summarize the results of your interview, and either make a brief presentation to your class or submit a brief written summary of your findings.

Next complete Skills Practice 7-2, Profiling a Great Leader. The purpose of the activity is to get you to formalize what you already know and believe about what it takes to be a good leader. This will provide a nice foundation on which to build as we move through the chapter.

Skills Practice 7-2
Profiling a Great Leader

Skill Level: **Basic**

Skill Objective

To develop a profile of the traits an individual should possess and the behaviors he/she should exhibit in order to be a great leader.

Procedure

1. Think of an individual you consider to be a truly great leader. This person may come from business, politics, religion, or any other field.
2. On a separate sheet of paper, write down the following information:
    a. Leader's name and position
    b. Leader's greatest accomplishment(s)
    c. The traits or qualities this individual possessed that make him/her a great leader
    d. The behaviors or actions of this individual that make him/her a great leader
3. Answer the following discussion questions.

Discussion Questions

1. If you had to select one or two things from the leadership profile you just prepared that you think are the most critical to effective leadership, what would they be? Why?
2. Would the leadership profile be effective in all types of situations? Why or why not?

EMERGING PERSPECTIVES ON LEADERSHIP

The field of leadership is dynamic. Recent decades have seen rather remarkable changes in how we think about leadership. Those changes reflect both continued development of leadership theory and practice and awareness of the need to adapt leadership to the demands of the modern workplace. Figure 7-1 presents some facets of the changing look of leadership.

FIGURE 7-1
The Changing Look of Leadership

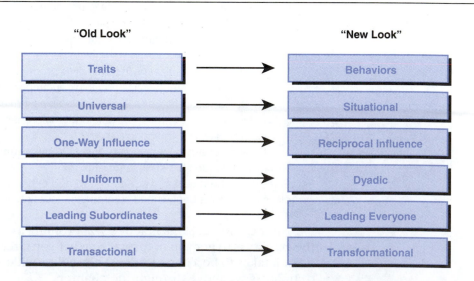

"Old Look"		"New Look"
Traits	→	Behaviors
Universal	→	Situational
One-Way Influence	→	Reciprocal Influence
Uniform	→	Dyadic
Leading Subordinates	→	Leading Everyone
Transactional	→	Transformational

Let's look at these in turn. First, while early leadership approaches emphasized the traits of successful leaders—who successful leaders *are*—newer approaches ask how successful leaders behave—what successful leaders *do*.

Second, early approaches to leadership tended to take a universalistic perspective, asking, "What works?" Newer approaches, recognizing that characteristics of the situation, such as followers' needs and skills, and various characteristics of the task must be considered, ask instead, "What works when?" Considering the situation may complicate the leader's life, but it is a necessary complication for effectiveness.

Third, early leadership approaches considered primarily one-way influence. In particular, they asked how a leader influences followers. Newer perspectives recognize that the influence process is reciprocal—just as leaders are influencing followers, followers are also influencing leaders. Effective leadership resides in the complex interplay of these mutual patterns of influence.

Fourth, while early leadership approaches tended to assume that leaders treat their various followers in similar ways—some leaders are nice, others "bossy," others strict, and so on—more recent approaches recognize that leaders may—for good or bad reasons—treat different followers differently. They may be more considerate with some followers than with others, give some more direction than others, let some participate more in decision making, and so on.

Fifth, while leadership approaches initially focused on the relationship of leaders to their subordinates, modern views of leadership are more inclusive. They recognize that the "others" whom leaders influence may include not just subordinates but also many others, including team members and perhaps even hierarchical superiors. Leadership does not have to face downward.

Finally, most early approaches to leadership tended to consider how a leader might influence others in a series of transactions. That is, they viewed leaders and followers as engaging in exchanges in which the leader would offer certain things—rewards, support, protection, or whatever—in return for desired follower behaviors. Newer leadership approaches recognize that, while important, this transactional view is incomplete. Leaders must take actions to transform followers and organizations by communicating values, inspiring, intellectually stimulating, and showing confidence in the face of crisis. Such transformational leader behaviors may often be critical to the life of an organization.

LEADER TRAITS

The earliest approach to the study of leadership was to try to identify characteristics, or traits, of successful leaders. For instance, one early study found links between leadership success and intelligence, education, preferences for high levels of risk, desire for independence, and other variables.[3] Literally thousands of studies have now explored leadership traits. Some of those traits relate to physical factors, some to ability, many to personality, and still others to social characteristics. Of the traits, activity, intelligence, knowledge, dominance, and self-confidence are most often found to be linked to leader success.

Unfortunately, most reviews of studies relating to leadership traits have concluded that the trait approach has not been fruitful.[4] One early survey of this literature noted that of all traits that showed up in one study or another as related to leadership effectiveness, only 5 percent were common to four or more studies.[5] In another early study, some high school students emerged as leaders on one type of task and others emerged on other tasks.[6] These findings suggest that the traits needed by leaders may depend on the situation. To illustrate how traits of successful leaders may vary, consider the following leaders: Mohandas Gandhi, Mary Kay Ash, Kemal Ataturk, Herb Kelleher, Henry Cisneros, Thomas Jefferson, Ho Chi Minh, Bill Gates, Margaret Thatcher, Cochise, Nelson Mandela, Lech Walesa, Winston Churchill. How are they similar? How do they differ?

Self-Assessment 7-2
Thinking About Yourself as a Leader

"He who knows others is wise; he who knows himself is enlightened." Lao-tzu (c. 604 – c. 531 B.C.)

"It is much more difficult to judge oneself than to judge others." Antoine de Saint-Exupéry (1900 – 1944), *The Little Prince* (1943)

If we are to understand and perhaps alter our leader behaviors, it's important to give some serious thought to our past leadership accomplishments, current leader behaviors, and leadership goals. Often, it is helpful to articulate our thoughts and feelings concerning these issues. With that in mind, answer the following questions.

1. Describe some leadership role you now hold or have held (at work, in a social organization, or wherever). How long have you been, or were you, in the position?
2. Describe some leadership situation for which you are especially proud of your performance. What about your leadership characteristics or behaviors do you think contributed to that accomplishment?
3. Is there some leadership quality you would like to have that you think you are now lacking? Describe that quality.
4. Consider a leader who has influenced you or motivated you. Describe the techniques he or she used to engage you as a follower.
5. Think of a situation where a leader disappointed you. What did he or she do, or not do, that was disappointing?
6. Suppose you were to retire from your firm tomorrow and one of your direct reports (or peers) was asked by your replacement to describe your leadership traits, behaviors, and/or effectiveness. What three or four words or phrases do you think they would be most likely to use?

A further concern with the trait approach relates to the question of how the findings can be used. Since traits are relatively stable, it is unlikely that leaders can develop them through training. So while information concerning traits of successful leaders might be useful to select leaders and place them in suitable positions, it is otherwise of limited value. In part, this is because the trait approach considers only characteristics of the leader while ignoring the characteristics of followers and situations.

Web Wise

The 20 Most Influential Leaders of the 20th Century

With the coming of the new millennium, *Time* magazine selected and profiled "100 remarkable people . . . who—for better or worse—most influenced the last 100 years." They were considered in five fields of endeavor. For the profiles of the 20 most influential leaders and revolutionaries, go to:

http://www.time.com/time/time100/

This doesn't mean that we should abandon the trait approach. For instance, it may be useful to determine which traits are associated with success in particular situations. However, it is safe at this point to say that more is likely to be gained by looking directly at what successful leaders *do* than at what they *are.*

DEVELOPING AND USING POWER BASES

We defined leadership as the ability to influence others toward the achievement of goals. But what exactly is influence? How does it relate to things such as authority, power, and control? How does a leader gain the ability to influence? These are among the topics we address in this section.

DEFINING TERMS

Let's first define some terms. *Authority* is the *right* to influence others. It is conferred by the organization. *Power* is the *ability* to influence others. People in organizations may have power without authority, and they may have authority without power. *Influence* is the actual exertion of force on others. Influence is power put into action; power is latent influence. *Control* is the exertion of enough influence to change others' behaviors. We may have a lot of power and exert a lot of influence without getting people to do what we want.

THE NATURE OF POWER

The definitions just given suggest that power is:

> **Latent**—Power is something that people have and may or may not choose to use. It is a weapon or tool; it may never be used, and just having it may make its use unnecessary.
> **Relative**—The power one person has over another depends largely on things such as the expertise of one person relative to another and the hierarchical level of one relative to the other. As such, a manager may have considerable power relative to one person and little or none relative to another.
> **Perceived**—Power is based on one person's belief that another has certain characteristics. If I believe you have power over me, you've got it!
> **Dynamic**—Power relationships evolve over time as individuals gain or lose certain types of power relative to others.

USES OF POWER

We often think of power as something we can use to get others to do what we want. While this view isn't necessarily wrong, it *is* incomplete. There are at least three general uses of power:[7]

1. **Power *over.*** This is power used to make another person act in a certain way; it may be called *dominance.*

2. **Power *to*.** This is power that gives others the means to act more freely themselves; it is sometimes called *empowerment.*
3. **Power *from*.** This is power that protects us from the power of others; it may be called *resistance.*

These uses of power suggest that power is more than just a way to change others' behaviors (though that function is certainly important). It may also be used to help others act more freely, or to prevent others from forcing us to do things we don't want.

FORMS OF COMPLIANCE TO POWER

We can also think of power in terms of *why* people comply with it. Three power types can be identified, based on the mechanism by which others accede to the power.[8]

> **Coercive power** involves forcing someone to comply with our wishes.
> With **utilitarian power,** compliance results from desires for rewards. For example, an employee may do what the boss asks in order to get a raise.
> **Normative power** rests on the employees' belief that the organization has the right to govern their behavior.

BASES OF POWER

If we're going to use power, we first have to get it. Traditionally, a distinction has been made between how *people* get power (termed *interpersonal power bases*) and how *groups* or *organizational subunits* get power (termed *subunit power bases*). Though we'll retain this distinction for now, we will point out that it is murky; people may use the so-called subunit power bases, and groups or subunits may use the so-called interpersonal power bases.

Interpersonal Power Bases John French and Bertram Raven have developed the best-known scheme for classifying bases of interpersonal power.[9] They have identified the following five power bases.

> **Legitimate power.** *Legitimate power* results when one person thinks it is legitimate, or right, for another to give orders or otherwise exert force. An employee who says "I ought to do as my boss says" is reflecting belief in legitimate power. Legitimate power may have a variety of sources:
>   • **It may be culturally specified.** In some cultures, it is considered right that older people or people of certain castes or with certain characteristics should be given respect and obedience. This has been called "the power of the eternal yesterday."
>   • **It may come from acceptance of the social structure.** If individuals accept the social structure as legitimate—whether it is the hierarchy of an organization, the status ranking in a street gang, or a

country's governance system—they are likely to accept demands of their "superiors" as legitimate.

- **It may be designated by a legitimizing agent.** Those with legitimate power may choose to share it with others. A firm's CEO may appoint an assistant. In democratic societies, the holders of legitimate power—we, the people—may pass on that power through elections.

Legitimate power sounds a lot like authority. The difference is that authority is the *right* to exert force, while legitimate power resides in an individual's belief that someone else *has* that right. These aren't the same. For example, unless subordinates accept authority, a boss has no legitimate power. On the other hand, someone may have legitimate power without formal authority, perhaps because of personal characteristics such as age and experience.

> **Reward power.** *Reward power* is power based on the perceived ability to reward. It depends on one person's ability to administer desired outcomes to another and to decrease or remove outcomes that are not desired.

> **Coercive power.** Coercive power (as discussed in our earlier presentation of types of power) is based on one person's perceived ability to affect punishment that another receives.

> **Referent power.** *Referent power* comes from the feeling of identity, or oneness, that one person has for another, or the desire for such identity. The commercial picturing Michael Jordan and saying "Be like Mike" is a concise and direct appeal to referent power.

> **Expert power.** *Expert power* is based on one person's perception that another has needed relevant knowledge in a given area. Doctors, lawyers, and computer specialists may all have expert power.

In addition to these interpersonal power bases, others have been suggested. For instance, possession of valuable information, persuasive abilities, and personal charisma may all be sources of power.[10] We'll touch on these potential sources later in the chapter, in our discussion of social influence.

The power bases aren't independent. For one thing, they may occur together; people at high levels in organizations are likely to simultaneously have a lot of legitimate, reward, and coercive power, and perhaps some other power bases, and thus can draw on an arsenal of power bases. The power bases are also interdependent, in the sense that reliance on one power base may influence levels of other power bases. For example, if we regularly coerce our subordinates, we're unlikely to have much referent power relative to them.

It may seem that some of the power bases we have identified are ethical and others are not. For instance, referent power seems fairly noble, while coercive power seems suspect and devious. However, this is an oversimplification; referent power may be used to get a teenager to use drugs or to induce a colleague to cheat on an expense account, and coercive power can be humanely employed as a last resort to stop an employee's drug use. Instead of asking which interpersonal power bases are ethical, it may be more useful to

FIGURE 7-2
Guidelines for Ethically Attaining and Using Interpersonal Power

Base of Power	Guidelines
Legitimate	1. Make polite requests 2. Make requests in a confident tone 3. Make clear requests and check for comprehension 4. Make sure that requests appear legitimate 5. Explain reasons for the request 6. Follow proper channels 7. Exercise authority regularly 8. Insist on compliance and check to verify it 9. Be responsive to subordinate concerns
Reward	1. Make sure compliance can be verified 2. Make sure the request is feasible 3. Provide an attractive incentive 4. Make it clear you can deliver on your promises 5. Make sure your requests are proper and ethical
Coercive	1. Inform subordinates about rules and penalties for violations 2. Administer discipline consistently and promptly 3. Provide sufficient warning before resorting to punishment 4. Get the facts before using reprimands or punishment 5. Stay calm and avoid appearing hostile 6. Maintain credibility 7. Use appropriate punishments 8. Administer warnings and punishments in private
Referent	1. Show consideration for subordinates' needs and feelings 2. Treat each subordinate fairly 3. Defend subordinates' interests when acting as a group representative 4. Select subordinates who identify with you 5. Show you would be personally pleased if the subordinate carried out a request for you 6. Model appropriate behavior
Expert	1. Promote an image of expertise 2. Maintain credibility 3. Act confident and decisive in a crisis 4. Keep informed 5. Recognize subordinate concerns 6. Avoid threatening the self-esteem of subordinates

ask how each power base can be ethically developed and employed. Some suggestions are summarized in Figure 7-2.[11]

Skills Practice 7-3 is designed to help you develop skill in analyzing a work situation and identifying specific strategies for enhancing your arsenal of power bases.

Skills Practice 7-3

Developing an Effective Power Base

Skill Objective

To develop skill in analyzing a work situation and identifying specific strategies for enhancing one's managerial power base.

Procedure

1. Read the case that follows.
2. Assume you were the supervisor in the case, and develop a set of strategies for enhancing your overall power base.
3. Discuss your recommendations with a classmate or present them to the class.
4. Identify and discuss the practical implications of this case for you as a future manager or supervisor.

Case—Power and the Green Supervisor*

You are a 22-year-old recent graduate of a major university on the West Coast. You have just been hired as a project supervisor in an advertising firm. Your job is to lead a staff of 12 somewhat rebellious advertising specialists and support staff in creating new advertising campaigns for your firm's clients.

The ages of your staff range from 25 to 40 years. These people have been with the firm for anywhere from 3 to 15 years. They've had no formal training in the development of advertising campaigns, but they do have 1–5 years of relevant advertising experience with the firm. Typically, the firm has followed a "promotion from within" policy, in which current employees are given preference over external candidates in filling position openings. However, the strength of your advertising training at the university, along with an advertising internship you completed while in school, impressed management at the firm so much that they offered you the job.

Your boss has arranged an initial meeting for you and your new staff. You walk into the room in which your staff has been chatting while waiting for you. Suddenly there is dead silence. Five pairs of eyes are now fixed on you. You know that (1) it is critical to start off on the right foot (avoiding a negative first impression), and (2) you need to establish your credibility as their boss.

How would you begin to build a power base in relation to your staff?

*This case is based on the actual experiences of recent college graduates who have assumed supervisory positions.

Subunit Power Bases In addition to these interpersonal power bases, at least two other power bases—control of critical resources and control over strategic contingencies—are important. As we said earlier, we will discuss these as sources of power for subunits, such as departments, but they apply to individuals and groups as well.

Resource Dependence Approach One source of subunit power is the ability to control the supply of important resources required by other subunits.[12] According to the resource dependence approach, those subunits that obtain the most critical and hard-to-get resources acquire the most power because of the dependencies that are developed. For instance, the power of a university department is related to its ability to secure outside grants and contracts, thus bringing critical funds into the university.[13] Similarly, those units that are at the "skin" of the firm, spanning the boundary between the organization and its

FIGURE 7-3
The Strategic Contingencies Model

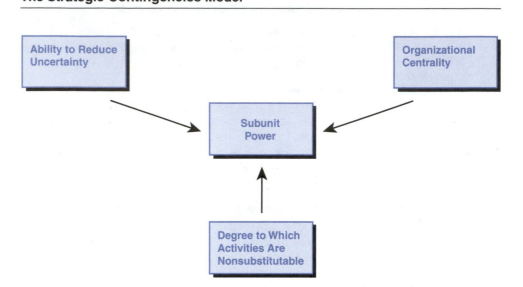

environment, derive power from their ability to obtain critical information from the environment.[14]

Strategic Contingencies Approach This approach is summarized in Figure 7-3. According to the strategic contingencies approach, a unit's power is based on the following three things.

1. A unit will have more power if it is able to *cope with uncertainty.* That is, if the unit can reduce uncertainties faced by other units, it has power relative to those units. For example, there may be uncertainties about supply of funds or personnel, about market preferences, about changes in laws, or about the ability to produce enough goods to meet customer demands.
2. The unit will have more power if it is *central* in the flow of information and work between units. Units are more central if they have an immediate effect on the organization or if they have an impact on most other units.
3. Power increases with *nonsubstitutability;* the harder it is for another unit to perform the activities of this unit, the more power this unit has.

This perspective helps explain the power of people such as departmental administrative assistants. Even though they may have little formal power, everyone knows that things would quickly grind to a halt if they left. They are the only ones who know where important documents are filed (so they cope with critical uncertainties), everyone depends on them (so they are central), and they keep all the information in their heads (so they can't be replaced).

The implications of the strategic contingencies approach for attaining power are straightforward:

1. Do something that is critical to the success of the organization.
2. Be in a position where many others depend on you.
3. And make sure you can't be replaced.

G L O B A L   P E R S P E C T I V E S

SIGNS OF POWER IN JAPAN

Signs of power may vary from one nation to another. For example, in Japanese organizations the appearance of equality is an important cultural value.* Because of this, salary, rank, and office space may have little to do with power. Instead, power can be gauged by studying patterns of interaction. Power flows from expertise, and those with power can be identified because others often consult with them.

*This discussion is drawn from J. Pfeffer, *Managing with Power* (Boston: Harvard Business School Press, 1992), pp. 64–66.

The *and* in this listing is critical. According to the strategic contingencies approach, if any of these three conditions is lacking, your power will decrease dramatically.

SIGNS OF POWER

You will often want to know where power lies in the organization. For example: How can you tell who has power in an organization? Job titles may help; so may status symbols. Still, we know that these things can be deceptive and that some people with a lot of power don't have fancy titles or big offices. Some other signs of managers' power include the following abilities: [15]

> To intercede favorably on behalf of someone in trouble with the organization
> To get a good placement for a talented subordinate
> To get approval for expenditures beyond the budget
> To get above-average salary increases for subordinates
> To get items on the agenda at policy meetings
> To get fast access to top decision makers
> To get regular, frequent access to top decision makers
> To get early information about decisions and policy shifts

SOCIAL INFLUENCE TACTICS

We said earlier that influence is power in action. *Social influence* is the use of power in interpersonal relationships. Here, we will discuss social influence approaches, consider how people might choose from among the approaches, and relate social influence to type of involvement.

SOCIAL INFLUENCE APPROACHES

People use a remarkable variety of approaches when attempting to influence others. Figure 7-4 lists some social influence tactics, arrayed from most popular to least popular.[16] It shows, for instance, that managers like to use participation, rational persuasion, and inspirational appeals to influence others. Tactics such as use of pressure and formation of coalitions are less popular. Finally, promising something in return for compliance is an influence tactic of last resort; it's costly and may create expectations that there will *always* be re-

FIGURE 7-4
Social Influence Tactics

Rank	Tactic	Description
1	Consultation	Seeking participation in making or planning implementation of a decision
2	Rational persuasion	Using logical arguments and facts to persuade another
3	Inspirational appeals	Making an emotional request or proposal that arouses enthusiasm by appealing to values and ideals or increasing confidence
4	Ingratiating tactics	Seeking to get someone in a good mood or to like you before asking for something
5	Coalition tactics	Seeking the aid of others to persuade someone, or using the support of others as an argument for agreement
6	Pressure tactics	Using demands, threats, or intimidation to get compliance
7	Upward appeals	Seeking to persuade someone that the request is approved at higher levels, or appealing to higher levels for help in getting compliance
8	Exchange tactics	Promising some rewards or benefits in exchange for compliance

wards for compliance and that compliance cannot be expected without such rewards. Let's look at some of the tactics in more detail.

Rational Persuasion One way to get what you want is to make a compelling, persuasive argument. Persuasive communicators are well liked and eloquent and have high credibility. They gain credibility by their apparent expertise and by giving the impression that their motives are honorable.[17] Persuasive messages are clear and intelligible and are moderately inconsistent with the message receiver's attitudes.[18] That is, a message that is entirely consistent with the receiver's prior attitudes makes no difference, while a message that is totally inconsistent with those attitudes is likely to be rejected out of hand.

Liking and Ingratiation Quite simply, we're more willing to do something for people we like. Liking may be based on such things as:

> Physical attractiveness
> Compliments and flattery
> Contact and cooperation (we tend to like people whom we know well, especially if we work with them on a common task or toward a cooperative goal)
> Association with other positive things (for instance, we like people who bring us good news and dislike those who bring us bad news)
> Social similarity (we like people who resemble us and are from the same social category)[19]

There may be a dark side to liking. For one thing, we said that people like others who are similar to them. This may put minorities and women at a disadvantage in organizations populated primarily by white males. Some sources of bias can be consciously recognized and addressed, but we probably don't spend a lot of time thinking about why we first came to like someone, so the resulting bias may be hard to overcome. Perhaps as diverse people spend more time together in organizations they will recognize more similarities than are immediately apparent, and they will also see that there are many other bases for liking.

Emotional Appeals Anyone with a small child knows that emotional appeals can be effective. First, friendly emotions are a useful influence approach.[20] Researchers have studied how flight attendants maintain a cheerful attitude with customers,[21] how "cast members" at Disney display friendliness with "guests,"[22] and how salespeople present a positive "emotional front" to customers.[23] Such research shows that recipients of good cheer repay those positive emotions. They want to prolong the positive interaction and to ensure future interactions. As such, they tend to comply with the wishes of the cheerful person, and they are likely to see the person as credible (which, you'll recall, should enhance persuasiveness).

Negative or unpleasant emotions can also be tools of social influence, especially when the person displaying the emotions has more power than the target of the influence. For instance, some leaders use expressions of hostility and irritation to intimidate subordinates.[24] Similarly, bill collectors use negative emotions such as anger, irritation, and mild disapproval to get payments. These emotions create anxiety in debtors, and the debtors try to escape that anxiety by meeting the collector's demands.[25]

Finally, emotional contrast is often helpful; the presence of a nasty person makes a warm and friendly person seem even warmer and friendlier and makes compliance with this kind person's requests more likely. This is evidenced in "good cop, bad cop" routines, in which a suspect who has been interrogated by a mean and hostile officer is then treated warmly by a "good cop." The suspect is anxious to repay the kindness and may even feel compelled to confess.

Social Proof Another way we can influence people to take some action is by convincing them that others are taking the same action; this is called *social proof.* People are apt to follow the lead of others; for one thing, the fact that others are doing something suggests that it is appropriate and socially acceptable. Many people are clearly aware of the principle of social proof. For example:

> *Our tendency to assume that an action is more correct if others are doing it is exploited in a variety of settings. Bartenders often salt their tip jars with a few dollar bills at the beginning of an evening to simulate tips left by customers and thereby to give the impression that tipping with folding money is proper barroom behavior. . . . Evangelical preachers are known to seed their audience with ringers, who are rehearsed to come forward at a specified time to give witness and donations . . . The producers of charity telethons devote inordinate amounts of time to the . . . listing of viewers who have already pledged contributions.[26]*

CHOOSING FROM AMONG INFLUENCE APPROACHES

We've already said that people generally prefer some influence approaches, such as participation, to others, such as promising something in return for compliance. People also select influence approaches to fit the situation. For instance, individuals responding to authoritarian managers tend to use approaches such as blocking and ingratiation, while those responding to participative managers are more likely to rely on rational persuasion. Also, employees use different influence attempts with their superiors depending on the goals they are seeking. When they are trying to secure personal benefits, such as career advancement, employees tend to use ingratiation with their superiors. When they are trying to achieve organizational goals, they use a broader range of influence tactics.[27] This all suggests that even though people may have preferred strategies, they still recognize the need to choose from a broader arsenal of strategies if the situation calls for it.

SOCIAL INFLUENCE AND TYPE OF INVOLVEMENT

People yield to influence through one of three processes—compliance, identification, and internalization.[28]

> **Compliance** occurs when people do something because they don't want to bear the costs of not doing it. For example, you may do what your boss tells you to do because you think you'll be punished if you don't.
> **Identification** results when influence flows from a person's attractiveness. Perhaps, for instance, the person is likable or charismatic or is in a position to which we aspire.
> **Internalization** takes place when we do something because we believe it is "the right thing to do."

This suggests that, while we may get what we want by relying on various power bases or employing diverse social influence tactics, we may get it in different forms and with different long-run consequences. While a leader may have to use each of these processes at times, it seems clear that identification and internalization will lead to better long-run consequences than compliance. Leaders who are credible and trustworthy are most likely to be able to use those processes.

Web Wise

Native American Leaders

The website of the Indigenous Peoples' Literature includes profiles of many Native American great chiefs and leaders. The profiles provide rich insights into the wide range of traits, behaviors, and motivations of these leaders.

http://www.indians.org/welker/leaders.htm

KEY LEADER BEHAVIORS AND SKILLS

The legendary Green Bay Packers coach Vince Lombardi is credited with once having said that leaders aren't born, they are made, and that they are made just like anything else, through hard work.

In the nearby Voice of Experience, Victor Allen, one of the leaders in the gourmet coffee industry, shares his insights and advice regarding effective leadership. He notes that he is self-trained, with an evolving style. What behaviors are evident in his leadership style?

In the search for leader behaviors that make a difference, several kinds of behaviors have been examined. In this section, we will first consider autocratic and democratic styles, reflecting the degree to which the leader lets followers participate in decision making. We will then address the degree to which the leader exhibits behaviors that are relationship oriented and/or task oriented. Following a look at these sets of behaviors, we will consider some characteristics of the situation that may help determine when those behaviors are needed.

VOICE OF EXPERIENCE

LEADING OTHERS

Victor Mondry,
Founder and President
Victor Allen's Coffee and Tea

1. What kind of leadership style do you use in the management of your organization?

Since I am self-trained, my style is constantly evolving. I have learned the importance of communication, even for what I'd consider to be small items. Things that would be easily known when we had one location and few staff are not communicated easily to multiple locations and a larger, spread-out staff. I don't know why, but I assumed they would, so it was quite surprising to learn that effort was required to get information circulated.

I have tried to lead by example and by being friendly to staff. It's become clear that individuals should have clear performance criteria and reviews, direction on company goals and goals for their own job. A combination of both structured meetings/reviews and informal communication works well to maintain a sense of direction, spirit, and participation toward the individual and common goals. A few minutes a week may be all that is required to make a world of difference in gluing the organization together.

2. What are the biggest leadership challenges you have faced in your business career? How did you handle them?

The biggest challenges were layoffs due to loss of a major account. I handled them with quick and sufficient action (in this case, letting some staff go), accompanied by honest explanations and reassurances, and, in some cases, pay increases to remaining staff.

3. What kind of advice would you give students regarding how to develop effective leadership skills for the "real world"?

Business leadership is not like organizing a camping trip or even a climb of Everest. Unlike those examples, business is ongoing. Therefore, it isn't just about planning, preparation, and division of labor, as might be the case for those. It's more like the experience of owning a car. Your car comes with a detailed owner's manual—it explains how things work, orients you to your task of driving, and teaches you how to maintain your car. Schedules are published for service at routine intervals. Warnings are posted and contacts listed for nonroutine maintenance and even for dangerous surprises. Basically, you're given clear instruction and training, a schedule of periodic reviews (service intervals), as well as procedures for "emergency situations." You have a clear idea of what to do in any circumstance and a clear idea of the difference between routine and emergency situations, along with the appropriate responses.

http://www.victorallen.com/

AUTOCRATIC AND DEMOCRATIC STYLES

An early approach to the study of leadership considered the degree to which leaders are autocratic or democratic. *Autocratic leaders* make decisions themselves, without inputs from subordinates. *Democratic leaders* let subordinates participate in decision making. Thus, as shown in Figure 7-5, autocratic and democratic styles are at opposite ends of a single continuum, differing in degree of delegation of decision-making authority. They differ *only* on this dimension, not necessarily on other variables, such as sensitivity and caring. There are "benevolent autocrats" and uncaring democrats, as well as their opposites.

Democratic style is consistently linked to higher levels of subordinate satisfaction. However, the relationship of style to performance is more complex. Democratic style is usually positively, but weakly, related to productivity.

FIGURE 7-5
Autocratic and Democratic Styles

Lower	Degree of Participation	Higher

→

| Autocratic | | Democratic |

There are many factors that determine whether a democratic style is appropriate, including the nature of the task and the personalities of subordinates. When tasks are simple and repetitive, participation has little effect, because "there is little to participate about."[29] When subordinates are intelligent and desire independence, participation is especially important.

Deciding on the appropriate level of participation is extremely important. Participation is empowering and satisfying, and it generates enthusiasm for the decisions that are reached. On the other hand, participation takes time away from other activities. Also, some people don't like to participate, and most people don't want to get involved in decisions they care little about. In Chapter 12, Managing Teams, we will more thoroughly address the question of when participation is most useful.

Also, we noted in Chapter 3 that people vary their behaviors depending on their perceptions of others; recall that this is a cause of the Pygmalion effect. So we might expect managers who see their subordinates as high performers to treat them differently, giving them more responsibility. As a result, the relationship between democratic style and performance could be due to the impact of performance on style rather than vice versa.

CONSIDERATION AND INITIATING STRUCTURE

For about half a century, researchers have examined a wide variety of leader behaviors, and one conclusion is clear: Effective leaders show concern for *both* the task and the people they lead. Without concern for the task, the job won't get done. Without concern for people, satisfaction, motivation, and team spirit will plummet and performance will ultimately suffer.

Two sets of leader behaviors—consideration and initiating structure—address these concerns.

> **Consideration** is behavior that shows friendship, mutual trust, respect, and warmth. Considerate leaders are friendly and approachable, look out for the personal welfare of team members, back up the members in their actions, and find time to listen to them.

> **Initiating structure** is behavior that helps clarify the task and get the job done. Initiating leaders provide definite standards of performance, set goals, organize work, emphasize meeting deadlines, and coordinate the work of team members.

It is easy—and wrong—to assume that these are somehow conflicting sets of behaviors. That is, it might seem that considerate leaders don't provide a lot of structure or that structuring leaders tend to be inconsiderate. In fact,

FIGURE 7-6
Consideration and Initiating Structure

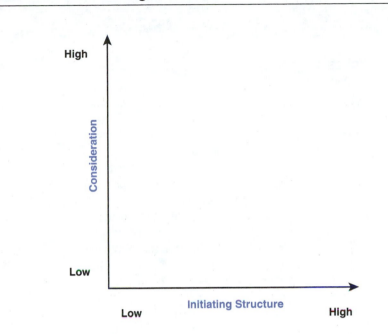

there is no trade-off between consideration and initiating structure. As shown in Figure 7-6, skillful leaders can exhibit *both* sets of behaviors. *Should* you as a leader exhibit both? The answer is that you should exhibit them *as needed.* For example, if team members are highly motivated, know their jobs, and have worked well together in the past, initiating structure may not help much. It may, in fact, be resented. The key is that you must show *concern* for people and the task, assess the situation, and then draw on your arsenal of behaviors as needed.

THE ROLE OF THE SITUATION

We have repeatedly said that leaders must fit their behaviors to the nature of the task, followers, and other characteristics of the situation. Many things may influence the way leader behaviors affect subordinate responses, including the following.[30]

> **Pressure.** When the situation involves stress, time pressures, task demands, and physical danger, subordinates view leaders' initiating structure more favorably than in calm, secure situations. Historically, subordinates have accepted autocratic, structuring leaders in times of war or other national emergency.
> **Task-related satisfaction.** When jobs are not intrinsically satisfying, leader-initiating structure may increase performance, but it leads to resentment and dissatisfaction. If subordinates don't like the job, they see little to gain from being told how to do it. Also, when the task is not

FOCUS ON MANAGEMENT

RECYCLING PEOPLE AT OMNI COMPUTER PRODUCTS*

Gerald Chamales is founder, President, and CEO of fast-growing Omni Computer Products, a company that manufactures printer ribbons and recycles toner cartridges under the Rhinotek brand. Chamales provides an example of a leader who cares about his employees as well as profits. A college dropout and a recovering drug and alcohol abuser who spent six months in a psychiatric facility and bottomed out as a homeless youth on the streets of Venice, California, 25 years ago, Chamales now recycles both people and laser cartridges.

In 1979, Chamales decided to rebuild his life. He set up a card table, borrowed $1,300 on his credit card, and started selling computer products. Now Chamales is inspired to help people with similar rough backgrounds. A full third of his 250 employees, including managers, are drawn from the welfare rolls and halfway houses of Los Angeles. Before Chamales will hire anyone with a troubled past, he demands 30 days of sobriety in a treatment program. After they join the payroll, Omni supports them with training programs, motivational seminars, and even short-term loans. A mentor is also assigned to each new employee— ex-addicts often need help with such basic etiquette as shaking hands and looking people in the eye.

This concern for people has been coupled with a strong focus on the bottom line. Chamales says, "When you get the right people, they give you 300 percent because they're so desperate to rebuild their lives. They're really hardworking people.

They're street smart. If their energies are channeled properly, they can be some of the best employees." Turnover of recovering alcoholics and drug addicts in Omni's workforce is significantly lower than that of other employees. Chamales has a "big hairy goal"—to increase Omni's sales eightfold, to $220 million, by the year 2002. Omni was recently named to *Industry Week*'s list of the Growing Companies 25— America's Most Successful Small Manufacturers.

http://rhinotek.com/index.html

*Based on E. Leibowitz, "Clean, Sober, and Good for Business," *Business Week*, March 1, 1999, p. ENT12; M. Marchetti, "Selling Saved Their Lives," *Sales and Marketing Management*, February 1999, pp. 36–42; and J. Maybury, "The Homeless CEO," *Forbes*, June 1, 1998, p. 32.

intrinsically satisfying, leader consideration becomes more important. A friendly, supportive boss may not be very important if you really enjoy your work, but a bit of warmth and comforting helps ease the pain of an unsatisfying job.

> **Subordinate need for information.** When subordinates lack knowledge about the task, perhaps because they are new on the job or because the job is very ambiguous, they like initiating structure. Quite simply, they are glad to get advice and structure when they need it.

> **Subordinate expectations.** Subordinates react more positively to levels of consideration and initiating structure that they expect than to unexpected levels of those behaviors. For instance, subordinates may even initially react warily to high levels of consideration from a usually inconsiderate boss. Perhaps they are suspicious about this unexpected behavior. This certainly doesn't mean the boss shouldn't show consideration, just that there may be a "feeling out" period after the changed behavior.

Together, these findings suggest some straightforward and logical guidelines for leaders. If the situation calls for structure, provide it. If it doesn't, subordinates will see structuring behaviors as redundant and bothersome. If subordinates clearly could use some support, consideration would be especially helpful. If not, consideration may be less important (though it rarely hurts). And subordinates (and others) value some predictability in behavior. If leaders behave erratically, subordinates are likely to react with suspicion and caution.

This recognition of the importance of the situation is reflected in theories of leadership that we will examine in the following sections. Each of these theories somehow considers the fit between the leader and the situation, and each gives the leader ways to achieve effective fit.

PATH–GOAL THEORY OF LEADERSHIP

Since so many things can affect the effectiveness of leader behaviors, it would be helpful to have a systematic framework in which to consider them. Path-goal theory provides one such framework. Robert House developed the *path–goal theory of leader effectiveness,* an extension and revision of the work of Martin Evans.[31] House based this approach on expectancy theory (discussed in Chapter 6). At base, the theory says leaders are effective because of their impact on subordinates' motivation, ability to perform effectively, and satisfaction. The theory is called path–goal because it focuses on how the leader influences the subordinates' perceptions of their goals and paths to goal attainment. According to path-goal theory, a leader's behavior is motivating or satisfying to the degree that it increases subordinate goal attainment and clarifies the paths to these goals. To couch these statements more explicitly in expectancy theory terms, the path–goal theory sees the leader as having the following three motivational functions.

> The leader can increase valences associated with work-goal attainment.
> The leader can increase instrumentalities of work-goal attainment for the acquisition of personal outcomes.
> The leader can increase the expectancy that effort will result in work-goal attainment.

In short, path-goal theory says leader behaviors are unlikely to have a positive effect unless they somehow help the subordinate attain desired outcomes.

Path-goal theory examines how the effectiveness of each of four sets of leader behaviors is influenced by two sets of contingency factors.

Path–Goal Leader Behaviors   The four kinds of leader behaviors considered by path-goal theory are as follows.

> **Directive leadership** is characterized by a leader who lets subordinates know what is expected of them and tells them how to do it. This is similar to initiating structure.
> **Supportive leadership** is characterized by a friendly and approachable leader who shows concern for the status, well-being, and needs of subordinates. This is much like consideration.
> **Participative leadership** is characterized by a leader who consults with subordinates and asks for their suggestions, which he or she seriously considers before making a decision.

> **Achievement-oriented leadership** is characterized by a leader who sets challenging goals, expects subordinates to perform at their highest level, and shows confidence that subordinates will meet such expectations.

Path–goal theory tries to explain how each of these types of leadership affects:

> The satisfaction of subordinates
> The subordinates' acceptance of the leader
> The degree to which subordinates feel their effort will result in performance (expectancy)
> And the degree to which subordinates feel their performance will result in rewards (instrumentalities)

Again, the theory essentially argues that subordinates will see each style of leadership as acceptable, satisfying, and motivating if they believe it either is an immediate source of desired outcomes or is useful in leading to such outcomes in the future.

Contingency Factors The model considers two contingency factors—personal characteristics of the subordinates and the nature of the task to be performed. As an example, subordinates who don't feel they have the ability to master their tasks will probably react positively to directive leadership. And if the job is highly structured, subordinates will see directive leadership as unnecessary and will resent it.

The elements of path–goal theory are shown in Figure 7-7.

Path–goal theory offers concrete guidelines concerning potentially important leader behaviors and situational variables and provides a logical framework to examine how they might interact to influence follower satisfaction and performance. Also, it emphasizes the need for leaders to be sensitive and flexible. That is, it encourages leaders to be sensitive to the characteristics of their subordinates and the task and to recognize that they may need to tailor their behaviors accordingly. This is a point we will stress again—the effective

FIGURE 7-7
Elements of Path–Goal Theory

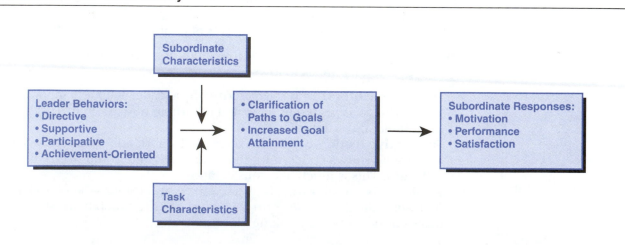

leader asks not "What works?" but "What works when?" The ability to adapt leader behaviors to the demands of the task and subordinates is a critical skill.

Skills Practice 7-4 is a group activity that will help you to see how path–goal theory works in action. After completing this exercise, you should have a much greater mastery of how to apply path–goal theory in an organizational context.

Skills Practice 7-4   **Skill Level: Challenging**
*Role Immersion Exercise—Using Path–Goal Theory
to Establish Leader–Situation Match*

Skill Objective
To develop skill in applying path–goal theory to a work situation.

Procedure
1. Form groups of 4–5 students each.
2. Assign one student to each of the following roles:
    a. Team Leader
    b. Employee 1
    c. Employee 2
    d. Employee 3
    e. Observer
    Note: If your group has only four members, you can eliminate the observer role.
3. Each student should read the following general scenario and their individual roles. Students should not read each other's role sheets.

a. The Setting
Williams & Associates is a leading advertising firm based in New York City. The firm specializes in the development of advertising campaigns for many Fortune 500 corporations. It employs approximately 75 advertising specialists and support staff at its main headquarters.

Williams & Associates faces fierce competition from other advertising firms from around the United States and the rest of the world. Speed and responsiveness to tough customer demands are critical for success in this industry. In the end, however, everything hinges on the effectiveness of advertising campaigns in generating business for their clients. This reality puts tremendous pressure on these firms to leverage every advantage they can find.

Recently, the firm has won a contract to develop an advertising campaign for Cobra Motor Corporation, a new luxury car manufacturer that aims to compete directly with world-class luxury car manufacturers such as Lexus, BMW, Mercedes, Audi, Jaguar, Cadillac, and Lincoln. Cobra is new to the luxury car market, so it needs to establish its name in the highly competitive U.S. market and enhance its name recognition. In the future, Cobra wants consumers to associate its name with the attributes of quality, exclusivity, elegance, performance, and sportiness.

The challenge for Williams & Associates is to create an advertising campaign that will make consumers remember the name of Cobra Motor Corporation.

b. Role 1—The Leader
You are the leader of the advertising development team that is in charge of the Cobra account. Your task is to effectively lead the various members of your team in completing the task of developing a high-quality advertising campaign for Cobra.

Use path–goal theory as your primary guide in helping you to lead your team through the process of developing the ad campaign.

Key Tips for Playing This Role

1. Remember that you want to develop an advertising campaign for Cobra that meets their requirements of establishing the name of the company and getting consumers to view it as a legitimate player in the luxury auto industry.
2. Apply the basic logic of path–goal theory in leading your team in this situation. That is, assess the needs of your employees and the nature of the task. Then match the appropriate leadership behavior (directive, supportive, achievement oriented, participative) to each employee.
3. Don't forget that you only have 30 minutes to develop your advertising campaign.

c. Role 2—Employee 1

You are one of the advertising specialists on the team that is developing an advertising campaign for Cobra Motor. You are a recent graduate of Billingsworth College, where you majored in English. You were an excellent student in college, maintaining a 3.7/4.0 GPA. However, you have had only one introductory course in advertising, and you have no prior work experience in the business world.

Key Tips for Playing This Role

1. Repeatedly state that you just started and that you don't have a clue what's going on or what you are supposed to be doing.
2. Ask for a lot of clarification on issues the leader brings up, and act confused by his/her explanations. The bottom line is that you need structure and direction from the leader.

d. Role 3—Employee 2

You are one of the advertising specialists on the team that is developing an advertising campaign for Cobra Motor. You have over 15 years of experience on the job, so you are a "seasoned veteran." You don't need direction from the leader, since you believe you already know how to perform your job. However, you have a strong need for recognition for your contributions to the project and to the firm in general.

Key Tips for Playing This Role

1. Emphasize repeatedly that you have bent over backwards for the firm in the past, but the firm has never shown any appreciation for your contributions.
2. Also state that the management has not provided enough support for advertising development teams in the past and that you feel like management doesn't really care much about its employees.

e. Role 4—Employee 3

You are one of the advertising specialists on the team that is developing an advertising campaign for Cobra Motor. You have been with the firm for about three years now. You are highly committed to the success of the firm, and you want to excel at your job in order to have a chance of being promoted in the future.

Key Tips for Playing This Role

1. You want the leader to inspire you, to "fire you up," and to lead the team to victory. The bottom line is that you demand strong leadership.
2. State that you expect the leader to communicate his or her vision or mission for the project to the team. Ask the leader why employees should give 150 percent of their

---

Web Wise

Big Dog's Leadership Page

Big Dog's Leadership page is part of the website called Big Dog's Bowl of Biscuits. The Bowl of Biscuits site contains information on training, leadership, and performance, as well as Big Dog's Library and other information. The Leadership Page provides information "for new supervisors, managers, leads, and anyone wishing to move up through the ranks as a leader. The first chapter, Concepts of Leadership, provides a basic background on leadership. The following chapters provide the skills and knowledge needed to implement effective leadership. The appendixes contain a basic lesson plan for implementing a leadership development program with several learning activities, definitions, quotes, references, and other tools."

http://www.nwlink.com/ ~donclark/leader/leader.html

effort to this project. You want your leader to be someone who has a clear sense of his/her goals and can get others to become committed to achieving those goals as well. Make "Why should we care?" or "Why is this important?" statements during the process.

f. Role 5—Process Observer
Your job is to observe the process and to document what the leader does to handle the situation and how employees react to the leader's behavior.

4. Each team will have 30 minutes to conduct the exercise.
5. When time has expired, each team should address the following discussion questions.

Discussion Questions
   a.   What were the characteristics of each of the employees and the task?
   b.   What types of behaviors was the leader using in dealing with each of the employees? Were they appropriate?
   c.   What suggestions would you make to the leader to enhance his/her effectiveness in this situation?
   d.   What are the practical implications of this simulation for you as future leaders in organizations?
6. *Optional:* The observer from each team can present a brief summary to the class of his/her impressions of the process, what the leader did, and how employees reacted.

The process model shown in the accompanying Bottom Line summarizes the basic steps associated with the application of the path-goal theory of leadership.

B O T T O M   L I N E

The Bottom Line: Applying Path–Goal Theory

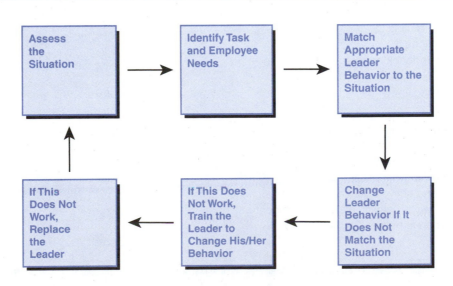

SUBSTITUTES FOR LEADERSHIP AND NEUTRALIZERS OF LEADERSHIP

We have said that particular leader behaviors are needed in particular situations. In other situations, those same behaviors may be useless or even harmful. This fact is the basis for the notions of *substitutes for leadership* and *neutralizers of leadership.* Figure 7-8 lists some of these substitutes and neutralizers. The figure indicates, for instance, that subordinates with high levels of ability or tasks that are well structured serve as substitutes for structuring leadership, while a considerable distance between the superior and subordinate neutralize the effects of such leadership. Similarly, relationship-oriented, supportive, considerate leadership will be neutralized when subordinates have high needs for independence, while tasks that are intrinsically satisfying and cohesive work groups serve as substitutes for such leadership.

The process model shown in the nearby Bottom Line summarizes the basic steps associated with the effective management of substitutes and neutralizers of leadership.

Skills Practice 7-5 will give you an opportunity to identify substitutes for leadership and neutralizers of leadership and to develop appropriate strategies in a work situation.

F I G U R E 7 - 8
Leadership Substitutes and Neutralizers

	SUBSTITUTE OR NEUTRALIZER ROLES	
Characteristic	**Relationship-Oriented Supportive, Considerate Leadership**	**Task-Oriented Directive, Structuring Leadership**
Of the Subordinate		
1. Ability, experience, training, knowledge		Substitute
2. Need for independence	Neutralizer	Neutralizer
3. "Professional" orientation	Substitute	Substitute
4. Indifference toward organizational rewards	Neutralizer	Neutralizer
Of the Task		
5. Unambiguous and routine		Substitute
6. Standardized methods		Substitute
7. Provides its own feedback concerning accomplishment		Substitute
8. Intrinsically satisfying	Substitute	
Of the Organization		
9. Formalization (explicit plans, goals, and areas of responsibility)		Substitute
10. Inflexibility (rigid, unbending rules and procedures)		Neutralizer
11. Closely knit, cohesive work groups	Substitute	Substitute
12. Highly specified and active advisory and staff functions		Substitute
13. Organizational rewards not within the leader's contract	Neutralizer	Neutralizer
14. Considerable distance between superior and subordinate	Neutralizer	Neutralizer

Source: S. Kerr and J. M. Jermier, "Substitutes for Leadership: Their Meaning and Measurement," *Organizational Behavior and Human Performance,* 1978, pp. 375–403.

B O T T O M   L I N E

The Bottom Line: Managing Substitutes and Neutralizers of Leadership

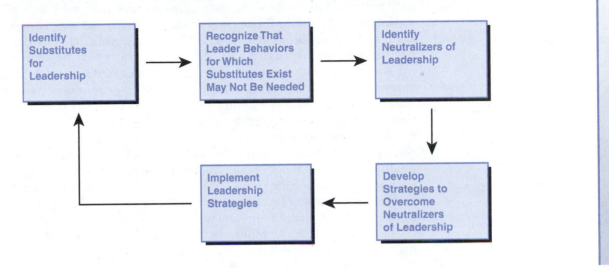

Skills Practice 7-5
Managing Substitutes for Leadership
and Neutralizers of Leadership

Skill Objective

To develop skill in identifying substitutes for leadership and neutralizers of leadership and to match appropriate leadership behaviors to these situations.

Procedure

1. Analyze the following information and identify the substitutes for leadership and the neutralizers of leadership for the employees in the scenario.

The Situation

You are the manager of a team of four video game developers for a major software company called X-GAMES based in California. Your team's task is to create highly innovative action and fighting games for the major video game systems in the industry. X-GAMES has a very informal and flexible operating structure that is designed to foster creativity in the organization. Information regarding your employees is summarized in the accompanying table.

Employee	Employee Experience and Qualifications	Need for Independence	Professional Orientation	Attitude Toward Organizational Rewards	Task Structure	Intrinsic Task Satisfaction
Josh Kanvik	High	Low	High	Positive	High	High
Blake Williams	Low	Low	Low	Positive	Low	Low
Kenisha Divine	High	High	High	Indifferent	High	High

---

2. Develop an action plan for managing the substitutes and neutralizers of leadership in this scenario. What type of leadership behavior, if any, is needed to effectively lead each individual?

LEADER–MEMBER EXCHANGE THEORY

We have already seen that leaders may appropriately behave differently in different situations. So asking whether a leader is autocratic or democratic, considerate or inconsiderate, is a bit simplistic. We have also seen that leaders may behave differently with some subordinates than with others. They may, for instance, let subordinates whom they feel are high performers have more say in decision making than others. There is a good deal of evidence that leaders do treat various subordinates differently. There may be some good reasons for this. Some subordinates may, for instance, need more guidance or reassurance or supervision than others. The *leader–member exchange (LMX) theory of leadership* examines other things that may cause leaders to treat some subordinates differently than others.

According to leader–member exchange theory, leaders establish a one-on-one relationship with each follower. These relationships vary in terms of the quality of the exchange. Some followers—members of the in-group—have a high-quality relationship with the leader, characterized by mutual trust, liking, and respect. These followers enjoy the confidence of their leader and are given interesting and challenging assignments. In exchange for the benefits of in-group status, these members have a role to carry out—to work hard, be loyal, and support the leader. Other followers—the out-group—have a lower-quality relationship with the leader. The leader tends to see them as lacking motivation or competence or loyalty, interacts with them less, and offers them few chances to demonstrate their capabilities. These out-group members, in turn, may "live down" to the leader's expectations, carrying out the tasks de-

FIGURE 7-9
Leader–Member Exchange Model

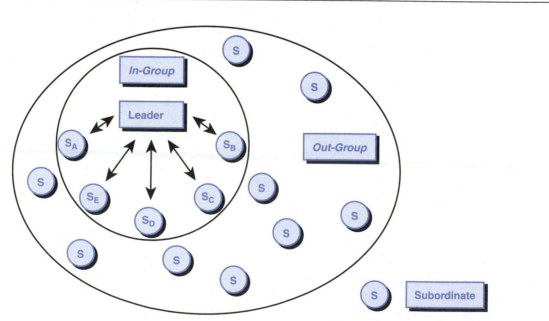

BOTTOM LINE

The Bottom Line: Applying the Leader–Member Exchange Model

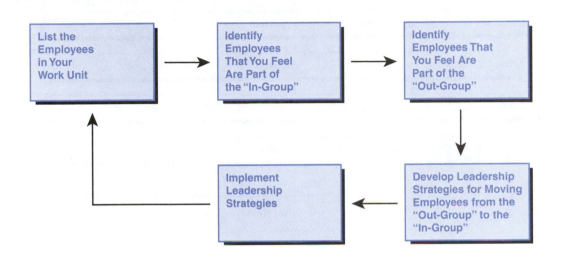

fined in their formal job descriptions and facing no real expectations of loyalty, creativity, or high performance. Figure 7-9 shows how the leader may treat some followers as members of an in-group and others as out-group members.

Life is full of self-fulfilling prophecies, and the relationships described by the leader–member exchange model certainly are among them. Members of the in-group are given support and opportunities and are viewed by the leader with a positive eye. Members of the out-group are—for whatever reason—placed in constraining boxes in which they have little chance or motivation to do well. Sadly, followers may sometimes find themselves as members of in-groups or out-groups due less to their abilities and potential than to favoritism, stereotypes, or personal conflicts.

In an ideal world, there would be no in-groups or out-groups—all followers would enjoy the rich exchange relationships of in-group status. In the real world, in-groups and out-groups are common and perhaps cannot be avoided. Nevertheless, leaders must do all they can to ensure that in-group membership is based on ability and motivation rather than favoritism or prejudice. They must also ensure that followers can move between the groups, having access to in-group membership when it is earned and falling from such status when it is no longer justified.

The process model in the nearby Bottom Line summarizes the basic steps associated with application of the leader–member exchange model. It emphasizes the ideal of moving all followers to in-group status.

The most recent focus of leader–member exchange theory is on how exchanges between leaders and followers can be used for "leadership making."[32] *Leadership making* is an approach to helping the leader develop high-

FIGURE 7-10
Phases in Leadership Making

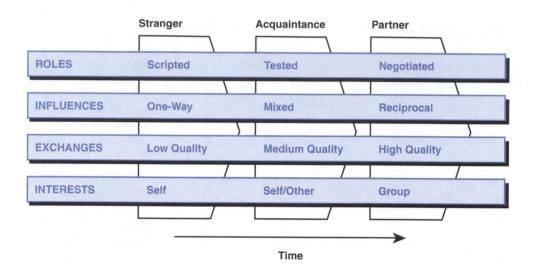

quality exchanges with all of his or her followers rather than just a few. It tries to make all followers feel like part of the in-group and thus to avoid the inequities and negative implications of being in an out-group. Leadership making seeks to promote the development of partnerships in which the leader tries to build effective dyads with all employees in the work unit as well as networks of partnerships throughout the organization.

As shown in Figure 7-10, leadership making develops over time in three phases: (a) the stranger phase, (b) the acquaintance phase, and (c) the mature phase. In the *stranger phase,* exchanges between the leader and follower are low in quality, like those of out-group members. The follower complies with the formal leader, who has hierarchical status, controls rewards, and is motivated primarily by self-interest rather than the good of the group. The *acquaintance phase* begins with an "offer" by the leader or follower for improved career-oriented social exchanges that involve sharing more resources and personal or work-related information. This phase is a testing-out period to see whether the follower is interested in taking on more roles and responsibilities and the leader is willing to offer new challenges. Quality of relations improves as leader–follower dyads develop trust and mutual respect and begin to focus more on the purposes and goals of the group rather than self-interest. Finally, the *mature phase* is characterized by high-quality leader–member exchanges. Relationships that have progressed to this stage show high levels of trust, mutual respect, and mutual obligation. The leader and follower have tested the relationship and found they can rely on each other. Each member of the dyad influences the other, and each may ask the other for favors and special assistance. The leader and follower are tied together in productive ways, and they move beyond their own self-interest to focus on the greater good of the team and organization.

TRANSFORMATIONAL LEADERSHIP

The behaviors we have discussed to this point are critical to the effective functioning of teams and organizations. When we think about great leaders, though, we usually picture something more; we expect inspiration, conviction, and vision. These are the essence of *transformational leadership.* Transformational leadership is based in the personal values, beliefs, and qualities of the leader. Transformational leaders broaden and elevate the interests of their followers, generate awareness and acceptance of the purposes and mission of the group, and stir followers to look beyond their own interests to the interests of others. Transformational leaders display the following five sets of behaviors.

> **Attributed charisma.** *Charisma* is a Greek word meaning "divinely inspired gift." More than 60 years ago, Max Weber wrote that charismatic leaders reveal a transcendent mission or course of action that may be itself appealing to the potential followers but that is acted upon because the followers believe their leader is extraordinarily gifted. Mary Kay Ash of Mary Kay Cosmetics, Jack Welch of General Electric, and Herb Kelleher at Southwest Airlines are known for their charisma. Leaders are seen as being charismatic when they display a sense of power and confidence, remain calm during crisis situations, and provide reassurance that obstacles can be overcome.

> **Idealized influence.** Walter Bagehot, a noted 19th century economist and editor, wrote that strong beliefs win strong men, and then make them stronger. Leaders display idealized influence when they talk about their important values and beliefs; consider the moral and ethical consequences of their decisions; display conviction in their ideals, beliefs, and values; and model values in their actions.

> **Intellectual stimulation.** Intellectually stimulating leaders help followers recognize problems and find ways to solve them. They encourage followers to challenge the status quo. They champion change and foster creative deviance.

> **Inspirational leadership.** Napoleon Bonaparte is reputed to have said that a leader is a dealer in hope. Inspirational leaders give followers hope, energizing them to pursue a vision. They envision exciting new possibilities, talk optimistically about the future, express confidence that goals can be met, and articulate a compelling vision of the future.

> **Individualized consideration.** Transformational leaders do more than just "be nice." They show personal interest and concern in their *individual* followers, and they promote their followers' self-development. They coach their followers, serve as their mentors, and focus them on developing their strengths.

Transformational leadership will require new sets of skills, including:[33]

> **Anticipatory skills**—the ability to intuitively and systematically scan the changing environment

> **Visioning skills**—the process of persuasion and example by which an individual or leadership team induces a group to take action that is in accord with the leader's purposes or, most likely, the shared purposes of all
> **Value-congruence skills**—the ability to be in touch with employees' needs so that they can engage employees on the basis of shared motives, values, and goals
> **Empowerment skills**—the ability to effectively share power with employees so that they can share the satisfaction derived from accomplishment
> **Self-understanding skills**—introspective skills as well as frameworks with which leaders understand both themselves and their employees

These are precisely the sorts of skills we seek to develop and reinforce throughout this text. For instance, we addressed anticipatory skills in Chapter 2, The Organizational Context, and value-congruence skills in Chapter 3, Understanding and Valuing Differences, and Chapter 6, Motivating Effectively. We consider visioning skills in this chapter and in Chapter 12, Managing Teams. We will address empowerment skills in Chapter 8, Organizing Culture, Empowerment, and Ethics. Finally, self-understanding skills are a focus of Chapter 9, Fostering Personal Growth, and of the self-assessment exercises found in each chapter.

We'll close this section with two important points. First, these ways of behaving have consistently been shown to influence team performance, the satisfaction and motivation of followers, and many other important outcomes. Second, these are all behaviors that you *can* change. You can, for example, choose to pay more attention to those who work for you, to set inspirational goals, to model the values you espouse, and to provide reassurance in the face of obstacles.

The process model in the nearby Bottom Line summarizes the basic steps associated with the application of transformational leadership.

Now assess your own transformational leader behaviors by completing Self-Assessment 7-3. Then complete Skills Practice 7-6 to develop skill in applying transformational leadership to a work situation.

FOCUS ON MANAGEMENT

TRANSFORMATIONAL LEADERSHIP AT GENERAL ELECTRIC

Jack Welch, CEO of General Electric, is a notable transformational leader. "We have found what we believe to be the distilled essence of competitiveness. It is the reservoir of talent and creativity and energy that can be found in each of our people. That essence is liberated when we make people believe that what they think and do is important—and then get out of their way while they do it." Welch describes his successor: "I want somebody with incredible energy who can excite others, who can define their vision, who finds change fun and doesn't get paralyzed by it. I want somebody who feels comfortable in Delhi or Denver."

http://www.ge.com/index.htm

BOTTOM LINE

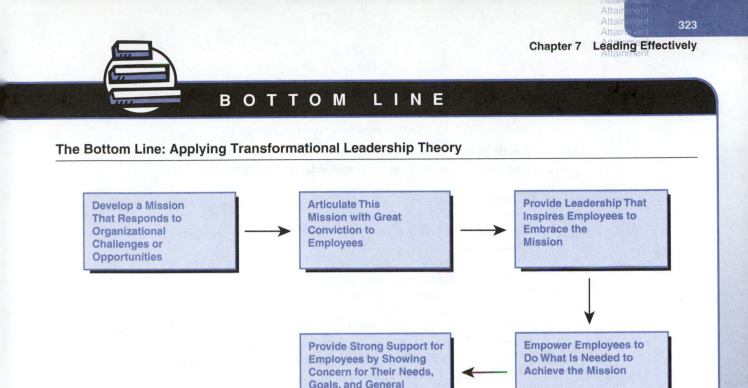

The Bottom Line: Applying Transformational Leadership Theory

Develop a Mission That Responds to Organizational Challenges or Opportunities → Articulate This Mission with Great Conviction to Employees → Provide Leadership That Inspires Employees to Embrace the Mission → Empower Employees to Do What Is Needed to Achieve the Mission → Provide Strong Support for Employees by Showing Concern for Their Needs, Goals, and General Welfare

Self-Assessment 7-3
Your Transformational Leader Behaviors

Indicate your degree of agreement with each of the following statements by using the following scale:

1 = Disagree Completely
2 = Disagree Somewhat
3 = Neither Agree nor Disagree
4 = Agree Somewhat
5 = Agree Completely

1. _____ I take stands on difficult issues.
2. _____ I am able to remain calm in difficult times.
3. _____ I encourage others to challenge the status quo.
4. _____ I treat others as individuals.
5. _____ I talk optimistically about the future.
6. _____ I assure others that obstacles can be overcome.
7. _____ I stand up for my beliefs and values.
8. _____ I look for multiple perspectives when solving problems.
9. _____ I coach others to develop their individual strengths.
10. _____ I am able to display an aura of power and confidence.
11. _____ I think about the ethical and moral aspects of my decisions.
12. _____ I encourage others to question assumptions.
13. _____ I present clear and persuasive visions of the future.
14. _____ I tailor my advice to others' particular needs.
15. _____ I talk about exciting new beginnings.

324

Awareness
Awareness
Awareness
Awareness

Chapter 7 Awareness **Leading Effectively**
Awareness

Skills Practice 7-6

Skill Level: **Challenging**

*Role Immersion Exercise—Using Transformational
Leadership to Support Organizational Change*

Skill Objective

To develop skill in applying transformational leadership to a work situation.

Procedure

1. Form groups of 4–5 students each.
2. Assign one student to each of the following roles:
   a. CEO
   b. Vice President of Marketing
   c. Vice President of Manufacturing
   d. Vice President of Finance
   e. Observer
   Note: If your group has only four members, the role of the observer can be eliminated.
3. Each student should read the following general scenario and his or her individual role. Students should not read each other's role sheets.

a. The Setting

GCX Computer Corporation is a manufacturer of mid-level to high-end desktop and laptop computers. The company established itself as a leader in the industry in the 1980s with its innovative product design, cutting-edge technology, value pricing, and outstanding technical support. The company is based in Denver, Colorado, where it employs 2,000 employees in administration, marketing, finance, and human resources. Manufacturing operations are located in Tuscaloosa, Alabama, where 1,000 production employees assemble its products on three separate shifts that run six days per week.

GCX sells its computer systems in more than 60 countries throughout the world. It is ranked fourth in the computer industry on the basis of market share.

In the past few years, GCX corporate performance has slipped significantly. Production costs have been increasing at 20 percent above the industry average, quality has declined dramatically, customer satisfaction has dropped 35 percent, and profitability has dropped by 70 percent. In addition, competition from other U.S. companies and foreign firms from Taiwan has intensified, and many customers have flocked to basic computer models that cost less than $1,000. In addition to these negative results, employee job satisfaction and retention throughout the company have decreased by 50 percent in just a couple of years.

b. Role 1—The Chief Executive Officer

You are the CEO and the leader of the senior management team at GCX. Your general objective is to lead your team by taking appropriate action to effectively turn around the organization's performance. Your specific task is to develop a turnaround plan for GCX that specifies the company's future goals and strategies for achieving them.

You should take specific actions that reflect the following behavioral dimensions of transformational leadership theory:

> *Attributed charisma*—Try to inspire your team by showing great confidence that a turnaround at the company is possible and that obstacles can be overcome.

> *Idealized influence*—Communicate your beliefs and values to the management team.
> *Intellectual stimulation*—Encourage team members to challenge the status quo and to support change.
> *Inspirational leadership*—Articulate a compelling vision of the future to your team.
> *Individualized consideration*—Show personal interest in and concern for each member of your team.

Don't forget that you only have 30 minutes to develop a turnaround plan for GCX Corporation.

c. Role 2—Vice President of Marketing

You are the Vice President of Marketing at GCX. You believe that the company's recent poor performance is just a fluke and that there is nothing fundamentally wrong with the company. You should focus your attention on the customer satisfaction data and emphasize that the numbers will improve over time. Your initial position should be that you don't see any point in developing a turnaround plan because the company is not in a crisis at all. If you think that the CEO does an effective job of convincing you otherwise, then feel free to modify your position. However, do not change your position unless you believe there is a compelling reason to do so.

d. Role 3—Vice President of Manufacturing

You are the Vice President of Manufacturing at CGX. Your major concern is with the product quality results that have declined significantly. Your initial position should be that you agree with the CEO that a turnaround plan is needed for the company, but you are not sure what it should look like. In short, you need direction and structure from the CEO regarding the specifics of the turnaround plan.

e. Role 4—Vice President of Finance

You are the Vice President of Finance at GCX Corporation. You are a "fence sitter" in that you haven't decided whether a turnaround plan for GCX is a good idea or not, but you are willing to discuss it with the other members of the team. You believe that the cause of the company's declining profitability is inefficiencies in the manufacturing plant.

f. Role 5—Process Observer

Your job is to observe the process and to document what the leader does to handle the situation and how employees react to the leader's behavior.

4. Each team will have 30 minutes to conduct the exercise.
5. When time has expired, each team should address the following discussion questions.

Discussion Questions

a. What types of behaviors was the leader using in dealing with each of the employees? Were they appropriate?
b. What suggestions would you make to the leader to enhance his/her effectiveness in this situation?
c. What are the practical implications of this simulation for you as future leaders in organizations?

6. *Optional:* The observer from each team can present a brief summary to the class of his/her impressions of the process, what the leader did, and how employees reacted.

FOCUS ON MANAGEMENT

REBUILDING THE GARAGE AT HEWLETT-PACKARD*

Carleton (Carly) Fiorina majored in medieval history and philosophy at Stanford University and later dropped out of UCLA's law school after one semester. In 1999, she was named CEO of Hewlett-Packard, the first outsider selected for a top position at the company. HP, started in a garage in 1938 by Bill Hewlett and Dave Packard with $538 in working capital, rode a history of innovation to become a leading global provider of computing and imaging solutions and services, with 86,500 employees worldwide and $42.4 billion in 1999 revenues. Fiorina became the first female CEO of one of America's 20 largest corporations and was ranked by *Fortune* magazine as the most powerful woman in American business (beating out Oprah Winfrey).

As a Stanford undergraduate, Fiorina worked as an HP temporary shipping clerk. After graduation, she joined AT&T and rose through many positions to ultimately lead the spin-off of Lucent Technologies from

AT&T. Her early success, high energy, fearless leadership, and a personal touch that inspires intense loyalty made Fiorina an American business legend.

When Fiorina took the reins, HP was awash in question marks, with lackluster financial performance and a dearth of recent innovative offerings. Fiorina saw the company as sick and endangered—slow, complacent, and risk averse. Seeking to reinvent HP, Fiorina evoked its original "garage" spirit and launched a $200 million brand and advertising campaign that included a new logo with the word "invent." Saying, "Preserve the best, reinvent the rest," Fiorina has pushed through more drastic changes in a short period of time than HP has ever seen before. She drew up a "rules of the garage," based on how the original HP operated. Among its mantras are "No politics, no bureaucracy" and "Radical ideas are not bad ideas." Along with many other changes, Fiorina has revamped salary structures to tie pay more closely to performance, rein-

forced key values, restructured the company to encourage independent product groups to work together, and realigned the upper ranks of the firm. She is seeking to make the company more agile, moving it to "Internet time."

In the first months of Fiorina's rein, HP has shown strong revenue growth, sharply increased its presence in the heavy-duty computing market, and won the admiration of Wall Street analysts. Fiorina has grand visions for the computer industry, predicting that "computer-driven appliances and services will be as pervasive as oxygen, as reliable as the sun and moon, and as invisible as radio waves."

http://www.hp.com/

*This discussion is based in part on "Business: Rebuilding the Garage," *The Economist,* July 15, 2000, pp. 59–50; "Wake-Up Call for HP," *Technology Review,* May/June 2000, pp. 94–100; N. Watson, "The Lists," *Fortune,* April 17, 2000, pp. 289–295; and Q. Hardy, "All Carly, All the Time," *Forbes,* December 13, 1999, pp. 138–144.

THE LANGUAGE OF LEADERSHIP

Transformational leaders must be able to inspire; communicate their vision, ideals, and beliefs; provide compelling reassurance; and challenge followers to think in new ways. To do all this, they must be masters of communication—they must "speak the language of leadership."

Two aspects of the language of leadership—framing and rhetorical crafting—are crucial.[34] *Framing* is presenting the message—defining the purpose in a meaningful way. *Rhetorical crafting* is using symbolic language to give emotional power to the message. That is, the message provides a sense of direction, and rhetoric heightens its emotional appeal and makes it memorable.

Two key elements of framing are amplifying values and belief amplification. *Amplifying values* is the process of identifying and elevating certain values as basic to the overall mission. *Belief amplification* is the process of emphasizing factors that support or impede actions taken to achieve desired values.

Rhetorical techniques of inspirational leaders include using metaphors, analogies, and stories, gearing language to the particular audience, and such speech techniques as alliteration, repetition, and rhythm.

Martin Luther King, in his famous "I Have a Dream" speech, delivered on the steps of the Lincoln Memorial in 1963, sculpted a masterpiece of language in service of transformational leadership. He spoke of values he held dear—"the inalienable rights of life, liberty, and the pursuit of happiness," "the riches of freedom and the security of justice," the need to "forever conduct our struggle on the high plane of dignity and discipline."

King envisioned exciting new possibilities, speaking with passion of the day when "on the red hills of Georgia the sons of former slaves and the sons of former slave owners will be able to sit down together at a table of brotherhood." He assured his listeners that "with this faith we will be able to hew out of the mountain of despair a stone of hope." He recognized the individual needs and perspectives of his audience members, speaking of the "marvelous new militancy that has engulfed the Negro community" but also of "our white brothers." "We cannot walk alone," he warned. He used words of inclusion, hope, and faith, ending with his vision of the day when "all of God's children . . . will be able to join hands and sing, in the words of the old Negro spiritual, 'Free at last! Free at last! Thank God Almighty, we are free at last!'" He repeated key phrases again and again, and his voice rose in volume and emotion as the speech progressed. Martin Luther King's famous speech can be found at many places on the Web, including:

http://www.ecsu.edu/sp/bowser/KingSpeech.html

GLOBAL PERSPECTIVES

WOMEN WORLD LEADERS

While there are relatively few female political leaders at top levels in the United States, Russia, China, and other large countries, many small developed, developing, and Third World countries have been pioneers. For example, women are serving, or have served in the recent past, as presidents (or an equivalent title) in Iceland, Malta, the Philippines, Haiti, Nicaragua, Ireland, Sri Lanka, Liberia, Switzerland, Latvia, Panama, Finland, and elsewhere. To read about more than 500 women presidents, prime ministers, governors general, and party leaders and those in other world leadership roles, go to:

http://www.terra.es/personal2/monolith/00women.htm

REFLECTIONS ON LEADERSHIP

The Top 25 Managers

According to *Business Week,* its Top Managers of 1999 "pushed their companies—and often their stock prices—to new highs. Some stood out by making smart decisions at lightning speed. Others were more patient, relentlessly pursuing a crucial deal or taking the time to right a once-sinking ship. In a year marked by hype, these execs' accomplishments were legit." To choose the year's 25 Top Managers, *Business Week* asked its staff of 149 writers and editors in 25 bureaus around the world to nominate candidates. They then pared the list to make sure each candidate's company's financial and stock performance outclassed the field.

Read about the top 25 managers, as well as "Managers to Watch" and "The Top Entrepreneurs," at:

http://www.businessweek.com/ 2000/00_02/b3663001.htm

As a manager or team member, you will often find yourself in positions of leadership or of potential leadership. Your leadership role will sometimes be formally prescribed, and at other times may develop informally. In either case, your actions may affect the performance and satisfaction of your subordinates and others. Give your leadership behaviors the attention they deserve.

To carry out your leadership duties, you will often need to draw on bases of power. Successful leaders draw on a variety of power bases. They recognize that referent power has a broad range and that heavy reliance on coercive power can be dangerous. As a leader, remember that control over resources, information, and the problem-solving process all serve to increase power.

When selecting people for leadership positions or assigning them to leadership tasks, it may be useful to consider such traits as intelligence, self-confidence, decisiveness, and need for occupational achievement. However, be sure to ask whether the position really calls for such traits. It is illegal to use selection criteria that are unrelated to task performance.

Remember that a leader must show concern for both task accomplishment and fulfillment of subordinate needs. This does not mean that as a leader you will always need to emphasize each of these factors. Often, the nature of tasks or of subordinates will take care of some concerns or make them less important. However, you must be ready to step in to see that these dual needs are somehow satisfied.

Remember too that the same style or behavior may not work in every situation. In deciding how to behave, consider the maturity and needs of your subordinates, the structure and other characteristics of the task, and the nature of the organization. The models discussed in this chapter should be useful in highlighting factors to keep in mind. Treat them as guides rather than as absolute rules. If you are using styles or behaviors that violate the suggestions of the models, ask yourself why. Do you disagree with the model? Is it ignoring variables that you feel are important, or are you somehow failing to assess the situation properly?

In general, behaviors reflecting consideration on the part of the leader are satisfying to subordinates and don't harm productivity. Further, consideration makes initiating structure more palatable. So if the situation is one that calls for a leader to initiate structure, consideration will be important.

Leadership can be frustrating. Structured tasks, separation of superiors and subordinates, bureaucratic constraints, and other factors can sometimes handcuff the leader. Try to be aware of such substitutes and neutralizers for leadership. If they seem helpful to the satisfaction and performance of your subordinates, it may be best to accept them. If you feel they are constraining performance or satisfaction, you may want to try to circumvent them. For instance, if your subordinates are indifferent toward organizational rewards, you may try to determine which rewards are important to them. You may also need to rely on alternatives to constrained power bases.

Also, as a leader you should not accept the situation as fixed. You may be able to change task structure, your power, relations with subordinates, and other dimensions. Before accepting the constraints, try to loosen them. Before fitting your behaviors to the situation, tailor the situation to your liking.

Perhaps more than anything else, the models reviewed in this chapter show that leader sensitivity, critical thinking, and flexibility are crucial. Leaders must be sensitive to the characteristics of tasks, workers, and other dimensions of the situation. They must choose suitable behaviors, avoiding those that are inappropriate or redundant. Finally, they must then have the flexibility to adopt those behaviors. These are difficult attributes to develop, but they will become increasingly important. You would be wise to try to cultivate them.

Finally, remember that vision and inspiration are important. Don't let a narrow focus on structuring of tasks and dealing with subordinates' needs on a day-to-day basis cause you to ignore broader, more transformational aspects of the leadership role.

Skills Practice 7-7 provides you with the opportunity to put the pieces of your leadership puzzle together and to think about leadership in an integrative manner based on the theories and concepts discussed in the chapter.

Skills Practice 7-7
Putting the Pieces Together—Developing
an Integrative Approach to Leadership

Skill Objective
To develop an effective leadership style based on an integrative (trait, behavioral, and situational) approach to leadership theories.

Procedure
1. Based on the leadership theories you read about in this chapter, identify the following on a separate piece of paper:
   a. The general traits or qualities you consider to be important for effective leadership.
   b. The general behaviors you believe an individual should exhibit in order to be an effective leader.
   c. Situational factors you think are important to consider for effective leadership.
   d. The general outcomes you see as measures of leadership effectiveness.
2. For each of the mini-cases that follow, discuss the type of leadership you believe would be needed to handle the situation effectively.

Integrative Leadership Case 1
You are the manager of a group of 20 recent college graduates who have been hired as sales representatives for your firm. Their job duties include selling computer networking software systems to corporate clients around the United States and the world. This job requires in-depth product knowledge and an understanding of customers' complex and constantly changing needs.

Your employees are bright, but they have little or no experience in sales. Each new hire is required to go through a six-week training program to provide him/her with the basics of sales techniques and product knowledge. However, many of them are still very intimidated by the thought of having to apply all of this knowledge in working with real clients.

How would you apply the leadership style you developed to the handling of this situation?

Integrative Leadership Case 2
You are the manager of a team of seven experienced food science researchers working for a consumer foods corporation. These scientists all have master's degrees or Ph.D.s in their

field. They possess an average of five years of work experience in the food industry, and they are highly competent at what they do.

The team works on a project basis in developing new products for the company. Members of the team have a strong need to "run their own show" with a minimal amount of guidance from management. Specifically, they maintain strong opinions about what should be done and how it should be done.

How would you apply the leadership style you developed to the handling of this situation?

Integrative Leadership Case 3

You are the manager of a team of 50 production workers at a consumer electronics company that manufactures TVs, boom boxes, and other stereo equipment. The team works together to assemble these products on a fairly traditional production line. The work is fairly routine, and your employees have enough experience to understand how to perform their jobs effectively. The challenge for you is that you were just promoted from production employee to manager. That is, until recently you were a coworker of the individuals whom you now must manage as their new boss. Some members of the team are happy for you and your promotion, while others resent that you were promoted over them and that you are now a member of "management" and not to be trusted.

How would you apply the leadership style you developed to the handling of this situation?

Integrative Leadership Case 4

You are the President of Premiere Hotels, a company that provides basic lodging and accommodations for business travelers at a reasonable price. Your company has over 500 locations throughout the United States and Canada. While your company has done well financially in the past 20 years, the hotel industry has become extremely competitive. Customers are more demanding now, and they expect more services and better accommodations for a lower price. Competition is intensifying, and new, more upscale hotels have been created that cater to consumers in your traditional niche.

These environmental changes are starting to affect Premiere Hotels' bottom line. In addition, a recent study of customer satisfaction with various hotels placed Premiere well below the industry average. Rumors are starting to circulate among employees that the company will announce mass employee layoffs in the near future and possibly close some of its hotels. These concerns are having a devastating effect on employee morale and job satisfaction.

How would you apply the leadership style you developed to the handling of this situation?

3.   Answer the following discussion questions.

Discussion Questions

1.   What do the various leadership theories have in common with each other? How do they differ from one another?
2.   Which leadership theory (or theories) was most valuable to you in developing your overall "leadership style"?
3.   To what degree did you modify the overall "leadership style" you developed, based on the scenarios in this exercise?
4.   What are the implications of this exercise for you as a future organizational leader?

Finally, read the scenario on leadership programs in the nearby Real-World Management Challenge and develop your own program to address this issue.

Later, you will be able to compare your program to those that major corporations are using to develop their leaders.

Real-World Management Challenge

Leadership Development Programs

The Leadership Challenge

One of the most significant challenges facing U.S. corporations has been the development of future leaders. Part of the challenge of addressing this issue is that the fundamental nature of leadership itself is constantly evolving in response to dynamic and complex external environments.

Some organizations have attempted to develop their own leadership development programs in response to the growing concern over a lack of future leadership talent. Unfortunately, many of these programs have failed to develop the right kinds of leadership skills among their management ranks. Edward Lawler, a leadership expert at the University of Southern California, says that the reason for this is that many of these leadership development programs focused on developing leadership competencies that were appropriate in the 1970s but not for the 1990s or for the 21st century.

What Would You Do?

If you were given the assignment of developing a leadership program for an organization, what would you do? Be as specific as possible in outlining the elements of your program, their objectives, and how you would implement them.

Source: "How Tomorrow's Best Leaders Are Learning Their Stuff," *Fortune*, November 27, 1995.

TOP TEN LIST: KEY POINTS TO REMEMBER
HOW TO LEAD EFFECTIVELY

10. Learn as much as you can about the work unit, organization, and industry associated with your leadership position.

9. Identify the needs of the leadership situation based on your goals and strategies, the motivation and skill of employees, and the complexity of the task.

8. Match the appropriate leadership style to the needs of the situation (that is, establish a leader–situation match).

7. Focus on developing and maintaining referent, expert, and reward bases of power rather than the more traditional emphasis on legitimate and coercive power.

6. Develop leaders by identifying individuals with leadership potential and providing them with formal and informal work and networking opportunities to develop relevant knowledge and skills.

5. Educate and guide your followers so that they understand their specific role in contributing to the success of the organization and are committed to it.

4. Establish and maintain good working relationships with your followers based on the principles of mutual trust and respect.

3. Measure the success of a leader in terms of employee outcomes such as motivation, satisfaction, and job performance as well as work unit or organizational outcomes.

2. Be aware that timing is critical and that you will only have a certain "window of opportunity" to establish the credibility of your leadership within an organization.

1. Remember that there is no single leadership style that is universally effective—effective leadership depends on the situation.

QUESTIONS FOR REVIEW AND REFLECTION

REVIEW QUESTIONS

1. What are five differences between the "old look" and the "new look" of leadership?
2. Which traits have been most consistently linked with effective leadership?
3. Define *authority, power, influence,* and *control.*
4. Identify five characteristics of power.
5. Cite three general uses of power.
6. Distinguish between coercive power, utilitarian power, and normative power.
7. List five interpersonal power bases.
8. Discuss the resource dependence approach and strategic contingencies approach to subunit power.
9. Identify five social influence approaches.
10. Define *consideration* and *initiating structure.*
11. Identify four characteristics of the situation that influence the way leader behaviors affect follower responses.
12. Discuss the path–goal theory of leadership, including the leader behaviors, contingency factors, and outcomes that it considers.
13. What are substitutes for leadership and neutralizers of leadership? Identify five substitutes or neutralizers, and indicate how each affects the role(s) of task-oriented and/or relationship-oriented leader behaviors.
14. Discuss leader–member exchange theory.
15. What is transformational leadership? Identify five transformational leader behaviors and five skills needed for transformational leadership.
16. What is meant by "the language of leadership"? What are four characteristics of the language of effective transformational leaders?
17. Give five guidelines for becoming a leader.

CRITICAL THINKING QUESTIONS

1. Take a position either for or against the following statement: "Different skills are needed to become a leader than to be successful once in a leadership role." Defend your position.
2. A colleague says to you, "I would never use coercive power, period." How would you respond?
3. We said in this chapter that transformational leadership requires five sets of skills. Which of those skills do you think is most difficult to develop? Easiest? Why?
4. Consider the various forms of emotional appeals discussed in this chapter (that is, friendly emotions, negative or unpleasant emotions, and emotional contrast). Give one example of how each of these might be used ethically and one example of how each might be used unethically.
5. When told about path–goal theory, a manager says, "They've got it backwards. The trick is to decide on what behavior I want to use and then to tailor the situation to fit those behaviors, not vice versa." What do you think of his argument?
6. When a supervisor is accused of treating some of her subordinates better than others, she says, "If some employees are in the in-group, it's because they've earned a place in the in-group." How would you respond to her statement?
7. A colleague says, "I really don't agree with the idea of substitutes for leadership. It never hurts to provide a little more guidance or to show a little more caring." Do you agree? Why or why not?
8. In accepting the Democratic Party's nomination for President of the United States, Al Gore spoke to criticisms that he lacked charisma, saying, "I know that sometimes people say I'm too serious, that I talk too much substance and policy. . . . But the presidency is more than a popularity contest. It's a day-to-day fight for people." Suppose you were a political advisor to Gore and wanted to make him appear more charismatic. What advice might you give him?
9. A manager says, "Don't give me this talk about the 'language of leadership.' That's putting style over substance. I want my employees to be swayed by the power of my arguments, not by speech tricks." How would you respond?

EXPERIENTIAL EXERCISES

WEB EXERCISE 7-1

TDIndustries, the premier construction and service company in the Southwest, is employee owned, debt free, and profitable. It was chosen national "Contractor of the Year" by Associated Builders and Contractors, a national construction association representing 18,000 firms across the United States. TDIndustries was ranked fourth in the year 2000 on *Fortune* magazine's "100 Best Companies to Work for in America." The company's CEO, Jack Lowe, Jr., attributes the company's success to a set of basic values that include concern for and belief in individual human beings and the valuing of individual differences, as well as to adherence to the philosophy of servant leadership. As described by Robert Greenleaf in *The Servant as Leader*,[35] the tenets of servant leadership include the views that leaders are people who have followers because they have earned recognition and respect and that leaders are first a servant of those they lead. Servant leadership sees the leader as a teacher, a source of information and knowledge, and a standard setter, more than a giver of directions and a disciplinarian. Jack Lowe is a noted proponent of the philosophy of servant leadership. Read more about servant leadership on the TDIndustries website at

http://www.tdindustries.com/About/values.asp

Then go to the website of the Robert K. Greenleaf Center for Servant-Leadership at

http://greenleaf.org/index.html

Read the sections entitled "Who is the servant leader?," "Who was Robert K. Greenleaf?," and "Servant-leadership in practice." Based on your reading on the two websites, answer the following questions.

1. Describe the servant leader in terms of the dimensions of consideration, initiating structure, and democratic versus autocratic style.
2. What power bases would the servant leader be likely to employ or avoid?
3. What might be primary social influence processes used by servant leaders?
4. Do you think the philosophy of servant leadership should be more widely adopted? Why or why not?

WEB EXERCISE 7-2

Go to the website of the Quotation Center at:

http://www.cyber-nation.com/victory/quotations/

At this site you will find links to thousands of quotations, searchable by subject, author, or keyword. Click on "View Quotes by Subject." You will see a listing of the letters of the alphabet. Click on "L" to get to a page showing subjects beginning with *L*. Then, click on "Leaders and Leadership." You will be shown more than 80 related quotes. Read through the quotes. Select five or more of the quotes that you think capture your views on leaders and leadership. Discuss those quotes and why you selected them.

CASE 7-1
GET WITH THE NEW POWER GAME

The Power Shift

A significant new trend in corporate America involves the very definition of *executive power* and what needs to be done to develop it and to use it to achieve business objectives. In short, the traditional leader who has relied on his/her formal authority and the ability to coerce or punish employees is considered to be a dying breed. That is, managers today simply cannot expect their employees to comply with their every request just because they are "the boss."

Drivers of the Trend

What accounts for this shift in the use of managerial power in organizations? First, employees today are better educated and much less tolerant of a traditional, authoritarian leader who barks out orders to subordinates. Second, organizational structures have changed fundamentally, in that there is a greater emphasis on decentralization. The result is that there is greater empowerment of front-line employees. This means that managers must increasingly share power with their employees. Third, unions and employment laws and regulations exist to protect employees against discrimination and mistreatment from their employers. In many cases, management in organizations is bending over backwards to avoid "crossing the line" on these issues due to concerns regarding potential lawsuits and the damage that could be done to their corporate images. Finally, employees today are more career oriented than ever. Simply put, they are less dependent on a single employer to support the achievement of their career objectives.

Strategies for Enhancing Managerial Power

The secret of the most successful power players is that they are open to talking about their formal authority and they are willing to share it or to give it away. For example, William J. Bratton, former police commissioner of New York City, made his employees accountable for achieving key objectives such as reducing crime and empowered them to do what was needed to achieve those objectives. In fact, Bratton believes that his power and influence actually increased as he shared power with others in his organization.

As formal authority and coercive power have declined in their relative significance to managers, other types of power have emerged to take their place. In a knowledge-based economy where the management of information is a key strategic issue, the expertise a manager possesses has become a critical source of power. In addition, many executives now go to great lengths to project an image of themselves as unintimidating and approachable to their employees. For example, at Lowes Cos., the giant discount retailer, CEO Robert Tillman tells his employees to just call him Bob. This emphasis on more egalitarianism in the workplace extends to the design of many work areas. Executive offices oftentimes are positioned in the middle of a floor and in the middle level of a corporate office building. The idea is to emphasize accessibility to senior management.

The design of executive offices themselves also reflects an emphasis on hiding rather than flaunting one's power and influence in organizations. The trend today is to make executive offices more casual and inviting and to de-emphasize power symbols such as marble floors, walnut desks and furniture, and scenic views.

Even an executive's attire has been affected by this trend toward de-emphasizing one's power. Many executives today dress casually for work. This helps to promote a more "down-to-earth" image of an executive in the eyes of employees.

Summary

While the mere mention of the word *power* makes many people bristle, it is clear that the development of an effective power base is critical to a manager's success in any organization and that the "rules of the power game" have fundamentally changed.

Discussion Questions

1. What is the trend today in terms of the bases of power that are being emphasized most by effective business leaders? What kinds of strategies are being used to develop these bases of power?

2. What is the trend today in terms of the bases of power that are being de-emphasized by effective business leaders? What kinds of strategies are being used to do this?

3. What are the practical implications of this case for you as a future manager?

Source: T. A. Stewart, "Get with the New Power Game," *Fortune*, January 13, 1997, pp. 58–62.

CASE 7-2
WHY CEOS FAIL

Causes of CEO Failure

If you were to look at a list of CEOs that have failed, what would they have in common with each other? Low IQ? Laziness? Lack of education? Unethical behavior? Actually, none of these factors is associated with the profile of a failed CEO. Some leadership research has revealed that there is one attribute of CEOs that is the dominant cause of failure—lack of execution. This includes CEO actions as basic as not getting things done, being indecisive, and not delivering on promises made to others. While no one would argue against the importance of strategy formulation, ineffective CEOs have a problem with implementing the elements of the strategic plan in order to achieve business objectives.

The cost of lack of execution is enormous as the business environment becomes more complex, global, and dynamic. In addition, speed in getting new products and services to market is a key source of competitive advantage today, and the effective execution of strategy is central to enhancing responsiveness to the market.

So, in what specific ways do CEOs fail to execute effectively in their jobs? The following list summarizes the most common mistakes that CEOs make on the job.

Common Causes of CEO Failure

> Failure to put the right people in the right jobs
> Denial
> Blind loyalty to poor performing subordinates
> Failure to fix problems on a timely basis
> Maintaining the belief that a talented subordinate cannot fail
> Keeping a poor-performing subordinate because he/she has important connections with constituents (e.g., customers, the press, Wall Street)
> Refusal to fire a poor-performing subordinate because it will make the CEO look bad
> Maintaining the belief that keeping a poor-performing subordinate is a lesser evil than the uncertainty associated with hiring from outside the firm
> Maintaining an attitude that implementation issues are boring

Profile of a Successful CEO

The successful CEO shares some things in common with failed CEOs, in that they are bright, work hard, make sacrifices, and develop strategy for their organizations. However, there are some critical differences that explain the gap in their level of performance as CEOs. The following list summarizes the profile of a highly effective CEO.

The Effective CEO Profile

> Takes quick action to fix problems
> Demonstrates a much deeper interest in developing and managing employees than failed CEOs

> Carefully nurtures employees and places them into jobs that are a good fit for them
> Believes in "people first, strategy second"
> Focuses on a few key initiatives that include clear objectives
> Ensures that initiatives become part of the company's DNA
> Does the "nitty-gritty" work of coordinating and following up on issues related to initiatives
> Possesses a drive to be competitive in an operational sense—highly committed to continuous improvement
> Constantly seeks information about markets using diverse sources

Summary

Clearly, strategy does matter in a big way. However, these listings emphasize the importance of the less sexy aspect of the management process—execution. And it is effective execution of strategy that differentiates successful CEOs from those who ultimately fail.

Discussion Questions

1. What are the most common causes of CEO failure? How would leadership theories discussed in the chapter explain why CEOs fail?
2. What kinds of strategies can be used to help a CEO avoid making these critical errors? What would leadership theories discussed in the chapter have to say about what CEOs need to do to be successful?
3. What are the practical implications of this case for you as a future manager?

Source: R. Charan, "Why CEOs Fail," *Fortune,* June 21, 1999, pp. 68–75.

VIDEO CASE
A STUDY OF SUNSHINE CLEANING SYSTEMS

 **Running Time: 11:50**

This video presents issues relating to leadership at SunShine Cleaning Systems, one of the largest contract cleaning companies in the state of Florida, with $10 million in annual sales and about 1,000 employees. SunShine's CEO, Larry Calufetti, and others discuss and demonstrate the nature and consequences of leadership at SunShine. Sun-

Shine has been financially successful and has maintained low turnover rates in an industry faced with unique challenges. After viewing the video, answer the following questions.

1. Based on information presented in the video and your own knowledge, what are likely to be some special

difficulties associated with leadership in the cleaning industry?

2. CEO Larry Calufetti was formerly a catcher and a manager with the New York Mets baseball team. How has his baseball experience influenced his leadership philosophy?

3. What are eight characteristics of the "coaching leadership style" at SunShine?

4. What are some examples of reward power at SunShine?

5. What does Steve Ketchum mean when he says, "I can't see the fences anymore?" What does this anecdote say about Larry Calufetti's leadership style?

6. The video states that all managers at SunShine have adopted Larry Calufetti's leadership style. Based on information presented in this chapter, what might be some benefits of a uniformity of leadership styles across all managers? What might be some costs?

7. What is the purpose of "Larry's Dream Team"?

LIGHTEN UP
THE LINK TO LINKS

In the continuing quest to understand leadership, researchers have linked leaders' effectiveness to their performance on the golf links. A recent study of golfing and leader effectiveness conducted by the *New York Times* compared golf handicaps of corporate heads to their companies' stock market performance over three years. The pattern was clear and statistically significant: The lower (that is, the better) the leader's golf handicap, the better his or her company's performance. For instance, executives whose companies were in the top performance group had handicaps that were about five strokes better than did executives whose firms showed the poorest performance.

What could explain such findings? Perhaps natural leaders also tend to be natural athletes. Perhaps perseverance or high need for achievement pays off in both golf and business. Perhaps early life experiences—such as caddying for executives—built golf skills while it provided exposure to business banter. Whatever the explanation, the study provides one more excuse for taking the time to improve one's golf game.

BOSSES FROM HELL[36]

In his *Dilbert* cartoons, Scott Adams lambastes "pointy-headed" bosses who are amazingly insensitive, unqualified, vindictive, fail to deliver on promises, or are simply clueless. While these bosses may seem too bad to be true,

Adams actually gets most of his ideas from the tens of thousands of messages he receives from readers of his strips. Annual "best boss/worst boss" contests also generate far more "worst boss" than "best boss" nominations.

DILBERT reprinted by permission of United Feature Syndicate, Inc.

Consider the following examples of actual bosses:

An elderly engineer passed away at his desk at approximately 3 o'clock. The boss told office workers not to call 911 until 5 o'clock because it would disrupt the routine and be nonproductive.

A boss told a programmer, "Give me a list of the unknown bugs in this system."

An employee's boss sent him a bouquet of balloons with words of praise on each one after closing a major account the company had romanced for months. But the message on the card said, "Good luck on your new job." When the employee, confused, asked, "What new job?" his boss replied, "The job you are looking for today. You're fired. I decided two months ago to cut overhead and let you go, but waited until our big account was secure."

An employee's father was scheduled for hip surgery, which had already been delayed by pneumonia. The employee's boss insisted that she call the surgeon and reschedule so she wouldn't miss work.

A supervisor for a Fortune 500 chemical manufacturer would announce at 3 p.m. that he was leaving early, say his good nights, and leave, only to sneak up the back stairway to hide in the supply closet with the lights off to spy on employees for two hours.

A boss who was a control freak imposed two-minute limits on his subordinates' bathroom visits—and went in after them if they remained overtime.

ORGANIZATIONAL CULTURE, EMPOWERMENT, AND ETHICS

CHAPTER *Eight*

SKILLS OBJECTIVES

> To be able to assess organizational cultures.
> To develop skill in designing and creating an organizational culture that supports the goals and strategies of the firm.
> To develop the tools and abilities to effectively empower others.
> To develop skill in encouraging ethical employee behavior.
> To effectively integrate ethical considerations into the managerial decision-making process.

KNOWLEDGE OBJECTIVES

> Understand the nature and functions of organizational culture.
> Identify elements of organizational culture and discuss ways in which organizations can use those elements to achieve desired organizational outcomes.
> Know how to assess organizational culture and bring about desired changes.
> Understand how organizational culture may be related to performance and other outcomes.
> Discuss the stages of the empowerment process.
> Recognize forms of unethical behavior in organizations and causes of such behaviors.
> Identify ways to enhance your ethical behavior and that of others.

We have seen that many changes in the modern workplace are likely to increase employees' levels of stress, insecurity, and frustration. It seems that many companies are chasing short-term financial gains at awful human costs. At the same time, other organizations are taking positive steps to ensure that they offer employees humane, supportive, empowering workplaces. Such firms may have strong competitive advantages in the new world of work. They will offer attractive environments, thus improving attraction and retention of good employees, and will have the potential for enhanced performance.

In this chapter, we address three critical elements of a humane and empowering work environment: organizational culture, empowerment, and ethics. We first address organizational culture, including its functions, elements, and impact on performance. We also offer guidelines for assessing culture and, as appropriate, for managing cultural change. We see how such companies as Southwest Airlines, Quad/Graphics, GE, and Disney have used organizational culture to foster employee satisfaction and motivation as well as organizational performance.

Next, we consider how organizational cultures can be designed to empower employees, unleashing their ability to achieve personal growth and exceptional performance. Finally, we examine a critical foundation stone of organizational culture: business ethics. We see that ethical violations can be devastating for organizations, while strong cultures of ethical behavior can foster employee morale, reputation, and performance. We offer guidelines both for fostering our own ethical behavior and for encouraging ethical behavior in others. Taken together, culture, empowerment, and ethics are absolutely critical to the ongoing success and health of organizations.

Read the Pre-Test Skills Assessment and develop an action plan for dealing with the situation effectively. This will help you to assess how much you know about handling the issues of culture, empowerment, and ethics in organizations.

Pre-Test Skills Assessment
Organizational Culture, Empowerment, and Ethics

You are a management consultant who has been hired by a major manufacturing company to help it to enhance its long-term effectiveness. This is a traditional organization in that its structure is very hierarchical, the culture of the firm values respect for authority, employee jobs are very narrowly defined, and communication flows from management to employees (i.e., from the top down) and not vice versa. In addition, management emphasizes a "bottom-line mentality" that puts tremendous pressure on employees to meet difficult production targets.

The result of this is an environment in which employees fear and mistrust management. Many employees resort to "cutting corners" in terms of quality and safety in order to meet their production targets. Employees do as they are directed by management and do not ask questions. Overall, the morale of employees is quite low.

The organization's performance has been in decline for some time now. Profits have fallen more than 70 percent this year. Product costs are up while quality is down dramatically.

Assessment
Assessment
Assessment
Assessment
Assessment
341
Chapter 8   Organizational Culture, Empowerment, and Ethics

D E V I L ' S   A D V O C A T E

Why do we need to be concerned with creating the right kind of "culture" in an organization? Isn't it more important to focus on developing a company's mission, strategies, structure, and processes?

Remember that organizational culture refers to the unique "personality" or ways of thinking and doing things in a given organization. Organizational culture plays a key role in determining how an organization goes about trying to accomplish its goals. It's important to note here that an organization's culture is shaped by the company's mission, structure, policies, and practices. Each is important, since you need to have in place the proper framework for action (e.g., mission, strategy, etc.) and the right kind of work environment (i.e., culture) to support management and employees in doing the kinds of things that will result in the success of the firm.

Doesn't "empowering employees" actually weaken the ability of a manager to get his/her job done?

Traditionally, a common approach to influencing and managing employees involved a reliance on the formal authority of the manager (i.e., "Do this because I am the boss") and the use of rewards and punishments. However, in today's business environment, management needs the "buy in" or commitment of employees to work toward achieving organizational goals. Management must now find ways to use as many of the skills and abilities of employees as possible in order to stay competitive. Given these needs, many managers have used employee empowerment as a strategy for providing employees with more responsibility to "call their own shots" when it comes to performing their jobs.

It's important to note that many managers who have empowered their employees have found that their overall power, influence, and credibility in the eyes of their employees have actually increased. So, the saying that "as you share it, you lose it" doesn't seem to hold true here.

Ethics can't be influenced, can they? Doesn't this have more to do with how someone has been raised and his/her personal value system?

There is some truth to what you say in that people's ethical beliefs and values are shaped by their upbringing and the culture they are from. However, there are still things that management can do to enhance the ethical behavior of employees in an organization. For example, an employer can "take a stand" and create a formal "code of ethics" for employees. This is a formal statement of what is considered to be appropriate behavior for managers and employees in the company. Managers can also be good "role models" for employees in terms of maintaining high ethical standards in the workplace. Finally, managers can attempt to foster an organizational culture that emphasizes high ethical standards in doing business.

Senior management recognizes the urgency of the situation. Specifically, they want you to assess the situation and to make specific recommendations regarding actions that should be taken to foster a more appropriate culture in the organization. This would be a culture that gives employees the authority to make decisions regarding their jobs and encourages them to meet efficiency goals without engaging in unethical behavior.

Develop an action plan for handling the key issues in the foregoing situation. Be specific.

Now, answer the questions in Self-Assessment 8-1 as a way to gauge your initial attitudes about organizational culture, empowerment, and ethics. The self-understanding you gain from doing this will be helpful to you as you read the rest of the chapter.

Self-Assessment 8-1
Attitudes Toward Organizational Culture, Empowerment, and Ethics

Answer the following questions regarding your attitudes toward organizational culture, empowerment, and ethics. Try to respond to each question as honestly as possible using the following response scale:

1 = Disagree Strongly
2 = Disagree Somewhat
3 = Neither Agree Nor Disagree
4 = Agree Somewhat
5 = Agree Strongly

1. _____ The culture of an organization is something that just naturally occurs—it cannot be managed.

2. _____ Organizational culture has little to do with the long-term performance of a firm.

3. _____ Organizational culture can be an important mechanism for shaping the behavior of employees.

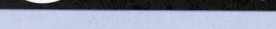

VOICE OF EXPERIENCE

ORGANIZATIONAL CULTURE, EMPOWERMENT, AND ETHICS

Annie Marschall
Employee Relations
Representative/
Production Supervisor
Cooper Power Systems Division

1. How would you describe the organizational culture at Cooper's?

Cooper Industries, a *Fortune 500* company, manufactures electrical distribution products and tools and hardware. The 165-year-old corporation is composed of eight divisions and 33,000 employees. The Cooper Power Systems Kyle Distribution Switchgear facility is over 50 years old. The organizational culture has been infiltrated over time as several different companies have taken ownership. Cooper is a centralized organization, as each of the corporation's eight divisions look to the corporate office for policies and procedures.

Cooper Power Systems has typically been conservative and

traditional in nature but is now focused on development. For quite some time, Cooper was the industry leader but is now up against competition overseas. Cooper must work to develop the most efficient product at a competitive price. Although Cooper has a reputation for quality, competition is forcing the company to differentiate its products to meet the needs of its customers.

2. What does management (or human resources) do to create an effective organizational culture at Cooper's?

In a time of development, Cooper's management team and human resources (HR) department work together to provide proper training to employees. With processes constantly changing, employees feel frustrated if they do not have the skills, tools, and knowledge to do their job well. Employees are used to being the best at what they do.

It is difficult to get each employee trained and up to speed

with the changes and even more challenging for current employees to train new employees joining the organization.

Cooper communicates a strong open-door policy to its employees. The facility is nonunion, and Cooper feels a union is not necessary. The company uses communication boards to post notices and roundtable meetings, department meetings, and newsletters to communicate with employees.

If employees have any questions, they can refer to the company's employee handbook or use the open-door policy. The employee should first see a supervisor. If further assistance is needed, the employee should then see the human resources manager and, finally, the vice president and general manager of the facility.

3. What does management (or HR) do to provide opportunities for employee empowerment at Cooper's?

Chapter 8   Organizational Culture, Empowerment, and Ethics

343

Assessment
Assessment
Assessment
Assessment
Assessment

4. _____ Most organizations have just one culture that prevails throughout the firm.
5. _____ Most employees do not want to be empowered in their jobs.
6. _____ Employee empowerment can have a significant, positive impact on an organization's performance.
7. _____ Empowerment programs are easy to implement and to make successful in organizations.
8. _____ The ethics of employees cannot be changed by managerial action or organizational policies and practices.
9. _____ Ethical principles can differ widely from one another, depending on the cultural background of employees.
10. _____ The degree to which employees behave in an ethical manner does not impact the organization's long-term financial performance.

In the nearby Voice of Experience, Annie Marschall discusses how the issues of organizational culture, empowerment, and ethics are handled at Cooper Industries.

Management and HR provide employees with opportunities for empowerment by soliciting their input through employee opinion surveys administered every two years. A customized, out-sourced survey gathers employee opinions and is followed up with feedback sessions and action plans. Cooper also uses a suggestion box, department meetings, and roundtable discussions to encourage employees to share issues.

Cooper's performance management system is set up to measure performance against accomplishing objectives set in line with the goals of the greater organization. Employees work with their supervisors to set these objectives. By accomplishing these objectives, employees see how their efforts work toward organizational goals.

There is no formal incentive program established that rewards employees for the contribution of ideas or productivity to the business. Employees have expressed concerns that their knowledge-able input is not taken into consideration by management. In employees' eyes, management has been rushing into decisions without taking employee input into consideration and without explaining the direction in which the organization is heading.

4. **What (if anything) does management (or HR) do to encourage ethical employee behavior at Cooper's?**

Cooper encourages ethical employee behavior. This is communicated by administering several policies, such as an electronic communications policy, a code of ethics, and a confidentiality agreement.

The electronic communications policy asks that employees use PC access for business purposes only. The confidentiality agreement notifies employees that what they learn while working at Cooper is not to be shared outside the organization and that all inventions will be property of the company. All employees are asked to sign the policies when they join the company.

5. **What kind of advice would you give students regarding the things that they should do to address the foregoing issues once they become managers in the real world?**

Organizations often get caught in a mindset of "this is the way we do it around here." Bringing in a diverse group of qualified employees helps to break this mindset and allows new perspectives to consider the issues mentioned. New students entering the real world should push themselves to come up with creative alternatives and set up action plans for their completion. Gathering as much information as possible from employees as well as other organizations will assist in evaluating possible options available and deciding on the best alternative.

BUILDING A CONSTRUCTIVE ORGANIZATIONAL CULTURE

Organizational culture consists of the values, symbols, stories, heroes, and rites that have special meaning for a company's employees. Culture represents the emotional, intangible part of the organization. If structure is the organization's skeleton, culture is its soul.

Many firms are now attempting to develop organizational cultures that are helpful in motivating their employees and keeping them committed to the firm. Companies such as Southwest Airlines, Quad/Graphics, Nordstrom, Disney, and General Electric credit their distinctive cultures for much of their success. Of 400 CEOs in North America and Europe interviewed by Price Waterhouse, 47 percent said that reshaping culture and related employee behavior took up a great deal of their time and was as important as monitoring financial information.[1] At General Motors, executives carry "culture cards" to remind them of their new missions. Japanese firms make heavy use of organizational culture for controlling member behavior through such things as songs, uniforms, and team-building exercises.

It is relatively easy to document a new machine's costs and benefits or even to demonstrate the short-term savings of slashing the workforce. Because these things can be measured, managers tend to focus on them.

But what are the true costs of a reorganization that leaves workers overburdened, angry, and stressed? What are the hidden costs of a merger that, while attractive "on paper," leads to internal clashes over core values and assumptions about "the right way to do things"? Conversely, what would be the benefits of a culture that instills values of cooperation and creativity, that fosters loyalty, and that people see as a "great place to be"? Because these things are difficult to measure, managers tend to overlook them. Culture, though, is real, and it is important. A recent study of 200 mergers found incompatible cultures to be *the* primary cause of failures.[2]

If something is to provide competitive advantage for a firm, it must be valuable, rare, and difficult to imitate. Unlike new technology, a pricing strategy, or a product design, an organizational culture is unique and impossible to duplicate. As such, it has the potential to yield great and enduring strategic advantage. But a strong culture can be destroyed overnight through an ill-advised redesign, an ill-planned merger, or a rash downsizing.

FUNCTIONS OF AN ORGANIZATIONAL CULTURE

Culture may serve many important functions in organizations, as shown in Figure 8-1:[3]

> **Cooperation.** By providing shared values and assumptions, culture may enhance goodwill and mutual trust, encouraging cooperation.
> **Decision making.** Shared beliefs and values give organizational members a consistent set of basic assumptions and preferences. This may lead to a more efficient decision-making process, since there are fewer disagreements about which premises should prevail.
> **Control.** Culture serves as a subtle organizational control system, informally approving or prohibiting some patterns of behavior. Control in organizations is provided by three mechanisms, referred to as *markets, bureaucracies,* and *clans.*[4] The *market control mechanism* relies on

Awareness
Awareness
Awareness
Awareness
Awareness

FIGURE 8-1
Functions of an Organizational Culture

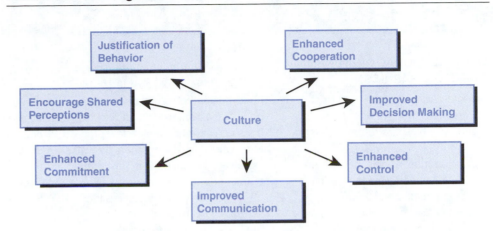

price. If results fall short of goals, prices (not only those charged to customers but those paid to suppliers and employees for the organization's inputs) are adjusted to stimulate necessary change. The *bureaucratic control mechanism* relies on formal authority. The control process consists of adjusting rules and regulations and issuing directives. Finally, the *clan control mechanism* relies on shared beliefs and values.[5] These shared beliefs and values essentially provide a map that members can rely on to choose appropriate courses of action. Clan control derives from culture.

> **Communication.** Culture reduces communication problems in at least two ways. First, there is no need to communicate in matters for which shared assumptions already exist; such things "go without saying." Second, shared assumptions provide guidelines and cues to help to interpret messages that are received.

> **Commitment.** People feel committed to an organization when they identify with it and feel emotional attachment to it. Strong cultures foster strong identification and feelings through beliefs and values that the employee can share with others.

> **Perception.** Organizational reality is socially constructed; what an individual sees is conditioned by what others sharing the same experience say they are seeing. Shared beliefs and values influence this process by providing organization members with shared interpretations of their experience.

> **Justification of behavior.** Finally, culture helps organization members to make sense of their behavior by providing justification for it. For example, it may be possible to justify expenditures on family-sensitive work practices on the basis of shared values relating to the value of people in the organization.

ELEMENTS OF ORGANIZATIONAL CULTURE

As a manager, you will be a creator, shaper, guardian, and communicator of organizational culture. You will play these roles through the behaviors you model, the things you expect and reward, the policies you set, the messages

FOCUS ON MANAGEMENT

ORGANIZATIONAL CULTURE AT QUAD/GRAPHICS*

Selected as one of the "100 Best Companies to Work for in America," Quad/Graphics is a remarkable success story. In 1971, Harry Quadracci bought a small, abandoned factory for $150,000 and paid for it with a rubber check for $10,000 as a deposit, a second mortgage on his home, and the hope that he could arrange more financing by the time the deal closed. Now, Quad/Graphics is the ninth-largest printer in the United States and has more than 10,000 employees at 16 plants in Wisconsin, New York, Georgia, California, Japan, and elsewhere. The company prints more than 100 million magazines a month.

The company's philosophy is "Have fun, make money, and don't do business with anyone you don't like." Quadracci, who has been called the P.T. Barnum of Printing, describes the company as a circus, a continuous performance of highly creative and individualistic troupes who have retained the childlike ability to be surprised and the flexibility to thrive on change.

Once a year, in May, the annual Quad University is held: Managers gather for a two-day conference, leaving nonmanagement personnel in charge. Others in the industry call this practice of leaving employees

unsupervised a huge gamble, since a small slip-up could cost the firm hundreds of thousands of dollars on a single print run. Quadracci disagrees. There have been few problems with this "management by walking away," he maintains. This attitude of trust permeates the company.

When Harry Quadracci founded the company, he said it would be "run by employees for employees," and one of his strongest beliefs is that people need to be free to do their best, without a lot of rules or fear of being punished if they make mistakes. When one unit spent three years and $1 million developing a new folding machine that didn't work, Quadracci threw a champagne party and awarded a medal to the project leader, saying "You've got to have a perfect zero once in a while as well as a perfect success if you've explored alternatives." When Quadracci was warned that giving employees full responsibility for their presses would fragment management, he responded, "I think that's a good idea. Let's fragment management."

Unlike other printers, there are no time clocks at Quad/Graphics—workers are trusted to show up and to fill out their own time cards. Quad/Graphics has never been unionized, and there are no rigid lines between management and workers. A com-

mon saying is, "No one is ever done learning at Quad/Graphics." More than three of every four employees attend training sessions annually, and customers are welcome to sit in as well.

The company offers a variety of benefits. Every Quad/Graphics location has a fitness center and child-care center. The company has a 40-acre nature preserve, lets employees purchase take-out food from its cafeterias (one of the nation's few company cafeterias with a liquor license), and maintains facilities for baseball, volleyball, basketball, and archery. Pay is augmented 15 percent by a combination of a profit-sharing plan and a savings program in which the company matches every dollar saved by an employee with 30 cents of its own, up to 6 percent of pay. There is even free popcorn that's always available. The popcorn is a constant reminder of Quadracci's philosophy that employees should generate a steady flow of new ideas, like kernels of corn in a popcorn popper.

http://www.qg.com/

*The discussion of Quad/Graphics is based on D. Kehrer, "The P. T. Barnum of Printing," *Across the Board,* May 1989, pp. 53–54; D. Kehrer, "The Miracle of Theory Q," *Business Month,* September 1989, pp. 44–49; and R. Ganzel, "Putting Out the Welcome Mat," *Training,* March 1998, pp. 54–62.

you send, and the cultural elements you employ. Let's consider some key elements of organizational culture.[6]

Values *Values* are deep-seated, personal standards that influence our moral judgments, responses to others, and commitment to personal and organizational goals. Values—the bedrock of organizational culture—let employees know how they are expected to behave and what actions are acceptable. For example, Procter & Gamble has core values of leadership, integrity, trust, passion for winning, and ownership, and it works to communicate those values and instill them in employees.

The sharing of values is key to the development of a successful organizational culture. The functions of culture listed earlier all relate somehow to the impact of shared values and assumptions. This suggests that the degree to which those values and assumptions are shared should be important. For instance, we might go into one organization and find that everyone shares the same values, tells the same stories, and points to the same heroes. Such a culture, in which there is sharing and acceptance of core values, is sometimes called a *strong culture*.[7]

In view of the various functions of culture, we might expect that the nature and strength of organizational culture would ultimately affect such things as quality, productivity, and profitability. This view was bolstered by the work of Tom Peters and Robert Waterman, described in their best seller, *In Search of Excellence*. Peters and Waterman concluded on the basis of their research on a variety of "excellent" companies that:

> *Without exception, the dominance and coherence of culture proved to be an essential quality of the excellent companies. Moreover, the stronger the culture and the more it was directed toward the marketplace, the less need was there for policy manuals, organization charts, or detailed procedures and rules. In these companies, people way down the line know what they are supposed to do in most situations because the handful of guiding values is crystal-clear.*[8]

We consider the impacts of organizational culture later in the chapter. However, it seems clear that a sharing of values may have important consequences for organizations and their members.[9]

Symbols *Symbols* are things that stand for or suggest something else. Office assignments signal status. Dress codes suggest the level of formality. A logo can influence customer and employee perceptions. Mary Kay Ash of Mary Kay Cosmetics chose the bumblebee as a symbol for her organization because "Aerodynamically the bumblebee shouldn't be able to fly, but the bumblebee doesn't know that so it goes on flying anyway."[10] And, an action can be symbolic. Consider the "Lambeau Leap," where a Green Bay Packers player leaps into the arms of hometown fans in the stands at Lambeau Field after scoring a touchdown, symbolizing oneness with the Green Bay faithful.

When General Motors decided to overhaul its organizational culture to regain competitiveness, GM President John F. Smith closed the executive dining room on the 14th floor of corporate headquarters and dispensed with neckties on Fridays—symbolic actions to reflect the company's moves toward being more democratic and responsive.[11]

Similarly, when Cincinnati Milacron wanted to regain its position as a world leader in factory machinery it adopted as its symbol the wolf pack. The company logo depicted a circle of wolves flanked on each side by a fierce wolf's head. "It's not a joke to us," said Milacron's President Daniel J. Meyer. "Wolves are survivors. They work in teams, and they go out to kill."[12] The wolf pack symbol was meant to convey an image both to the company's employees and to its external constituencies.

Web Wise

The Land O'Lakes Logo

The importance of company symbols to those outside the firm is seen in a study of customers' ratings of 47 firms on such things as quality and reputation.* Six hundred customers were asked to rate the firms on the basis of their names, and 600 others were provided with the company logos. Those logos often had a strong influence on the ratings. For example, Motorola's logo improved its score by 55 percent and Buick's by 53 percent. But the Travelers umbrella reduced the insurer's score by 6 percent, and Land O'Lakes' kneeling Native American woman—perhaps because of its "politically incorrect" connotations—dropped the company's approval rating by 12 percent. To see the Land O'Lakes logo and read its history, go to:

http://www.landolakes.com/new/ourCompany/LandOLakesHistory.cfm

*"When Company Logos Detract From Image," *The Wall Street Journal*, June 18, 1993, p. B1.

FOCUS ON MANAGEMENT

VALUES AT HEWLETT-PACKARD

At Hewlett-Packard, there is a clear focus on the five values of the "HP Way":

> We have trust and respect for individuals.

> We focus on a high level of achievement and contribution.

> We conduct our business with uncompromising integrity.

> We achieve our common objectives through teamwork.

> We encourage flexibility and innovation.

If values are to have a positive impact on the culture of the organization, they must become part of the daily working lives of employees. At Hewlett-Packard, units are kept small. There are no time clocks. Employees can choose which shift to work. Offices are separated by open partitions to increase accessibility and foster teamwork. In addition, Hewlett-Packard has an unwritten policy never to lay people off.* Thus, the company's policies and practices support its values.

Carly Fiorina, the president and CEO of Hewlett-Packard and the first woman to head a company listed on the Dow Jones Industrial Average, addressed the COMDEX convention on November 15, 1999. In her address, Fiorina said, "I will argue that the challenge for the Net, as we enter the new millennium, the challenge to make the Net warm, intimate, friendly, pervasive, personal, is not about technology. It's first about culture, and the culture in our companies, in all of our companies, as we wrestle with what's next on the Net. I believe companies to succeed in this new era, to really fulfill the promise of the Net, must build a new culture." Fiorina envisions that culture as being based on radical ideas, inventiveness, and synthesis of "the best of the old and the new, of the dot-com and the bricks and mortar, of the young Turks and the old guard." To read Fiorina's full speech to Comdex, and to view a video of the speech, go to:

http://www.hp.com/ghp/ceo/
speeches/comdex99.html

To visit the Hewlett-Packard website, go to:

http://www.hp.com/

*See R. Levering, M. Moskowitz, and M. Katz, *The Hundred Best Companies to Work For in America* (Reading, MA: Addison-Wesley, 1984), pp. 143–144; "Best Practices at Hewlett-Packard," *Dealerscope*, March 2000, p. 57; and E. Nee, "Hewlett-Packard's New E-vangelist," *Fortune*, January 10, 2000, pp. 166–167.

Narratives *Narratives* are written or spoken accounts used by members of the organization to make sense of their experiences and express their feelings and beliefs. Narratives may take a variety of forms, including stories, legends, myths, and sagas.[13]

Stories dramatize relatively ordinary, everyday events within organizations in order to convey important cultural meanings. They often combine truth and fiction, are spread by word of mouth, and convey important values. Stories often reflect basic themes—whether, for example, the organizational culture supports equality or inequality, security or insecurity, and control or lack of control.

As an example, a story widely repeated at IBM tells of how founder and CEO Tom Watson praised a security guard who required him to go back for his identification. A similar story is told at Revlon, differing in just one detail: When a Revlon receptionist refused to let CEO Charles Revson walk off with a sign-in sheet, he fired her. The first story conveys a sense of egalitarianism, saying, "We all obey the rules." The second conveys the opposite, saying, "We obey the rulers."[14]

Legends are more uplifting than stories and portray events that defy explanation by ordinary circumstances. Here's a legend at Procter & Gamble:

> *Just before the turn of the century, Harley Procter, a son of the founders of Procter & Gamble Company, became concerned that the company's candle business was declining. One Sunday morning, while attending church services, he had a revelation as the minister read a passage about ivory palaces from the 45th Psalm. He went to the company's board of directors, composed of very religious men, and told them of his revelation. Using it, he persuaded them to call a new white bath soap* Ivory.[15]

Myths are dramatic, unquestioned narratives about imagined events. They are often used to explain the origins or transformations of things of great importance. The explanations are placed beyond doubt and argument. While myths are largely inventions, they have a kind of ingrained integrity and truth; they have been called "things that never happened, but always are." [16]

Finally, *sagas* are a form of narrative that describes heroic exploits performed in the face of adversity. They help to perpetuate culture by anchoring the present in the past and lending meaning to the future. They intermix historical facts (sometimes in embellished and altered form), justifications of past events, and wishful thinking. Many sagas celebrate the organization's founders and their ideas. The tale of how Bill Hewlett and Dave Packard began Hewlett-Packard in Hewlett's garage using Hewlett's oven and of how they subsequently dealt with adversity without laying off workers is such a saga.

FOCUS ON MANAGEMENT

STORIES AT 3M

The eleventh commandment at 3M is "Never kill a new product idea." The importance of innovation as a 3M value is supported by a story often repeated throughout the organization. According to the story, an employee accidentally developed cellophane tape but was unable to get his superiors to accept the idea. Persistent in his belief in the new product, the employee found a way to sneak into the corporate boardroom and tape down the board members' copies of the minutes with the transparent tape. The board was impressed enough with the novelty to give it a try, and the product was incredibly successful.* This story not only reinforces the importance of innovation but encourages 3M employees who believe strongly in their ideas never to take no as a final answer.

3M's website introduces its "Innovation Chronicles" as follows: "Stories have always been an important part of 3M's culture. This compilation presents some of the important milestones in 3M's history, based on recollections of those who were major participants in these milestones. Stories such as these can help us in understanding the many sources of our innovative culture—and the importance of our continuing desire to challenge and encourage each other as we look for innovative new ways to meet customer needs and solve customer problems. They can help to inspire all 3Mers to participate in the stories of our future." Go to the "Innovation Chronicles" at the following address to read more about the importance of stories to 3M's culture and tales about the invention of masking tape, cellophane tape, and Post-It Notes and about 20 other 3M stories:

http://www.3m.com/about3M/pioneers/list.html

*A. Wilkins, "The Creation of Company Cultures: The Role of Stories and Human Resource Systems," *Human Resource Management*, 1984, 23, p. 21.

Heroes *Heroes* are company role models. In their actions, character, and support of the existing organizational culture, they highlight the values a company wishes to reinforce. Heroes are often the main characters of organizational narratives. CEOs such as Herb Kelleher at Southwest Airlines, Anita Roddick at the Body Shop, and Jack Welch at GE are heroes in their firms. But, heroes may come from all levels, such as an employee who persevered to champion an important new product or who provided extraordinary effort when the company faced a crisis.

Rites *Rites* combine cultural forms into a public performance. *Rites of passage* mark important transitions. For instance, employees who complete a rigorous management training program off site may be welcomed back with a speech, a certificate, and perhaps a cocktail party.

Rites of enhancement celebrate accomplishments of members, enhancing their status. The enhanced individuals often receive some concrete symbol of their enhanced status. Mary Kay Cosmetics (http://www.marykay.com/) is famous for its rites of enhancement. It gives its high-performing members a variety of awards and titles. Diamond pins, furs, and pink Cadillacs (and other luxury cars) are awarded to its top performers at elaborate meetings called *Mary Kay Seminars*. Participants, dressed in fancy evening clothes, receive

FOCUS ON MANAGEMENT

HERB KELLEHER OF SOUTHWEST AIRLINES*

Herb Kelleher is cofounder, chairman of the board, president, and CEO of Southwest Airlines. Irreverent, Elvis-impersonating, arm-wrestling, chain-smoking, bear-hugging, rap tune–singing, Harley Davidson–riding, Wild Turkey–drinking Kelleher plays many roles, among them coach, quarterback, cheerleader, sage, cultural icon, father figure, friend, and legend. Much of Southwest's folklore recounts Kelleher's outrageous antics and comments. Kelleher may be found singing "Tea for Two" for Southwest employees, walking plane aisles dressed as the Easter Bunny, tossing luggage with baggage handlers, or having a beer with an off-hours flight crew. Under his guidance, Southwest has been remarkably

successful. It has been profitable every year since 1973 (the only airline able to make that claim), yet maintains the lowest fares. It is the safest airline in the world and ranks number one in the industry for service, on-time performance, and lowest employee turnover rate. It has been named the most admired airline and the best place to work in the United States by *Fortune* magazine. $1,000 invested in Southwest in 1971 is worth more than $250,000 today. Kelleher's take on Southwest's recipe for success: "First, employees are number one. The way you treat your employees is the way they will treat your customers. Second, have fun at work. Third, take the competition seriously but not yourself. Fourth, think of the company as a service organization that happens to be in the airline business. Last, al-

ways practice the Golden Rule, internally and externally." Kelleher has crafted a unique culture at Southwest Airlines through a mix of humor, altruism, concern for others, and straight talk. He looks for these qualities in prospective employees, saying "But what are their values? We'll take the one with the less experience if he has the values we're looking for, someone else can take the expert." Learn more about Kelleher and Southwest at:

http://www.iflyswa.com/

*Based on J. C. Quick, "Crafting an Organizational Culture: Herb's Hand at Southwest Airlines," *Organizational Dynamics,* Autumn 1992, pp. 45–56; K. Melymuka, "Sky King: Down-to-Earth Technology Helps Make Herb Kelleher's Southwest Airlines a Soaring Success," *Computerworld,* September 28, 1998, pp. 68–71, and other sources.

FOCUS ON MANAGEMENT

CULTURE AT WALT DISNEY COMPANY

Walt Disney Company is a good example of an organization in which elements of culture are apparent. The employees in Disney's theme parks—primarily high-school and college students—are critical to the company's success. Disney's challenge is to get them to convey the Disney fantasy and create happiness while carrying out repetitive work at low pay. To make the challenge even greater, Disney is heavily unionized, with 24 unions at Disneyland alone. Disney meets this challenge by careful attention to its organizational culture.

For one thing, Disney uses language to reinforce the culture. Employees are called *cast members*, and they don't work—they're "cast" in "roles." Cast members are employed "onstage" or "backstage," and they wear "costumes" rather than uniforms.

Further, Disney uses selection, training, and socialization to create a sense of community and shared values. The company's clean-cut and conservative image generally attracts the kind of employees Disney wants. In addition, the company shows prospective employees a film about the kind of discipline, grooming, and dress code the company demands. Cast members participate in an ongoing orientation program that continually reinforces the firm's values, philosophies, and guest service standards. During orientation, teachers at Disney University dress in full uniform as they lead new employees through the park.

To encourage commitment and enthusiasm, Disney uses service recognition awards, peer recognition programs, and banquets for 10, 15, or 20 years of service. Informal recognition parties help to boost morale. During the Christmas holiday, the parks open one night just for cast members and their families, and management dresses in costumes and operates the parks. All events are designed to build a sense of camaraderie and identification with the Disney organization.*

http://disney.go.com/ disneycareers/index.html

*Based on C. M. Solomon, "How Does Disney Do It?" *Personnel Journal*, December 1989, pp. 50–57; G. F. Grates, "Building a World-Class Organization," *Communication World*, June/July 1998, pp. 41–43; and L. Rubis, "Show and Tell," *HR Magazine*, April 1998, pp. 110–117. See also, H. Allerton, "Professional Development the Disney Way," *Training and Development*, May 1997, pp. 50–56; and M. Gunther, "Eisner's Mouse Trap," *Fortune*, September 6, 1999, pp. 106–118.

Web Wise

Harley Owners Group (HOG)

A good example of rites of integration is the "meetings" of Harley-Davidson's HOG (Harley Owners Group) chapters, where "the bond is metal" as hundreds of Harley riders hit the road together to help out worthy causes or just "share the awareness." Learn more about the Harley Owners Group at

http://www.hog.com/home.asp

their awards on the stage of an auditorium to the cheers of a large audience.[17] Rites of enhancement both provide public recognition of a person's personal accomplishments and serve to motivate others to similar efforts.

Rites of integration bring people together to revive shared feelings that bind and commit them to the organization. An annual holiday party is a rite of integration. So is the Wal-Mart annual meeting, where 20,000 shareholders come together to see featured celebrities, hear inspiring stories, watch videos about Wal-Mart's accomplishments, and join in the Wal-Mart cheer.[18]

Rituals *Rituals* are relatively simple combinations of repetitive behaviors, often carried out without much thought and often brief in duration. Rituals guide behavior in daily organizational life. There may be rituals, for instance, about how organizational members greet one another, how visitors are met at airports, who eats where and with whom, and how a phone conversation should proceed. These rituals often are more important for their expressive, emotional consequences than for more practical reasons.

Complete Skills Practice 8-1. This will help you to better describe the culture of an organization by thinking about its characteristics in a variety of unusual ways.

Skills Practice 8-1
Images of Organizations

Skill Level: Challenging

Skill Objective

To develop skill in describing an organizational culture by thinking about its characteristics in a variety of unusual ways.

Procedure

Answer the following questions regarding an organization of which you are currently a member or some other organization of which you have been a member. Use a separate piece of paper to document your work.

1. What are the principal *images* or *metaphors* that people use to describe your organization? Provide *at least three such images or metaphors*.
2. What does your organization *look like?* Sketch a picture that represents your view of your organization. You don't need to be an artist to do this. Just draw something that conveys to you what the organization is like. Does the organization seem to you like a vehicle? An animal or mix of animals? A person or persons?
3. What does your organization *sound like?* Give the name of a song or songs or some song lyrics (or write your own lyrics) that represent your organization.
4. What does your organization *feel like?* List words or phrases (happy, comfortable, frightening, exciting, or whatever) that best capture what your organization feels like.

ASSESSING CULTURE

If we are to describe, understand, and perhaps influence culture, we need to be able to somehow assess it. For example, how do we tell whether we are likely to "fit" well in a culture or whether the culture seems to foster healthy interactions among employees? One way to do this is with careful observation and questioning. This yields a rich, relatively unconstrained view of the organization's culture and provides compelling, concrete examples.

Here are some suggestions for learning about an organization's culture:

> Look around—what do the headquarters and other buildings look like? How are people dressed? Is there much interaction? Who is talking with whom? How does the place "feel"?

> Ask to see newsletters and other internal documents. What values are emphasized? Who are the heroes held up for praise? Are parties, celebrations, or other ceremonies mentioned? What sorts of things are discussed?

> Look at annual reports or other communications to those outside the firm. What "face" is being presented to the world?

> Ask, "Can you tell me anything about what the culture is like here? Are there any stories that people here tell about the firm?"

> Ask, "What values are stressed here? How are they communicated? How are they reinforced?"

> Ask, "Who is looked up to here?"

> See what you can learn about rites and ceremonies in the organization. What happens when people accomplish something? Are there rites of passage, such as promotion ceremonies and retirement parties? Are there regular get-togethers, such as holiday parties, social events, and company sporting events?

Awareness
Awareness
Awareness
Awareness
Awareness
353

Chapter 8   Organizational Culture, Empowerment, and Ethics

> Ask, "What sorts of behaviors are expected and rewarded here? What sorts of behaviors are punished?
> Ask people outside the firm what they think of it.
> Check magazines, newspapers, and other sources to get clues about the culture of the organization.

These sorts of steps to assess culture are valuable, but observation alone cannot answer some important questions about culture. For instance, observation doesn't permit systematic examination of the strength of relationships among culture-related variables or rigorous comparisons across cultures. Further, it is difficult with observation to sort out the relative roles of multiple variables. A complementary approach to observation is to score culture on various dimensions using questionnaires. Such measures permit comparison of culture across organizations. They also make it possible to assess relationships between characteristics of culture and other organizational characteristics, including performance and other outcomes.

Now let's get out into the "real world" and examine organizational culture in an actual organization. By completing Skills Practice 8-2, you will be able to better see the role of organizational culture in determining the success of a firm.

Skills Practice 8-2   **Skill Level: Challenging**
Fieldwork Experience: Assessing
Organizational Culture

Skill Objective
To develop skill in assessing organizational culture.

Procedure
1. Identify an organization in your local community. Try to use an organization in which you already know someone, if possible. This will facilitate gaining access to the organization.
2. Visit your organization and take a tour of its operations. Again, this part of the process will be greatly enhanced if you have a contact in the organization. As you conduct your tour, look for the following types of things (review the section on assessing organizational culture for more ideas):
   > Use of corporate symbols
   > The corporate mission statement
   > The physical work environment
   > Attire worn by employees versus management
   > The employee parking lot: Are there reserved spots for executives?

In addition, ask your contact at the organization the following questions:

   > How would you describe the culture in this organization?
   > Can you give me specific examples of things that reflect the culture of this organization (e.g., employee handbook, general policy statements, annual company events)?

Discussion Questions
1. Do you feel that the culture of this organization supports the overall mission and goals of the firm? Why or why not?

2. If you could change the culture of this organization, what would you do?

3. What kinds of barriers to change might you experience if you attempted to change the culture of the organization you analyzed for this exercise?

4. What are the implications of this exercise for you as a future manager?

SUBCULTURES AND COUNTERCULTURES

Our discussion of organizational culture to this point may give the impression that a single culture pervades an entire organization. In fact, though, there will almost certainly be many *subcultures:* distinctive clusters of ideologies, cultural forms, and other practices within the larger culture. Subcultures may develop among members of the organization who have common training or duties, similar personal characteristics, frequent interaction, or shared experiences.

In fact, there may even be countercultures in organizations. *Countercultures* are subcultures that contradict the dominant culture. The dominant culture and these countercultures may exist in uneasy symbiosis, taking opposite positions on value issues that are critically important to each of them.[19] There are several situations that may give rise to countercultures.[20] For example, determined innovators in old, established organizations may feel they must oppose the dominant culture to permit change. Or, a counterculture may arise as a way to handle severe, shared employee discontents, as when employees oppose a threatening new program or policy. Further, when firms with differing cultures combine through mergers or acquisitions, the culture of the acquired organization may represent a counterculture for the acquiring firm.

It may seem that a single, strong culture would be best, as suggested by the earlier quotation by Peters and Waterman. There are certainly costs to subcultures and countercultures. For example, differences in perspectives and goals may lead to conflict and misunderstanding. Nevertheless, subcultures may be useful.

John Jermier and his colleagues have provided a fascinating glimpse into subcultures of a police organization.[21] They used questionnaires, participant observation, and interviews to identify five distinct subcultures of the organization, such as "crime-fighting commandos," "peace-keeping moral entrepreneurs," and "anti-military social workers." The subcultures differed in how they were organized and acted and in their performance and commitment to the organization; only one of the subcultures seemed in close conformance with the "official" culture. The researchers concluded that the police organization was actually a "soft bureaucracy," with a rigid exterior appearance symbolizing what key stakeholders expect but with less rigid internal practices. In this way, an external face could be presented while subcultures were free to develop and meet specific demands.

Just as subcultures may have value to the organization, countercultures may serve useful functions for the dominant culture. For example, countercultures may help to clarify the boundaries between acceptable and unacceptable behavior and may provide a safe haven for the development of innovative ideas.[22] Further, countercultures may encourage the questioning of old, and perhaps outmoded, values.

FIGURE 8-2
Views of How Organizational Culture Affects Performance

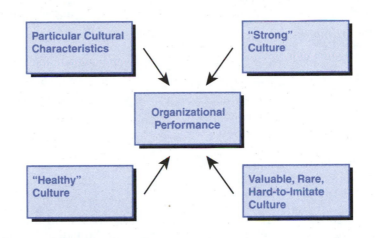

CULTURE AND EFFECTIVENESS

Does organizational culture affect important organizational outcomes, such as quality and productivity? The many functions of organizational culture we discussed at the beginning of the chapter would certainly suggest that culture is important and that it could reasonably be expected to influence organizational outcomes. Further, much of the tremendous interest in organizational cultures was spawned by a few best-selling business books that provided prescriptions for "effective" cultures that would lead to quality and productivity. As shown in Figure 8-2, there are at least four positions concerning how culture might influence organization performance.[23]

The first of these approaches attempts to identify particular cultural characteristics that are associated with success. For example, William Ouchi in his book, *Theory Z,* presented comparative studies of Japanese and American management techniques. Ouchi reported that many successful Japanese companies have strong cultures that emphasize such values as employee participation, open communication, security, and equality.[24] Ouchi's comparison of typical Japanese (type J), typical American (type A), and type Z American organizational cultures is presented in Figure 8-3. Ouchi saw the type Z culture as incorporating individual achievement and advancement but as having a dedication to developing a sense of community in the workplace. He believed the type Z organization's emphasis on new cultural values in the work environment would reduce the negative influences of norms by fostering individuality and individual responsibility. Ouchi argued that the cultures of Japanese firms and American type Z firms would help them to outperform type A firms. Such arguments led managers and consultants to embrace many Japanese ideas and practices, such as quality circles. While, as we discuss in other chapters, there are many potential benefits to such approaches, their success has been mixed.[25]

The most popular writing on the relationship between organizational culture and effectiveness was presented by Tom Peters and Robert Waterman in

FIGURE 8-3

Type A, Type J, and Type Z Organizations

Cultural Value	U.S. (Type A)	Japan (Type J)	U.S. (Type Z)
Commitment to Employees	Short-term employment	Lifetime employment	Long-term employment
Decision Making	Individual	Group and consensus	Group and consensus
Responsibility	Individual	Collective	Individual
Evaluation	Rapid and quantitative	Slow and qualitative	Slow and qualitative
Control	Explicit and formal	Implicit and informal	Implicit and informal
Career Paths	Narrow	Broad	Moderately broad
Concern for People	Narrow	Holistic	Holistic

In Search of Excellence.[26] Based on their observation of 62 successful firms, including Hewlett-Packard, McDonald's, Disney Productions, Levi Strauss, and Johnson & Johnson, the authors concluded that eight key attributes of the organizational culture contributed to their success:

1. *A bias for action.* While the companies may be analytical in their approach to decision making, they prefer to "do it, fix it, try it." That is, problems are not talked to death nor is time wasted in developing elaborate models for solving problems.

2. *Closeness to the customer.* Learning from customers is important for success. Customer satisfaction becomes a dominant value and can be achieved through excellent customer service and high product quality and reliability.

3. *Autonomy and entrepreneurship.* Excellent companies encourage innovativeness through the development of structures that foster innovation and change. Work units are kept small so that employees have a sense of belonging and feel comfortable about making suggestions.

4. *Productivity through people.* Rank-and-file employees are viewed as valued resources of the organization, the main source of quality and productivity. "We-versus-them" labor attitudes are avoided.

5. *Hands-on, value-driven.* Managers of excellent companies have clearly defined the value system of the firm. Both managers and employees understand what values guide the activities of the firm. For example, McDonald's incorporates quality, service, cleanliness, and value in all aspects of the company's activities.

6. *Stick to the knitting.* Successful companies will stay close to the business they know. This may mean a focus on a single product line or a related group of product lines rather than a diverse mix of products.

7. *Simple form, lean staff.* Keeping the company simple in its structure with few staff positions was found to be important to company success. In general, no more than five layers of management are encouraged. When the company increases in size, divisions are broken down into subdivisions to avoid additional layers of management.

8. *Simultaneous loose-tight properties.* Excellent companies are both centralized and decentralized. They apply centralized or tight controls to

the company's core values. In other areas, such as innovation and creativity, controls on employees are loose or decentralized.

Not every company studied by Peters and Waterman scored high on all eight attributes. However, success in promoting some of the attributes and a desire to score well on others were part of the organization culture.

While the Peters and Waterman findings have received widespread attention, they have not gone without challenge.[27] For example, Peters and Waterman focused on successful companies, but what if the characteristics of "excellent" companies were also found in companies that are poor performers? Also, measures of excellence were limited to the financial performance of the company.[28] Were the organizations also successful in terms of customer satisfaction and social responsibility? Subsequent developments haven't been encouraging. For instance, in the years following publication of *In Search of Excellence,* several of the "excellent" companies suffered financially.[29] Further, one study found no significant five-year performance differences between a representative subset of 14 of the Peters and Waterman "excellent" companies and 162 firms representative of the *Fortune 1,000* industrials.[30] In fact, average performance was lower for the "excellent" firms than for the comparison group. Further, there were no significant differences between the two groups of firms in the extent to which they adhered to measured attributes that Peters and Waterman said were associated with excellence. And, there were no significant relationships between the degree to which firms in either group adhered to those attributes and their performance.[31]

Perhaps such findings shouldn't be too surprising. After all, organizations operate in different environments, under different strategic conditions, and with different structures and technologies. It seems unreasonable that the same type of culture would be appropriate for all these differing conditions. Continuing to search for "one best way" may be futile. Instead, it may be more important to ensure that cultural elements are internally consistent and in tune with demands of particular internal and external environments.[32]

A second position concerning the relationship of culture to performance is that strong cultures lead to success. This approach focuses not just on the nature of cultural characteristics but also (or instead) on their strength. The term *strong culture* is sometimes used in different ways. Some see strong cultures as cultures where values and ideologies are widely shared and clearly ordered in terms of their relative importance. Others use the term to mean extremity of culture, with a strong culture reflecting strong commitment to certain positions, such as strong emphasis on personal worth. In general, it seems simplistic to assume that strength of culture per se would necessarily lead to success. There are certainly some strong cultures that are inconsistent with the demands of their environments, and a strong culture may discourage change. So, it may be necessary that a culture be "right"—fitting the needs of its members and the demands of its environment—as well as strong.

A third position, as seen in Figure 8-4, focuses on sick cultures.[33] This view sees some cultures as deriving unhealthy modes of functioning from the psychopathological problems of their chief executives. Such "neurotic" firms would be unlikely to attain long-term success.

The fourth position on the relationship of culture to performance tries to identify conditions under which cultures are more important for and con-

FIGURE 8-4
Neurotic Leaders and Their Firms

Form of Neurosis	Chief Executive	Culture
Dramatic	Needs attention, excitement; feels a sense of entitlement	Dependency needs of subordinates complement "strong leader" tendencies of chief executive
Suspicious	Vigilantly prepared to counter attacks and personal threats	"Fight-or-flight" culture, including dependency, fear of attack, lack of trust
Detached	Withdrawn and not involved; lacks interest in present or future	Lack of warmth or emotions; conflicts; jockeying for power; insecurity
Depressed	Lacks self-esteem, self-confidence, or initiative; fears success and tolerates mediocrity or failure	Lack of initiative; passivity; negativity; lack of motivation; ignorance of markets; leadership vacuum
Compulsive	Tends to dominate organization from top to bottom; dogmatic or obstinate; perfectionist	Rigid, inward-directed, insular; subordinates are submissive, uncreative, insecure

ducive to success. For instance, if a culture is to contribute to sustained financial performance (as we suggested earlier in the chapter), it must (1) be valuable in the sense that it leads the firm to behave in ways that result in high sales, low costs, high margins, and other factors adding financial value to the firm; (2) be rare in the sense that other firms don't have the same or very similar cultures; and (3) be difficult to imitate so that competitors can't readily change their cultures to include the same advantageous characteristics.[34] A strategic advantage of a unique and valuable culture, once developed, is that the third of these conditions is likely to follow: Competitors are likely to find it impossible to duplicate.

The nearby Bottom Line presents a process model summarizing the basic steps associated with development of an effective organizational culture.

CHANGING CULTURES

Our discussion of managing culture may give the impression that culture can easily be molded to fit some image. In fact, though, change may be very difficult; values, stories, heroes, and rituals develop over time and are enduring. This is nicely illustrated by the case of a *Fortune 500* manufacturer saddled with a history of low productivity, poor quality, and hostile labor relations.[35] When a consultant hired by the company began talking with the employees, they told him many stories about Sam, the 300-pound plant manager with the personality of King Kong. When Sam saw a transmission that displeased him, he smashed it with a sledgehammer. A worker called to Sam's office vomited on the way. Once, Sam drove his car into the plant, got on the roof, and began screaming at his workers. One fed-up worker poured a line of gasoline to Sam's car and lit it. Hearing these stories, the stunned consultant made an appointment to see the plant manager. When he entered the plant manager's office, the consultant was surprised to see a slim, pleasant-looking man behind the desk; his name was Paul. "Where's Sam?" the consultant asked. Paul, look-

Attainment
Attainment
Attainment
Attainment
Attainment
Attainment
359

Chapter 8   Organizational Culture, Empowerment, and Ethics

BOTTOM LINE

The Bottom Line: Developing an Effective Organizational Culture

ing puzzled, replied, "Sam has been dead for nine years." Paul's claim notwith-standing, Sam was clearly very much alive in the minds of the employees. Paul's efforts of almost a decade to instill a sense of fairness and participation were thwarted by the plant's nightmarish history. To change company culture, leaders in an organization should consider these recommendations:[36]

> **Understand the current culture.** It is hard to chart a course without knowing where you are now. Similarly, it is folly to attempt to change culture without first understanding the current culture.

> **Change at the right time.** Culture change is most likely to be successful when, as with any other change, there is a felt need. This may occur when there is a problem (a "burning platform"), opportunity, or change in circumstances.

> **Value diversity.** We often hear that the cure for a rare disease may be found in the cells of an obscure creature in the depths of a rain forest or that a threatened plant may prove to be an unimagined energy source. We are warned that loss of ecological variety may forever cut off opportunities: Diversity offers potential. Similarly, organizations with many distinct subcultures may have better chances for successful change. Rather than starting from scratch, such organizations can select subcultures that best fit the vision of the desired culture, nourish them, and diffuse them throughout the organization. Similarly, those employees who have been bucking the old culture and who have ideas for a better one can be encouraged.

> **Understand resistance to culture change.** People resist changes for many reasons, such as fear of the unknown, threats to personal security, habit, threats to power and influence, lack of trust, and disruption of social relationships. Whether or not these fears and concerns are justified, their impact is real. Sources of resistance to culture change must be recognized and sensitively dealt with; we'll address this issue in Chapter 8.

> **Recognize the importance of implementation.** Many change efforts fail because of flaws in implementation. Quite simply, changes don't implement themselves. It is critical that adequate human and financial resources be provided for implementation and that those who are responsible for the implementation accept the need for change and are motivated to enthusiastically pursue their task. Such acceptance and enthusiasm are unlikely unless top management clearly and visibly supports the cultural change.

> **Use appropriate cultural forms.** Cultural change can be facilitated by appropriate use of symbols, rites, narratives, and other cultural forms. For example, managers can employ symbolic tools, such as being present at meetings relating to the change and visibly spending time related to the values they preach. New logos and slogans can be developed. Rites can be modified to incorporate new values, or new rites can combine elements of the old and the new. Stories reinforcing the change can be publicized.

> **Give it some time.** Everything we've said suggests that changing organizational culture will be difficult and time-consuming. There will almost certainly be resistance. Those who resist the change will be quick to point to problems that arise during the change process, and there will always be a period during which costs of change are obvious but benefits are still on the horizon. However, as Rosabeth Moss Kanter has said, "Everything looks like a failure in the middle." It is critical to focus on the horizon and to recognize that it takes time to reach it. Significant, organization-wide improvements may take five to ten years.[37]

The nearby Bottom Line presents a process model summarizing the basic steps associated with changing the culture of an organization.

A major challenge facing many managers is how to change the existing culture at a firm to one that better supports the mission, goals, and strategies of the organization. Completing Skills Practice 8-3 will help you to develop skill in creating action plans for transforming the culture of an organization.

Skills Practice 8-3   Skill Level: **Challenging**
Transforming Organizational Cultures

Skill Objective
To develop skill in formulating action plans for changing organizational culture.

Procedure
1. This exercise can be completed on an individual basis or in groups of 3–5 students.
2. Read the descriptions of organizational cultures that follow. Select one of the organizations to focus on for this exercise.
3. Develop an action plan for changing the culture of the selected firm.

Awareness
Awareness
Awareness
Awareness
Awareness
Awareness

361

Chapter 8   Organizational Culture, Empowerment, and Ethics

BOTTOM LINE

The Bottom Line: Changing the Culture of an Organization

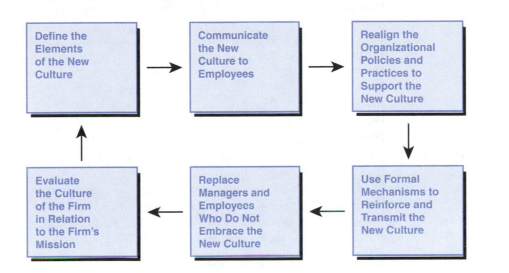

4.   *Optional:* Present your action plan to the class and defend its logic. Be sure to discuss why you feel your plan would work.
5.   Answer the discussion questions that follow.

Discussion Questions
1.   Which guidelines for changing organizational culture (from the chapter) did you incorporate into your action plan? Why?
2.   What are some general obstacles to changing an organization's culture? What would you do to address these obstacles?
3.   What are the implications of this exercise for you as a future manager?

Organizational Cultures: Mini-scenarios
Note: The scenarios below are based on actual companies.

Scenario 1—Creating a "Team-Based" Culture
The Micro-X Corporation, a major computer hardware manufacturer, is a very traditional organization in many ways. It is very hierarchical, and managers tend to be highly authoritarian in their leadership styles. The organization is "functionally" structured, meaning that work tends to be organized by functional area (e.g., marketing, human resources, finance, etc.). Owing to this structure, there is little interaction across functional areas in the company. Employees' jobs tend to be highly specialized and relatively narrow.

In response to competitive pressures and the need to design and manufacture better computer components more efficiently, the company has adopted a "team-based" approach in which cross-functional teams are formed and given the responsibility for product development. Early indications from the new team-based approach are that its employees are not embracing it. A key barrier is that the culture of the organization still emphasizes "functional" thinking and individual effort as opposed to the cross-functional and team-oriented mentality needed now.

What would you do to change the culture of Micro-X?

Scenario 2—Creating a "Learning Organization" Culture

Wilson Motor Company, a global leader in the design and manufacture of a full line of sport-utility vehicles and trucks, is experiencing extreme competitive pressures from other automotive companies in the United States and in Germany and Japan. A major problem for the company has been that it seems to make the same mistakes over and over again. For example, the redesigns of its current models tend to be consistently off in relation to the needs and desires of its target customers. The exterior styling of the vehicles themselves is viewed as being "weird" or "boring." The interiors of many vehicles use an excessive amount of cheap-looking plastic material.

One of the major reasons for the company's inability to learn from its mistakes is an ingrained corporate culture that emphasizes "good news": Management is not interested in hearing about problems or weaknesses in the organization. Positive results tend to be emphasized at management meetings. Bad news results in a "shoot-the-messenger" ritual that makes people fearful of discussing anything negative with management. Although management perceives that everything is okay, their view does not match reality.

If you were a consultant, what would you do to change the culture at Wilson Motor in order to create a "learning organization" that learns from good and bad news?

Scenario No. 3: Creating a "Merit-Based Culture"

North American Air, one of the major airlines in the United States, has always possessed a culture that emphasized being a family and taking care of employees. Traditionally, this was reflected in the company's employment practices, such as pay and promotion-from-within policies based on length of service to the company. This has led to the creation of an "entitlement" culture in which employees felt that it was their right to receive generous pay increases each year independent of actual job performance.

Unfortunately, North American Air's performance has dropped significantly in the last three years. Profitability, customer satisfaction, and operating efficiency have all declined.

The CEO of North American Air realizes that the company must focus more on achieving bottom-line results. This will require a major cultural shift for the company in terms of moving from an entitlement culture to a "merit-based" culture that emphasizes and rewards employees on the basis of their actual contributions to the success of the company.

What would you do to create a merit-based culture in this firm?

EMPOWERING OTHERS

As discussed, an organizational culture influences how employees communicate, cooperate, and make decisions. To foster a creative and productive environment where employees are motivated to achieve exceptional performance, the organization's culture needs to empower its employees. Let's take a look at the need for empowerment and the process involved in establishing an empowered workforce.

POWERLESSNESS

Carl Sandburg wrote, "I am the people—the mob—the crowd—the mass. Do you know that all the great work of the world is done through me?"[38] If the people are to do the world's work, they must have the power to do so. Unfortunately, many characteristics of traditional organizations create feelings of powerlessness and *learned helplessness* among employees; learned helplessness is a condition that occurs when it appears that one's behaviors simply don't make a difference.[39] Rules won't change, and we are bound to them. Bosses are set in their ways, and we must obey them. Things have always been done a certain way, and that's how we must do them. The assembly line is relentless, and we must follow it. And it seems there's nothing we can do about it. It's not surprising that many employees feel powerless and helpless.

Even high-level executives may feel that they are helpless. For instance, managers are often encouraged to emulate successful behavior, even though it isn't clear to them (and perhaps to anyone else) why that behavior was successful. If the behavior turns out to work well, the manager still doesn't know why. If it fails, the manager is punished, even if he or she competently carried it out.[40] This is a prescription for powerlessness.

Powerlessness has many important and unfortunate consequences. For example, learned helplessness has been proposed as a mechanism resulting in—among other things—depression, burnout, academic failure, and susceptibility to illness.[41] Also, powerlessness leads to lowered self-efficacy. As we discussed in Chapter 3, self-efficacy is the belief that one can master a task, and it is critical for successful task accomplishment. Since powerlessness is pervasive in organizations, empowerment is a rallying cry of the new millennium.

THE EMPOWERMENT PROCESS

Empowerment seeks to break the spiral of powerlessness by giving employees a sense of real control. Empowerment gives people in organizations the ability to get things done, often at levels of the hierarchy where the power can be most directly and effectively applied. To gain a better understanding of empowerment, consider the empowerment process shown in Figure 8-5.[42]

Leaders empower by removing chains, developing subordinates' self-sufficiency, and employing empowering leadership practices. There are five stages to the empowerment process.

Stage 1 represents those conditions—bureaucratic climate; autocratic supervision; rewards that aren't tied to performance; and routine, simplified jobs—that lead to powerlessness. In stage 1, the direct causes of powerlessness are identified. For example, unnecessary rules, supervisors who give employees no discretion, reward systems that are unrelated to things that employees can influence, and stultifying jobs are recognized as potential causes of powerlessness.

In *stage 2,* the manager draws on an arsenal of empowering managerial practices. We consider each of these approaches, including participative management, goal setting, feedback, modeling, rewards based on behavior and competence, and job enrichment, in other chapters. For example:

> Let the people who work for you participate in decision making. They will gain a sense of control over their work lives, and they will be more enthusiastic about implementing the decisions and selling them to others.

> Offer control over work processes. Toyota, Saturn, and Jaguar let workers on their assembly lines stop the lines at any time if they have a prob-

FIGURE 8-5
The Empowerment Process

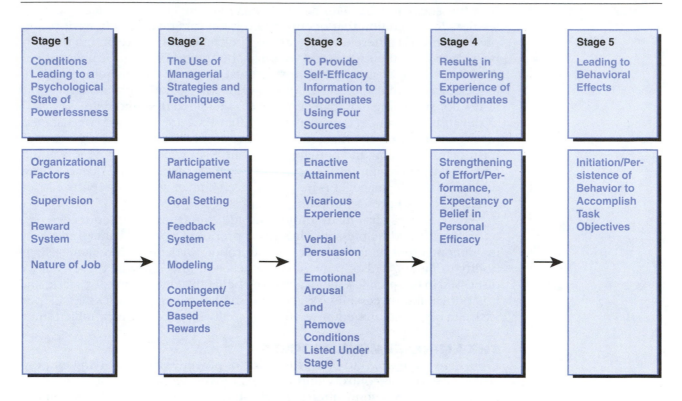

Stage 1	Stage 2	Stage 3	Stage 4	Stage 5
Conditions Leading to a Psychological State of Powerlessness	The Use of Managerial Strategies and Techniques	To Provide Self-Efficacy Information to Subordinates Using Four Sources	Results in Empowering Experience of Subordinates	Leading to Behavioral Effects
Organizational Factors Supervision Reward System Nature of Job	Participative Management Goal Setting Feedback System Modeling Contingent/Competence-Based Rewards	Enactive Attainment Vicarious Experience Verbal Persuasion Emotional Arousal and Remove Conditions Listed Under Stage 1	Strengthening of Effort/Performance, Expectancy or Belief in Personal Efficacy	Initiation/Persistence of Behavior to Accomplish Task Objectives

lem, immediately correcting errors and reducing the number of faulty products. Similarly, many hotels now let their desk clerks respond directly to customers' concerns without having to get supervisors' approval; they can even void customers' bills, granting them a free stay to compensate for a bad experience. Similarly, Disney World gives employees the authority to do whatever is necessary to deal with problems on the spot in order to make customers happy. Disney World believes front-line employees should be the first—and the last—contact with customers.[43]

> Tie rewards to performance. Employees naturally feel powerless when they see that they aren't allowed to make a difference. When they see that their actions directly influence things they care about, they gain a sense of control—and they're more likely to do it again.

> Express confidence, encouragement, and support. Celebrate "small wins" and provide assurances that obstacles can be overcome.

Stage 3 is used to provide information to subordinates to increase their self-efficacies. This can be done in a variety of ways:[44]

> First, people may gain self-efficacy by actually mastering a task (called *enactive attainment*); initial success experiences make people feel more capable and strengthen their belief that they can handle more

FOCUS ON MANAGEMENT

AN EMPOWERING CULTURE AT SATURN CORP.

Saturn employees at plants in Spring Hill, Tennessee and Wilmington, Delaware don't punch time clocks. Labor and management (all called *team members* rather than *labor* and *management*) share the same cafeteria. Thanks to a unique agreement with the United Auto Workers union at the time of Saturn's creation, the union gave up rigid work rules, and GM (Saturn's parent corporation) abandoned most of its rigid hierarchy. Saturn employees were grouped into small teams and given responsibility for everything from covering absent members to major production decisions.* The cooperative environment, focus on quality, and such concepts as no-haggle pricing have built a loyal customer base and provided an empowering work environment. When Cynthia Trudell, Saturn's chair and president, walks down the line, smiling workers ask her to pose with them for souvenir photos. The culture of Saturn is so unusual that a special team, called *Saturn Consulting Services,* is available to provide consulting and training expertise to organizations wanting to learn from the Saturn experience. Go to the following site and click on "A Different Kind of Company" to learn more about Saturn's values, mission statement, philosophy, policies, and community activities.

http://www.saturn.com/

*To read more about Saturn and the challenges it currently faces, see I. Austen, "Problem Child," *Canadian Business,* March 26, 1999, pp. 22–31.

complex and difficult tasks. So, giving employees goals they can successfully attain may be helpful.

> Second, *vicarious experience*—seeing that others who are similar can master a task—may enhance self-efficacy. As such, job training may involve showing someone completing the task.

> Third, employees may simply be convinced through *verbal persuasion,* words of encouragement and feedback that they can master tasks.

> Finally, techniques that create emotional support or foster a supportive and trusting group atmosphere may reduce the *emotional arousal* states that result from stress, fear, anxiety, and depression and that lower self-efficacy.

In addition to these approaches, self-efficacy may be enhanced by removing the stage 1 conditions that led to powerlessness.[45] There is an old Abbott and Costello routine in which Costello, playing a patient, raises his arm and says to Abbott, playing a doctor, "Doc, it hurts when I do this." Abbott replies, "Don't *do* that!" So, it is important to find the chains that are binding employees and then don't *do* that. Cut unnecessary red tape, rethink stifling rules, back off on overly close supervision, and treat your employees as capable and mature individuals.

In *stage 4,* the benefits of stages 2 and 3 are reaped as employees' self-efficacy is actually enhanced and employees gain a sense of power. Finally, in *stage 5,* the behavioral consequences of enhanced self-efficacy are seen: Empowered employees engage in task-oriented behavior.

The process model presented in the nearby Bottom Line summarizes the basic steps associated with empowering employees in an organization.

EMPOWERMENT AT FEDERAL EXPRESS

The goal of Fred Smith, chairman and president of Federal Express, was to create a "power environment."* Smith calls empowerment "the most important element in managing an organization."† To create a power environment, Federal Express has a corporate philosophy that fosters respect for human dignity, ingenuity, and potential. There is a job-secure environment in which people aren't afraid to take risks. Jobs have been redesigned to increase employee power, and there are many opportunities for promotion from within. Further, at Federal Express, there are many programs and processes designed to empower employees. An annual employee attitude survey, called *Survey Feedback Action,* is followed by an action phase in which managers meet with their staffs to develop an action plan for dealing with every concern. A *Guaranteed Fair Treatment* process is a three-stage avenue for airing employee grievances. An *Open-Door* process directs employees' questions to the people in the company best qualified to answer them. Unlike many such programs, the process at Federal Express is monitored to ensure that each question is answered within 14 working days. A *Circle of Excellence* award is presented monthly to the best performing Federal Express station, underscoring teamwork, and other awards encourage employee service and achievement of quality. A *Bravo Zulu* (Navy talk for "well done") program gives managers the chance to award dinner, theater tickets, or cash to any employee who has done an outstanding job. These philosophies, policies, and practices work together to create an environment in which employees feel valued and believe they can make a difference.

http://fedex.com/us/careers/

*F. W. Smith, "Empowering Employees," *Small Business Reports,* January 1991, pp. 15–20.

†F. W. Smith, "Empowering Employees," *Small Business Reports,* January 1991, p. 15.

The Bottom Line: Empowering Employees

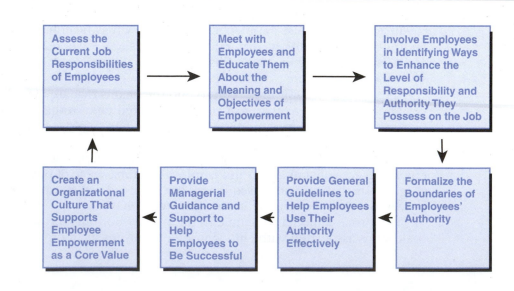

Now use relevant material from this chapter to complete Skills Practice 8-4. Remember that your focus should be on how to translate the concept of empowerment into specific managerial action.

***

Skills Practice 8-4
Empowering Employees

Skill Objective

To develop skill in empowering employees in order to enhance their job satisfaction, work motivation, and job performance.

Procedure

1. This exercise may be done individually or in groups of three to five students.
2. Select a scenario from below on which to focus for this exercise.
3. Develop an action plan for empowering the employees in the scenario. Be specific and action oriented (i.e., indicate exactly what needs to be done).
4. Optional: Present the action plan to the class and defend it.
5. Discuss the questions that follow.

Discussion Questions

1. What are the general strengths and weaknesses of employee empowerment?
2. When is it most appropriate to use employee empowerment? When is it not appropriate?
3. What are the implications of this exercise for you as a future manager or supervisor?

Scenario 1—An Administrative Assistant

Beth Martin is the administrative assistant for Stacey Long, the director of human resources at the Marqwell Corporation. Beth's job is very routine but requires a tremendous amount of detail work (e.g., completing forms, typing letters and reports, answering the phone, filing, organizing, etc.). Unfortunately, Beth feels powerless in her job, since she is told that everything must be done in a certain way. In addition, Beth must constantly get authorizations from Stacey before doing many things. Sometimes this creates inefficiencies when Stacey is out of the office or in meetings all day.

Beth is becoming increasingly dissatisfied with her job. She feels that she can just "check her brain at the door" when she comes to work each day.

What advice would you give to Stacey Long regarding strategies for empowering Beth?

Scenario 2—Sales Associates

Mike Anderson is the sales manager at Lord Foggington's Jewelry Store. Fifteen sales associates work for Mike. Their job duties include working with customers to identify their needs and to develop a variety of product options for satisfying these needs. Given that Lord Foggington's is in the business of selling jewelry, many customers come into the store wanting to negotiate or barter the best price possible for a given piece of jewelry. One problem with this is that the sales associates do not have the authority to negotiate prices with customers. Only Mike can authorize a price reduction from the official price on the tag attached to a given item.

Another problem is that the sales associates deal only with the sales process itself. After a purchase has been made, customers deal with the customer service department in getting jewelry repaired or cleaned. Sales associates feel that this robs them of the opportunity to develop the long-term relationship with customers needed for repeat purchases and loyalty.

What advice would you give Mike Anderson regarding strategies for empowering the sales associates?

ENCOURAGING ETHICAL BEHAVIOR

Ethics are principles of morality or rules of conduct. *Business ethics* are rules about how businesses and their employees ought to behave. Ethical behavior conforms to these rules; unethical behavior violates them. Business ethics help to guide an organization's efforts and offer a foundation for its culture.

The need for ethical behavior in organizations has been dramatized by some very visible ethical violations, including use of kickbacks, bribes, and myriad other forms of corruption.

Consider these facts:

> In one study, 65 percent of managers claimed to have personally seen or had direct evidence of fraud, waste, or mismanagement within their organizations. Of these people, however, only 50 percent reported what they had seen to appropriate authorities.[46]

> In a survey of more than 1,000 randomly selected adults, 24 percent reported that they had been asked to do something at work that went against their ethical standards. Of those, 41 percent reported carrying out the order.[47]

> The U.S. Chamber of Commerce estimates that workplace theft costs U.S. businesses up to $40 billion each year and that employees are thought to be responsible for much of the theft.

GLOBAL PERSPECTIVES

BRIBES, QUANXI, AND SOKAIYA

In some countries, gifts and gratuities are seen as an acceptable part of doing business—much as we give tips for good service—and aren't viewed as bribes. However, in other cases, ethical and legal violations are more clear-cut. Bribery in overseas dealings has increased sharply in the last two decades. It has been estimated that bribes paid to acquire large contracts in developing countries now exceed 15 percent of the contracts' value.* Outright bribes and payments for *quanxi,* or "connections," total $3 billion to $5 billion in China, costs that are largely borne by consumers.†

Japan has been rocked by evidence that corporate leaders have made large payments to *yakuza,* or gangsters, to secure favors and pre-vent retribution from the yakuza. In one case, the chairman and two other top executives of the Kirin Brewery Company, Japan's largest beer producer and a member of the powerful Mitsubishi group, resigned after four corporate officers were arrested on charges of making payoffs to *sokaiya,* gangsters who specialize in corporate extortion. The *sokaiya* obtain information about illicit corporate activities and threaten to disclose it; they also threaten to disrupt annual meetings.‡ *Sokaiya* activity in recent years has moved Japan's financial system to the brink of disaster, with large banks and security houses paying huge sums to the *sokaiya* and with many high-level executives resigning in related scandals. Now, companies, the police, and public opinion are turning against the *sokaiya,* whose number is decreasing. However, the *sokaiya* who remain have been toughened by the harsher climate, are using less subtle tactics, and are charging higher fees.§

*"A War on Global Corruption," *The New York Times,* May 11, 1993, p. D2.

†See, for instance, "The Destructive Costs of Greasing Palms," *Business Week,* December 6, 1993, pp. 133, 136, and 138.

‡J. Sterngold, "3 Kirin Executives to Resign," *The New York Times,* July 19, 1993, p. D7.

§See N. Montagu-Smith, "You'll Be Hearing From My Bengoshi," *International Commercial Litigation,* July/August 1997, pp. 10–15; M. Ishizuka, "Japanese Firms' Sokaiya Ties Run Deep," *Asian Business,* August 1997, pp. 18–20; R. Dale, "Tokyo's Confidence Crisis," *Financial Regulation Report,* March 1998, pp. 1–2; and "Business: Question Time in Japan," *The Economist,* May 1, 1999, p. 61.

> **Bribes**—payments "up front" to influence a transaction—have reached such epidemic proportions that 34 industrial nations have forged a multinational treaty to address them.

> **Kickbacks,** which occur when someone who has won a contract or made a sale through favorable treatment gives back part of the profits from the transaction to the party providing the favor, are proliferating.[48] For example, in the "IBM affair," the computer giant's arm in Argentina was charged with paying $37 million in kickbacks and bribes to land a $250 million contract to supply a computer network to state-run Banco de la Nación.[49]

> Many U.S. companies have been charged with running inhumane sweatshops, most of them in the Third World, with low wages, long hours, and unhealthy conditions and often employing children or forced labor. In late 1999, more than 50,000 protesters descended on the meetings of the World Trade Organization in Seattle to protest sweatshops (as well as such issues as human rights violations, environmental degradation, and genetically engineered food).[50] John Sweeney, president of the AFL-CIO, said that corporate interests are well looked after "while 250 million children around the world go to work, not school, and tens of thousands of workers are chained into forced labor and prison camps."[51] Activists charge that many of the products sold by the Gap and Nike, among others, are made in such Third World sweatshops.[52]

> The Association of Certified Fraud Examiners estimates that U.S. industry loses about $400 billion annually to unethical or criminal behavior.[53]

ETHICS AND FIRM PERFORMANCE

It is very difficult to document the relationship of ethical behavior to organizational performance. There are many reasons for this, including disagreements over what behavior is ethical. However, some attempts have been made to explore the relationship. For instance, one recent study found that companies that had an "ethical commitment"—as evidenced by the inclusion of ethics codes in the management reports within annual reports—had much higher levels of financial performance than did those without such codes in the reports. Also, those companies with an "ethical commitment" had higher scores on *Fortune* reputation ratings.[54] In addition, as we discuss a bit later, committing specific unethical acts may have disastrous consequences for organizations and their officers.

THE WHISTLE-BLOWING RESPONSE TO UNETHICAL BEHAVIOR

An employee who learns that his or her company engages in an illegal or unethical activity can keep quiet, report the incident to others in the firm, or go outside the firm with the information. By going outside the firm, the employee is said to be "blowing the whistle." *Whistle blowers,* those individuals who report to the press, government, or other parties outside the firm illegal activity occurring in a firm, may find their jobs and careers threatened. About 35 states now have laws protecting whistle blowers.[55]

Also, the federal False Claims Act allows whistle blowers to sue government wrongdoers in the name of the United States. The False Claims Act was strengthened in 1986, bolstering whistle blowers in three important ways. It gave them more power to initiate and prosecute claims, offered them up to

25 percent of any money recovered by the government, and provided protection against employer retaliation. Since enactment of the act, the number of whistle blower complaints received by the Department of Justice has skyrocketed, and the government has recovered more than $1.8 billion in false claims cases.[56]

Those favoring whistle-blower protection note that without protection, those reporting wrongdoing may face (and have faced) harassment, demotion, firing, or other retribution (including death). Without protection, they would never be willing to expose important wrongdoing. Those opposing such protection argue that whistle blowing causes employees to circumvent companies' internal mechanisms for ethical resolution, may encourage malcontents who will take every opportunity to complain, and may lead to abuse of the law. For instance, they argue, a marginal employee who is afraid of being dismissed because of poor performance may find gossip about someone in the firm (or make some up), report it outside the firm, and then evoke whistle-blower protection laws when the company threatens dismissal. Opponents of protection laws also argue that they may encourage "dialing-for-dollars" whistle blowers who care more about personal gain than about justice. For instance, whistle blowers have received awards of more than $20 million for reporting on illegal activities in their firms.

Whatever the merits of whistle blowing and of whistle blowers' protection laws, there is little doubt that whistle blowing can have devastating consequences for the targeted firms. Further, the need for whistle blowing generally suggests both that unethical behaviors have reached unacceptable levels within the firm and that appropriate internal mechanisms to correct such behaviors are lacking.

LEGAL REMEDIES FOR UNETHICAL BEHAVIOR

For millennia, we have turned to legal codes to help to provide guidelines for dealing with unethical behavior. One of the earliest of these was the Code of Hammurabi, a code consisting of 282 rules outlining all aspects of public involvement and sorted into groups such as family, labor, personal property, real estate, trade, and business.[57]

In more recent years, this search for legal guidance has continued. A 19th-century English judge, Edward Baron Thurlow, lamented in a court decision: "Did you ever expect a corporation to have a conscience when it has no soul to be damned and no body to be kicked?" Then he whispered, "By God, it ought to have both."[58] Increasingly, governments are finding a "body to be kicked." They are applying criminal laws to companies and company executives. For example, the Foreign Corrupt Practices Act of 1977 was enacted in response to disclosures that American corporations were paying bribes to high governmental officials in foreign countries in an attempt to win contracts and sell products and services.

Further, Congress created a U.S. Sentencing Commission to issue new guidelines for white-collar crime, such as bribery, fraud, and tax evasion. The commission's guidelines—the 1991 Sentencing Guidelines for Organizations—provide tougher sanctions, including jail sentences and fines in the millions of dollars, for those convicted of corporate lawbreaking. Many business people who paid small fines, if anything, for wrongdoing are now often serving mandatory prison terms.[59] Sentencing under the guidelines for an offense committed by an organization depends on such things as the nature of the crime, the amount of loss suffered by victims of the crime, and the amount of planning evidenced by the offense. In addition, such factors as the organization's history of criminal activity and whether high-level organizational personnel were involved in or tolerated the activity are considered in determining a penalty. Depending on such considerations, a $25,000 bribe paid to a city official could result in fines ranging from $17,500 to $1.4 million.[60]

Companies must do more than rely on whistle blowing and legal mechanisms to ensure ethical behavior (and having corporate sins publicized or corporate officers thrown in jail are rather drastic and painful approaches to ethical compliance). If they are really serious about encouraging ethical behaviors, managers and companies must take concrete actions, establishing and following guidelines for ethical behavior.

GUIDELINES FOR ETHICAL BEHAVIOR

Mark Twain advised, "Always do right. This will gratify some people, and astonish the rest." As a manager, it is absolutely critical that you behave ethically. One reason is obvious and overwhelming: It is the right thing to do. Another is perhaps less evident; if you do not, you will lose respect of yourself and others as well as credibility and trust and, as you do, you will lose the power to lead. Here are some guidelines for ethical behavior:

> Be *honest,* direct, and open in your dealings with others. Jim Kouzes and Barry Posner, authors of *The Leadership Challenge,* surveyed more than 20,000 people on four continents to identify the characteristics they most look for and admire in a leader. Only four characteristics were identified by more than 50 percent: competent (63 percent), inspiring (68 percent), forward-looking (75 percent), and honest (88 percent). Honesty's top rating suggests that it is perhaps *the* essential ingredient of successful leadership.[61]

> *Take ethical stands* on difficult issues. Confucius said, "The superior man understands what is right; the inferior man understands what will sell." The willingness to stand up for your beliefs is one mark of a transformational leader.

> Ask whether your actions reflect the *rights of others,* including such rights as due process, free speech, and privacy.

> Ask whether your actions are *just.* An act is unjust if it involves unequal treatment of individuals or inconsistent administration of rules.

> Ask how you would feel if the act was done to you.

> Use your power in ethical ways. If you use legitimate power, make polite requests. If you use reward power, deliver on your promises. If you use coercive power, fully inform people who work for you of the rules and penalties for violations, provide warning before punishing, and administer discipline consistently and promptly. If you use referent power, take actions that justify and maintain that power: Treat people fairly, be considerate of their needs and feelings, show your appreciation when they do things that please you, and defend their interests when acting as a group representative. If you use expert power, do nothing to endanger those relying on your expertise.

> Apply the *sunlight test.* How would you feel if your actions were brought to the light of day? Would you be proud to have your children read about them in the newspaper?

Now, complete Skills Practice 8-5. The exercise will help to raise your awareness of ethical issues and how to deal with them more effectively in the future.

Skills Practice 8-5
Ethical Reflections

Consider each of the following questions and respond as honestly as possible. There are no "right" or "wrong" answers. Instead, these "reflections" are intended to encourage you to think about some important ethical issues facing people in businesses today. Use a separate piece of paper to document your work.

1. Think of a situation in which you had to make an important ethical choice (at school, at work, with friends, or whatever). Describe the choice and identify why you made the choice you did.

2. Thinking back on your choice, are you now satisfied with it? Was there anything you wish you had done differently? Were there things that others could have done that would have helped you "do the right thing"?

3. What lessons do you draw from your answers to questions 1 and 2?

4. Identify a situation (preferably, one in which you were personally involved) in which someone did something that you felt was unethical. Describe the situation and indicate why you feel the behavior was unethical.

5. What do you think were some causes of the unethical behavior you just described? Try to think of as many feasible causes as you can. For instance, did the behavior reflect the values or personalities (or both) of the person or people involved? Demands of the situation? The sorts of things that were rewarded? A culture that encouraged the behavior? A lack of mechanisms to prevent the behavior? Other things?

6. What happened to the person who engaged in the unethical behavior you have described? Did he or she gain or lose by engaging in the behavior? Should anyone have done anything differently to ensure that the individual wouldn't profit from the behavior?

7. The following list contains a series of questions about ethical behavior. Answer each of these questions. Then, meet with at least one other student in your class and compare your answers. Explore reasons why you may have had different answers. Use the following scale when responding:

1 = Disagree Strongly
2 = Disagree Somewhat
3 = Neither Agree nor Disagree
4 = Agree Somewhat
5 = Agree Strongly

1. _____ In general, people who engage in unethical behavior get ahead in organizations.

2. _____ Most organizations encourage unethical behavior if it helps profits.

3. _____ Things that are considered to be unethical in one culture (e.g., bribery or child labor) may be considered to be ethical in another.

4. _____ Whether a behavior is ethical or unethical is in the eyes of the beholder.

5. _____ When dealing with people from other cultures, we shouldn't try to impose our ethical standards on them.

6. _____ Most people try to be ethical.

7. _____ In general, I believe worthwhile ends may justify some cutting of ethical corners.

8. _____ Ethical behavior pays off on the "bottom line."

9. _____ If I see people engaging in unethical behavior, such as stealing office supplies or making inappropriate use of company resources, I am morally obligated to report it.

10. _____ Virtually everyone will do unethical things if the situation demands it.

11. _____ When people behave in unethical ways, it is more often due to the situations in which they find themselves than to their values or personalities.

12. _____ The degree to which employees behave ethically should be part of formal performance reviews.

13. _____ Ethics isn't something that can be taught.

14. _____ I wouldn't work in a company if I thought it would require me to engage in unethical acts.

15. _____ Some people are inherently unethical.

16. _____ It's generally not possible to decide what is or isn't ethical.

17. _____ If I worked in a company at which I saw people breaking the law in ways that endangered public safety, I would report the wrongdoing to law enforcement officials or others outside the firm if necessary.

18. _____ It's not the company's responsibility to encourage ethical behavior; employees have the responsibility to be ethical.

19. _____ Companies should have a "zero-tolerance" policy for unethical behavior; any unethical behavior should be grounds for dismissal.

20. _____ Employees shouldn't be held responsible for unethical behaviors that aren't explicitly addressed in the company's code of ethics.

ENCOURAGING ETHICAL BEHAVIOR IN OTHERS

It is not enough that managers behave ethically; they must also encourage ethical behavior in others. To do this, you can:

> **Promote, communicate, and reward** ethical behavior as a key value.

> **Model ethical behavior.** Both in public and private, act in ways you hope and expect others to act. If others see that you don't walk the talk, your speeches about ethics will be dismissed as hypocrisy.

> **Speak out** against unethical behavior when you see it. Don't wink at it or ignore it, and certainly don't reward it. Remember that if employees can get ahead by acting in unethical ways and nothing is done about it, that behavior is being rewarded and will probably be repeated.

> **Communicate expectations** regarding ethical behavior. For instance, make sure employees are aware of the firm's *code of ethics.* The code of ethics should be a living document that embodies principles that show up in performance appraisals and the reward system. A code of ethics is most meaningful when employees help to draft and revise it. For instance, Herron Communications Corporation had the company lawyers draft a code of ethics to govern many facets of employee behav-

ior. The employees' response to the many "thou shalt nots" was so negative that the code was never implemented. The company then got employees involved in developing a new code. It was worded in terms of acceptable behavior rather than forbidden actions, and response was much more favorable.[62]

However, companies should do more than just remind employees of the code of ethics. Employees should regularly receive messages of various sorts concerning the importance of ethical behavior. Unfortunately, one study found that regardless of organizational rank, no more than one-third of employees of *Fortune 1,000* firms received any sort of message regarding ethics, other than a reminder of the code, more than once a year.[63]

> Make sure that goals don't push employees into unethical behavior. Unreasonable goals are often the motivation for lying, cheating, and stealing.

> Encourage *ethics training.* Tie ethics training to the legal, behavioral, and policy needs of organizations and their members.[64] Make sure employees know about laws, policies, and expectations regarding ethical behavior. Ethics training is most often used to address conflicts of interest, personal conduct, public conduct, use of official information, and responsibilities to those in authority.[65] It can also reinforce codes of ethics so employees can see how the generality of codes can be used in specific, day-to-day situations.[66] Ethics training might include such things as video material, role-playing, board games with ethical scenarios, conferences on ethical issues, and use of current newspaper reports of real-life occurrences relating to ethical issues.[67] At GE, videos and seminars are used to encourage employees to report ethical violations. Employees are even subjected to pop quizzes in hallways with questions such as, "What are the three ways to report wrongdoing?" A correct answer wins a coffee mug.[68] Unfortunately, no more than one-fourth of all employees in *Fortune 1,000* firms receive ethics training and education at least once a year. About the same number receive no ethics training or education of any sort.

> Give employees ways to voice their ethical questions and concerns. Don't force employees to ignore unethical behavior, to accept it, or to jeopardize their careers by going outside the firm with their concerns (that is, by whistle blowing).

For instance, IBM has had a "Speak Up!" program for more than 25 years. It allows an employee to appeal any supervisory action and get a mailed response without having his or her name communicated to the supervisor. A meeting between the employee and management is arranged if necessary. About one-half of the *Fortune 1,000* firms have adopted some kind of *ethics hot lines*—telephone-based systems employees can use (anonymously if they prefer) for ethics and compliance complaints and questions. For example, Sundstrand Corporation has an ethics hot line that receives an average of 1,500 calls per year.[69]

In addition, many firms, including Rockwell, Johnson & Johnson, Herman Miller, Inc., and Volvo, encourage workers to report ethical problems to ombudsmen's offices. The *ombudsman*—an old Norse term for "people's representative"—is a neutral third party designated

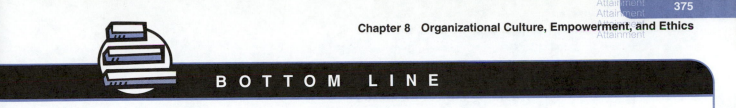

BOTTOM LINE

The Bottom Line: Encouraging Ethical Employee Behavior

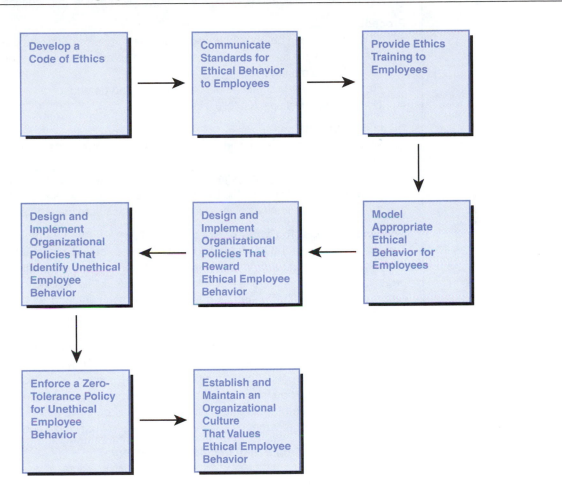

by the firm to check out and help to resolve employee complaints. Ombudsmen are also helpful in preventing miscommunication and misunderstanding between management and employees.[70]

> Set up internal programs to resolve ethical conflicts. Develop clear routines and procedures for dealing with any complaints or allegations brought against employees under the ethics policies of the firm.

The nearby Bottom Line presents a process model summarizing the basic steps associated with encouraging ethical behavior in organizations.

Now complete Skills Practice 8-6. The focus of this activity is to help you develop skill in thinking about and dealing with difficult ethical dilemmas in various managerial situations.

Skills Practice 8-6
Handling Ethical Dilemmas

Skill Level: **Basic**

Skill Objective
To develop skill in evaluating managerial situations with ethical implications.

Procedure
1. This exercise can be completed individually or in groups of three to five students.
2. Select one of the following scenarios and develop an action plan for dealing with it effectively as a manager.
3. Optional: Present your action plan to the class and defend it.
4. Discuss the questions that follow as a class.

Discussion Questions
1. Why is it important to consider the ethical implications of decisions made by managers?
2. To what extent should managers make tradeoffs between handling ethical issues appropriately and achieving "bottom-line" business objectives and results?
3. What are the implications of this exercise for you as future managers and supervisors?

Scenario 1—Jobs: To Export or Not to Export?
The Americana Corporation, a leading United States–based manufacturer of a variety of consumer electronics products, such as personal digital assistants, digital phones, pagers, and digital cameras, has taken great pride in its tradition of being an "All-American" company committed to designing and manufacturing all its products in the United States of America. This strategic emphasis has been incorporated into the company's mission statement and its product advertising.

Recently, the company's financial performance has begun to decline, owing to intense foreign competition, value-oriented consumers, and severe upward pressure on costs. For the first time, you are contemplating the idea of moving some or all of your production overseas to a developing country with cheap labor. However, you don't know how such a move will be received by employees and customers who may perceive this as being unethical or irresponsible given the company's All-American image. What would you do?

Scenario 2—Managing a Staff of Financial Advisors
Linda Jones is the manager of a group of financial advisors at a mutual fund company based in New York. Her staff does a lot of its work out in the field, meeting directly with customers to develop appropriate investment plans for achieving their financial goals. The relationship between the financial advisor and the client is critical for the long-term success and profitability of the firm. This relationship must be based on mutual trust and respect.

The financial advisors receive a base salary, but a major portion of their overall compensation comes from sales commissions. For her financial advisors, Linda sets specific sales targets that they are expected to meet. Failure to do so on a consistent basis leads to disciplinary action or termination.

The environment at the firm clearly stresses the importance of prospecting customers and selling as a core activity. Recently, it has come to Linda's attention that some of her staff have been using high-pressure sales tactics on elderly individuals and recent widows in order to get them to invest in high-risk mutual funds that generate large commissions for themselves. The problem here is that the very aggressive and volatile high-risk mutual funds are generally not a good investment option for elderly people and recent widows.

Given this situation, what would you do?

Scenario 3—Does Integrity Matter?

Keisha Anderson, the CEO of Austin Corporation, needs to fill the position of vice president of marketing. The candidate that he likes is named Bill Scott. Bill has been with the firm for 15 years and is viewed as being highly competent. He possesses excellent technical skills. Bill is very outgoing and personable. He has tremendous energy and charisma, and he would bring a lot of experience and expertise to the position.

One concern that Keisha has is that though Bill is married and has two children, he has developed a reputation in the company for being a "womanizer." In fact, rumors have been circulated about all kinds of affairs that he has had with female employees.

Given the family-oriented and very conservative culture that prevails in the firm, this issue could be problematic in terms of giving the job to Bill. What would you do?

Finally, read the nearby Real-World Management Challenge and develop an action plan for handling the situation. This was an actual challenge that a company had to deal with, so you will be able to compare what you come up with against the actions that management actually took to handle this situation.

Real-World Management Challenge

Implementing an Employee Ethics Program at Quorum Health Group

The Situation

Quorum Health Group, Inc. owns and operates 21 acute care hospitals and local/regional health care systems in nine states in the United States. Quorum employs a workforce of over 20,000 employees. The basic mission of the company is as follows:

> Quorum Health Group, Inc. owns and manages health care systems and is committed to meeting the needs of consumers and providers through innovative services that enhance the delivery of quality healthcare.

One of the key values at Quorum is "personal and business integrity." This issue has become increasingly important to health care organizations as regulation of the overall industry intensifies and the business practices of health care providers are subjected to greater scrutiny by the federal government and payers of health care services.

Given the concern for compliance with complex regulation, Quorum identified the need to develop a comprehensive business ethics program for its management and employees.

The purpose of the program was to reinforce the values of the company and to ensure that employees possessed the knowledge and tools to make ethical decisions in performing their jobs on a day-to-day basis.

What Would You Do?

Suppose that you were put in charge of developing the business ethics program at Quorum. What would you do? Be as specific as possible in developing the various elements of your program.

http://www.quorumhealth.com/

Source: C. F. Batts, "Making Ethics an Organization Priority," *The Healthcare Forum Journal*, January/February 1998, pp. 38–41.

The topics addressed in this chapter—organizational culture, empowerment, and ethics—may be dismissed by some as "soft" and idealistic. They are not. You say you don't have the time to deal with such issues? Jack Welch,

CEO of General Electric, has gone to Crotonville, GE's Leadership Development Center, *every two weeks for more than 15 years* to run leadership training programs, teach the GE Management Values statement, and reinforce the GE culture. Jack Welch finds the time.

TOP TEN LIST: KEY POINTS TO REMEMBER
ORGANIZATIONAL CULTURE, EMPOWERMENT, AND ETHICS

10. Develop and maintain an organizational culture that reinforces the core values of the firm.

9. Align the culture of an organization with its mission and strategic objectives.

8. Use a variety of methods (e.g., stories, rites and ceremonies, and symbols) to communicate organizational culture to employees.

7. Allow subcultures and even countercultures to co-exist with the dominant corporate culture when they support the strategic objectives of the firm.

6. Assess the current culture of a firm as the first step in developing a plan for changing it.

5. Identify the underlying causes of resistance to changing corporate culture as a basis for developing a plan for ultimately transforming it. Recognize that cultural change in organizations will take time.

4. Ensure that employees possess the job-specific knowledge, skills, and abilities as well as the maturity to benefit from an empowerment program.

3. Remember that sharing power with employees (i.e., empowerment) actually enhances the power of a manager in many cases as opposed to diminishing it.

2. Establish what "ethical behavior" means for your firm and communicate these standards to employees using a variety of mechanisms (e.g., employee handbooks, mission statements, annual reports, memos).

1. Develop a "system" and a culture that emphasize the importance of ethical behavior in the workplace. Use managerial policies and practices to reward ethical behavior and to punish unethical behavior.

QUESTIONS FOR REVIEW AND REFLECTION
REVIEW QUESTIONS

1. What is organizational culture?

2. Discuss seven important functions of organizational culture.

3. Define values, symbols, narratives, heroes, rites, and rituals.

4. What is a strong culture? Why does it matter?

5. Discuss four types of narratives.

6. Provide guidelines for assessing organizational culture.

7. What are subcultures and countercultures? Why are they important?

8. Discuss how organizational culture is related to performance and other organizational outcomes.

9. Provide seven guidelines for changing organizational cultures.

10. Identify causes and consequences of powerlessness.

11. Describe each of the five stages of the empowerment process.

12. Define business ethics. How are ethical behaviors related to organizational performance?

13. What is whistle blowing?

14. Identify seven guidelines for enhancing your own ethical behavior.

15. Discuss eight guidelines for encouraging ethical behavior in others.

CRITICAL THINKING QUESTIONS

1. Do you think organizational cultures are more important in some types of firms than others? Defend your position. If your answer is yes, describe the characteristics of the firm, environment, employees, or other factors that might influence the importance of organizational culture.

2. A CEO tells her top management team, "I want a strong, unified culture. There's no place for subcul-

Chapter 8   Organizational Culture, Empowerment, and Ethics

379

Skills Application
Skills Application
Skills Application
Skills Application
Skills Application

tures in this organization." Do you agree that subcultures are inconsistent with a strong culture? Why or why not?

3. The chapter has considered four perspectives concerning how organizational culture might affect a firm's performance. Which of these perspectives do you feel is most useful? To what extent can the perspectives complement one another? Be as specific as possible.

4. A colleague says, "I can understand how having a strong culture might help management. Still, words such as *brainwashed* and *robot* come to mind when I think of cultures where everyone is encouraged to think alike. That doesn't sound like a place I want to be." What might you say to reassure your colleague?

5. After listening to his CEO talk about the company's planned efforts to empower the workforce, an employee says, "It seems to me that we're just getting a lot more responsibility and work and are being told we should be glad because we're 'empowered.' What if I don't want to be empowered? Am I empowered to turn down empowerment?" How might you respond?

6. Consider the following argument: "We can't change people's ethical values; those are learned early in life. As a company, we should simply expect complete integrity from our employees and then promptly and appropriately punish unethical behavior." Do you agree? Why or why not?

7. A concern is sometimes raised that by focusing on issues, such as culture, empowerment, and ethics, companies may lose sight of "the bottom line." Based on the material presented in this chapter and your own experience and perspectives, discuss ways that *failure to pay attention* to organizational culture, empowerment, and ethics may harm a firm's financial performance.

EXPERIENTIAL EXERCISES

WEB EXERCISE 8-1: ORGANIZATIONAL CULTURES

1. Do a Web search, using a search engine such as Google or Excite, to find information about a firm's corporate culture. In the search engine, type "corporate culture" and the name of the firm for which you'd like information. Some firms with noteworthy cultures, and for which there are many Web resources, include GE, Disney, IBM, Apple, Nike, Harley-Davidson, Southwest Airlines, and Johnson & Johnson, but you do not have to limit your search to those companies. Select at least four websites that provide information about the corporate culture of the firm you have chosen.

2. In addition, do a Web search to find the company's Web page (some of these are given in this chapter). Go to that page and find links to information about the company's culture.

3. Based on the information on the company's Web page and the other four (or more) sites, how would you describe the company's culture? Do you expect it to be effective? Would you like to work for the company? Are there things about the culture that need to be changed or that should be zealously reinforced? In your answers, be sure to note any inconsistencies between the culture as described on the company's Web page and on the other sites you have selected.

WEB EXERCISE 8-2: CODES OF ETHICS

The website of the Centre for Applied Ethics at the University of British Columbia (UBC) offers a wide variety of ethics resources. Click on the following link to find a selection of codes of ethics for such companies as Johnson & Johnson, Northern Telecom, Texas Instruments, and several others. There is also a link to more codes of ethics on the Illinois Institute for Technology (IIT) website:

1. Select **three** company codes of ethics from the UBC or IIT (or both) sites (or from other websites that you identify).

2. Identify **one** topic that is covered in **each** of the three codes of ethics (e.g., conflicts of interest, accepting gifts, or use of company facilities). Provide summaries of each of the relevant sections.

3. Compare and contrast the coverage of the topic across the three codes of ethics. What might account for similarities and differences? Do you think one of the codes would be more effective than the others? Why or why not?

*http://www.ethics.ubc.ca/resources/business/
codes.html*

CASE 8-1
UP FROM THE ASHES AT MALDEN MILLS: COMMITMENT TO EMPLOYEES AND THE COMMUNITY

The Company

Malden Mills Industries, Inc. is a privately held textile manufacturing firm based in Lawrence, Massachusetts. The company was founded in 1906 by Henry Feuerstein. Today, the firm is run by Aaron Feuerstein, grandson of the founder. The company is known for its Polarfleece and Polartec fabrics that are used in more than 50 countries. The company's major customers include manufacturers of athletic and outdoor apparel such as Eddie Bauer, L.L. Bean, and Polo Ralph Lauren (USA).

Malden Mills maintains a workforce of 3,100 employees in its Lawrence textile mill. Its sales revenues in 1998 were $400 million.

An Organizational Crisis and Management's Reaction

In December 1995, a massive fire completely destroyed Malden Mill's textile facilities in Lawrence. While some thought that this would be an ideal opportunity for Aaron Feuerstein to collect the very substantial insurance payment and to move Malden Mills to the south or abroad to a low-wage country, this is not what he did. Aaron Feuerstein made an announcement that not only would he rebuild a new textile plant in Lawrence, he would keep all employees on the payroll for the next month. Later, he extended this same offer two more times. The cost of covering all of Malden Mills' employees' pay and benefits for three months was approximately $10 million.

These actions by Aaron Feuerstein earned him the names of "new patron saint of working Americans" and the "Mensch of Malden Mills" (man with a heart).[71] Feuerstein's rationale for his decisions was based on a number of beliefs and principles. First, he believed in an old Jewish saying, "When there is moral chaos, try to be a person of the highest principles."[72] Second, he believed that business leaders have lost their allegiance to workers and communities in order to achieve short-term profits. He saw employees as an asset, not an expense, and felt a strong sense of responsibility to employees and the community. "It was the right thing to do and there's a moral imperative to do it irrespective of the consequences. U.S. companies can only be successful if they invest in a workforce capable of creating innovative and high-quality products," said Feuerstein.

The human resources department at Malden Mills also played a key role in helping employees to get through the crisis. It created a "workers' center" where employees could be updated on rebuilding efforts, pick up pay checks, and receive job training (e.g., computer). It also worked with the local chamber of commerce to get food vouchers for displaced workers.[73]

Results

The rebuilt textile production facility is a $130 million state-of-the-art plant. Approximately 80 percent of the displaced employees were back to work by April 1996, with the groundbreaking on a new facility which began in early 1997. This new mill has become a symbol of what loyalty to employees and community can build. When the new plant was officially dedicated, 15,000 employees and family members attended the event.

In terms of business results, the new textile facility has been generating some impressive numbers. Some of the key outcomes are listed next:[74]

> The overall business has grown over 200 percent for the decade.

> Sales have increased 40 percent since the new facility opened.

> Customer retention is 95 percent.

> Employee retention is 95 percent.

> Employee motivation and commitment to Malden Mills has increased significantly.

> Product quality and efficiency have improved (the defect rate dropped from 6–7 percent to 2 percent).

Discussion Questions

1. To what extent do you agree with Aaron Feuerstein's decision to rebuild the textile facility in Lawrence and to continue to pay his employees for three months? Why?

2. What are the advantages of Aaron Feuerstein's decisions in this case? Why?

3. What are the disadvantages of Aaron Feuerstein's decisions in this case? Why?

4. To what extent should Aaron Feuerstein's management philosophy be a model for management in public corporations that must focus on enhancing shareholder value? Why?

5. What are the practical implications of this case for you as a future manager?

http://www.polartec.com/

381

Chapter 8   Organizational Culture, Empowerment, and Ethics

Skills Application
Skills Application
Skills Application
Skills Application
Skills Application

CASE 8-2
GLOBALIZING THE GE WAY

The Company

General Electric was founded by Thomas Edison as the Edison Electric Light Company on October 15, 1878. In its early years, the company played a key leadership role by creating the lighting and power generation businesses. Since that time, General Electric, or "GE," has grown into a diversified services, technology, and manufacturing company in businesses including aircraft engines, appliances, commercial equipment, financial services, medical systems, plastics, and entertainment. In 1999, its total revenues were $111.6 billion. The company operates in over 100 countries around the world. It employs a workforce of 340,000 employees (197,000 in the United States). The chairman and chief executive officer since 1981 has been Jack Welch.

General Electric has developed and maintained a reputation for being one of the best corporations in the world. It won *Fortune* magazine's "World's Most Admired Company" award in 1998 and 1999. It was also awarded the *Financial Times* World's Most Respected Company award in 1998 and 1999.

Strategic Initiatives

General Electric's business strategy focuses on four key "Growth Initiatives":

> Globalization
> Services
> Six Sigma Quality
> e-Business

The GE Culture

The core values that provide the foundation for GE's culture are:

> Unyielding integrity
> A passionate focus on customer service
> Insistence on excellence and intolerance for bureaucracy
> Act in a boundaryless fashion (search for and apply the best regardless of their source)
> Prize global intellectual capital and the people that provide it . . . build it to maximize it
> See change for the growth opportunities it brings (i.e., "e-business")
> Create a clear, simple customer-centered vision . . . and continually refresh its execution

> Create an environment of "stretch," excitement, informality and trust improvements . . . and celebrate results
> Demonstrate . . . always with infectious enthusiasm for the customer of GE leadership: the personal energy to welcome and deal with the change . . . the ability to create an atmosphere that energizes others, make difficult decisions . . . and the ability to consistently execute

Business Strategies[75]

The most significant long-term challenge facing GE is how to transform itself into a truly global corporation that embraces the GE culture or "GE Way" (i.e., its value system) throughout all of its businesses, managers, and employees around the world. A major area of focus in achieving this objective has been GE's multitude of businesses throughout Asia. The strategy GE has been implementing in recent years in Asia has emphasized taking GE's universal corporate culture, transplanting it in a range of Asian countries, nurturing the development of local talent, and letting the businesses evolve and grow to suit local market conditions.

Each GE business group possesses a strategic plan for the Asian countries in which it operates. However, GE's overall organizational structure for Asia is based on business needs and not geographic location.

GE maintains a highly centralized organizational structure in terms of the key elements of its business model (e.g., core values, financial targets, performance evaluation and promotion, globalization, six sigma quality). Beyond these issues, GE's system emphasizes adapting business and management practices to local conditions. For example, when GE made acquisitions of such firms as Toho Mutual Life Insurance in Japan, it changed the Japanese company's books to the "GE format" and eliminated the "seniority-based" employment system. The rest of the company, however, tailored much of its strategy and operations to the Japanese market.

GE provides employees in its Asian business units with opportunities to "have a voice" in identifying opportunities for additional revenue growth. For example, one manager at its GE Capital operations in Thailand felt that there was a huge opportunity for the company to finance consumer auto loans. Although Jack Welch was initially skeptical, the employee made a compelling case to support his proposal and it was supported. The bottom line is that many of the best ideas at GE are initiated by lower-level employees.

GE has used American expatriates to staff key positions in Asian operations in the past. However, the company has been sending many of these American expatriates home and replacing them with Asian managers and executives. The rationale for this practice has been to empower local managers who understand their home markets with the authority to manage their businesses effectively. In addition, using expatriates was not viewed as an appropriate strategy for supporting the company's overall globalization strategic initiative.

Results and Future Challenges

So far, General Electric's various Asian businesses have been growing twice as fast as those in other parts of the company. In addition, GE has achieved superior margins in its Asian operations.

According to Jack Welch, one of the most critical challenges facing GE is what he calls the "globalization of intellect." This will require the creation of a system and corporate culture that fully leverage the knowledge and expertise of GE employees in the United States as well as in the diversity of countries where GE does business. One

example of an attempt to move in this direction was the creation of a corporate research and development unit in Bangalore, India, that may eventually employ 1,000 scientists and engineers. The company's only other research and development unit is based in Schenectady, New York, where it employs about 1,600 professionals. Other similar types of actions will be needed if GE is truly serious about realizing its vision of becoming a global corporation.

Discussion Questions

1. Describe the organizational culture at General Electric.
2. Evaluate the effectiveness of the organizational culture at General Electric.
3. What recommendations would you make to Jack Welch regarding how to address the globalization of intellect challenge?
4. In the near future Jack Welch will retire as CEO of GE and will be replaced by Jeffrey Immelt, now head of GE's medical systems business. What recommendations would you make to Immelt in terms of how to handle the challenges facing GE?
5. What are the practical implications of this case for you as a future manager?

http://www.ge.com

VIDEO CASE
CULTURE IN AN ORGANIZATION:
W. B. DONER & CO.

Running Time: 15:30

W. B. Doner & Company is an international advertising agency with offices worldwide. The company, which has won awards for its work for such clients as Red Roof Inns and British Petroleum, prides itself on its creative work. However, as a medium-sized agency in an industry dominated by huge firms, Doner had to develop a unique culture. The video shows Doner CEO Alan Kalter and others as they discuss the nature and purposes of this culture. After viewing the video, answer the following questions:

1. What behaviors does the Doner culture aim to stimulate and enhance?
2. How does Doner's culture contribute to its success?
3. What does Doner look for in employees who would

best "fit" the culture? What sorts of people would be unlikely to fit well in the Doner culture?
4. What are some important characteristics of the Doner culture?
5. What are the core values established by the company's founder, Broad Doner?
6. What are some unacceptable behaviors in the Doner culture?
7. What is the purpose of the Head, Heart, and Funny Bone Award?
8. Based on the Doner experience, what role can a strong culture play in a time of crisis?

CHAPTER *Nine*

SKILLS OBJECTIVES

> To be able to apply self-management principles to enhance personal and work effectiveness.
> To develop skills in dealing with your own stress and in designing and implementing stress management programs for employees.
> To be able to design a protean career.
> To manage key challenges associated with the stages of employee career development.
> To develop skill in fostering career development of women and minorities.
> To develop the ability to be an effective mentor.

KNOWLEDGE OBJECTIVES

> Recognize the need for self-management and the consequences of its use.
> Understand guidelines for behavioral and cognitive self-management.
> Discuss the prevalence and nature of stress, identify key stressors, recognize signs of stress, and understand personal and organizational approaches to managing stress.
> Understand the nature of a career and contrast the protean and traditional careers.
> Discuss career stages in organizations, including associated roles and developmental needs.
> Identify forms of career mobility and discuss how people may "fit" to careers and career mobility patterns.
> Describe ways in which companies are fostering career development of women and minorities.
> Identify stages of the mentoring relationship and discuss the benefits and costs of mentoring for mentors and protégés.

There is an old Chinese curse, "May you live through interesting times." These are certainly interesting times in organizations, and you are about to live through them. Heraclitus wrote in 500 B.C. that "All is flux, nothing stays still" and "Nothing endures but change." These statements are especially true today, as change invades all areas of our lives and at a dramatically accelerating rate. This is one reflection of what Richard Bolles, author of the popular *What Color Is Your Parachute?*—an annual guide to job hunting and career changing—has called a *workquake,* an ongoing restructuring of the world's entire workplace.[1] To survive and prosper in this workquake, you will need to be alert, skilled, and proactive. You will have to learn to take charge of your life, effectively deal with stressors, and actively manage your career. This chapter addresses each of these critical skills. We discuss the need for self-management, consequences of self-management, and guidelines for behavioral and cognitive approaches to self-management. We then examine stress and burnout, including the nature of stress, primary stressors, signs of stress, the characteristics of burnout, and personal and organizational approaches to stress management. Finally, we examine approaches to managing your career. We discuss the protean career, career stages in organizations, fitting people to careers, and guidelines for self-management of careers, and we close with a focus on career issues relating to diversity and mentoring. Together, these sets of skills will prove extremely valuable in the dynamic modern workplace.

Take a few minutes now and complete Self-Assessment 9-1. You will learn more from this chapter if you start off with a good awareness of your beliefs and feelings regarding your personal growth in terms of self-management, stress, and career development.

Self-Assessment 9-1
Attitudes Toward Personal Growth

Please answer the following questions regarding your attitudes toward self-management, careers, and stress. Answer each question as honestly as possible using the response scale that follows.

1 = Disagree Strongly
2 = Disagree Somewhat
3 = Neither Agree nor Disagree
4 = Agree Somewhat
5 = Agree Strongly

1. _____ Organizations generally don't place much value on employees with the ability to work in an autonomous and self-directed manner.
2. _____ A good boss should provide enough guidance and direction so that an employee does not really need self-management skills.
3. _____ Good self-management is basically just a matter of systematically setting goals for oneself.
4. _____ Approximately 33 percent of all visits people make to doctors are related to stress.
5. _____ Employee stress is an internal psychological process that cannot be influenced by management.

DEVIL'S ADVOCATE

I'm still not clear regarding what self-management is and why it's important. Isn't management my boss's job?

A major trend in organizations today is to give lower-level managers and employees more authority to make their own decisions about how to perform their jobs. Sometimes, this is called employee empowerment. Even at the team level, there are new approaches, such as "self-managing work teams," that give employees a lot of work autonomy.

Given this emphasis on autonomy and empowerment, it is even more critical that managers and employees be able to manage themselves effectively. This can be a lot harder than you might think, since many people struggle with going from a situation in which someone else provides a lot of direction and structure for employees to a situation now in which the employees have to figure this out for themselves.

Aren't a fast-paced business world and the high job stress that goes with it part of the "nature of the beast"? Can we do anything about this?

While it is generally true that today's business and work environment are indeed very fast-paced, it is not true that we can't do anything about the stress we experience in relation to that environment. Stress management strategies can help you to better cope with the stress associated with your work situation. This is critical given all the adverse psychological and physiological effects associated with high stress.

Why is it important to take a lifelong view of my career?

A "life cycle" view of careers is important because the career issues and challenges you will face will differ, depending on whether you are in the early, middle, or late stages of your career. The key, even if you are

still in school, is to think long term about your career regarding your goals and the type of work, company, and industry of which you see yourself being a part in the future.

Why should we take so much responsibility for managing our careers? Shouldn't a good employer or my boss be doing that for me?

Well, a good manager or employer (or both) will probably discuss with you or offer you various career opportunities to promote your professional development. However, it is important to take the ultimate responsibility for your career. With very few exceptions, nobody else will care as much about your career as you do. So, you need to be proactive and take the initiative to explore and to identify appropriate job and career opportunities for yourself.

6. _____ Worker stress is important in terms of its impact on employees but has little real financial impact on organizations.

7. _____ The most common cause of worker stress today is working with new technologies on the job.

8. _____ The most important concern of workers who are in the early stages of their careers is job security.

9. _____ The most significant problem for workers in the late stages of their careers is that they reach a point where it is unlikely that they will be promoted any further in their organizations.

10. _____ Mentoring has not been shown to be an effective method for fostering the career development of workers.

As a way to assess your initial level of skill in managing issues related to personal growth in organizations, read the Pre-Test Skills Assessment and develop an action plan for handling this situation. Be as specific as possible in stating your recommendations.

Assessment
Assessment
Assessment
Assessment
Assessment

Pre-Test Skills Assessment
Fostering Personal Growth

You are the head nurse supervisor for the evening shift in the emergency room at a large hospital located in Atlanta, Georgia. You oversee 15 nurses who work from 11 p.m. until 6 p.m. Because the hospital is located in a large city, there is a high volume of patients coming in for various reasons. The work environment is fast-paced, and the workload is tremendous. In fact, some of your nurses have worked double shifts in order to help care for the flow of patients who come into the hospital.

In the last year, the morale of the nurses in the emergency room has plummeted. The absenteeism rate for the night shift has tripled, as many nurses are calling in sick. Turnover has risen to 70 percent per year as well. Some nurses have left for other nursing jobs that provide better working hours, a more reasonable workload, and greater opportunities for personal and professional development. Other nurses have left to pursue careers in different fields. All this comes at a bad time, as there is a national shortage of nurses.

As the supervisor of this work unit, develop an action plan for handling this situation. Be specific and focus on action.

MASTERING SELF-MANAGEMENT

The first-century Roman philosopher, author, and statesman Lucius Annaeus Seneca wrote that, "He is most powerful who has power over himself." As a manager and in other roles in organizations, you must be able to motivate yourself and to teach others this critical skill. *Self-management* is the process of managing oneself. Instead of relying on others to reward and punish, to direct, to set goals, and to provide feedback, we must learn to use these tools to manage our own behavior.

Before reading on, complete Self-Assessment 9-2. It will give you some baseline information as a foundation for your later self-management goals.

Self-Assessment 9-2
Self-Management Attitudes and Practices

Answer each of the questions in this section using the following scale:

1 = Disagree Strongly
2 = Disagree Somewhat
3 = Neither Agree nor Disagree
4 = Agree Somewhat
5 = Agree Strongly

1. _____ I regularly set goals for myself.
2. _____ I keep track of how well I've been doing.
3. _____ I generally keep the resolutions that I make.
4. _____ I often seek feedback about my performance.
5. _____ I am able to focus on positive aspects of my work.
6. _____ I'll sometimes deny myself something I want until I've met my goals.
7. _____ I use a "to do" list to plan my activities.
8. _____ I have trouble working without supervision.

9. _____ When I set my mind on some goal, I persevere until it's accomplished.
10. _____ I'm a self-starter.
11. _____ I make lists of things I need to do.
12. _____ I'm good at time management.
13. _____ I'm usually confident that I can reach my goals.
14. _____ I am careful about how I manage my time.
15. _____ I always plan my day.
16. _____ I often find I spend my time on trivial things and put off doing what's really important.
17. _____ Unless someone pushes me a bit, I have trouble getting motivated.
18. _____ I reward myself when I meet my goals.
19. _____ I tend to dwell on unpleasant aspects of the things I need to do.
20. _____ I tend to deal with life as it comes rather than to try to plan things.
21. _____ I generally try to find a place to work where I'll be free from interruptions.
22. _____ I'm pretty disorganized.
23. _____ The goals I set are quite specific.
24. _____ Distractions often interfere with my performance.
25. _____ I sometimes give myself a treat if I've done something well.
26. _____ I am able to focus on positive aspects of my activities.
27. _____ I use notes or other prompts to remind myself of things I should be doing.
28. _____ I seem to waste a lot of time.
29. _____ I use a day planner or other aids to keep track of schedules and deadlines.
30. _____ I often think about how I can improve my performance.
31. _____ I tend to lose track of the goals I've set for myself.
32. _____ I tend to set difficult goals for myself.
33. _____ I plan things for weeks in advance.
34. _____ I try to make a visible commitment to my goals.
35. _____ I set aside blocks of time for important activities.

In the nearby Voice of Experience, Ann and Jim Cue discuss the challenges and strategies related to self-management.

THE NEED FOR SELF-MANAGEMENT

Self-management is needed particularly when employees are relatively isolated, such as with telecommuting. It may also be useful when supervision is lacking or when employees must be self-directing, as with enriched jobs and self-managed work teams.[2] In such cases, self-management may serve as a potent "substitute for leadership."[3] The movement in organizations toward what some have called *self-organization*—freeing employees to figure out how to get the job done without central planning or control—assumes that employees will have the skills to proactively deal with workplace uncertainties and demands.[4] As we have discussed in other chapters, such companies as General Electric, Xerox, Hallmark, Ben & Jerry's, and Eastman Kodak are abandoning traditional top-down organization and moving toward self-organization.[5]

In addition, self-management may be less expensive than reliance on organizational reward-and-control systems and, once self-management skills have been learned, they are transferable across a vast array of tasks and settings. Finally, self-reinforced behavior is generally maintained more effectively than if it had been externally regulated.[6] In view of all these potential benefits, it

SELF-MANAGEMENT

Ann and Jim Cue,
Multilevel Distributors
Sunrider International

1. What are the most significant challenges you face in managing yourselves in running a Sunrider distributorship?

We are a Multi-Level Distributor for Sunrider International, a major direct marketer of personal health care products. We have approximately 3,000 distributors that operate under our umbrella. In setting up our business operations over 10 years ago, we decided to locate our business office in one section of our home.

One of the biggest challenges we face regarding self-management is the issue of deciding how much time to give to our business. We are the owners of our distributorship so we really don't report to anyone in the Sunrider hierarchy. Given this, we have to decide for ourselves what our business hours will be and how we will operate. It can be really tough trying to figure out exactly where to "draw the line" between your personal and business lives.

A second big challenge we have encountered is deciding how to balance the need to have some structure and formalization in our system versus the need for flexibility. This is especially difficult since we need to set some guidelines for ourselves about procedures or policies for things like ordering products and documenting business transactions. On the other hand, we need the flexibility to be able to handle a wide variety of issues that come up on a day-to-day basis as well as to help us strike some balance between work and family.

2. What kinds of self-management strategies have been effective for you?

Given that our business office is actually part of our home, space management is critical. We keep all our business and personal issues completely separate from each other. For example, we only do business with our distributors in the business area of our home. When the mail comes each day, we physically separate it into work vs. personal piles and put them in different parts of the house. We have two computers—one for all of our Sunrider business and the other for personal stuff.

We have learned that you must have some formal policies and procedures so that you ensure that key tasks get accomplished and you have time for your personal life. For example, we have created policies for ourselves that specify that we will not do business on Sundays and that the deadline for our distributors to place orders is 2 p.m. on the Thursday of each week

Ongoing planning meetings are absolutely critical for us to manage ourselves. Every Monday morning, we hold a planning session where we set goals for the week and a list of things to do. This is the basis for focusing our time and effort throughout the week. Every three months or so, we hold a planning meeting that focuses more on the overall direction and long-term goals of our business.

We feel that a big part of self-management is rewarding yourself for your accomplishments. When we meet or exceed our sales goals for a given period of time, we make a point of doing something to reward ourselves (e.g., buying new software for our personal computer).

3. What kinds of advice would you give students regarding the best ways to develop self-management skills?

First of all, recognize that this is not common sense and it is not easy to do. You must become a master of the fundamental skills of goal setting, time management, and self-motivation. Take courses, read books, or go to seminars to learn these critical skills. It's not enough to just learn these skills, though. You must actually apply these principles and make them work in terms of your job. How can you do this? Write the key principles of success down on a piece of paper and post it in a place where you will see it every day. Think about how everything you do in your job can be related back to these principles. The bottom line here is to keep these principles visual and salient for yourself.

http://www.sunrider.com

isn't surprising that self-management is often presented as a distinguishing characteristic of "best" and "most admired" firms.[7] It's also no surprise that self-motivation is among the key characteristics sought by employers.

CONSEQUENCES OF SELF-MANAGEMENT

Self-management works. Early evidence came from clinical settings, where self-management techniques have been very successful in programs dealing with weight loss, smoking cessation, and phobia reduction.[8] In academic settings, they have led to improved study habits and enhanced academic performance. In organizational settings, they have reduced absenteeism, increased satisfaction with work, enhanced commitment to the organization, and improved task performance.[9]

FORMS OF SELF-MANAGEMENT

There are two broad approaches to self-management. The first, termed *behavioral self-management,* is to learn to manage our own behaviors, deciding what we want to achieve and setting up appropriate systems of goals, rewards, and controls. The second, termed *cognitive self-management,* involves the development of effective thinking patterns. These approaches can best be used together to achieve effective and satisfying patterns of thought and behavior.

GUIDELINES FOR BEHAVIORAL SELF-MANAGEMENT

Here are concrete steps to take to change or maintain behaviors:

> *Pinpoint* the specific behavior you want to change or maintain. One way to do this is through self-observation. You may decide, for instance, that you are working on jobs that you should delegate to others, that you need to lose weight, or that you spend too much time chatting with people who walk into your office.

> Set *specific* goals for behavioral change. As we discussed in Chapter 6, effective goals should be specific, difficult, and measurable. Further, if the goals are to be effective, our acceptance of and commitment to them must be sincere. Some specific goals might include:
> • Exercise at least four days a week for at least 30 minutes per day.[10]
> • Spend at least two hours with my children every evening.
> • Quit smoking for three months.

> **Keep track** of the frequency, duration, and any other dimensions of interest, such as the time and place at which the behavior occurs. Use diaries, graphs, or timing devices as needed. Sometimes, self-monitoring itself is sufficient to change the behavior. For instance, if you really identify how much time you spend watching television, you may simply watch less. Here are some examples of monitoring techniques:
> • Weigh in once a week at the gym.
> • Each time I eat fast food, write down what I ate and how much the meal cost me.
> • Write on my Daytimer what time I arrive at school each day.
> • Put project due dates on a calendar and track what has been done for projects each week leading up to the due date.

> **Modify cues.** Sometimes the behavior we want to change is preceded by other events that serve as cues or signals for the behavior. By altering or controlling the cues, you may be able to change the behavior. For example, you may find that you can't get your work done because you're constantly answering the phone. A solution might be to activate your voice mail or have an assistant hold calls. Or, you may increase desired behaviors by as simple a prompt as a to-do list. Some cue modifications might include:

- Plan a menu for the week ahead.
- Bring my work-out clothes to school so I can work out immediately after class.
- Eat small meals throughout the day so I don't get very hungry and "pig out."
- Study on the second floor of the library so I don't see my friends who study on the first floor.
- Keep low-fat snacks in my office so I don't get snack food from the vending machine.

> **Modify consequences.** This can involve self-reward or self-punishment (or both). You might, for example, reward yourself for quitting smoking by spending the savings on purchases of musical CDs. Or, you may decide that you'll skip a concert if you don't meet your goal. Here are some consequences that may serve as rewards or punishments:

- Each time I complete a project before it's due, I'll buy myself a new CD.
- If I get up on time, I can have my favorite breakfast (raspberry toaster strudel).
- I will award myself four hours of "free time" on Sunday night to spend having fun if I complete all my tasks.
- I will save the money I would have spent on cigarettes for six months and apply it to a trip to Negril, Jamaica.
- I will have pictures of me with a flabby belly if I don't keep up my exercise routine.

Some consequences, such as the CD purchase, are relatively immediate whereas others, such as the trip to Jamaica, must wait until the behavior has been exhibited for a lengthy period of time. It is generally best to use a combination of such consequences, such as a reward for each week you don't smoke with a longer-term reward, such as the Jamaica trip.

> **Reorder behavior.** We often do relatively enjoyable tasks in order to put off others we don't care for. As a result, the things we put off may never get done or may get done poorly. To prevent this, make pleasant behaviors depend on completion of the noxious task. For instance, if you enjoy reading your mail but find writing reports to be unpleasant, put off reading the mail until you have finished the project reports. Here are further examples:

- Exercise before dinner rather than after.
- Make lunch the night before, rather than in the morning as I usually do, and read the paper in the morning, so I'll be sure to have lunch.
- Eat my vegetables before I eat the meat. This way, I should be more full before I eat the meat.

> Write a *contract* with yourself (see Skills Practice 9-1 for a sample contract). In the contract, specify the behavior you will change, the length of the contract, how you will monitor progress, the rewards or punishments you will use, and so on. Write the contract clearly and post it in a conspicuous spot. Have others witness the contract, sign it, and agree to help to monitor your behaviors.

> *Rehearse.* Physically or mentally practice activities before you actually perform them. Rehearsal may suggest that you should rethink your goals.

> *Check* your progress on a regular basis. If you're not doing as well as you'd like, take corrective action, such as changing prompts or rewards or making sure that you are rewarding yourself promptly.

> Plan strategies to *maintain* a successful change. If not, you may fall back into your old habits. But don't become wedded to the same system of rewards and punishments on which you relied to bring about the change. Consider something such as a maintenance diet or give yourself a bit more slack regarding leisure activities.

Use Skills Practice 9-1 to apply self-management to your own behaviors. Try it first with a behavior that you can easily observe and in which you may quickly see results, such as an exercise schedule or a program to cut down on distractions at work. Then, apply it to a longer-term goal, such as learning a new skill. Once you master these techniques, you can draw on them to help with almost any task.

Skills Practice 9-1
Applying Self-Management

Skill Level: Basic

Skill Objective
To apply behavioral self-management to two behaviors.

Procedure
Apply the self-management guidelines we have discussed to your own behaviors. Start by pinpointing two behaviors you would like to change. One of these should be short term, such as your physical exercise or eating habits or time spent on the telephone during the next week. The other should be for a longer period, such as the amount of work you will take home at night over the next six months. For each pinpointed behavior, go through the steps we have discussed. It may help to have friends or colleagues provide support with the self-management process. For example, they may sign your contract and check on a regular basis to see that you are maintaining the desired behaviors.

1. *Self-analysis*
    A. Pinpointing
        (i)   What is a short-term behavior you would like to change?
        (ii) What is a longer-term behavior you would like to change?
    B. Self-set goals: For each of the selected behaviors, set a specific goal.
    C. Self-monitoring: How do you plan to monitor each of these behaviors?
2. *Modifying antecedents:* For each of the behaviors to be changed, identify events that precede and serve as cues or signals for the behavior and which might be altered. For

example, if leaving your door open leads to your spending excessive time talking with friends, you might keep your door closed. If you smoke when in certain settings, you might want to avoid those settings.

3. *Modifying consequences:* What rewards or punishments will you use to alter each of the behaviors identified?

4. *Reordering of behavior:* For each behavior, identify one or more ways that reordering of behaviors may help. For example, if you put off an unpleasant task until you have completed more pleasant tasks, can you change the order so that the pleasant task becomes a reward for completion of the unpleasant task?

5. *Contracting:* For each of the behaviors you have selected, write a brief contract specifying the behavior to be changed, how you will monitor the behaviors, what rewards and punishments you will use to encourage desired behaviors, and so on. In addition, if feasible, identify an individual or individuals who might help to monitor the behaviors. A contract follows for your use with the short-term behavior you have chosen. Develop a similar contract for your selected long-term behavior.

6. *Evaluating program effectiveness*

7. *Maintaining the desired change:* How will you know whether your behavioral change program was effective? If your change attempts aren't initially successful, what steps will you take? Also, how do you plan to maintain the desired behaviors once they are attained?

Web Wise

Self-Management at W. L. Gore

W. L. Gore & Associates has been in business for more than 40 years and has more than $1.25 billion in annual global sales. While some large, mature firms might become bureaucratic and rigid, Gore has maintained a remarkable record of creativity and innovation. Ranked in the top 10 of the "100 Best Companies to Work for in America," Gore is best known for its GORE-TEX fabrics but has products in hundreds of markets and locales. For instance, the company has advanced the science of regenerating tissues destroyed by disease or traumatic injuries, developed next-generation materials for printed circuit boards and fiber optics, and pioneered new methods to detect and control environmental pollution. Gore was a pioneer in worker autonomy and self-management. Read Gore's philosophy regarding these issues on its website at:

http://www.gore.com/

SELF-MANAGEMENT CONTRACT
Short-Term Behavior

Effective Dates: From _____ to _____

The following behavior will be monitored by: _____

Behavior: _____

Monitoring will occur: _____
(when or in what situations)

Whenever _____ ***occurs at*** _____
(behavior)   (specified level)

_____ ***will award*** _____
(self or other)   (consequence)

Whenever the behavior does not occur at the specified level, the following consequence will occur: _____

Contract may be revised on: _____
(date)

Signatures: _____

_____

_____

The nearby Bottom Line presents a process model that summarizes the basic steps associated with implementation of the self-management process.

B O T T O M   L I N E

The Bottom Line: The Self-Management Process

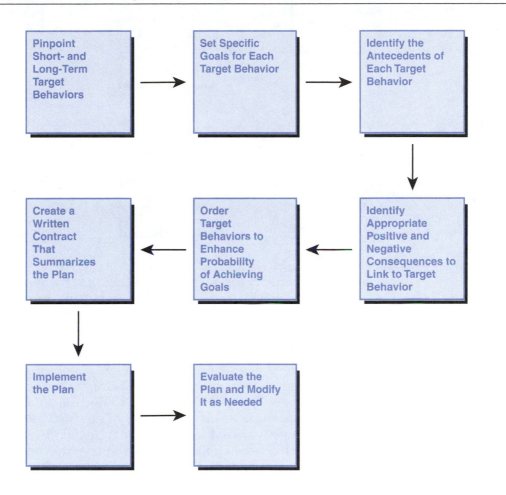

- Pinpoint Short- and Long-Term Target Behaviors
- Set Specific Goals for Each Target Behavior
- Identify the Antecedents of Each Target Behavior
- Identify Appropriate Positive and Negative Consequences to Link to Target Behavior
- Order Target Behaviors to Enhance Probability of Achieving Goals
- Create a Written Contract That Summarizes the Plan
- Implement the Plan
- Evaluate the Plan and Modify It as Needed

COGNITIVE-FOCUSED STRATEGIES FOR SELF-MANAGEMENT

Behavioral self-management works best when accompanied by effective thinking, as shown in Figure 9-1.[11] One step to effective thinking is to physically and mentally redesign tasks to make them more naturally rewarding. This involves creating ways to do tasks so that the enjoyment of performing the task itself creates significant natural reward value. Natural rewards come from performing tasks in a way that allows us to experience a sense of competence, a sense of self-control, and a sense of purpose. In addition, effective thinking is fostered by establishment of constructive and effective habits of thinking, such as "opportunity thinking" as opposed to "obstacle thinking." By studying and managing our beliefs and assumptions, we can start to develop the ability to find opportunities in new work challenges. Use of mental imagery tech-

FIGURE 9-1
Strategies That Promote Effective Thinking

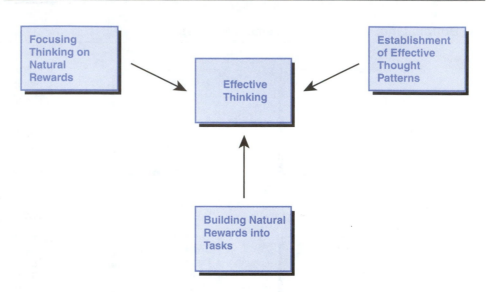

niques and positive internal self-talk aids this process. Effective, positive thinking patterns are necessary for successful self-management and are also helpful for effectively dealing with stress, the topic to which we turn next.[12]

MANAGING STRESS AND BURNOUT

Why care about stress? It is a cause of psychological problems as well as physical reactions, such as ulcers, high blood pressure, backaches, and heart disease; an estimated 75 to 90 percent of visits to doctors are somehow stress-related.[13] Stress is associated with high levels of dissatisfaction, absenteeism, turnover, lost productivity, and lawsuits. It may also result in a climate that stifles creativity. It has been implicated in workplace violence and employee suicide.[14] Total stress-related costs to U.S. business are estimated at $200 to $300 billion annually.[15]

The Microsoft Lexicon is an online "compilation of slang peculiar to the Microsoft working environment." Here is the lexicon's definition of "Death March":

Death March: The long, lingering final countdown to a ship date, involving 16–25-hour days, catnaps on couches, and plenty of "flat food" (food, mostly from vending machines, that you can slip under people's doors so they can keep working).

While the term "death march" is used in a tongue-in-cheek fashion at Microsoft to refer to the stress of meeting looming deadlines, stress is, in fact, a very real killer. Let's consider the nature of stress and methods to recognize and manage stress at both a personal and an organizational level.

Take a few minutes now to complete Self-Assessment 9-3. It will provide you with information about the degree to which you currently experience symptoms of stress.

GLOBAL PERSPECTIVES

KAROSHI

Karoshi, three Japanese characters that literally mean "excessive," "labor," and "death," is a term given by the Japanese to sudden death from heart attack or stroke induced by job stress.* Japanese work, on average, 225 hours, or six work-weeks, more per year than their American counterparts. One in six male Japanese workers puts in more than 3,100 hours annually—or about 60 hours a week, 52 weeks a year. Their overwork is driven in part by employers' demands and expected loyalty to the company and by the weakness of Japan's labor unions and the country's strong work ethic. It appears that karoshi results primarily from feelings of depression and helplessness combined with over-work. Karoshi is now recognized by the Japanese government as a cause of death under the country's worker compensation law. Dentsu, Japan's largest advertising agency, was ordered to pay the equivalent of $1.2 million to the family of Ichiro Oshima, an employee who killed himself after working exceptionally long hours. In the eight months before his death, Oshima, a radio-commercial planner, had worked from early in the morning until well past 2 a.m. for 105 days and beyond 4 p.m. for 49 days. While only about 75 Japanese per year have been for-mally identified under the law as suc-cumbing to karoshi, some estimates place karoshi deaths at 10,000 to 30,000 annually, with tens of thou-sands of others suffering serious physical and mental health conse-quences. Recognizing the dangers of karoshi, the Japanese Labor Ministry has asked the Japan Federation of Employers' Associations, Nikkerien, to join in efforts to prevent stress-death, in part through reduced over-time demands. In addition, Japan's prime minister has proposed legisla-tion aimed at encouraging Japan's citizens to reduce their work hours and to take more holidays.

*This section is based on K. L. Miller, "Now, Japan Is Admitting It: Work Kills Executives," *Business Week,* August 3, 1992, p. 35; S. Arai, "Rethinking Japan's Work Ethic," *Japan 21st,* June 1994, p. 25; Z. Abdoolcarim, "Executive Stress: A Company Killer," *Asian Business,* August 1995, pp. 22–26; P. Smith, "Tougher Than the Rest," *Management,* March 1998, pp. 42–47; and S. Long, "Culture of Long Hours Inexcusable," *Australian Financial Review,* October 20, 1999, p. 19.

Self-Assessment 9-3
Tension and Anxiety

Answer each of the questions in this section using the following scale:

1 = Disagree Strongly
2 = Disagree Somewhat
3 = Neither Agree nor Disagree
4 = Agree Somewhat
5 = Agree Strongly

1. _____ I have trouble relaxing at home.
2. _____ My workload is under control.
3. _____ I use alcohol or other drugs to help me relax.
4. _____ I have trouble sleeping.
5. _____ When I get up in the morning, I look forward to the day.
6. _____ I feel nervous under pressure.
7. _____ I have a constant fear of failure.
8. _____ I feel short-tempered and irritable.
9. _____ I find myself being angry with people I care about.
10. _____ At the end of the day, I usually have a sense of accomplishment.
11. _____ I find fault with all sorts of things.
12. _____ I don't find much pleasure in life.

13. _____ I haven't been happy lately.
14. _____ I'm not exercising as much as I used to.
15. _____ I often feel extreme irritation over small things.
16. _____ I look forward to meeting new people and doing new things.
17. _____ I often feel hounded, cornered, or trapped.
18. _____ I lack energy.
19. _____ I often feel that I just can't cope.
20. _____ I sometimes have feelings of hopelessness.
21. _____ I am unable to stop thinking about my problems.
22. _____ I often feel preoccupied and indecisive.
23. _____ My muscles often feel tense and "achy."
24. _____ I often feel that I can't do anything right.
25. _____ I engage in a variety of pleasant hobbies and other activities.

THE NATURE OF STRESS

As shown in Figure 9-2, three concepts—stressors, stress, and stress reactions—must be considered when trying to effectively deal with stress.

Stressors are environmental factors (deadlines, noise, rules, demanding bosses, and the like) that raise stress levels. *Stress* is a physiological state resulting from stressors.

As shown in Figure 9-3, when faced with stressors, our body undergoes a complex set of reactions aimed at preparing us to be able to effectively engage in "fight or flight"—striking back at the stressor or escaping it.

Finally, as we discuss later in the chapter, *stress reactions* are mental and physical responses to stress.

While the processes involved in stress may be effective in countering immediate threats, they also burden the body's resources. Hans Selye has described a *general adaptation syndrome* of the body's responses to a stressor. As shown in Figure 9-4, there are three stages to the general adaptation syndrome. First, in the alarm stage, the body "gears up" for action. Then, in the resistance stage, the body tries to fight back at the stressor. Finally, in the exhaustion stage, the body's resources are drained, and resistance is no longer possible.

STRESS REACTIONS

As suggested by the general adaptation syndrome, not all stress is bad; stress may help us to prepare for a challenge. However, prolonged exposure to stressors may be debilitating. As shown in Figure 9-5, at low levels stress is an activating force, called *eustress* from the Greek "eu", meaning good. However, excessive levels of stress, called *distress,* have negative consequences. Most employees already face at least moderate levels of stress. American doctors

F I G U R E   9 - 2
Concepts Involved in Stress Management

FIGURE 9-3
Physiological Reactions in Stress

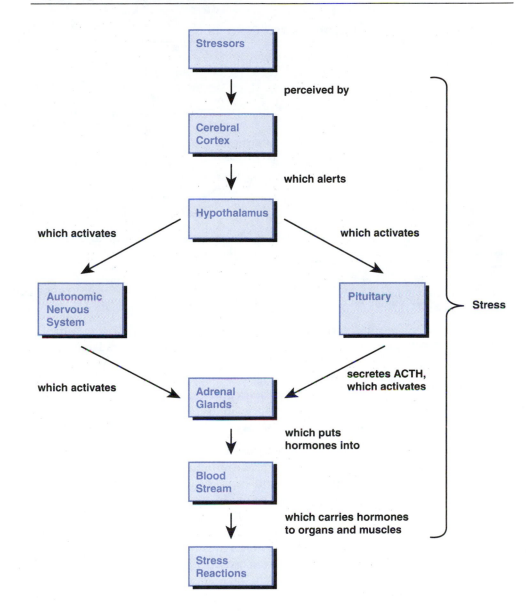

FIGURE 9-4
The General Adaptation Syndrome

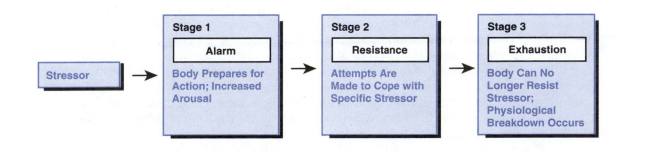

FIGURE 9-5
Eustress and Distress

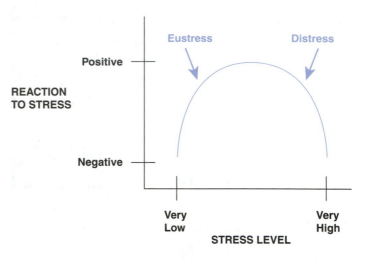

write 25 million prescriptions a year for sedatives such as Valium.[16] So, almost any increase in organizational stressors is likely to cause distress.

STRESSORS

Almost anything can be a stressor: job insecurity, poor working conditions, excessive responsibility, job loss, office politics, family concerns, and so on. In this section, we consider some primary stressors.

Work Environment   The key stressors faced by our early ancestors came from the physical environment, such as hostile weather, threatening animals, and uncertain food supplies. While civilization has expanded the range of stressors, the work environment continues to provide challenges. For instance, some jobs are by their nature risky. In the United States, commercial fishing is the most dangerous job, with Alaskan crab fishing topping the list; in recent years, it has had an average of one injury per employee per year (a figure rendered more remarkable by the fact that the crab-fishing season lasts only a few weeks), and the fatal accident rate is 100 times the national average.[17] Police work, fire fighting, and timber cutting are other highest-risk jobs.

Many other jobs pose subtler dangers, such as prolonged noise, glaring or inadequate lighting, excessive temperature variations, poor air quality, or required repetitive motions. For instance, building-related illness and sick building syndrome[18] are now being cited as major stressors. After the energy crisis of the 1970s, buildings were made "tight." Windows were sealed in commercial buildings, and the buildings became solely dependent on mechanical ventilation to supply heating, cooling, and humidity. Now, mildew, fungi, viruses, and bacteria abound, as do chemicals from carpet, paint, photocopier toner, radon and its decay products, and many other contaminants.[19] Now, indoor air is much more seriously polluted than outdoor air in even the largest and most industrialized cities.[20] Building-related illness and sick building syndrome have been implicated in respiratory/lung problems; asthma; stroke; eye, ear, nose, and throat irritation; headaches, dizziness, and fatigue; emphysema; heart disease; cancer; organ damage; and acute toxicity.[21]

Interpersonal Conflict We have all encountered people with whom we simply can't get along; we find them to be somehow offensive or irritating. Generally, we try to avoid such people. In the workplace, though, we may have coworkers, subordinates, or even superiors whom we can't stand and with whom we must deal on a daily basis—and may have to do so for years into the future. Worse, we may have to depend on such people for our jobs, salary increases, promotions, or other things. It's not surprising that this can serve as a very debilitating stressor.[22]

Specific Job Demands By their nature, managerial jobs and many other jobs in organizations require specific activities that may be stressors for many people. For instance, the manager's job is full of demands to communicate with individuals or groups. When people are asked to list their greatest fears, death usually shows up somewhere in the top five.[23] For many people, public speaking is at the top rung on the fear ladder. The thought of standing in front of others, possibly looking nervous, boring the audience, being laughed at, or saying something foolish paralyzes many people. Generally, audience members aren't aware of a speaker's stage fright, and nervousness may actually enhance the vitality and enthusiasm brought to the situation.[24] Nevertheless, the stress induced by the fear of speaking is very real.

Emotional Labor Imagine you are in a bad time in your life. Perhaps a loved one has died or your child has a chronic illness or you're concerned about the emotional health of a friend. Suppose, too, that you have to go to work every day during those hard times and that your job demands that you be upbeat; you must smile at customers, greet them enthusiastically, interact with them warmly, and leave them with the admonition to "have a nice day." Such work requires *emotional labor,* the required public display of emotions that employees may not privately feel.[25] The consequences of this emotional labor include a deadened emotional state, burnout, and loss of "voice." [26]

Life Events Another stressor is life change (or even imagined change).[27] Our bodies see changes, whether good or bad, as stressors requiring some reaction. As shown in Figure 9-6, many common organizational actions—geographical reassignments, promotions, early retirements, reprimands, firings—can have tremendous cumulative life impacts. Note that the stressors listed in Figure 9-6 aren't all "bad." Even desirable changes, such as a promotion or vacation, are stress-inducing. Research shows that people experiencing very high levels of life change as measured by this scale experienced much higher levels of stress and were more likely to have health problems than were those with low levels of life change.[28]

Hassles While "big" things, such as deaths and disasters, are clearly stress-inducing, so are daily hassles. Such things as a troublesome neighbor, home renovations, a long daily commute, financing children's education, and even dealing with a malfunctioning teller machine can all add to one's stress levels.[29] What these things lack in severity they make up in frequency.

Web Wise

Toastmasters

Toastmasters International is an organization dedicated to helping people to develop better listening, thinking, and speaking skills. At Toastmasters, members learn by speaking to groups and working with others in a supportive environment. A typical Toastmasters club is made up of 20 to 30 people who meet once a week for about an hour. Each meeting gives everyone an opportunity to practice various activities:

> Conducting meetings. Meetings usually begin with a short business session that helps members learn basic meeting procedures.

> Giving impromptu speeches. Members present one- to two-minute impromptu speeches on assigned topics.

> Presenting prepared speeches. Three or more members present speeches based on projects from the Toastmasters International Communication and Leadership Program manuals. Projects cover such topics as speech organization, voice, language, gestures, and persuasion.

> Offering constructive evaluation. Every prepared speaker is assigned an evaluator who points out speech strengths and offers suggestions for improvement.

Visit the Toastmasters site at:

http://www.toastmasters.org/

FIGURE 9-6
Stressful Life Events

Event	Relative Stressfulness
Death of a spouse	100
Divorce	73
Marital separation	65
Jail term	63
Death of a close family member	63
Personal injury or illness	53
Marriage	50
Firing from a job	47
Retirement	45
Pregnancy	40
Death of a close friend	37
Son or daughter leaving home	29
Trouble with in-laws	28
Trouble with boss	23
Change in residence	20
Vacation	13
Christmas	12
Minor violations of the law	11

Role Stressors Jobs with conflicting expectations (called *role conflict*) or unclear expectations (called *role ambiguity*) about what an employee is supposed to do at work serve as major stressors. Role conflict and role ambiguity have been shown to lead to dissatisfaction, absenteeism, turnover, poor performance, and a host of other undesirable outcomes.

Role ambiguity occurs when people:

> lack clear information about what they are expected to accomplish;
> know what outcomes are expected but don't know how to achieve those outcomes; or
> don't know what personal costs or benefits are associated with meeting particular expectations.

Role conflict may take many forms:

> **Intersender role conflict** results from conflicting expectations of different role senders. For example, supervisors sometimes find that their subordinates expect them to identify with labor while their superiors expect them to see themselves as part of management.
> **Intrasender role conflict** occurs when a single role sender transmits incompatible expectations. This might occur, for instance, if a boss says to place more emphasis on quality while at the same time demanding greater quantity.
> **Inter-role conflict** comes about through incompatible demands of different roles. A person's role as operations manager of a company that

needs wetlands to expand production capacity may conflict with her role as officer of a local conservation group.[30]

> **Person-role conflict** results from clashes between role demands and personal values and expectations. A police officer who is called on to evict an aging tenant, or a manager who must fire loyal employees because of budget cuts may experience person-role conflict. Or, consider shelter workers at the ASPCA. People are drawn to work at the shelters because they love animals, but they must often kill young, healthy animals. It's not surprising that shelter workers suffer a wide range of distressing reactions, including grief, anger, nightmares, and depression.[31]

In addition, when the level or nature of job demands is inconsistent with an employee's capabilities and interests, *role overload* or *role underload* may occur. As shown in Figure 9-7, either role overload or role underload may be quantitative or qualitative. We may be overwhelmed with too much to do (quantitative overload) or bored with too little to do (quantitative underload). Similarly, we may be frustrated by being given types of tasks that are beyond our capabilities (qualitative overload) or by being faced with simple, tedious, perhaps demeaning work (qualitative underload).

Responsibility for Others It is often stressful enough to have to take care of ourselves. When we must also accept responsibility for the welfare of others, the level of our stressors escalates. Managers may feel responsible for the welfare of their subordinates and mentors for the welfare of their protégés. Similarly, employees may have to care for children at home or for elderly relatives. The latter set of responsibilities—called *eldercare*—is a growing problem both for employees and employers. A study by the American Association of Retired Persons found that people with heavy eldercare responsibilities reported feelings of depression about six times the national average.[32]

Dealing with Others' Stress: The Toxic Handlers In the Martin Scorsese movie "Bringing Out the Dead," Nicholas Cage plays a New York paramedic working the graveyard shift in Hell's Kitchen.[33] The nightly horrors of his job take an exhausting toll on his life; he cannot bring himself to eat, and his sleep is haunted by visions of a young woman who died as he tried to revive her. Cage's character is one form of *toxic handler,* someone who must regularly

F I G U R E   9 - 7
Role Overload and Underload

| | | Nature of Mismatch | |
		Work Amount	Work Type
Level of Mismatch	Insufficient	Quantitative Underload	Qualitative Underload
	Excessive	Quantitative Overload	Qualitative Overload

deal with the sorrows and ill fortune of others as part of the job. Many managers in organizations also are toxic handlers, voluntarily shouldering the sadness, frustration, bitterness, and anger of others to help the organization to accomplish its goals.[34]

PERSONAL INFLUENCES ON STRESS

Some people "bounce back" better in the face of stressors than do others. These resilient individuals tend to share some personality characteristics, including low levels of the type A behavior pattern, high levels of hardiness and optimism, and rapid tension discharge rate.

> **Type A behavior pattern.** As we discussed in Chapter 3, the *type A behavior pattern* is characterized by feelings of great time pressure and impatience. Type A persons work aggressively, speak explosively, and find themselves constantly struggling. The opposite pattern—relaxed, steady-paced, and easygoing—is called the *type B behavior pattern.* The type A is much more likely than the type B to experience high stress levels and to suffer negative stress reactions, including fatal heart attacks. It appears that one dimension of type A behavior—hostility—is the key culprit in leading to negative stress reactions.

> **Hardiness.** Hardy individuals have high levels of commitment to their jobs, believe they can control their outcomes, and see stress as a challenge. These three components of commitment, control, and challenge combine to provide resistance to the adverse effects of stress.

> **Tension discharge rate.** Suppose your boss has humiliated you in front of your coworkers, blaming you for the department's failure to meet a critical deadline. You feel the missed deadline is the boss's fault but know you can't strike back at him. Instead, you keep quiet, silently seething. What then? Would you continue to dwell on this injustice, replaying it in your mind and getting more and more angry, or would you be able to "let it go"? Those who can let it go—who have high *tension discharge rates*—deal better with stress.[35]

> **Optimism.** Someone has said, "Whether you believe you can succeed or that you can't, you're right." Life is often a self-fulfilling prophecy. People who believe things will turn out well are more self-confident, set higher personal goals, adopt problem-focused coping styles, persist in the face of difficulties, and generate enthusiasm in others. As a result, they do better than those who anticipate bad outcomes. Optimists assume their troubles are temporary ("I'm tired today") rather than permanent ("I'm washed up") and specific ("I have a bad habit") rather than universal ("I'm a bad person"). Also, they give themselves credit when things go right and often externalize their failures ("That was a tough audience" rather than "I gave a bad speech").[36]

SIGNS OF STRESS

There are many signs of stress. They include:

> Trouble in concentrating.
> Working excessively but not effectively.
> Feeling that you've lost perspective on what's important in life.

F I G U R E   9 - 8
Major Components of Burnout

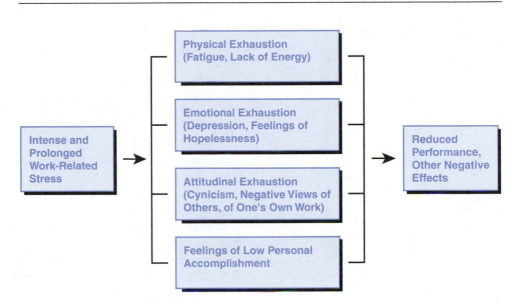

> Angry outbursts.
> Changes in sleeping patterns.
> Loss of interest in social and recreational activities.
> Prolonged fatigue.
> Increases in smoking, drinking, and eating.
> A feeling that you just can't face the day.

BURNOUT

The constellation of stress reactions is sometimes called *burnout. Burnout* is a process of emotional exhaustion, depersonalization, and diminished accomplishment, with low job satisfaction and a reduced sense of competence.[37] As shown in Figure 9-8, there are four major components to burnout: physical exhaustion, emotional exhaustion, attitudinal exhaustion, and feelings of low personal accomplishment.

Now, complete Self-Assessment 9-4: Coping with Stress. It will help to identify the ways you tend to deal with stressful situations. We address coping styles later in this section.

Self-Assessment 9-4
Coping with Stress

Answer each of the questions in this section using the following scale:

1 = Disagree Strongly
2 = Disagree Somewhat
3 = Neither Agree nor Disagree
4 = Agree Somewhat
5 = Agree Strongly

When I am faced with a stressful situation, I:

1. _____ Do my best to get out of the situation gracefully.
2. _____ Try to address the situation directly and promptly.
3. _____ Try to get additional people involved in the situation.
4. _____ Tell myself that I can probably work things out to my advantage.
5. _____ Avoid being in this situation if I can.
6. _____ Try to see this situation as an opportunity to learn and develop new skills.
7. _____ Work on changing the things that caused this situation.
8. _____ Try to think of myself as a winner—as someone who always comes through.
9. _____ Try to be very organized so I can keep up on things.
10. _____ Turn to others for support.
11. _____ Tell myself that time takes care of situations like this.
12. _____ Ask others to help out.
13. _____ Separate myself as much as possible from the people who created this situation.
14. _____ Remind myself that other people have been in this situation and that I can probably do as well as they did.
15. _____ Seek help or advice from friends or colleagues.
16. _____ Think of ways to use this situation to show what I can do.
17. _____ Work hard to resolve it.
18. _____ Request help from other people who have the power to do something for me.
19. _____ Devote more time and energy to dealing with the situation.
20. _____ Accept the situation because there is nothing I can do to change it.

GUIDELINES FOR MANAGING PERSONAL STRESS

What can you do about stress?

> **Take it seriously.** Act as if stress is a matter of life and death—because it is.

> **Manage your time.** Here are some guidelines for time management:[38]

  • **Conduct a time analysis.** Make a list of all the routine activities you perform and record the time you spend on each activity. After a month, add up the totals and see what things are making the greatest demands on your time. You'll probably find time-consuming activities that can be trimmed.[39]

  • **Set priorities and plan a time budget.** Schedule activities, being sure to leave some slack time (perhaps 10 to 15 percent of your time) for unexpected emergencies and opportunities. Plan your work and work your plan.

  • **Schedule leisure activities.** Build time into your schedule for relaxation and recuperation. If not, they'll be driven out by other things.

  • **Ask which tasks can be curtailed.** Categorize tasks in terms of their urgency and importance. Sort mail and other tasks into A = urgent and important; B = not urgent but important; C = urgent but not important; and D = neither urgent nor important. Focus on your *A*s and *B*s.

  • **Try to accumulate similar tasks and handle them together.** For instance, set aside one block of time to write letters, another to return phone calls, and so on.

- **Learn to say no.** Trying to do everything for everyone will hurt both you and others. Unless you learn to say no, you'll be overwhelmed, and the work you do will suffer.
- **Don't procrastinate.** Procrastination may be the single most common time management problem. Apply self-management tools to overcome tendencies to procrastinate.[40]
- **Learn to delegate.** Often, we are overwhelmed because we are reluctant to pass on work to others. Delegating work is a key component of effective management. It permits you to help to develop team members' skills while concentrating on matters of importance.[41]

> **Develop effective coping strategies.** People cope with stress in very different ways. Some "run away" from stressors, either physically or mentally. Some turn to colleagues or friends for help. Others roll up their sleeves and do their best to deal with the stressor. Still others re-think the stressors, finding ways to view them as opportunities. And some turn to alcohol or other drugs to ease the pain. In general, coping strategies that deal directly with the stressor work better than those that rely on avoidance or treatment of symptoms.[42]

> **Get fit and stay fit.** Exercise reduces tension and strengthens the cardiovascular system. Physically fit individuals are better able to master stressful situations.

> **Let it go.** As we said earlier, people who have high tension discharge rates (i.e., who can quickly "let go" of a stressful situation) suffer fewer negative stress reactions. Letting go of stress is often difficult. If someone has cut us off in traffic or yelled at us at work, we often continue to stew about it. The more we do this, though, the worse we feel and the greater the likely health consequences. While it's hard to "let it go," we can at least tell ourselves that the longer we dwell on the stressor, the more we let the person or thing that is bothering us "win." Living well is the best revenge.

> **Get a little help from your friends.** Individuals who have the support of colleagues, friends, families, and loved ones experience far fewer symptoms of stress than do those without social support. Social support helps in at least two ways. First, it can directly reduce the impact of stress by fulfilling critical human needs, such as security and social contact, and by emphasizing positive life and work aspects, such as affiliation and approval. Social support may also buffer the impact of stressors, since members of the social support network provide resources to help the individual cope with them.[43] If you are lacking social support, seek it out. Work on friendships, keep family ties strong, and find a place to belong: Social groups, churches or synagogues, and local support organizations are possibilities.

> **Think positively.** Don't dwell on the worst possible scenario. Treat a stressful situation as an opportunity to show your skills and abilities.

> **Learn to relax.** Such relaxation techniques as the relaxation response and transcendental meditation have been shown to reduce muscle tension, heart rate, and blood pressure. Such techniques may entail selecting a quiet setting, sitting comfortably with closed eyes, and repeating a sound or phrase, or they may involve muscle relaxation techniques.

Web Wise

Dale Carnegie Training

Dale Carnegie's book, *How to Win Friends and Influence People*, inspired generations of salespeople and others with its messages about the power of positive thinking. Dale Carnegie Training teaches selling and public speaking skills and continues to publish *How to Win Friends and Influence People* and *How to Stop Worrying and Start Living* and other books. It has more than 4 million graduates, 2,700 professional instructors, and courses in 70 countries and 20 languages. Check out its website at:

http://www.dale-carnegie.com/

> **Manage change.** Avoid unnecessary change and think through the cumulative impact of planned changes.
> **Avoid self-medication.** Those who deal with stress by treating its symptoms—especially by use of alcohol or other drugs—often find themselves in a downward spiral.[44]
> **Practice self-management.** The self-management techniques discussed at the beginning of this chapter can effectively be applied to stress management. You could, for instance, use self-management to modify stressors, build social support networks, improve coping styles, or better deal with stress reactions.
> **Get professional help.** Especially if stress is severe, seek out professional guidance. Most campuses and many firms have people whose key role is to provide assistance in times of crisis. Take advantage of them.

ORGANIZATIONAL POLICIES AND PRACTICES FOR MANAGING WORKPLACE STRESS

As a leader, you can do more than manage your own stress; you can help to develop a less stressful work environment. You can do this by clarifying expectations, providing needed coaching and social support, empowering, encouraging family-sensitive work practices (such as on-site child care facilities and flextime), and teaching stress-management skills. We address family-sensitive work practices later in this chapter and elsewhere in the book. Let's now consider some other company policies and practices that help to manage employees' stress.

Stress-Management Programs Many companies now offer programs specifically directed toward stress management. For instance, when Chase Manhattan Corporation was anticipating a 12 percent workforce reduction, it initiated a program of lunchtime support groups, led by professional therapists, for employees feeling stress. Ovation Marketing Inc. even provides an in-house professional masseuse to reduce employees' stress and increase their creativity. Ovation also offers a complete exercise room, a sauna, warm yellow lighting, and a large office filled with nothing but soft feather beds and huge down cushions. That area, called *The Pillow Room,* is used for collective brainstorming, solitary daydreaming, and afternoon napping.[45]

Wellness Programs Today's health care costs are astounding. In the United States, they now total more than $1 trillion annually, or 14 percent of the gross national product. This works out to about $3,900 per employee, and costs are expected to double by 2007. It is estimated that over 50 percent of corporate profits go to health care costs versus only 7 percent three decades ago.[46] For every 100 workers in the country, an average of 27 have cardiovascular disease, 24 have high blood pressure, 50 or more have high cholesterol, 26 are classified as being obese, 26 smoke, 10 are heavy drinkers, 60 don't wear seat belts regularly, 50 don't get adequate exercise, and 44 suffer from excessive levels of stress.[47] A study at Steelcase Corporation determined that for every employee who had excessive alcohol consumption, the company paid $597 more per year in health care. The corresponding figures were $488 more for sedentary employees, $327 more for employees with hypertension, and $285 more for smokers.[48] Partly as a result of such figures, 91 percent of organizations now have some sort of health promotion program in place.[49]

FOCUS ON MANAGEMENT

SUCCESSFUL WELLNESS PROGRAMS*

Two notably successful wellness programs are offered by Sentara Healthcare (http://www.sentara.com) and Chevron Corporation (http://www.chevron.com). Both programs were winners of the 1998 C. Everett Koop National Health Award. Chevron has an on-site fitness center, coaches who lead stretching exercises during breaks in the offices, and staff specialists who facilitate such "energizers" as stretches and

laughter before meetings. Employees can also set "ergonomic breaks" every 15, 30, or 60 minutes on their computers to remind them to take a break and stretch. The company provides healthy choices for snacks and meals at all-day meetings. Sentara began its Healthy Edge program in 1995 for employees at its 60-plus hospitals, nursing homes, and pharmacies. The program incorporates awareness of health risks, handbooks about common disorders and how to treat them, and between

50 and 100 fitness programs on site each month, including aerobics and stretching. Sentara also encourages "power naps" during work hours. To read about wellness programs of these and other award winners, go to:

http://healthproject.stanford.edu/koop/

*This box is based on W. Atkinson, "Employee Fatigue," *Management Review,* October 1999, pp. 56–60.

Web Wise

Resources for Fostering Personal Growth

The Medical Basis for Stress and Stress Reactions. Find a clear and detailed discussion of the medical basis for stress and stress reactions at:

http://www.teachhealth.com/

The Occupational Safety & Health Administration (OSHA). OSHA, in the U.S. Department of Labor, is charged with enforcing the Occupational Safety and Health Act. Visit the OSHA site at:

http://www.osha.gov/

Read the full Occupational Safety and Health Act at:

http://www.osha-slc.gov/OshAct_toc/OshAct_toc_by_sect.html

Health Questions and Answers. Go Ask Alice! is the health question and answer Internet site produced by Alice!, Columbia

(continued on following page)

As suggested by the foregoing examples, wellness programs take a variety of forms:[50]

> **Assessment activities.** Assessment activities help employees to learn their fitness levels and health risks, often through a health screening whereby people have their height, weight, cholesterol, and blood pressure checked. Assessment may also include a computerized analysis, called a *health risk appraisal.* This consists of a confidential questionnaire in which employees report their smoking and alcohol consumption levels, weight, age, family history of various illnesses, and so on. This is used to compute a "health age"—the actual age adjusted up or down by health risks and healthy lifestyle practices—as well as specific suggestions for change.

> **Communication materials.** These include such publications as newsletters, paycheck stuffers, posters, and other communications regarding wellness.

> **Self-help materials.** The advantage of self-help is that people can alter their behavior on their own time and in the privacy of their own homes. Some wellness vendors also provide toll-free counseling for employees trying to quit smoking, lose weight, or manage stress on their own. A study conducted for Ford Motor Company by the American Institute of Preventive Medicine showed a 45 percent quit rate for 622 employees who participated in a self-help smoking cessation program. All Ford employees were able to request a self-help kit and, in the materials, were given a toll-free number that they could call to speak at any time with a health educator regarding questions or problems with quitting.

> **Group programs.** Group programs are classes conducted by an instructor who comes on site to a union hall or the workplace. These programs permit interaction with a professional and other attendees. Unfortunately, participation rates tend to be low for such programs.

Web Wise
(continued)

University's Health Education Program, a division of the **Columbia University Health Service.** There are sections on relationships; sexuality; sexual health; emotional health; fitness and nutrition; alcohol, nicotine, and other drugs; and general health.

http://www.goaskalice
.columbia.edu/index.html

Progressive Muscle Relaxation Exercise. To learn the steps in progressive muscle relaxation, go to:

http://ourworld.compuserve
.com/homepages/har/les1.htm

Alcohol and Drug Resources. The National Clearinghouse for Alcohol and Drug Information (NCADI) is the world's largest resource for current information and materials concerning substance abuse. Visit NCADI at:

http://www.health.org/
aboutn.htm

(continued on facing page)

> **Medical self-care instruction.** It is estimated that about 25 percent of the 735 million annual visits to physicians in the United States are unnecessary, as are more than half of the 90 million emergency room visits. As such, medical self-care—teaching employees to become wiser consumers of the health care system—is a promising way to reduce health care costs. Medical self-care programs often include a self-care guide, self-care workshops, a nurse advice line, and promotional materials to reinforce self-care recognition and behaviors.

Wellness programs often incorporate incentives for healthy behavior. These might take the form of charging less for health plan contributions, offering lower coverage levels, providing reimbursement for wellness programs, giving premium discounts to employees who engage in healthy lifestyles, and giving gifts such as T-shirts, water bottles, or golf equipment, to participants in wellness programs.[51] At Pitney-Bowes, about 40 percent of employees earn credits each year by participating in wellness programs. These employees get a 5 percent reduction in their health insurance costs. The company estimates that each employee who participates in the program saves the company from $291 to $375 in annual health care costs versus a $40 annual cost to administer the program.[52]

Employee Assistance Programs The line between wellness programs and employee assistance programs (EAPs) is now blurring. However, EAPs have historically been used to help employees with serious personal and organizational problems, often relating to alcoholism and substance abuse. The programs now touch on other serious stressors, including sexual harassment, financial planning, child care and eldercare, depression, and domestic violence.[53] Several organizations now educate their employees about domestic violence and provide in-house assistance programs, including counseling and referrals to community domestic violence programs. Both Polaroid Corporation and Liz Claiborne, Inc., have EAPs that offer treatment and support to employees facing violence in their homes.[54]

FOCUS ON MANAGEMENT

HEALTH INCENTIVE PROGRAMS AT HOME DEPOT

Ruth Flott, an audit and controls specialist for the Atlanta-based Home Depot, used to feel stressed during much of her first seven years working for this hardware giant. According to a study by the New York Business Group on Health, each employee who, like Flott, suffers from stress, anxiety, or depression misses 16 days of work per year.

Listening to Flott testify to the success of the company's health incentive programs is like listening to an evangelist preach at the pulpit. Thanks to the company's stress management, nutrition enhancement, and exercise programs, she is not only less stressed but has lost 62 pounds. "There is no excuse for anyone to be overweight or unhealthy at Home Depot," she says. Her productivity has also improved.

"Now I have all this energy. I'm zipping around. I'm alert. I told my boss since I've been working out I'm getting double the work done so how about double the salary," she jokes.*

http://www.homedepot.com/
cgi-bin/prel80/index.jsp

*K. Hein, "The Boiling Point," *Incentive,* September 1998, pp. 26–32.

BOTTOM LINE

The Bottom Line: The Stress Management Process

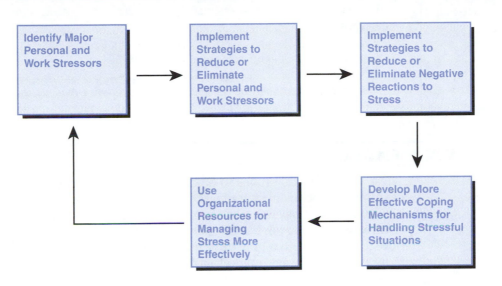

The process model in the nearby Bottom Line summarizes the basic steps associated with implementation of the stress-management process.

Now, complete Skills Practice 9-2 on developing a personal stress management program. This activity should help you to think systematically about the management of the stress process and to develop action steps based on your stress analysis.

Web Wise
(continued)

Mental Health. For a free encyclopedia of mental health information, visit Internet Mental Health at the following Web address. Internet Mental Health provides information on mental disorders, treatments, research, and diagnosis and an online Mental Health Magazine.

http://www.mentalhealth.com/fr01.html

Skills Practice 9-2   **Skill Level: Basic**
Developing a Personal Stress-Management Program

Skill Objective
To develop skill in designing and implementing a personal stress-management program.

Procedure
1. Follow the steps that follow to identify the stressors in your current situation and to develop an action plan for reducing these stressors and managing them more effectively. Use a separate piece of paper to record your work for this activity.

    Step 1: Using a simple 10 point scale with 1 = "no stress at all" to 10 = "extremely stressed out," rate your current situation in terms of the overall level of stress you are experiencing currently. Write down your overall rating.

    Step 2: List the major stressors you are experiencing in relation to your work.

    Step 3: List the major stressors that you are experiencing in relation to your life in general.

    Step 4: How do you tend to respond to the stress you experience in your work and in your life in general? Note some of your most common physical and psychological reactions to the stressors you listed in steps 2 and 3.

Step 5: Develop a list of actions you might take to reduce the level of life and work stressors you identified.

Step 6: Identify a list of actions you might take to deal with or cope with stressful situations more effectively.

Discussion Questions

1. Evaluate your personal stress-management plan. What are its strengths and weaknesses?

2. If you were to implement your personal stress-management plan, what would you need to do in order for it to be successful?

3. What factors would create barriers to the success of your personal stress-management plan? What could you do, if anything, to overcome these barriers?

4. What are the implications of this exercise for you as a future manager or supervisor?

MANAGING YOUR CAREER

These are interesting times to be embarking on a career. Each year, hundreds of thousands of business graduates enter the job market. Fortunately, business is one field that offers a rich diversity of interesting job opportunities and a relatively favorable job market. Nevertheless, as we have seen throughout this book, business is changing rapidly, and jobs and careers are changing with it. Downsizing, mergers, market and technological changes, new perspectives on the psychological contract, and changing patterns and levels of global competition are creating unprecedented levels of uncertainty, challenge, and opportunity.

In the midst of this new world of work, individuals are rethinking the meaning of careers and of career success, and they are less inclined than in the past to pursue a lifelong career with a single firm. Only about a third of all careers in the United States are traditional (i.e., vertical careers in corporations), and this figure continues to fall.[55] Employees regularly report concerns about losing their jobs. Remarkably, Labor Department statistics project that the average person entering the workforce in the United States will have three and a half careers and work for 10 employers, keeping each job for only about three and a half years. Given this reality, employees must prepare themselves for a *portfolio career:* one in which people develop a portfolio of their accomplishments in different companies. They can then "carry" that portfolio with them to help to secure new jobs.[56] These are times that call for energy, careful and intelligent career planning, and active career self-management.

THE PROTEAN CAREER

Let's begin by discussing what we mean by a career. Certainly, a career has something to do with getting jobs, and perhaps with moving between jobs, places, and levels of responsibility and challenge. However, a career means more than that.

Proteus was a character in Greek mythology who could change shape in any way he wanted—from fire to lion to dragon to tree. Only when Proteus was held down was such change impossible. Douglas Hall has drawn on this myth to coin the term *protean career.* According to this view of careers, there is much more to a career than just moving up the hierarchies of organizations:

The protean career is a process which the person, not the organiza-tion, is managing. It consists of all of the person's varied experiences in education, training, work in several organizations, change in oc-cupational field, etc. The protean career is not what happens to the person in any one organization. The protean person's own personal career choices and search for fulfillment are the unifying or integra-tive elements in his or her life. The criterion of success is internal (psychological success), not external.[57]

Viewed in this light, a career is an ongoing sequence of events, some of which may have little or nothing to do with money or prestige. Also, accord-ing to this view, a career extends over the entire work life. What happens in one year or in one corporation is just a small piece of the rich career mosaic. Finally, determining whether a career is successful is up to the individual. If people are happy with the way their careers turn out, how can anyone say that their careers are failures? Figure 9-9 summarizes key differences between the traditional view of careers and the protean view.

Career Identity   The protean view of careers also highlights the fact that much more than one's company and hierarchical level change throughout a career. There may, for instance, be changes in career identity, the integration of individuals with the requirements of their career environments. Our iden-tities define who we are, and the sort of work we do plays a large part in es-tablishing an identity. Hall points out that "The question, 'What do you do?' is often a more acceptable way of asking, 'Who are you?'"[58] As such, one mea-sure of career success is whether our work is consistent with our self-identity. If you think of yourself as a creative, responsible individual but you spend your days doing routine, low-level tasks, you probably don't think of your ca-reer as successful.

F I G U R E   9 - 9

The Protean Versus the Traditional Career

Issue	Protean Career	Traditional Career
Who's in charge?	Person	Organization
Core values	Freedom; growth	Advancement; power
Degree of mobility	High	Lower
Important performance dimensions	Psychological success	Position level; salary
Important attitude dimensions	Work satisfaction; professional commitment	Work satisfaction; organizational commitment
Important personality dimensions	Do I respect myself? (self-esteem); What do I want to do? (self-awareness)	Am I respected in this organization? (esteem from others); What should I do? (organizational awareness)
Important adaptability dimensions	Work-related flexibility; current competence (measure: marketability)	Organization-related flexibility (measure: organizational survival)

Career Adaptability Similarly, *career adaptability* may change over the course of one's career. Such terms as *managerial obsolescence* suggest that, after a while on the job, managers may become inflexible in their attitudes, outdated in their knowledge, and less intrinsically motivated to do the job. As such, career adaptability is the ability to successfully respond to new job demands. Adaptability may result from such things as training in technical and interpersonal skills; working with new, young employees who provide a fresh perspective and knowledge of new concepts; job rotation; and independent study. Another measure of career success, then, is the degree to which you have been able to stay current, fresh, and responsive.

Career Attitudes Finally, *career attitudes* may change over the course of careers. These attitudes, such as satisfaction with work and commitment to the organization, are shaped by many factors inside and outside the organization. Clearly, if you are dissatisfied with your job and company, you probably don't think of your career as successful.

Complete Skills Practice 9-3 on protean careers. This activity will help you to think about your career in terms of the factors that provide you with self-fulfillment and enrichment in your work.

Skills Practice 9-3   Skill Level: **Basic**
Designing a Protean Career Using Your "Dream Job"

Skill Objective
To develop skill in designing and implementing a protean career.

Procedure
Use the following steps in order to develop a view of your career from a protean perspective. Use a separate piece of paper to record your work.

Step 1: If you could have your "dream job," what would it be? Describe your dream job.
Step 2: Describe why you feel that the job that you identified in step 1 would be your dream job.
Step 3: Now, think about how you would define your career success solely in terms of how you feel about your job and career. How would you define "career success"?
Step 4: What actions could you take to achieve your protean career? Be as specific as possible.

Discussion Questions
1. Evaluate your protean career. How does the job you described reflect the core elements of a protean career discussed in the chapter?
2. Now compare your protean view of a career with the more traditional view of careers that emphasizes moving up the corporate hierarchy and achieving an attractive salary. Are these two perspectives of a career incompatible with each other? Why? If you were a manager in a company, what kinds of things could you do to integrate the protean and traditional perspectives?
3. What are the implications of this exercise for you as a future manager or supervisor?

CAREER STAGES IN ORGANIZATIONS

Many writers have drawn parallels between the life cycle and career stages. While many social changes are calling into question whether such a perspective is appropriate, it probably is the case that careers do have a series of stages and that those stages are linked in part to life stages. Figure 9-10 shows roles associated with four career stages.

As an apprentice, the individual is directed by others and is concerned with helping and learning. Colleagues become independent contributors to the organization. At the mentor stage, individuals assume responsibility for others, spending time on such activities as training and guidance. Finally, sponsors are concerned with directing the organization as a whole and shaping its direction. As people pass through these stages in their early, middle, and late careers, their task needs and socioemotional needs change. Figure 9-11 presents a summary of these evolving needs. Let's consider some important aspects of each of these stages.

FIGURE 9-10
Roles Associated with Four Career Stages

	Stage 1	Stage 2	Stage 3	Stage 4
Central Activity	Helping Learning Following directions	Independent contributor	Training Interfacing	Shaping the direction of the organization
Primary Relationship	Apprentice	Colleague	Mentor	Sponsor
Major Psychological Issues	Dependence	Independence	Assuming responsibility for others	Exercising power

FIGURE 9-11
Developmental Needs in Careers

Stage	Task Needs	Socioemotional Needs
Early Career	• Develop action skills • Develop a specialty • Develop creativity, innovation • Rotate into a new area after 3–5 years	• Support • Autonomy • Deal with feelings of rivalry, competition
Middle Career	• Develop skills in training and coaching others (younger employees) • Train for updating and integrating skills • Develop broader view of work and organization • Job rotation into new job requiring new skills	• Opportunity to express feelings about midlife (anguish, defeat, limited time, restlessness) • Reorganize thinking about self (mortality, values, family, work) • Reduce self-indulgence and competitiveness • Support and mutual problem solving for coping with midcareer stress
Late Career	• Shift from power role to one of consultation, guidance, wisdom • Begin to establish self in activities outside the organization (start on a part-time basis)	• Support and counseling to help see integrated life experiences as a platform for others • Acceptance of one's one-and-only life cycle • Gradual detachment from organization

EARLY CAREER ISSUES

Early in their careers, people often experience great uncertainty about their competence and performance potential.[59] They are likely to need guidance and support to get their careers moving. This stressful time can have a major influence on the remainder of their careers.

Career Problems of Young Managers   Young managers commonly face a variety of problems. An awareness of these problems may help you to deal with them when they occur.

> **Early frustration and dissatisfaction.** As our discussion of socialization processes suggested, young managers' job expectations often exceed reality. Their academic training may have focused on cases in which they took the roles of top-level executives. So, they may now expect to get a lot of responsibility quickly. Instead, they are often placed in routine, boring jobs until they have proven themselves. As a result, young managers may experience severe reality shock, become frustrated, and perhaps leave the firm. If the company has painted an overly bright picture when recruiting, this reality shock may be especially great.

> **Insensitivity and passivity.** Organizations are political. Young managers often are insensitive to the political aspects of organizations and may resent them. They may also be passive, hoping that things will turn out for the best. As a result, they may not actively explore the organizational environment to understand relationships and attitudes and to clarify their own positions.

> **Loyalty dilemmas.** Most people in authority value subordinates' loyalty. One survey asked chief executives what they value most in subordinates. Fully 86 percent said they value loyalty most, distantly followed by sense of humor (6 percent), capacity for hard work (5 percent), and integrity (3 percent).[60] However, there are many versions of loyalty. Some see loyalty as obedience: Subordinates are loyal if they do what they are told. Others interpret loyalty as putting in effort and long hours to prove concern for the company. To still others, loyalty is successful completion of tasks or protection of the superior from ridicule and adverse evaluation by others or giving the superior honest information about mistakes and potential failures. Unfortunately, young managers often do not know which version of loyalty the organization or superior expects. These uncertainties and conflicts may cause the young manager to conform to power and authority, to try to change the superior's expectations, or to leave.

> **Personal anxiety.** Young managers may experience anxiety. They often find that just at the time they are beginning to reap the rewards of their jobs, they question the value of what they are doing. They may say, "I am making $70,000 a year, but I don't think what the company produces has much value to society." As a result, young managers may fear that they are "selling out." Young managers may also feel anxiety about commitment to the organization. They may feel they would benefit from conforming to the norms of the organization and having a sense of certainty about their careers, but they don't want to close doors and shatter illusions about possibilities. Finally, young managers may feel anxious about being dependent on others in the organization or they may also

feel anxiety because others in the organization—subordinates, peers, and even superiors—are dependent on them.

> **Ethical dilemmas.** Most young managers face unexpected career dilemmas that force them to think about what is ethical and unethical. In one survey, 30 percent of new employees admitted to feeling pressure to compromise their company's ethical standards because of deadlines, overly aggressive goals, concerns about the company's survival, and other factors. Thirty percent reported personally observing conduct that violated the law or their company's standards in the last year. Frequently mentioned types of misconduct included falsifying reports or records, lying to supervisors, theft, and sexual harassment. However, less than half the employees said they tried to report what they saw to others in the company.[61] In trying to resolve ethical dilemmas, the young manager may consider economic self-interest, obedience to the law, observance of religious principles, obedience to a superior, or doing the greatest good for the greatest number.

> **Job security.** Job security has always been a concern for new managers. Recognizing this, some companies are using security as a lure. For example, Northern Telecom Ltd. is providing a three-year employment guarantee to new hires. Similarly, Electronic Data Systems offers three-year contracts, though it requires a payback of a portion of new hires' training costs if they bail out early.[62] Similarly, there are probably few careers that offer less job security than professional sports, where an injury or poor year can mean the end of a promising career. The Cleveland Indians have used this knowledge as part of their rebuilding strategy. The Indians signed on more than a dozen young players at less pay than they might get elsewhere but with assurances that they'll be employed for at least two or three years.[63]

> **Organizational seduction.** Anyone who has read John Grisham's novel, *The Firm,* or has seen the movie knows about another early-career danger: organizational seduction.[64] This occurs when the organization provides new employees with jobs that are very enticing, in terms of pleasant work environment, stimulating tasks, chances to satisfy status needs, and so on. When this happens, employees sometimes become so committed to the organization that their longer-term career interests—and perhaps their nonwork lives—are hurt. The employees may, for instance, feel guilt about leaving the firm for a better opportunity, may "burn out" through overwork, may pass up professional development opportunities, may neglect their families, and so on. Seduction is, of course, difficult to deal with precisely because it's so pleasant. However, employees in early career would be wise to listen to the counsel of others about whether the energy and focus they are giving the job are appropriate and to ask whether the short-term pleasures of organizational seduction are worth the longer-term costs.

The Importance of Early Career Challenge and Success   Our discussion of organizational seduction suggests that stimulating, challenging jobs may have some inherent dangers. At the same time, though, there is considerable evidence that, kept in proper balance, early job challenge can be very helpful. A model of the career-growth cycle suggests the importance of this early career

FIGURE 9-12
The Career-Growth Cycle

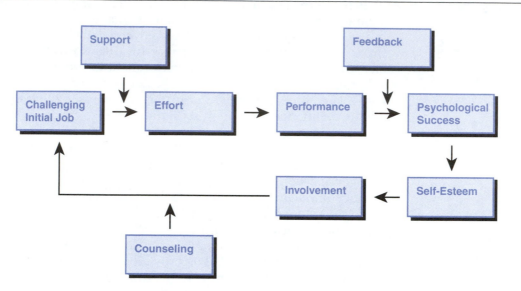

challenge.[65] According to this model, shown in Figure 9-12, a job that provides challenging, stretching goals triggers the process of career growth. The clearer and more challenging the goals and the more support the job provides, the more effort the employee will exert and the greater will be the chance of good performance. A person who does a good job and receives positive feedback will feel successful. These feelings of psychological success will enhance self-esteem and increase job involvement. This will lead, in turn, to the setting of future stretching goals and continued career growth.[66]

MIDDLE CAREER ISSUES

By midcareer, individuals are becoming fully independent contributors. They have learned the ropes of organizational life and focus on exposure and advancement. There can be many new stresses at this stage, and some individuals may find their movement thwarted.

Coping with Midcareer Stress[67] At midcareer, the employee experiences many physiological, attitudinal, occupational, and family changes. There is an awareness of aging and a recognition that many ambitious career goals will never be attained. New life goals may be sought. A disturbing sense of obsolescence may develop, coupled with a feeling that one is becoming less mobile and less attractive in the job market.

Having realistic expectations about midcareer crises and transitions seems to ease the stress and pain of this period. In addition, midcareer employees can receive training to provide exposure to new skills and ideas. They may also be trained to help younger employees, thereby remaining fresh and up-to-date. Midcareer employees can be encouraged to face their feelings of restlessness and insecurity, to re-examine their values and life goals, and to set new goals or recommit themselves to old ones. Life-planning and career-planning exercises may be especially valuable. The company can take steps to deal with

FIGURE 9-13
Performance and Promotability

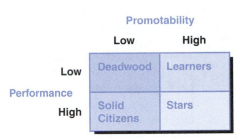

obsolescence through seminars, workshops, degree programs, and other forms of "retreading." It can also try to prevent obsolescence in the first place by providing challenging job assignments that force the individual to build new skills and learn about new developments in the professional field.

The Career Plateau   The *career plateau* is the point in a career where the likelihood of further promotions is very low.[68] Employees often experience this plateau at midcareer. Some people may plateau because they simply don't want any more promotions. Perhaps they enjoy their current jobs, do them well, and simply don't want to move out of them. Or perhaps they just don't want more responsibility at this point in their lives. Others may have plateaued because of poor performance. Still others find there is no place they can go; there are no openings at higher levels. So, the fact that an employee is plateaued doesn't necessarily say anything about his or her performance.

Figure 9-13 presents a model of managerial career states. The model classifies four principal career states on the basis of current performance and likelihood of future promotion.

Learners have high potential for advancement but are now performing below standards. Trainees or employees recently promoted into new positions that they have not yet mastered would be examples. Stars, performing well and having high potential for continued advancement, are on a "fast track." Solid citizens have good current performance but little promotion potential. Finally, deadwood are poor performers with little potential for advancement.

The solid citizens and deadwood have plateaued, though for different reasons. Deadwood are "ineffective plateauees." Solid citizens are "effective plateauees." Some are organizationally plateaued because of lack of openings. Because organizations are typically pyramid-shaped, such organizational plateauing is common. Others are personally plateaued either because they do not desire higher level jobs or because they are not seen as having the abilities needed for such jobs.

This model raises some interesting issues. For instance, firms may want to take steps to ensure that their solid citizens are not neglected. They can appraise, counsel, and develop career paths for solid citizens and provide them with training, skill upgrading, and development. They can try to identify deadwood early and act to restore performance through a variety of means. For instance, they might employ education programs to upgrade technical skill; development programs focusing on emotional and intellectual recharging; and job rotation through new duties, skill demands, or location.

Workers who have plateaued because of slack demand for labor or because of poor performance often have little to do. Japanese white-collar excess workers are called *madogiwazoku,* or "sitting by the window tribe," because they have little to do but stare out the window. They may be assigned to lawn or maintenance work. In the United States, executives whose careers have stagnated have been called *shelf-sitters;* they have been "put on the shelf" in make-work, dead-end positions.[69]

Research about managers who describe themselves as plateaued finds them to show surprisingly little dissatisfaction with their careers, lives, and the promotion policies of their firms and to generally be well adjusted.[70] Apparently, many plateaued managers can cope with and adapt to the career plateau. As we have said, some genuinely may not want promotions. Others who did not receive desired promotions may rationalize, emphasizing the longer hours and increased pressure that promotions would bring. Still others may divert their energies to activities outside the job. Finally, some plateaued managers may move to new jobs within the firm to hide their embarrassment from their peers.

Whatever the satisfaction level of plateaued managers, plateauing may cause problems for more than just the plateaued employee. One survey found that younger employees were often demoralized by the stalled careers of older, plateaued employees, thinking that this might be a vision of what the future holds for them. Plateaued employees were also seen as clogging promotion channels, lowering morale of coworkers and subordinates, and harming relationships with customers and clients.[71]

Further, there is some disturbing evidence about the health consequences of plateauing. For example, one study (which examined data for subjects tracked over a period of 70 years, from 1922 to 1992!) found mortality rates to be significantly higher for men whose careers plateaued after early rapid progress than for those whose career progress continued unabated.[72] While the causes of such mortality may be complex, the findings provide further evidence that career plateaus should be taken very seriously.

LATE CAREER ISSUES

By late career, many individuals have already experienced considerable advancement and may turn their attentions to aiding and developing others. If their careers have been fulfilling, this can be a satisfying and rewarding time. If the career was frustrating, this can be a difficult period of trying to cope with disappointments. In late career, individuals also begin to turn their thoughts toward separation from the organization.

Mentoring In late career, many older, more experienced managers serve as mentors for less experienced protégés and contribute to their career development. We consider mentoring in more depth later in the chapter.

Adjustment into Retirement Retirement gives some individuals a sense of loss and finality. Many workers fantasize that they will die soon after retirement. For other people, retirement is a chance to escape a frustrating or high-pressure job and to enjoy free time and pursue hobbies. In any case, this is a major transition. As we discussed earlier in the chapter, life change—whether desirable or undesirable—is stressful. Retirement combines changes in work patterns with personal, financial, and perhaps health changes. Those happiest in retirement have prepared for it over time and have made plans for their retirement years.

Now, complete Skills Practice 9-4. The purpose of the activity is to help you to develop skill in analyzing employee career situations and formulating appropriate courses of action.

Skills Practice 9-4

Managing Employees in Different Stages of Career Development

Skill Level: Challenging

Skill Objective

To develop skill in developing action plans for managing employees in different stages of career development.

Procedure

Note: This activity can be done individually or in groups of three to five students.

1. Read the descriptions of each of the following three employees. Identify at which stage of career development each employee is currently.

Employee No. 1

Bill Scott, 59 years old, is the director of marketing at a very-fast-growing computer software company based in California. Bill has 27 years of experience working in the computer industry and 20 years of experience working with this company. He has been a solid performer for the company and has been very loyal to the organization in many ways. Overall, he is content with his current job, but his motivation has been declining as he is preparing for retirement in 3 to 5 years.

Employee No. 2

Kiersten Williams, 22, is a recent bachelor's degree graduate from a major state university in North Carolina. She was a marketing major in college and earned an overall grade point average of 3.0 (B). Although Kiersten did not have any marketing-related internship experience during college, she was very active in the school's marketing student association. Her current job is serving as a sales representative for a medical systems manufacturer in Austin, Texas. She has held this position for 9 months.

Employee No. 3

Giselle Fernandez, 42 years old, is a product design engineer at a plastics company based in Cleveland, Ohio. She has held her current position for about 8 years. Giselle possesses excellent research capabilities, but the company feels that she does not possess the competencies needed to become a departmental supervisor. Giselle has been an outstanding performer in terms of her current technical position.

2. For each employee, develop an action plan for managing career issues effectively. Be specific. Use a separate piece of paper to record your answers.

Discussion Questions

1. Evaluate your action plans for the three employees. What are their strengths and weaknesses?
2. What would have to be done in order to implement these action plans effectively?
3. What would be the barriers to the success of your action plans? How might you overcome these barriers?
4. What are the implications of this exercise for you as a future manager or supervisor?

MOVING UP AND DOWN, IN AND OUT, AND AROUND

The view of stages we have just considered focused primarily on upward movement in the organization. However, movement may be more complex. As shown in the model seen in Figure 9-14, movement through the organization may take place in three dimensions, making up a *career cone*.[73]

> **Vertical.** Vertical movement is up and down the organizational hierarchy, such as a promotion or demotion. This is the traditional way to view movement in organizations.

> **Radial.** Radial career movement includes moves toward or away from the inner circle or the core of the system. Radial movement takes the individual closer to or further from central tasks, people, or power. Generally, radial movement will be related to vertical movement. However, some individuals may experience vertical movement while remaining on the periphery. Others may stay on a level but move closer to the core as they gain experience and trust.

> **Circumferential.** Circumferential movement means moving to a different function, program, or product in the organization, such as to production from sales. Such moves may be a useful broadening experience, providing the base for future vertical moves.

FIGURE 9-14
The Career Cone

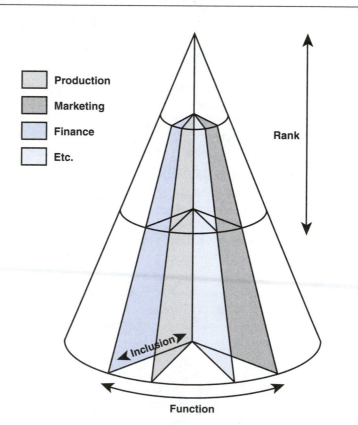

Different organizations have different structures and boundaries relating to these dimensions and, thus, offer different types of mobility to employees. The boundaries that correspond to the types of movement are three:

> **Hierarchical boundaries,** separating the hierarchical levels from one another
> **Inclusion boundaries,** separating individuals or groups who differ in their degree of centrality
> **Functional or departmental boundaries,** separating departments or different functional groupings from each other.

Organizations differ in terms of the number of each type of boundary, how difficult it is for members to cross those boundaries, and the criteria for movement across boundaries.

This view has some important implications. It suggests, for instance, that promotions may actually hinder subsequent career progress if they result in moves away from the core (as when people are "kicked upstairs," receiving "promotions" to powerless, peripheral—and perhaps newly created—positions). On the other hand, lateral moves toward the core or across functions to gain visibility and expertise or to get out of a clogged channel may be valuable.

As employees and companies recognize this, more attention is being given to lateral moves, and many large firms, including American Greetings, Corning, and Eastman Kodak, are encouraging them.[74] At some firms, such as FMC Corporation and Whirlpool Inc., cross-functional training—including international experience—is being touted as critical.[75] Similarly, companies are trying some interesting new approaches to lateral moves. For example, Corning Inc., which has long attracted recruits by promising them they can "change careers without changing companies," now offers a 5 percent raise to managers who make lateral moves, and it encourages managers not to block subordinates' lateral moves. Also, American Greetings Corporation redesigned 400 jobs in its creative division and asked workers and managers to reapply. Everyone was guaranteed a job, without a pay cut. With the restructuring completed, employees work in teams instead of assembly-line fashion, and they can freely transfer between teams that make different products.[76]

FITTING PEOPLE TO CAREERS

We have discussed what careers are, and we have explored some of the key issues you may face at various career stages. But how do people choose careers and then make other career-related decisions? Several theories try to answer these questions by examining the fit of individuals to careers. Such theories might help organizations to select appropriate individuals and tailor programs to their particular needs. They might also help individuals to find suitable positions. Let's consider three models that focus on individual differences in the way people view occupations or jobs: career anchors, occupational personality types, and career concept types. As we review models, think about the things that you value and find of interest and how those values and interests may shape your career.

Career Anchors   On the basis of his research, Edgar Schein has presented the idea of career anchors.[77] These anchors are "a syndrome of motives, values, and self-perceived competencies which function to guide and constrain an individual's entire career."[78] An anchor can be thought of as a "master motive" or the thing the person will not give up under any circumstances. Schein's study led him to conclude there are at least five career anchors, as follows.

> **Anchor 1: managerial competence.** The career is organized around the competencies and values inherent in the management process. The most important components of this concept are the ability to influence and supervise, the ability to analyze and solve complex problems, and emotional stability.

> **Anchor 2: technical-functional competence.** The career is organized around the challenge of the actual work being done, whether it is related to marketing, financial analysis, corporate planning, or some other area. The anchor is the technical field or functional area rather than the managerial process itself. Individuals with this anchor don't want to be promoted out of the kind of work they are doing.

> **Anchor 3: security.** The individual has an underlying need for security and tries to stabilize the career by tying it to the given organization. More than others, individuals with this anchor are likely to let the organization define their careers. They rely on the organization to recognize their needs and competencies and to do what is best for them.

> **Anchor 4: creativity.** Individuals with this anchor have a strong need to create something. This anchor is most evident among entrepreneurs, but corporate employees may also hold it.

> **Anchor 5: autonomy and independence.** The concern is with freedom and autonomy. Individuals with this anchor often find organizational life too restrictive or intrusive into their personal lives and seek careers that offer more autonomy.

Can you think of people who appear to hold each of these career anchors? The anchors reflect predominant concerns. An employee may still care about other things, but the anchor is overriding. It is important that companies recognize these anchors and create appropriate career opportunities. For example, a person with a technical-functional anchor may not welcome a promotion to a management position. Organizations must think about the contributions that people with various anchors can make. They will also have to develop multiple reward systems and career paths to permit the full development of diverse kinds of individuals. Recognizing this, some companies—such as Texas Instruments at its information systems and services division—now use career anchors for counseling and evaluation in their career development programs.[79]

Now, identify your career anchors by completing Self-Assessment 9-5: Career Anchors.

Self-Assessment 9-5
Career Anchors

Use the following scale to rate the importance of each of the 25 career characteristics listed. First, find the career characteristic that you think is **least** important and write its number in the left-hand box (in the "1" column). Then, find the characteristic you think is **most** important and place its number in the right-hand box (in the "7" column). Next, select the

three characteristics that you feel are the **least important of those that remain** and place their numbers in boxes in the "2" column. Then, select the **three** characteristics that you feel are the **most important of those that remain** and place their numbers in boxes in the "6" column. Continue this process until the number of each characteristic is in a box in the column corresponding to its relative importance to your career:

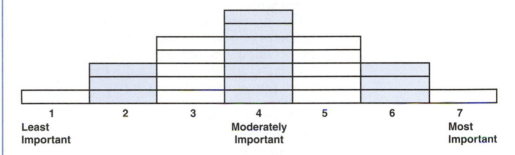

1	2	3	4	5	6	7
Least Important			Moderately Important			Most Important

A Career Offering

1. The autonomy and independence to choose my own work hours and activities
2. Positions of leadership and influence
3. The chance to concentrate on what I do best
4. The opportunity to remain in my specialized area rather than being promoted out of my area of expertise
5. Long-term job stability
6. The chance to invent things
7. The opportunity to rise to a general management position
8. The ability to supervise, influence, and lead people
9. The opportunity to act without dealing with a lot of rules and regulations
10. Life-long job security
11. The chance to focus on my particular functional or technical area of expertise
12. Independence
13. The chance to create something entirely new
14. The chance to hone my technical and functional skills
15. The chance to rise to positions where my decisions really make a difference
16. The chance to develop new things
17. The ability to stay in positions in my area of expertise
18. Guaranteed work, pension, and other benefits
19. The chance to work without fear of losing my job
20. The ability to fully use my creativity
21. The chance to be in positions of control
22. The ability to act without needing approval from others
23. The chance to bring new things into being
24. Great security
25. Great freedom

Occupational Personality Types John Holland reasoned that people gravitate toward environments that match their personal orientations. He proposed a hexagonal model, with six personality types and six matching occupational environments:[80]

> **Realistic.** Involves aggressive behavior and physical activities requiring skill, strength, and coordination. Examples include forestry, trucking, and farming.

> **Investigative.** Involves cognitive (thinking, organizing, understanding) rather than affective (feeling, acting, or interpersonal and emotional) activities. Examples include biology, mathematics, and oceanography.
> **Social.** Involves interpersonal rather than intellectual or physical activities. Examples include clinical psychology, foreign service, and social work.
> **Conventional.** Involves structural, rule-regulated activities and subordination of personal needs to an organization or person of power and status. Examples include accounting and finance.
> **Enterprising.** Involves verbal activities to influence others and to attain power and status. Examples include management, law, and public relations.
> **Artistic.** Involves self-expression, artistic creation, expression of emotions, and individualistic activities. Examples include art and music education.

Research shows that when people choose a career consistent with their personality, they are more likely to be satisfied with their career choice and not to change professions. They are also more likely to remain excited by the nature of the work they do and to be satisfied with their colleagues at work.[81]

Career Concept Types We all know that people differ in terms of how they move from job to job and the degree to which they are active or passive in that movement, initiating moves or "going with the flow." Michael Driver described four basic career concept types:[82]

> **Transitory.** There is no clear pattern of career movement. Some transitory individuals may drift in a relatively passive way from job to job. Others may be entrepreneurial types who innovate new activities but move on as soon as stabilization sets in.
> **Steady-state.** The individual chooses a lifetime occupation. Steady-state types settle into an organization and prefer stability rather than change.
> **Linear.** Career choice is made early, and there is emphasis on steady upward movement on a career ladder.
> **Spiral.** There is a planned search for increasing self-development and creative growth. The career choice may change periodically.

Driver has linked his career concept types to Schein's career anchors. For instance, individuals having security as the career anchor might fit the steady-state career concept. Those with autonomy as the career anchor might adhere to the transitory or spiral career concepts.

Driver reasons that organizations might be categorized in terms of the four career concept types. A transitory organization is loose, temporary, and entrepreneurial, with few formal procedures. Both linear and steady-state organizations have classic pyramidal structures with tight controls. However, there is stress on vertical movement in linear organizations and units of great stability in steady state organizations. Some high-technology or artistic organizations may show spiral patterns. Some departments in linear or steady-state organizations may also operate in a spiral mode.

An employee would generally best fit into an organization of a corresponding type—a transitory individual in a transitory organization, and so on. A linear individual, for instance, would be uncomfortable in a transitory organiza-

BOTTOM LINE

The Bottom Line: Managing the Career Development Process

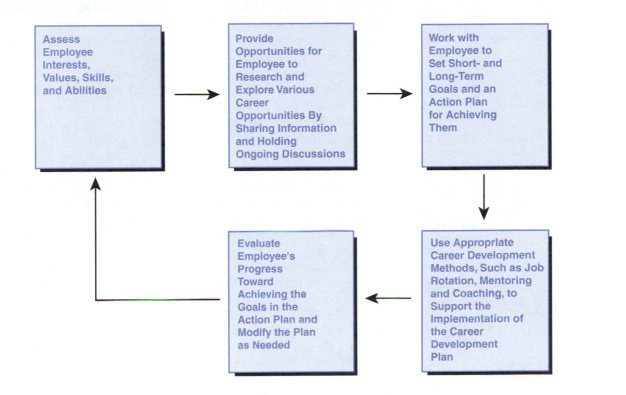

Assess Employee Interests, Values, Skills, and Abilities → Provide Opportunities for Employee to Research and Explore Various Career Opportunities By Sharing Information and Holding Ongoing Discussions → Work with Employee to Set Short- and Long-Term Goals and an Action Plan for Achieving Them → Use Appropriate Career Development Methods, Such as Job Rotation, Mentoring and Coaching, to Support the Implementation of the Career Development Plan → Evaluate Employee's Progress Toward Achieving the Goals in the Action Plan and Modify the Plan as Needed

tion. However, Driver also takes a dynamic view of the career concept types. He reasons that career concepts may evolve during a lifetime, owing to work or other social learning or to the inner dynamic of human development. Therefore, organizations must do more than simply be concerned with fit to an unchanging employee; they must also cultivate staff planning systems, employee development programs, and even strategies and structures that recognize transitions between career concept types.

SELF-MANAGEMENT OF CAREERS

Many forces affect career development. Organizational practices clearly play a role, and luck may even be important.[83] Certainly, though, as the workplace becomes more dynamic and uncertain, employees are forced to be more proactive, acting to manage their own careers.

Guidelines for Self-Management of Careers   Here are some guidelines for the self-management of careers:[84]

> **Develop basic career competencies.** There are at least five basic career competencies, and each can be developed:[85]

- **Self-appraisal.** Successful career development requires self-awareness. The counseling, guidance, career planning, or personnel offices on most campuses can help at this stage. Counseling interviews, aptitude and interest tests, and career-planning exercises may all be useful. Also, just asking others, such as an instructor or boss, to give you feedback about your performance can be enlightening.

- **Occupational information.** Career development requires a fit between you and your job, so it's important to learn about potential jobs. Some sources that provide information about types of work, skill requirements, occupational developments, worker trait requirements, and other relevant factors include the *Dictionary of Occupational Titles,* the U.S. Department of Labor's *Occupational Outlook Handbook,* and the *Occupational Outlook Quarterly.* Also, some interactive computer methods for providing career information are now available.

- **Goal selection.** Career success, according to the approach taken in this chapter, means achieving one's goals, so the process of properly setting goals is crucial. It is generally best if goals are challenging, consistent with career capabilities, set by the individual (alone or in collaboration with another), and implemented by the person's independent effort.

- **Planning.** Once a goal is set, it is necessary to specify the steps to meet that goal and to determine the order of those steps. Both counseling and career-planning exercises may be helpful at the planning stage.

- **Problem solving.** Because problems constantly arise during careers, competence in problem solving can be crucial to successful movement through a career.

> **Choose an organization carefully.** Your choice of an organization to work for is extremely important. The organization will control many important rewards, may determine where you live, and may even influence the sorts of competencies you develop and the kinds of skills you exercise. Also, your initial choice of an employer may have lasting consequences in terms of your chances for future moves to other organizations.

> **Get a challenging initial job.** In choosing a first job, you should generally give such short-term considerations as starting salary and location less weight than that given to challenge and potential for career growth. If you do take a job that offers little challenge, you should probably try either to make a later job change or to redefine your job to assume more responsibility.

> **Be an outstanding performer.** Good performance enhances your esteem both in the eyes of others, such as your boss, and in your own eyes. Ask your boss to help you to set challenging goals, to give feedback, and to coach you.

> **Develop professional mobility.** More options are better than fewer. Mobility and potential mobility (not just upward mobility, but mobility of all kinds) are crucial to career success.

> **Plan your own and your spouse's careers collaboratively.** If both spouses are working or may work, severe strains can result unless careful career planning takes place. It is unrealistic and unfair to assume

that one partner will go along passively when the other takes a job transfer.

> **Get help in career management.** Seek advice from experts in your school or organization. Consider using professional job counselors or placement specialists.

> **Anticipate chance events.** No matter how precisely you plan, chance will play a role. Develop contingency plans that specify what you will do if various things—good or bad—happen.

> **Continually reassess your career.** Midcourse corrections may be needed. You will have to make career choices all your life, not just when you first leave school. Continually ask where you are, where you want to be, and how you are going to get there.

The process model presented in the nearby Bottom Line summarizes the basic steps associated with implementation of the general career development process.

Complete Skills Practice 9-5 on self-managing your career. The activity will help you to think more systematically about how to motivate and direct yourself in the management of your career.

Skills Practice 9-5
Self-Managing Your Career

Skill Level: **Basic**

Skill Objective
To use self-management principles to enhance the effectiveness of your career management.

Procedure
Apply the steps that follow to develop a self-management plan for handling career issues. Use a separate piece of paper to record your answers. For each of the career self-management guidelines, brainstorm a list of specific actions you could take to address it effectively. Leave blank any guidelines that you feel are not applicable to you.

Guideline 1: Conduct a self-appraisal of your knowledge and skills and job performance
Guideline 2: Obtain occupational information through research
Guideline 3: Set short-term and long-term career goals
Guideline 4: Choose an organization (employer) carefully
Guideline 5: Get a challenging initial job
Guideline 6: Become an outstanding performer
Guideline 7: Develop professional mobility
Guideline 8: Plan your own and your spouse's careers collaboratively
Guideline 9: Get help in career management
Guideline 10: Anticipate chance events
Guideline 11: Continually reassess your career

Discussion Questions
1. Evaluate your plan in terms of its strengths and weaknesses.
2. What kinds of things would you need to do to make this plan successful if you were to actually implement it?
3. What would the barriers to success be for making your plan successful? What could you do to overcome these barriers?
4. What are the implications of this exercise for you as a future manager or supervisor?

FIGURE 9-15
Questions Asked by AT&T When Screening Candidates for Overseas Transfer

- Would your spouse be interrupting a career to accompany you on an international assignment? If so, how do you think this will [affect] your spouse and your relationship with each other?
- Do you enjoy the challenge of making your own way in new situations?
- Securing a job on re-entry will be primarily your responsibility. How do you feel about networking and being your own advocate?
- How able are you in initiating new social contacts?
- Can you imagine living without television?
- How important is it for you to spend significant amounts of time with people of your own ethnic, racial, religious, and national background?
- As you look into your personal history, can you isolate any episodes that indicate a real interest in learning about other peoples and cultures?
- Has it been your habit to vacation in foreign countries?
- Do you enjoy sampling foreign cuisine?
- What is your tolerance for waiting for repairs?

Source: "Consultants for International Living," *The Wall Street Journal,* January 9, 1992, p. B1.

Web Wise

The Monster Board International Pages

The international pages of the Monster Board contain information both for U.S. citizens thinking of working abroad and for foreign nationals considering work in the United States. Information on work abroad includes advice on work permits, job search, and various other work-abroad resources. There are also international jobs message boards and career network sites for specific countries, including Australia, Belgium, Canada, France, the Netherlands, New Zealand, Singapore, and the United Kingdom.

http://international.monster
.com/index.asp

GLOBAL PERSPECTIVES ON CAREERS

As companies take seriously the fact that business is becoming more global, they must also develop global perspectives on careers. For one thing, as firms increasingly enter global markets and send employees to foreign assignments, they must consider whether prospects for transfer have the skills, flexibility, and tolerance for uncertainty required to successfully perform in foreign settings. Also, the costs of maintaining an employee abroad are typically two to three times the cost of salary and benefits in the United States, so mistakes are expensive.[86] Figure 9-15 presents some questions asked by AT&T when screening candidates for overseas transfer. How would you respond to the questions?

Also, multinational firms must recognize that foreign nationals may have different career experiences, expectations, and aspirations than U.S. workers. National cultures shape the way in which people think of careers and the way in which they perceive the world of work.[87]

VALUING DIVERSITY: ENHANCING CAREERS FOR WOMEN AND MINORITIES

Women and minorities may still face an invisible but real glass ceiling that acts as a subtle barrier to promotions into high-level executive jobs.[88] According to the Bureau of Labor Statistics, women now account for more than 43 percent of managerial and related employment, up from 22 percent in 1975.[89] However, of the *Fortune 50* companies, only 1.3 percent of corporate officers are women, while 1.7 percent are women within the *Fortune 500* companies.[90] And, as if glass ceilings aren't bad enough, there may be "glass walls" as well.[91] The glass walls keep women and minorities in staff or support positions in such areas as public relations and human resources and away from jobs in such core areas as marketing, production, and sales. As such, women face hierarchical, functional, and inclusion barriers.[92]

There are some signs of change. As noted, the percentage of management jobs held by women has increased dramatically over the last quarter century. In addition, annual earnings of full-time women workers are now about 75 percent of comparable male earnings, up from 60 percent in 1979.[93] Still, companies recognize that there is a long way to go and that they must take active steps to further the career development of women and minorities. In this section, we consider some of the steps now being taken.

Women's Career Development   The growing number of women in management presents opportunities and challenges to organizations. If women's potential is to be fully realized and used, companies must take active steps to foster their career development. As shown in Figure 9-16, companies have chosen several routes to such development.

Some of these routes take traditional forms, such as posting of job opportunities, career counseling, and training programs. Training programs and other developmental opportunities are crucial, and there is evidence that women have fewer developmental opportunities relating to high-responsibility positions than do men.[94] Others approaches are more innovative, such as opportunities for part-time jobs at advanced levels in the hierarchy and a variety of family-sensitive work practices, which we discuss next. Mentoring also can be critical to women's career development and is discussed later in the chapter.

Family-Sensitive Work Practices   Many companies are using a variety of family-sensitive work practices to permit managers to better balance work and family demands. Some of these practices, such as flexible work hours, job sharing, compressed workweeks, family-leave policies, and work-at-home arrangements, provide needed flexibility. Others, such as on-site child care facilities, reduce distraction and concerns over such things as baby-sitting.

Research shows that firms that use family-sensitive practices often reap gains in greater loyalty, increased job satisfaction, and lower turnover.[95] Some

FIGURE 9-16
Company Practices to Enhance Women's Career Development

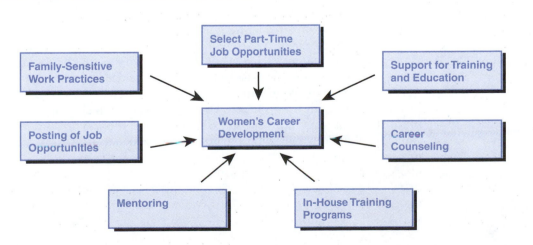

firms also report productivity increases, and family-sensitive practices are a powerful recruiting tool.[96]

Ironically, though, it appears that firms offering family-friendly policies are sometimes the slowest in promoting women to management positions.[97] Further, some women feel that if they use such family-friendly policies as flex-time, their chances of promotion are reduced. Some observers feel that family-sensitive work practices may emphasize the differences between genders, making it harder for women to overcome stereotypes and get serious consideration for top jobs.

Job-Pathing *Job-pathing* involves a carefully planned sequence of job assignments aimed at developing certain job-related skills.[98] The paths are designed to ensure that important skill-building experiences are provided in increments small enough not to overwhelm the individual but large enough to require stretching. The goal is to minimize the career time needed to reach a target job. Through the use of job-pathing, one large retail organization feels it can reduce the time to develop a store manager from 15 years to five. Plotting career paths not only speeds employee growth but forces the organization to think about the career paths it is now using. It may find that some potential paths are not being used and perhaps that paths can be plotted through different functional areas to develop managers with broader views.

Talent Development Among Hourly Employees Companies are trying to find new ways to attract more female and minority hourly workers into presupervisory programs. One problem is perceptual: Females and minorities sometimes feel that opportunities for upward mobility are lacking or that barriers exist to their upward mobility. Some also do not perceive themselves as fitting into supervisory roles. Firms must act to alter these perceptions. Some firms are also relying on training programs conducted by professional or trade organizations to develop female and minority employees. Many of these employees see training provided by such associations as being less competitive and more supportive than company-sponsored programs.

Layoff Policies Women and minorities have historically faced a major hurdle in corporations. Since the movement of women and minorities in management positions has been primarily a recent phenomenon, they have suffered from companies' "last hired, first fired" rules. That is, when layoffs have occurred, white men, with longer tenure, have been most likely to keep their jobs. As such, promising women and minorities have often found their management careers cut short. Now, many large firms, such as Du Pont, AT&T, and Honeywell, are using criteria other than seniority to make job-cut decisions.[99] For example, Honeywell bases its decisions on performance appraisals, and AT&T has used early-retirement sweeteners to encourage older managers— primarily white men—to leave. These policies are welcomed by women and minorities but often are very stressful for white men, who sometimes say that they feel abandoned.[100] As such, companies are in a precarious situation, hoping to increase diversity but wanting to avoid a white male backlash and charges of reverse discrimination. At some firms such courses as one at AT&T titled "White Males: The Label, the Dilemma" are offered in which employees, male and female, white and minority, learn about workforce changes and can express their feelings.

Special Programs for Minorities[101] Many firms have developed special programs for minorities. For example, American Airlines offers English as a second language for minority employees, and it sponsors an Asian Cultural Association and an Organization of African Americans. To encourage minority development, American has a Walk-a-Mile Program, a systematic method of establishing career goals and receiving guidance in choosing career paths. In the program, minority employees can nominate themselves for a position and then work for a day in that position with the person currently holding the job.

American Express Company has a Black Employee Network and the East-West Exchange (an Asian employee network), which act as support groups to aid in networking and self-help programs. The organizations bring in speakers and sponsor events around Black History Month and other special holidays.

McDonald's offers career development programs tailored to its diverse workforce, including seminars on such topics as black career development, Hispanic career development, and managing cultural differences. In addition, affirmative action training is given to almost 3,000 employees each year at McDonald's employee management training school, Hamburger University. The company also supports organized minority employee networking groups that have representatives meet periodically with company management. McDonald's maintains close ties to minority colleges and students through its scholarships and contributions. It also has a program that develops minority entrepreneurs.

MENTORING

In Homer's *The Odyssey,* Mentor was the trusted advisor of Odysseus, king of Ithaca. When Odysseus went to fight in the Trojan War, he entrusted the care of his kingdom to Mentor who served as the teacher and overseer of Odysseus's son, Telemachus. Now, a *mentor* is defined as one who is an experienced, well-established member of a profession or firm and takes a personal interest in the career of a less-experienced member and attempts to facilitate that individual's career advancement.

PHASES IN THE MENTORING RELATIONSHIP[102]

There are four phases in the mentoring relationship:

> **Initiation.** This is a period of 6 months to a year during which the relationship gets started and begins to take on importance for both individuals. Both parties develop expectations and engage in work-related interactions. The mentor coaches and provides challenging work and visibility. The protégé provides technical assistance, shows respect, and demonstrates the desire and willingness to be coached. It is important to recognize that the relationship between mentor and protégé may be initiated by the protégé. Indeed, it may be increasingly important for protégés to take proactive roles, seeking out appropriate mentors. Research shows that protégés do influence the nature and amounts of mentoring they receive and that protégés who have internal loci of control, are high self-monitors, and have high emotional stability are especially likely to initiate mentoring relationships.[103]

> **Cultivation.** After initiation, there is a phase of 2 to 5 years during which the mentor provides many career-related and psychosocial functions. There are frequent interactions and many mutual benefits. Both parties become emotionally linked.

> **Separation.** This phase may begin when the protégé feels it is time to assert autonomy and independence or when something external to the relationship, such as a promotion for the protégé or a transfer for the mentor, is marked by significant changes in the functions provided by the mentor relationship and in the affective experiences of the mentor and protégé. There may be feelings of turmoil, anxiety, and loss, and both parties reassess the value of the relationship as it becomes a less central part of their work lives. The period is especially stressful if the protégé feels abandoned by the mentor or if the mentor resents the protégé's growing independence. Nevertheless, this phase is critical to development; it gives the young manager a chance to demonstrate the ability to perform independently from the mentor, and it enables the mentor to demonstrate success in developing new management talent.

> **Redefinition.** If the separation stage has been negotiated successfully, the relationship enters a final, redefinition stage characterized primarily by friendship. The parties continue to have some informal contact and to provide mutual support. The relationship takes on a more equal footing, though the mentor may continue to take pride in the protégé's accomplishments and the protégé may continue to feels gratitude and appreciation for the support of earlier years.

BENEFITS AND COSTS OF MENTORING [104]

The mentoring relationship is critical to career development. Precisely because it is so important, mentoring may generate both costs and benefits for both the mentor and protégé.

Benefits and Costs to Protégés Benefits and costs of mentoring from the perspective of the protégé are shown in Figure 9-17. There are clearly many potential benefits of the mentoring relationship to protégés. Mentors bring the strengths and accomplishments of their protégés to the attention of others, nominating them for positions and increasing their visibility. They take protégés under their wing, helping to protect them from various consequences of errors and warning them of the dangers associated with certain actions. They provide valuable emotional support and guidance. In general, evidence suggests that mentoring is crucial to protégés' career development. [105]

At the same time, mentoring may entail costs for protégés. For one thing, protégés may have an increased workload and work under heightened scrutiny on their jobs. Further, if the mentor lacks talent or has mistaken ideas about the company, the protégé may be hurt. The protégé may also toil in the shadow of the mentor and thus fail to receive proper credit for his or her contributions. Further, being attached to a mentor may be a problem if the mentor loses in a major political contest. Also, others may misperceive the nature of the relationship. For example, if the mentor is of the opposite gender, others may assume that the professional relationship has turned personal. Protégés may also run risks if they terminate the relationship but stay with the or-

FIGURE 9-17
Benefits and Costs of Mentoring for the Protégé

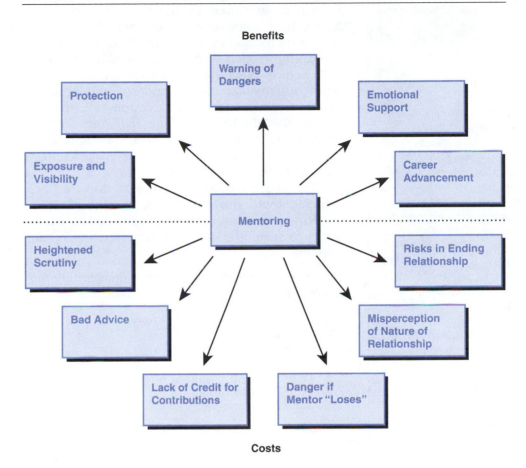

ganization. Further, if coworkers think the protégé is getting special treatment that they are not, resentment is likely. As one manager noted, "No one likes the teacher's pet." [106]

Benefits and Costs to Mentors Mentors also face various benefits and costs in the mentoring relationship. On the plus side, protégés are generally loyal to mentors and put in time and effort on assigned tasks. Mentors receive recognition from others in the firm for their mentoring efforts, and they are associated with achievements of the protégé. Further, many mentors get great personal satisfaction from mentoring: It causes them to feel needed and gives them a sense of accomplishment.

On the other hand, mentoring demands considerable time and effort. Further, if the protégé lacks talent or motivation and fails to perform well, the mentor may be blamed. And, like the protégé, the mentor may suffer from others' misperceptions of the basis of a mixed-gender relationship. Finally, mentors often feel deserted and betrayed when a protégé breaks off the mentoring relationship.

Web Wise

Systers

Thousands of women and minorities are using a new, high-tech approach to mentoring: the personal computer.* They seek informal career guidance—virtual mentors—from online bulletin boards, in-house electronic mail, or websites. For example, when one female computer scientist grew frustrated trying to get male coworkers to pay attention to her at meetings, she posted her complaints on Systers, an electronic mailing list (and now a website) for women. The list, begun in 1987, now has over 2,500 members in 38 countries. The scientist quickly got several answers, providing concrete suggestions. Visit Systers at:

http://www.systers.org

*J. E. Rigdon, "You're Not All Alone If There's a Mentor Just a Keyboard Away," *The Wall Street Journal,* December 1, 1993, p. B1; N. D. King, J. F. Alexander, D. E. McCorkle, and R. Martinez, "Preparing for Careers in Global Business: Strategies for Female College Students," *American Business Review,* June 1999, pp. 34–42; and D. Radcliff, "Champions of Women in Technology," *Computerworld,* January 18, 1999, pp. 46–48.

ISSUES IN MENTORING OF WOMEN AND MINORITIES[107]

Firms are taking formal steps to ensure that qualified women and minorities have mentors. Dozens of large firms, including AT&T, Johnson & Johnson, and Xerox, have hired full-time "diversity managers," one of whose roles is to establish mentoring relationships.[108] At many companies, such as Pacific Bell, promising women—often nominated by their department heads—are paired with senior executives who offer one-to-one career counseling. And many women who attain high positions reach out to help younger women—some of them still in school. For example, a University of Pennsylvania alumnae group called the *Trustees' Council of Penn Women* gives female students a list of about 70 distinguished women on whom they can call for career advice. The council also runs a "shadowing" program that lets students spend a workday with a female executive.

The process model in the nearby Bottom Line summarizes the basic steps associated with the implementation of the formal mentoring process.

Now, complete Skills Practice 9-6. The exercise will give you an opportunity to develop skill in designing an effective mentoring process for another person.

Skills Practice 9-6
Becoming an Effective Mentor

Skill Level: Basic

Skill Objective
To develop skill in being a mentor to others.

Procedure
Apply the steps that follow to develop a plan for being an effective mentor as an upper-class student mentoring an incoming freshman student.

1. **Your role in this exercise is to be a student mentor.** This is an appropriate role for you since you have the experience needed to be a student mentor (you have been in college). In addition, the basic mentoring process for a student is not fundamentally different from a typical mentoring process in a corporate setting.

    In this exercise, your task is to design a mentoring process for an incoming freshman student who is attending your college or university. You should design your mentoring process based on your own experience as a college student in terms of what you think a new student needs to know about surviving at your school.

2. **The structure of the mentoring process.** List the issues that you would discuss with your student "protégé." Be as specific as possible and record your answers on a separate page.

3. **The mentoring process itself.** Describe how you would implement your mentoring process with your student protégé (e.g., how often to meet, how long to meet, etc.).

4. **Evaluation of the mentoring process.** Describe how you would assess the effectiveness of your mentoring process. Be as specific as possible.

Discussion Questions
1. How can a good mentor make a difference in terms of helping other people?
2. What are some of the most important things to do when mentoring someone?
3. What would have to be done if you wanted to create a large-scale mentoring system that matches upper-class students with incoming freshmen?
4. What are the implications of this exercise for you as a future manager or supervisor?

BOTTOM LINE

The Bottom Line: The Formal Mentoring Process

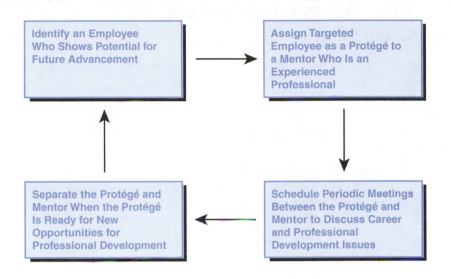

Identify an Employee Who Shows Potential for Future Advancement → Assign Targeted Employee as a Protégé to a Mentor Who Is an Experienced Professional

Separate the Protégé and Mentor When the Protégé Is Ready for New Opportunities for Professional Development ← Schedule Periodic Meetings Between the Protégé and Mentor to Discuss Career and Professional Development Issues

We began this chapter by warning you to prepare for the workquake, and we hope we have helped with that preparation. Those who will survive and prosper in the workquake will actively seek to understand their organizations and professions and their own career goals and capabilities and will be proactive in managing their work lives and careers. We encourage you not only to take seriously the information in this chapter when thinking about and planning for your career but to continue to seek information about careers and career management. Good luck in the coming interesting times.

Now, read the Real-World Management Challenge and develop specific strategies for addressing the problem. Later, you can compare your recommendations to those of a group of management consultants.

Real-World Management Challenge

STRESS MANAGEMENT PROGRAMS

The Situation

The Kensington Technology Group recently conducted a survey of employee stress and found that worker stress levels are on the increase. The specific stressors facing employees include the use of technology, such as voice mail and e-mail, and heavier work loads for employees.

Given the employee stress that has resulted from these work trends, some companies are developing specific programs and policies to help employees to strike a better balance between work and personal time and to promote a high quality of life.

What Would You Do?

If you were a senior manager in a firm, what specific strategies would you implement to reduce your employees' stress?

Source: M. A. Verespej, "Stressed Out," *Industry Week,* February 21, 2000, pp. 30–34.

TOP TEN LIST: KEY POINTS TO REMEMBER

FOSTERING PERSONAL GROWTH

10. Develop and implement personal and job-related strategies for managing yourself more effectively.
9. Always seek to achieve some balance between work and leisure in your life.
8. Enhance your ability to cope with stress by eating right and exercising on a regular basis.
7. Develop and maintain a personal and professional support network.
6. Maintain a fundamentally positive outlook on your career and life.
5. Take personal responsibility for managing your own career.
4. Define career success in terms beyond just job title and pay.
3. Identify a mentor who is willing to share his/her wisdom and expertise with you.
2. Assess your career progress and satisfaction on a regular basis.
1. Develop and implement special programs to advance the career development of women and minorities in your organization.

QUESTIONS FOR REVIEW AND REFLECTION

REVIEW QUESTIONS

1. What is behavioral self-management? Present 10 guidelines for behavioral self-management.
2. What is cognitive self-management? Discuss three strategies to promote effective thinking.
3. Define stressors, stress, and stress reactions and discuss the series of physiological reactions in stress.
4. Identify nine primary stressors.
5. Discuss four personal influences on stress.
6. What are the major components of burnout?
7. Present 12 guidelines for managing personal stress.
8. Discuss company stress-management programs, wellness programs, and employee assistance programs.
9. What is the protean career? Discuss differences between the protean career and the traditional career.
10. Describe four career stages in organizations. Then, discuss developmental needs in early, middle, and late career.
11. Discuss the career cone, career anchors, and career concept types.
12. Identify nine guidelines for self-management of careers.
13. Discuss approaches that companies are taking to enhance careers for women and minorities.
14. Define mentoring. Identify phases in the mentoring relationship and identify potential benefits and costs of mentoring for the mentor and protégé.

CRITICAL THINKING QUESTIONS

1. For decades, many people have questioned attempts to use learning theory to motivate employees. Now, some people are raising similar concerns about company efforts to teach employees behavioral self-management. They reason that, "It's bad enough that we try to drive employees to work beyond their limits.

Now we're teaching them to push themselves. Where will it all end?" Do you agree? Why or why not?

2. After listening to a presentation on company programs for managing stress, your boss says, "This really bothers me. Stress is a natural part of any job. When employees take a job as a telemarketer or customer service representative or manager or whatever, they know that the job's demands are likely to be stressful. If people can't handle the stress, they should look for other jobs. The company shouldn't have to spend time and money to compensate for employees' weaknesses." Defend a position for or against your boss's arguments.

3. A colleague says, "I just can't accept the idea that desirable changes are stressful. They're exciting and stimulating, but I see that as something very different from stress." How would you respond?

4. Some companies are now giving incentives to employees who engage in healthy behaviors. Consider the following argument: "What matters to employees and companies is the state of the employees' health, not just whether they're currently engaging in certain types of healthy behaviors. Companies should be rewarding employees for their health status, not their healthy behaviors." Present your views on this argument.

5. You overhear the following comments: "This talk about the protean career is a cop-out. People who can't succeed by conventional criteria say, 'That's not important to me. What I care about is personal growth and fulfillment.' Who do these losers think they're kidding?" What do you think of this view?

6. A friend says, "When people talk about the Japanese *madogiwazoku*—the 'sitting by the window tribe'— they act like these workers are just excess fat to be trimmed and discarded. If those people don't have productive work to do now, it's the fault of the company. Those employees have put in many years for their companies. They've earned their view out the window." Do you agree? Why or why not?

7. A colleague says, "This talk about self-management of careers sounds really Machiavellian to me. The next thing we know, we'll be seeing "Survivor" episodes set in corporate offices. I think employees should just do their best at their jobs, and cream will rise to the top. In my opinion, the best employees should be promoted, not those who are the best self-marketers." Present arguments against this position.

8. Some people have expressed concerns about whether it is ethical to have special career management programs for women and minorities. They argue that such programs are unfair to other employees, including white men who may have been economically or educationally disadvantaged. Defend a position for or against this view.

9. A manager in your department is near retirement. He says to you, "The company is pressing me to do more mentoring of our new employees. I'm just not going to do it. Mentoring these days is a minefield. If the protégé fails, I take the blame. I need to devote my time and energy to wrapping up my career and preparing for retirement. I just see a lot of costs to mentoring with very little gain." How would you respond?

EXPERIENTIAL EXERCISES

WEB EXERCISE 9-1: STRESS MANAGEMENT AND EMOTIONAL WELLNESS LINKS

The following website offers hundreds of links to stress management and emotional wellness resources, including cognitive approaches to stress management, humor and health, relaxation techniques, time management strategies, approaches to increasing social support networks, nutritional approaches to stress management, exercise and stress management, emotional self-help, and much more:

http://imt.net/~randolfi/StressLinks.html

Visit the site and then complete the following tasks:

1. Select three links from the site that seem potentially useful and/or interesting to you (for instance, Biofeedback Webzine, Mantra Meditation, and Panic Coping Skills).

2. Visit those three sites and examine the resources, providing a short (two-paragraph) discussion of each.

3. Provide your reactions to each of the sites. Were they interesting? Useful? Would you use them again? How might they help you as a manager?

WEB EXERCISE 9-2: CAREER RESOURCES ON THE WEB

Listed next are four major career-related websites:

America's Job Bank: The America's Job Bank is a partnership between the U.S. Department of Labor and the state-operated Public Employment Service. It offers computerized links to the 2,000 state Employment Services offices and provides listings of about 1 million job seekers and more than 1 million available jobs. The site also provides a wide range of occupational and economic information.

http://www.ajb.dni.us/

CareerMosaic: CareerMosaic offers a wealth of information regarding job openings, cooperative opportunities, résumé preparation, career planning books, online job fairs, the Fortune Career Resource Center, the International Gateway, and more.

http://www.careermosaic.com/cm/

Job Hunt: Job Hunt is a large compilation of Internet-accessible job search resources and services. These include job search-retrieval systems and places to which you may submit your résumé. There are many links, including a link to *Career Magazine* and links to most of the other major career boards.

http://www.job-hunt.org

Monster Board: The Monster Board provides an interactive database that permits you to list and locate job opportunities. You can research companies, store your résumé on the database, read listings of career events and information, visit various "career zones" (such as health care, international, and HR), and more.

http://www.monster.com/

1. Visit each of the job sites and find one feature from each that you think is especially interesting or useful.
2. Write a one- or two-paragraph description of the feature from each site that you have selected.
3. Select two of the four features and use them (i.e., post a résumé, do a job search, etc.).
4. Discuss your reactions to the two features you used. Were they helpful? Were they easy to use? Were there things you found frustrating? Would you use the feature in the future?

CASE 9-1
THE WORK/LIFE BALANCE PROGRAM AT DELOITTE & TOUCHE

The Organization

Deloitte & Touche is a leading professional services firm that offers assurance and advisory, tax, and management consulting services to clients through a professional staff of more than 30,000 people working at approximately 100 U.S. offices. The firm works with clients in a wide range of industries, including financial services, energy/utilities, technology, communications, manufacturing, and transportation. On a global scale, Deloitte & Touche is part of Deloitte Touche Tohmatsu, a professional services firm with more than 90,000 employees who work with clients in more than 130 countries.

The corporate mission of Deloitte & Touche is "To Help Our Clients and Our People Excel." The core values of the firm include the following: outstanding value to clients, commitment to each other, integrity, strength from cultural diversity, and recognition of the importance of people.

The Situation

In 1992, Deloitte & Touche identified two alarming realities with respect to its workforce. First, the turnover rate for women at the firm was much higher than for men. Female employees perceived that the firm was male-dominated and that there were limited opportunities for advancement. Second, both men and women reported that they were experiencing major challenges in balancing work with their personal commitments.[109]

The Work/Life Balance Program

One of the key human resource standards at the firm is "respecting the personal lives of our people and supporting them in balancing multiple commitments and interests." On the basis of this principle and the results of the 1992 surveys, Deloitte & Touche implemented a work/life balance program in 1993 to enable its employees to establish and maintain high-quality professional and personal lives. The rationale behind this was that employees who have more meaningful and satisfying personal lives would be more effective at work.

The major feature of the work/life balance program is flexibility. The firm offers flexible work schedules to employees so that they have greater control over which days they work and how many hours they work on those days. Flextime provides workers with the option of starting their workday earlier and finishing earlier. This enables some employees to pick their children up after school or to have time to handle business during the day. The telecommuting component of the program makes it possible for employees to work at home and to have the flexibility to pursue other personal interests, such as writing a book, running for public office, or training to compete in a sporting event.

Another unique component of the program is called *LifeWorks*. This program is administered by Ceridian Performance Partners. It provides resource and referral services that help employees with child care and eldercare, school selection, adoption assistance, and locating a variety of personal and convenience services.

Results

In 1997, at least 650 employees were using flexible work arrangements. Over 70 percent of the employees using these arrangements indicated that they would have left the firm if these options were not available to them. Deloitte & Touche estimates that the increased retention of administrative professionals due to the work/life balance program has saved it over $11 million. The program has also helped the firm to hire high-quality professionals. Specifically, 76 percent of women and 60 percent of men said that the work/life balance program strongly influenced their decision to accept a job offer with Deloitte & Touche.

Finally, the results of the 1999 Human Resource Standards Survey and Flexible Work Arrangements Survey indicated that the work/life balance program at Deloitte & Touche has been highly beneficial for its employees, its clients, and the firm as a whole. The 1999 results of these surveys showed that an all-time high of 83 percent of the firm's employees said that they would recommend Deloitte & Touche to their friends as a place to work.

Discussion Questions

1. Why has the issue of work/life balance in organizations become so significant in the last decade?
2. From a business perspective, what is the case that can be made in support of implementing work/life balance programs in organizations?
3. What are the strengths of the work/life program at Deloitte & Touche? What about weaknesses?
4. What are the short-term and long-term challenges associated with the success of the work/life program at Deloitte & Touche?
5. What are the practical implications of this case for you as future managers?

http://www.dttus.com

Source: Deloitte & Touche website, http://www.dttus.com

CASE 9-2
CREATING A SELF-DIRECTED WORKFORCE AT THE HOSPITAL FOR SPECIAL CARE

The Organization

The Hospital for Special Care (HSC) is a private, not-for-profit hospital located in New Britain, Connecticut. HSC is licensed by the state of Connecticut and affiliated with the University of Connecticut as a teaching hospital. The 200-bed facility focuses on providing rehabilitation services for individuals suffering from stroke, spinal cord injury, brain injury, or other related conditions. In short, the mission of HSC is "to rebuild lives."

The medical staff at HSC consists of specialists in internal medicine, infectious diseases, psychiatry, pulmonology, psychology, and pediatrics.

HSC maintains strong ties with its local community. It is strongly committed to the professional development of its employees and to sharing its expertise with other medical professionals and the public.

The Situation

Senior administrators at HSC concluded that being the most cost-effective provider of health care services would be the key to ensuring that the hospital would remain financially strong and profitable in the long term. In 1992, HSC reorganized itself into three service lines: pediatrics, rehabilitation, and respiratory care. A clinical resources department was created at this time. This new department was staffed with experts from different disciplines who were responsible for providing clinical resources, supervision, education, and support to other units at HSC. It was managed by a clinical resources director who was also a member of the senior administration.[110]

In 1996, as part of an ongoing evaluation, HSC identified the need to reengineer the clinical resources department in order to better align it with the needs of its customers. The new design for the department used a self-directed work team approach that gave full responsibility for managing all aspects of clinical services to a team of medical professionals. The objectives of the self-directed work team approach were to enhance employee empowerment, build commitment to organizational change, and create a sense of ownership in the organization. This approach was a significant deviation from the traditional approach in which employees worked toward achieving individual performance objectives under the direction of the clinical resources director.

In 1997, the clinical resources department was renamed the *clinical resources self-directed work team* (CRSDWT). The clinical resources director position was formally eliminated under this new structure. The team members (clinical resources consultants) assumed responsibility for 70 percent of the clinical resources director's position.

The mission of the CRSDWT was "To provide clinical leadership to the organization in terms of meeting staff educational needs as well as contributing to the clinical body of knowledge of the larger professional community." The CRSDWT educational efforts also reflect the organizational goal to provide care that is appropriate for the patient's age and developmental level and takes into account the individual's cultural and spiritual needs.

The team worked with a facilitator to establish ground rules and to develop a communication system. Later in the year, the team conducted its own evaluation of its performance. This was based on the pre-existing merit pay system that focuses on individual team-member performance in clinical expertise and education.

Results

A midyear evaluation of the team revealed the following problems areas: (1) The organization did not understand

the purpose or role of the clinical resources consultant; (2) team members did not feel that their needs were being met; and (3) team response time was too slow. In addition, coordination problems existed in terms of linking customer inquiries to consultants, and the consultants themselves did not fully understand the scope of their roles and how they overlapped within the self-management framework.

The CRSDWT developed an action plan to address the issues raised in their self-evaluation process. This included maintaining ongoing contact between members of the team and internal customers. In addition, a communication effort was implemented to educate the clinical resources consultants about their roles in the organization.

Up to this point, the CRSDWT has produced many benefits for HSC in terms of dealing with complex patient cases, increasing quality, education, and reducing costs.

Discussion Questions

1. How did HSC apply the principles of effective self-management?
2. Evaluate HSC in terms of the overall self-directed work-team approach it implemented. What were its strengths and weaknesses?
3. What needs to be done to ensure the long-term success of self-managing work teams at HSC?
4. What are the practical implications of this case for you as a future manager?

http://www.hfsc.org/

Source: Website for HSC: http://www.hfsc.org

VIDEO CASE
A CASE STUDY IN CAREER MANAGEMENT: LABELLE MANAGEMENT

Running Time: 12:05

LaBelle Management was founded in 1948 when the late Norman LaBelle opened the Pixie Restaurant. Complete with carhop waitresses and inexpensive food, the Pixie quickly became a popular place with both the local population and the students of Central Michigan University. Now, LaBelle Management owns and operates 30 hotel,

resort, conference center, and restaurant properties in the Midwest. These include the Grand Beach Resort Hotel, Pixie Restaurants, franchises of Comfort Inn, Fairfield Inn, Big Boy Restaurants, Bennigan's, and Ponderosa Steakhouse, and other properties.

The video shows owner Bart LaBelle and others as

they discuss career management at LaBelle. After viewing the video, answer the following questions:

1. What are the dual goals of LaBelle Management's comprehensive career management program? How successful has LaBelle been in achieving those goals?

2. Why does LaBelle pay such close attention to its new employees during their first 90 days on the job?

3. How does LaBelle encourage its managers to develop people beneath them?

4. What is LaBelle's Adopt an Employee program?

5. What are the elements of Tier Management at LaBelle?

6. How does the fact that LaBelle Management owns a variety of different types of properties affect its career management efforts?

http://www.labellemgt.com/

LIGHTEN UP
THE MICROSOFT LEXICON

We wrote earlier in the chapter about jargon at Microsoft. To learn more about the special language of Microsoft, access The Microsoft Lexicon:

http://www.members.tripod.com/jeeem/mslex.htm

There, you'll find the definitions of *buzzword bingo, dogfood, facemail, klugey, open the kimono, permatemp, self-toast, weasel user,* and about 150 more Microsoft terms.

MANAGING POLITICS, CONFLICT, AND CHANGE

SKILLS OBJECTIVES

> To apply political strategies and tactics to effectively manage work situations.
> To apply strategies for reducing political activity in an organization.
> To use various conflict-handling styles for dealing with different types of situations.
> To effectively design and implement organizational change.
> To apply strategies for handling various forms of resistance to change.

KNOWLEDGE OBJECTIVES

> Identify causes and consequences—including costs and benefits— of political behaviors.
> Recognize political strategies and tactics and learn guidelines for minimizing political activities.
> Understand the causes and characteristics of organizational conflict.
> Understand conflict management, including ways to resolve conflict and to generate productive conflict.
> Identify forces for change, the nature of the change process, and targets of change.
> Understand sources of resistance to change and approaches to overcoming resistance.
> Describe organization development (OD), including OD assumptions, the OD process, and conditions for OD success.
> Describe the learning organization, including the disciplines, learning disabilities, and approaches to applying the disciplines.

Politics, conflict, and change are real, pervasive, and important. They create uncertainty, turmoil, and stress. Your success as a manager will depend on your ability to deal with them. Further, we see that some similar things, such as resource scarcity, cause them. They each foster more of the same: Politics leads to more politics, conflict to more conflict, change to more change. They may also breed one another. Politics and change are likely to engender conflict. Conflict may foster change, and it may lead to political behaviors. Finally, while politics, conflict, and change aren't often listed in job descriptions, they involve critical skills. You have to get ready for them.

In this chapter, we first address organizational politics. We consider causes of political behaviors and the costs and benefits of politics. We then discuss specific political strategies and tactics and suggest guidelines for minimizing levels of political activity. We next examine organizational conflict, including its causes and characteristics. We see how conflict premises influence conflict processes and outcomes and discuss conflict management, including ways to resolve conflict and to generate productive conflict. We next turn to a discussion of organizational change, including forces for change, the nature of the change process, and targets for change. We consider sources of resistance to change and approaches that can be taken to effectively deal with such resistance. Then, we examine the set of change approaches known as *organization development* and conclude with a discussion of ways to develop change-oriented learning organizations.

Take a few minutes now and answer the self-assessment questions that follow. You will learn more from this chapter if you start off with a greater awareness of your beliefs and feelings about how to manage power, conflict, and organizational change.

Self-Assessment 10-1
Attitudes Toward Managing Politics, Conflict, and Change

Please answer the following questions regarding your attitudes toward managing politics, conflict, and change in organizations. Answer each question as honestly as possible using the response scale that follows.

1 = Disagree Strongly
2 = Disagree Somewhat
3 = Neither Agree nor Disagree
4 = Agree Somewhat
5 = Agree Strongly

1. _____ Effective managers do not use political tactics to get their jobs done in organizations.
2. _____ The best strategy for responding to people who behave in a highly political manner is to ignore them.
3. _____ Political factors are not important to my personal success in an organization as long as I perform my job well and mind my own business.
4. _____ Too little conflict in an organization can be a problem rather than a strength.
5. _____ Compromising is always the best approach to use when dealing with conflict in organizations.
6. _____ Avoiding the conflict is always the least effective approach for handling conflict in organizations.
7. _____ Management must take specific actions to prevent or overcome employee resistance to organizational change.

445

Chapter 10   Managing Politics, Conflict, and Change

Assessment
Assessment
Assessment
Assessment

DEVIL'S ADVOCATE

I am really turned off by the idea of corporate politics, and I refuse to play this "game." As long as I do a good job and not worry about politics at all, I will be fine.

It's a bit naive to think that all you need to do to be effective in the "real world" is to put your head down and focus exclusively on just doing your job well. Although this is certainly important, if you do this, you will be much more likely to stay in your current job for a long time. The reason for this is that you have not done anything to cultivate your credibility and a favorable impression in the eyes of others. In order to be successful in your organization, you will need to show management that you possess skills and expertise needed by the firm and that you have the ability to "fit in" in relation to the company's way of thinking and doing things (i.e., its culture). All these things require the use of basic political strategies and tactics. You may not like playing "corporate politics," but it is an essential part of being successful in the real world.

How can conflict possibly be a good thing?

If you are a manager or team leader and nobody ever questions anybody else regarding the goals of your work unit or your plan for achieving them, you should be suspicious. This may mean that your staff is not really

working together in terms of thoroughly analyzing problems and getting all the important issues out on the table. This can lead to poor decision making on the part of the manager and team. Many good managers attempt to stimulate "healthy conflict" (constructive discussion and disagreement) in order to increase the team's chances of coming up with the best ideas or the best plan of action. The bottom line is that although too much conflict is usually a bad thing, no conflict whatsoever may also be a bad thing.

In terms of handling conflict, my style is my style. It's not realistic to expect me to change my approach for every conflict situation I encounter.

Clearly, many people have dominant styles or characteristic ways of handling such issues as conflict. However, research on managing conflict shows that a manager should match his/her approach for handling conflict to the situation. For example, you may be a "collaborator" by nature, but if you find yourself in a conflict with a "competer," your style may not be very appropriate or effective in that situation. So, while you may have one general style for handling conflict, it will be beneficial to you in the long run to be flexible in terms of how you handle conflict in specific situations.

Why is organizational change so difficult to implement? So long as management is very clear about telling employees how they need to change the performance of their jobs, isn't it a "no-brainer"?

Implementing change in today's business environment is much more involved than simply telling people that they are going to be doing things differently and here's how to do it. Today, management needs the "buy in" or commitment of employees when it comes to working toward achieving organizational objectives: Management needs employees to exert 100 percent of their effort toward helping the company to be successful. This, combined with the fact that many people simply do not like change, makes it even more important to plan and implement organizational change in a very systematic fashion. Specifically, managers need to take the time to explain to employees why a given change is needed. In addition, managers must provide support (e.g., guidance and training) for employees adopting new changes so that they can make a smooth transition to the new way of doing things. Finally, managers need to make sure that changes "stick" in the sense that employees continue to implement a change appropriately over time.

8. _____ Organizational change often fails because management does not provide support to employees in implementing the change.

9. _____ Organizations today operate in external environments that are fairly simple and stable.

10. _____ It is possible to make individual employees "smarter" but not the organization as a whole.

As a way to assess your initial level of skill in managing politics, conflict, and change in organizations, complete the Pre-Test Skills Assessment. Read the scenario and develop an action plan for how you would handle this situation. Be as specific as possible in stating your recommendations.

Pre-Test Skills Assessment
Managing Politics, Conflict, and Change

You are the director of marketing at XBKE, a company that designs and manufactures high-end racing bicycles. You lead a team of seven bright but relatively inexperienced marketing specialists who are responsible for building the sporty image of the brand through a variety of promotional campaigns. In the past, your team was fairly successful with the marketing of the company's products when it only had three basic models. However, the company's explosive growth, changing customer preferences (desire for greater off-road capability and for a wider variety of styles and colors), and intense foreign competition have made your team's job infinitely more complex.

The company recently announced a new empowerment program in which employees are to be given greater freedom to work in teams to manage themselves. Your job as the leader is to serve more as a coach or resource person as opposed to serving as a manager providing specific direction to the team. When you announce this to your team, the reaction is very mixed. While a couple of employees like the idea, others are not comfortable with the lack of structure that will be associated with the new program. A major concern of everyone is that they don't really understand what empowerment means or how they are supposed to behave under such a program. In addition, you are concerned that some of the personality differences between your employees will become problematic without a clear structure for the team. Specifically, some employees have been very competitive with each other in trying to outshine each other on the job so that they may increase their chances for a promotion in the company.

As the manager of this work unit, develop an action plan for handling this situation. Be specific and focus on action.

Skills Practice 10-1 will give you an opportunity to interview a management professional and to learn more about specific examples of effective and ineffective handling of politics in organizations.

Skills Practice 10-1
Field Work: Organizational Politics in the Real World

Skill Level: **Basic**

Skill Objective
To develop skill in analyzing political factors as they exist in actual organizational situations.

Procedure
1. Interview someone you know who is working in a managerial position. In your interview, be sure to ask the following questions:
    a. What is the most challenging political issue you have had to deal with on your job? How did you handle it, and what was the outcome?
    b. What is the biggest political mistake that you or someone you know has made in your organization? Why was this such a serious mistake?

   c. Describe the person who you feel is the most effective at managing political issues in your organization. What is it about this person that makes him/her so skilled at organizational politics?

   d. What advice would you give to students about how to handle organizational politics when they start their first jobs in organizations after graduation?

2. *(Optional)* Present a summary of your findings to the class.

3. Answer the following discussion questions.

Discussion Questions

1. Discuss the things that you feel are associated with effective political players in organizations.

2. Discuss the things that you feel are associated with ineffective political players in organizations.

3. What are the implications of this exercise for you as a future manager?

MANAGING POLITICS

When we hear someone speak of organizational politics, we probably think of such things as "passing the buck," "apple polishing," "backstabbing," and other "dirty tricks" we use to further our selfish interests. We use the term *organizational politics* more broadly, to refer to activities that people perform to acquire, enhance, and use power and other resources to obtain their preferred outcomes in a situation where there is uncertainty or disagreement.[1] Since the focus is on people's preferred outcomes, rather than organizational outcomes, this may or may not involve activities that are contrary to the best interests of the organization.

It is easy to condemn organizational politics as unethical (and we explore the ethics of politics later in the chapter). We need to remember, though, that the way in which an activity is labeled influences whether we see it as political. For example, what one person labels *blaming others* another may label *fixing responsibility;* passing the buck may be called *delegating responsibility;* forming coalitions may be labeled *facilitating teamwork;* apple polishing may be seen as *demonstrating loyalty.*[2] So, we should be careful about condemning behavior as political until we ask whether the labeling itself was a political act![3]

People's ambivalence toward organizational politics is reflected in Figure 10-1. That figure shows, for example, that almost 90 percent of managers believe that successful executives must be good politicians, but only about 40 percent feel politics helps the organization to function effectively. The figure also reflects a dilemma of sorts: Most managers believe that those at the top got there because of politics, but about half want those at the top to get rid of politics. However, people like to dance with the one they came with; they aren't likely to abandon the keys to their success.

Further, even though you may be justifiably reluctant to use political tactics, it's probably true that everyone wants to avoid political gaffes, such as criticizing your boss in public, losing control of your emotions during meetings, or challenging sacred beliefs or values of the organization. So, sensitivity to politics may be important, if only to be alert for the political actions of others and to avoid personal embarrassment. In the nearby Voice of Experience,

FIGURE 10-1

Managers' Feelings About Workplace Politics

Statement	% Expressing Strong or Moderate Agreement
The existence of workplace politics is common in most organizations.	93.2
Successful executives must be good politicians.	89.0
The higher you go in organizations, the more political the climate becomes.	76.2
Powerful executives don't act politically.	15.7
You have to be political to get ahead in organizations.	69.8
Top management should try to get rid of politics in organizations.	48.6
Politics helps organizations function effectively.	42.1
Organizations free of politics are happier than those where there is a lot of politics.	59.1
Politics in organizations is detrimental to efficiency.	55.1

J. Gandz and V. V. Murray, "The Experience of Workplace Politics," *Academy of Management Journal*, 1980, *23*, p. 244.

Scott Finkelmeyer, an account executive at Siemens Medical Systems, provides suggestions for dealing with politics in organizations.

In this section, we discuss factors that encourage political behavior and examine political strategies and tactics. We then consider some political games that are played in organizations. Next, we look at the ethics of political behavior and its costs and benefits. If you decide that particular behaviors are self-serving at the expense of the organization or that the behaviors cost the organization more than they are worth, you can consider some guidelines that we provide for minimizing political behavior.

FACTORS ENCOURAGING POLITICAL BEHAVIOR

Why does political behavior occur? It seems that there are some people who are prone to political behavior and some situations that seem to foster such behavior. These are summarized in Figure 10-2.

FIGURE 10-2

Some Determinants of Organizational Politics

Individual Determinants
- Machiavellianism
- Self-Monitoring
- Need for Power
- Individual Values

Organizational Politics

Organizational Determinants
- Organizational Values
- Ambiguity
- Counternorms
- Competition
- Level in Organization

VOICE OF EXPERIENCE

POLITICS AND CONFLICT

Scott Finkelmeyer,
Account Executive
Siemens Medical Systems

1. What kinds of political issues do you face on your job and in your organization?

In my organization I was hired at the same time as six other individuals who had just graduated from college. We are all very achievement-oriented and want to be successful and to move up at Siemens. So, we are competitive with each other in trying to make a good impression on our boss. This does not involve dirty tactics where we try to undermine each other, but rather a healthy sense of competitiveness that pushes each of us to be better.

At Siemens, the trainees in the account executive training program are strongly encouraged to work as a team and to do things that will reflect positively on the team as a whole because that is how we are viewed by others in the company. Two of my team members made some serious political errors during the first week on the job. First, when they arrived for a meeting at one of the corporate offices, one of them was rude to a receptionist. This receptionist informed management of how she was treated, and it really tarnished the image of the entire team. What a way to start! Second, at a company-sponsored social event that week, another trainee from my team drank way too much beer, and it showed. This did not impress management very much, either.

2. What advice would you give students regarding the effective handling of organizational politics in the real world?

First, always conduct yourself in a professional manner at all times when you are at work, including social events where people from your company are present. Never ever let your hair down! Remember that you are always being evaluated by others in your company, not just by your boss. Also, be aware of the grapevine in your organization. It can be nasty. Don't give people anything that can be processed through the "rumor mill." Finally, I would say that you should treat everyone in your organization as a customer, whether they are actually a customer or not.

3. What types of conflicts do you encounter in your job? How do you handle them?

I face two types of conflict that can occur on my job. First, there is conflict with customers, where they call me and say that the system I sold them does not meet their needs in some way or that the system they received was not the one they ordered. Second, I experience conflict with the technical people at my company, where a technician will call me and say that I shouldn't have sold a customer some combination of features or components with a system.

I try to handle conflict with customers by using a collaborative approach. We must keep the customers happy or they won't come back to us again in the future. I use more of a collaborative approach when dealing with people within the company, because we can't serve our customers well unless we work together as a team.

4. What advice would you give students regarding the effective handling of conflict in the real world?

First, you need to communicate with each other a lot. Be open with each other, and lay all the cards on the table. Make sure that everyone who is affected by the issue is involved in the process of resolving it. Finally, emphasize to the person(s) you have the conflict with that you want to resolve the issue but also maintain a good working relationship with them.

http://sms.siemens.com/

Individual Factors Four individual characteristics that influence political behavior are Machiavellianism, self-monitoring, need for power, and individual values. All have been discussed in previous chapters, so we look here only at their relationships to political behavior.

> **Machiavellianism.** Since, as discussed in Chapter 3, Machiavellians believe that ends justify means and that they should always "look out for number one," it's not surprising that they are highly political. Al Neuharth, the founder of *USA Today* and author of *Confessions of an SOB,* has defended his view that "winning is the most important thing in life" by stating that "I'm simply describing a combination of techniques that most successful CEOs use but don't admit to" and adding, "Being Machiavellian, as a general offense, is not all bad." As these statements suggest, Machiavellians see political behavior as pragmatic and, as such, as appropriate. As an example, research has shown Machiavellianism to be related to the decision to offer illegal kickbacks to purchasing agents.[4] Students scoring higher on Machiavellianism have been shown to score lower on measures of ethical orientation and lower on corporate social responsibility orientation.[5] Further, marketers scoring higher on Machiavellianism have been shown to be less likely to consider ethical aspects of situations.[6]

> **Self-Monitoring.** Recall that high self-monitors are chameleon-like, adjusting their behaviors in ways to induce positive reactions from others. High self-monitors have been shown to be more apt than low self-monitors to engage in manipulation and filtering of the information that they transmit upward in order to create a favorable impression. For instance, they are more likely to transmit information that reflects positively on their decision processes and more likely to try to shift the blame for mistakes to others.[7]

> **Need for Power.** Since politics is about the use of power, it makes sense that need for power should be related to political activity. In Chapter 6, we said that the need for power is the desire to control other persons, to influence their behavior, and to be responsible for them. However, David McClelland identified two types of need for power.[8] *Personalized power seekers* try to dominate others for the sake of dominating, and they derive satisfaction from conquering others. *Socialized power seekers* satisfy their power needs in ways that help the organization. They may show concern for group goals, find goals to motivate others, and work with a group to develop and achieve goals. So, we would probably expect more political behavior from personalized power seekers than from socialized power seekers.

> Finally, *individual values* may affect the levels of political behaviors or at least of unethical political behaviors. For example, the degree to which individuals have economic value orientations (interested in the production and consumption of goods and the uses or creation of wealth) or political value orientations (focusing on power, influence, and recognition) predicts unethical behavior.[9]

Organizational Factors Several organizational factors are known to influence organization politics. These include organizational values, ambiguity, counternorms, competition among employees, and level in the organization.

> **Organizational Values.** One organizational influence on political behavior is the set of values dominant in the organization. As we discussed in Chapter 8, these values are central to organizational culture. The values of some organizations condemn political behavior. In these organiza-

tions, it is felt that "hard facts," "cool logic," and "objective criteria" should rule. In other organizations, political behavior is seen as valuable and necessary in the real world and as entirely appropriate. To the extent that these values are widely accepted and communicated, political behavior is likely to vary accordingly. Some specific managerial values have been viewed as causes of unethical aspects of political activity:[10]

- A *bottom-line mentality* sees financial success as the only value to be considered; rules of morality are simply obstacles on the way to the bottom line.
- An *exploitative mentality* is a selfish perspective that encourages using people to benefit one's own immediate interests.
- A *Madison Avenue mentality* says, "It's right if I can convince you that it's right." This public relations–oriented mentality focuses on making others believe that our actions are moral, perhaps by hiding unethical behaviors or rationalizing them. As such, this mentality is a kind of organizational impression management; we look more at impression management later in the chapter.

> **Ambiguity.** Another key organizational determinant of political behavior is ambiguity. Politics thrives in ambiguous, uncertain situations. For instance, if goals are unclear, people may use political behaviors to define those goals to their advantage. If there is a lot of change in the organization, its markets, or its technology, people may exploit the resulting uncertainty to gain territory or otherwise serve self-interests. If there is ambiguity surrounding a decision, there is room for political maneuvering to define the decision and decision process to fit one's interests. Also, if there are limited resources, political behaviors may be used to maximize one's share of the pie.[11]

> **Counternorms.** Further, organizations may develop counternorms. *Counternorms* are accepted organizational practices that are contrary to the more explicit norms of the organization.[12] They are examples of the organization's "talking out of both sides of its mouth," saying that one thing is appropriate but expecting another. Some of these counternorms are shown in Figure 10-3.[13]

FIGURE 10-3
Norms and Counternorms

Norms	Counternorms
Openness, honesty, candor	Secrecy and lying; "play your cards close to your chest"
Follow the rules	Break the rules to get the job done
Be cost-effective	"Spend it or burn it"
Take responsibility	Avoid responsibility; "pass the buck"
"All for one and one for all"	Achieve your goals at the expense of others
Maintain an appearance of consensus; support the team	Maintain high visibility; "grandstanding"
Take timely action	"Never do today what you can put off until tomorrow"

> **Competition.** In addition, political behavior is nurtured by competition among employees. Competition fosters a zero-sum atmosphere, in which one person's gain is another's loss. In such an atmosphere, there is little incentive for cooperation and openness.

> **Level in the Organization.** Finally, people at all levels of organizations share the view that political behavior increases with organizational level.[14] This may reflect the fact that at higher levels in organizations, the stakes are higher and decisions are often more ambiguous.

POLITICAL STRATEGIES AND TACTICS

Jeffrey Pfeffer has described a variety of political strategies and tactics.[15] The strategies are general guidelines for the effective use of power for one's purposes. The tactics are specific ways in which those strategies can be carried out.

Political Strategies   Pfeffer identifies three general political strategies:

> **Make power unobtrusive.** Power is most effective when it is subtle. Blatantly employing power may create a backlash and use up "credits." It has been said of Michael Ovitz, founder of Creative Artists Agency, former president of Disney, and recognized Hollywood "power broker," that he "exercises power like a Zen brush painter: delicate, deliberate strokes."[16] Ovitz realizes that a key to successful power use is not to appear to be using power.

> **Build legitimacy.** Power is most effective when the power itself and the decision process and outcomes that flow from it appear to be legitimate. For instance, if it can be shown that actions are consistent with the values of the organization or that they were initiated by appropriate organizational actors (such as a committee broadly representing affected parties), legitimacy will be enhanced.

> **Build a base of support.** A final power strategy is to act in ways that either increase the actor's own power or obtain support or acquiescence from other powerful actors in the organization.

Political Tactics   The three strategies outlined by Pfeffer are general guidelines for effective power use. Here are some specific political tactics that are often employed to successfully carry out those strategies.

> **Selectively use objective criteria.** We've said that political tactics are likely to be employed in ambiguous, uncertain situations. In those situations, there is often room for disagreement over an appropriate criterion: Should we minimize cost, maximize quality, or what? In such cases, it's possible to decide which criterion makes your preferred alternative look best and then argue for that criterion. This is less obtrusive than simply arguing for the alternative; if the criterion is accepted, choice of the alternative will follow. Of course, in cases where you can simply specify criteria, you can essentially guarantee choice of your preferred alternative. For instance, you can say, "We need someone with at least 10 years of experience in this industry, and with an MBA, and with production experience, and who's familiar with our company. Go find the

best person." Of course, you have through your specification of those criteria made the choice.

> **Use outside experts.** The ability to hire an outside expert, such as a consultant, has many benefits. The expert is credible and authoritative since he or she appears objective, clearly has expertise, and is expensive—it's hard to disagree with someone whose advice costs thousands of dollars. However, Pfeffer sees outside experts as hired guns, brought in to support the position of the person who hired them. While they appear objective, they in fact are not. They were selected on the basis of their past recommendations and views, they are fed information by the people who hired them, and they want to be hired again. As such, the appearance of objectivity is an illusion.

> **Control the agenda.** Those who control an agenda can take advantage of their position in at least three ways. First, they can simply decide what will and won't be considered. Second, they can decide what gets discussed when. Things placed early on an agenda tend to be carefully considered and endlessly debated. Things placed late tend to be considered casually, if at all; people are so tired of being in a meeting that they just want to get it over with. Third, the relative placement of proposals makes a difference. For instance, suppose you have a stronger and a weaker proposal. Which should you place first? The evidence suggests that the weaker proposal should be placed first: It will be carefully considered and, if it is accepted, the stronger proposal will look even better and is also likely to be accepted. If the weaker proposal is rejected, the stronger proposal benefits in three ways: Its later placement means it will get less scrutiny, its placement after the weaker proposal lets it profit from contrast effects, and it may benefit from sympathy since the other proposal was defeated and you should get something. But, what if you don't have a weaker proposal to place before the stronger proposal? Invent one! A weak dummy proposal may be designed and used specifically to make the later, real proposal look better, receive less scrutiny, and capture some sympathy.

> **Form coalitions.** A *coalition* is a set of individuals or organizations who join together to pursue a specific goal. For instance, people may pool their votes to defeat a common foe. In laboratory experiments, the coalition containing the fewest resources (dollars, votes, shares, or whatever) needed to win often forms. This is explained by the *minimum-resource theory,* which says the smaller the winning coalition, the more leverage you get from your resources (e.g., you may be able to win in a particular voting situation by having a plurality of perhaps 30 percent of the votes). And, with a small coalition, you don't have to share the "spoils" with so many others. In contrast to these laboratory findings, Pfeffer argues that real-world coalitions are often as large as possible—a *maximum-resource theory.* By forming a large coalition, there is a broader base of support and fewer losers who may hold grudges in the future. Further, this larger coalition may not really be costly; some members will be happy just to be on the winning side, and some may accept promises of future benefits.

Coalitions may be external or internal. An *external coalition* is formed with outside groups in contact with the organization, such as

Web Wise

Building Coalitions

The Ohio State University Extension website provides information about coalition benefits and costs, coalition functioning and goal setting, communication in coalitions, construction of a coalition, turf issues, working with diverse cultures, networking, and other issues. Visit the site at:

http://ohioline.ag.ohio-state.edu/index.html

(Click on Search in the lefthand column and type "Coalition")

suppliers, creditors, or customers. An external coalition has the benefits of bringing in new resources and may have less conflict of interest with internal subunits. However, forming such coalitions may be seen as disloyal to the organization and its goals. An *internal coalition* is formed with others inside the organization with common interests. Internal allies are closer to the decision process and, therefore, may be more valuable in influencing decision outcomes.

One interesting internal coalition is formed through promotions. Suppose you're in a position to make or recommend a promotion. Of the handful of individuals who could possibly be selected, one seems clearly best qualified. Whom do you choose? Not that person. The reason: If you select the best-qualified candidate, he or she will think, "I was chosen because I'm best qualified. I deserved it." If, on the other hand, you select someone who is a surprise, he or she will think, "I have this position because you gave it to me. I owe you." You have gained an ally. So, the rule here is "promote the nonobvious choice."

Another innovative approach to formation of internal alliances is "everybody's a winner." With this tactic, people who don't get what they want may be given a fancy title or moved into a newly created, "higher-level" position as a consolation prize. This lets everyone save face, and the win-lose aspects of politics are downplayed.

> **Co-opt others.** With co-optation, some dissenting element is brought into the unit. *Co-optation* involves giving a representative of the organization or subunit whose support is sought a position on the board, committee, or other body of the unit seeking the support. For example, a student who is constantly challenging decisions of a university committee may be asked to join the committee. The student will then be exposed to the social influence of the committee members and to conformity pressures and will be forced to justify his or her statements and actions. Also, the student will begin to have a stake in the success of the committee and begin to think about it differently.

When Douglas Fraser, then president of the AFL-CIO, was put on the board of directors of Chrysler, many hailed the event as a victory for labor. Others, though, felt that Fraser had been co-opted and that he would now begin to identify more with management. One observer noted that "Fraser is now neither fish nor fowl." Of course, co-optation has its costs. For example, secrecy may be lost. In addition, the person who is co-opted may actually persuade others.

> **Use committees.** Suppose I know whom I want chosen to fill a new position; let's say it's Janet. I know, though, that if I just appoint Janet, there may be some rumblings of dissent: I have been obtrusive, haven't developed an aura of legitimacy, and haven't built a base of support. Instead, I'll appoint a search-and-screen committee, made up of respected representatives of all the areas affected by the position to be filled. I'll widely publicize the committee and its distinguished members, and I'll give the committee the charge of providing me with a list of suitable candidates for the position. I'll somehow make sure that Janet becomes one of those candidates (perhaps one of the committee members will be a "plant" who will argue for Janet's presence on the list, or perhaps I'll have to ask the committee to generate more names if Janet's is-

n't initially included). When the committee gives me its list, I will thank them profusely, will broadly and visibly praise the committee members for their efforts, and will note the time and effort and expertise they have devoted to this important task. Then I'll pick Janet! Use of committees in this way nicely satisfies each of the aforementioned general strategies: It is unobtrusive, it is seen as legitimate, and it builds a base of support.

QUESTIONING THE TACTICS

What makes Pfeffer's tactics so interesting is that they are all widely used and often appear socially desirable. And, of course, they may each be used for perfectly good and selfless reasons. Nevertheless, the discussion encourages us to at least question such tactics when they are used. We might ask, for instance:

> Why were these criteria specified in the posting of job requirements?
> Who selected the outside consultant who was brought in to make recommendations regarding changes in the reward system?
> Why wasn't a discussion of the proposed job redesign program on the agenda?
> Is this committee to which I've been appointed for real or is the decision it's dealing with a "done deal"?

The purpose of Skills Practice 10-2 is to give you a chance to apply the political strategies and tactics discussed in this section to a realistic organizational situation. Remember that this is the area where recent graduates have consistently indicated that they wish they had learned more while still in college, so challenge yourself and see what you can do.

Skills Practice 10-2   **Skill Level: Challenging**
Applying Political Strategies and Tactics

Skill Objective

To develop skill in formulating and implementing action plans for using political strategies and tactics effectively.

Procedure

1. This exercise can be done individually or in groups of three to five students.
2. Read the following scenario regarding a situation involving organizational politics.

You are the vice president of marketing at a major insurance company based in Chicago, Illinois. The company offers a full line of insurance products for home, auto, business, and personal coverage. The company has approximately 5,000 employees in its corporate offices and another 2,500 insurance agents who serve as independent contractors to the company.

The firm's financial performance has been very strong in the last five years, in particular. Although this is very encouraging, a major concern you have is that the growth potential for the markets in which your company operates is fairly limited. Given this, the strategic emphasis of the company has shifted from seeking new customers to retaining current customers.

One of the keys to successfully retaining customers is the relationship between the agent and the customer. Specifically, agents who are especially good at building and maintaining a relationship with their customers tend to have much higher customer retention rates.

On the basis of this situation, you would like to conduct a study of the service practices of agents to identify which service practices tend to be associated with higher customer retention. Although this sounds like a no-brainer in that the importance and value of the study would go unquestioned, you know that you will encounter significant political hurdles if you pursue this study. For example, the agents are independent contractors (not employees), so they may resent the company "checking up on them." The strained relationship between the company and the agent force in recent years will not help the situation either. In addition, the culture of the company tends to react very negatively to unfavorable results or information. This could also be a major problem in that some people may not see the need for the study while others don't want the study conducted because they are fearful of the results.

Suppose that you decided to move forward with your study of agent service practices despite concerns about the political ramifications. What actions could you take to effectively manage the political factors associated with this scenario?

3. Develop an action plan for applying political strategies and tactics effectively to this scenario. Be very systematic and specific in your recommendations.
4. Present your action plan to your class (optional).
5. Answer the discussion questions that follow.

Discussion Questions

1. Why is it important to manage political factors in organizations?
2. Evaluate your action plan. Why do you feel it would work? What are the barriers to its successful implementation? What could you do to overcome these barriers?
3. What are the implications of this exercise for you as a future manager?

Other Political Tactics In addition to the tactics Pfeffer has presented, at least two others—defensive behaviors and impression management—deserve mention.

> **Defensive behaviors.** Just as power may be used to resist the influence attempts of others, political behavior may involve protecting one's self-interest.[17] As such, people may engage in *defensive behaviors* to avoid action, blame, or change. Some of these defensive behaviors are presented in Figure 10-4.

You have probably seen people use many of these defensive behaviors. Some of the behaviors, such as overconforming, passing the buck, depersonalizing, and buffing, probably come to mind when you think of a bureaucracy. Certainly, such behaviors are associated with many of the worst characteristics of bureaucratic organizations.

> **Impression management.** *Impression management* is behavior that people direct toward others to create and maintain desired perceptions of themselves.[18] The most prominent type of impression management behavior is self-presentation, which involves the manipulation of information about oneself.[19] Self-presentation can be verbal or nonverbal or involve displays of artifacts. There are at least eight types of verbal self-presentations, shown in Figure 10-5. One of those types—descriptions of the organization—is included because glowing descriptions of our organization are often used to reflect positively on ourselves. What the

FIGURE 10-4
Defensive Behaviors

To Avoid Action

Overconforming—Avoiding action by resorting to a strict interpretation of one's responsibility ("The rules clearly say") and perhaps citing supportive precedents ("It's always been done this way")

Passing the buck—Foisting responsibility for execution of a task on another person ("I'm too busy"; "That's not my job")

Playing dumb—Attempting to avoid an unwanted task by falsely pleading ignorance or inability; "strategic helplessness"

Depersonalizing—Avoiding unwanted demands from others by treating them as objects or numbers rather than people

Smoothing and stretching—Smoothing refers to masking fluctuations in effort and output; fluctuations suggest inconsistency since peaks in performance suggest what is attainable and troughs thereby suggest a decline. Stretching refers to prolonging a task so one appears occupied.

Stalling—Appearing more or less supportive publicly while doing little or nothing privately; "foot-dragging"

To Avoid Blame

Buffing—Rigorously documenting activity or fabricating documents to project an image of competence and thoroughness

Playing safe—Evading situations that may reflect unfavorably on oneself

Justifying—Providing accounts that lessen one's responsibility for an event or apologies acknowledging at least partial responsibility for an event and including some expression of remorse

Scapegoating—Assigning blame for a negative outcome to someone or something that is not entirely (or not at all) blameworthy

Misrepresenting—Manipulating information about one's intentions, action, knowledge, performance, and so forth

Escalating commitment—"Throwing good money after bad" in an attempt to recoup losses and vindicate the initial decision

To Avoid Change

Resisting change—A catch-all for a variety of behaviors, including some of the above behaviors such as overconforming, stalling, playing safe, and misrepresenting, when they are used to avoid change

Protecting turf—Defending the task domain against the encroachment of others in order to protect one's prestige and power

Adapted from B. E. Ashforth and R. T. Lee, "Defensive Behavior in Organizations: A Preliminary Model," *Human Relations,* 1990, *43,* pp. 621–648.

types have in common is that they each are intended to make us look better. Have you seen people use each of these impression management approaches? Do you think they worked?

In addition to verbal self-presentations, impression management may involve nonverbal behaviors. For example, erect body posture, a steady gaze, a confident tone of voice, facial expression, and gestures may all be used for impression management.[20] We might also try to create a favorable impression by the clothes we wear or how we decorate our offices.

Impression management may also involve creating other forms of impressions. For instance, Clark Molstad took a job as a brewery worker and studied how his coworkers reacted to the repetition and boredom of their jobs and to the total lack of freedom associated with being

FIGURE 10-5
Verbal Self-Presentational Behaviors

Behavior	Definition	Example
Self-Descriptions	Statements describing oneself.	A job applicant tells a recruiter, "I'm a real go-getter. I tend to be a bit aggressive, but I always get results."
Organization Descriptions	Statements about the organization to which one belongs.	An acquaintance says, "I work for the best-respected firm in the industry."
Opinion Conformity	Expressions of agreement with the opinions of a target audience in order to gain audience approval.	A manager says to his boss, "You're absolutely right. Government regulation is stifling industrial growth. I couldn't agree with you more."
Accounts	Explanations of a predicament-causing event that are designed to minimize the apparent severity of the predicament. Accounts may involve excuses, defenses of innocence, or justifications.	A worker complains to a supervisor, "I don't know what happened to the hydraulic press. I've kept up with maintenance, but it's not working correctly. It must have been defective."
Apologies	Admissions of blameworthiness for an undesirable event that are coupled with an attempt to obtain a pardon from the audience.	A broker tells a client, "I'm sorry I'm late for our appointment. I'm almost always on time, but today's been an unusually hectic day. Please forgive me."
Acclaiming	Expressions of favorable events that are designed to maximize the desirable implications for the speaker.	A salesman informs a peer, "The sales in our division have nearly doubled since I was hired."
Other Enhancement	Efforts to increase one's attractiveness to an audience through the use of favorable evaluations of the target's attributes.	A junior executive tells a superior, "I really admire your style of management. You're decisive, fair, and opportunistic. It's a pleasure to work with you."
Rendering Favors	Doing something nice for a target audience in order to gain the target's approval.	A salesman informs a prospective client over lunch, "This is my treat. Order anything you like. Consider it a token of our esteem for your firm."

Source: Gardner and Martinko, p. 332.

closely controlled by supervisors. Here is his description of the workers' impression management techniques:

The most effective of these worker tactics combine the acts of looking busy and disappearing into one process. When a worker is on foot and being observed, this procedure requires appearing busy and active, even preoccupied and harassed, and then managing to drop out of the supervisor's sight, either by going into the distance or by disappearing behind obstacles, such as machinery. The idea is to look intense and involved to the point that one can't be bothered with more work or with silly questions and conversation. . . . These ploys will not necessarily fool all experienced supervisors but, by dis-

459

Chapter 10   Managing Politics, Conflict, and Change

Awareness
Awareness
Awareness
Awareness
Awareness
Awareness

appearing, the worker can hope that something else will distract the supervisor's attention.[21]

For better or worse, there is evidence that impression management works. For example, one study showed that those who engaged in impression management techniques, including other-enhancement, favorable self-descriptions, opinion conformity, and rendering favors, were given higher performance ratings than those who did not. Also, those who engaged in impression management had more supportive, positive communications with their supervisors than did others.[22] In addition, it has been shown that subordinates' engagement in various self-enhancing and other-enhancing impression management tactics with their superiors was related to greater liking by the superior, which in turn was related to more positive exchanges between the superior and subordinate.[23] Liking and the quality of the exchange relationship are often related to positive consequences for subordinates, such as greater influence in decisions and more supervisor support and guidance. Taken together, these findings show that impression management can have important consequences.

The purpose of Skills Practice 10-3 is to give you some practice in applying to management situations the impression management strategies discussed in the chapter.

Skills Practice 10-3
Applying Impression Management Strategies

Skill Level: Challenging

Skill Objective
To develop skill in applying impression management strategies in different types of organizational situations.

Procedure
1. This exercise can be done on an individual basis or in groups of three to five students.
2. Read the following organizational scenarios.

Scenario 1—Customer Rage at the Airport
You are the lead flight attendant for a major airline based in Chicago. It is the holiday season right now, and the number of air travelers is at an all-time high. At the worst time possible, your plane experiences a mechanical problem that will delay its departure for an unknown amount of time. You know that the 300 passengers waiting impatiently at the gate will be absolutely furious when they hear the news.

What would you say to your customers in order to attempt to create a positive impression of you and your employer in handling this situation? Base your answer on the impression management techniques discussed in the chapter and be action-oriented in terms of your recommendations.

Scenario 2—The New Employee
You are a brand new employee working as merchandise trainee for a major retailer based in Cleveland. Although you graduated from an excellent university, majored in retail management, and earned a 3.9/4.0 GPA in school, you know that this will not be enough for you to be successful in your real-world job.

As you start your new job, what kinds of strategies could you use to create and maintain a positive impression of yourself in the eyes of your boss and coworkers? Base your answer on the impression management techniques discussed in the chapter and be action-oriented in terms of your recommendations.

3. Identify actions that could be taken to effectively implement impression management strategies for each scenario. Be sure to base your action steps on the impression management strategies discussed in this chapter.

4. Answer the following discussion questions as a class.

Discussion Questions

1. Which strategies did you recommend for handling each scenario? Why do you feel they would be effective?
2. How would you respond to critics of impression management techniques who say that they focus too much on appearance and image and not on the key issue of the real substance of what a person or company does?
3. What are the implications of this exercise for you as future managers?

POLITICAL GAMES

Our discussion of politics may suggest the picture of one or two political actors calmly choosing from among alternative strategies and tactics. In fact, politics often is going on *all over the place* in organizations. Henry Mintzberg has suggested that organizational politics is a "collection of goings on, a set of 'games' taking place . . . a kind of three ring circus."[24] He has identified four types of these games, as shown in Figure 10-6.[25]

FIGURE 10-6
Political Games

Game	Typical Players	Purpose
Authority Games		
Insurgency Game	Lower-level participants	To resist formal authority
Counterinsurgency Game	Upper-level managers	To fight back against resistance to formal authority
Power Base Games		
Sponsorship Game	Subordinate employees	To enhance power base by using superiors as sponsors
Alliance-Building Game	Peers — often line managers	To enhance power base using peers to build alliances
Empire-Building Game	Line managers	To enhance power base using subordinates to build empire
Rivalry Games		
Line vs. Staff Game	Line managers and staff personnel	To defeat each other in the quest for power
Rival Camps Game	Any groups at the same level	To defeat each other in the quest for power
Change Games		
Whistle-Blowing Game	Usually lower-level participant	To correct questionable or illegal behavior
Young Turks Game	Upper-level managers close to but not at center of power	To throw legitimate power into question, perhaps even overthrow it, and institute major power shift

It's clear that these games differ in many ways, such as their actors and purposes and their consequences for the organization. Also, some of the games, such as sponsorship games and whistle-blowing games, may be consistent with goals of the organizations; others, such as insurgency games and Young Turks games, may not. Further, some of the games appear to be more ethical than are others. This is the issue to which we turn next.

Skills Practice 10-4 deals with an interesting way of looking at organizational politics—as a circus. It will also help you to understand how metaphors can be useful in conceptualizing such organizational phenomena as political behavior.

Skills Practice 10-4
Politics as Circus

Skill Level: **Advanced**

Skill Objective
To explore the metaphor of the organization as a circus.

Procedure
Henry Mintzberg compared organizational politics to a three-ring circus. Explore the metaphor of the organization as a circus. In particular, respond to each of the following questions.

1. What audiences is the circus trying to satisfy? How will it determine whether it has been successful?
2. What acts are playing in each of the three rings?
3. What mix of skills is needed in the circus?
4. Which acts require coordination?
5. What lions need to be tamed? What horses must be trained?
6. Who are the jugglers? The trapeze artists? The tightrope walkers? The animal trainers? The costume makers? The fire eaters?
7. Who are the clowns? Why are they clowning? Are they really happy?
8. Who wear masks? What are they covering up?
9. Who drives the circus train? Who cleans up after the elephants?
10. What acts are in the sideshow? Who is the shill?

THE ETHICS OF ORGANIZATIONAL POLITICS

We began this section by saying that it is hard to decide whether something is a political behavior and that the labeling of the behavior sometimes implies whether it is unethical. It's not surprising, then, that there is so much disagreement over the ethics of political behavior in general and of specific political tactics in particular. To some extent, "dirty" politics is like someone's definition of pornography: "I know it when I see it." And some behaviors—such as lying to or cheating others—would be labeled as unethical by almost anyone. Still, it would be nice to have some guidelines that we could apply to ask whether particular political behaviors are ethical. One set of such guidelines is presented in Figure 10-7.[26] According to those guidelines, an act must satisfy three conditions to be ethical. First, the act must improve the *welfare* of various parties involved rather than just favor narrow interests. Second, the act must respect the *rights* of all those involved, such as the rights of due process, free speech, and privacy. Finally, the act must be *just.* For instance, the

FIGURE 10-7
Asking Whether a Political Act Is Ethical

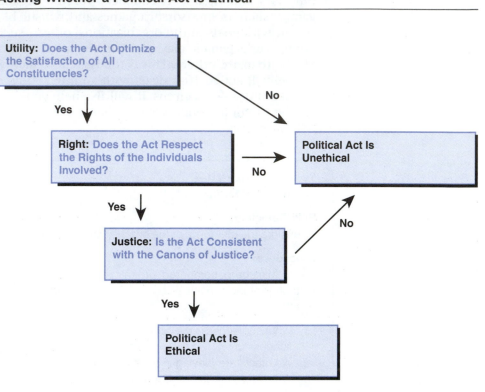

act is unjust if it involves unequal treatment of individuals or inconsistent administration of rules. If any of these conditions are not satisfied, the act is unethical.[27]

These are useful guidelines, though they may be hard to apply. For instance, we may honestly believe that an action considers everyone's interests, but others may see things very differently. Perhaps the best we can do is to try to consciously and honestly ask and answer these questions when considering our own actions—and we would do well to remember that self-serving biases and other perceptual errors may color our answers.

COSTS AND BENEFITS OF ORGANIZATIONAL POLITICS

In view of all that has been said, we could easily make the case that we should just try to get rid of organizational politics. For instance, Henry Mintzberg has stated:

> *Politics is divisive and costly; it burns up energies that could go into operations. It can also lead to all kinds of aberrations. Politics is often used to sustain outmoded systems of power, and sometimes to introduce new ones that are not justified. Politics can also paralyze an organization to the point where its effective functioning comes to a halt and nobody benefits. The purpose of an organization, after all, is to produce goods and services, not to provide an arena in which people can fight with one another.*[28]

Politics often does lead to such negative outcomes. For instance, it has been shown that political behaviors among managers are related to reduced interpersonal trust and enhanced feelings of alienation.[29] Also, perceptions of politics are related to reduced job satisfaction and increased job anxiety, stress levels, and intent to leave the firm.[30]

Nevertheless, before we address ways in which to get rid of political activity, we should recognize that it may have some benefits. For example, Henry Mintzberg argues that political activity may:[31]

> act in a Darwinian way to ensure that the strongest members of an organization are brought into positions of leadership.
> ensure that all sides of an issue are fully debated. Politics encourages a variety of voices to be heard on any issue, and each voice is forced to justify its conclusions in terms of the broader good.
> stimulate necessary change that is blocked by those currently in power. Since internal change is often blocked by the legitimate systems of influence, political power may be needed to bring it about.
> ease the path for the execution of decisions. Managers may use politics to persuade, negotiate, and build alliances to smooth the path for the decisions they wish to make.

MINIMIZING POLITICAL ACTIVITY

Whatever you think of these potential benefits, you'll probably find yourself in situations in which you will want to minimize political activity. Here are some guidelines that follow from our discussion:

> **Don't close your eyes to politics.** Politics is important and pervasive; ignoring it doesn't make it less real. Think about the strategies and tactics we have discussed and ask whether, why, and by whom they are being used.
> **Challenge political behaviors.** We said in our discussion of learning theory in Chapter 6 that failure to respond to behaviors may be reinforcing. If we see behaviors that we think are inappropriate, we should deal with them. If we have been rewarding them without meaning to, we should stop doing so. If it seems that employees believe that only political behaviors can meet their objectives, we should try to help them to find other, more legitimate ways to reach their goals. If we ask employees to stop certain behaviors and they don't, we may have to use punishment; this, though, should be our last resort.
> **Reduce ambiguity.** Uncertainty fosters politics, so it follows that clarifying goals, minimizing unnecessary change, making decision processes clear, or otherwise minimizing ambiguity may discourage political activity.[32]
> **Make things visible.** Politics thrives in darkness, like mushrooms—and may have similar nutrients. So, bringing activities out into the open may make some people more reluctant to play politics. Open meetings, published minutes of meetings, and public votes may all help. The key is to ensure that political activity can't be hidden.
> **Walk the talk.** If you argue against political behaviors but use them yourself, you're going to lose credibility. Instead, subordinates will as-

sume that, whatever the talk, there are actually counternorms favoring politics.

> **Recognize that others may interpret your behaviors as political, even if you really weren't being political.** This reinforces the need for openness. Keep your actions visible and clearly explain them.

> **Reduce your own and others' vulnerability to political behavior.** People are often helpless in the face of political behavior because they lack options. They can't challenge such behavior because they can't afford to lose their jobs or jeopardize their careers. This suggests that we should try to minimize our own vulnerability. We can do this by keeping our options open, minimizing secrecy, and fostering a climate in which politics is neither ignored nor rewarded. We should also do all we can to ensure that others have ways to voice their concerns about politics without fear of reprisal and that they are not placed in situations in which they have no choice but to submit to political pressures.

The purpose of Skills Practice 10-5 is to provide an opportunity to develop skill in analyzing situations involving political factors and developing strategies for reducing their influence on organizational effectiveness.

Skills Practice 10-5
Reducing Political Activity

Skill Level: Challenging

Skill Objective

To develop skill in reducing the level of political activity in an organization.

Procedure

1. This exercise can be completed on an individual basis or in groups of three to five students.
2. Read the following scenario.

Management Development Specialists is a training firm that specializes in offering a variety of continuing education programs for business professionals in the areas of management, accounting, finance, and marketing. The company has been in existence for only 2 years, but it has quickly established itself as a high-quality provider of professional training services for many Fortune 500 clients.

The president of the company is Allison Warren, a training professional with a Ph.D. in business administration and 20 years of corporate experience. Allison started the company on her own in 1997. As her customer base increased, the number of her employees has grown to over 25 training professionals.

Allison has a very informal but detail-oriented style of leading the company. She does not believe in creating structures and formalizing things, as she feels that these things will stifle the creativity of the organization. This approach is reflected in the lack of job descriptions, policies, and standard operating procedures in the company. Rather, employee responsibilities tend to blur together or overlap with each other in many cases. Oftentimes, this creates confusion and frustration among employees and engenders conflict over who has ownership of certain tasks.

Allison tends to be very guarded in terms of sharing information with her employees regarding issues related to the company. In addition, she is involved in all significant decisions that affect the company. Because she uses her intuition ("gut feeling") as a key driver of her decision-making process, this tends to promote a lot of competition and conflict among her employees who are fighting for her approval and financial support for their projects and programs. In many cases, the projects that were approved by Allison were not necessarily the best projects but rather the projects that were supported by the most skilled politicians in the company.

Recently, a growing number of employees have been complaining about the company's "hostile and back-stabbing culture." Employee morale has been declining, stress levels have increased dramatically, and many employees are talking about leaving the company if things don't change.

Using the general guidelines for reducing political activity discussed in the chapter, develop an action plan for Allison regarding the handling of this situation.

3.   Discuss the following questions as a class.

Discussion Questions

1.   What actions did you recommend that management take in order to reduce the level of political activity in the scenario? Why?
2.   What barriers to success might exist in terms of implementing your recommendations?
3.   Why is it problematic for a firm to have an excessively high level of political activity (i.e., what are the costs of political behavior in organizations)?
4.   What are the implications of this exercise for you as future managers?

The process model presented in the nearby Bottom Line summarizes the basic steps associated with the general process of managing organizational politics effectively.

B O T T O M   L I N E

The Bottom Line: Managing Organizational Politics Effectively

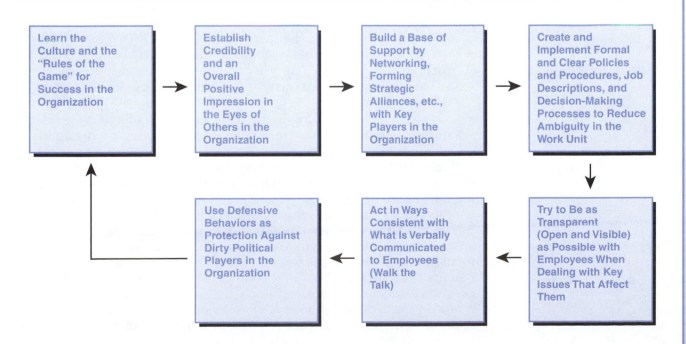

Learn the Culture and the "Rules of the Game" for Success in the Organization → Establish Credibility and an Overall Positive Impression in the Eyes of Others in the Organization → Build a Base of Support by Networking, Forming Strategic Alliances, etc., with Key Players in the Organization → Create and Implement Formal and Clear Policies and Procedures, Job Descriptions, and Decision-Making Processes to Reduce Ambiguity in the Work Unit ↓

Use Defensive Behaviors as Protection Against Dirty Political Players in the Organization ← Act in Ways Consistent with What Is Verbally Communicated to Employees (Walk the Talk) ← Try to Be as Transparent (Open and Visible) as Possible with Employees When Dealing with Key Issues That Affect Them

MANAGING CONFLICT

Because managers are often the hub of organizational communications—in the "middle of things"—they must regularly deal with conflict. All organizations experience conflict. The way in which conflict is managed determines whether it is motivating or destructive. As we will see, there are many costs, but also many benefits, to conflict. The challenge, then, is not to eliminate conflict but to make sure that conflict is successfully managed.

CONFLICT PREMISES

Conflict situations are generally emotion-laden and, as such, they call for emotional intelligence. Here are some things to keep in mind as you think about and deal with conflict.

> **Conflict and disagreement are normal** in human relationships. Because of different life experiences, including things such as upbringing, culture, education, and previous experience in relationships, people inevitably see the world in a variety of ways. Most of us think that our view is the "correct" one, for we interpret the world though our limited experience.

> **Conflict may be good.** Conflict helps to diagnose sources of problems and it motivates the search for new approaches. It provides an opportunity for people to recognize and value differences of opinion, open up their world-view, expand their perspective, and solve problems. It gives both parties the opportunity to learn, to improve, to practice tolerance, and to achieve satisfactory resolution of emotional tension that often hampers their creativity, productivity, trust, and communications both on and off the job.[33]

> The way in which conflict is framed may influence its nature and outcomes. *Framing* of conflict appears to vary along three dimensions, as follows:

   • **Relationship/task.** First, do the parties to conflict focus on their relationships with the other party or on the task itself?

   • **Emotional/intellectual.** Second, do the parties to conflict direct their attention to the emotional components of the dispute, such as hatred, anger, and jealousy, or to the actions that occur apart from those emotions?

   • **Cooperate/win.** Finally, do the parties to conflict focus on maximizing joint outcomes or on maximizing their own gain, regardless of consequences for the other party?

   While it is hard to fully sort out how these perceptions influence outcomes, research provides some clues. For example, those parties adopting intellectual or relationship frames tend to be more satisfied with the conflict resolution process than do those adopting task or emotional frames. Also, those parties adopting task or cooperation frames tend to attain higher personal and joint outcomes than those adopting a win-focused frame.[34] It is important to realize, then, that our framing of the conflict situation is likely to affect both satisfaction with the conflict process and conflict outcomes.

> A mutually acceptable solution can often be found. If one can adopt an abundance mentality and communicate in an honest but considerate and

respectful manner, people can often move from disagreement to compromise to collaboration to synergy.

> Any of the parties in conflict can contribute to its resolution by taking personal responsibility and initiating communications. Consider the following:

- Your contribution to relationships is under your control; the part others choose to play is not under your control.
- When you change, your relationships change.
- Waiting for other persons or situations to change so that you can change equals no change.
- The way you are treated by others depends partly on how you "train" them to treat you.
- Risk-taking is part of conflict management. You may be rejected.

> *Trusting behavior* can evoke trusting behavior.[35] The principle of social reciprocity stipulates that you get back what you give to others: "What goes around, comes around." If you want others to trust you, listen to you, care for you, respect you, and the like, you must give these qualities first. You then stand a better chance of having them returned. You demonstrate trusting behavior by empowering others, being open to influence, taking some risks, and being willing to change when faced with new information. As Sitting Bull once said, "Offer your opponent the peace pipe first."

> *Consensus and synergy* are likely only when people choose to cooperate in a win-win relationship rather than compete. Sometimes, one must accommodate; other times, one must compete with all you have. Because of past experiences (often deprivations, rejections, and other painful emotional experiences), some people cannot *not* try to compete, to win at all costs, even that of personal relationships. When dealing with a battler on an unimportant issue, let him or her win so you can gather social credits for later use. When dealing with a critical issue, as Sitting Bull continued, "Fight them with everything you have. And when it is over, let bygones be bygones."

> Some conflicts may *never be resolved* because of fear, rigidity, intolerance, anger, paranoia, or other emotional impairment. Most often, it is best to sidestep others' negativity, sarcasm, and malicious ridicule. Often, people with low self-esteem ridicule others so they can feel better about themselves. Rather than taking such stuff personally, be assertive and be honest regarding your convictions and your rights to be treated with respect.

CAUSES OF CONFLICT

There are many potential causes of conflict. Some of these, as we have suggested, are due to our perceptions, assumptions, and framing of conflict. Others, as we discuss next, are characteristics of the situation.

> **Competition over scarce resources.** The limit of resources in most organizations increases the potential for conflict. Individuals or units want to obtain the necessary money, facilities, personnel, and information to attain their goals. If it appears that resources are scarce, efforts will be made to secure resources, often to the detriment of the goals of others. Inflating budgets, challenging the legitimacy of activities by oth-

ers, and covert efforts to prevent budget cuts may all result from conflict over scarce resources.

> **Ambiguity over responsibility or jurisdiction.** When it is not clear who is responsible for what, some things may "slip through the cracks" or there may be duplication of efforts.

> **Task interdependence.** Task interdependence refers to the nature of the dependence among units for information or for financial, material, or human resources. The greater the interdependence among units, the greater the potential for conflict.

There is substantial interdependence when units provide one another with inputs (this is called *reciprocal interdependence*). For example, a legal department at a savings and loan may review borrowers' applications that have been submitted to the loan department. After an application has been reviewed, it is sent back to the loan department so the request or denial of the loan can be processed. The output of the loan department becomes the input for the legal department, and the output of the legal department becomes the input of the loan department. That is, there is a two-way flow between departments.

Task interdependence is greatest in the case of team interdependence. *Team interdependence* exists when work is interactive, or acted on jointly by members of different units rather than simply being transferred back and forth. Teamwork is the most important method of coordination in team interdependence.

> **Goal incompatibility.** Different individuals or units may have different, and perhaps incompatible, goals. Such differences may lead to conflict even when both parties agree on some overall goal for the organization. In the aftermath of a hijacking or bombing, for example, personnel responsible for airport security may institute more stringent and time-consuming procedures at security checkpoints. At the same time, personnel in the control tower are committed to the goal of maintaining take-off and landing schedules. The delays caused by security may cause conflict between the two groups.

> **Competitive reward systems.** If individuals or units are given incentives that will reward the attainment of the organizational goal, cooperation is likely to result. However, if the incentives are designed to reward those who attain their specific assigned goals without regard to coordination or the "big picture," political behaviors are likely. For example, Ted Noble, vice president of sales at The Harter Group, an office furniture manufacturer, was offered a job by a fast-growing competitor. The proposal was that he would manage the New York region, another new hire would manage the Washington, D.C., region, and a third would manage a territory in Boston. The person with the most sales at the end of a designated period would become head of the Northeast division and oversee the other two. Noble declined the offer, reasoning that "Instead of engendering team work and camaraderie, it would create a divisive atmosphere, planning against the other guy. You wouldn't want to share information because it could forecast your own downfall. It would be a nice company to work for, but this would be like a gladiator pit, with all of us going after a piece of raw meat."[36]

FOCUS ON MANAGEMENT

DIFFERENTIATION AT LITTON ENTERPRISE SYSTEMS*

Litton Enterprise Solutions, a division of Litton Industries that provides information and technology services, provides a good example of the impact of differentiation. When Jeffrey Erle took over as president, the division was a loose confederation of east and west coast operations that needed to be integrated in order to provide customers with a full range of services. The west coast opera-

tion had been running call centers for more than 30 years, was hard working but resistant to change, and was led by an executive who thought he deserved Erle's position. The east coast operation was pasted together from recent acquisitions and specialized in enterprise process consulting. The operation was led by a general manager who felt that she should have been given the presidency. Her group was freewheeling and risk-taking and cared little about

Litton's culture and tradition. Because of these many differences, there was virtually no communication between the two operations, and there was no unified sense of direction. Both sides routinely engaged in covert sabotage in order to dilute the other's effectiveness.

http://www.litton.com/

*H. M. Guttman, "Conflict at the Top," *Management Review*, November 1999, pp. 49–53.

> **Differentiation.** As each unit or department in an organization tries to cope with the unique demands of its own environment, it necessarily develops its own types of procedures, cherished values, and points of view. For example, a research department in a chemical firm might be run very democratically, and its personnel might develop a long-term time perspective, since most of the things on which they are working will not reach fruition for years. On the other hand, the production department might be run more autocratically, and its managers might be expected to put a much greater emphasis on immediate results. Because of these differences, communication and agreements about the sharing of resources will be difficult. Differentiation is a major source of conflict in mergers and acquisitions, since the joined units may have different histories, values, time perspectives, risk preferences, and much else.

A CONFLICT MODEL

Suppose someone says, "In a healthy company, you won't see conflict." We have already seen one reason to challenge such a statement: Some conflict is needed to enhance creativity and seed change. Another basis for challenge is that the lack of visible conflict (i.e., that which is manifested) doesn't imply that there are no tensions, hostilities, uncertainties, disagreements, or pressures. It simply means that they have not been allowed to air. In a healthy relationship, we're likely to see some conflict from time to time. Such conflict, if not allowed to get out of control, can help to vent frustrations, air concerns, and "clear the air." It is when conflict gets out of hand or when a relationship is so fragile that people are afraid to voice their concerns that things become unhealthy.

A model of the conflict process is presented in Figure 10-8. The model shows that there are several steps in the process and that a variety of things may determine whether conflict ever becomes overt or manifest.[37]

FIGURE 10-8
The Conflict Process

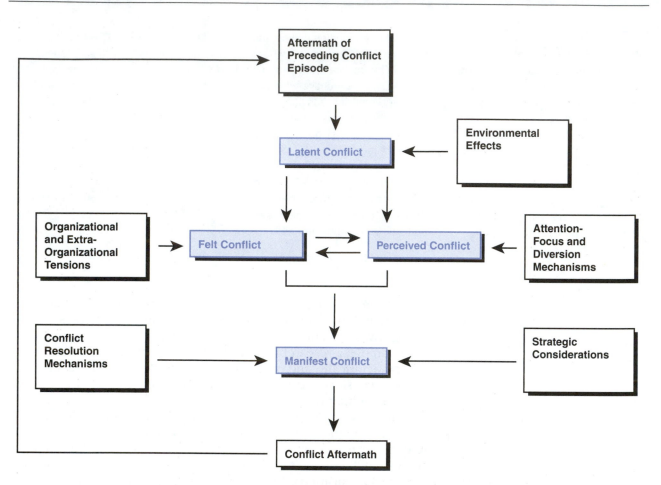

Latent Conflict Latent conflict is essentially conflict waiting to happen. It is a situation in which the conditions are right for open conflict to develop. Latent conflict is influenced by the aftermath of preceding conflict situations and by environmental effects. The latter are the conflict causes we discussed earlier, including scarcity of resources, ambiguous jurisdictions, incompatible goals, task interdependence, competitive reward systems, and differentiation.

Felt Conflict Felt conflict is experienced as discomfort and tension. The party experiencing felt conflict is motivated to reduce those negative feelings. Felt conflict may be heightened by other tensions inside or outside the organization. For example, if we are also experiencing pressures at home or are worried about losing our jobs, we may already be "sore." As such, we may feel even greater tension from further irritants.

Perceived Conflict Perceived conflict is the awareness that we are in a conflict situation. For example, when we learn that there will be budget cuts, we may realize that a struggle over scarce resources is likely. Perceived conflict depends in part on mechanisms that may exist to direct attention to or away from the conflict. For example, a sudden crisis may shift our attention from the current conflict situation. Conversely, if we know that others are watching to see how we will do, we may be more conscious of the conflict. Note that felt conflict and perceived conflict are mutually reinforcing. When we perceive conflict, we are likely to experience tension, and when we feel conflict, we are likely to think about it.

Manifest Conflict   After conflict is perceived and felt, it may or may not become open, or manifest. As seen in Figure 10-8, whether conflict becomes manifest depends on whether mechanisms are in place to resolve conflict as well as whether engaging in open conflict seems wise. Conflict resolution mechanisms might include such things as a focus on larger goals, use of mediators, separation of parties, or use of negotiating techniques, as discussed later. Strategic considerations might include, for instance, a decision that the conflict "just isn't worth it." While we may want a bigger share of the budget, we may decide that fighting for it would lead to more costs than benefits.

Conflict Aftermath   Conflict is likely to breed more conflict and, when it does, that conflict is likely to take on a life of its own. Witness, for instance, longstanding feuds for which the original insult, misdeed, or misunderstanding has been long forgotten but for which bitterness and even hatred are unabated.

FOCUS ON MANAGEMENT

THE LEGACY OF CONFLICT AT THE DART GROUP*

The legacy of conflict is seen in the saga of the Hafts, once called the "most feared family in retailing." Herbert Haft had founded the Dart Group (a retail empire including the Dart Drugs and Crown Books chains and Trak Auto, a national network of auto supply stores) in the 1950s. He was serving as CEO when, in early 1993, he read a newspaper article suggesting that his clout was on the wane and that his son, Robert, had become Dart's de facto head. Haft, a flamboyant executive whose small stature, trademark white pompadour, and feisty manner earned him comparison to "a cockatoo with a limo and driver," decided to make sure that wasn't going to happen. He quickly fired his corporate secretary (his wife, Gloria) and his president (his son,

Robert), installing as president his younger son, Ronald, a shopping center developer with no experience in the business. His wife then filed for divorce, alleging—among many other things—that Herbert was responsible for shady dealings designed to cheat her out of her share of the company's wealth. Robert sued for breach of contract and won, receiving a settlement of $40 million, and joined his sister, Linda, in a suit against Ronald. Then, Herbert had a falling out with Ronald. Ronald, who had purchased his father's voting shares to shelter them from Gloria in the divorce settlement, then sold those shares back to the company. The family subsequently battled for control of the empire, diverting attention from running the businesses and finally declaring bankruptcy and dismantling the company. In 1998, Rich-

food Holdings agreed to take over the financially troubled Dart Group. The feud, though, hasn't ended. After Herbert announced that he was going to start an online health products venture, Healthquick.com, Robert started his own online business, Vitamins.com. The battle moves to cyberspace:

http://www.healthquick.com and *http://www.vitamins.com.*

*This example is based on M. Lewyn, "This Week on The Hafts . . . ," *Business Week,* November 22, 1993, p. 96; B. McMenamin, "Family Matters," *Forbes,* September 13, 1993, pp. 236–237; B. Dumaine, "America's Toughest Bosses," *Fortune,* October 18, 1993, pp. 38–45; K. Holland and A. Barrett, "Relief for a Poisoned Dart Group," *Business Week,* May 5, 1997, p. 48; D. Sparks, "Good Riddance, Herb," *Financial World,* May 20, 1997, pp. 32–34; S. Stoughton, "Writing a New Story Line for Crown Books," *The Washington Post,* December 13, 1999, p. F18; and S. Henry, "The Name Game," *The Washington Post,* November 11, 1999, p. E01.

CONFLICT STYLES

Recall that in Chapter 4 we discussed a set of five conflict styles that varied in terms of the degree to which they emphasized concern for satisfying our own needs and concerns for satisfying needs of the other party. In that chapter, we focused specifically on one of the styles: collaborating. Here, we consider situations in which each style may be most appropriate.

> **Competing.** The competing, or forcing, conflict style involves trying to win at the other party's expense. The competing style generally leads to antagonism and festering resentment. It may be necessary when time is of the essence and we are sure we are correct or when the other party would take advantage of a more collaborative approach. In each of these cases, though, we should be sure to question our assumptions before resorting to competition. That is, is there really a time constraint? How can we be sure we are correct? What evidence do we have that the other party cannot be trusted?

> **Avoiding.** The avoiding style attempts to avoid or smooth over conflict situations. While this style is generally unproductive, it may be appropriate when conflicts are trivial. It may also be useful as a temporary tactic, to let parties cool down during heated disputes.

> **Accommodating.** The accommodating style involves acceding completely to the other party's wishes or at least co-operating with little or no attention to one's own interests. This style may be acceptable when the other party has great power or the issue isn't really important to us. However, appeasement may be seen as a sign of weakness and may lead to even greater demands rather than to "peace in our times." In the long term, it may generate rather than resolve conflict.

> **Compromising.** Compromising involves an attempt to find a satisfactory middle ground (i.e., to "split the difference" by reaching an agreement that, while not ideal for either party, seems equitable). Compromise may be necessary when there is little chance of agreement, both parties have equal power, and there are time constraints. Even when such conditions exist (and again, we should be sure to question whether they really do), compromising is unlikely to yield more than an equally unsatisfactory outcome.

> **Collaborating.** This problem-solving style is mutually beneficial, when a "win-win" solution is sought that fully satisfies the interests of both parties. This style (discussed in detail in Chapter 4) requires trust, open sharing of information, and creativity. This is the "ideal" style and should be sought unless the parties to conflict have perfectly opposing interests. Even in the latter case, though, we should be sure to examine whether those interests are truly opposing or whether in fact the apparent incompatibility is due to misperceptions or failure to see the "big picture."

As we've just discussed, some of these approaches generally work better than do others, but each may be appropriate in certain situations. The situations in which each style may be appropriate are summarized in Figure 10-9.

Now complete Self-Assessment 10-2. The purpose of the exercise is to help you better understand your conflict style.

FIGURE 10-9
Fitting Conflict Style to the Situation

Conflict Style	Appropriate Situation(s)
Competing	> Time is short and we're sure we are correct.
	> The other party would take advantage of a collaborative approach.
Avoiding	> The conflict is trivial.
	> We need a temporary, cooling-off tactic.
Accommodating	> The other party has great power.
	> The issue isn't important to us.
Compromising	> There is little chance of agreement, both parties have equal power, and there are time constraints.
Collaborating	> This is the "ideal" style to be sought unless the parties to conflict have perfectly opposing interests.

Self-Assessment 10-2
Conflict Style

Answer each of the questions in this section using the following scale:

1 = Disagree Strongly
2 = Disagree Somewhat
3 = Neither Agree nor Disagree
4 = Agree Somewhat
5 = Agree Strongly

When I'm faced with a conflict/bargaining situation:

1. _____ I generally try to keep a low profile.
2. _____ I find it's often best to seek the middle ground.
3. _____ I go for the win.
4. _____ I often focus more on satisfying the other person than on getting what I need.
5. _____ I'll back off rather than embarrass the other party.
6. _____ I usually try to "split the difference," giving a little to get a little.
7. _____ I insist that my position be accepted.
8. _____ I treat it as a mutual problem to be solved.
9. _____ I usually try to avoid controversial positions.
10. _____ I argue for my position as strongly as possible.
11. _____ I seek a solution that meets all our needs.
12. _____ I assume that it wasn't important and back off.
13. _____ I'm willing to compromise if others will meet me halfway.
14. _____ I start by asking how we both can achieve our goals.
15. _____ I work hard to make sure that there is a friendly, harmonious outcome.

FIGURE 10-10
Approaches to Conflict Resolution

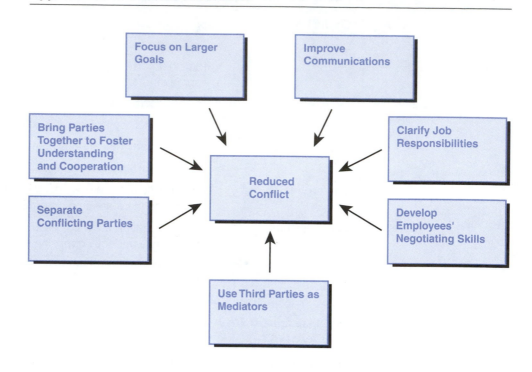

APPROACHES TO CONFLICT RESOLUTION

Several approaches to conflict resolution are shown in Figure 10-10. As we will see, some of these approaches involve changes to organizational processes, such as improving communications. Others entail specific actions in the conflict episode, such as using third parties. Still others focus on developing employees' skills, such as their negotiation skills.

Focus on Larger Goals Larger goals can often shift focus from conflict to cooperation. Threats of bankruptcy, loss of jobs, or deterioration of product quality can often encourage conflicting parties to cooperate to achieve a mutually beneficial goal. The need to "save the company" or to pull together to capture an opportunity encourages people to set aside hostilities.

Improve Communications Because conflict often results from lack of communication or miscommunications, it follows that improving communications, in ways such as those discussed in Chapter 5, may help to prevent or reduce conflict. Communication is also critical in the midst of conflict. Here are some guidelines for communicating in a conflict situation. Try to come to agreement with your conflicting party to follow these guidelines to build more positive and productive, less stressful relationships.[38]

> Be honest; say what's on your mind now. Be open.
> Be specific; provide examples.
> Don't use the words *never* and *always*.
> Listen in depth; reflect and paraphrase what you hear.
> Ask questions to clarify the meaning of what the other person is saying.
> Focus on behavior that the other person controls.

> Maintain good eye contact.
> Focus on only one specific issue or behavior at a time.
> Don't interrupt.
> Stay there. Don't walk away mentally, emotionally, physically, or psychologically.
> Be direct but tactful.
> Use *I* statements rather than *you* statements (e.g., "When this happens, I feel . . ." rather than "When you do this, it makes me feel . . .").
> Don't attack the other person by ridiculing, taunting, or otherwise being rude and hostile.
> Don't defend yourself by blaming others, avoiding, or withdrawing.

Develop Employees' Negotiating Skills[39] With training, employees can gain skills in reaching constructive agreements. They can learn to look beyond their own positions to consider the other party's interests, to seek "win-win" solutions, and to try to get past emotions when facing difficult decisions.[40]

Use Third Parties as Mediators A neutral third party with expertise in human behavior can often facilitate the reduction of conflict. The third party can meet with both individuals or with representatives of both groups and help to work out an agreement that is acceptable to both. Third parties can be especially useful when suspicion between groups has resulted in a deadlock. Because third parties have no vested interest in the conflict, the disputants are often willing to trust and abide by their recommendations.

Separate Conflicting Parties The physical separation of conflicting parties is a quick and direct way to reduce conflict. Though it doesn't necessarily reduce the hostility felt between individuals or deal with the underlying causes of conflict, it prevents the conflict from flaring up. Obviously, this isn't an option when parties have to cooperate on a joint task.

GLOBAL PERSPECTIVES

KOREAN CONFLICT MANAGEMENT*

While managers in all societies recognize that conflict must be managed, the way it is managed depends on many cultural factors. For example, Koreans feel that harmony is essential in all relationships and situations. This belief is founded in Confucianism, which has influenced Korean thinking and culture for centuries. To help to achieve harmony, the Confucians laid out a hierarchical societal structure and prescribed that individuals should maintain their position. Further, individuals should

exhibit piety toward parents, render loyalty to superiors, and preserve harmony with group members. Since harmony is an important goal, all parties should strive to attain it and, when it is disturbed, it should be restored through compromise. Those higher in status have an obligation to maintain or restore harmony among those below them, and they reap respect when they do so. Research shows that Korean leaders actively manage conflict, often intervening in their subordinates' disputes, and are quite assertive when dealing with their own subordinates.

Korean subordinates tend to serve as deferential liaisons between the parties when assisting in their leaders' disputes.

*This example is based on N.-H. Kim, D. W. Sohn, and J. A. Wall, Jr., "Korean Leaders' (and Subordinates') Conflict Management," *International Journal of Conflict Management*, April 1999, pp. 130–152. For more on cross-cultural comparison of conflict resolution tactics, see R. Cropanzano, H. Aguinas, M. Schminke, and D. L. Denham, "Disputant Reactions to Managerial Conflict Resolution Tactics: A Comparison Among Argentina, the Dominican Republic, Mexico, and the United States," *Group and Organization Management*, June 1999, pp. 124–154.

Bring Conflicting Parties Together While separating conflicting parties is often useful, it may also be helpful to do just the opposite: bringing the parties together so that they can get to know each other's perspectives and practice cooperation. Two Pacific Northwest nonprofit groups used this approach to smooth the waters between environmental and timber interests, battling over preservation of timberland for the spotted owl. Ten men who were central to the fight, including a mill owner, a logger, a scientist, and a government official, agreed to spend three days guiding an old wooden sailboat through the San Juan Islands in Puget Sound. According to one of the organizers, "It's a cooperative effort to be on the boat, and that spills over into any kind of discussion."[41]

APPROACHES TO GENERATING PRODUCTIVE CONFLICT

Sometimes there is employee complacency, lethargy, and overconfidence in an organization. In such cases, it may be useful to generate productive conflict. For example, sales contests create competition among marketing employees. Uncertainty can be induced by assigning different tasks, hiring new personnel, or changing the reward system. A *devil's advocate* can be given the task of finding faults in proposed solutions so as to avoid a situation in which a group fails to evaluate its choices critically. A *scapegoat*—someone who bears the blame for an unpopular action—may be needed to introduce needed changes. For example, a CEO who feels that employees in one department are doing just enough to get by may assign a tough boss to the department, to "shake things up." The new boss would introduce needed changes and "take the heat" from employees who may be upset. Once the changes have been implemented, the boss may be replaced.

The nearby Bottom Line presents a process model that summarizes the basic steps associated with the general conflict management process.

BOTTOM LINE

The Bottom Line: Applying the General Conflict Management Process

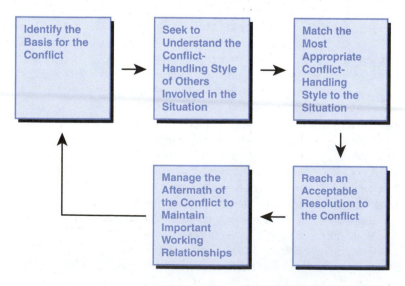

Identify the Basis for the Conflict → Seek to Understand the Conflict-Handling Style of Others Involved in the Situation → Match the Most Appropriate Conflict-Handling Style to the Situation → Reach an Acceptable Resolution to the Conflict → Manage the Aftermath of the Conflict to Maintain Important Working Relationships →

Skills Practice 10-6 requires you to find a partner. The purpose of the exercise is to give you an opportunity to practice the management of conflict by creating a simulation of an actual work situation and then applying different strategies for handling the conflict issues in the simulation.

Skills Practice 10-6
Skill Level: Challenging

Role Immersion Simulation: Managing the Conflict Process

Skill Objective
To develop skill in matching the appropriate conflict-handling style to different types of situations.

Procedure
1. Form pairs for this exercise.
2. Select one of the scenarios that follow. Each person should select one of the two roles in the situation being used for this exercise.
3. Each student should read the description for the role he/she selected and the overview of the situation. Students should not read the role descriptions being played by other members of the group.

Scenario 1—The Strained Relationship
StarCorp is a toy company that designs, manufactures, and markets educational toys for children between the ages of 0-15 years. The company's main headquarters are based in San Diego, California. Its current workforce consists of 25,000 employees in the United States and another 5,000 in Latin America, Asia, and Europe. The company does the vast majority of its design and marketing work in the United States and outsources its manufacturing function to suppliers in low wage countries in Asia and Latin America. The company's key strategic priorities are to support production innovation, customer service, and value.

StarCorp is a major player in the toy industry in terms of its product mix, distribution, and marketing expertise. However, the industry is intensely competitive with cost being the critical source of competitive advantage.

Role Description 1—Director of Marketing
You are the director of marketing. You have just been informed that you will be working with the Director of Finance on a project that involves studying the cost-effectiveness of a new process for distribution of your firm's products to retailers and individual consumers. You believe that the new system may reduce costs, but that it will create huge inefficiencies and bottlenecks in the distribution process. This increases the risk that retailers and consumers may experience delays in obtaining hot-selling products that you offer. Speed is critical in this industry, and with strong product offerings from other toy companies, StarCorp could lose out big if it can't be responsive to the demands of the market.

Your position is to keep the current distribution system because it is more flexible and responsive, although more costly to maintain. Your key concern is the customer and the market with a secondary concern for cost reduction. Use a *competing conflict-handling style* (demonstrate concern for your position, but little concern for the position of the Director of Finance). You may alter your conflict-handling style if you feel that there is a legitimate basis for doing so, but do not give in easily!

Role Description 2—Director of Finance
You are the Director of Finance. You have a strong "bottom-line mentality" that stresses reducing costs and maximizing profits. You are a strong supporter of the new distribution system because you believe that it will enable StarCorp to reduce costs and operate more efficiently. Inflation, product development costs, and new competitors are driving costs up at

an alarming rate (20% per year), and you must do something to reverse this trend. Although you are most concerned about costs, you recognize that the company needs to be responsive to its customer base as well. You should attempt to use a *collaborating style* with the Director of Marketing. Try to find a common ground between your positions in which you both can fully achieve your objectives. See if there is a way to get the Director of Marketing to support the new system for its ability to reduce costs, but also attempt to get the marketing director's support by arguing that the new system will not cause excessive inefficiencies in distribution. You may alter your conflict-handling style only if you feel that there is a legitimate basis for doing so, but do not give in easily!

Scenario 2—Hard-Headed and Pressed for Time

The Arlington assembly facility is owned by COMPELL, a major consumer electronics firm that designs and manufactures televisions, VCRs, DVD players, and stereo systems. This plant employs 1,500 employees who assemble various electronic products on assembly lines. COMPELL is known for innovative product design and superior product quality and durability. This reputation for quality has taken years for the company to establish so it is critical that the company's high quality standards be maintained. However, as the company has taken action to improve product quality, its manufacturing processes have become more complex and costs have increased dramatically. This is a major concern for COMPELL management because the consumer electronics industry is extremely price sensitive.

Recently, COMPELL implemented a total quality management program that involved training managers and employees to use various quality tools (e.g., flow charts, scatter diagrams) and measures (e.g., customer satisfaction, process efficiency).

Role Description 1—Production Supervisor

You are the first-shift production supervisor for one of the assembly lines. You manage a team of 40 production employees. This has been your job for five years. The key measure of quality in your unit has always been the "defect rate" associated with products assembled in your area. You are not a big fan of the new total quality management program and you think that measures such as customer satisfaction and process efficiency are not nearly as critical as the defect rate measure. You should use an *avoiding style of conflict* in responding to anyone who questions your position on this issue. Tell others that you are doing fine on the defect measure and that there is no problem as far as you are concerned. Although some of your employees have deviated from standard operating procedures in order to reduce product defects, you believe that this is justified. The key here is to avoid acknowledging that any quality problem exists in your unit.

Role Description 2—Quality Supervisor Scenario

You are the quality supervisor at COMPELL's Arlington production facility. Your job is to implement total quality management principles in order to further enhance the company's reputation for product quality and durability. You have established a quality measurement system composed of 12 critical measures of quality that you monitor on an ongoing basis. In reviewing the last six months of quality data, you have identified one production line that is well below average (25% below the plant average) on all of the quality measures (e.g., customer satisfaction, process efficiency, costs, productivity) except the defect measure. You decide to go and discuss this issue with the production supervisor. You should use a *competing conflict-handling style* in dealing with the production supervisor by insisting that the quality data clearly shows that there are serious quality problems on his or her line. Insist that the production supervisor improve on the other measures of quality and tell him or her that you are not interested in excuses. Explain to the production supervisor that he or she must improve quality on all 12 measures and that this is part of the company's overall quality strategy. Maintain your position and do not give in!

4. Start the simulation and let it run for approximately 10–15 minutes.

5. After the simulation has been completed, answer the following questions as a group.

Discussion Questions

1. Which conflict-handling style was each person using in the simulation? How did you know this?

2. Evaluate each person's handling of the conflict in the simulation. What could have been done differently to handle the conflict more effectively?

3. What are the implications of this exercise for you as a future manager?

MANAGING CHANGE

Leaders make change happen, initiate improvements, make the world different. Most people tend to seek pleasure and avoid pain, but almost all change involves disruption of safe, comfortable routines. That's why leaders meet resistance.

The ability to manage change is a valuable skill. Change is a critical uncertainty facing the organization. Environments of organizations are becoming increasingly dynamic. Organizations are becoming more change-oriented, responding to various forces. Still, change is difficult, and not all change is good. Change may often be necessary, but it shouldn't be pursued blindly. It may be rewarding, but it may also be painful. Further, people may differ in the degree to which they resist change and in their motivations to change.

There are currently many visible examples of companies (e.g., Toys "R" Us, Eastman Kodak, and Northwest Airlines) that are seeking to successfully undergo major change. In addition, many traditional "brick-and-mortar" companies, such as Barnes & Noble, are trying to establish an Internet presence as well.

FORCES FOR CHANGE

We discussed in Chapter 1 and elsewhere the many forces for change in the modern workplace. Globalization, the growing diversity of the workforce, the explosion of the Internet, the changing psychological contract, new legislation, political changes, changing consumer and employee desires and expectations, and heightened levels of competition are among the many external forces for change. Internal forces for change might include performance gaps, new leadership, a new mission, and employee pressures. These forces for change are pervasive and are accelerating in both frequency and magnitude. They demand that companies and their employees develop the capability, motivation, and mindset to succeed in a radically changed—and radically changing—new world of work.

PLANNED VERSUS REACTIVE CHANGE

Managers can respond to pressures for change either by planning or reacting. *Planned change* occurs when managers develop and install a program that serves to alter organizational activities in a timely and orderly way. In many instances, planned change is instigated because managers expect the development of a force for change and thus seek to prepare the organization to adjust activities with minimal disruption. *Reactive change* occurs when managers simply respond to the pressure for change when that pressure comes to their attention. Usually, this is a piecemeal approach because managers are facing problems that need immediate resolution.

Planned change is typically regarded as superior to reactive change. It is often used when change in the organization is to be extensive and lengthy. As

FIGURE 10-11

The Change Process—Lewin's Change Model

Phase 1   **Unfreezing**

- Create High Felt Need for Change
- Minimize Resistance to Change

Phase 2   **Changing**

- Change People, Tasks, and Structure
- Encourage Ongoing Support

Phase 3   **Refreezing**

- Reinforce Outcomes
- Constructive Modification

such, it requires a greater commitment of time and resources and additional expertise in formulating and implementing the change. However, planned change can also be very effective when only modest change in organizational activities is required. The key to planned change is that managers must be able to anticipate the types of change that will be necessary.

Reactive change is usually hurried and less expensive to carry out than is planned change. It is most effective when applied to small or day-to-day problems in the organization. Examples would include postponing production activities in response to shipping delays, altering a dress code policy to enable office workers to help to move belongings to new headquarters, or deciding to hire computer consultants on learning that recently purchased computers are in some ways incompatible with current systems. These changes usually require minimal planning and are best handled by managers when a problem occurs. Other instances in which reactive change may be appropriate occur when external and internal forces are themselves changing so rapidly that planning is virtually impossible.

THE CHANGE PROCESS

Whether managers engage in planned or reactive change, understanding and implementing the steps in the change process will increase the chances for success. Kurt Lewin's change model includes three general stages of the change process, as shown in Figure 10-11.

As seen in Figure 10-11, successful change requires first creating a situation in which change is seen as necessary and desirable, then taking steps to bring about the change, and finally ensuring that conditions are appropriate to reinforce the change. Clearly, change isn't a "one-shot" thing. We address these steps throughout the remainder of the chapter.

Skills Practice 10-7 will help you to develop skill in applying Lewin's change process model to a realistic organizational situation. Remember to address all three phases.

Skills Practice 10-7
Applying Lewin's Change Process Model

Skill Level: Challenging

Skill Objective

To develop skill in applying Lewin's change process model in order to effectively manage the overall change process in an organization.

Procedure

1. This exercise may be completed on an individual basis or in groups of three to five students.
2. Read the scenario that follows.

Coopers owns and operates 75 department stores in North America, Europe, Latin America, and Asia. It specializes in high-end apparel and accessories for adults and children. It employs over 50,000 people across its worldwide operations.

Coopers entered the retail business in 1890 when it opened its first store in New York City. Since then, Coopers has been a dominant force in the retail industry, as reflected in its status as the largest retailer in the world. Its name has always been synonymous with the concepts of value, variety, quality, and service.

In recent years, Coopers' overall performance measured in terms of sales, profits, and customer satisfaction has declined significantly as aggressive new competitors have entered the retailing industry. Some industry analysts now view Coopers as a retailer whose merchandise mix and service concept are "out of touch" with its customer base.

Other analysts have said that Coopers is too slow and conservative to compete in today's volatile and dynamic retailing environment. Finally, customers are becoming increasingly dissatisfied with the unprofessional service they are receiving in Coopers stores by sales associates who are rude and don't know anything about the products they are selling.

Despite these warning signs regarding the current state of affairs at Coopers, senior management appears to be unfazed. Their attitude is that "Coopers is still the number one retailer in the world and it will come back." They have explained away criticism of the company's performance as being attributable to unforeseen changes in market conditions or to weak economies in some countries in which Coopers does business. The bottom line is that senior management intends to continue to "do business as usual."

3.   Use Lewin's change process model to develop an action plan for addressing the key challenges in the situation above.
4.   Answer the following discussion questions.

Discussion Questions
1.   What are the key activities and outcomes associated with the three phases of Lewin's change process model?
2.   How does your action plan successfully apply Lewin's change process model? Be specific.
3.   What kinds of problems or "barriers to success" might you encounter in implementing your action plan? What steps could you take to overcome them?
4.   What are the implications of this exercise for you as a future manager?

TARGETS OF CHANGE

As shown in Figure 10-12, there are many things we might want to change in organizations, including people's attitudes or behaviors, the nature of technology, structural relationships, and even ultimate goals.

Structural Change Structural change involves altering a firm's formal authority structure or job definitions. Examples include changes in communication patterns, the way in which rewards are given, how the firm is departmentalized, or the decisions that employees can make.

At the aircraft engine factories of Rolls Royce, workshop managers were not allowed to change shop assignments or give out rewards. Therefore, workers tended to ignore the workshop managers. The factory managers, who made the decisions and gave out rewards, spent very little time in the

FIGURE 10-12
Targets of Change

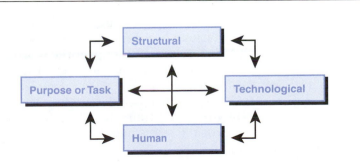

workshops and could not make good decisions on giving rewards. When upper management decided to let workshop managers determine shop assignments and give out rewards, productivity and quality increased dramatically.

Technological Change A *technological change* occurs when a new method is used to transform resources into a product or service. An organization's technology consists of machinery, knowledge, tools, techniques, and actions necessary to complete the transformation process. The installation of robots on an automobile assembly line is a good example of a technological change.

Human Change *Human change* involves changing employee attitudes, skills, knowledge, or behavior. Persuading employees to support the United Way or view diversity more positively, to learn how to use a computer, or to prepare for a new team assignment requires human change. We consider human approaches to change in the next chapter. In addition, organization development, discussed later in this chapter, relies heavily on human change.

Purpose or Task Change With a *purpose* or *task change,* the goal of the organization is changed. At one time, the goal of the March of Dimes was to conquer polio. When an effective polio vaccine was introduced, the March of Dimes changed its organizational goal to conquering birth defects.

SOURCES OF RESISTANCE TO CHANGE

Niccolo Machiavelli wrote, "There is nothing so difficult as to implement change, since those in favor of the change will be small in number and those opposing the change will be numerous and enthusiastic in their resistance to change." As such, it is important to recognize that resistance to change is likely and to prepare to deal with it.

It is often tempting to dismiss resistance to change as irrational or petty. In fact, though, people often have many reasons to resist a particular change, some of them very reasonable. Sources of resistance to change are shown in Figure 10-13.

Self Interest It is natural for organization members to have interests in benefiting themselves directly. Recall that the theories of motivation we have considered, such as expectancy theory and learning theory, are based on the idea that we seek positive outcomes and try to avoid negative outcomes. Resistance is likely to occur if a proposed change threatens those interests. Being assigned to manage a new product may increase one's prestige while lessening the prestige of those who did not receive the assignment. Changes may threaten—among other things—skills, power, relationships with others, social status, and self-esteem.

Uncertainty With change comes uncertainty. Organization members may resist a change because they cannot see how the change will affect their work and lives. Often, they expect the worst. And they know that change may predict future change. As such, even those who expect to emerge unscathed from a major change (e.g., a reorganization, merger, or implementation of new technology) may wonder about what further changes it may precipitate and how they will be affected. This can lead to a dogged resistance and a preference for the status quo.

FIGURE 10-13
Sources of Resistance to Change

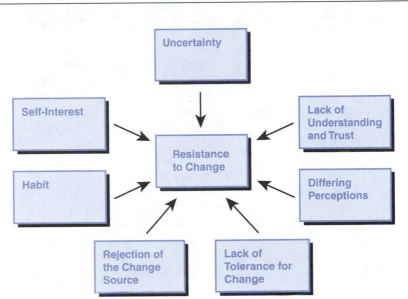

Lack of Understanding and Trust Many proposed changes are not adequately explained to those who will be affected by the change. For example, Ciba Geigy employees learned as they drove to work one day that their company was merging with Sandoz and that the combined company would probably employ at least 10 percent fewer workers. Failure to understand the change increases the chances that members or departments will resist the change. Unfortunately, in a recent study, only 28 percent of surveyed workers reported that their managers do a good job of explaining decisions to them, and only 27 percent reported that they're involved in decisions that affect them.[42]

Lack of trust can also support resistance to change. Prior experiences with those supporting or initiating change may have involved misrepresentations or deceit. In this case, resistance may be based simply on who supports the proposed change in the organization.

Differing Perceptions Differences of opinion about the need for change and what the change will accomplish can be a cause of resistance. People tend to see situations and events differently because of prior experiences and training. An engineer is likely to view a change in the production process differently than an accountant views it. The engineer may perceive the change in terms of increasing efficiency in the production of a good. The accountant may perceive the change in terms of the cost increase that will be reflected in the price of the product. Thus, resistance may result from legitimate disagreements over the outcome of change based on the differing perceptions.

Lack of Tolerance for Change Some people feel comfortable with change while others feel uncomfortable. Even when organization members are shown that the change will not threaten their self-interest, that the results are certain, that full understanding and trust exist, and that perceptions agree, they may still resist change. For example, some people prefer to drive the same route

FOCUS ON MANAGEMENT

TRUST BUILDING AT EASTMAN CHEMICAL*

Earnest Deavenport, CEO of Eastman Chemical, a spin-off from Eastman Kodak, credits the company's substantial success to the way in which Eastman has retooled the traditional contract between company and employees. Deavenport says, "We have to capture the heart and spirit of the individual before we can capture market share or our competition's customers." Eastman has pursued a trust-building strategy by

moving decision making farther down in the organization, enhancing the company's role as a provider of information, and developing an incentive and compensation program that encourages employees worldwide to become stewards of the company. Through the latter program, called the *Eastman Performance Plan,* Eastman employees will soon own 20 percent of the company's stock. Eastman Chemical was a winner of the 1993 Malcolm Baldrige National Quality Award. It is

the only major chemical company to receive the award. "The Eastman Way" states that Eastman people are the key to the company's success and that its values and principles are aimed at treating them with fairness and respect. Read about those values and principles at:

http://www.eastman.com/About_ Eastman/Our_Commitment_To_ You/The_Eastman_Way.htm

*See K. Ohlson, "Leadership in an Age of Mistrust," *Industry Week,* February 2, 1998, pp. 37–46.

to work even when they agree that a different route is quicker, safer, and less crowded. They are unwilling to change because they like the comfortable familiarity of the old route.

APPROACHES TO OVERCOMING RESISTANCE TO CHANGE

What can leaders do to reduce human inertia and encourage participation, cooperation, or at least compliance? Some primary approaches to dealing with resistance to change are summarized in Figure 10-14.

FIGURE 10-14
Change Approaches

Tactic	Characteristics
Education and Communication	Explaining the need for and logic of the change
Participation and Involvement	Having members participate in the planning and implementation of the change
Facilitation and Support	Gradual introduction of the change process and provision of support to people affected by the change
Negotiation and Agreement	Negotiating or bargaining to win acceptance or reduce resistance to change
Manipulation and Co-optation	Covertly steering individuals or groups away from resistance to change through selective use of information, or assigning potential resisters to a desired position in the change process.
Coercion	Demanding that members support the change or be threatened with the loss of rewards and resources

FIGURE 10-15
The Rhetorical Triangle

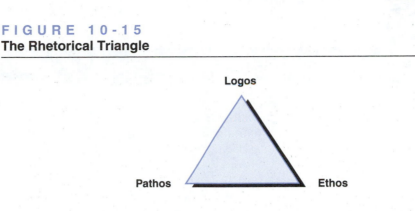

Aristotle argued that all attempts to encourage others to change their minds, feelings, and behavior can be summarized in terms of the *rhetorical triangle,* shown in Figure 10-15. It is useful to consider the change approaches in the context of the rhetorical triangle.

Here, *logos* refers to convincing another person to accept a change through reason, logic, and data; *ethos* through the strength of your moral character and the trust that followers have in you; and *pathos* through appeals to your target audience's emotional and psychological needs.

Logos When people are told about a change at work that will affect them, they normally react by first asking "Why?" When you initiate change, be prepared to provide a clear rationale in a direct, well-supported manner, using education and communication as your persuasive method. To accomplish this:

> **Do your homework,** gathering relevant facts that prove that a real problem exists. Identify potential causes and pinpoint probable causes. Thoroughly describe on paper the problem or opportunity, its causes, the need to do something about it, alternative solutions, and the cost-benefits of each. Communicate clearly the advantages and disadvantages of the change that you are selling.

> **Identify sources of help.** Who could help you sell the change? Staff, managers, inside/outside experts? Idea champions, venture teams, and innovation departments (each discussed in Chapter 4) may all prove useful, as may external change agents (to be discussed later in this chapter).

> **Anticipate questions and objections.** Think about the change from others' point of view. Identify the questions that you would have and the objections that you would raise if you were the target of this change.

> **Sell the benefits** of the change in terms of the perspective of those who will have to go through it. How will the change help to make things better and avoid or reduce bad consequences? It is easiest to sell the need for change when there is a *"burning platform,"* a dramatic, vivid demonstration that the current situation is unacceptable. Plummeting profits, competitive threats, irate customers, or lawsuits may all serve as burning platforms.

General Dennis Reimer, the U.S. Army's Chief of Staff, recently spoke of the Army's attempts at change. He explained that with the end of the Cold War and the fall of the Berlin Wall, the Army is in a different world and that it has to be able to change to serve the nation's needs. However, General Reimer noted that the Army is a conservative organization

FOCUS ON MANAGEMENT

THE BURNING PLATFORM AT ALLIEDSIGNAL

Larry Bossidy, former CEO of Allied-Signal, said about that company's burning platform, "In 1991, we were hemorrhaging cash. That was the issue that needed focus. I traveled all over the company with the same message and the same charts, over and over. 'Here's what I think is good about us. Here's what I'm worried about. Here's what we have to do about it. And if we don't fix this cash problem, none of us is going to be around. You can keep it simple: We're spending more than we're taking in. If you do that at home, there will be a day of reckoning.' In the first 60 days, I talked to probably 5,000 employees. . . . Also, there was a context to our burning platform . . . People here had observed difficulties at IBM, Kodak, and other companies, so the environment was ripe for change."* Bossidy capped his career at AlliedSignal in grand fashion, retiring in April 2000 after completing another major change effort—the acquisition of Honeywell.†

http://www.honeywell.com/

*"Bossidy's Burning Platform," *The Journal of Business Strategy,* September/October 1996, p. 10. See also S. Sherman, "A Master Class in Radical Change," *Fortune,* December 13, 1993, pp. 82–86; and M. Z. Strub, "Quality at Warp Speed: Reengineering at AT&T," *Bulletin of the American Society for Information Science,* April/May 1994, pp. 17–19.

†J. P. Donlon, "The CEO's CEO," *Chief Executive,* July/August 1998, pp. 28–37; and T. A. Stewart, "How to Leave It All Behind," *Fortune,* December 6, 1999, pp. 345–348.

---

and that it believes in the "first rule of wingwalking: You don't let go of what you've got in your hands until you've got something else in your hands."[43] As such, change can best be "sold" when the present situation is unacceptable and there is something else to hold on to—some promising new beginning.

> **Use catalytic mechanisms** to reinforce the change.[44] *Catalytic mechanisms* help to translate objectives into performance by making "stretch" goals reachable. They generally involve a dramatic policy that turns normal corporate practice on its head, requiring people to act in new ways that further the overarching corporate goal.[45]
> **Listen in depth** to concerns, questions, and fears.
> **Create an implementation plan** that answers the key questions most people have when faced with change: who, what, where, when, why, and how.

Ethos People tend to cooperate with a leader who has high credibility, a combination of competence and trustworthiness.

People tend to believe someone who demonstrates *expertise* and *authoritativeness,* has the requisite qualifications, and comes across to them as experienced, informed, skilled, and intelligent. When faced with a persuasive argument, the audience asks, "Does this person *know* the truth?" The other dimension is *trustworthiness:* one's character, moral fiber, and personal integrity. When faced with a persuasive argument, the audience asks, "Does this person *tell* the truth?"

Pathos You may have a rational idea for change, one that has a great cost-benefit ratio. You also may be seen as a trusted person of strong moral character and technical competence. That's not enough to persuade people to change, however. You also must attend to your target audience's emotional and psychological needs.

If the change that you are initiating threatens people's emotional safety and security—if it lowers their self-confidence or self-esteem—you may get begrudging compliance or none at all. One effective way to satisfy people's emotional needs and to stimulate high motivation is to get them actively involved in the change itself. When people feel that they have had a voice and a hand in shaping the change and its implementation, they tend to adopt ownership of it. Now, it isn't just you; *I* has turned to *we*. Such participation and involvement can be sought at stages in the process or throughout, depending on the skills and interests of the players and the needs of the situation.

Using *participation* in planning and implementing changes simultaneously enriches people's work, raises self-esteem and self-confidence, and hones their problem-solving skills. In this way, you may turn what at first looks like win-lose into a win-win proposition for all.

Some changes, however—despite your best efforts—create winners and losers. Productivity improvements, for example, sometimes result in unneeded staff. You initiate such painful change by providing *facilitation and emotional support* and by *negotiating, compromising, and compensating* the individuals for their loss. Here the leader pays special attention to people's emotional needs and concerns and to their pocketbooks. Eliminating a job but transferring the person to a less desirable but higher-paying job is an example. Providing a generous severance-pay package is another.

Manipulation and Coercion   As a leader, you can use other forms of persuasion: that of manipulating people through misinformation and downright lies; demanding change in a forceful, dictatorial manner; or threatening people with punishments if they fail to comply. Do these tactics work? Sometimes, but usually at high costs to morale, to positive working relationships, to willing cooperation, and to your trustworthiness as a leader. The best advice? Sit closer to Aristotle.

F O C U S   O N   M A N A G E M E N T

SHORT PAY AT GRANITE ROCK

As an example of a catalytic mechanism, Granite Rock is a century-old California company that sells crushed gravel, concrete, sand, and asphalt. A dozen years ago, the company's copresidents, Bruce and Steve Woolpert, set an audacious goal for the company: Granite Rock would provide total customer satisfaction and achieve a reputation for service that met or exceeded that of Nordstrom, an upscale department store that is world-famous for delighting its customers. To achieve this goal, the Woolperts implemented a radical new policy: "short pay." The bottom of every Granite Rock invoice contains the words, "If you are not satisfied for any reason, don't pay us for it. Simply scratch out the line item, write a brief note about the problem, and return a copy of this invoice along with your check for the balance." Note that Granite Rock customers don't have to ask for a refund or return the product or even call and complain. They have the complete discretion to decide whether and how much to pay based on their satisfaction level. Short pay serves as a warning system, providing specific feedback about quality. It impels managers to track down the root causes of problems to prevent repeated short payments. It signals to employees and customers the sincerity of the company's commitment to customer satisfaction. Since Granite Rock implemented "short pay," it has had remarkable success. The small firm has been able to compete successfully with huge rivals, has significantly improved its profit margins, and won the 1992 Malcolm Baldrige Quality Award.

http://www.graniterock.com/

FIGURE 10-16
Deciding When to Use the Change Approaches

Tactic	Best when
Education and Communication	Resistance to change is due to lack of information or inaccurate information and analysis.
Participation and Involvement	The initiators of change don't have all the information they need to design the change, and others have considerable power to resist.
Facilitation and Support	People are resisting change because of fear or adjustment problems.
Negotiation and Agreement	Someone or some group will clearly lose out in the change and that party has considerable power to resist.
Manipulation and Co-optation	Other tactics won't work or are too expensive.
Coercion	The initiator of change has power, and change must occur quickly.

Figure 10-16 provides a summary of situations in which the various change approaches are likely to be selected.

Skills Practice 10-8 is designed to give you some practice in analyzing situations in which employee resistance to change exists and in developing action plans for dealing with these issues appropriately.

Skills Practice 10-8
Overcoming Resistance to Change

Skill Level: Challenging

Skill Objective
To develop skill in effectively managing and overcoming employee resistance to change.

Procedure
1. This exercise can be done individually or in groups of three to five students.
2. Select and read one of the following scenarios.

Scenario 1—Total Quality Management
Meritron Corporation is a major provider of wireless communication services based in Palo Alto, California. It employs about 2,000 workers at its world headquarters and another 1,200 workers at various regional offices around the United States. Owing to concerns regarding inefficiencies and ineffectiveness (e.g., poor quality) in administrative processes at the corporate office (e.g., customer service, order processing, etc.), senior management has decided to implement a "total quality management" (TQM) program. This new initiative will entail the implementation of fundamentally new ways of thinking and doing things, including (1) a process orientation, (2) identifying and tracking critical measures of success, (3) benchmarking, and (4) the use of data-based decision making.

When senior management sent out a brief memo to employees informing them of the new TQM program, the response was one of skepticism and frustration. Many employees felt that this was just another "management fad" that would pass quickly. Others felt that TQM was applicable only to manufacturing settings. One employee even commented that he thought TQM was a "Japanese management method" and therefore could not work in a very different culture such as that of the United States.

Scenario 2 — Teamwork

TBM Medical Products is a major manufacturer of medical diagnostic equipment used for performing computed axial tomographic (CAT) scans, ultrasounds, and blood analysis. The product development process at the firm involves researchers, engineers, and marketing professionals working independently to develop appropriate technologies and then to design products that use these technologies. This means that there tends to be little interaction between the three groups of individuals during the overall product development process.

A recent internal evaluation of the firm's operations revealed that the product development process was inefficient relative to other companies in the industry. Senior management has concluded that transitioning into a "team-based organization" would help to enhance the efficiency and effectiveness of the product development process. However, the problem with this was that the researchers, engineers, and marketing people involved in the process were accustomed to working only with others in their area; they did not like the idea of having to work in "cross- functional teams." In addition, the work styles of the researchers, engineers, and marketers all differed from one another in fundamental ways. For example, while the concepts of "customers" and "markets" were critical to marketers, many engineers and researchers did not focus on them. Moreover, the marketers did not understand the technical aspects of the products as the researchers and engineers did.

3. Develop an action plan for dealing with the employee resistance to change in the scenario you selected. Be sure to base your plan on the strategies for dealing with resistance to change discussed in the chapter.
4. Answer the following discussion questions as a class.

Discussion Questions

1. What were the causes of the resistance to change in your scenario?
2. Which strategies did you propose to use to handle the resistance to change in your scenario? Why do you feel that they will be effective?
3. What barriers to success would your action plan face in relation to the scenario? What could you do to overcome them?
4. What are the implications of this exercise for you as a future manager?

ORGANIZATION DEVELOPMENT

Organization development (OD) has been defined as "an effort (1) planned, (2) organization-wide, and (3) managed from the top, to (4) increase organizational effectiveness and health through (5) planned interventions in the organization's 'process,' using behavioral science knowledge."[46] In this definition, we find the key ideas to the organization development approach to change. First, the OD approach is planned. Change is based not on spontaneity but on careful consideration of the goal of the change and the methods that will lead to the achievement of that goal. Second, OD is an approach to human change that considers and includes all members of the organization, not just certain individuals or groups. Third, OD is a change approach supported by top management. Generally, this requires a firm commitment of resources to the change process. Fourth, the change is designed to increase organizational effectiveness and to improve the working conditions of its members. Increased effectiveness at the cost of deteriorating working conditions is to be avoided. Finally, OD uses behavioral science approaches to create a more open and honest atmosphere in organizations. Emphasis is on the use of techniques that facilitate communication and problem solving among members.

OD Assumptions and Values The practice of OD is based on several assumptions about people as individuals, as group members, and as members of the organization. These assumptions guide OD practitioners in their efforts to bring about change in the organization.

> **People as individuals.** OD practitioners make three basic assumptions concerning people as individuals. First, people in the organization seek to satisfy higher needs, such as personal development and growth in their jobs. Second, people desire to make a contribution to the organization. Third, people have not only the desire to contribute to the organization but the potential to do so. The OD approach seeks to overcome organizational barriers that discourage members from satisfying higher needs and making a contribution to the organization through their work.

> **People as group members.** OD practitioners assume that the nature of group relationships will determine the satisfaction and contribution of the individual members of the group. It is important to the OD approach that group members feel that acceptance in a work group is meaningful and that the group is capable of generating trust, support, and cooperation among the members. Finally, the nature of the group should be such that members are capable of acting both as leaders and as followers in the group when necessary.

> **People as members of the organization.** OD practitioners assume that organizational structures have an impact on member attitudes and behaviors. For instance, if a new policy on dress were communicated to organizational members, there would be an effort to abide by the policy. A second assumption is that win-lose conflict strategies—in which one member wins at the expense of another—are not healthy in the organization. A third assumption is that upper management must have a long-term commitment to change within the organization.

These assumptions of the OD approach are critical to the OD practitioner's success. If a practitioner of OD were to try to improve the effectiveness and health of an organization in which members did not want to participate in the change and upper management did not support the change, the chances of success would be slim.

The OD Process Several important steps can be identified in the OD process. OD is usually started by what is termed a *change agent,* usually an individual outside the organization who intervenes to start the change process. The steps involved in the intervention are to identify a need for change, to select a technique for change, to gather top management support, to overcome resistance to change, and to evaluate the change process. While we have already discussed some of these steps, it is useful to consider them in the OD context.

> **Identify a need for change.** The first step of an OD intervention occurs when the change agent identifies a need for change. This may, for example, be the result of work with managers or employees in trying to understand why productivity or satisfaction is low. The change agent

must determine whether the situation is temporary or may have long-lasting effects on organization and member effectiveness. If the situation appears to be long-lasting, the change agent will want to identify a change process that will solve the problem.

> **Select a technique for change.**[47] A broad arsenal of intervention techniques is available to change agents.

- **Diagnostic techniques.** Once the change agent has identified a need for change, an effort to get more information about the situation is necessary. This can be accomplished through diagnostic techniques that may include such methods as administering questionnaires and surveys, conducting interviews, attending meetings, or reviewing reports and minutes of the organization.

- **Team building.** Team building (discussed in Chapter 12) consists of a series of activities designed to help individuals who work in groups to develop a sense of teamwork. Teams may consist of members who work alongside one another daily or are together on a project only for a short time. The change agent introduces exercises that help communication among members of the team and teaches problem-solving techniques (as discussed in Chapter 4).

- **Survey feedback.** The survey feedback technique of organization development starts with administering a questionnaire designed to gauge attitudes and perceptions of members. The information is then collected by the change agent and is fed back to members. The feedback may present the results of the survey with time set aside for the group to discuss their meaning and explore possible interpretations. Members may be actively involved in the solution to problems through the use of the survey feedback technique.

- **Education.** Educational techniques usually consist of classroom training. The classroom can be used for both the development of skills in relating to others and the exploration of material on specific topics. Emphasis is on the development of human skills rather than of technical skills.

- **Intergroup activities.** The change agent may want to focus on techniques designed to improve relationships between groups. These may include techniques that increase communication between groups, develop understanding of one another's goals and problems, and promote cooperation.

- **Third-party peacemaking.** The change agent may want to use mediation or negotiation between parties engaged in conflict (as discussed earlier in this chapter). The parties to conflict may be groups, individuals, or organizations or a mix of the three.

- **Sociotechnical activities.** The term *sociotechnical* refers to the way in which members relate to the organization technology. The change agent may examine the technology of the organization to see whether it is compatible with existing structures. If not, a structural change, such as a move toward decentralization, may be necessary. Or the change agent may want to change the number and composition of tasks for which an employee has responsibility.

- **Process consultation.** Process consultation is a popular technique in which the change agent observes individuals or groups in the organization to develop an understanding of their attitudes and behaviors. The change agent provides immediate feedback to members so that they can readily understand how certain processes shape their relationships.

- **Life and career planning.** Life and career planning is particularly useful when the goals of members and the goals of the organization are incompatible. The change agent may help individuals to formulate personal goals that mesh with those of the organization or to identify specific career maps and training opportunities.
- **Coaching.** Coaching is an effective technique when individuals need feedback to understand how others are responding to them. The information provided is usually nonevaluative and constructive.
- **Planning and goal setting.** Time management, goal setting, and activity planning are important managerial tasks. The change agent can help managers to improve their performance in these areas. Increasingly, computer software is being made available to managers for these purposes.

> **Gather top management support.** The successful implementation of any OD technique directed at human change requires the support of top management. Top management should communicate support of the OD change technique to those organizational members who will be involved in the change process. Communication from top management should identify the goals, purpose, and expected results of the change effort. In this way, members will more fully understand why the change effort is taking place and know that top management supports its implementation. Without the support of top management or in situations in which top management has not announced its support, members are likely to treat the change effort as frivolous or inconsequential. If this occurs, the change effort is doomed.

> **Plan the change process.** The change process must be well conceived from start to finish. The change agent should break down the change process into subparts, and then each subpart should be carried out sequentially. This will enable the change agent to check and evaluate progress. If some techniques do not work, the change agent can substitute a more effective technique without a large loss of organizational resources invested in the change process.

> **Overcome resistance to change.** As noted earlier in the chapter, resistance to change may come from many directions. Top management may get cold feet partway through the change process and begin to withdraw support. Managers of divisions or departments directly affected by the change may feel that their competence or power is under attack. In addition, managers of divisions or departments left out of the change process may, because of uncertainty, feel that the change will weaken their position. Employees may feel that the change process is an effort to increase their work performance without a commensurate increase in pay. Or they may feel that the change is simply an effort to check their work and that management will use the information to decide about firings or layoffs. Whatever the source or nature of the resistance, the change agent should have a well-thought-out plan to counter the resistance and to apply the techniques for overcoming resistance to change (discussed earlier).

> **Evaluate the change process.** Evaluation of the change process is the final step in an OD program. Measures of the effectiveness of the program can be established through observation of activities, discussions with participants and nonparticipants, and collection of performance data to determine whether the change process achieved its goal. Evaluation of the change process can be difficult. Many factors outside the control of the change agent may affect the intended outcome of the process. As such, change agents should look beyond their own efforts in evaluating the causes of success or failure of the change process.

Conditions for Successful OD Programs While many factors may contribute to the success or failure of an OD program, there are several important conditions thought to be necessary for an OD program to succeed:[48]

> **Recognition by managers and members that the organization has problems.** Without such recognition, it is unlikely that a change process will receive the required resources to make the effort successful.
> **Use of an external change agent to start the process.** The change agent should not be a member of the organization. Internal change agents often lack the objectivity and autonomy to carry out necessary changes, and their efforts may be hampered by political infighting.
> **Support from top management for the change process.** As noted, the lack of top management support can seriously jeopardize the successful implementation of a change program.
> **Involvement of work group leaders.** Where change is directed at work groups or teams, it is important that the work group leaders have an active role in the change process. Without their involvement, implementation of the change process is unlikely to occur.
> **Early success with the OD effort.** Success breeds success. Generally, change agents should strive initially to carry out a change process that has a high chance of success. Success motivates members to continue with the process and gives them confidence that more ambitious efforts can also be successful.
> **Understanding of the change process and its goals.** Generally, people will not respond positively to a change process unless they understand why the change is being made. Articulation of the purpose and goals of the change process should be made frequently.
> **Support of managerial strengths.** Change agents often become so focused on the process that they ignore the positives that exist in the organization. Effective managers should be acknowledged and reinforced. The change agent should be wary of overplaying the "expert" role in an organization.
> **Inclusion of human resource managers in the OD program.** The change agent should include managers from the personnel or human resources department in the planning and implementation of the change process. Human resources managers can provide valuable information and insight into members' performance, development, and rewards.
> **Development of internal OD resources.** One goal of an OD program is to make change an ongoing and comfortable process in the organization. The change agent should involve and train organization managers at all levels in OD skills and techniques so that managers of the organization can plan and carry out change long after the change agent has left.

> **Effective management of the OD program.** The change agent should watch and respond to situations to optimize the chances of success. This often requires careful coordination and control of activities to ensure that the change process is correctly carried out and that members support the program.

> **Measurement and evaluation of results.** Measurement and evaluation of results provide the change agent and members of the organization with important information about the effectiveness of the change program. This information can be the basis for planning and implementing future change programs.

THE LEARNING ORGANIZATION

As organizations face environments that are increasingly competitive, complex, uncertain, and dynamic, they must develop the capacity to change on an ongoing basis. Adaptability and flexibility require the ability to continually learn. According to Arie De Geus, head of planning for Royal Dutch/Shell, "The ability to learn faster than your competitors may be the only sustainable competitive advantage." Peter Senge, in his book, *The Fifth Discipline,* discusses learning organizations. According to Senge, in *learning organizations* "people continually expand their capacity to create the results they truly desire, where new and expansive patterns of thinking are nurtured, where collective aspiration is set free, and where people are continually learning how to learn together."[49] Learning organizations develop specific learning capabilities not present in traditional organizations.[50] The five disciplines of the learning organization are presented in Figure 10-17.

Senge argues that these five disciplines must develop as an ensemble. Systems thinking is the "fifth discipline" that integrates the disciplines, fusing them into a coherent body of theory and practice. Without systems thinking, Senge reasons, the other disciplines may become "separate gimmicks or the latest organization change fads."[51] For example, unless we adopt a systems perspective, vision paints enticing pictures of the future without adequate regard for the forces that must be mastered to achieve them.

The Seven Learning Disabilities Senge has identified seven "learning disabilities" that interfere with organizational learning. Before these disabilities can be cured, we must recognize them.[52]

1. "I am my position." People often identify with their jobs rather than with the purpose of the larger enterprise of which they are a part. They tend to see themselves as having little or no influence over the larger system and thus see their responsibilities as limited to the boundaries of their position. As a result, they have little sense of responsibility for overall results.

2. "The enemy is out there." We have a tendency to "externalize"—to find someone or something outside ourselves to blame when things go wrong. So, when a company loses market share, it is tempted to blame foreign governments, unions, unfair competitors, disloyal customers, or anyone but itself. Unfortunately, if we refuse to consider that our actions—our failure to stay focused on our customers, to take actions to retain our valued employees, or to treat our suppliers with respect— may be the true source of our problems, we will never learn from our

Awareness
Awareness
Awareness
Awareness
Awareness

F I G U R E   1 0 - 1 7

The Five Disciplines of Learning Organizations

Discipline	Description
Personal Mastery	This discipline of aspiration involves formulating a coherent picture of results that people most desire (their personal vision) alongside a realistic assessment of the current state of their lives (their current reality).
Mental Models	This discipline of reflection and inquiry skills focuses on being aware of the personal attitudes and perceptions that influence thought and interaction. By reflecting upon, discussing, and reconsidering these internal pictures, people gain capability in governing their actions and decisions.
Shared Vision	This collective discipline involves building a common sense of purpose. People learn to nourish a sense of commitment by developing shared images of the future that they seek to create and the principles and guiding practices by which they hope to get there.
Team Learning	This discipline of group interaction requires reflecting on action as a team and transforming collective thinking skills so the team can develop intelligence and ability greater than the sum of the individual members' talents.
Systems Thinking	This discipline involves understanding the language of interrelationships that shape the behavior of the systems in which people exist and thereby being better able to deal with the forces that shape the consequences of our actions.

P. Senge, A. Kleiner, C. Roberts, R. Ross, G. Roth, and B. Smith, *The Dance of Change: The Challenges to Sustaining Momentum in Learning Organizations* (New York: Doubleday, 1999), pp. 32–33. These disciplines are discussed in detail in P. M. Senge, *The Fifth Discipline: The Art & Practice of the Learning Organization* (New York: Doubleday, 1990), pp. 139–269.

mistakes and never correct them. We would do well to remember the words of Pogo, "We have met the enemy and he is us."

3. "The illusion of taking charge." According to Senge, all too often, "proactiveness" is just reactiveness in disguise; people just become more aggressive in fighting the "enemy out there." True proactiveness, he argues, requires seeing how we contribute to our own problems; it is a product of our way of thinking rather than of an emotional state.

4. "The fixation on events." We are conditioned to see life as a series of events and to believe that there is one obvious cause for each event. However, Senge argues, "Today, the primary threats to our survival, both of our organizations and of our society, come not from sudden events but from slow, gradual processes. . . ."[53]

5. "The parable of the boiled frog." A frog placed in a pot of boiling water will quickly try to jump out. However, if the frog is placed in water at room temperature and the heat is very gradually turned up to the point of boiling, the frog will stay in place and ultimately be killed. The reason: Its internal apparatus for sensing threats to survival is geared to sudden

changes in the environment, not to gradual changes. Similarly, the U.S. auto industry initially paid little attention to Japanese competition because Japanese market share eased up gradually. Thus, it is critical to remain attuned to the gradual processes that often pose the greatest threats.[54]

6. "The delusion of learning from experience." We learn best from experience. Unfortunately, we never experience the consequences of our most important decisions. The most important decisions made in organizations have system-wide consequences that play out over years or decades.

7. "The myth of the management team." Senge argues that members of management teams, instead of working together to battle these disabilities, fight for turf, try to avoid blame, and work to give the appearance of a cohesive team. They squelch disagreement, discourage questioning, and reward those who express their views rather than inquire into complex issues. This all leads to a situation that psychologist Chris Argyris calls "skilled incompetence," teams full of people who are very proficient at keeping themselves from learning.

Developing Learning Organizations To successfully develop a learning organization, it is necessary to instill the five disciplines while overcoming learning disabilities. This requires a variety of elements:

> **Learning leaders.** Leadership in a learning organization begins with the principle of creative tension.[55] Creative tension comes from recognizing the gap between where we want to be—our "vision"—and the truth about where we are—our "current reality." The leadership task of generating creative tension without causing defensiveness requires that leaders be able to see leaps of abstraction, to balance inquiry and advocacy, to recognize the difference between the views that they espouse and those that they act out, and to recognize and defuse defensive routines. Learning leaders must also help others to see the big picture. To do this, they must see interrelationships rather than things and processes rather than snapshots. They must be able to move beyond blame, using systems-thinking to see how the cause of problems is part of an interrelated system. They must focus on areas of high leverage, using small, focused actions to produce significant, enduring improvements. That is, properly placed small actions may serve as levers, bringing important change with a minimum of effort. In addition, learning leaders must look beyond symptoms to underlying causes in the system.

> **Leadership communities.**[56] In learning organizations, the leaders are those building the new organization and its capabilities.[57] Such leadership is collective, and it is based on the idea of *servant leadership:* People lead because they want to serve one another as well as a higher purpose. In addition to executive leaders, two other types of leaders are important in these leadership communities. These are local line leaders and internal networkers, or community builders. Local line leaders are individuals with significant business responsibility and "bottom-line" focus. They have units that are large enough to be meaningful microcosms of the organization, yet they have enough autonomy to undertake meaningful change. Local line leaders create subcultures that may be quite dif-

ferent from the mainstream culture. They sanction significant practical experiments aimed at connecting new learning capabilities to business results. Internal networkers, or community builders, have no positional authority, but they bring about change through the strength of their convictions and the clarity of their ideas. Internal networkers understand informal networks, and they move freely, with high accessibility. They identify local line managers who have the power to take action and who are inclined to develop new learning capabilities. Internal networkers then serve as "seed carriers," linking people of like minds in varied settings to one another's learning efforts. They may subsequently help to develop formal coordination and steering mechanisms needed to leverage from local experiments to organization-wide learning. Executive leaders, local line leaders, and internal networkers are all important parts of leadership communities in learning organizations.

> **Learning infrastructures.**[58] Learning organizations weave basic tools and methods for reflective thinking throughout the firm. They create virtual learning spaces or "managerial practice fields" in which learning arises through performance and practice.[59] For example, such companies as Royal Dutch/Shell, AT&T, Federal Express, and Ford Motor Company use such tools as scenario planning, learning laboratories, and learning forums. At Shell, planners produce multiple plans for multiple possible scenarios. As they plan for multiple futures, assumptions have to be articulated. and mental models become explicit. At Ford Motor Company, learning laboratories are part of the product development process. Groups involved in product design ask how the design process can be redesigned so they are not just designing new products but continually developing better ways to develop products. In this way, the learning process and the product development process are interwoven. At AT&T, teams meet on a regular basis in learning sessions called *forums* to discuss strategic issues. At the chairman's forum, the top 150 people meet twice a year to discuss basis strategy of the firm. In a sense, these various learning tools are all experiments sharing common elements: (1) they connect the learning agenda to core management processes and business imperatives; (2) they involve key players; and (3) they respect freedom of choice, permitting learning to occur in different ways.

> **Learning cultures.**[60] A learning organization represents a shift in culture. The learning organization embodies new capabilities and is grounded in a reinforcing culture based on transcendent human values of love, wonder, humility, and compassion. The culture of a learning organization treats surprises as opportunities to grow and differing behaviors, assumptions, and viewpoints as valid. In addition, it is a culture that recognizes the limitations of our knowledge and perspectives and thus the need and opportunity for improvement.

We began this chapter by saying that politics, conflict, and change are real, pervasive, and important. We said, as well, that these things aren't often listed in job descriptions but that they involve critical skills and that you must be ready to deal with them. In many ways, this chapter presents some of the greatest difficulties you will face in the workplace. These issues involve situations in which it is often unclear how an act may affect the various parties it touches, whether it is really well intentioned or manipulative, how others will view it, and whether its short-term impact may yield unforeseen long-term consequences. We've seen cases in which prescriptions could even be seen— at least on the surface—as opposing (e.g., use of outside experts may be viewed as a political tactic, yet it is central to OD). We hope the skills exercises in this chapter will help you to think about and prepare for some difficult situations in the workplace. At base, this chapter gives you a set of tools that, if used with integrity, respect, and trust, may foster a healthier, more open work environment. If misused, the tools may lead to inequities, hostility, stress, and a generally poisoned and unproductive climate. It will be your responsibility as a manager not only to understand these tools but to help to ensure that you and others use them properly. Your ability to do so is likely to be a major factor in your success as a manager and in the sort of place in which you will spend your working life.

Now, here's a tough challenge for you. In the nearby Real-World Management Challenge, read the scenario about the problems that the Xerox Corporation is experiencing and develop a plan for what you think it should do to turn itself around. Use material from the chapter as much as possible in formulating your recommendations. Later, you can compare your recommendations with what management is actually doing and with the recommendations of experts in the field.

Real-World Management Challenge

Fixing Xerox Corporation

The Company

Xerox Corporation, based in Stamford, Connecticut, is a leading provider of document-related products (copiers, printers, fax machines) and services on a worldwide basis. The company's formal mission statement is as follows:

Our strategic intent is to be the leader in the global document market, providing document solutions that enhance business productivity.[†]

The corporate values at the company are as follows:

> We succeed through satisfied customers.
> We value and empower employees.
> We deliver quality and excellence in all we do.
> We provide superior return to our shareholders.
> We use technology to deliver market leadership.
> We behave responsibly as a corporate citizen.

Xerox has 94,600 employees around the world. Its 1999 revenues were $19.2 billion.

The Problem

Xerox, once respected for its technological prowess and dominant position in many markets, has fallen on hard times in recent years. Its sales have been growing at an anemic pace of 3 to 4 percent per year. Competition from Canon, Ricoh, Hewlett-Packard, and others has enabled printers to perform many of the functions of a traditional copier machine, thereby eroding Xerox's position. A recent large-scale reorganization of the company has demoralized its sales force. This has contributed to a growing number of customer defections.

Chapter 10   Managing Politics, Conflict, and Change

Skills Application
Skills Application
Skills Application
Skills Application
Skills Application
Skills Application

499

According to James Gartner, a former Xerox employee who became a management consultant, one of the biggest and most challenging problems facing Xerox is an attitude that prevails in the company that Xerox is just "a copier company that sells copiers."

What Would You Do?

If you were the CEO of Xerox Corporation, what would you do to turn around the company? Be as specific as possible.

Source: P. L. Moore, "If I Were Running Xerox . . . ," *Business Week*, June 19, 2000, p. 220.

† www.xerox.com.

TOP TEN LIST: KEY POINTS TO REMEMBER
MANAGING POLITICS, CONFLICT, AND CHANGE

10. Recognize that politics is a reality of organizations. The key is to manage it effectively.

9. Be sensitive to how your behavior influences others' impressions of you.

8. Consider the ethics of your political behavior by applying the utility, right, and justice tests.

7. Be proactive in taking actions to reduce political activity in your work unit or organization.

6. Recognize that some conflict may be good and that no conflict at all may be very bad. Take action to stimulate healthy conflict in your work unit.

5. Adapt your approach for handling conflict to the nature of the situation.

4. View conflict situations as opportunities to learn. Take steps to achieve positive outcomes in the conflict aftermath (e.g., improved working relationships).

3. Remember the steps of the change process. Be sure to identify the need for change and to provide appropriate support during change efforts. Take steps to reinforce change so that it becomes a natural part of how work is performed in the organization.

2. Involve all key organizational players (e.g., senior management, line managers, human resources personnel, and affected employees) in the design and implementation of any OD program.

1. Work to build learning organizations. A key is the "Fifth Discipline": the ability to view and manage organizations as systems of interrelated parts.

QUESTIONS FOR REVIEW AND REFLECTION
REVIEW QUESTIONS

1. Do managers feel that successful executives must be good politicians? Do they feel that politics helps the organization to function effectively?

2. What are four individual determinants of organizational politics? What are four organizational determinants of organizational politics?

3. Discuss three organizational values that may cause unethical political activity.

4. Identify at least five norms and their corresponding counternorms.

5. Discuss three general strategies for the effective use of power for one's own purposes.

6. Discuss six political tactics that may be used to carry out the general political strategies.

7. Identify defensive behaviors used to avoid action, avoid blame, and avoid change.

8. Describe at least five verbal self-presentational behaviors.

9. Discuss four types of political games, including their typical players and purposes.

10. What are three guidelines for determining whether a political act is ethical?

11. Discuss costs and benefits of organizational politics.

12. State seven guidelines for minimizing political activity.

13. Discuss eight conflict premises.
14. Discuss six causes of conflict.
15. Explain the stages of the conflict process.
16. Describe five conflict styles and indicate when each might be most effective.
17. Discuss seven approaches to conflict resolution.
18. Identify approaches to generating productive conflict.
19. Differentiate between planned and reactive change.
20. Discuss the three stages of the change process.
21. Describe four primary targets of change.
22. Discuss seven sources of resistance to change.
23. Discuss six approaches to overcoming resistance to change, including when each is most effective.
24. What is the rhetorical triangle? What are the three points on that triangle?
25. What is organization development (OD)? What are its assumptions and values?
26. Discuss the stages of the OD process.
27. Identify factors that contribute to success or failure of OD programs.
28. What is a learning organization? What are the five disciplines of learning organizations? What are the seven learning disabilities?
29. Discuss four approaches to developing learning organizations.

CRITICAL THINKING QUESTIONS

1. Pactiv Advanced Packaging Solutions (formerly Tenneco Packaging) is a world leader in packaging and automotive parts. Its credo is "Management with no fear, egos, or politics." Do you think this credo is feasible? Is it desirable? Defend your position.

2. Suppose you have a good test that could be used to determine which job candidates were likely to be Machiavellian. Would you use the measure as part of your selection process? Why or why not? If you would use the measure, what would you do with the information it provides?

3. As an employee of a management consulting firm, you have been assigned to a project involving a major corporation that is concerned about destructively high levels of political activity. After conducting interviews and focus groups with managers and other employees of the corporation, you have determined that a set of counternorms is in place. Those counternorms, which encourage secrecy, avoiding responsibility, and placing blame on others, are apparently widespread in the organization rather than being isolated in one or two units. What steps might you take to provide guidance to management on dealing with the counternorms?

4. Your golfing partner, the CEO of a local manufacturing firm, says to you, "I'm proud to say you won't see any conflict in our organization." How might you respond?

5. Defend a position for or against the following statement: "There is really no such thing as productive conflict. Any benefits potentially gained through conflict could have been achieved equally well in other, less destructive ways."

6. After a serious disagreement about proposed changes in the company's pay systems, your boss announced in a meeting that, "I've decided to call in an outside expert to get some objective advice on how we should proceed." What would you say or do in response to this announcement?

7. You have led a task force to propose changes in company policies in order to make the workplace more "family-friendly." While you feel the task force did a thorough job in soliciting inputs and gathering other information to ensure that the proposed changes were feasible and in line with employee preferences, the task force's recommendations were met with widespread foot shuffling and comments of "flavor of the day." What would be your next steps?

8. As part of a discussion of a proposed major restructuring, you point out that major change attempts work best when there is a "burning platform." Your boss disagrees, saying, "That's motivating with fear. We need to change before the platform is on fire." Take a position for or against your boss's argument.

9. After a presentation on targets of change, your colleague says to you, "Any attempt to directly change people is unethical, period. What right does management have to try to toy with people's values or attitudes? What's next?" Do you agree with your colleague? Why or why not?

Chapter 10   Managing Politics, Conflict, and Change

501

Skills Application
Skills Application
Skills Application
Skills Application
Skills Application

10. Consider the rhetorical triangle. Think about a particular change with which you are quite familiar that affected more than one person; this could be a personal change, a change at work, or any other sort of change that interests you. Discuss how logos, pathos, and ethos did or did not play roles in the change process. Were there ways in which these elements of the triangle could have been used to make the change process more successful?

EXPERIENTIAL EXERCISES

WEB EXERCISE 10-1

Go to the *Fortune Small Business* articles site at:

http://www.pathfinder.com/fortunesb/articles/

You will see a Search box. Conduct searches on one or more terms from this chapter, such as *politics, conflict,* or *change.* For each search, you will be given a listing of recent *Fortune* articles dealing with the topic you have chosen. For instance, you may find such related articles as "Conflict Doesn't Kill Companies; It Makes Them Stronger"; "Should You Lie?"; "Managing By Endurance"; "Surviving in the Shadow of Microsoft"; and "Keep an Eye on the Competition." Select any two of those articles. For each article, write a one-page executive summary:

1. State the topic of the article and why that topic is important.
2. Summarize the author's key arguments.
3. Indicate what you see as key management implications of the article.

WEB EXERCISE 10-2

Go to the "United Parcel Service and the Management of Change" site at:

http://cpba.louisville.edu/bruce/cases/ups/htm/ups.htm

The case presented on the site is a student team project, written for a management class of Professor Reginald Bruce at the University of Louisville. It provides a comprehensive discussion of successful and unsuccessful change efforts at UPS. Read the case and answer the following questions:

1. What were the "burning platforms" that convinced UPS of the need for change?
2. What were the change efforts? Why was each change effort undertaken?
3. What were some of the sources of resistance to change at UPS? How were they addressed?
4. Which change efforts were successful and which were unsuccessful? What factors contributed to the success, or lack of success, of each effort?
5. Overall, how would you characterize the effectiveness of attempts to change at UPS?

http://www.ups.com

CASE 10-1
THE ARTHUR ANDERSEN—ANDERSEN CONSULTING BREAKUP

Go to the Arthur Andersen home page at:

http://www.arthurandersen.com/

Go to the Andersen Consulting (now Accenture) home page at:

http://www.ac.com/

The Companies
Arthur Andersen is a leading U.S. accounting firm that operates 385 offices in 83 countries around the world with a workforce of over 70,000 professionals. Its mission is "to build relationships and develop innovative solutions which help dynamic people and organizations to create and realize value." In 1999, the firm had over $7.2 billion in revenues.

In 1989, the Andersen Organization created Andersen Consulting as a separate entity with a focus on business and technology consulting. This decision was driven by the fact that major differences existed between the consulting and accounting markets in terms of client needs, preferences, strategies, and the like. As part of the creation of this new organization, the consulting partners had to give up their ownership in Arthur Andersen and become a part of Andersen Consulting. Since then, Andersen Consulting has established itself as a leading provider of management consulting services in 48 countries with a global workforce of approximately 65,000. Its 1998 revenues were $8.3 billion.[61]

The Situation

It wasn't long before problems began to emerge between Arthur Andersen and Andersen Consulting. In 1991, Arthur Andersen started to offer professional services that were similar to those provided by Andersen Consulting. Then in 1994, Arthur Andersen created its own business consulting unit, further straining the relationship between the two firms. Tensions came to a head in 1996 when Arthur Andersen opened a North American technology innovation center that was very similar to the technology and integration centers at Andersen Consulting.[62]

In addition to these events, the original agreement between the two firms required the more profitable firm to make transfer payments of up to 15 percent of their annual revenue to the less profitable firm each year. Andersen Consulting, with its 20 percent revenue growth per year compared with 8 percent for Arthur Andersen, has had to make the vast majority of these payments totaling almost $1 billion per year.

In addition, the original agreement specified that Arthur Andersen was to focus on providing consulting services to smaller organizations (less than $175 million in revenue per year) while Andersen Consulting was to target larger companies. Andersen Consulting alleged that over time, Arthur Andersen increasingly overstepped these boundaries and used the transfer payments made to it to build its own consulting business.

In 1998, the two firms took their "irreconcilable differences" to the International Chamber of Commerce to let an arbitrator determine whether Arthur Andersen had violated the terms of its agreement with Andersen Consulting.

The Resolution

On August 6, 2000, international arbitrator Guillermo Gamba ordered the split up of Andersen Consulting from Arthur Andersen. He blamed the breakup on Andersen Worldwide, the parent company of the two firms, stating that it had failed to live up to its obligation to run the organization effectively.

As part of the terms of the breakup, Andersen Consulting will be required to give up the Andersen name (as of January 1, 2001, its new name is Accenture) and some of the technology owned by Arthur Andersen. It must also make payments totaling $1 billion to Arthur Andersen according to a schedule of payments.[63]

Although the 10-year battle between Andersen Consulting and Arthur Andersen has been resolved, the costs have been high as well. Many corporate clients of the firms lost confidence in them during the ordeal, the overlapping consulting businesses created great confusion for clients, and employee dissatisfaction and turnover at the firms increased, making it more difficult to attract and retain the very best professionals so critical to their long-term success.[64]

Discussion Questions

1. What factors contributed to the conflict between Arthur Andersen and Andersen Consulting?
2. Which style for handling conflict did each firm use in attempting to resolve its differences with the other? Were these appropriate given the situation?
3. Do you agree with the arbitrator's ruling on the issues of conflict between Arthur Andersen and Andersen Consulting?
4. What actions could management at Andersen Worldwide have taken to prevent this conflict from occurring?
5. What are the critical challenges associated with the conflict aftermath for Arthur Andersen and Andersen Consulting? What should management at the firms do to address these issues?
6. What are the practical implications of this case for you as future managers?

CASE 10-2
TRANSFORMATION AT FORD MOTOR COMPANY

Go to the Ford Motor Company home page at:

http://www.ford.com/

The Company

Ford Motor Company, headquartered in Dearborn, Michigan, was started in 1903 by Henry Ford. Since then, it has grown to become the second-largest company in the automotive industry, behind General Motors. Ford's portfolio of auto marquees includes Ford, Mercury, Mazda, Lincoln, Volvo, Jaguar, Land Rover, and Aston Martin. It sells its cars and trucks in more than 200 markets around the world with its workforce of approximately 400,000 employees. The company also owns Hertz, a rental car company; the Ford Credit financial services unit; the service organization Quality Care; and Visteon, its auto parts unit.

Ford Motor's vision for the 21st century is to become a consumer company that continuously changes and improves the cars and trucks it manufactures to maximize shareholder returns.

Ford is the most profitable and, many argue, the best-managed company in the auto industry. It is a dominant player in the fast-growing sport-utility vehicle (e.g., Explorer and Expedition) and pickup trucks (e.g., F-Series) segments and has recently scored major hits with the Ford Focus small car, redesigned Ford Taurus, and recently unveiled Ford Escape mini-sport-utility vehicle. In 2001, the much anticipated, retrostyled Ford Thunderbird will also go on sale. In short, Ford is a red-hot company with tremendous sales momentum.

The Situation

In early 1999, Jacques Nasser, a Lebanon-born Australian who started with Ford in 1968 and worked his way up through the organization, became the new CEO of Ford Motor Company. Nasser's goal since becoming CEO has focused on transforming Ford from a traditional manufacturer of cars and trucks into a fast, flexible, high-growth consumer company that places a greater emphasis on the auto maintenance and financing businesses.

The pace of change that Nasser has been implementing at Ford has been relentless, causing some analysts to question whether other managers and employees may "burn out" from pure exhaustion. For example, Nasser has reduced employee headcount, eliminated "deadwood" (low-performing employees or employees who don't embrace the new philosophy and value system at the company), and bureaucracy throughout the organization. Also, he has hired and promoted non-Americans, such as Wolfgang Reitzle, formerly of BMW, to high-level positions in the company. He has also taken what some may call "radical" actions by outsourcing subassembly work to suppliers.[65]

Nasser's plan is to give brand unit heads more autonomy and accountability in meeting their target customers' needs and preferences. This is being done to help the company to design cars and trucks that are better tailored to the desires of younger consumers who have favored imports in the past. To a large degree, this new direction is the opposite of the approach emphasized under former CEO Alex Trotman's Ford 2000 Program.

Ford's traditional organizational culture was slow, fragmented, rigid, and not particularly customer-oriented. Nasser has sought to transform this culture into one that is entrepreneurial, aggressive, fast, flexible, and customer-driven. Since 1996, when he was the President of Ford, Jac has spent countless hours in classrooms and lecture halls teaching approximately 50,000 employees the meaning of basic business concepts, such as shareholder value and price/earnings ratios. Many of these sessions were intense, and Nasser developed a reputation for his aggressive style of running them.

To further support his goal of transforming Ford, Nasser sends out a personal e-mail to 89,000 employees worldwide every Friday. These e-mail messages provide updates to employees regarding news and events in the company that concern them. Hundreds of employees respond to Nasser's e-mails, and he reads each response.[66]

Challenges

Despite its tremendous success, Ford Motor is not without some significant challenges. First, there is growing overcapacity in the global auto industry, and many European and Asian manufacturers are focusing on the competitive U.S. market, where Ford has its strongest position, to support their sales growth strategies. Second, such competitors as Toyota and Nissan are starting to build better sport-utility vehicles and pickup trucks that could put additional competitive pressure on Ford. Third, many consumers are starting to favor sport-utility vehicles that are based on car platforms, such as the Honda CR-V or Toyota RAV4. Until the fall of 2000, Ford did not have a viable entry for this hot segment. Fourth, Ford's profits are highly dependent on sales of pickup trucks and sport-utility vehicles. The company needs more strong entries in the car segments, such as the Focus, that will attract consumers and be profitable as well. Finally, there is the problem of turning around Ford's global operations in Europe, Latin America, and Asia, where many auto markets and economic conditions in general have not been favorable.[67]

Discussion Questions

1. What are the environmental forces driving change at Ford Motor Company?
2. What does CEO Jacques Nasser do to implement change?
3. Evaluate Jacques Nasser's plan to transform Ford into a consumer company. What are its strengths? Weaknesses?
4. What would you recommend that Jacques Nasser do to support change at Ford Motor Company?
5. What are the practical implications of this case for you as a future manager?

www.ford.com

VIDEO CASE
MANAGING CHANGE: A STUDY OF
CENTRAL MICHIGAN COMMUNITY HOSPITAL

Running Time: 12:00

Central Michigan Community Hospital (CMCH), named one of the top 100 hospitals in the United States, is riding a tidal wave of change. Faced with growing governmental regulation and scrutiny, heightened competition, controls on costs, increased patient load, and many other fundamental changes, CMCH must respond quickly and appropriately if it is to survive and prosper.

The video shows the hospital's president/CEO, medical director, patient care services administrator, chief financial officer, surgeons, and others as they discuss the situation at CMCH. After viewing the video, answer the following questions:

1. What are specific environmental changes to which CMCH must respond?
2. What are some of the constraints CMCH faces as it attempts to deal with change?

3. What are some of the changes CMCH is undertaking to meet environmental challenges?
4. How does the traditional nature and training of health care workers impact on resistance to change at CMCH?
5. What are some specific things CMCH is doing to help to make its change efforts successful?
6. Do the various actions CMCH is taking to deal with its changing environment appear to be consistent with the guidelines for managing change presented in this chapter? Why or why not?

http://www.cmhs.org/cmhsframe.asp?action= cmchinfo

LIGHTEN UP
HUMOR AND CONFLICT

Humor can often defuse a tense situation. Sigmund Freud saw humor as an outlet for discharging psychic energy, thus providing relief from tension and rendering potentially damaging conflicts harmless. In addition, witty people are perceived to be more relaxed, better able to cope with stress, better able to change behaviors when necessary, far more intelligent, better problem solvers, and even more analytical. They are generally more articulate, better communicators, better as motivators and decision makers, and more forgiving. And finally, those gifted with a sense of humor tend to be more open-minded, less rigid in their beliefs, more hopeful and optimistic, more likely to see both sides of an issue, and far more accessible.[68] Here are two sites with humor resources on the Web:

BAD FADS

While change is often desirable, people may also implement change for questionable reasons. For example, some change efforts are essentially impression management, attempts to give the appearance of progress or to detract attention from other problems. In addition, change may sometimes take the form of blind following of fads.[69] In a Dilbert cartoon, when the boss announces at a meeting that ". . . companies must learn to embrace change," the employees sitting around the conference table collectively

Joke Central: http://www.joke-central.com
Lots of Jokes: http://www.lotsofjokes.com/cat_101
.htm

think, "Uh-oh. It's another management fad. Will it pass quickly or will it linger like the stench of a dead woodchuck under the porch?" When the boss continues with "I think we should do a 'change' newsletter," they collectively think "woodchuck." Check out fashion, collectible, activity, and event fads of the last 100 years:

http://www.badfads.com

ATTRACTING, SELECTING, AND DEVELOPING EMPLOYEES

CHAPTER *Eleven*

SKILLS OBJECTIVES

> To design effective recruiting plans for filling job openings.
> To design an effective selection process for hiring qualified employees.
> To develop job-interviewing skills needed to assess job applicant qualifications.
> To conduct orientation training programs for new employees.
> To conduct efficient and humane termination sessions with employees.
> To design effective employee training programs to enhance job performance.
> To conduct effective performance appraisal sessions that provide appropriate feedback and identify goals and strategies for enhancing employee job performance.

KNOWLEDGE OBJECTIVES

> Describe the three stages of staffing.
> Discuss the trade-off between recruiting, selection, and placement on the one hand and training and development on the other.
> Identify sources of job applicants and describe the realistic job preview.
> Identify approaches to selection and hiring and explain their relative benefits and problems.
> Define placement and indicate what it includes.
> Discuss the need for training and development and identify training and development methods.
> Discuss why performance appraisal is important to the firm and how employee performance can be measured.
> Describe how job worth, employee performance, labor market conditions, and pay systems determine levels of employee compensation.

From the local delicatessen to the largest international bank, business firms are made up of people. It is critical to get good people into the right jobs and then to develop them properly. Recognizing this, companies have developed some novel staffing methods. For instance, it is said that retailer J. C. Penney invited candidates to breakfast and served them eggs. If a candidate salted or peppered the eggs before tasting them, Penney concluded that he or she was inclined to make decisions without enough information and was not suitable for the company.[1] As we will see, such salt-and-pepper approaches to human resources management are no longer viewed as acceptable or successful.

In a workplace that is dynamic, uncertain, stressful, and increasingly litigious, human resource skills are especially crucial. It is important, for instance, to maintain diversity in the workforce, to find good employees in a tight labor market, to keep up with a bewildering array of employment laws relating to issues such as racial discrimination, sexual harassment, and advance notification of layoffs, and to see that employees continue to master new skills. Further, these activities are not solely the responsibility of human resource managers. Increasingly, line managers are working in partnership with HR managers and employees to ensure that the firm's human resource needs are met. In this chapter, we will explore skills associated with attracting, selecting, and developing employees. We will examine staffing and training and development. We will also discuss approaches to appraising employee performance and to compensating employees.

Take a couple of minutes now to answer the questions in Self-Assessment 11-1. You will learn more from this chapter if you start off with a greater awareness of your beliefs and feelings about how to attract, select, and develop employees.

Self-Assessment 11-1
Attitudes Toward Attracting, Selecting, and Developing Employees

Answer the questions that follow regarding your attitudes toward leading others in organizations. Answer each question as honestly as possible using the following response scale:

1 = Disagree Strongly
2 = Disagree Somewhat
3 = Neither Agree nor Disagree
4 = Agree Somewhat
5 = Agree Strongly

1. _____ An abundance of high-quality workers is available in the external labor market.
2. _____ Promoting employees from within the organization is always the best approach to filling higher-level management positions.
3. _____ Job interviews have low validity as selection methods.
4. _____ Managers can ask just about any question they want to in a job interview.
5. _____ Managers should not check the work references of individuals who have applied for jobs with their organizations.
6. _____ Classroom training is generally the best training method for enhancing employee performance.
7. _____ The basis of a training program is its training objectives.

D E V I L ' S   A D V O C A T E

I am not interested in being a human resources professional, so why should I worry about HR issues?
You will need to deal with a variety of HR issues even if you don't work in the human resources department in your company. Remember that HR is a support function, so its purpose is to help managers and employees deal with a variety of issues, including hiring, firing, training, compensation, and performance evaluation.

As a manager, you will need to be able to attract, train, motivate, and retain good employees in your work unit. This will require an understanding of basic human resources principles. In addition, there are many employment laws and regulations covering issues related to sexual harassment, discrimination based on race, disability, age, and so on. You may end up with a lawsuit on your hands if you do not understand these laws and their implications for how you perform your job as a manager.

If the goal of the staffing process is to hire people to fill jobs, then we should do whatever we can in order to find a qualified person and then get him/her to accept our job offer. Given this, why is it so important to provide a realistic job preview?
It is important to provide job candidates with realistic job previews in order to ensure that you are establishing a good fit between the person you hire and the requirements of the job, as well as a good fit between the person you hire and the culture of the organization. If you don't provide a balanced view of what it would be like to perform a given job or to be an employee in the company, you run the risk of having the employee realize later that the job and the company aren't what the employee thought they were going to be. This can lead to frustration, job dissatisfaction, and employee turnover.

Is it realistic to expect a manager to make the time to conduct orientations for new employees? This seems like a waste of time to me.
The new-employee orientation is a critical part of the employment process. It is an opportunity to address many of the questions that new employees may have about benefits, company policies, etc. It's also an opportunity to start socializing new employees into the firm's corporate culture.

I know a lot of people who are working in the "real world" who have told me that the performance appraisal process at their companies is not very effective. Does this mean that performance appraisal simply is a bad idea because it doesn't work?
On the contrary, performance appraisal is a very important concept that has the potential to make a significant difference in the motivation and performance of employees. Unfortunately, there are many companies that have poorly designed performance appraisal systems and/or weak implementation of their performance appraisal systems.

8. _____ An employee's manager is the only person who can legally evaluate the performance of that employee.

9. _____ Most managers do not need training in the conduct of performance appraisals.

10. _____ It is not critical for managers to develop an action plan for employees based on the performance appraisal.

As a way to assess your initial level of skill in attracting, selecting, and developing employees, read the scenario in the Pre-Test Skills Assessment and develop an action plan for how you would handle this situation. Be as specific as possible in stating your recommendations.

Pre-Test Skills Assessment
Attracting, Selecting, and Developing Employees

You are the manager of a rental car company located near a major international airport on the East Coast of the United States. Your job is to manage overall operations and the 70 employees who work in customer service, maintenance, administration, etc.

You are experiencing some significant challenges associated with your workforce. It has become extremely difficult to find an adequate supply of qualified labor to fill position openings in your growing firm. You have been shocked by the low level of work skills (e.g., analytical, quantitative, computer) and poor attitudes (e.g., work ethic) exhibited by job applicants. You have also found it difficult to make the idea of working for a rental car company appealing to younger workers.

Many of the younger employees in their 20s feel that working for your company is a "dead-end job" with few opportunities to grow or advance in terms of a career. A recent employee attitude survey revealed that employees are not receiving any feedback on their job performance, and they feel that management is not providing any support for them in terms of mastering new computer systems being integrated into their jobs and in understanding the company's new customer service concept.

Finally, the annual turnover rate for employees is 80 percent. This indicates that you are not doing an effective job of finding the right kinds of people to fill various jobs. This has been especially problematic for customer service jobs.

As the manager of this work unit, develop an action plan for handling this situation. Be specific, and focus on action.

STAFFING THE FIRM

Staffing is a vital part of human resource management. It involves bringing new people into the organization and then moving them through, and perhaps out of, the firm. Staffing consists of three stages: recruiting, selection and hiring, and placement. These staffing activities are coupled with the training and development function to match the abilities of the job candidate with the needs of the firm. This matching process is most clearly seen when the new employee enters the firm or when the requirements of the job change.

STAFFING OR TRAINING?

Figure 11-1 illustrates the balancing act necessary between the staffing activities of recruiting, selection, and placement on the one hand and training and development on the other. In its personnel practices, should a firm tip the balance to one side or the other? More specifically, should a firm hire people who are ready to step into their jobs, or should it "groom" them through training programs?

Careful selection and placement certainly have their advantages. The new employees can begin work immediately, showing results right away rather than in six months, after a training program. For example, offshore drilling companies such as SEDCO hire undersea welders who are already competent and can do their jobs safely. Acquiring these skills takes years of experience. Individuals are hired because they already have proven skills; the firm does not have to gamble that they will learn them properly. Brokerage companies such as Prudential-Bache Securities offer big bonuses to brokers who come

FIGURE 11-1

The Staffing/Training Balancing Act

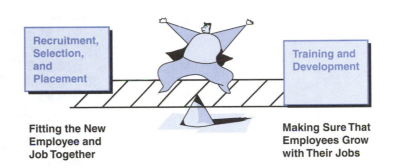

Recruitment, Selection, and Placement

Training and Development

Fitting the New Employee and Job Together

Making Sure That Employees Grow with Their Jobs

from other companies.[2] These brokers already have the needed skills and have proven their ability.

Training and development also has its advantages. For one thing, people can be hired at lower rates of pay if they come to the firm untrained. Also, training and development can be tailored exactly to the company's needs. For example, Westinghouse hires students with degrees in advertising and then retrains them completely. Ford, Bell Telephone, and McDonald's have similar training programs for employees who need special skills that cannot be

VOICE OF EXPERIENCE

ATTRACTING, SELECTING, AND DEVELOPING EMPLOYEES

Jane Schumann,
Corporate Recruiter,
Kohl's Department Store

1. **Why is HR important to the success of an organization in the "real world?"**
   All organizations have employees—and the HR function plays a key role in the acquisition, development, and productivity of those employees. How well the employee group performs is directly related to the success of the business.

2. **What do you feel are the most difficult HR challenges that line**

   managers face in today's business environment?
   The most difficult challenges relate to the tight labor market—hiring individuals whom they might not have hired and having to train and make them productive employees.

3. **There is a lot of talk about how HR professionals and line managers need to work together in a partnership in order to effectively handle HR issues. In terms of putting this idea into practice, what actions do line managers and HR professionals need to take to create and maintain an effective partnership?**

   They need to develop clear and productive lines of communication—as well as trust. Line managers have to trust the advice and assistance that HR provides.

4. **What general advice would you give to new managers regarding the handling of HR issues?**
   New managers always try to give an immediate answer. They need to stop and consult HR. They should not feel pressure to give an answer right away—listen first and tell them they will get back to them. Then take the time to access a policy and procedure manual and human resources.

   http://www.kohls.com/

FIGURE 11-2
Bankers Trust Ad in Chess Magazines Seeking Currency and Bond Traders

HERE'S A MOVE THAT COULD CHANGE YOUR LIFE.

Chess at its top level requires certain finely-honed skills.

The ability to predict an opponent's future moves.

Courage to take short-term risks for long-term gains.

Patience to assess every option available and strike accordingly.

Interestingly enough, these are the exact skills necessary to succeed as a trader in the global currency and securities markets.

Allow us to introduce ourselves.

We're Bankers Trust and this is basically a fancy 'Help Wanted' ad.

Bankers Trust is one of the most successful traders of foreign exchange and debt securities in the world.

Every day we trade over $35 billion in volume and we've made money doing this every year for the past twenty years.

Most of our competitors just hire MBAs right out of school but we're predicting that "a few good chess players" have what it takes to win in our highly competitive world.

The idea came to us from several of our best traders who are themselves, games players, one of our most successful in particular being an international master.

He is still moving pieces to form a calculated game plan, but now it is Yen and Deutchmarks as well as Rooks and Knights.

If you are interested in this quite unique job opportunity, send your resumé and/or a letter about yourself to Allen R. Beyer, Bankers Trust New York Corporation, 31st floor, One Bankers Trust Plaza, New York, New York, 10006. It doesn't really matter what your background is and it could be the best move you'll ever make.

obtained elsewhere. In addition, people trained by a firm often feel loyal to it. Sales and service personnel trained by IBM feel strong loyalty to their company; they are renowned for their dedication to IBM's interests. Bankers Trust New York Corp. placed ads in magazines for chess and bridge enthusiasts, in order to recruit trainees for bond trading positions. The company reasoned that bond traders, like bridge and chess players, make moves as part of a calculated game plan. One of the ads is shown in Figure 11-2. Bankers Trust believes that it can teach individuals with these skills the specifics of bond trading.

In the remainder of this section, we will examine the three stages of staffing: recruiting, selection and hiring, and placement. In the next section, we will examine training and development.

RECRUITING

The first of staffing's three stages is recruiting. The term *recruiting* refers to all activities involved in finding interested and qualified applicants for a job opening. No matter how employees are later selected, trained, and motivated, it is important to start out with a good group of job applicants. The greater the number of applicants and the better their qualifications, the more likely it is that the firm will build a solid personnel base.

GLOBAL PERSPECTIVES

THE GLOBAL TALENT SEARCH*

International staffing has become increasingly common as companies become more global in their operations and strategic thinking. Firms once looked only as far as their national borders to find qualified managerial talent, but they now look beyond. For instance, Gillette's International Graduate Trainee Program has helped groom local talent in the countries where the company has business operations. Training includes an 18-month term at the company's Boston headquarters, followed by an entry-level management position at the division in the home country. While at the headquarters, the trainee focuses on two major disciplines, such as marketing and finance or manufacturing and market-

ing. An executive mentor is responsible for overseeing his or her training and education in Gillette's operations. About half of the trainees have moved into executive positions, and many have returned to the United States or moved to other countries to pursue international careers.

Almost 70 percent of Colgate-Palmolive's $7 billion in sales come from overseas. The company has been operating internationally for more than 50 years, and 60 percent of its expatriates (employees operating outside their home countries) come from places other than the United States. Two of the last four CEOs were from outside the United States. All top executives speak at least two languages, and important meetings routinely take place all over

the globe. Because of its reputation, Colgate-Palmolive attracts people who want to seek global skills so that they can have international careers anywhere in the world. In 1991 a global team of Colgate human resource leaders and senior-level managers began a year-long quest to develop global human resource policies that would mesh with business goals. These efforts culminated in 1992 in a Global Human Resources conference, with more than 200 human resource leaders from more than 35 countries in attendance.

*Based on "The Global Talent Search," by Jennifer Laabs, *Personnel Journal*, August 1991; and C. M. Solomon, "Staff Selection Impacts Global Success," *Personnel Journal*, January 1994, pp. 88–100.

Sources of Applicants Job applicants can be found in many ways. Sources of applicants differ in ease of use, cost, and the quality of applicants obtained. Some primary sources are summarized in Figure 11-3.

CREATIVE RECRUITING

In the current tight job market, companies are trying some creative approaches to recruiting. Consider the following.

> How tough is it to get high-tech help these days? Tough enough to send IBM to the beach. Big Blue is hitting three spring-break hot spots to get a jump on computer rivals in recruiting techno-savvy 18–20-year-olds. The company set up a booth at a job fair on the beach—even building a giant sand sculpture of an IBM ThinkPad and flying a plane over the beach with a banner promoting Big Blue's job website. At Lake Havasu in Arizona, IBM recruiters have rented jet skis to reach students tooling around in the water. Others will rollerblade along the shore, giving out lava lamps and brochures to students.

> Where might companies find employees who were thinking about leaving their companies? Many firms—especially in high-tech industries— are linking their Web pages to the Dilbert Zone, the busiest site for frustrated programmers looking for a job change.[3] Check out the Dilbert List

FIGURE 11-3
Sources of Applicants

Source	Benefits and Costs
Walk-ins to the company	Company must assign a contact person to greet walk-ins and set up procedures to store and use applications.
Newspaper and magazine ads	These bring in many applicants, but don't screen out unqualified applicants.
Referrals from current and past employees	Referring employees understand the firm's needs and may know good people in the industry.
Private employment agencies	These agencies are in the business of matching job seekers with suitable jobs. They charge a fee for their services.
Public employment agencies	Most cities have an office of the state employment agency. It finds jobs for unemployed people and may offer training programs.
Educational institutions	Universities, colleges, high schools, and other educational institutions are good sources of applicants. Companies may send recruiters to campus.
Labor unions	These are good sources of jobs for blue-collar and some professional jobs. Some have hiring halls where employers and job seekers are brought together.
Social service agencies	Various social service agencies provide training and assistance for the homeless, including help with job seeking.
Coops and internships	Students currently attending school may be available to work through coops and internships. With a coop arrangement, the student attends school full time and works full time on an alternating basis. With an internship, the student works for an employer for a specified period of time, such as a summer.
Temporary help agencies	Contingent workers are workers who are employed by a firm on a temporary basis. Some are self-employed and others work for an agency that provides temporary workers to firms. They are used when work is of short duration and may give companies flexibility in responding to economic fluctuations.

of the Day, a month of Dilbert, the Dilbert Travel Zone, Catbert's Anti-Career Zone, and other features at *http://www.dilbert.com.*

> The Internet is the hottest tool for recruiting. Search engines such as Yahoo! and Excite as well as bulletin board systems and news groups provide job information. Job banks (which we'll discuss further in our discussion of careers) include the Career Resource Center, Career Mosaic, Job Trak, Monster Board, America's Job Bank, and many more. Cisco Systems, a computer network equipment manufacturer, hires as many as 1,200 people every three months. Its Internet job pages record as many as 500,000 hits a month.[4] Cisco gets 81 percent of its résumés from the net, making 66 percent of its hires from the Net. Texas Instruments has updated its popular website with additional career development tools for engineering students and prospective hires. Brand new to the site is "Ask the Cyber Recruiter," an interactive area where students can ask for career advice, post questions about TI, and learn how to use the Web for job searches. Cyber Recruiter also includes a "Career Mapper" that asks questions designed to uncover what type of company or corporate

culture would best suit an individual and "Fit Check" for assessing whether a user would be a good fit with the TI culture.

Merits of Internal and External Recruiting Sources There are costs and benefits to internal recruiting methods (such as internal job postings, referrals, and identifying internal candidates for promotion or transfer through skills inventories) and the various external recruiting methods. Internal sources generally benefit from the facts that employees are familiar with the organization, recruiting and training costs are relatively low, and internal recruiting enhances employee morale and motivation since it gives a signal that the organization offers opportunities for advancement. On the other hand, internal recruiting may lead to political infighting for promotions, inbreeding, and morale problems for those not promoted. External sources generally reverse these lists. They introduce new ideas and approaches, provide knowledge and skill not currently available in the organization, and permit new hires to start with clean slates. However, there may be less fit between the new hire and the organization, an increased adjustment period for the individual, and reduced morale and commitment for current employees.

Skills Practice 11-1 gives you the opportunity to develop a recruiting plan for a specific job. Remember to think strategically! That is, stay focused on using recruiting methods and sources that are appropriate to the job you are seeking to fill.

Skills Practice 11-1   **Skill Level: Challenging**
Developing a Strategic Recruiting Plan

Skill Objective
To develop skill in designing and implementing a recruiting plan for a specific job.

Procedure
1. Select one of the following scenarios (or you can select a job based on your current "real-world" job).

Scenario 1—Recruiting Web Page Designers at an Internet Retailer
You work at an upstart Internet retailer that sells books, videos, CDs, etc. Due to the explosive growth of your firm, you have a strong need to hire 10 high-level Web page designers who can continuously develop and maintain the company's website in order to attract, satisfy, and retain customers. Currently, there are only two people performing this function. No formal job description yet exists for this job, but you need experienced people who are creative, enthusiastic, and team-oriented and can work in a self-directed manner.
    What would you do to recruit people for this job?

Scenario 2—Recruiting New Agents at an Insurance Company
You work as a district manager at a major insurance company based in the Midwest. Your company sells a full line of insurance through an agent force that works as an independent contractor for the company. Recently, you have noticed the following few trends.
   a. The company's long-term growth potential in current and new markets is excellent.
   b. The five-year success rate (agents who are profitable after five years of operation) has plummeted to below 50 percent.
   c. Interest in becoming an insurance agent has fallen to an all-time low among people in their 20s.

In terms of the job of insurance agent, ideally you need someone with:

> Excellent interpersonal skills
> Good management and organizational skills
> The ability to develop trust in the eyes of customers
> Strong ties with the local community in which he/she is doing business
> The ability to work in a self-directed manner
> Perseverance and the ability to delay gratification

You need to hire a large number of new agents who can support the company's expansion strategy. Given this situation, develop a recruiting plan to increase the recruitment of new insurance agents at the company.

2. Develop a plan for recruiting qualified candidates to fill the job openings in the scenario you selected. This plan should include the following elements:
   a. The job that needs to be filled
   b. The objectives of this recruiting initiative
   c. Job requirements (duties and responsibilities)
   d. Desired applicant qualifications
   e. Where you will look for appropriate candidates to fill this job (recruiting sources)
   f. The methods you will use to recruit from the sources you have selected
   g. How you will evaluate the effectiveness of your recruiting process
3. Answer the following discussion questions.

Discussion Questions
1. Evaluate your recruiting plan in terms of its relative strengths and weaknesses.
2. What are the key things to do in terms of effective implementation of your recruiting plan?
3. What are the barriers to the success of your recruiting plan? What steps would you take to overcome these barriers?
4. What are the implications of this exercise for you as a future manager or supervisor?

The Outsourcing Alternative As noted earlier in the chapter, outsourcing is one alternative available to firms.[5] In the face of increased demand, evolving needs, or cost considerations firms may use outside parties to perform tasks that would otherwise be handled in-house.[6] This is a popular, rapidly growing option. In 1996, American firms spent over $100 billion in outsourced business activities.[7] By outsourcing some activities, firms can concentrate their resources on their core competencies, those things that they do particularly well. A new biotechnology firm, for instance, may choose to outsource routine payroll functions since those functions do not require the firm's specialized expertise.

The scenario in the Real-World Management Challenge deals with the challenges associated with "e-recruiting." Put on your management consultant's hat and develop some recommendations for creating a good e-recruiting system. Later, you can compare your recommendations with those offered by experts in the field.

Real-World Management Challenge

In Search of More Effective E-Recruiting Strategies

The Problem
Tight labor markets have created a "War for Talent" among employers as they scramble to develop creative recruiting strategies to attract and retain high-quality employees. A key

recruiting strategy that is being implemented by many employers today is "cyber-recruiting," or "e-recruiting." This method enables job seekers to research and identify appropriate job opportunities from a company's website. In many cases, a user can submit a résumé and actually apply for a given job opening online as well.

Despite the appeal of the Internet as a recruiting method, a recent study by Nielsen Norman Group, a management consulting firm, found that job seekers were unable to complete a job application at selected corporate websites 74 percent of the time. This suggests that the e-recruiting sections of many corporate websites possess serious deficiencies.

What Would You Do?

If you were given the assignment of developing an e-recruiting Web page for a company, what steps would you take to ensure that it is effective? Be as specific as possible.

Source: S. H. Wildstrom, "Wanted: Better Job Listings," *Business Week,* September 20, 1999, p. 19.

Realistic Job Preview Most companies present a rosy picture of themselves and their job openings in order to attract job applicants. Partly as a result, many new employees experience "entry shock" and are dissatisfied when they learn the "truth" about the company. Many even quit after a short time. In addition, courts in recent years have ruled that employees can sue their companies if exaggerated claims or promises lured them into accepting a job.[8]

To avoid such outcomes, many companies now use realistic job previews. The aim of the *realistic job preview (RJP)* is to give the recruit an accurate picture of what the company and the job are like.[9] For example, films of people on the job and uncensored comments of current employees may be used to acquaint new employees with the day-to-day reality of the job. Exxon prints brochures describing the kinds of jobs available for people with varying educational backgrounds, the promotion and salary opportunities of the jobs, and where in the world an individual might work. Because of its highly developed preview, Exxon has one of the lowest employee turnover rates in the petroleum industry. Research shows that RJPs lead to higher levels of employee satisfaction and lower levels of turnover. Further, presenting an honest, balanced picture doesn't appear to reduce the acceptance rate of jobs.

Try completing Skills Practice 11-2 on providing realistic job previews. Although as a concept this is not difficult to grasp, it takes real skill to present a balanced view of a job within the context of the recruiting process, where you are trying to attract prospective employees.

Skills Practice 11-2
Conducting Realistic Job Previews

Skill Level: **Basic**

Skill Objective

To develop skill in identifying and effectively communicating a balanced perspective (positive and negative characteristics) of a job to candidates during the recruiting process.

Procedure

1. Find a partner for this exercise.
2. Select a job you are familiar with. This can be your current part-time job or a job you held in the past.
3. Make a list of the things you believe are the *positive aspects of the job* (e.g., type of work, compensation, work environment, coworkers, opportunities for advancement, benefits).

4. Make a list of the things you believe are the *negative aspects of the job* (e.g., type of work, compensation, work environment, coworkers, opportunities for advancement, benefits).

5. Practice communicating the positive and negative aspects of the job to your partner as if you were interviewing that person for your job. Be careful not to oversell the positive aspects of the job. Also, take care not to be overly negative about the less desirable aspects of the job either.

Discussion Questions

1. Although this may be a basic exercise, why is it important to provide realistic job previews during the recruiting process? What are the costs of not doing this?

2. What could you do to further apply the concept of a realistic job preview in other aspects of the hiring process? Try to be as specific as possible.

3. What should the appropriate balance be in terms of discussing the positive and negative aspects of a position with job candidates?

4. What are the practical implications of this exercise for you as a future manager or supervisor?

The nearby Bottom Line presents a process model summarizing the basic steps associated with implementation of the recruiting process.

SELECTION

The role of recruiting is to locate job candidates; the role of *selection* is to evaluate each candidate's qualifications and pick the one whose skills and interests best match requirements of the job and company. Some firms use informal selection procedures, such as reviewing application blanks and ré-

BOTTOM LINE

The Bottom Line: The Recruiting Process

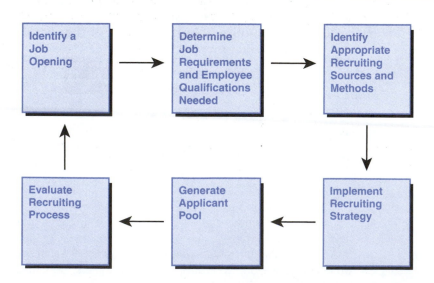

FOCUS ON MANAGEMENT

THE DIRECTOR OF ROMANCE

Consider the case of Korbel Champagne Cellars. Since consumption of champagne is often associated with romantic situations, Korbel has a Romance, Weddings, and Entertainment Department, presided over by a Director of Romance. When the Director of Romance resigned, the company was faced with the task of selecting a successor. The ideal candidate, according to a company spokesperson, should "personify romance in some highly visible or glamorous way."* How might you go about selecting such a person?

*"Only Effervescent Personalities Need Apply," *Business Week,* July 10, 1989, p. 36.

sumés. Others ask their job candidates to take personality and ability tests. Still others have assessment centers, where procedures for selecting and hiring new employees are very systematic.

Careful selection procedures can be time consuming and costly. However, they are worthwhile if the costs of a wrong decision are high, if there are many applicants and few openings, and if selection tools are accurate. Some companies now use expensive selection procedures even for positions that would traditionally have been filled without much screening. Let's look at some of the ways in which firms determine whether the qualifications of a job candidate are in line with the requirements of the job.

Application Forms The first source of information about a potential employee is the *application form.* It provides the hiring firm with information about educational background, work experience, and outside interests. Much of this information is especially useful for screening purposes. For example, an applicant for a position as a computer analyst should have had courses in data processing. The application form would tell the employer right away whether the applicant had the needed training.

However, there are at least three problems with application forms as sources of information about potential employees. First, the information pro-

FOCUS ON MANAGEMENT

SELECTION AT TOYOTA

When Toyota Motor Corp. wanted to fill positions at its new auto assembly plant in Kentucky, it received 90,000 applications from 120 countries for its 2,700 production jobs and thousands more for the 300 office jobs. The company wanted to select workers who would conform to its emphasis on teamwork, loyalty, and versatility. Toyota required applicants to spend as much as 25 hours completing written tests, workplace simulations, and interviews, in addition to undergoing a physical examination and a drug test. The tests examined not only literacy and technical knowledge, but also interpersonal skills and attitudes toward work. At each stage of the selection process, more applicants were screened out. Only 1 in 20 made it to the interview.*

http://www.toyota.com/

*R. Koenig, "Toyota Takes Pains, and Time, Filling Jobs at Its Kentucky Plant," *Wall Street Journal,* December 1, 1987, p. 1. See also N. Templin, "Dr. Goodwrench: Auto Plants, Hiring Again, Are Demanding Higher-Skilled Labor," *Wall Street Journal,* March 11, 1994, pp. A1, A4.

FIGURE 11-4
Some Unfair Pre-Employment Inquiries

> Any inquiry that implies a preference for people under 40 years of age
> Whether applicant is a citizen; any inquiry into citizenship that tends to divulge applicant's lineage, ancestry, national origin, descent, or birthplace
> All inquiries relating to arrests
> Inquiries that would divulge convictions that do not reasonably relate to fitness to perform the particular job or that relate to convictions for which the date of conviction or prison release was more than seven years before the date of application
> Specific inquiries concerning spouse, spouse's employment or salary, children, child care arrangements, or dependents
> Any inquiries concerning handicaps, height, or weight that do not relate to the job requirements
> Whether the applicant is married, single, divorced, engaged, widowed, etc.
> Type or condition of military discharge
> Request that applicant submit a photograph
> Gender
> Any inquiry concerning race or color of skin, hair, eyes, etc.
> All questions as to pregnancy, and medical history concerning pregnancy and related matters
> Any inquiry concerning religious denomination, affiliations, holidays observed, etc.
> Requirement that applicant list all organizations, clubs, societies, and lodges to which the applicant belongs
> Inquiry into original name where it has been changed by court order or marriage

Web Wise

National Labor Relations Board

The National Labor Relations Board (NLRB) is the independent federal agency that administers U.S. labor law. The NLRB's website includes an information locator, rules and regulations, and summaries of its recent decisions.

http://www.nlrb.gov/

vided by the applicant may not be relevant to performance on the job. Second, job applicants may give incorrect or misleading information on the forms or in résumés. The National Credit Verification Service has found that about one-third of the job applicants whose credentials it has investigated somehow misrepresented their educational backgrounds.[10] One survey found that 95 percent of college students are willing to make at least one false statement to get a job, and 41 percent have already done so.[11] Sometimes these misrepresentations are discovered many years later when employees are considered for promotion. Third, the law places many restrictions on what can and cannot be asked on a job application. Figure 11-4 lists questions considered to be unfair by the Washington State Human Rights Commission. Clearly, firms must be careful to avoid questions on application forms that violate state or federal law.

References   References are another popular selection tool. *References* are information provided by previous employers, coworkers, teachers, or acquaintances concerning an applicant's credentials, past performance, or qualifications for the current position. The reference givers may be contacted in person, by phone, or by mail. The evidence suggests that references are generally of little value in the employee selection process. The people asked to provide references sometimes do not really know much about the person for whom they are providing the reference. Sometimes they are not frank because they do not want to say anything uncomplimentary about a person, especially in writing. And applicants usually carefully select references whom they think will write positive letters. As a result, references are generally biased in the applicant's favor.

References are probably most useful if a structured form is used so that all people providing references give the same information for each applicant. Also, standardized scoring keys can be used to arrive at quantitative scores relating to such things as the applicant's mental ability, cooperation, dependability, and vigor.[12] In addition, it is often helpful to ask the references to in turn suggest other references. While the job candidate might consciously choose references that would be likely to make positive comments, these secondary references may respond in a more balanced fashion.

Interviews The hiring firm generally asks candidates that pass the initial screening process to participate in an interview. In an *interview,* a representative of the hiring firm asks the candidate a series of questions. The goal of the interview is to determine how well the candidate's skills and interests match the job requirements. The interviewer may be a member of the firm's human resources department or a supervisor, team leader, or manager who has an open position. Some firms, such as Virginia Natural Gas and Philip Morris U.S.A., use panel interviewing, in which from two to six interviewers meet with job candidates as a team.[13]

Interviews can be conducted in many ways. Two types often used are structured interviews and unstructured interviews. In a *structured interview,* all candidates are asked the same list of questions in the same order. A structured interview helps ensure that all questions are related exclusively to job duties and requirements critical to job performance. By sticking to the questions in the structured interview, the interviewer gives each applicant the same chance as every other and makes it easier to compare candidates. The fact that all applicants are treated the same also makes it less likely that the company will be sued for discrimination in hiring.

An *unstructured interview,* on the other hand, is a looser exchange between the interviewer and the job candidate. The interviewer often asks questions that are not on the planned list to follow up on the candidate's comments. This sometimes results in a more complete picture than would otherwise be possible.

Advantages of Interviews Interviews are widely used. More than 90 percent of all people hired for industrial positions are interviewed at least once. There are many reasons for the popularity of interviews, including the following.

> It is easier to ask someone a series of questions than to develop a test.
> Interviewing makes the selection process more personal and gives the interviewer an overall idea as to whether the applicant is right for the job.
> Companies may use interviews to give the applicant information about the duties of the position to be filled and about the organization in general.
> Interviews may be used to "sell" the company to the applicant.
> Interviews may also be used to complete the information about job candidates.
> Good candidates might be unwilling to consider a job seriously unless they had the chance to ask questions and gather information.

Problems with Interviews Despite the popularity of interviews, a successful interview does not always mean that the recruit will perform well on the job.

FIGURE 11-5
Discriminating Questions

Legal

1. Do you have 20/20 corrected vision?
2. How well can you handle stress?
3. Can you perform this function with or without reasonable accommodation?
4. How many days were you absent from work last year?
5. Are you currently illegally using drugs?
6. Do you regularly eat three meals a day?
7. Do you drink alcohol?

Illegal

1. What is your corrected vision?
2. Does stress ever affect your ability to be productive?
3. Would you need reasonable accommodation to do this job?
4. How many days were you sick last year?
5. What medications are you currently using?
6. Do you need to eat a small number of snacks at regular intervals throughout the day in order to maintain your energy level?
7. How much alcohol do you drink per week?

Interviewers sometimes show many biases, disagree with one another over which recruits are likely to do best, and ignore much of the information available. The success of an interview in identifying the best candidate for the job depends on the skill and good judgment of the individual interviewer.

Further, as with application forms, there are rather severe legal restrictions on what can be asked in interviews. These restrictions became even more severe after implementation of the Americans with Disabilities Act (ADA) in 1992.[14] For instance, questions about disabilities or medical histories are banned unless the applicant brings them up. The U.S. Equal Employment Opportunity Commission attempted in 1994 to clarify matters relating to the ADA by presenting lists of legal and illegal versions of similar interview questions. The legal versions are intended to focus on the ability to carry out the job rather than on disability per se. Unfortunately, as the questions presented in Figure 11-5 suggest, these distinctions are subtle and, some argue, confusing.[15]

There have been widely publicized cases in recent years relating to alleged discriminatory interview tactics, and studies show that most interviewers are unaware that certain types of questions may be discriminatory. For instance, questions about arrest records are inappropriate, since an individual must be considered innocent unless actually convicted of a crime. Even questions about the applicant's willingness to work on weekends could be seen as betraying religious discrimination, since orthodox Jews can't travel on Saturdays.

Improving Interviews Steps can be taken to increase the likelihood of a successful interview. For example:

> Interviewers should always prepare for an interview by making a list of specific topics to be covered and/or specific questions to be asked.

> Interviewers should be trained in preparing questions that relate to the job requirements, probing for details, listening carefully, and avoiding discriminatory questions.
> Interviewers should use behavioral and situational questions. Behavioral questions ask candidates to recall and describe a specific behavior, such as a time when they had to deal with a hostile customer. Situational questions present a situation and ask how the candidate would deal with it. For instance, a question might be "Suppose a colleague yelled at you in front of a customer. What would you do?"
> Written records of the interview should be kept.
> Whenever possible, multiple interviewers should be used so that the selection will depend on the judgment of more than one person.
> Interviews should never be the sole basis for selection of a candidate. They should be used along with other selection devices to provide additional information on candidates' strengths and weaknesses.[16]

Find a partner and complete Skills Practice 11-3, a role-immersion simulation exercise on job interviewing. The purpose of the exercise is to give you an opportunity to practice designing an interview process and developing interviewing skills. Remember to be systematic and focused in the questions you ask during the interview.

Skills Practice 11-3

Skill Level: **Challenging**

Role-Immersion Simulation Exercise: Conducting an Effective Job Interview

Skill Objective

To develop skill in designing and implementing an effective job interview.

Procedure

1. Select one of the following scenarios *or* a job you are familiar with to use for this exercise.

Situation 1

You are the manager of customer sales and service for a major catalog retail firm based in northern Wisconsin. It is time to start hiring help for the holiday season. You are interested in hiring customer service representatives who can answer customer calls, take orders accurately, answer questions about catalog merchandise intelligently, and provide service to customers in a friendly and professional manner. You need people who are hard working, trustworthy, and dependable. You will be interviewing job applicants for these positions.

Situation 2

You are the current president of the general management student organization at your university. It is the end of the school year and time to select your successor. When you took over as president of the organization last year, it was literally in shambles. There was only a handful of active members, low attendance at meetings, no funds in the organization's bank account, and very few activities in terms of speakers and social events. Since then, you have rebuilt the membership to more than 100. The organization has over $2,000 in the bank, it has sponsored many events and socials, which have been a great success, and it was even recognized by the university as the best student organization of the year. Your goal at this point is to maintain the positive momentum of the organization by selecting a "strong leader" who can build on what you have done. You have decided to interview a person who has indicated an interest in being president of the organization.

2. Design your interview process. Make sure that you address the following issues.
   a. List the key duties and responsibilities of this job.
   b. List the key employee qualifications (knowledge and skills) needed for this job.
   c. Given the job responsibilities and applicant qualifications you just listed, what kinds of behavioral or situational interview questions would be appropriate for assessing the degree to which the candidate is qualified for the job? Try to make a list of 4–6 interview questions.

3. Conduct a mock interview with a partner in the class, with you playing the role of the interviewer. Your job is to assess the qualifications of the interviewee with respect to the job you are using for this exercise. Summarize your evaluation of the candidate in terms of the following three areas:
   a. Strengths of the candidate
   b. Weaknesses of the candidate
   c. Overall evaluation of the candidate
   The person being interviewed (your partner) should play him- or herself and use his or her own background as a basis for answering the interview questions.

4. Switch roles and repeat Steps 1–3. When you are done, answer the following discussion questions.

Discussion Questions

1. Evaluate the effectiveness of the interviews you and your partner conducted with each other. What went well? What didn't go so well?
2. If you were to conduct your interviews again, what would each of you do differently?
3. What are the practical implications of this exercise for you as a future manager or supervisor?

The nearby Bottom Line presents a process model summarizing the basic steps associated with implementation of the job interviewing process.

Testing A *test* is a systematic and standardized procedure for obtaining information from individuals. Testing is a relatively objective way to determine how well a person may do on the job. Many human resources experts and personnel managers believe that testing is the single best selection tool. Tests yield more information about a person than does a completed application form, and they are generally less biased than interviews.[17]

Types of Tests Human resources managers use many types of tests today. Let's examine seven types: ability tests, personality tests, interest tests, work sample tests, integrity tests, drug and impairment tests, and genetic testing.

> **Ability tests** measure whether the applicant has certain skills required to perform the job tasks. Mental ability tests assess memory, problem-solving speed, verbal comprehension, ability to deal with numbers, and so on. Mechanical ability tests measure spatial relations—the ability to see how parts fit together into a whole. Such spatial relations skills might be useful, for instance, in putting a carburetor back together or for drafting or interpreting blueprints. Psychomotor ability tests assess reaction time and dexterity. They might assess speed of limb movement, coordination, or finger dexterity. Psychomotor ability tests are given to people applying for jobs involving mostly physical tasks. Professional football teams use them to assess athletes.

BOTTOM LINE

The Bottom Line: The Job Interviewing Process

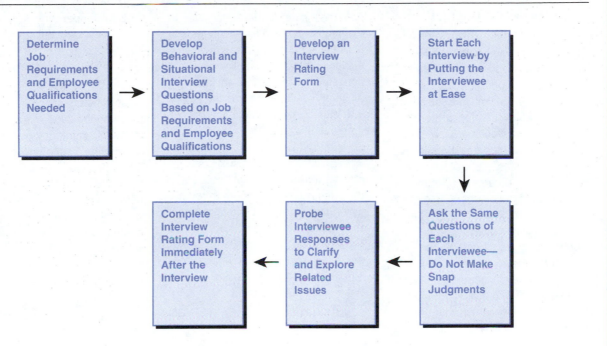

> **Personality tests** measure the strength or weakness of personality characteristics that are considered important for good performance on the job. Job applicants are asked to describe themselves in terms of traits or behavior.
>
> Personality tests have been used for managerial jobs for a long time. They are now becoming more popular when hiring people for entry-level jobs, such as customer sales representatives and sales clerks, and for blue-collar positions. This is especially true at companies that practice participatory management, where workers are given responsibility in running operations. Also, many financial service and insurance firms, trying to improve service in the face of competition, are looking harder for workers with "people" skills such as empathy, the ability to communicate, and motivation to please others. The "Big 5" personality measures discussed in Chapter 3 have been shown to predict success across a variety of job types.
>
> **Interest tests** measure a person's likes and dislikes for various activities. A person whose interests don't fit well with the characteristics of a particular job would probably find the job boring and unsatisfying.
>
> **Work sample tests** measure how well applicants perform selected job tasks. An applicant for a job that requires typing skills is usually given a typing test; a police officer candidate might be given judgment tasks involving realistic job situations. Work sample tests generally predict subsequent job performance quite well.

FOCUS ON MANAGEMENT

TOO SMART FOR THE NEW LONDON POLICE DEPARTMENT*

The former whaling village of New London, Connecticut, refused to grant Robert J. Jordan a job interview. The reason: He was *too* smart. The City of New London contends that applicants who score too high on a pre-employment test are likely to become bored in patrol jobs and will leave the force soon after the city has paid to train them. In 1996 Jordan scored 33 out of 50 on the exam, published by Wonderlic, Inc. The exam is used by 40,000 employers across the country, including the National Football League, and has been given to 125 million people since 1937. However, Jordan "failed" the test since his score was 8 points *above* the New London cutoff. Upon learning that he had been denied an interview because of his high score,

he sued the department. However, in September 1999, a federal judge in New Haven ruled that the practice of excluding too-bright applicants was constitutional, since the city treats all smart would-be officers the same and thus did not discriminate against Jordan.

The Wonderlic "User's Manual" warns clients about the costs of replacing workers who quit because they become dissatisfied with repetitive work, stating that "simply hiring the highest-scoring employee can be self-defeating." It offers the following suggested minimum and maximum cutoffs for selected professions, based on a scale from 1 to 50:

Profession	Cutoff
Administrator	27–35
Editor	29–35
Industrial engineer	28–34
Reporter	27–34
Teacher	27–34
Bookkeeper	24–29
Police, patrol officer	22–27
Telephone operator	22–26
Driver, bus or truck	20–24
Warehouseperson	17–21

Jordan has used up his savings in pursuing the case. He now supplements his insurance business by working as a state prison guard for $26,000 a year—$15,000 less than he would make as a New London patrol officer. New London says it will continue to use the test to screen out the overqualified. So "while those with badges and guns are called New York's finest, they will continue to be New London's fair to middling."†

*Based on M. Allen, "Ideas and Trends: Invoking the Not-Too-High-IQ Test," *New York Times,* September 19, 1999, Sec. 4, p. 4.

†Ibid.

> **Integrity tests** measure an applicant's honesty. Dishonesty and theft can be major expenses for many firms. One form of honesty test is a polygraph (or "lie detector") test, an electronic device used to detect lying. As a result of concerns about validity and invasion of privacy, a 1988 federal law outlawed most private uses of pre-employment polygraph tests aimed at assessing employee honesty.[18] Written "honesty" or "integrity" tests are now often given instead. These contain items concerning one's attitudes toward theft and other forms of dishonesty (such as "Do you ever think about cheating people?" or "Are there times when it's OK to be dishonest?") or about personality characteristics believed to be related to theft (such as "Do you consider yourself to be a trustworthy person?"). However, many of these written honesty tests may be even less valid than the polygraph tests they replace.[19] Further, it makes sense that dishonest employees might also be dishonest in responding to integrity test items. Further, many individuals are offended when asked to take such tests. As a result, integrity testing should probably only be considered when the potential costs of dishonesty are very high.[20]

Many firms, including Abbott Laboratories, J. C. Penney, and Nordstrom Inc., are also trying to judge the integrity of applicants by performing credit checks.[21] Critics question the validity of credit checks and charge that firms may use them to obtain personal information they aren't supposed to consider, such as age or marital status.[22] Further, the Federal Fair Employment Reporting Act requires that if a company denies an applicant or employee a job or promotion based wholly or in part on information from a credit report, it must notify the person of the fact. The individual then has the right to review the entire report, demand a reinvestigation, and give his or her own version of statements in the report. In the case of some extensive credit checks, requirements are even stricter. Further, beginning in late 1997, employers were no longer able to obtain credit reports on employees without first advising them in writing and obtaining a written acknowledgment. Employees must then be informed that the credit check is being performed for purposes of retention.[23] Violations of the Fair Employment Reporting Act can result in civil and/or criminal penalties for the employer.[24]

> **Drug and impairment tests** measure abuse of alcohol or other drugs. The cost of alcohol and other drug abuse in the United States is estimated to be $60 billion per year. Substance abuse has been shown to be related to such behaviors at work as spending work time on personal matters, falling asleep, extra-long lunch and rest breaks, and theft.[25] Substance abuse also results in huge costs for sick time and health care. As a result, more than 80 percent of major U.S. corporations use drug tests, spending in excess of $250 million annually on the practice.[26] The tests may involve examination of body fluids, such as urine and blood, of hair, or of the reaction of the pupil to light.

In response to concerns that drug testing violates rights of privacy and that there may be errors in the testing process, many firms have decided to use impairment testing. Impairment testing involves the use of activities similar to a video game to measure an employee's ability to work.[27] One such test works on a PC coupled with a control panel and special software. During the test, a bar is centered on the computer screen. Below the bar is a vertical arrow that the computer sweeps back and forth at increasingly rapid speeds. Using a control knob, the employee tries to keep the arrow under the center mark of the bar. The focus of such tests is on actual impairment of motor skills and hand–eye coordination rather than on detecting chemicals. This permits employers to immediately see whether or not an employee is able to work on a given day. Further, impairment tests detect impairment due to things such as illness, sleep deprivation, and emotional preoccupation that would be missed by drug tests.[28]

> **Genetic testing**—a relatively new form of testing—may exclude employees with certain genetic characteristics.[29] Full of promise and peril, it applies the expanding science of genetics to the testing of workers for chromosomal damage or susceptibility to disease. Genetic testing of workers comes in two varieties: monitoring and screening. They differ in their purposes and in the way they have been received.

Genetic monitoring involves periodically testing groups of employees to see whether they are showing any alarming chromosomal abnormalities that might have been caused by their environment. Monitoring has the approval of most observers, including labor leaders. It provides an early warning of danger from the work environment and indicates when workplaces need cleaning up.

Genetic screening is the one-time analysis of DNA taken from blood or other body fluids. It is aimed at finding genetic "markers" that indicate that a person may be especially susceptible to harm from a particular substance. Advocates of genetic screening say that screening could identify those with a special susceptibility to a disease and steer them away from work with dust or fumes that might trigger it. But screening worries many critics. They argue that if employers know that certain workers are susceptible to a disease caused by workplace hazards, they will simply get rid of those workers rather than clean up the workplace. Critics also warn that such screening could be used to screen out employees who are likely to develop a debilitating or fatal genetic disease such as Huntington's chorea or Alzheimer's. If so, susceptible workers may find their privacy violated, their careers ruined, and their health insurance terminated.[30] Because of such concerns, some states, including Michigan and California, have passed legislation restricting the use of genetic testing for employment purposes.[31]

Test Validity Although testing works well, it is not perfect. First, the value of a test is based on its validity. *Validity* is the degree to which predictions from selection information are supported by evidence. Thus, a test that accurately predicts employee performance is valid, while one that does not is invalid.[32] Valid tests are expensive to develop. Also, some jobs, such as those of top management, are hard to describe, and the abilities and interests required may be all but impossible to predict on the basis of test results. In general, ability tests and work sample tests are more valid than other selection tools.[33]

The issue of validity is demonstrated by the use of *graphology,* or handwriting analysis, to predict job performance. While still not widely used in the United States, graphology is very popular in western European countries, such as Britain and France. Most French companies require job applicants to provide handwritten letters. These are sent to graphologists, who analyze the handwriting and determine if the applicant is right for the job and has the proper character. Companies usually follow the graphologist's advice. The theory behind graphology is that handwriting reflects personality. For example, a high bar used to cross lowercase *t*'s is seen as reflecting strong willpower; a low bar is interpreted as revealing lack of self-confidence. Unfortunately, while graphology is difficult to fake, there is no solid evidence that it actually predicts job performance.[34]

Faking Tests There is also the danger that tests can be faked (as we suggested may be the case with integrity tests). Tests are easiest to fake when it is obvious what they are measuring (that is, when the tests are "transparent"). As such, one way to discourage faking on tests is to make it hard to tell what the test is assessing. Unfortunately, tests that are not transparent tend to lack "face validity." That is, since it isn't obvious what the test is measuring, people may be reluctant to accept its results.

Test Fairness Some tests may be unfair to certain groups, such as women and blacks. Everyone agrees that tests should be fair, but few agree on a definition of fairness. To some people, a test is unfair if it includes questions about things that might be unfamiliar to some people because of their race or ethnic origin. For example, consider the following item to assess math skills: "Arnie bogeys all the odd-numbered holes and eagles all the even ones. What's Arnie's score for the entire round?"[35] Such an item reflects cultural bias, presuming background knowledge more likely in some social groups than in others. To other people, a test is unfair if it measures things that aren't needed on the job but that serve to block some people from being hired. In the eyes of the law, a fair test is one that does not underpredict or overpredict performance of one group of employees relative to another. For instance, if a test predicts that white males will do better than black males on the job, when in fact both groups do equally well, the test is unfair.

Assessment Centers Instead of just using an interview or a test, about 2,000 large companies approach the employee selection process more systematically. They use various procedures, combined in the form of an *assessment center.* Assessment centers are part of the firm; they are a collection of systematic procedures rather than a physical place. The centers employ psychologists and other experts on human behavior as well as providing tests, interviews, group discussions, and other approaches for evaluating job candidates. Often, managers from within the firm serve as assessors.

One approach used in assessment centers is *role playing,* where job recruits pretend to be actual employees in a real decision situation. Another approach to discovering how recruits hold up under fire is the *in-basket.* The recruit is given a basket piled high with memos, phone messages, letters, and other matters requiring attention. Each person's performance is evaluated in terms of how the tasks are sequenced, how promptly they are completed, whether the most important ones in the pile are finished, and how good the proposed solutions are.

Assessment centers have many uses besides selection. They may help to spot management potential early. They may pinpoint areas of weakness where employees should improve to enhance their career prospects. When the assessors are managers within the firm, the training they receive on how to run assessment centers is also valuable in helping them understand the firm, observe and rate behavior, and make judgments.

Assessment centers are expensive, but they may be worth the cost to the large firms that use them, such as AT&T, IBM, and General Electric, which can spread the costs over many employees. AT&T alone runs more than 40,000 people through its center each year. Sprint created the University of Excellence, a corporate training operation combining assessment centers with executive development programs and other activities. The assessment centers establish an employee's readiness to accept initial or additional management responsibilities. The centers include challenging "day-in-the-life" simulations and then feed into management curricula.[36] Studies of assessment centers show them to make better predictions of employee performance than other approaches to selection. Also, employees usually report that assessment centers have given them a fair chance to show their abilities.[37]

FOCUS ON MANAGEMENT

SELECTION FOR SELF-DIRECTED TEAMS AT C&S GROCERS

At C&S Grocers, Inc., of Brattleboro, Vermont, the warehouse crew has worked in self-directed teams since 1989, a move credited with boosting employee morale and the company's profit margin.* Team members are involved in all hiring decisions, and they can recruit members from other teams, get rid of team members, or reassign job responsibilities. Teams with openings look to other teams for potential members. Employees are paid for each case order filled, and top-producing teams can handle 9,000 cases a day, which translates to about $20 an hour per employee. When a highly productive, and thus well-compensated, team finds that one member is not carrying his or her weight, it usually tries to help increase that member's productivity. If this fails, the team has the authority to pass the low performer off to another, typically less productive, team.

For example, a team earning $20 an hour may trade a member who is producing at a level of $16 per hour to a team earning $14 an hour. The lower-performing team benefits, and the $20-per-hour team can then seek a superstar elsewhere in the firm.

*Based on S. Caudron, "Team Staffing Requires New HR Role," *Personnel Journal*, May 1994, pp. 88–94.

Selecting for Teams As organizations rely more heavily on teams, they must carefully screen team candidates for their ability to work with other team members.[38] For example, at Delta Dental Plan, a self-directed team provides services for a contract providing dental insurance for 31,000 employees. This is Delta Dental's biggest contract, and it is important that the team be staffed with qualified, motivated individuals. The Human Resources department spent more than six months recruiting and selecting team members. To ensure that the team had balance, the company used a personality test called the Myers–Briggs Type Inventory to find members with complementary personality types. Also, since some customers of the new account were not English speaking, the company selected some bilingual team members. Finally, because Delta Dental wanted some team members who were familiar with the business and the company's culture and some who would bring fresh insight and perspectives, it selected members from both inside and outside the company. After ensuring that the mix of potential team members met these requirements for balance, candidates' interpersonal skills were assessed by interviews with members of the Human Resources department and other employees and managers.

The process model shown in the nearby Bottom Line summarizes the basic steps associated with implementation of the selection process.

PLACEMENT

Placement means fitting people and jobs together after the people have become employees of the firm. It includes everything from helping new employees feel at home in the firm to promoting them to positions of greater pay and responsibility or demoting them to less demanding positions when necessary.

Orientation *Orientation* involves introducing new employees to their jobs and to the company. It is their first "inside" look at the company, and it can make an important impression. The job orientation reduces uncertainties, makes company policies and expectations clear, and provides a good idea of what the firm, plant, and coworkers are like. Also, a thorough orientation sends a signal that the new employee has an important role to play in the organization.[39] Orientation also offers a bonding opportunity, ensuring that new hires don't feel alienated and helping to instill in them a sense of pride and opportunity.[40]

Often, both the human resource department and the new employee's supervisor are involved in the orientation efforts. Orientation may include such elements as an explanation of job procedures and responsibilities, criteria for performance appraisal, organization and work unit rules, safety regulations, the chain of command for reporting purposes, and where to turn with problems or questions. Often, the new employee is given an orientation packet containing organization charts, maps of the facility, the company policy handbook, copies of performance appraisal forms, lists of holidays and employee benefits, phone numbers of key personnel, and copies of insurance plans.

Skills Practice 11-4 will give you a chance to develop an orientation program for new employees. Remember that this is an important part of the socialization process for new employees, for it sets the tone for the subsequent working relationship between the company and the employee.

BOTTOM LINE

The Bottom Line: The Selection Process

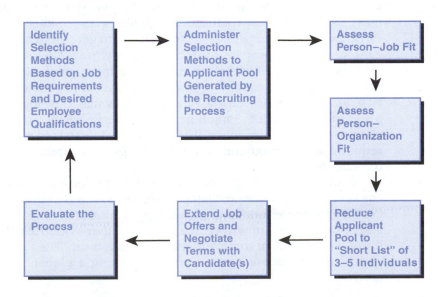

Skills Practice 11-4
Conducting New Employee Orientations

Skill Level: **Basic**

Skill Objective
To develop skill in designing orientation programs for new employees.

Procedure
1. Select a job and organization you are familiar with. This may be your current job or a job you had in the past.
2. Develop a plan for conducting an effective new-employee orientation for this job and the company as a whole. At a minimum, be sure to address parts a, b, and c that follow.
    a. List the major issues the employee needs to be informed of about the *job* (e.g., duties, responsibilities, procedures, policies, performance standards and expectations)
    b. List the major issues the employee needs to be informed of about the *work unit* (e.g., breaks, procedures, policies, meeting coworkers, meetings, culture)
    c. List the major issues the employee needs to be informed of about the *organization* (e.g., company history, mission, culture, benefits, general policies)
3. Answer the following discussion questions.

Discussion Questions
1. Describe the process you would use for implementing your orientation program.
2. What is the value of conducting new-employee orientation programs? What is the cost of not providing an orientation for new employees?
3. Why do so many companies fail to conduct any kind of orientation program for new employees? What kinds of problems may result from not having an orientation program?
4. What are the practical implications of this exercise for you as a future supervisor or manager?

Lateral Move Firms sometimes move employees laterally—that is, neither up nor down in the organizational hierarchy, but sideways. One type of lateral move, systematic job rotation, may build worker skills. At Union Carbide, three executive vice presidents traded jobs to get a better feel for the total organization and to prepare for the presidency. Such lateral moves can provide valuable learning experiences, building a more solid base for later promotions.[41] Employees may welcome the change of pace and duties of job rotation, and those who learn a variety of skills may develop a greater sense of pride and self-worth.[42] Sometimes lateral moves are dictated by organizational changes. For instance, when IBM reorganized its staff to reduce costs, its plan required several thousand people to change jobs, often from staff positions to the sales force.

W. R. Grace & Company, a chemical and consumer products company, has been moving managers laterally for years, some to special projects for the company's future, others to fill slots at locations far from their current posts, and still others to newly created jobs in other countries. According to the firm's vice president for corporate administration, "They get new challenges, and we get broadened managers—something a global, decentralized company must have."[43]

Promotion The most pleasant job move is the promotion. A *promotion* is a move up, generally to a new title, more responsibility, and greater financial rewards. Most employees would like more status, challenge, and pay, so promotions are attractive to them. But good promotion decisions also benefit the firm. An individual who has demonstrated competence and loyalty to the firm and shows promise for further accomplishment is moved to a position with greater impact on the firm's success. Promotions also demonstrate to other employees that good performance and potential are rewarded, thus serving as a motivating device.

Promotions must be handled carefully. For one thing, the fact that the promoted individual did well at the old job is no guarantee that he or she will do well at the higher-level job. Jobs at different levels may require vastly different skills and interests. All too often, a good salesperson or engineer becomes a poor manager. This tendency is called the *Peter Principle,* which asserts that good workers are repeatedly promoted to positions of greater authority. Eventually, they reach their "level of incompetence" and will not be promoted again. Most managers can point to examples of the Peter Principle in their firms. Good promotion decisions prevent capable salespersons or engineers from becoming poor managers.

Promotions can also cause problems for the people promoted. Some employees may be happier in their current jobs than they would be in positions requiring greater responsibility, new skills, and geographic moves. Such changes can cause stress. To make the move a bit less scary, some firms have instituted fallback positions. Employees accepting promotions are guaranteed that if they are unhappy, they can "fall back" to their old positions or positions of equal stature.

However, most people certainly welcome promotions. Many employees may even experience an "inverse Peter Principle," performing better as they take on increased responsibility and challenge.

Demotion A move down in the organizational hierarchy to a lower title, less responsibility, and lower salary is called a *demotion.* Demotions are stressful for employees, of course, and they are likely to be resisted by unions. Still, demotions are often necessary. For example, companies may demote individuals who are performing poorly rather than fire them. Also, especially during recessions, employees may prefer demotion to unemployment. Some companies have experimented with demoting employees temporarily so that they can relate better to their subordinates. Also, some employees ask for their old jobs back if they are unhappy with their promotions.

Termination Another painful reality in business is the need to fire employees. Sometimes firings are necessary because employees have continued to perform poorly or because they have been unmotivated or uncooperative. Firings are traumatic for the terminated individual and costly for the firm. For instance, the firm will have to bear the costs of recruiting and training a replacement. Therefore, employees who are performing below standards should be counseled and given written performance goals and plans for meeting them. They should have a probationary period and should receive regular feedback over that period. Firing should be used only if such corrective efforts fail, as a last resort.

In recent years, many employees have been fired as a result of things having little to do with their motivation or performance. Due to technological changes, restructuring, mergers, changes in strategy, foreign competition, or other factors, firms may have to cut costs by reducing the size of their workforce. As we have discussed in earlier chapters, such downsizing is taking place at unprecedented levels and rates.

It was probably inevitable that companies would come up with some innovative jargon to avoid using terms such as "firing" and "layoff." Employees who are terminated are now likely to hear that their firms are engaging in a "skill mix readjustment," "rightsizing," or "workforce imbalance correction." Other workers may find that they have been subjected to "indefinite idling," "outplacing," "dehiring," "degrowing," "decruiting," or a "career-change opportunity."[44] Whatever they are called, firings are extremely stressful to individuals and firms. In some cases, the firm hires outplacement companies to assist people who are affected. These firms help the employer with the dismissal—offering advice and sometimes getting involved in the termination interview—and then counsel the individual on how to carry out a job search and cope with the period of transition between jobs. They may also actually help the individual find a job.

Due to recent changes in the law and its interpretation by the courts, companies can no longer fire employees anytime they want (called "termination at will"). Although courts generally recognize management's right to terminate employees who are incompetent, lazy, or uncooperative, they are increasingly attacking firings for certain other reasons. For instance, courts have challenged firings for reasons of convenience, to make the employee a scapegoat, or to avoid pension costs. Also, the Worker Adjustment and Training Notification (WARN) Act requires U.S. employers with 100 or more employees to give 60 days' notice to employees who will be laid off as a result of a plant closing or a mass separation of 50 or more workers.

In some cases, terminated employees are claiming that firings defame their character, and they are filing defamation suits as well as claiming unlawful termination. For instance, a Texas jury awarded Don Hagler, a 41-year veteran of Procter & Gamble Co., $15.6 million in such a defamation case. Hagler said P&G fired him after publicly accusing him of stealing a $35 company telephone and posting notices accusing him of theft on company bulletin boards.[45] Clearly, companies planning to terminate employees should be certain of the facts in the case, avoid innuendo when discussing a firing, tell only those with a need to know the details of the firing, and avoid making an example of the fired employee. Here are some guidelines for effective termination.[46]

> Give as much warning as possible for mass layoffs.
> Be sure the employee hears of the termination from a manager, not a colleague.
> Sit down one-on-one in a private office with the individual to be terminated.
> Tell the individual in the first sentence that he or she is terminated; leave no room for confusion.
> Express appreciation for the employee's past contributions if appropriate.
> Complete the firing session within 15 minutes. Make the session brief and to the point, not an opportunity for debate.

> Keep the conversation professional, avoiding personal comments.
> Briefly explain how much severance pay will be provided and for how long; provide written explanations of severance benefits.
> Provide outplacement services away from company headquarters.
> Unless security is an issue, don't rush the employee off site.

Skills Practice 11-5 will help you gain skill in what many managers say is the *most* challenging task they have had to perform in their jobs—terminating an employee. Most managers never receive any training whatsoever in how to terminate an employee in an appropriate, legal, and humane manner, so this exercise is important preparation for your future career.

Skills Practice 11-5

Skill Level: Challenging

Role-Immersion Simulation:
Conducting Effective Employee Terminations

Skill Objective

To develop skill in conducting employee terminations in a professional, humane, and legal manner.

Procedure

1. Find a partner for this exercise. One person should assume the role of the "manager" while the other person should play the role of the "employee."
2. Read the following scenario to provide a context for the exercise.

The Manager Role

You are a sales manager for a struggling construction equipment manufacturing firm based in Indiana. Top management has issued a directive for all managers to reduce their staff by 20 percent effective immediately. After a grueling decision-making process, you have decided to lay off an employee who has been a solid performer as a sales representative and has been with the company for over 20 years.

The Employee Role

Your role is to listen to what the manager has to say and to evaluate it after he/she has completed the termination meeting. Try to react as you would if this were actually happening to you.

3. The manager should now conduct the employee termination. After it is completed, the two partners should evaluate the process in terms of how effectively the student playing the manager role applied the managerial guidelines for handling employee terminations.
4. *Optional:* Once this round of the exercise has been completed, the two partners can change roles and repeat the process.

Discussion Questions

1. What did you find most difficult about conducting your mock employee termination?
2. If you were to do this exercise again, what would you do the same in terms of conducting the employee termination? What would you do differently?
3. Many "real-world managers" do a poor job of handling employee terminations. Why do you think this is the case? What can companies do to better support managers in handling this difficult issue?
4. What are the practical implications of this exercise for you as a future supervisor or manager?

TRAINING AND DEVELOPMENT

The training of employees and the development of their skills and careers have many advantages for the firm. First, training and development helps the firm meet its immediate human resource needs. Over the long run, training and development ensures that the firm's employees are ready to meet future challenges. As we'll see, training and development take a variety of forms.

It is estimated that firms in the United States spend $30 billion a year to train employees.[47] Nevertheless, workers in the United States often receive far less training than their Japanese counterparts. For example, new production workers in Japan receive 380 hours of training, and new workers in Japanese-owned plants in the United States receive 370 hours. In contrast, new workers in U.S.-owned plants in North America receive only 47 hours of training, or about one-eighth as much.[48]

DETERMINING TRAINING AND DEVELOPMENT NEEDS

Training and development needs may arise for many reasons. In general, training and development should follow a systematic needs assessment. The needs assessment should consider three sets of factors:

1. *The organization.* What is the environment for training in terms of the organization's goals, resources, and climate for training?
2. *The task.* What is the work to be performed and the conditions under which it will be performed?
3. *The person.* What personal capabilities are needed to do the job, and what are the people like who will do the job?

The needs assessment may indicate a requirement for specific skills that are not readily available, such as computer programming, accounting, or mechanical skills. Or it may suggest needs for future career development among employees. Also, firms often set up special training programs for women, minorities, and the handicapped, in order to correct imbalances in management positions and meet affirmative action goals.[49]

ON-THE-JOB TRAINING

As the name says, *on-the-job training* is conducted while employees perform job-related tasks. They are not taken out of the workplace or put in a classroom. Employees learn the job by doing it, with coaching and feedback from a supervisor or more experienced employees. On-the-job training is the most direct approach to training and development. It offers both employer and employee the quickest return in terms of improved performance. Such training is also conducted in anticipation of future job requirements. For example, many large companies rotate their employees through a variety of positions to broaden their knowledge of the company so that they will be equipped to handle jobs in other areas. Other on-the-job training for employees includes regular coaching by a superior, committee assignments to involve individuals in decision-making activities, and staff meetings to broaden employee understanding of company activities outside their immediate areas.

OFF-THE-JOB TRAINING

It is often necessary to train employees away from the workplace. Such off-the-job training may take place elsewhere within the firm or outside the company. Role playing and in-baskets, which we discussed in conjunction with assessment centers, are often used for training purposes. Let's consider other popular off-the-job training techniques.

Classroom Training Some large organizations have sophisticated classrooms for training purposes; films, videotapes, and other audiovisual media are used. Classroom training might also include case studies. With case studies information is presented about a business problem, such as how to finance the expansion of a new plant, and trainees are then asked to analyze the material and present recommendations. This may enhance their knowledge about specific issues and improve their decision-making skills.

Programmed Instruction With *programmed instruction,* subject matter is broken down into organized, logical sequences. The trainee is presented with a segment of the information and responds by writing an answer or by pushing a button on a machine. When a correct response is given, the trainee is presented with the next segment of material. An incorrect response is met with an explanation and the suggestion to "try again." Computer-assisted instruction (CAI) is a more sophisticated version of programmed instruction in which the memory and computational ability of computers permit more complex topics to be taught.

Management Games *Management games* present trainees with a simulated business situation. Trainees make a series of decisions, such as how much of a product to manufacture and what price to charge. Generally, trainees are members of teams competing with other teams. The performance of each team is evaluated, and trainees get feedback, often from a computer. The games give a feeling of "real" decision making and generate considerable enthusiasm. For example, in a three-day seminar on strategic planning, teams of four or five participants compete against each other in a simulation developed by Strategic Management Group.[50] Each team makes strategic business decisions that team members key into a computer. The computer calculates the effects of the decisions on bottom-line measures such as market share. Teams then adjust their strategies based on the feedback.

Sensitivity Training *Sensitivity training* is used with small groups, called "T" (training) groups. In extended sessions, group members share their feelings and learn to be open to the views of others. Sensitivity training is designed to develop participants' sensitivity, self-insight, and awareness of group processes. However, it has not been conclusively proved that sensitivity training leads to improvements in performance on the job. Also, some people feel stressed when asked to "open up" to others. Sensitivity training is still a part of many training programs (sometimes under other names), but its popularity has faded since the 1970s.

Behavior Modeling With *behavior modeling,* trainees view videotapes in which a model supervisor is shown attempting to improve or maintain an employee's performance. The model shows specifically how to deal with the situation. Trainees then take the role of the supervisor and practice, in front of the trainer and other group members, the behaviors demonstrated by the models. As the trainee's behavior comes closer to that of the model, the trainer and other trainees provide praise, approval, encouragement, and attention. The behavior is videotaped to add feedback and reinforcement.

CORPORATE UNIVERSITIES

A major new development in company training is the growth of corporate universities. Corporate universities are educational organizations established and run by a corporation to educate employees, customers, and suppliers.[51] There were an estimated 1,600 corporate universities in April 1999, up from 400 in 1998. These take a variety of forms. For instance, Dow Chemical—which has training expenditures of more than $90 million annually—is developing online learning over its company's intranet. In the first nine months, the company developed 31 classes across a broad range of topics, and over one-quarter of its 40,000 employees completed one or more classes. Dow expects to save more than $20 million in the first three years of the online university. We discuss corporate universities further in Chapter 13.

HIGH-TECH TRAINING

Web Wise

The Virtual Environment Technology Laboratory

The Virtual Environment Technology Laboratory (VETL), a joint enterprise of the University of Houston and NASA/Johnson Space Center, performs research and development focused on virtual environments for training, education, and scientific/engineering data visualization. Visit the VETL at:

http://www.vetl.uh.edu/

Sophisticated new tools are being used in training.[52] For instance, simulation in training once meant using expensive replicas of job situations. Now, 300 law enforcement agencies across the country use complex computer-based simulations. On a 10-foot video screen, patrol officers watch criminals "respond" to their actions. If officers use their laser guns to shoot a criminal, the attacker can die on the screen. If not, the suspect might escape or even shoot back, "killing" the officer. After the simulation is completed, the computer rates the officer on the accuracy of any shooting and the wisdom of the decision. Other computerized simulations are used as part of the training of airline pilots and operators of nuclear power plants.[53]

The newest simulations employ virtual reality. *Virtual reality* immerses the trainee in a simulated setting through the use of computer peripherals and stereographic imaging.[54] In one form of virtual reality, trainees wear fiber-optic helmets. They see 3-D images through the lenses of the helmet and hear stereophonic sound. As the trainee's head moves, the computer senses it and adjusts the image accordingly. In December 1993, NASA mounted an ambitious effort to repair the Hubble space telescope. The mission required six trips outside the space shuttle, each lasting more than six hours, during which astronauts removed, replaced, and repaired many telescope components. Their confidence and success were due in part to the fact that they had done it all before—in a virtual reality simulation back on Earth.[55] Although virtual reality techniques are expensive, they typically cost much less than training on real equipment.[56] Further, the cost of such technology is dropping while its sophistication is improving dramatically. In fact, using a specialized display system called a *haptic interface,* virtual reality can now simulate not just appearance but also touch.[57] The haptic interface transmits forces to the hand or fingers in a way that mimics the sensation of touching real objects. The trainee—such as a prospective surgeon—can actually "feel" objects created by the computer.

TRAINING FOR TOLERANCE

Some of the techniques we have already discussed, such as sensitivity training, may be used to enhance tolerance toward minority group members and others. However, firms are adopting many other approaches to training for tolerance. As one example, at Hoechst Celanese the top 26 officers are each required to join two organizations in which they are a minority. For another example, IBM's Systems Storage Division in San Jose, California (a city where 33 languages are spoken), launched an annual diversity day in 1993.[58] Employees dress in various ethnic costumes, perform traditional dances, and prepare authentic dishes for fellow workers. The festival has been so successful in defusing tensions that the plant's diversity council now prepares a monthly bulletin that lists diversity events in the city. The council will also produce a series of videos featuring a different culture monthly, to be played at gathering spots in the plant.

Firms are also providing training to integrate sexual orientation into ongoing diversity efforts. In this training, they tell employees that the reasons for valuing gay and lesbian employees are basically the same as for valuing women, religious minorities, and people of color: so that all employees can contribute to their fullest potential, unhampered by prejudice, stereotypes, and discrimination.[59] In addition, many firms are "gender training" to promote tolerance between the sexes.[60]

CROSS-TRAINING

As firms make more use of cross-functional teams and generally seek employees with multiple skills, they are increasingly employing cross-training. *Cross-training* is training of employees to master one or more tasks in addition to their primary duties. Cross-training develops a versatile, flexible workforce that is qualified and willing to work where the need arises.[61]

Often, cross-training includes training not just across multiple jobs but across jobs in different functional areas, such as accounting and sales. With such training, workers develop broader perspectives, enhancing cooperation and communication across functions.[62] As they develop breadth and their career prospects are enhanced, they often become more committed to the goals of the company as well as better able to provide quality service to customers.[63]

EVALUATING TRAINING OUTCOMES

Firms often fail to assess whether training programs have been effective in meeting their goals. Measures of training effectiveness might include participants' reactions to the training, learning of the content of the training, and use of new skills and knowledge on the job. It could also include the company's return on the training investment. For instance, personnel responsible for training at Allied Signal's Garrett Engine Division assessed its effectiveness on these dimensions. In assessing the return on training investment for programs aimed at maintenance workers, they considered such things as the cost of the training and how equipment downtime subsequently differed between trained and untrained groups of workers. Using these figures, Garrett estimated that the training yielded a 126 percent return on investment.[64]

The process model shown in the nearby Bottom Line summarizes the basic steps associated with the implementation of the general training process.

The purpose of Skills Practice 11-6 is to give you a very "hands-on" activity to practice applying the basic steps in the training process. Remember to base everything on the training objectives!

Web Wise

Training Net

The Training Net is an online marketplace of training materials that provides human resource professionals with links to books, classes, videos, CDs, and other training resources. Visit the Training Net at:

http://www.trainingnet.com/

BOTTOM LINE

The Bottom Line: The Training Process

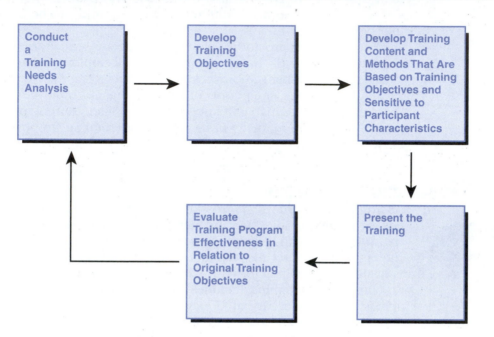

Skills Practice 11-6
Developing a Training Program

Skill Level: Basic

Skill Objective

To develop skill in designing a training program for a job.

Procedure

1. Select a job you are familiar with. This may be, for instance, a current or previous part-time job, a summer job, or an internship.
2. Design a training program for new employees in this job. This should consist of:
   a. Training objectives (1–3) for your training program
   b. Training content for the training program
   c. Training methods for delivering your content
   d. An evaluation plan for assessing the effectiveness of your training program
3. Present a brief summary of your training program to the class.

APPRAISING PERFORMANCE

Performance appraisal is the process of measuring employee performance against established goals and expectations. Before we look at techniques for performance appraisal, let's consider why performance should be appraised in the first place.

WHY APPRAISE PERFORMANCE?

There are many reasons to measure how well employees are performing. First, if companies don't have good performance appraisals, they may make poor promotion, salary, and termination decisions. They may also find themselves vulnerable to lawsuits claiming unfair action on the part of the firm. Second, if employees are to do their jobs better in the future, they need to know how well they have done them in the past. Then they can make adjustments in their work patterns as necessary. Third, appraisal can have powerful motivating effects. When employees know that their performance will be evaluated, they try harder to meet performance goals. For example, Northern States Power Company is committed to achieving the benefits of workplace diversity. As a result, its annual performance reviews now include an assessment of how well an individual creates an environment that cultivates workforce diversity and measures each person's active participation in meeting departmental diversity goals.[65]

Finally, performance appraisal is necessary as a check on new policies and programs. For example, if a new pay system has been put into effect, it is useful to see whether it has had a positive effect on employee performance.

IMPROVING PERFORMANCE APPRAISALS

While performance appraisals are clearly very important, many managers find the performance appraisal process to be difficult and unpleasant. They often have had little training or experience in conducting performance appraisals, and they are reluctant to make critical comments about their subordinates. Here are some suggestions for improving performance appraisals.

> Ensure that the performance appraisal measure is reliable and valid. For example, make sure that the performance rating captures all the important aspects of performance and that it is not contaminated by nonperformance factors, such as personal liking.
> Provide training for raters. Such training can make the rater more knowledgeable and more comfortable with the process, and it may help reduce specific rating errors (such as halo error, discussed in Chapter 3).
> Involve employees in the process.
> Make sure that performance ratings are discussed.
> Develop an action plan based on the discussion.
> Attempt to link merit increases to performance ratings.
> Integrate performance evaluation into the broader process of day-to-day performance management.

Some managers are turning to computer software programs to help make their appraisals more effective and constructive.[66] A typical program permits managers to type in goals they would like addressed and to select from categories to be included, such as professionalism, leadership, and job knowledge. Managers then grade employees by applying ratings to statements that appear on screen. Some programs also permit the manager to type in comments to be added to the employee's file and, if the comments are negative or contain inappropriate language, may suggest changes or call for more specific information.

Controversy has developed in recent years concerning the use of performance appraisals. For instance, W. Edwards Deming argued that performance appraisal and Total Quality Management are incompatible.[67] However, while it is true that some performance appraisals are poorly planned or executed, there is much evidence of their value. Indeed, all companies somehow appraise employees' performance; some just do it more systematically and openly than others. In fact, one survey showed that more than 20 percent of firms are tying performance appraisal directly to their Total Quality Management efforts.[68]

TYPES OF PERFORMANCE MEASURES

Performance may be appraised in at least three major ways. Appraisal can focus on employee traits, behavior, or accomplishments.

Trait Approaches Under these approaches, a manager or performance appraiser rates an employee on such traits as friendliness, efficiency, and punctuality. The assumption is that these traits are related to performance. One such approach asks the appraiser to check the word or phrase (such as *outstanding, average,* or *poor*) that best describes how an employee rates on each trait.

Trait approaches are widely used in business, but they suffer from a number of problems. For instance, words such as *superior* and *average* may mean different things to different people. Also, the people appraising performance are sometimes biased in their ratings. They may also feel uncomfortable giving a coworker a low score on efficiency, decisiveness, or supervisory ability, especially if the ratings will be shown to the person being rated. As these problems suggest, trait approaches should never be used alone, if at all.

Behavioral Approaches These approaches involve the rating or recording of specific employee actions. In the critical incidents method, for example, the performance appraiser keeps a list of all the employee's actions that were especially good or bad. A newer approach, the *behaviorally anchored rating scale,* presents a list of possible employee actions, rated on a scale ranging from very desirable to very undesirable. The rater checks the action on the scale in which the employee would be most likely to engage. By focusing on specific actions, this approach improves on the earlier trait approaches. However, behavioral approaches sometimes give employees the feeling that the rater is always looking over their shoulders.

Outcome Approaches Rather than considering traits or actions, some appraisal techniques rate what the employee is supposed to accomplish on the job. This approach is time consuming and may cause people to focus only on objectives that can be easily expressed in numbers. However, it does get directly at the things that the company cares most about.[69]

Increasingly, firms are including a broad array of outcomes in their performance appraisal systems. As already noted, for example, some firms are tying performance appraisal to their efforts to increase diversity. At chemical giant Hoechst Celanese four sets of outcomes are equally weighted in performance appraisals: attainment of workforce diversity goals, financial success, customer satisfaction, and environmental and safety improvements.[70] As a result, managers at Hoechst Celanese pay attention to diversity, knowing the success of their diversity efforts will be reflected in their salaries and bonuses.

360-DEGREE FEEDBACK

In the past, the employee's immediate supervisor conducted the performance appraisal. Now firms such as British Airways, AT&T, Otis Elevator, and General Electric are increasingly using 360-degree feedback.[71] With 360-degree feedback, the employee receives performance feedback from four sources: the supervisor, subordinates, peers or coworkers, and self-ratings. 360-degree feedback can potentially provide a fuller, more realistic picture of the employee's overall performance. However, implementation of 360-degree feedback must be done carefully, since, for instance, subordinates may be afraid to provide honest answers about their superiors' performance.[72]

Skills Practice 11-7 will give you a chance to experience the performance appraisal process from the perspective of the manager and the employee. This is a challenging process, so be prepared!

Skills Practice 11-7

Skill Level: Challenging

Role-Immersion Simulation: Conducting an Effective Employee Performance Appraisal

Skill Objective

To develop skill in conducting an effective employee performance review.

Procedure

1. Find a partner for this exercise. One person will play the role of the "manager." The other person will play the role of "Lisa, the employee."
2. Read the following role descriptions.

Role 1—The Manager

You are the supervisor of a team of sales associates who work in the TV and video department at a major consumer electronics retailer. The sales associates all work on a sales commission. An ideal sales associate is one who has a strong customer service orientation, excellent sales figures, and consistent attendance, comes to work on time, works well with others, and is mature and professional.

It is time for Lisa's performance review. She has been working in her current job as a sales associate for about three years now. Lisa's sales per day average $1,200. The average daily sales figure for all of your sales associates is $1,000.

Lisa used a total of seven sick days this year. She was also marked "late" (more than 30 minutes late for the beginning of her shift) twice.

Lisa tries to help others out with their work (e.g., stocking merchandise, cleaning) when she is not busy. Generally, she has a positive attitude, although sometimes she is rather moody and short with her coworkers and even with customers on occasion.

Lisa has demonstrated an excellent understanding of the products you carry in your department.

How would you rate Lisa's performance based on the performance evaluation form that follows?

Performance Appraisal Form

PERFORMANCE EVALUATION FORM—SALES ASSOCIATE
DEPARTMENT: TV/Video
EMPLOYEE: Lisa

		Poor	Fair	Satisfactory	Good	Excellent
1.	Customer Orientation	1	2	3	4	5
2.	Sales Productivity	1	2	3	4	5
3.	Attendance	1	2	3	4	5
4.	Punctuality	1	2	3	4	5
5.	Teamwork	1	2	3	4	5
6.	Attitude	1	2	3	4	5

Role 2—Lisa, the Employee

Your job is to listen to what the manager says to you about your job performance and to react as you would if this were actually happening to you. Be sure to read the foregoing information about Lisa to guide you in determining what to do and say during this exercise.

3. The manager should now sit down with the employee and conduct a performance appraisal session in which Lisa's performance ratings are discussed.

4. After the performance ratings have been discussed, the manager and Lisa should develop an action plan. This plan should include the following:
   a. *Performance goals*—specific ends that the employee should accomplish in the next year
   b. *Supporting action steps*—specific actions that should be taken to support the achievement of the performance goals
   c. *Training needs*—any training needed to support the achievement of the performance goals

Discussion Questions

1. Evaluate the performance appraisal process that was conducted by the manager. What was done well? How could the process have been improved?
2. What are the practical implications of this exercise for you as a future supervisor or manager?

The nearby Bottom Line presents a process model summarizing the basic steps associated with implementation of the general performance appraisal process.

COMPENSATING EMPLOYEES

The wages paid to employees, as well as other job benefits, depend in part on how well those employees perform on the job. Other factors influencing employee compensation are the relative worth of each job within the firm, labor market conditions and prevailing wage rates, and the type of pay system used. Let's take a closer look at these determinants of employee compensation.

JOB ANALYSIS, SPECIFICATION, AND DESCRIPTION

The systematic study of a job to determine its characteristics is called *job analysis.* One common method of gathering information about a job is to observe workers on the job, noting which tasks they perform, the order in

BOTTOM LINE

The Bottom Line: The Performance Appraisal Process

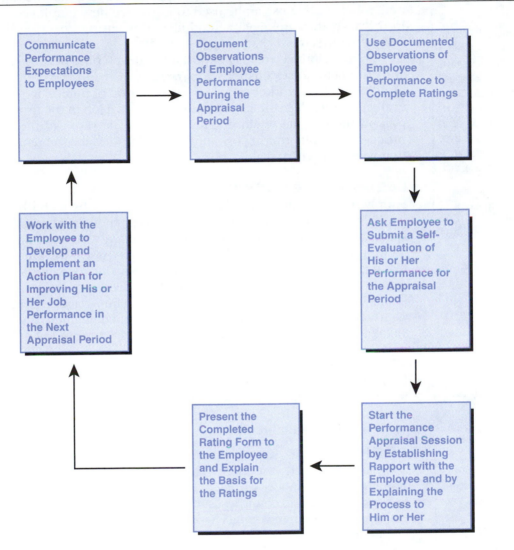

which the tasks are done, and the time it takes to perform each one. Another method is to interview employees about the nature of their work. Sometimes employees are asked to supply the needed information by filling out written questionnaires. The value of this information is that it allows a job specification and job description to be written. A *job specification* is a summary of the qualifications needed in a worker for a specific job. It is especially useful in recruiting job applicants and making hiring decisions. A *job description* is a short summary of the basic tasks making up a job. A job description usually includes the title of the job, the supervisor to whom the employee re-

ports, all major categories of work activities involved in the job, and working conditions.

Job descriptions serve a number of important functions. First, they clarify organizational structure by specifying who is to perform each task. This also minimizes job overlap (in which two people are assigned the same task). Second, job descriptions can be used to introduce new employees to their jobs. In this way, they are given a good idea of what to expect on the job before they actually start work.

Job descriptions are also important in developing performance standards and criteria for job evaluations. *Performance standards* define the goals to be achieved by a worker over a specified period of time. The purpose of a job evaluation is to determine the relative worth of a job in the firm. The more important the job, the higher the level of pay. The result of the job evaluation process is a rank ordering or rating of job importance, which is useful in setting wage and salary scales.

LABOR MARKET CONDITIONS

Supply and demand cause the wages for some jobs to be higher than the wages for others, even though the jobs may be of similar difficulty and responsibility. For example, in an area where many teachers but few nurses are looking for work, employers may have to pay more to hire a nurse than a teacher, even if the jobs are considered equally responsible. The level of wages is also influenced by what other local firms pay. For example, machine shops in the same town will tend to pay the same wage, especially if a union contract is in effect. Because of this tendency, some companies conduct surveys of local wage rates to make sure that their own are in line.

PAY SYSTEMS

Even after the value of a job is determined and the local and regional wage differences are taken into consideration, one person may be paid more for the same job than another person. We can identify at least five other factors that account for wage differentials.

Seniority The term *seniority* refers to the number of years spent with the company. Generally, the more years of service, the greater the level of pay. The idea is that seniority reflects loyalty to the company as well as valuable experience. In some countries, such as China, factories traditionally pay older employees more than younger workers on the same job, regardless of performance levels. When Volkswagen entered into a joint venture with Shanghai Automotive Industrial Corporation to form Shanghai Volkswagen Automotive Company, it found that it had to adapt to this practice. So performance is not considered in setting pay, though it is a factor in promotion decisions.[73]

Individual Performance How much individual employees are paid is often based largely on how well they do on the job. Under a *piece-rate system* of compensation, total wages paid are tied directly to output. For example, a worker in a toy factory may get one dollar for every puppet produced. Piece-rate systems are often justified because they motivate employees. As we discussed in Chapter 6, rewards that are directly based on desired outcomes have the strongest motivating effects. Performance may be defined in various ways in compensation plans. For instance, at firms such as GTE and Sony, customer service representatives are rewarded on the basis of the speed and courtesy with which they respond to phone calls from customers.[74]

Group Performance Workers performing similar or related tasks are sometimes organized into work groups, or teams. In such situations, pay scales are often tied to group performance. How much each person takes home is based on how well the group as a whole does. Such group performance systems encourage cooperation. Also, because wages for one worker are determined by the efforts of others, group members have an incentive to push slow workers to do better.

If rewards are to be based on individual or group performance, keep in mind the following guidelines.[75]

> Appropriately link pay and performance. Ensure that pay really is tied to performance that is under control of the individual or group and that performance is fully assessed. For instance, it would make little sense to base pay on quantity produced for an assembly worker whose level of output is controlled by an assembly line. It would also be unwise to reward just one aspect of performance, such as quantity produced, if several aspects, including quality, are important.

> Use pay-for-performance as part of a broader human resources management system. Make sure that performance appraisal systems are accurate and that those conducting the appraisals are well trained.

> Build employee trust and promote the belief that performance makes a difference. Unless employees believe that rewards will really be linked to good performance, they're unlikely to take pay-for-performance seriously.

> Use multiple layers of rewards. Pay based on individual performance lets employees see how their personal contributions lead to direct rewards, but it may encourage internal competition rather than cooperation. As such, it may help to base rewards on multiple performance measures. For instance, at AT&T credit bonuses are based on 12 measures, reflecting the performance of both regional teams and the entire business unit. Team members must meet their individual performance goals to be eligible for the bonuses.[76]

> Increase employee involvement. Since employees must view a pay plan as legitimate if they are to take it seriously, it helps to let employees participate in the design of the plan. This increases acceptance of the plan and provides a better fit of the plan to individual needs.

> Include nonfinancial incentives. While pay is certainly important, remember that praise, honorary titles, increased job responsibility, and other nonfinancial incentives can also be provided as rewards for good performance.

Plantwide or Companywide Productivity Employee pay rates can be based in part on the productivity of the entire plant or organization. For instance, at Borden, 28,000 workers at 180 plants had the opportunity to win bonuses ranging from $250 to $800 each, depending on how their individual plants performed in relation to measures of attendance, safety, quality, production, and financial goals.[77]

At Monsanto's chemical plant in Luling, Louisiana, workers earned bonuses of $760 each when the plant met goals for reducing injuries and preventing pollutants from escaping into the outside air.[78] One form of productivity plan is the *Scanlon Plan,* under which groups of employees suggest to management how productivity might be improved. Then, at regular intervals, the productivity of the organization is evaluated. If productivity is up, each worker is rewarded with a bonus.[79] Some Japanese companies have adopted an interesting variation of this plan. They have annual picnics at which new ideas, inventions, and improvements devised by the employees are exhibited and demonstrated by the company president.

Organization-Based Plans Many companies today feature *profit-sharing plans.* Under such plans, employees are given a bonus if company profits are high.[80] While profit-sharing plans are sometimes associated with large companies, they can also be useful at small firms. For instance, the Artful Framer Gallery, a small company in Fort Lauderdale, Florida, began a profit-sharing plan in 1987 when it employed only five people, and by 1993 the plan had amassed $150,000. The owner of the gallery states that "the plan makes employees happier and more committed to the company, which helps us produce better results than if they were uncertain about their benefits packages."[81]

Another way to link rewards to company performance is through employee stock option plans (ESOPs). *ESOPs* reward employees with company stock, either as an outright grant or at a price below market value. ESOPs give employees actual ownership of the firm. While ESOPs were initially an executive perk, companies such as Procter & Gamble, General Electric, and Chase Manhattan now grant them at all levels.[82] Research shows that firms that have adopted ESOPs have subsequently done well, with total shareholder returns that averaged almost 7 percent annually above those of similar companies without ESOPs.[83] In some firms, employees' returns from ESOPs have been extraordinary. For instance, in the past 12 years alone, Charles Schwab and Co. has contributed an average of 8,109 shares to each of its employees' ESOPs,

FIGURE 11-6
The Wage Determination Process

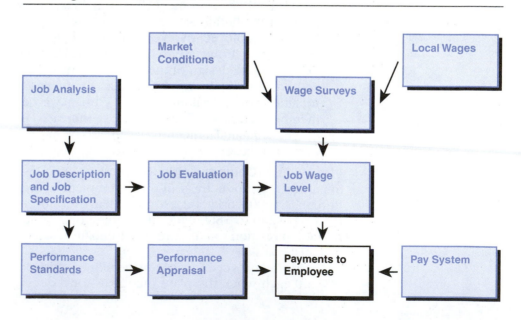

which translates into $1.26 million *per employee* as of the April 1999 high of $155. As such, Schwab has produced an estimated 2,000 new millionaires, many of whom have taken early retirement.[84]

A desirable feature of organization-based plans is that firms make payments only when the firm can best afford them. However, a problem with such plans is that employees are not rewarded on the basis of individual performance. Research clearly shows that the more closely rewards are tied to individual performance, the more strongly the employee will be motivated. Also, employees do not like to be penalized for things outside their control, such as low company productivity or profit or a fickle stock market. For instance, Du Pont introduced an ambitious "achievement sharing" plan, involving nearly 20,000 employees in its fiber plants. However, poor performance of Du Pont's fiber business, primarily due to a weak economy, caused employees to face pay losses, and the plan was ended two years later.[85] In general, plantwide productivity plans, profit-sharing plans, and ESOPs may result in more positive employee attitudes toward the company, but they may not have much impact on individual performance.

Figure 11-6 shows where each of the factors we have discussed fits into the process of setting employee wage and salary rates.

TOP TEN LIST: KEY POINTS TO REMEMBER

ATTRACTING, SELECTING, AND DEVELOPING EMPLOYEES

10. Make sure that your recruiting strategy is based on a clear understanding of the requirements of the job and the type of person who is qualified for that job.

9. Use external recruiting methods when hiring for entry-level positions and internal recruiting methods (whenever possible) when hiring for higher-level positions.

8. Structure your job interview process so that the questions are job-related and legal.

7. Focus on asking behavioral and/or situational types of interview questions, which have been shown to be more valid in assessing the qualifications of job candidates.

6. Continually evaluate your recruiting and selection processes in order to enhance their effectiveness.

5. Use multiple valid selection methods in evaluating job candidates.

4. Be professional and humane when terminating employees.

3. Think strategically about training issues in your work unit by identifying specific training needs that support the achievement of your work unit's goals and objectives.

2. Make sure that the performance appraisal method used reflects the key performance dimensions of the job performed by an employee.

1. Take steps to ensure that every performance appraisal leads to the development of a clear action plan for helping an employee to improve his/her job performance.

QUESTIONS FOR REVIEW AND REFLECTION

REVIEW QUESTIONS

1. What are the three stages of staffing?

2. What are the relative benefits of recruitment, selection, and placement versus training and development?

3. What is recruiting? Identify primary sources of job applicants.

4. Discuss relative costs and benefits of internal recruiting methods and external recruiting methods.

5. What is a realistic job preview?

6. What is the role of selection?

7. Discuss benefits and costs of alternative selection

tools, including application forms, references, interviews, tests, and assessment centers.

8. Provide guidelines for improving interviews.

9. Identify and discuss seven types of tests.

10. Discuss each of the following aspects of testing: validity, faking, and fairness.

11. What is placement?

12. Explain the importance of orientation, lateral moves, promotions, and demotions.

13. Provide guidelines for effective termination.

14. What three sets of factors should be considered in a training and development needs analysis?

15. Discuss five types of off-the-job training.

16. What are the reasons for appraising performance?

17. Identify guidelines for improving performance appraisals.

18. What are the relative merits of trait approaches, behavioral approaches, and outcome approaches to performance appraisal?

19. What is 360-degree feedback? How does it differ from traditional approaches to performance appraisal?

20. Define *job analysis, job specification,* and *job description.*

21. Identify guidelines for linking rewards to individual or group performance.

22. What are the relative benefits and costs of individual- or group-based rewards versus rewards based on plantwide or companywide outcomes?

23. Discuss the steps in the wage determination process.

CRITICAL THINKING QUESTIONS

1. A colleague states, "It's simply unfair to deprive people of jobs on the basis of their answers to some paper-and-pencil test." How would you respond?

2. As stated in the chapter, about one-third of job applicants whose credentials have been investigated by the National Credit Verification Service somehow misrepresented their educational backgrounds. You have learned that a current employee who was hired in large part on the basis of her educational background, including a master's degree, falsified her application materials; she began a master's program but dropped out in the first semester. The employee has been doing extremely well on the job. What do you think should be done? Why?

3. A human resource manager presents the following argument: "The purpose of a rigorous selection process is to ensure that we hire employees who will perform best on the job. When we use an ability test, for instance, we're looking for individuals who have the highest levels of skills required to do the job. It's not our concern *why* candidates developed, or didn't develop, those skills. They may have had a bad childhood, inadequate education, poor training, or whatever, but the bottom line is that they haven't acquired needed skills. If that's the case, why should we be required to hire people that genetic screening shows are likely to develop health problems that will harm their productivity and sap company profits?" Take and defend a position for or against this argument.

4. Which of the various forms of integrity tests (e.g., polygraph tests, written honesty tests, credit checks) do you think is most defensible for selection purposes? Least defensible? Why?

5. The Peter Principle asserts that workers are promoted to positions of greater authority and responsibility as long as they perform well and that these promotions will continue until they reach their "level of incompetence." Taken to the extreme, the Peter Principle predicts that at steady state everyone in an organization will be incompetent. Present four arguments *against* this prediction of the Peter Principle.

6. Take and defend a position for or against the following statement: Performance appraisal is demeaning and has no place in modern organizations.

7. Your boss says, "In this environment, we have to become a team-based organization. To provide a clear and consistent message, all of our rewards will be team based." Discuss the potential benefits and costs of following your boss's suggestion.

8. An employee says, "Profit-sharing plans are just a way to shift risk from the company to employees. We accept lower pay with the promise of a share of profits, but if profits are poor for reasons that are out of our control, we're the ones left holding the bag." Do you agree? Why or why not?

EXPERIENTIAL EXERCISES

WEB EXERCISE 11-1

The Society for Human Resource Management (SHRM) is the world's largest human resource management association. It provides education and information services, conferences and seminars, government and media representation, online services, and publications to more than 120,000 professional and student members throughout the world. Go to the SHRM website at:

http://www.shrm.org/

The site contains a vast array of human resource information (some of it restricted to members). In the left-hand column, click on "HR Magazine." You will have access to articles in the latest issue of the magazine as well as articles from previous issues, a searchable index, and other features. Click on "Articles from Previous Issues." You will see articles arranged by category, such as Benefits, Compensation, Contingent Personnel, Diversity, Legal Issues, and Training and Development. Select any two articles. Write a two-page summary of each article, being sure to highlight how the article contributes to your knowledge as a potential manager.

WEB EXERCISE 11-2

HR-guide.com is a very extensive HR website. It provides a wide variety of materials relating to such topics as personnel selection, job analysis, compensation, education programs, training and development, legal issues, and much more. Go to the site at:

http://www.hr-guide.com/

Click on "Personnel Selection." This will take you to a page with information about tests, interviews, and other selection procedures and issues. At the bottom of the page are categories of interview questions (e.g., achievement, behaviors, creativity, interests, leadership, loyalty, self)—1,700 questions in total. Click on the "self" category (you will see 75 questions listed). Select five questions from the category that you think are particularly interesting or challenging. How would you answer each question?

CASE 11-1
WORLD-CLASS PERFORMANCE APPRAISAL SYSTEMS

Overview

It is a well-known fact that the performance appraisal systems in many organizations are simply not effective. In fact, it is not uncommon for managers and employees to refer to their performance appraisal process as a "joke." Why is this the case? In some organizations, employees don't even receive a performance appraisal. And even if they do, many managers do not possess sufficient knowledge and skill to do a good job of conducting employee performance appraisals. The list of reasons for the failure of performance appraisal systems could go on and on.

Performance Appraisal Best Practices

Fortunately, not all performance appraisal systems are ineffective. In fact, an examination of the performance appraisal systems at some of America's best companies reveals that they share some common characteristics that represent "best practices," or benchmarks that other systems can hopefully emulate in the future.

Best Practice 1—They Get Tough

A key element of great performance appraisal systems is that they set very clear and demanding performance standards, and they hold employees accountable for meeting those standards. For example, companies such as Ford, Intel, Microsoft, and General Electric all possess tough performance appraisal systems that identify poor or marginal performers and "weed them out" of the organization. These systems are brutally frank in the evaluation of employee performance. Critics of this approach argue that employees become demoralized under such a "survival of the fittest" approach. However, top-performing employees tend to react very favorably to a system that effectively differentiates between truly outstanding employees and the rest of the pack.

Best Practice 2—They Cut to the Core

Outstanding performance appraisal systems focus on reinforcing the "core competencies" (knowledge, skills, behaviors, and abilities) needed of all employees in order for an organization to be successful in the long term. Examples of core competencies include leadership, customer service, integrity, and teamwork. The process of narrowing an overall list of competencies to a subset of core competencies can be difficult. For example, management at TManage started with a list of 21 different competencies, but identified almost all of them as critical for organizational success. In-depth analysis and discussion was needed in order to finally narrow this list to a handful of critical competencies.

Best Practice 3—They Seek Mastery

A common problem with performance appraisal systems is that they do not provide sufficient specificity in terms of defining high levels of employee performance. That is, what does it mean in behavioral terms to be a "team player" or "customer-oriented"?

The best performance appraisal systems not only define each dimension of employee performance but also develop a list of specific, observable behaviors that demonstrate a high level of performance with respect to each dimension.

Best Practice 4—They Check for Frequency

Once the core competencies of employee performance and their supporting behaviors have been identified, an appropriate measurement scheme is needed. The best performance appraisal systems emphasize the use of "behavioral frequency" scales that assess how often employees exhibit certain key behaviors. A common behavioral frequency scale may include the following points: "rarely," "occasionally," "frequently," and "regularly." The advantage of this approach is that it enables managers to provide much more specific feedback to employees regarding what they do well and where they need to improve. It also helps to reduce the perception of some employ-

ees that their performance evaluations are based on the "fuzzy, global impressions" of their managers.

Best Practice 5—They Realize That Objectivity Is a Myth

One of the most common criticisms of performance appraisal is that employees feel that they are not objective enough and are based just on the subjective opinions of their managers. The problem with this argument is that it would be inappropriate to assess employee performance for many jobs in terms of "objective measures." For example, the evaluation of a software programmer's performance should not be based on an objective measure such as "number of lines of code written." The bottom line here is that the best performance appraisal systems recognize that complete "objectivity" in the performance appraisal process is an elusive goal. Rather, it is the professional judgment and evaluation of employees by their managers that is the most beneficial to employees. To support this, these companies also provide training for managers so that they have the knowledge and skills to perform these employee evaluations effectively.

Discussion Questions

1. How do the performance appraisal best practices discussed in this case apply the strategies for improving performance appraisals covered in the chapter? Do you agree with each of the best practices?

2. Why is it so difficult for many organizations to create performance appraisal systems that apply the best practices identified in this case?

3. What are the practical implications of this case for you as a future manager or supervisor?

Source: D. Grote, "The Secrets of Performance Appraisal: Best Practices from the Masters," *Across the Board,* May 2000, pp. 14–20.

CASE 11-2
CREATIVE RECRUITING AT EDS CORPORATION

The Company

EDS is a major provider of management consulting, information, and technology services that help clients to enhance their long-term performance in terms of customer service, quality, and product development. It is a global leader in providing these services to 9,000 business and

government clients in 55 countries around the world. Its business clients come from industries such as communications, health care, financial services, energy and chemicals, and retailing.

The company is headquartered in Plano, Texas, and employs more than 121,000 worldwide.

Recruiting Practices

EDS has developed a reputation for being especially adept at using innovative strategies to recruit high-quality employees, even in an increasingly tight labor market. For example, EDS was a major sponsor for the U.S. Sunrayce, an intercollegiate competition involving the design and racing of solar-powered cars. The company provides equipment and its own engineers to support the competition. In the end, this has proven to be an extremely valuable strategy for attracting top-notch college graduates to fill a variety of technical positions within the company.

EDS also recruits employees by sending company representatives to ski lodges around the country and passing out flyers and T-shirts to skiers as they are flying down the slopes. This has helped the company to build name recognition among its target populations.

The company maintains a strong commitment to developing long-term partnerships with 50 colleges and universities throughout the United States. This includes offering résumé writing and other career services to college students and a national case study competition in which EDS executives serve as judges and finalists earn the opportunity to visit EDS corporate headquarters and to win scholarships.

EDS has a large college internship program that hires 500–700 students each year. Interns are given numerous opportunities to learn about the company and its culture. If a manager is sufficiently impressed with an intern, he/she may offer that individual a job up to 9–10 months before graduation.

An employee referral program is also a major component of the EDS overall recruiting system. Employees receive a variety of rewards for making referrals. In addition, any employee who makes a referral gets his/her name placed in a hat from which names are drawn to win prizes such as vacations and laptop computers.

When it comes to career fairs, EDS differentiates itself from other employers by using a traveling EDS mobile station equipped with interview rooms and satellite links to the Internet. The company even inserts its recruiting ads into a direct-mail envelope called "Val Pak" that includes coupons for discounts on products and services.

Finally, EDS hires a large number of college graduates with backgrounds in music and the humanities and then trains them through its own development programs.

Summary

Clearly, EDS uses a multifaceted recruiting strategy that enhances its attractiveness as an employer among students at leading colleges and universities. It also effectively develops long-term partnerships with sources of qualified labor and uses creative recruiting methods to tap into nontraditional populations.

Discussion Questions

1. Evaluate EDS's various recruiting strategies. What are their strengths? Weaknesses?
2. What recommendations would you make to EDS to improve its recruiting efforts?
3. What are the practical implications of this case for you as a future manager?

http://www.eds.com

Source: C. M. Solomon, "Stellar Recruiting for a Tight Labor Market," *Workforce,* August 1998, pp. 66–70.

VIDEO CASE
MANAGING HUMAN RESOURCES:
A STUDY OF NEXT DOOR FOOD STORE

Running Time: 14:09

Headquartered in Mount Pleasant, Michigan, Next Door Food Store is a family-run business with more than 30 outlets in Michigan and Indiana. The stores sell gasoline and a wide variety of grocery and general merchandise items. Along with many other challenges, Next Door must deal with a diverse customer base as well as the convenience store industry's remarkable 100 percent average annual turnover rate.

The video shows Next Door Food Store's President and CEO, Dave Johnson, as well as Human Resource managers Barry Chapman and Diane McKenna, Training Director Rich Evanoff, and other Next Door Food Store personnel as they discuss how Next Door seeks to develop loyal and competent employees while controlling costs. After viewing the video, answer the following questions.

1. What does Next Door Food Store see as its target market? How does the nature of that target market influence the sorts of employees needed by Next Door?
2. What are some costs of turnover to Next Door? According to the video, what has been a primary cause

of employee turnover at Next Door? What are the four main elements of Next Door's efforts to reduce turnover?

3. What is Next Door doing to facilitate hiring of qualified employees?

4. What are the goals of training at Next Door? What is the nature of that training?

5. What is the nature of the compensation system at Next Door?

6. What is the purpose of the performance evaluation system at Next Door? What is the company doing to help ensure that performance evaluations are carried out on a timely basis?

7. What factors does Next Door weigh in deciding whether to offer particular benefits, such as medical benefits for all employees?

http://www.nextdoor1.com/

LIGHTEN UP
ROTTEN RÉSUMÉS

Here are some unintentional bloopers from actual job seekers' résumés:

> "I am extremely loyal to my present firm, so please don't let them know of my immediate availability."

> "Note: Please don't misconstrue my 14 jobs as 'job hopping.' I have never quit a job."

> "Marital status: Often. Children: Various."

> "Wholly responsible for two (2) failed institutions."

> "Terminated after saying, 'It would be a blessing to be fired.'"

> "I am writing to you, as I have written to all Fortune 1000 companies every year for the past three years, to solicit employment."

> "Insufficient writing skills, thought processes have slowed down some. If I am not one of the best, I will look for another opportunity."

> "It's best for employers that I not work with people."

> "Excellent memory; strong math aptitude; excellent memory; effective management skills; and very good at math."

To check out more résumé bloopers and other résumé information, go to Resumania at:

http://www.resumania.com

YO! I'M YOUR CEO

When Ben & Jerry's Homemade Inc. wanted to find a successor for cofounder and CEO Ben Cohen, it held a "Yo! I'm your CEO" essay contest. Aspiring CEOs were asked to mail in 100-word essays on "Why I Would Be a Great CEO for Ben & Jerry's." The first-place finisher got to run Ben & Jerry's; the runner-up got a lifetime supply of ice cream. Even the losers were to receive rejection letters "suitable for framing." While the approach is whimsical, the task is a serious one. Cohen, who will stay on as chairman, said, "I feel really stretched trying to run an organization this size." To make the job more attractive, the company lifted a salary cap that limited the CEO's pay to seven times that of the lowest-paid employee.

Response to the contest was overwhelming, with 22,500 entries arriving in less than two months from as far away as London and India. One applicant took out a full-page ad in the *New York Times* offering his services. Another attached his résumé to a Superman costume.

To help make the decision regarding the new CEO, Ben & Jerry's hired an executive search firm. Fourteen search firms were considered. The winning firm, Russell Reynolds Associates Inc., included a list of employees' 19 favorite Ben & Jerry's flavors with its presentation. The firm learned of the victory with the arrival of 19 gallons of those ice cream flavors.[86]

The choice for CEO, Robert Holland, subsequently supervised Ben & Jerry's expansion into France and helped professionalize the company's management. He has since left Ben & Jerry's to purchase WorkPlace Interiors, an office-furniture dealership established by Steelcase Inc.[87] To learn about Ben & Jerry's success under its latest CEO, Perry Odak, visit Ben & Jerry's on the Web at:[88]

http://www.benandjerrys.com/

UNUSUAL INTERVIEWS

Human resource professionals at 100 major American corporations were asked for stories of unusual job applicant behavior they had experienced. Here are some they shared.

> Said he was so well qualified that if he didn't get the job, it would prove the company's management was incompetent.

> She wore a Walkman and said she could listen to music and me at the same time.

> Balding candidate abruptly excused himself, returned to office a few minutes later wearing a hairpiece.

> Asked to see interviewer's résumé to see if the personnel executive was qualified to judge the candidate.

> Said if he were hired, he would demonstrate his loyalty by having the corporate logo tattooed on his forearm.

> Interrupted to phone his therapist for advice on answering specific interview questions.

> Wouldn't get out of chair until I would hire him. I had to call the police.

> Took a brush out of my purse, brushed his hair, and left.

> Candidate asked me if I would put on a suit jacket to ensure that the offer was formal.

> Candidate said he didn't really want the job, but the unemployment office needed proof that he was looking for one.

> Asked if I wanted some cocaine before starting the interview.

SKILLS OBJECTIVES

> To build and maintain a highly cohesive team.
> To manage a team through the stages of group development.
> To evaluate a team's process in terms of progress toward achieving its goals.
> To design and lead effective team meetings.
> To make effective team decisions.

KNOWLEDGE OBJECTIVES

> Discuss the importance of teams in the workplace.
> Identify and discuss the strengths and weaknesses of teams.
> Discuss when teams may be most useful and when they may not be needed.
> Identify and define the characteristics of teams and discuss what managers can do to realize the benefits of teams while avoiding team pitfalls.
> Identify and discuss guidelines for effectively running team meetings.
> Identify and describe special-purpose group techniques.

At Harley-Davidson Motor Company, teams of workers machine aluminum castings into cylinder heads for motorcycles. The teams supervise themselves, with no bosses giving orders. The teams have the authority to purchase machines costing hundreds of thousands of dollars, to bargain with suppliers, and to decide the physical layout of the workplace. They set their own schedules and budgets, and they inspect the quality of their finished products. They hold meetings relating to productivity, quality, and other matters. In short, they manage themselves. These self-managing teams were a key factor in Harley's dramatic turnaround from the brink of bankruptcy in the early 1980s.[1] They represent a major trend in the modern workplace. Today, there are teams everywhere, taking many forms, and handling many tasks. By one estimate, 80 percent of *Fortune* 500 companies now have half of their employees on teams.[2] Team-management skills are increasingly critical.

The purpose of this chapter is to explore the management skills that you will need to create and lead teams. You will learn the role of teams in today's business environment and strategies for building effective teams. Next, we will present techniques for running effective team meetings. We will conclude the chapter by discussing self-managing teams and providing guidelines for use of special-purpose group techniques.

Answer the questions in Self-Assessment 12-1 as a way to assess your initial attitudes about teams. The self-understanding you gain from doing this will be helpful to you as you read the rest of the chapter.

Self-Assessment 12-1
Attitudes Toward Teams

Answer the questions that follow regarding your attitudes toward working in teams. Try to respond to each question as honestly as possible using the following response scale:

1 = Disagree Strongly
2 = Disagree Somewhat
3 = Neither Agree nor Disagree
4 = Agree Somewhat
5 = Agree Strongly

1. _____ Individuals are better than teams in generating creative solutions to business problems.
2. _____ Teams make better decisions than individuals when the task at hand is complex.
3. _____ Teams must have formal leaders in order to be successful.
4. _____ Teams should be used to complete all type of tasks and projects in organizations.
5. _____ Effective team management is primarily a matter of providing direction regarding the tasks that a team must complete.
6. _____ There is little need to actively manage a well-designed team.
7. _____ All team meetings should have a written agenda.
8. _____ It is important for team members to get acquainted with one another when a new team is formed.
9. _____ Conflict between team members is always a bad thing.
10. _____ Teams should have a clear idea of how they will evaluate their own effectiveness.

DEVIL'S ADVOCATE

I hate working in teams! It's not fair to evaluate my job performance based on what other people do!

You may not like working in teams, *but* many organizations today are moving toward a "team-based" approach to work. This means that working in teams is the basic method used to get work done in these organizations. As a result, many employers actively look for a person's ability to work in teams when they are interviewing job candidates.

This stuff seems so basic. Teamwork is just common sense, anyway.

If you think managing teams is just a matter of having "common sense," then a lot of managers must lack common sense. Many managers don't even take the time to do basic things like have an agenda at a meeting, set clear goals for the team, and provide feedback to the team regarding progress toward its goals. Moreover, good team man-

agers in the "real world" would probably not agree that managing teams, in actual practice, is "basic." They would say that it takes a *lot* of work, time, and skill!

I'm not a management major, so why should I care about teamwork? It doesn't relate to me!

Oh yes it does! No matter what kind of organization you work in, what industry the firm is in, your functional area (e.g., marketing, finance), or even the country your company operates in, you will be required to work in and manage teams at some point in the future. Teamwork is just one of those things that is an important issue in *every* organization!

I'm a doer, not a thinker! Why do I need to think about managing teams? Just do it!

How do you "do" without thinking first? Is managing teams a reflexive response like blinking your eyes or kicking your knee up when the doctor taps it with that little hammer?

The point is, you must understand what you are trying to accomplish and how you are going to get there *before* you can do anything. Managing teams effectively is a process that must be driven by an understanding of where you want to go as a team and how you are going to get there.

Why do I need to learn concepts and theories about managing teams? They don't have any relevance in the "real world!"

You may not realize it, but *you* possess your own set of theories that you carry around with you. These "personal theories" give you guides for things such as how to get a good grade in a class, how to throw a great party, and even how to get someone to go on a date with you! The point here is that good theories have a lot of relevance in the "real world" because they provide you with frameworks for action in terms of how to manage a team effectively.

Before reading on, complete Skills Practice 12-1 to provide a "real-world" foundation for the topics to be discussed in this chapter.

Skills Practice 12-1

Skill Level: Challenging

Field Experience in Diagnosing Team Functioning

Skill Objectives

1. To provide exposure to the challenges facing real teams in organizations.
2. To develop the ability to systematically evaluate the functioning of a team.
3. To develop the ability to make recommendations for enhancing the functioning of a team.

Procedure

1. Identify the leader or manager of a work team in a local organization. Ask the manager or team leader if you can interview him/her for approximately 20–30 minutes. If possible, interview one or two members of the team as well in order to obtain an employee perspective.

2. When you meet with the manager or team leader, ask the following questions.
   a. What does your team do? What is the composition of the team membership?
   b. What are the major strengths of the team?
   c. What are the key areas where the team could improve?
3. Summarize the results of your interview(s).

Discussion Questions

1. What are some things that surprised you when conducting your interviews?
2. Identify some specific recommendations you could make to enhance the effectiveness of this team.
3. What did you learn about teams from doing this exercise?

TEAMS IN THE WORKPLACE

While teams may hold great promise in the workplace, it is important to recognize that teams can take different forms, depending on their purpose, and that the use of teams is not without its costs. In this section we will first consider types of teams. Then we will explore a variety of potential advantages and disadvantages of teams and provide guidelines for choosing between teams and individuals for addressing business issues.

TYPES OF TEAMS

You will be a member of many types of teams during your career. The teams will have a variety of purposes, forms, and members. Some of the teams will be functional, others cross-functional, and still others self-managing.

A *functional team,* also called a *command team* or *vertical team,* consists of a supervisor and his or her subordinates in the chain of command. This may be a manager and his or her direct reports, but it could also include members from more than two levels in the chain of command.

A *cross-functional team* is made up of members from different functional departments in the organization.[3] Such teams are formed to monitor, standardize, and improve work processes that cut across different parts of the organization, to develop products, or to otherwise address issues that call for broad representation and expertise. For example, representatives from the order-entry, order-processing, invoicing, inventory-control, and shipping departments might form a cross-functional team to find ways to avoid delays in filling customers' orders. Cross-functional teams are becoming much more common as companies try to remove barriers that separate functions such as accounting, marketing, and production. In the quest to become "boundaryless," companies are focusing on key processes and are drawing team members from all over the organization to achieve process goals.

A *self-managing team*—such as the Harley-Davidson team in our chapter-opening example—is able to make key decisions about how its work is done. Members learn all tasks and rotate from job to job. Self-managing teams actually take over managerial duties, such as work and vacation scheduling, hiring new members, and ordering materials. Self-managing teams are increasingly important as companies must respond in prompt and creative ways to changes in customer demands, technology, economic conditions, and other factors. As we'll discuss later in this chapter, they also pose special challenges and require special skills.

VOICE OF EXPERIENCE

**WORKING IN
"REAL-WORLD" TEAMS**

*Elizabeth Oberpriller,
Assistant Buyer
Target Corporation,
Minneapolis, MN*

1. What have you learned about working effectively in teams in the real world?

I've learned that to make a team effective in the real world, the key ingredient is communication. Each party must communicate thoughts and feelings about what is happening, to make a team work. Each party must also be perceptive not only to the environment surrounding them, but to the other parties as well. This will create an understanding and make the team more effective. Also, each party must value the opinions of others. Each party must ask for input from others even if she/he thinks her/his own idea is the best. Each party must accept responsibility and allow for other leaders in the group instead of leading all the time. This will make everyone more comfortable, and ultimately the team will be the most effective.

2. What are the most challenging team experiences you have had so far?

Sometimes it's difficult to work with others when they don't share the same view as you do. Target is a very team-oriented organization and therefore I work with a lot of different people every day. I think the key to working with different views is to remain open minded and to understand that others have not had the same experiences you have had—that's why their opinions differ. In most cases, difference of opinion is good in a team because it makes you really concentrate on the issue or issues at hand and forces you to think outside of the box. This is especially helpful in a retail-oriented environment, where being different is good—it separates you from the competition.

3. What kinds of things is your company doing to promote teamwork?

Target has come up with a few ways to help people work more effectively and successfully in teams. They have an individual incentive program as well as a group incentive program. Bonuses are given once a year on the company's performance as a whole, your particular department's performance, and individual performance. There are three bonuses total. This helps people work toward a common goal but also leaves room for individual achievement.

In the nearby Voice of Experience, Elizabeth Oberpriller discusses what she has learned about teams from her real-world experience.

Before proceeding, read the scenario in the Pre-Test Skills Assessment and develop an action plan for dealing with the situation effectively. This will help you to get a better sense of how much you already know about managing teams.

Pre-Test Skills Assessment
Managing Teams

You are the new manager of customer service at a mutual fund company based in San Francisco, California. This firm has just completed a major restructuring that resulted in a significant realignment of employees in terms of where they are working now. Your Customer Service Department was just created as part of the company's reorganization. Consequently, you have 25 employees who are new to their jobs and new to the firm as well. Most of these new employees are inexperienced, and they do not know each other at all.

Your first task is going to focus on transforming this group of individuals into a high-performing team that will provide exceptional service to the company's customers. Develop an action plan for building your team in this situation. Be specific.

THE ADVANTAGES OF TEAMS

Teams offer a variety of *potential* benefits. As we'll see later, these benefits will be realized only if the teams are properly managed. Some potential benefits include the following.

> Teams provide many perspectives, skills, and resources. This is especially true if the group has diverse membership.
> Participation increases acceptance and understanding of the team's outcomes. When individuals feel they are real participants in the team, they are more willing to carry out the team's decisions and to enthusiastically endorse them to others.
> Participation is empowering. It is easy to feel helpless when you have little say in decisions that affect things that are important to you. Being part of a team that is making important decisions or carrying out other important tasks builds confidence and self-esteem, and it helps prevent a sense of powerlessness.
> Working in teams is stimulating. When we work in the presence of others, our adrenaline levels increase, stimulating us to greater performance. This phenomenon—first noticed more than a century ago—is known as *social presence effects.* IDEO Product Development, an organization that specializes in innovation, has a constant stream of "backstage" visitors, including clients, reporters, students, and others, even inviting them to join brainstorming sessions. IDEO believes this constant stimulation through social presence enhances the company's creative work.[4]
> Team decisions tend to be more reliable than those of individuals. Pooled judgments capture broader knowledge and dampen a variety of biases. For example, some people may be overconfident and others less confident than is appropriate. Team decisions may help balance out these biases. Reliable decisions are also likely to be better decisions.
> Participation in teams is a developmental experience. Just as a backup quarterback may be put into a football game to gain valuable playing time and experience, an individual may be given "playing time" on a team to gain team-related skills.

These various potential benefits of teams are sometimes called *process gains.* That is, they are gains that may be realized by appropriate use of group processes. When managing or participating in teams, we want to do all we can to capture these process gains.

THE DISADVANTAGES OF TEAMS

The benefits just presented help explain the tremendous appeal, and growing use, of teams in today's organizations. Note, though, that we were careful to call them *potential* benefits. Unfortunately, teams often suffer from serious drawbacks that may prevent those benefits from ever being realized. For example, in teams:

> Dominant or stubborn members may control the process.
> Some members may be reluctant to participate.

Attainment
Attainment
Attainment
Attainment
Attainment
563

Chapter 12 Managing Teams

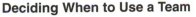

FIGURE 12-1
Deciding When to Use a Team

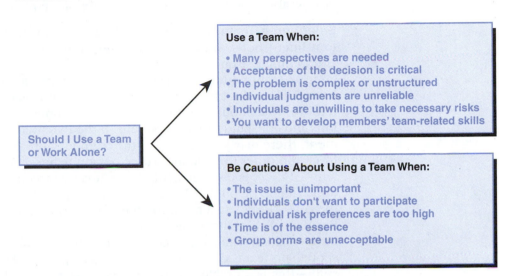

> Some members may focus on personal goals. They may, for instance, try to use the meeting to gain resources for themselves, or they may simply want to win arguments, show off their knowledge, or bully another team member.

> Time and resources are taken from other activities.

> Some members may rely on others to carry the load, called *social loafing.* This not only loses the contributions of those members, but angers others on the team who feel that they're being treated as "suckers."[5]

> Team members may be afraid to "rock the boat." That is, they may not want to seem like troublemakers, so they may suppress their concerns and simply agree with others.

These various potential drawbacks are sometimes called *process losses.* These are losses that may result from using group processes. Clearly, we want to minimize process losses.[6]

WHEN ARE TEAMS NEEDED?

When deciding whether or not to use a team to solve a business problem or achieve an organizational objective, managers will want to consider these advantages and disadvantages. Figure 12-1 offers guidelines—some of them based on material presented later in the chapter—for choosing between teams or individuals to address business issues.

BUILDING EFFECTIVE TEAMS

Once a decision has been made to use a team, there are several things to keep in mind in order to enhance team effectiveness. These include choosing team size and membership, encouraging effective team-member roles, defining the team's assignment, planning the team effort, developing productive norms, recognizing the impact of polarization, and building team spirit.

CHOOSING A TEAM SIZE AND MEMBERS

A basic issue facing teams is the selection of its membership. This requires decisions about both team size and the mix of members.

Selecting a Team Size How big should a team be? We'll start with the bottom line: Choose a five-person or seven-person team unless there are very compelling reasons to do otherwise.

Any team with fewer than five members has its own unique set of problems. The smallest team, with two members, is called a *dyad.* People in dyads tend to be anxious and uncomfortable. Members are reluctant to give opinions and constantly ask for opinions. If the two members can't reach an agreement, there may be a stalemate, the team may break up, or one member may force the other to "give in." Three-person teams, *triads,* have a special problem—if there is disagreement, the split is two to one. While people generally don't like to be on the "losing" side, it is especially upsetting to be an isolate, the *only* "loser." In a triad, the member in the minority is *always* an isolate. Because of this, either one member is very unhappy or coalitions constantly have to shift, with associated tension and political activity. Four-person and six-person teams can lead to stalemates or power plays if the team is equally split—this is a problem with any even-sized group, but an even split is less likely as teams get larger.

Beyond size seven, team management becomes much more difficult. There are many reasons for this. For example:

> It becomes harder to coordinate the team. The number of members who must interact and whose actions must be synchronized becomes unwieldy.
> Members may be tempted to engage in social loafing in large teams, figuring their slacking off won't be noticed.
> We tend to have a limit of about seven to many of our perceptual and cognitive abilities (psychologists call this "the magic number seven"). For example, we can only keep about seven "chunks" of information in our short-term memories, can only distinguish about seven levels of sound, and can only discern about seven levels of saltiness of a drink. When we are in a group of more than seven people, we tend to stop treating them all as individuals, treating them instead as members of clusters. We see Paul as part of the group that sits at the back of the room, Donna as one of the people who was in the group that stayed after class to talk, and so on.

We said you should use five- or seven-member teams unless you have a compelling reason to do otherwise. What might be such compelling reasons? Quite simply, there are times when the problem or task isn't important enough to involve five members, or five people simply aren't available. Conversely, there may be political reasons for involving more than seven persons, or the problem or task may demand broad participation because of its great complexity. However, the problems associated with large teams are so great that we encourage you to do all you can to keep teams small. This may require breaking the team into subteams, or using a technique (such as the nominal group technique, which we'll discuss later in the chapter) that restricts the degree of member interaction and the related problems.

Staffing the Team The team's composition can have a major impact on how well it achieves its goals and how satisfied its members feel. Keep the following suggestions in mind.

> Vary team membership across tasks.
> Ensure availability of key information, skills, and resources.
> Ensure participation of affected parties.
> If you will not be leading the team, appoint a task-oriented leader with sufficient power to keep the team on track.
> Consider varying membership over the course of the task.

ENCOURAGING EFFECTIVE TEAM-MEMBER ROLES

We all wear many "hats" in life. We may be—at the same time—friends, neighbors, students, siblings, lovers, employees, and much more. Each of these hats carries with it a set of expectations for its wearer. Someone in a parent hat is expected to show concern for his or her children, to provide them with love, guidance, food, and shelter. Someone in a student hat is expected to attend classes, to complete assignments, and to be an active participant in class activities. These various hats are called *roles*.

As shown in Figure 12-2, team members can adopt many roles, not all of them positive. Two sets of roles—task-oriented roles and relations-oriented roles—are vital if the team is to be effective on a continuing basis. *Task-oriented roles* are needed to get the job done. Team members who initiate tasks, gather information for use by the team, offer suggestions, and help motivate others would be performing task-oriented roles. *Relations-oriented roles* are needed to keep the team healthy and its members satisfied. Team members who help keep the group harmonious, assist in helping members resolve disputes, and encourage members as they face barriers are engaging in relations-oriented roles. However, team members may also assume other, self-serving roles. *Self-oriented roles* are roles the member adopts for personal gain. These roles may often hamper team performance and cohesiveness. For

FIGURE 12-2
Team Roles

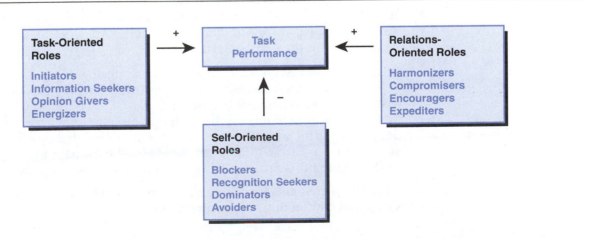

instance, some team members gain a sense of power by dominating others or blocking others' attempts to get things done.

We said that roles carry with them sets of expectations. Sometimes, as discussed in Chapter 9, those expectations are unclear, conflicting, or overwhelming in number. Unclear expectations cause *role ambiguity.* Role ambiguity results when team members simply don't know what is expected of them. Conflicting expectations cause *role conflict.*[7] For example, you may experience role conflict if two colleagues tell you to do opposite things, or if your boss tells you to do one thing one day and the opposite the next. You may even feel role conflict if your own values—which carry their own role expectations—conflict with demands of a role. If, for instance, you are told to fire a long-term employee who is near retirement and this is contrary to your values, role conflict may result. Finally, when role expectations are simply overwhelming—we're expected to do too many things—*role overload* occurs. Role ambiguity, role conflict, and role overload cause *role stress.* Role stress causes dissatisfaction, absenteeism, turnover, a host of illnesses, and many other problems.

Managers can increase a team's productivity by understanding these different roles and adhering to the following guidelines.

> Encourage and reward members who adopt positive roles.
> Recognize that both task-oriented and relations-oriented roles are critical to team performance. A team that focuses only on relations-oriented roles may never get the job done. A team that emphasizes only task roles is likely to face growing member dissatisfaction, to lose team spirit, and to breed disruptive conflicts.
> Identify and discourage negative roles. Team leaders—and other team members—have a responsibility to make it clear that disruptive, self-serving behaviors will not be tolerated.
> Understand the roles you must play as a team leader—and those you need not play.
> Do all you can to minimize role ambiguity and role conflict. Make sure that assignments are clear, that messages are consistent and unambiguous, and that responsibilities are not overwhelming.

DEFINING THE TEAM'S ASSIGNMENT

Defining the team's assignment involves specifying—preferably, in writing—the team's purpose, responsibilities, and needs. Answers to the following questions make up the team's assignment.

> What is the issue with which the team must deal? What is its scope?
> What is the team's responsibility? To perform a specific task? To make a decision? To exchange information?
> What are the constraints on the group? For example, what are its deadlines? What is its budget? What other resources (such as administrative support) are available to it? What should be the format of its final report or the nature of its final product? Will it have to give progress reports?

Now complete Skills Practice 12-2 in order to help develop basic skills in designing and conducting an effective team meeting.

Skills Practice 12-2
Facilitating Effective Team Meetings

Skill Objective

To develop the skills needed to plan, facilitate, and evaluate a team meeting.

Procedure

1. Form groups of 5 to 7 students.
2. Read the following brief overview of tips for running effective team meetings.

Brief Overview of Tips for Running Effective Team Meetings

    a. Assign one person to each of the following roles:

    Meeting Leader: This person is responsible for leading the team through the agenda.

    Facilitator: This person participates as a regular team member but also pays attention to the group process and ensures that the ground rules are being followed (e.g., making sure everyone participates and that the meeting starts and finishes on time).

    Scribe: This person takes notes regarding what was done in the meeting (e.g., issues discussed, decisions made).

    b. As a team, set specific ground rules that everyone on the team agrees to follow. These must be enforced consistently!

    Examples of Common Ground Rules

       > All meetings start and end on time.
       > All team members must come prepared.
       > One person talks at a time.
       > Everyone must participate.
       > Differences in opinion should be valued and respected.

    c. Criteria for evaluating a team process include:

       > Did the team stay on the agenda?
       > Were the meeting objectives achieved?
       > Were the ground rules followed?
       > Did all team members contribute to the team meeting?

3. Plan an agenda for a brief 15–20-minute meeting to complete a task or achieve an objective that the group selects (e.g., planning a social get-together, creating a study group for an upcoming exam, etc.). Make sure your agenda has the following elements:
    > Clear objectives
    > An itemized listing of the issues to be covered
    > A specific amount of time allocated for each agenda item
4. Conduct the meeting according to your agenda.
5. Evaluate your meeting process, and identify specific actions for improving future team meetings.

Discussion Questions

1. Why is it critical to plan meetings and to actively manage them?
2. What do you think are the key things that need to be done in order to conduct an effective team meeting?

PLANNING THE TEAM EFFORT

Once the team assignment is defined, the overall team effort should be planned. This includes the following steps.

> Divide the team's overall assignment into parts. This overcomes psychological hurdles and makes it easier to develop estimates of time and resource needs.

> Estimate the time and resources needed to complete each part of the assignment and the overall assignment.

> Determine the time and resources needed, and take necessary actions to reduce any gaps between what is needed and what is available. This may involve changing the assignment, getting deadlines extended, adding members to the team, seeking additional resources, or making other adjustments.

DEVELOPING PRODUCTIVE NORMS

Norms are the unwritten rules of the team. They are shared expectations about how team members should behave. For example, the team may have norms about how members should dress, how hard they should work, how much members should help one another, or whether team members should keep secrets from others in the organization. Norms may be *prescriptive* — dictating what should be done — or *proscriptive* — dictating what should not be done.

Norms are powerful. Because we want to meet the expectations of our team members, norms control our behavior. This is sometimes called *clan control,* and such control may be even stronger than the control imposed by rules and orders. Further, once a team develops norms, those norms tend to persist — often, even after all the original members have eventually left the team and been replaced by new members.

Team members may "import" norms when they join the team. For example, members may bring with them the norms of their professions, or they may import the norms of other teams of which they've been members. For instance, if someone has been on a team that valued working extra hours to get a job done, she may bring that norm with her to a new team. Norms may also develop because of some critical event in the life of the team. For example, if a major client stops doing business with a firm because he was upset by an employee's rude behavior, norms may develop about the nature of appropriate interaction with clients. Often, though, norms develop gradually in the life of the team. In fact, there are distinct stages of group development. As shown in Figure 12-3 and described in this section, these stages are called *forming, storming, norming, performing,* and *adjourning.*[8] As the names suggest, norms do not become well developed until the team has experienced a lot of jockeying for position, testing of boundaries, and conflict.

In the *forming* stage of group development, team members are getting acquainted and becoming oriented to the task. There is great uncertainty because expectations are unclear. Team members attempt to learn which behaviors are acceptable and which are not. At this stage, leaders can help members become comfortable and feel like part of the team. They can encourage quiet members to build relationships with others and can generally encourage communication and interaction among members.

During the *storming* stage, conflict and disagreement among group members are likely. Members become more assertive in their roles, and their personalities begin to become clearer. The team lacks cohesiveness as there is jockeying for positions and subgroups form. This stage may be necessary to

FIGURE 12-3
Stages of Group Development

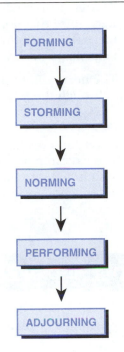

permit team members to resolve disagreements, uncertainties, and conflicts and to permit agreement and a common vision to develop. However, if the team doesn't get past the storming stage, it cannot become productive. As such, the leader must help the team work through this stage in ways that are ultimately constructive.

By the *norming* stage, conflicts have largely been resolved, and the team becomes more cohesive. Members settle into roles, and team norms, values, and expectations develop. The leader should encourage communication among members at this stage and help team members as they agree on roles, values, and norms.

In the *performing* stage the team is mature. Members have learned the bounds of acceptable behavior, worked through their disagreements, developed norms, and settled in their roles. The focus now is on performance as team members constructively face new challenges, coordinate their activities, and pursue the team's vision. When the team is at this stage, it can largely manage its own affairs. The leader can step back a bit, concentrating on helping the team with its self-management. Later in the chapter, we'll explore how the leader might do this.

Finally, in the *adjourning* stage the team dissolves, having accomplished its purposes or breaking up because of internal or external forces.

Our discussion of norms suggests the following guidelines for team management.

> Recognize the power of norms. While unwritten, norms are just as real as, just as powerful as, and perhaps more enduring than written rules and regulations.

> Identify team norms; reinforce positive norms.
> Communicate expectations concerning performance and other goals.
> Recognize that norms develop gradually and are resistant to change.
> Recognize that norming takes place relatively late in the team development process; until that point, norms are quite fluid. So it is important to help shape positive norms as early in the life of the team as possible.

The nearby Bottom Line presents the basic steps involved in managing a team through the stages of group development.

UNDERSTANDING POLARIZATION

Some very interesting things happen when people interact in groups. One that can have important consequences is called the *risky shift phenomenon.* Risky shift—said to be the most studied phenomenon in social psychology— is the tendency for groups to make riskier decisions than individuals. There are a number of reasons for this. For one, when we're in a group, we no longer

BOTTOM LINE

The Bottom Line: Managing the Stages of Team Development

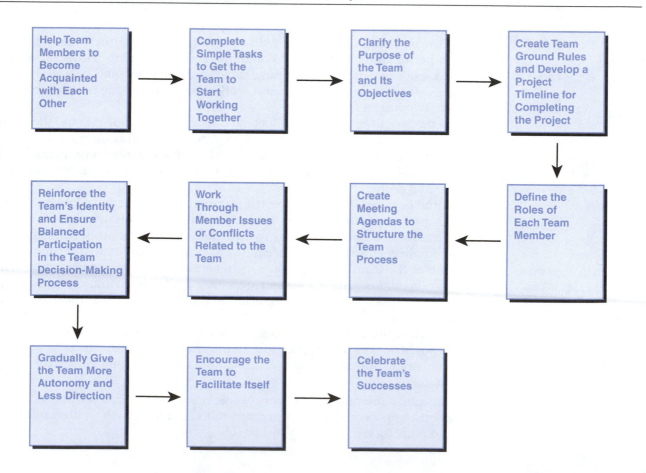

Help Team Members to Become Acquainted with Each Other	→ Complete Simple Tasks to Get the Team to Start Working Together	→ Clarify the Purpose of the Team and Its Objectives	→ Create Team Ground Rules and Develop a Project Timeline for Completing the Project
Reinforce the Team's Identity and Ensure Balanced Participation in the Team Decision-Making Process	← Work Through Member Issues or Conflicts Related to the Team	← Create Meeting Agendas to Structure the Team Process	← Define the Roles of Each Team Member
↓ Gradually Give the Team More Autonomy and Less Direction	→ Encourage the Team to Facilitate Itself	→ Celebrate the Team's Successes	

HOT GROUPS

Extremely high levels of team spirit, excitement, and energy characterize what have been called "hot groups."* According to Jean Lipman-Blumen and Harold Leavitt, "A hot group is a special state of mind. It's not a name for some new team, task force, or committee. The hot group state of mind is task obsessed and full of passion, coupled with a distinctive way of behaving, a style that is intense, sharply focused, and full-bore. Any group can become a hot group— if it can get into that distinctive state of mind. . . . It is not the name, but that contagious single-mindedness, that all-out dedication to doing something important, that distinguishes a hot group from all others." Hot groups abound in Silicon Valley; the team that created the Macintosh computer is cited as a classic example. To encourage hot groups, according to Lipman-Blumen and Leavitt, it is important to make room for spontaneity, break down barriers, encourage intellectual exchange, select talented people and respect their self-motivation and ability, use information technology to build relationships, and value truth and the speaking of it.

*J. Lipman-Blumen and H. J. Leavitt, "*Hot Groups* (New York: Oxford University Press, 1999). See also J. Lipman-Blumen and H. J. Leavitt, "Hot Groups 'with Attitude': A New Organizational State of Mind," *Organizational Dynamics,* 1999, *27(4),* pp. 63–72; and H. J. Leavitt and J. Lipman-Blumen, "Hot Groups: The Rebirth of Individualism," *Ivey Business Journal,* 2000, *65(1),* pp. 60–65.

have to accept the entire "risk pie." Since others are sharing responsibility with us, we only have to accept a slice of that pie and, as such, might not mind a bigger pie. Also, we tend to look up to people who are willing to take at least moderate levels of risk, and we tend to overestimate our own risk preferences relative to those of others—only a very small percentage of people think they're more risk averse than the average person. As a result, when we interact in a team we tend to see that we've overestimated our relative risk preferences, and we adjust them upward. The risky shift phenomenon is one manifestation of a more general phenomenon known as group polarization. *Polarization* is the tendency of groups to make initial group tendencies more polar—that is, more extreme.[9]

CROSS-FUNCTIONAL, CROSS-CULTURAL TEAMS AT MAXUS ENERGY

Maxus Energy, a subsidiary of Madrid, Spain-based Repsol-YPF S.A., the world's eighth largest oil company, is an example of a company that has built cross-functional teams that comprise different cultures, languages, sites, and even time zones.* Maxus views cross-cultural differences and cross-functional skills as strengths. A team at Maxus may consist of geophysicists, geologists, engineers, oil-drilling experts, and production experts. It may have members from the United States, Holland, Great Britain, and Indonesia. Team members may come from different religious, political, cultural, and functional backgrounds. This diversity brings in many perspectives and encourages creativity. Members must develop cross-cultural competencies and must learn to respect, trust, and value others' contributions.

http://www.repsol-ypf.com/

Note that this is a Spanish-language website.

*For a good discussion of teams at Maxus, see Charlene M. Solomon, "Global Teams: The Ultimate Collaboration," *Personnel Journal,* September 1995, pp. 49–53.

BUILDING TEAM SPIRIT

Some teams "stick together" better than others. There is a real sense of team spirit, and members are proud to be associated with each other and with the team. Teams with high levels of this team spirit—also called *cohesiveness*—generally are more effective in achieving their goals than teams that lack team spirit.[10] Members of cohesive teams also communicate relatively better with one another, are more satisfied, and feel less tension and anxiety.

Note that we said that cohesive teams are more effective in achieving *their* goals. Since their goals may not always foster the best interests of the organization, it is important to make sure that team members are aiming for the right sorts of things. If not, increasing team cohesiveness may help attain undesirable goals. So if a team has goals of high performance, creativity, and an honest day's work, greater cohesiveness is probably helpful. If it has goals of leaving work early, pilfering, doing as little as possible on the job, or padding the budget, increased cohesiveness may not be a good thing.

Several things help make teams more cohesive. For example, cohesiveness rises with increases in team status and team goal achievement. Cohesiveness also tends to increase when there is a clear outside threat that requires the team to pull together to meet the challenge. As teams get bigger, cohesiveness declines.

These characteristics suggest the following concrete guidelines for building team cohesiveness.

> Make it attractive to be a member of the team: Use logos and team names as appropriate. Emphasize team status. Make team membership an honor.
> Praise and publicize team accomplishments. Go for some "small wins." That is, make sure the team has some projects and goals that can have clear, short-term consequences. Success on these may build cohesiveness and confidence as the team tackles larger tasks.
> Keep the team small.
> Identify outside threats and pressures. Communicate them to the team, and emphasize how teamwork can counter them.

FOCUS ON MANAGEMENT

BUILDING TEAM SPIRIT AT GE PLASTICS

When GE Plastics, a division of General Electric Company, acquired rival company Borg-Warner Chemicals, the company faced the formidable task of integrating two very different work cultures. It was decided that some form of team-building experi-ence was needed to make a lasting impression on the participants while serving some larger purpose. A project called "Share to Gain" was started in which GE Plastics employ-ees from different departments and from the acquired company worked together to renovate five nonprofit fa-cilities in San Diego. The project was credited with building corporate loy-alty, enhancing team spirit, and smoothing the pains of integration.*

http://www.geplastics.com/

*See David Bollier, "Building Corporate Loyalty While Rebuilding the Community," *Management Review*, October 1996, pp. 17–22.

The Bottom Line: Developing Team Cohesion

The process model presented in the nearby Bottom Line provides a summary of the basic steps involved in developing team cohesion.

DEALING WITH PROBLEM TEAM MEMBERS

Teams will never realize their potential if some team members fail to cooperate.[11] Unfortunately, team members sometimes behave in ways that detract from overall team performance.

TYPES OF PROBLEM BEHAVIORS

There are many forms of problem behaviors in teams. We will consider four types of problem team members: freeloaders, complainers, bullies, and martyrs.

> **Freeloaders.** Some team members simply don't carry their fair share of the team's workload; they engage in social loafing. Such freeloaders detract directly from team performance by their lack of contribution. In addition, they may provoke conflict in the team as other members refuse to carry an unproductive member.

> **Complainers.** These members constantly complain about the team's scheduling, activities, progress, or other matters. They see the project as a waste of time, feel they aren't being treated well, or simply hate to work in teams. Complainers damage team morale, and other members often spend an inordinate amount of time and energy trying to placate them.

> **Bullies.** Some members actively disrupt the team by pushing their opinions on others. Bullies seem to revel in making others feel inadequate or unintelligent. They may be better prepared or more knowledgeable than others and anxious to display their expertise, or they may use bullying to cover up their inadequacies. In either case, their insistence on controlling the team process leads to ill will and lack of team coordination.

> **Martyrs.** These are members who feel they are carrying the load for the team. They see themselves as being forced to cover for incompetent team members, as having all the worst assignments, and as doing far more than their fair share. Unlike complainers, they really don't want anything to change; they just want others to feel guilty and to acknowledge their burden. This often creates conflict as other team members chafe at the martyr's claims, attributions, and attitudes.

GUIDELINES FOR DEALING WITH PROBLEM BEHAVIORS

Many of these problem behaviors can be avoided or alleviated through proper planning and team management. For example:

> **Choose team members carefully.** Take team membership seriously. Think about whether potential members are likely to get along. Pick members who have a genuine interest in the task outcome. Make clear to each member why he or she is needed on the team.

> **Offer training.** Give members guidance on how to deal with problem behaviors. Members can, for instance, be shown videotapes of teams successfully dealing with problem members. Such videos may describe forms of potential problem behaviors, show team members' disappointment with such behaviors, make role expectations clear, and suggest specific ways to address problem behaviors.[12]

> **Provide clear goals.** Make sure the team knows what it is expected to do and why its task is important. Emphasize clear, well-defined goals and the consequences of the team's decision. Direction provided at the first team meeting is crucial and will establish lasting precedents for the team.

> **Clearly define member responsibilities.** Many problems in teams occur because members' responsibilities are unclear. Early agreement on a clear and equitable division of responsibilities will work wonders in preventing future conflict.

> **Use peer evaluations.** Team members and leaders must be willing and able to provide—and accept—honest feedback about their individual behaviors and the final outcome of the team's work.[13] Members are more willing to do their fair share and to curtail other problem behaviors if they know their contributions will be evaluated. 360-degree feedback and other approaches that employ peer evaluations are helpful in this regard.

> **Reward superior performance.** Team members who excel should somehow be rewarded for their contributions. This can take the form of positive peer evaluations, praise, or celebrations of accomplishments.

> **Don't let social considerations overwhelm concern with the task.** Many teams develop norms of peaceful coexistence—members are reluctant to openly confront others and to generate hurt feelings. As a result, social loafing and complaining is never challenged. Members

must be willing to appeal to norms of fair participation and to openly deal with problem team members.

> **Appeal to the "shadow of the future."** Remind team members that they are likely to be working together on future tasks and that inappropriate behavior on this task won't be forgotten.

> **Remove problem team members.** As a last resort, it may be necessary to remove an intransigent member from the team. While this may be unpleasant, problem behaviors that sap team morale and performance cannot be allowed to continue unabated.

RUNNING TEAM MEETINGS

Meetings are a big part of the workday, and unless properly managed they can be frustrating, boring, and generally a waste of time. Alternatively, well-run meetings can reap the tremendous potential benefits of teams. As such, the ability to run a meeting well is a valuable skill. In this section, we will provide guidelines for helping team members become acquainted, providing a facilitating setting, considering spatial arrangements, and giving structure to meetings.

HELPING TEAM MEMBERS BECOME ACQUAINTED

It's very important for team members to know and be comfortable with one another. If they aren't, meetings will be tense.

> Before the first meeting, distribute members' biographical sketches, along with the team's assignment and other relevant materials.
> Before each meeting, give members a chance to socialize.
> At the first meeting, introduce each member or have the members introduce themselves.
> Use appropriate "icebreaker" exercises.[14] This might involve stories, exercises, or even jokes. Icebreakers can help overcome initial discomfort in teams. Until team members know whom they are dealing with, they are uncomfortable and perhaps suspicious. However, icebreakers themselves can make team members nervous and uncomfortable if they

FOCUS ON MANAGEMENT

aren't handled well.[15] The nearby skill-development exercise (Skills Practice 12-3) provides concrete suggestions for icebreaking.

> During long meetings, provide breaks.

Now, complete Skills Practice 12-3 with a group of your classmates as a way to explore some basic strategies for getting acquainted with the other members of a new group.

Skills Practice 12-3
Team Management Skills: Breaking the Ice

Skill Level: Basic

Learning Objectives
1. To obtain information from your fellow team members so you can work more effectively with them during the course of the project.
2. To get acquainted with your fellow team members so that you can begin to develop positive working relationships with one another.
3. To develop a sense of team identity by selecting a name for your team.

Procedure
1. Get into groups of four to six students each. Ideally, each group will work together for an actual class project. However, each group may be formed just for this exercise.
2. Go around the group and provide the following information to one another: your name, year in school, major, and where you are from.
3. Select one of the following ice-breaking activities to complete as a group.

   a. The Q & A Exercise
      Step 1: State any one of the following questions to the team:
      > What's your favorite movie of all time? Why?
      > What's your favorite dessert? Why?
      > What's your favorite thing to do for relaxation? Why?
      Step 2: Give your team members 10 minutes to obtain the answers to the chosen question from each other.

   b. The "Let's Do Lunch" Exercise
      Step 1: Tell your team that you would like to have an informal team meeting at a local restaurant.
      Step 2: Ask your team for suggestions as to where to have lunch. Select the restaurant by vote or consensus.
      Step 3: During the lunch, don't talk about the project you are working on. Rather, make "small talk" and try to get to know your team members as people.

   c. The Pictionary Challenge Exercise
      Note: Your instructor will need to bring the materials needed to conduct this exercise.
      Step 1: Select a team leader for the exercise.
      Step 2: Ask the team leader to take a marker or piece of chalk to the chalkboard (or dry erase board).
      Step 3: The team leader will be given a Pictionary card from the instructor and told which item or concept to focus on for the exercise.
      Step 4: When the instructor says, "Go," the leader should attempt to draw the item or concept given to him/her without talking. The team should try to guess the correct answer.
      Step 5: Team performance is based on the number of seconds it takes a team to guess the answer. This exercise can be repeated, if time permits.

4. Now brainstorm some ideas for a team name. Try to be creative.
5. Decide on a team name based on the list you generated.

Discussion Questions

1. What is the value of these simple activities? How do they help a group to develop itself?
2. What are the practical implications of this exercise for you as a future manager?

PROVIDING A FACILITATIVE SETTING

Make sure the team can work in a comfortable space without distractions. Use a room that is large enough to accommodate the number of participants, but not so large as to make them feel "lost." Provide flipcharts, whiteboards, and other writing surfaces. Avoid long, narrow tables, since they restrict eye contact and communication. Offer flexibility in how team members can arrange themselves and their work.[16]

CONSIDERING SPATIAL ARRANGEMENTS

Sometimes the "little things" can make a big difference in teams. For example, when people come into a conference room for a meeting, they usually sit wherever they want. The team leader may—or may not—consciously choose a seat at the head of a conference table or in front of the group, but everything else is often left to chance. In fact, though, the way team members are arranged can make a big difference in how interaction takes place and, in turn, how well the team performs.

At least three aspects of spatial arrangements are important in teams: (1) how far apart team members are; (2) who is sitting in high-status positions; (3) how team members are arranged relative to one another. Let's look at these aspects in turn.

Interpersonal Distance Suppose you meet a friend in the hallway and stop to chat. How close would you be likely to stand to your friend? Chances are you'd stand just far enough away that you could reach out and put your thumb in your friend's ear (Note: don't do this!). The point is that we have certain "comfortable" distances for particular types of interactions. When people are too close to us or too far away, we tend to feel uneasy. Put another way, we have a sense of *personal space,* an area around us that we treat as an extension of ourselves, and we want people to be in specific parts—or zones—

FOCUS ON MANAGEMENT

UNITED TECHNOLOGIES AUTOMOTIVE'S IDEA CENTER

In 1997 United Technologies Automotive, a subsidiary of Lear Corporation, added an Idea Center to its Dearborn, Michigan, headquarters. The center is a focal point for brainstorming and systems development, incorporating the latest technology and designed to stimulate the free flow of ideas. The center allows members from various product teams to meet in a supportive setting and is aimed at reducing costs, improving quality, and speeding up product-development time.*

http://www.lear.com/

*See Dale Jewett, "Supplier Builds Itself an Incubator for Ideas," *Automotive News,* December 16, 1996, p. 20.

FIGURE 12-4
Zones of Personal Space

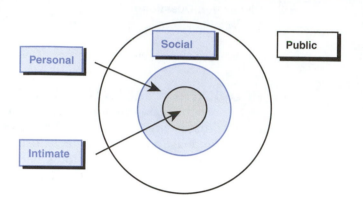

of that personal space for particular activities. There are four zones of personal space, as shown in Figure 12-4.[17]

The *intimate zone* is a bubble extending, for Americans, to about 19 inches from the skin. As the name suggests, we let others enter this zone only for the very best of reasons, such as lovemaking, protecting, and comforting. When other circumstances—such as a crowded elevator—force us to allow people into the intimate zone, we tend to treat them as objects rather than persons.

The *personal zone* ranges from about one and a half to four feet from the person. It is used for comfortable interaction with others and connotes closeness and friendship.

The *social zone,* from 4 to 12 feet, is used for most impersonal business. People working together use the inner part of the zone. The outer part is used for more formal interactions.

Finally, the *public zone,* more than 12 feet from the body, is beyond the range of comfortable interaction.

As discussed in the nearby Global Perspective, these distances vary by culture. Businesspersons entering other cultures must be especially careful to learn appropriate zones for various interactions. Typically, people experience discomfort when their personal space is inappropriately entered. They may protest or leave the situation rather than accept it.

Eye Contact When leaders enter a room, where do they go? Often, they choose a position at the front of the room, or an elevated position, or a position at the head of a conference table. These positions have one thing in common: They each give the leader the chance to make direct eye contact with as many others as possible. In general, leaders tend to position themselves in a way that gives them a lot of potential eye contact with others. In turn, people who are in such positions (again, at the head of a conference table, in a central position in a room, or in an elevated position) are more likely to be seen as leaders. They are perceived (other things equal) to have more status and to be more "leaderlike," and they have more communications directed toward them, than if they were in less visible positions.

INTERPERSONAL DISTANCES ACROSS CULTURES

Interpersonal distances corresponding to the zones of personal space vary dramatically across cultures. For instance, in northern Europe, the "bubbles" tend to be quite large and people keep their distance. In southern France, Italy, Greece, and Spain, the bubbles are smaller. A distance seen as intimate in northern Europe overlaps normal conversational distance in southern Europe. As a result, Mediterranean Europeans "get too close" for the comfort of Germans, Scandinavians, English persons, and Americans of northern European ancestry.*

*See Edward T. Hall and Mildred Reed Hall, *Understanding Cultural Differences* (Yarmouth, ME: Intercultural Press, 1990).

Seating Arrangements Suppose you and another individual were about to sit down at a conference table. Where would the two of you sit? Across from each other? Side by side? Corner to corner? Far apart? Your response probably depends on how the two of you would expect to be interacting, if at all. As shown in Figure 12-5, this is just what happens. If people expect to cooperate, they tend to sit side by side. If they expect to be in conflict, as in many bargaining situations, they tend to sit face to face. If they plan to engage in casual conversation, they sit corner to corner. If they don't plan to interact at all (for example, if they are each going to be working on their own homework) they tend to sit distant opposite.

Here's the more interesting finding: If people are *randomly* seated in these relative positions, they are more likely to interact in these ways than if seated differently. For example, people seated across from each other are more likely to get into an argument than if seated next to each other or corner to corner.

GIVING STRUCTURE TO MEETINGS

Team leaders are sometimes reluctant to provide structure. They don't want to be seen as "bossy," and they believe (or hope) that things will somehow

FIGURE 12-5
Seating Arrangements for Different Activities

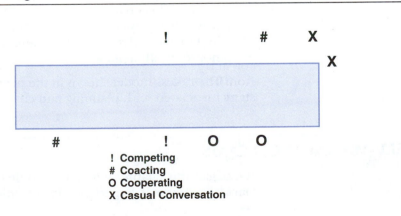

! Competing
Coacting
O Cooperating
X Casual Conversation

Web Wise

The Virtual Meeting Assistant

Visit the Virtual Meeting Assistant website, constructed and maintained by the Department of Communication Studies of the University of Kansas, for a rich array of tips on running meetings, links to articles on meeting management and to videoconferencing sites, and much more:

http://www.ukans.edu/cwis/ units/coms2/vma/vms.htm

"work themselves out." This is unfortunate, since meetings need—and team members welcome—structure. The key point here is that providing appropriate structure does not mean dominating the process. Instead, it gives team members clear bounds within which to operate.

> Prior to the meeting, distribute an agenda to all team members.
> At the beginning of the meeting, review progress to date and establish the task of the meeting.
> Early in the meeting, get a report from each member with a pre-assigned task.
> Manage the discussion to ensure fair participation. The team leader—and other team members—must make sure that all members have the opportunity to participate. If one or a few members dominate the process, the benefits of using a team will quickly evaporate. Here are some tips for encouraging fair participation:
>   a. Establish norms for fair participation. For example, state early in the meeting: "Let's make sure we all have a chance to make our views known. I hope we'll all feel free to speak up, but also that we'll let others have their say."
>   b. Provide guiding comments. If someone has been dominating the process, say something to the effect of "Janet, I think you've done a good job of stating your position. Let's see if someone else has any comments." If someone hasn't been contributing, say something like "Donna, is there anything you'd like to add?" Often, people are anxious to make a point but are reluctant to say anything unless they're directly asked to participate.
>   c. Use a *round-robin process,* asking members to give their comments in turn. For example, the leader may simply say, "Let's go around the table and see what each of us has to say." Sometimes, as when team members have made up lists of ideas, the round-robin technique may be used to have each member in turn give his or her first idea, then in turn give his or her second idea, and so on.
>   d. Ask members to write down their ideas. This will result in more unique, clearly stated ideas.
> At the end of the meeting, summarize what was accomplished, where the group is on its schedule, and what will be the team's task at the next meeting. This gives the team a sense of movement and accomplishment.
> Also, make public and clear each member's assignment for the next meeting. This creates a sense of responsibility. It also makes sure people know what they're expected to do, and that tasks don't either get duplicated by more than one team member or "fall through the cracks," being ignored by all members.

The process model shown in the nearby Bottom Line displays the general steps associated with planning and conducting an effective team meeting.

SELF-MANAGING TEAMS

We began this chapter with an example of the self-managing teams at Harley-Davidson. Harley's experience is not unique. According to one survey, more

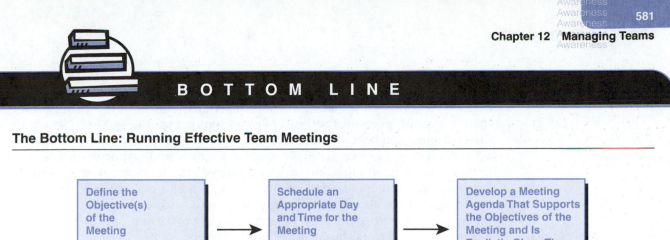

BOTTOM LINE

The Bottom Line: Running Effective Team Meetings

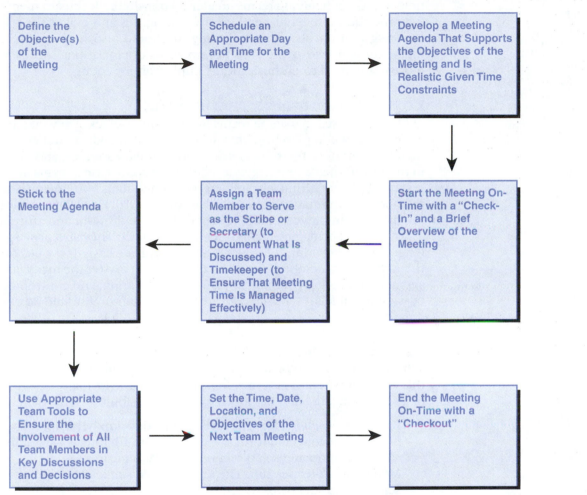

Define the Objective(s) of the Meeting → Schedule an Appropriate Day and Time for the Meeting → Develop a Meeting Agenda That Supports the Objectives of the Meeting and Is Realistic Given Time Constraints

Stick to the Meeting Agenda ← Assign a Team Member to Serve as the Scribe or Secretary (to Document What Is Discussed) and Timekeeper (to Ensure That Meeting Time Is Managed Effectively) ← Start the Meeting On-Time with a "Check-In" and a Brief Overview of the Meeting

Use Appropriate Team Tools to Ensure the Involvement of All Team Members in Key Discussions and Decisions → Set the Time, Date, Location, and Objectives of the Next Team Meeting → End the Meeting On-Time with a "Checkout"

than two-thirds of *Fortune* 1000 firms use self-managing teams with at least some employees, and they are one of the fastest-growing forms of employee involvement.[18] Self-managing teams are common at such companies as Procter & Gamble, General Motors, Motorola, Ford, General Electric, AT&T, Xerox, American Express, and Prudential.[19]

WHY USE SELF-MANAGING TEAMS?

Everything about the new workplace suggests that self-managing teams will become increasingly important. For example, as organizations become flatter and more decentralized, decision making is pushed down to lower levels. With fewer supervisors, employees must learn to manage themselves. In addition, the modern work environment is dynamic and uncertain. In such an environment, firms must be agile, able to respond quickly to changes in markets and technologies. Placing responsibility at the level of the team, rather than at higher levels in the firm, permits rapid response—those closest to the customer and best able to meet customer demands have the authority to act. Further, employees generally value autonomy and opportunities to participate. As such, giving teams greater responsibility lets team members more fully use their intellectual and creative capacities and makes the job more interesting and intrinsically motivating. It should also help ensure that team members will take ownership of important organizational decisions and be more committed to enthusiastically implementing them.

HOW SELF-MANAGING TEAMS WORK

Quite simply, self-managing teams manage themselves. They take responsibility for their work, plan how they will carry it out, allocate duties among team members, monitor their own performance, seek resources, and make changes in their performance strategies as needed. In some cases, teams may also have responsibility for hiring, disciplining, and scheduling.[20] At Boeing, for instance, members of self-managing teams elect their own team leaders and interview prospective employees, looking especially for culture fit and attitude.[21]

While self-managing teams offer great promise, they also pose special challenges. For one thing, of course, managing isn't easy. It would be naïve to think that team members would be able to easily master the many tasks of management, including planning, organizing, motivating, and controlling. Our discussion of guidelines for self-management in Chapter 9 should be useful in this regard.

LEADER ROLES IN SELF-MANAGING TEAMS

What does it mean to be in charge of a self-managing team? It might seem that this is a contradiction in terms. In fact, though, the formally designated leader of a self-managing team has a variety of responsibilities. These include:[22]

> Becoming a self-leader. The leader must develop behavioral and cognitive self-management skills—discussed in Chapter 9—to achieve the self-motivation and self-direction needed to perform.

> Modeling self-leadership. The leader's own self-leadership behaviors serve as a model from which others can learn. When, for instance, self-managing team members see the leader setting goals for behavioral change, using self-reward to foster goal attainment, self-monitoring his or her performance, and then attaining the self-set goals, they are likely to initiate their own self-leadership actions.

> Encouraging self-set goals. As discussed in Chapter 6, goal setting is critical for effective motivation. Consistent with that discussion, leaders should encourage team members to set specific and challenging goals for themselves.

> Creating positive thought patterns. Constructive thought patterns are central to effective self-leadership. Leaders can attempt to transmit positive thought patterns to team members, and they can encourage positive self-expectations in them. Especially in the early stages of a new job or assignment, employees have doubts and fears, and a leader's words of

confidence, praise, and support are crucial. This behavior often results in a self-fulfilling prophecy; those who believe they can do well are more likely to excel because of constructive thought patterns.

> Developing self-leadership through reward and constructive reprimand. Leaders of self-managing teams may use conventional rewards and reprimands to encourage self-leadership behaviors. However, use of reprimands is likely to discourage employees as they are in the transition to self-leadership and should be used only as a last resort for severe and chronic carelessness or underperformance. Beyond this, leaders should encourage and teach team members to reward themselves and build self-rewards into their work. That is, the leader should de-emphasize externally administered rewards, emphasizing self-administered and natural rewards.

> Promoting self-leadership through teamwork. Quite simply, team members learn self-leadership through regular and varied experiences in team settings that place them in positions where self-management is necessary.

> Facilitating a self-leadership culture. Leaders must play a part in developing pervasive, integrated organizational cultures—as discussed in Chapter 8—which are conducive to high levels of self-management and performance.

Xerox uses many self-managing teams in its customer service division. Research on the teams has identified several factors that seem to characterize leaders of the most successful self-managing teams. For instance, leaders of the most successful teams give first priority to getting the team set up correctly and to arranging organizational support for it before turning to coaching.[23]

USING SPECIAL-PURPOSE GROUP TECHNIQUES

When we think of bringing people together to deal with problems, we probably envision a committee meeting, with people arranged—notebooks open and pens poised—around a conference table. In fact, though, there are more entrees on the group menu than just the committee du jour. Here, we will present four specific alternatives to traditional interacting groups: the devil's advocate, brainstorming, the affinity technique, and the nominal group technique. Each of these techniques is easy and effective to use, can be completed in a single session, and serves a specific purpose. Your mastery of these techniques can add valuable skills to your management arsenal.

TO ENCOURAGE HEALTHY DISSENT: THE DEVIL'S ADVOCATE

Beginning in the 12th century, the Roman Catholic Church instituted strict procedures to determine who was, or wasn't, worthy of sainthood. One barrier on the road to sainthood was the devil's advocate. The devil's advocate—a position that wasn't abolished until 1983—was a church officer whose role was to spot flaws in the arguments on behalf of a candidate for sainthood. Now the *devil's advocate* refers to an individual or group given the responsibility for challenging a proposal. The idea is to find flaws while they may still be remedied, or to recognize that they are fatal, before competitors, customers, or others become aware of them.

The devil's advocate's role is to make sure that the group takes a hard second look at its preferred alternative. Designating a devil's advocate makes it clear that dissent is legitimate. It brings out criticisms that might not otherwise be aired, and it highlights underlying assumptions.

However, devil's advocates must be used with caution. If they are employed too often or if they are overly severe in their criticisms, they may cause problems. Some people may become demoralized if their views are constantly criticized. As a result, they may come up with safe solutions, not especially risky or creative but able to stand up to criticism. Also, if the devil's advocate is successful in finding fatal problems with a plan or alternative, there is no new plan or alternative to take its place. That is, the devil's advocate approach focuses on what is wrong without pointing out what is right.

TO GENERATE CREATIVE IDEAS: GROUP BRAINSTORMING

People sometimes use the term *brainstorming* any time they sit around and try to come up with ideas. In fact, though, brainstorming is a specific technique with a set of rules. *Group brainstorming* seeks to create the right atmosphere for relaxed, spontaneous thinking. A small group of employees is brought together, presented with the problem, and told to follow four rules:

> Don't criticize any ideas. This creates a climate of psychological safety, reducing inhibitions.
> Freewheel. Any idea, no matter how wild, is fine.
> Try to come up with as many ideas as possible. The more ideas, the better.
> Try to combine and improve. "Hitchhiking" on others' ideas may create a chain of inspiration.

Many companies are using brainstorming to develop new product ideas, marketing approaches, and creative advertising strategies. For example, Honda's engineering team used a brainstorming approach to develop the highly fuel-efficient engine for the 1992 Honda Civic. Hallmark Cards has regular brainstorming sessions for its greeting-card writers. Adaptec's experience with brainstorming is highlighted in the nearby Focus on Management. Diverse brainstorming groups, or groups that include members who hold minority views, typically produce not only more ideas but also higher-quality ideas than homogeneous groups.

New electronic tools promise to make brainstorming even more effective. At IBM, meeting rooms are equipped with personal computers for each participant, and a large color monitor is located where everyone can see it. Participants type in their ideas, comments, or reactions on their keyboards. Their input, which is anonymous, appears simultaneously on the monitor as well as on each computer screen. Everyone gets a chance to contribute, and no one can dominate the process. One popular electronic tool for facilitating brainstorming and other group decision processes is Ventana Corporation's GroupSystems, described in the nearby Web Wise box.[24]

As befits a technique meant to enhance creativity, there are some creative variants of brainstorming. With *stop-and-go brainstorming,* short periods of brainstorming (10 minutes or so) are interspersed with short periods of evaluation. *Reverse brainstorming* brings fresh approaches by turning the problem around. How could we stifle creativity? How could we decrease morale?

Web Wise

Ventana Corporation's GroupSystems

GroupSystems is a suite of team-based, decision-support software tools that can be used for strategic planning, innovative problem solving, business process reengineering, and other purposes. It includes electronic tools for brainstorming, information gathering, voting, organizing, prioritizing, and consensus building. GroupSystems is used by such organizations as American Express, IBM, the Canadian Imperial Bank of Commerce, Statoil of Norway, and the U.S. Federal Aviation Administration.

http://www.ventana.com

FOCUS ON MANAGEMENT

BRAINSTORMING AT ADAPTEC

Adaptec, a California semiconductor firm, believes it is difficult to build real consensus on important corporate decisions without an empathetic business organization. Employees at all levels of the organization attend interdepartmental brainstorming sessions. These sessions usually produce ideas that reflect the company's overall competencies better than ideas arising from any single department. Adaptec also engages in interdepartmental communications programs so that each department is exposed to the elementary concepts used in other departments. For example, finance people attend sessions in marketing and operations. Employees at all levels appreciate seeing the "whole picture" and feeling involved.*

http://www.adaptec.com

*See Paul G. Hansen, "Getting Your Team On the Same Side," *Financial Executive*, March/ April 1994, pp. 43−45+.

How could we lower productivity? With large groups, the *Phillips 66 technique* can be used. Once the problem is clearly understood, small groups of six members brainstorm for six minutes. Then a member of each group presents the best ideas or all ideas to the larger group.

TO GENERATE CREATIVE IDEAS: THE AFFINITY TECHNIQUE

Brainstorming is a simple and useful tool for generating creative ideas. Another good creativity-enhancement tool is the *affinity technique.* The affinity technique is a simple but powerful technique that a team can use to enhance the effectiveness of its decision making. It can be used whenever a team is attempting to identify creative solutions to a problem. For example, the affinity technique can be used to identify ideas for improving customer service, product quality, or productivity. The affinity technique achieves its purpose by requiring a team to systematically generate potential solutions to a problem, clustering them in terms of their similarities, naming the clusters, and then using a voting procedure to identify which ideas should be given the highest priority.

Now use Skills Practice 12-4 to work in a group to apply the affinity technique for group decision making. Again, this is an excellent tool for addressing problems that require creative solutions.

Skills Practice 12-4
Applying the Affinity Technique

Skill Level: Challenging

Skill Objective

To develop skill in using the affinity technique to support team decision making.

Procedure

1. Form groups of four to six students each for this exercise.
2. Obtain the following items from your instructor:
    > 1–2 pieces of flipchart paper
    > 1 pad of Post-It notes for each team member
    > 1 large felt tip marker
    > 4 pieces of masking tape

3. Identify a problem or issue that requires a creative solution. Some examples might include:
    > How can a student organization increase the involvement of its members in its activities?
    > How can a fast food restaurant make itself more attractive as a place of employment for college students?
    > How can an organization improve its customer service?
    > How can students best prepare themselves for a job in the "real world"?

4. Using the issue you just identified, follow the steps associated with the affinity technique:

    Step 1: *State the problem:* The first step is to state the problem by writing it on a flipchart or whiteboard that is clearly visible to the team. The problem should be an issue for which creative solutions are needed based on team member input. The team leader should make sure that all team members understand the problem.

    Step 2: *Silent generation of ideas:* Now each team member should be given a packet of "Post-It" notes. The team leader should instruct each team member to silently generate ideas or potential solutions to the problem. Team members should use one Post-It note for each idea. Again, this should be done with no discussion between team members.

    Step 3: *Posting Ideas:* Once all team members have finished generating ideas on Post-It notes, they should stick them on a whiteboard or large piece of flipchart paper at the front of the room. They do not have to be put up in any order at this point. The key is simply to get all the team members' ideas together in one area.

    Step 4: *Clustering:* Now team members should take a few steps back from the area with all the ideas posted and start looking for "clusters" of ideas. A cluster exists when the same or a highly similar idea is identified by two or more team members. When this happens, a team member (it makes no difference who) should put the Post-It notes together (i.e., stick them next to each other). This should be done for all other ideas that are considered to be the same. Individual ideas that do not fit into any cluster should be placed to the side for potential action later. A team may find any number of idea clusters, depending on their problem and the number of ideas initially generated.

    Step 5: *Naming:* Finally, the team leader should draw a circle around each cluster and ask the team to name it. When all the clusters have been named, the team leader should check to ensure that all team members understand the meaning of every cluster. The final outcome from the affinity technique is a set of potential solutions (represented by the named clusters) for the problem in question.

    Follow-up: Although not part of the formal affinity technique, team members are now in a position to vote for their favorite idea(s). This is useful in helping the team to prioritize problem solutions in terms of which ones should be pursued first. A simple voting procedure could be used here: Each team member puts a checkmark next to the three to five problem solutions he/she likes the most (the team leader should decide the number to vote on based on the number of problem solutions that have been identified). The problem solutions with the highest number of votes are the ones the team should consider implementing first.

5. Discuss the following questions as a class.
    > How does this technique help a team to make better decisions?
    > What are some other problems or issues that could be addressed with this technique?
    > What are the keys to applying this technique effectively?

TO GENERATE A GROUP SOLUTION: THE NOMINAL GROUP TECHNIQUE

Earlier in this chapter we pointed out benefits and drawbacks associated with using teams. Here's an important thing to recognize in looking at those lists—the benefits generally result simply from the many perspectives, skills, and resources brought to a group by its members, while the drawbacks usually result from the interaction of team members. For example, interaction may permit some people to dominate others, to block others' ideas, or to bully. Of course, interaction is often needed—we want the chance to air our views and to get others' ideas and reactions, and we often simply like to be able to talk with our colleagues. Still, there may be times when interaction really isn't needed and when, therefore, we might want to restrict it.

A nominal group (a group "in name only") is another name for a coacting (that is, noninteracting) group. For instance, if you and your roommates were all sitting around a table and writing down ideas on how to cut down on your food costs, without discussing your ideas or interacting in other ways, you would be members of a coacting group. With a coacting group, members are working together on the same task, but they aren't talking with one another or communicating in other ways.

The *nominal group technique* uses a blend of coacting and interacting stages in order to capture the benefits of groups while minimizing potential problems. It seeks:

> To encourage all members to make inputs
> To prevent dominant members from controlling the process
> To ensure that all ideas get a fair hearing
> To allow members to evaluate alternatives without fear of retribution.

To do all this, the nominal group technique uses the steps shown in Figure 12-6.

FIGURE 12-6
Steps in the Nominal Group Technique

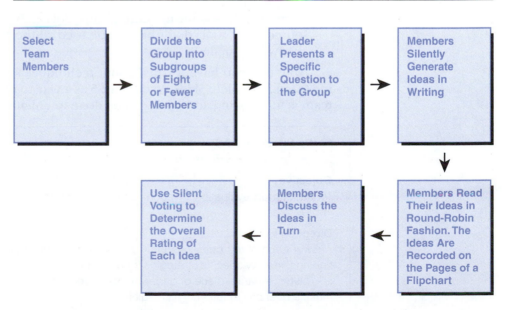

Each of the steps in the figure is important, but one of them—the silent generation of ideas in writing without interaction—deserves further comment. By taking just 15 minutes or so to complete this step, you can achieve the following benefits:

> Ideas are generated without being evaluated.
> Members focus their time directly on the search for ideas.
> Nobody can dominate the process.
> Everyone makes inputs.
> Ideas are put in writing.

GAINING ACCEPTANCE OF NEW TECHNIQUES

Each of the tools we've just discussed works well and is widely used in modern organizations. Still, it sometimes seems difficult to try something different; people know what to expect in committees, and they're comfortable with them even as they lament the time they're wasting in one meeting after another. Here are some tips for gaining acceptance of new group processes.

> Just do it. Take charge and announce that you're going to handle the meeting differently today. Your assurance in presenting and using these tools will go a long way toward ensuring their acceptance and enthusiastic use. As we discussed in Chapter 7, a leader who is forceful and assured is seen as charismatic and is likely to have enthusiastic followers.
> Explain why you're doing something different. Point out that the tool you're going to use is the best available for the task you're about to undertake—coming up with good ideas, making sure concerns are aired, or coming up with a creative solution.
> Point out that these are widely used, effective techniques. Give specific examples of how they're used in companies such as IBM, American Express, Xerox, and Adaptec.
> Treat this as a skill-building experience both for yourself and for your colleagues. Point out to team members that they will all be team leaders, formal or informal, and that learning these techniques may be of great value to them.
> Point out that mastering more group tools adds further to the team's resources. The tools don't have to be used all the time, but they're available when needed.

Now that you have learned about techniques for developing and managing teams, complete Skills Practice 12-5 as a way to understand how well your team is functioning and what can be done to enhance its effectiveness.

Skills Practice 12-5
Team Process Evaluation

Skill Level: Basic

Objective

To perform an evaluation of each team's process in order to identify opportunities for improvement.

Directions

Answer each of the questions individually, then discuss them as a team. Based on your findings, identify specific strategies for enhancing the effectiveness of your team process.

Use a separate piece of paper to record your answers. If possible, each team should make a brief presentation of its results.

Team Diagnostic Questions

1. List the specific things your team has been doing well so far in terms of managing its team process.
2. List the specific things your team has *not* been doing well so far in terms of managing its team process.
3. List the specific team concepts, tools, or principles discussed in this chapter that you have applied to the management of your team process (e.g., agendas, timelines, ground rules). Have they been effective? Why or why not?
4. What opportunities for improvement exist in terms of enhancing the effectiveness of your team process? Be as specific as possible.

Finally, read the scenario in the Real-World Management Challenge and develop an action plan for handling the situation. This was an actual challenge that a company had to deal with so you will be able to compare what you come up against the actions that management actually took to handle this situation.

Real-World Management Challenge

Transitioning to a Team-Based Approach

The Team Challenge

CR Bard Inc. is a worldwide developer and manufacturer of medical devices. Its Glenn Falls, New York, manufacturing facility employs approximately 500 employees. The performance of the facility is measured in terms of costs, schedule performance, and quality.

During the early 1990s, the organization had carried out a total of four employee lay-offs. At the same time, management was implementing a variety of new initiatives to increase the work expectations of employees in order to increase efficiency. This resulted in frustration, negativity, and low morale among employees. The bottom line for employees was maintaining their employment.

Within this scenario, management announced a proposal to implement a team-based approach across the organization. The objective of doing this was to empower teams to develop a "results-oriented culture" (as opposed to the current process-oriented culture) and to realize continuous improvements in business results over time.

What Would You Do?

If you were assigned the responsibility of implementing the transition of the manufacturing facility to a team-based approach, how would you proceed, given the situation? Be as specific as possible.

Source: "The Gradual Transition to a Team-based Environment: The Success Story of a Medium-sized Manufacturing Facility," *Hospital Material Management Quarterly,* August 1999.

TOP TEN LIST: KEY POINTS TO REMEMBER

HOW TO MANAGE TEAMS EFFECTIVELY

10. Identify the objective(s) of your team.
9. Identify the expertise you will need on your team.
8. Select the members of your team based on the expertise needed *and* an appropriate diversity of team-member work and personality styles.

7. Take the time to "break the ice" between team members in order to facilitate positive working relationships.
6. Work with team members to develop a timeline for achieving the goals of the project.

5. Define a role for each team member that aligns his/her needs and goals with those of the team.

4. Use ground rules and meeting agendas to structure the team process.

3. Ensure that all team members are participating in the team process.

2. Build quality checks into the team process that assess team progress in relation to the project timeline, and make adjustments as needed.

1. Balance the concerns for tasks and for people throughout all phases of the team process.

QUESTIONS FOR REVIEW AND REFLECTION

REVIEW QUESTIONS

1. Identify and describe three types of teams.
2. Discuss potential advantages and disadvantages of teams.
3. Discuss factors that help decide when a team should be used.
4. Provide guidelines for determining team size and membership.
5. Identify types of team roles, and indicate guidelines for enhancing a team's productivity by understanding these roles.
6. Give guidelines for defining the team's assignment and planning the team's effort.
7. Discuss ways to develop productive norms.
8. Describe team polarization and why it is important.
9. Identify causes and consequences of team cohesiveness.
10. Set out guidelines for helping team members become acquainted and for providing a facilitative setting for team meetings.
11. Discuss ways to give structure to meetings, including techniques to encourage fair participation.
12. Discuss how team member eye contact and seating arrangements influence team processes and outcomes.
13. Identify potential benefits of self-managing teams, as well as leader roles in self-managing teams.
14. Discuss special-purpose group techniques, including the devil's advocate, group brainstorming, the affinity technique, and the nominal group technique.
15. Provide guidelines for gaining acceptance of new techniques.

CRITICAL THINKING QUESTIONS

1. A manager says, "If I need a team, I'll form it. I don't want my employees to form informal groups, and I break up informal groups when I can." What might be some unintended consequences of the manager's actions?
2. Considering the potential advantages and disadvantages of teams, describe a situation in which a team would be *most* useful. Then describe a situation in which use of a team would clearly be undesirable.
3. Consider a group of which you are a member. Identify four norms of the group. How do you think each of those norms developed? Discuss what you see as the consequences of each norm.
4. A colleague complains that every team he is in seems to start out fighting, stating, "I'm about to give up on teams." How might you respond?
5. Discuss how implementation of self-managing work teams might affect each of the following in organizations:
   a. Power relationships
   b. Selection and training
   c. Career mobility
6. Recall that polarization causes initial group tendencies to become more extreme. Discuss situations in which polarization might be desirable, as well as situations in which polarization is clearly undesirable. Are there any types of group tendencies for which polarization would *always* be harmful or would *always* be helpful?
7. The nominal group technique has been found to be very useful for generating large numbers of unique and creative ideas. What characteristics of the technique might limit the degree to which it is used?
8. Do you think the growing use of teams in organizations will continue? Why or why not?

EXPERIENTIAL EXERCISES

WEB EXERCISE 12-1

Go to the following URL and read the *ComputerWorld* article titled "Xerox: A Tough Culture to Duplicate."

http://www.computerworld.com/cwi/story/0,1199, NAV47_STO33384,00.html

Answer the following questions relating to the article.

1. How is dissent treated in Xerox Corp.'s information systems department? What are some consequences of that treatment?

2. How is diversity viewed in the department? What are some apparent benefits of diversity for the department?

3. What is the role of the annual employee motivation and satisfaction survey?

4. What might be some costs of the steps taken by the department to encourage expression of dissent?

WEB EXERCISE 12-2

Use a search engine to find websites containing the word *teamwork* as well as the name of a specific company of your choice. Review the selected sites to find material discussing teamwork (types, benefits, special characteristics, etc.) at the company. Write a one-page summary of your findings.

CASE 12-1
SELF-MANAGING WORK TEAMS AT CHEVRON

The Company

The Chevron Corporation is a global petroleum company that is engaged in oil exploration, production, transportation, refining, retail marketing, and chemical manufacturing and sales. It operates in more than 100 countries, with a workforce of 31,000 employees.

The mission of Chevron is as follows:

We are an international company providing energy and chemical products vital to the growth of the world's economies. Our mission is to create superior value for our stockholders, our customers and our employees.

The vision of the company is to be "Better than the Best." The supporting elements of this vision include:

> Employees are proud of their success as a team.
> Customers, suppliers, and governments prefer us.
> Competitors respect us.
> Communities welcome us.
> Investors are eager to invest in us.

The primary strategic objective of the firm is to be No. 1 in total stockholder return for the period 2000–2004.

The Situation

The Kern River Asset Team (KRAT) is part of Chevron's Western Production Business Unit and South Valley Profit Center. Its primary job is to produce oil from Chevron facilities in Bakersfield, California. In the past, the KRAT was composed of many asset teams that functioned within a traditional, hierarchical organization. Some of the problems associated with this approach included:

> The teams had difficulty relating the processes associated with their asset to broad objectives.
> Teams had trouble developing a "big picture" perspective of the processes they managed.
> The small asset team structure encouraged accountability or ownership at the micro level. This resulted in redundancy of work processes.

The Self-Managing Work Team Structure

The new structure implemented at the Kern River Profit Center involved the organization of teams around specific work processes and quality management principles. Employee empowerment and labor–management cooperation were also important parts of the process.

To initiate the development of the self-managing work team concept at Chevron, a team of employees who represented various parts of the organization was formed. The objective of this team was to work with an external management consultant to identify and organize tasks into meaningful groupings and to define specific boundaries for each team. This design team kept employees updated regarding their progress on designing the new system.

The composition of the self-managing teams that were formed was diversified in terms of technical, interpersonal, and leadership skills. Each team had five to eight members. All the processes that the teams would be managing were formally flowcharted as well.

At this point, the organization implemented a training program to help teams to prioritize their tasks in relation to assigned business processes and external constituents (suppliers, customers, etc.).

A coach was also assigned to each team to provide leadership support. The main purpose of this person was to monitor the progress of the team and to offer guidance as needed. Additional training was provided in the areas of general team building, problem solving, communication, conflict resolution, etc.

In the beginning, the coach and each team made decisions together. However, the goal for the future was to transfer authority and responsibility for the business process from the coach to the team.

Some problems that occurred after the administration of the new team system included: (1) employee frustration resulting from a lack of understanding of the system, (2) adopting a new system that required a fundamentally different mentality and way of doing things, and (3) personality and interpersonal conflicts.

Results

Preliminary evaluations of the self-managing work team system:

> Product cycle time was reduced.

> Process improvements were identified and implemented.

> The use of process measures has helped the teams to enhance their knowledge and mastery of their process.

Discussion Questions

1. To what extent do you feel that self-managing work teams are appropriate for this situation?

2. What were the strengths of the process for designing and implementing the self-managing work teams approach?

3. What were the weaknesses of the process for designing and implementing the self-managing work teams approach?

4. What recommendations would you give to Chevron regarding the handling of this situation?

http://www.chevron.com

Source: M. Attaran, "Succeeding with Self-Managed Work Teams," *Industrial Management,* July/August 1999, pp. 24–28.

CASE 12-2
DA CHICAGO BULLS . . . THE GREATEST BASKETBALL TEAM OF ALL TIME?

For the official website of the Chicago Bulls, visit:

http://www.nba.com/bulls/

From the *Quotations* file of IdeaBank:

There are plenty of teams in every sport that have great players and never win titles. Most of the time, those players aren't willing to sacrifice for the greater good of the team. The funny thing is, in the end, their unwillingness to sacrifice only makes individual goals more difficult to achieve. One thing I believe to the fullest is that if you think and achieve as a team, the individual accolades will take care of themselves. Talent wins games, but teamwork and intelligence win championships.

—Michael Jordan (1963–), American professional basketball player with the Chicago Bulls, in *I Can't*

Accept Not Trying (San Francisco: Harper San Francisco, 1994).

The 1996–1997 NBA Champions

The Overall Team

The "starting five" of the Chicago Bulls consisted of Michael Jordan, Scottie Pippen, Dennis Rodman, Luc Longley, and Ron Harper. The supporting cast included Tony Kukoc, Steve Kerr, and Jud Buechler.

Many sports analysts and journalists have noted that as individuals, the Chicago Bulls players were, for the most part, not "all-star" or "dream-team" material. In fact, Sun-Times journalist Rick Telander even referred to the Chicago Bulls as a "bunch of overachievers."* Overachievers?! Telander's point was that the one thing that made the Chicago Bulls great was that "the sum was greater than the whole." That is, they were truly a superior team.

The Power Trio

Michael Jordan, Scottie Pippen, and Dennis Rodman. Together they formed the heart of the Chicago Bulls NBA championship team. This colorful and unconventional threesome enabled the Chicago Bulls to win five NBA championships in seven years. Why was this threesome considered to be one of the very best of all time? What was the secret of their success?

Team Roles

The success of the Jordan-Pippen-Rodman trio was based to a large degree on the unique roles each one played on the team and how they complemented one another so well. Jordan was the phenomenal shooting guard, the inside driver who was "airborne" so often, and the undisputed leader of the Chicago Bulls team. Pippen was the forward who worked with Jordan so skillfully to set up countless game-winning plays. Pippen was an outstanding offensive player in his own right as well. His scoring capabilities helped to keep defensive players from focusing solely on Jordan. Finally, Rodman, the power forward, although not a gifted offensive player, did what he could to contribute in the scoring column and distinguished himself in his defensive play.

Many people considered Jordan and Pippen to be the best players in the NBA and Rodman the best rebounder. Together they helped the Chicago Bulls to achieve a 85.1% winning percentage during their first two years playing together. In fact, in their first year together, the team won 72 games for the season, setting an NBA record.

In the 1996–1997 NBA season, Jordan averaged over 29 points per game, with Pippen scoring over 20 points. Dennis Rodman excelled on defense by averaging over 16 rebounds per game.

On the defensive side of the ball, Jordan and Pippen were strong players as well. In fact, all three members of the "Power Trio" were consistently named to the first-team all-defensive squads of the NBA, and Rodman won the NBA defensive player of the year two times.

Personality Factors

Jordan, Pippen, and Rodman all possessed different personalities. Jordan provided strong leadership and inspiration to his teammates through his amazing feats and the extraordinary effort he exerted in every game. Clearly,

Jordan was an individual who "led by example." Scottie Pippen was a strong team player, although he sometimes felt overshadowed by Jordan. This dissatisfaction, at times, led to rumors that Pippen had asked to be traded to another team. Rodman exhibited a wide range of problem behaviors, including an incident in which he headbutted a referee. Other incidents that many perceived as "crossing the line" in terms of what was appropriate included anti-Mormon comments he directed toward Utah Jazz fans, and his participation in a World Wrestling Federation match. Moreover, Rodman's orange hair always drew attention and controversy to himself.

Teamwork at Its Best: Game Six of the 1996–1997 Championship Series

One of the very best examples of the ability of the Chicago Bulls to come together to get the job done as a team was in game six of the 1996–1997 NBA championship series with the Utah Jazz. In that game, the Bulls struggled for the first three quarters. They looked sluggish and sloppy and they were shooting poorly. However, in classic Bulls fashion, they fought their way back to tie the game with less than 28 seconds left in the game.

In a dramatic sequence, Scottie Pippen set up the play and passed it off to Jordan, who drove inside and set up for a mid-range jump shot. However, as Jordan was literally airborne, he dumped the ball off to his wide-open teammate Steve Kerr, who was the team's best outside shooter. Kerr sank the shot, putting the Bulls ahead with just a few seconds left in the game. As Utah made one last desperate attempt at a comeback, Tony Kukoc, Chicago's "sixth man," stole the ball, sprinted downcourt, and slam-dunked the ball, sealing the victory and the NBA championship for the Chicago Bulls.

Summary

The Chicago Bulls will go down in history as one of the greatest NBA teams of all time. They dominated the NBA for much of the 1990s. And NBA fans will never forget the excitement, passion, and inspirational play of the amazing "Power Trio" of Michael Jordan, Scottie Pippen, and Dennis Rodman.

Discussion Questions

1. Describe the key roles played by Jordan, Pippen, and Rodman in helping the Chicago Bulls to become so successful in the 1990s.
2. What characteristics of a good team are illustrated by the Chicago Bulls Power Trio?

3. Use your knowledge of team formation and composition to evaluate the decision of Chicago Bulls' management to break up this team. Given the more recent performance of the Chicago Bulls, do you feel that this decision was a good long-term course of action?

4. What recommendations would you give to the management and coaching staff of the Chicago Bulls in order to rebuild the team?

5. What are the practical implications of this article for teams in the corporate world?

---

*Telander, R. *Chicago Sun-Times,* April 22, 1996, p. 2.

Source: http://sportsillustrated.cnn.com/features/1997/bull/powertrio.html

VIDEO CASE
A STUDY OF SELF-DIRECTED WORK TEAMS
AT NEXT DOOR FOOD STORE

Running Time: 11:36

Headquartered in Mount Pleasant, Michigan, Next Door Food Store is a family-run business with more than 30 outlets in Michigan and Indiana. The stores sell gasoline and a wide variety of grocery and general merchandise items. Next Door management faces many challenges, including a high turnover rate. Management believes it can address these challenges by motivating and empowering employees through the use of self-directed work teams. It is using self-directed work teams to encourage employees to shift from narrow individual goals to a focus on the business as a whole.

The video shows the first team in place at company headquarters, the audit department (called the DGIT Team). Next Door Food Store's Training Director, Brenda Henry-Coan, members of the DGIT Team, and others discuss the company's use of self-directed teams. After viewing the video, answer the following questions.

1. Why was the audit department selected as the company's first self-directed work team?

2. What are concerns that would interfere with DGIT Team members' motivation and ability to create a successful self-directed work team?

3. According to members of the DGIT Team, what are some things the team must do to be successful?

4. Why are team-building exercises used at Next Door Food Store?

5. Is there any evidence that the DGIT Team has been successful?

6. How would being part of a self-directed work team, such as the DGIT Team, increase motivation?

7. The DGIT Team members are seeking ways to eliminate their own jobs. What would motivate them to do this?

8. According to DGIT Team members, what are the advantages of "being out in the field"?

http://www.nextdoor1.com/

LIGHTEN UP
"NORMS"

"Norm" is likely to bring to mind Norm Peterson, the jovial, rotund regular on *Cheers. Cheers,* a long-running television program set in a Boston pub, had a cast of characters that exchanged jokes, stories, and insults in the comfort of "a place where everybody knows your name." The characters on *Cheers* did, in fact, share a variety of norms. For example, members shared expectations about where the regulars should sit, how regulars entering the bar

should be greeted, what subjects were acceptable for discussion, and how Cheers' patrons should react to challenges from outsiders. An ongoing gag was the "Normisms," Norm's replies to those greeting him when he entered the bar. For a collection of "Normisms," go to:

http://home1.gte.net/badger85/norm!.htm

CONCRETE CANOES AND SUBSURFACE PAINTBALL

Some teambuilding approaches move outside the office. For instance, many companies send their employees to outdoor "challenge courses" where team members must work together to complete tasks such as climbing walls, weaving their ways through webs of rope, and passing a hula hoop around a circle while holding hands. Other firms send their teams on caving, camping, sailing, or rock climbing outings. Some activities are even more innovative. Companies may, for instance, dispatch their teams to battle in a subsurface paintball complex or have them build and race concrete canoes.[25] The idea of these exercises is to encourage team members to develop team spirit by jointly facing adversity and overcoming challenges. Facilitators work with the teams to point out how the activities parallel the work environment.

Thirteen

CHAPTER

SKILLS OBJECTIVES

> To perform a self-evaluation of the management skills acquired in this book.
> To develop a personal management skills mastery plan for the future.
> To apply management skills from a systematic and integrated approach.

KNOWLEDGE OBJECTIVES

> Explain steps involved in planning ongoing skills learning.
> Identify opportunities for management skills learning while still in school.
> Explain how an organization is a marketplace for skills.
> Discuss how reading of popular management books and journals can enhance learning.
> Understand how professional associations, participation in local business and community activities, and networking can facilitate ongoing skill development.
> Describe some approaches to finding stretching assignments at work.
> Identify alternative ways to foster your formal continuing education.

Now that you are nearing completion of this course, you may be tempted to believe that you can put aside thoughts of developing management skills and move onto other things. Resist the temptation. Management skills require lifelong learning and constant practice. The growing importance and awareness of lifelong skills learning is becoming increasingly clear, as seen in Al Gore's proposal during his presidential campaign for a tax credit to foster "lifelong learning accounts" for education and training.[1]

Recall that this text has used as its foundation a social learning approach, consisting of skills assessment, skills awareness, skills attainment, and skills application. This approach differs from that of many conventional texts in its strong skills emphasis and from experiential exercise texts in its provision of conceptual underpinnings for skills. The text's strong skills emphasis is consistent with a chorus of calls from businesspersons, educators, and politicians for greater skills focus in business education. As we have discussed in previous chapters, social learning approaches have been used very successfully in business and other settings. In addition, experimental evidence in classroom settings shows social learning approaches to be superior to experiential education that emphasizes applying skills before learning about their conceptual foundations.[2]

We have used the social learning process to help you to develop an array of important management skills. To be successful in the workplace, you will both have to properly apply those skills and to continually update your skills portfolio. To facilitate that process, we use this chapter to encourage you to look ahead toward your career and its associated opportunities and demands. We begin with a discussion of planning for ongoing skills learning, offer tips for how you can continue to develop management skills while still in school, and encourage you to think of organizations as skills marketplaces and incubators. We then provide some guidelines for continued reading for ongoing skills development and give you suggestions for participating in professional associations and networks. We conclude with advice for seeking stretching assignments at work, making use of Web resources, and exploring continuing education options.

PLAN FOR ONGOING SKILLS LEARNING

When asked about his presidential ambitions, former New York governor Mario Cuomo once said, "I have no plans, and no plans to plan." If you are going to build a strong and sustaining management skills portfolio, you will need to plan, and to plan to plan on an ongoing basis.

MAP AND TRACK YOUR SKILLS PORTFOLIO

Your skills portfolio will be critical to your career. Be aware of what is in the portfolio and what is needed. On a regular basis, stop and conduct a self-assessment of your management skills. As a starter, complete Self-Assessment 13-1. Then, go back and redo the Self-Assessment Exercises in previous chapters to see whether your "before" and "after" scores differ and to pinpoint those areas that need more work. Maintain a written record of your skill development activities and of skills in which you are proficient. When writing or updating your résumé, be sure to highlight your skill proficiencies.

599

Chapter 13   Looking Ahead: Maintaining and Enhancing Your Management Skills Portfolio

Assessment
Assessment
Assessment
Assessment
Assessment

DEVIL'S ADVOCATE

We covered a *lot* of information in this course. How can we possibly remember all this?

First of all, it's not realistic or appropriate to expect you to simply memorize all the information in this book. Remember that one objective of this book was to stretch your mind in terms of exposing you to key management concepts, models, and principles. You can't be an effective "doer" until you have a solid foundation of general management and organizational behavior knowledge. In other words, you need to develop an effective personal management philosophy that helps you to think through the tough issues and dilemmas you will face in the "real world."

The second focus of this book was to provide you with as many opportunities to develop actual management skills as possible. The skill activities and assignments were designed to reinforce the knowledge you acquired and to link it to specific skill applications.

So, although there was a lot of information that was covered, view it as part of the process of developing the way of thinking about management that you will need and the translation of that knowledge into application in terms of the management skills that are critical for success.

There are so many "differences" that you say we need to acknowledge to be effective managers. How can we adapt to so many differences effectively?

Yes, there are a lot of differences to worry about. We have talked about personality factors, communication styles, perceptual differences, decision-making styles, attitudes, and conflict-handling styles, not to mention differences due to such demographic variables as age, gender, race, and nationality. Although this is a lot to remember, the underlying management principle is that understanding people with whom you work or whom you manage puts you in a better position to work with them. For example, suppose that you know that the CEO of your company has a finance background, is numbers-oriented, and emphasizes the bottom line (i.e., financial performance) of the organization. This would then suggest to you that any presentation you make to that CEO had better provide financial data or a cost analysis associated with any recommendations you make as well as an analysis of the impact that implementation of your ideas would have on the firm in financial terms (e.g., increased profits, lower costs). If you did not do this, the CEO probably would not be very happy with you.

So remember: Everyone with whom you deal in an organization has a unique style. The challenge for you is to adapt your style (within limits, of course) in a way that is compatible with those with whom you deal on your job as manager.

What advice would you give students regarding ways in which they can develop their management skills further?

This is a great question. The best step that you can take is to get involved in activities outside the class-

room at your college or university. Student organizations are a logical choice. If you join, remember that it doesn't do you any good to just pay your membership dues and then not get involved at all. Many employers are attracted to job candidates who are "well rounded" and have demonstrated an ability to juggle multiple responsibilities in their lives (e.g., going to school, holding a part-time job, and being the president of a student organization). So, if you join, seek out a leadership position (e.g., committee leader) that will give you responsibility for a project or activity (e.g., fund raising, social events, speakers) and the opportunity to manage a team of committee members. The experience you can gain from this kind of involvement can be invaluable! You can also perform volunteer work at a local not-for-profit organization or work on an independent research project with a faculty member that will give you a chance to do some "hands-on" work with an organization. For example, some students have evaluated various policies, programs, or systems in real-world organizations and have made recommendations to management regarding things that can be done to enhance employee or organizational effectiveness. These kinds of projects not only show students how the things that they are learning in the classroom relate to the real world but provide exactly the kind of challenge that students need to develop real management skills.

Self-Assessment 13-1
Skills Portfolio

Answer each of the questions in this section using the following scale:

1 = Disagree Strongly
2 = Disagree Somewhat
3 = Neither Agree nor Disagree
4 = Agree Somewhat
5 = Agree Strongly

I have a good basic mastery of the following skills:

1. _____ Active listening
2. _____ Time management
3. _____ Developing an action plan
4. _____ Self-management
5. _____ Developing a strategic plan
6. _____ Using tools for creativity enhancement
7. _____ Setting goals
8. _____ Developing a power base
9. _____ Applying the general problem-solving process
10. _____ Managing informal communication
11. _____ Empowering employees
12. _____ Managing undesired employee behaviors
13. _____ Assessing organizational culture
14. _____ Designing and implementing employee attitude surveys
15. _____ Handling ethical dilemmas
16. _____ Applying job design principles to enhance employee motivation
17. _____ Personal stress management
18. _____ Effective speaking
19. _____ Using transformational leader behaviors
20. _____ Becoming an effective mentor
21. _____ Reducing political activity
22. _____ Conflict management
23. _____ Managing change
24. _____ Evaluating a team process
25. _____ Developing a mission statement
26. _____ Assessing employee job satisfaction
27. _____ Sensitivity to cross-cultural differences
28. _____ Applying the balanced scorecard
29. _____ Understanding and managing nonverbal communications
30. _____ Conducting a job interview
31. _____ Conducting a performance appraisal
32. _____ Critical thinking
33. _____ Facilitating effective team meetings
34. _____ Diagnosing team functioning
35. _____ Applying impression management techniques

DEVELOP A SKILLS ACTION PLAN

Develop a plan for maintaining and reinforcing your current skills and for developing new skills. In developing your plan, recognize that you have to be aiming at a moving target. In an interview, one young woman was asked what she thought she would be doing in 20 years. She replied, "That job hasn't been invented yet." [3] Hockey great Wayne Gretzky is credited with explaining his success by saying, "I skate to where the puck is going, not to where it is." [4] Similarly, Margaret Schweer, director of human resources for information systems at Kraft Foods, says of training programs that "It's not just giving people skills for where they are now but for where they're going." [5] You will need to learn the skills "where the puck is going." Fortunately, the puck appears to be going in generally predictable directions, although with increasing speed. For example, demands for interpersonal skills, problem-solving skills, and communication skills will almost certainly become even more important in future decades. Nevertheless, be alert to new developments in your company, industry, or society in general that may place value on new, perhaps now unimaginable, skills and perspectives.

IDENTIFY ROLE MODELS

One good way in which to recognize desirable skills and behaviors is to identify role models whose skills you would like to emulate. A role model could be anyone whose behaviors and accomplishments you've admired, such as a boss, a famous executive, someone from an annual listing of "best managers," a teacher, or a parent. Once you've decided you want to "be like Mike" or like Steve, or Fiorina, or Jack, focus on the behaviors of the role model. Recall from our discussions of social learning in previous chapters that when modeling others, you do not want to simply mimic them; rather, you want to learn *from* them. They may be in different contexts, have different backgrounds, be attending to different goals, and so on. Your task is to develop skills based on their examples and to apply those skills in the ways that are required in your unique situation.

USE SELF-MANAGEMENT FOR SKILL LEARNING

Once you have identified skills that you would like to develop or maintain, apply the self-management principles you learned in Chapter 9. That is, treat each skill as a behavior to be changed or reinforced. Pinpoint the specific behavior, set specific goals for behavior change, and set up a system of rewards to reinforce skill learning. Systematically monitor the behavior to track your progress and develop contingency plans in case your initial attempts at skill learning or maintenance are unsuccessful.

PRACTICE, PRACTICE, PRACTICE

There is an old joke about a person who gets into a cab in New York City and asks the driver, "Do you know how to get to Carnegie Hall?" The driver's reply of "Practice, practice, practice" also provides the directions to mastering a job, moving toward the executive suite, or having a fulfilling career. Use every chance you get to practice your management skills.

COORDINATE YOUR SKILLS

We have talked about skills as being in a portfolio or tool kit. As with any tools, it is important not just that you learn how to use them but that you use them together in proper ways. For one thing, resist the temptation to simply apply a new skill to every problem you find: It has been said that "If all you have is a hammer, everything looks like a nail." Just as each construction job requires a specific combination of tools, often used in a particular order and in concert with one another, organizational tasks require a proper balance and combination of skills. This suggests that you should take advantage of opportunities for learning, practicing, and using management skills that require you to employ them together.

Skills Practice 13-1 is an in-class activity that will give you the opportunity to immerse yourself in a fun and "hands-on" activity that requires the use of a variety of management skills.

Skills Practice 13-1
You Be the Manager!

Skill Level: **Challenging**

Skill Objective
To develop an integrated and systematic approach for using personal, interpersonal, and management skills for the completion of an unstructured group task.

Procedure
1. You will need to work in groups of six to eight students for this exercise.
2. After you have formed your groups, your instructor will randomly select a formal leader for this exercise.
3. Once the leader has been selected, read the description of the group task that follows.

Overview of the Group's Task
Your task is to work with your team leader to develop and present a *highly creative 20- to 30-second TV advertisement to sell a product or service* with which you all are familiar. Some teams in the past have selected cars, famous restaurants, airlines, hotels, food, or beverages for this activity. The specific product or service you select is not critical so long as at least some of the members of the team have some familiarity with it. *Note that every member of your team must play some role or part in the presentation of the advertisement.*

Your instructor will have flip chart paper and markers if you want to use them for your advertisement.

You will have 30 minutes to develop and practice your advertisement before you must present it to the class. Your classmates will evaluate the quality of your advertisement in terms of whether the length of your advertisement was within the 20- to 30-second range, the degree to which all members of the team participated in the advertisement, and the degree of originality reflected in your advertisement.

Good luck and have fun!!

4. Your instructor will now tell you to start working on your task. He or she will keep track of time and stop you after 30 minutes, so watch your time!
5. Remember that you will need to develop *and* present your advertisement to the class and that everyone on the team must be involved in presenting the advertisement to the rest of the class.
6. After time has been called, present your advertisement to the class, ask your classmates to evaluate it, and then discuss the following questions as a class.

Discussion Questions
1. Describe your team's process in terms of how you approached the task that you were given to complete. What were the key challenges that you faced in completing this task? What did you do to try to overcome them?

2. Evaluate your team's process. In what ways was it effective? Ineffective? What did the team leader do to try to facilitate the process?
3. What types of general skills were needed to be successful in completing this task? Why?
4. What types of management skills were needed to be successful in completing this task?
5. Suppose that you were asked to repeat this exercise again by developing another creative advertisement for the same product or service you used the first time. What would you do the same to enhance your success the second time? What would you do differently?
6. What are the practical implications of this exercise for you as a future manager?

SEEK OUT LEARNING OPPORTUNITIES WHILE IN SCHOOL

While much of your ongoing skill learning will take place once you've entered a work environment, there are also many good opportunities to acquire management skills while in school. Here are some options to consider:

Internships[6] Most business schools have internship opportunities to give students the chance to experience realistic business environments. According to the National Society for Internships and Experiential Education, an internship is "any carefully monitored work or service experience in which an individual has intentional learning goals and reflects actively on what he or she is learning throughout the experience."[7] Individuals participating in internships receive hands-on training while contributing real, productive work to the organization. Often, the internship serves as a "trying out" period in which companies and individuals see whether they fit one another before making a longer-term commitment. Some internships now provide competitive salaries and benefits.[8]

Independent Studies Many colleges and universities offer students the opportunity to take independent studies. These typically permit students to earn credits for working one-to-one with a faculty member to explore an interesting issue. If, for example, you want to learn more about team building or conflict management, you might approach a faculty member who has an interest in one of those areas. Requirements for the independent study will vary but generally are tailored to fit a student's particular needs and interests.

Student Organizations Student organizations provide the opportunity to participate in many management-related activities, develop management skills, and adopt leadership roles. Two such organizations are Sigma Iota Epsilon and AIESEC. Sigma Iota Epsilon is both an honorary and a professional management society. Its goals are to stimulate interest and achievement in the field of management, to stimulate scholarship in management, and to gain recognition of the contribution and value of scholastic achievement in the management discipline.

http://www.fsu.edu/~sie/

The world's largest student organization, AIESEC is a global network of 50,000 members across more than 85 countries and territories at more than

Web Wise

InternReview.com*

In considering internship options, learn all you can about what you will be doing. While some internships offer challenge, responsibility, and the opportunity to develop important skills, others are filled with "make-work" assignments. One group of Carnegie Mellon business and computer science students, many of whom had poor internship experiences, founded a website called *InternReview.com*. The site contains students' reports of their internship experiences, permits searching for internship reviews by company, lets students submit résumés to apply for internships, and has other links.

http://www.InternReview.com/

* J. Dash, "Student Interns Hand Out Mixed Grades to Employers," *Computerworld*, October 2, 2000, p. 42.

800 universities worldwide.[9] AIESEC's primary activity is facilitation of work-abroad exchange programs between its member countries. AIESEC in the United States sends students from the United States to work abroad and receives students from around the world to work for companies in the United States.

http://www.aiesec.org/

Team Projects   Treat team projects as a chance to practice management skills. After all, a team project is in many ways typical of the project management tasks that you will face in the work environment. Think of the team project as a relatively low-risk way to try out your skills at motivating team members, exhibiting leader behaviors, managing conflicts, and communicating effectively.

In the nearby Voice of Experience, Maria Bahr and Amie Crohn, two seniors majoring in management at the University of Wisconsin-Madison, talk about how they have developed valuable "real-world" management skills and how you can do the same.

VOICE OF EXPERIENCE

THINGS WE HAVE LEARNED ABOUT MANAGEMENT IN COLLEGE

*Maria Bahr,
Undergraduate
Management Student,
University of Wisconsin-Madison*

*Amie Crohn,
Undergraduate
Management Student,
University of Wisconsin-Madison*

1. What are the most valuable concepts you have learned (knowledge) about management during your college experience?

(Maria) I would say that my management classes have taught me the importance of teamwork, developing a systematic approach, and maintaining a strategic focus on achieving desired outcomes. Everything must be driven by your "bottom-line" objectives.

(Amie) I feel that I learned the importance of understanding the mission statement of an organization and thinking about how to achieve that mission on an ongoing basis. The principles of effective teamwork have also been emphasized in my classes. I also have learned a lot about the emphasis on decentralized organizations and employee empowerment as a popular organizational model. Finally, I would say that I really recognize the importance of managing employee satisfaction effectively since it has such an important influence on retention.

2. What are the most valuable real-world management skills that you have acquired during your college experience?

(Maria) I have really developed skills in the areas of managing conflict effectively, working with a diverse group of individuals, and giving and accepting feedback (both positive and negative). I have also developed the skill of being able to lead peers through my leadership roles in student organizations and other extracurricular activities. Related to this, I have really learned how to delegate. Although this sounds like an easy thing to do, it is not. The tendency is to want to do it all yourself, but you learn that you have to trust other people to handle certain responsibilities. This helps you to focus on issues that are more critical to your personal success. Finally, I feel that I have developed the skills of recognizing and rewarding people effectively. Sometimes you do this in small ways (such as just saying "Thanks"), but it really matters to people, and it is a great motivator.

(Amie) I think that the ability to effectively manage a project has been a critical skill I have acquired in college. The numerous group projects I had to complete in my classes, my involvement in the Students in Free Enterprise

Skills Practice 13-2 is actually a "project" that gives you an opportunity to step out into the real world and examine how many of the issues related to management exist in actual organizations. This will require some extra work on your part, but it will definitely be worth it when you see how many management concepts and issues discussed earlier in this book "come to life." In addition, completing this project will help you to develop self-management skills (and teamwork skills, if you do this project with another student).

Skills Practice 13-2
Field Work Experiences in Management and Organizational Behavior

Skill Level: Challenging

Skill Objectives

1. To use management knowledge and analytical skills to study and evaluate management problems and challenges in real-world organizational settings.
2. To develop the management skills needed to complete complex projects.

---

competition team, and a management consulting project I completed for a class were all extremely helpful in developing this skill. I think that I have developed skill in understanding the needs of "internal customers" and how to satisfy those needs using a strategic approach. I also have learned how to link data with the identification of specific action steps. Finally, I would echo Maria in that I have developed skills in the areas of leadership and delegation.

3. **Which specific learning experiences during your college careers have been the most valuable in helping you to learn about management and to development of real-world management skills?**

    (Maria) For me, being the president of a student organization, doing a semester-long management consulting project with the

University Health Service, my internships with South Central Wisconsin Center and Firstar Bank, and my role as vice president of my sorority have been the most valuable learning experiences.

(Amie) I would say the same kinds of things have been the most beneficial to me. Again, my involvement in the Students in Free Enterprise team, my management consulting project with the Wisconsin Union, my role as president of a student organization, and my internship at Cargill have all been truly fantastic learning experiences.

4. **What advice would you give other students regarding the things that they can do to learn about management and to develop management skills in preparation for the real world?**

    (Maria) Get an internship and obtain some relevant work experience! In your internship, be as-

sertive and ask for more responsibility and challenge. Join a student organization and get involved. Ask yourself, "How can I add value to this organization?" The key is to take advantage of opportunities for learning and developing leadership skills outside the classroom.

(Amie) Recognize that it's not just what you know but also whom you know. You need to develop relationships with people who can help you to develop yourself professionally. This would include academic advisors, professors, teaching assistants, career advisors, business professionals, and your fellow students! Also, don't burn bridges with people. This can come back to haunt you in the future. Finally, think "outside the box" by creating opportunities for yourself. Don't wait for them to fall into your lap. Get out there and make a difference!

Procedure

1. Decide whether you want to complete this project as an individual or in a group. (Many students in the past have preferred working in teams.)

2. Identify a manager who might be willing to work with you for this project. If you don't know someone personally, ask your instructors, alumni office, career placement service, friends, and family for the names of working managers who might be willing to help you out. Not-for-profit organizations are often very willing to work with students on these kinds of projects as well.

3. Once you have found a manager who is willing to work with you, discuss what you would like to do with that individual. Some examples of projects that students have completed in the past include:

   > Evaluating the functioning of a work team and developing recommendations for enhancing its effectiveness.

   > Evaluating the design and implementation of a specific change in an organization and making recommendations for improving the process in the future.

   > Assessing employee job satisfaction, identifying key areas of dissatisfaction, and developing recommendations for enhancing job satisfaction.

   > Assessing the culture of an organization and evaluating its effectiveness in relation to the organization's mission and objectives.

   > Assessing levels of job stress of employees and formulating action steps to reduce or eliminate the causes of stress,

   > Analyzing the reasons why employees choose to leave an organization and developing recommendations for increasing retention behavior.

   > Evaluating a management process or system (e.g., customer service, sales, production, product development) and developing recommendations for enhancing its effectiveness.

   Note that these are just examples of the types of projects that students have completed in the past. The best one for you will be based on what you and the manager with whom you are working are interested in and the amount of time that you are expected to devote to this project by your instructor.

4. Once you have selected an appropriate topic and focus for your project, work with your instructor and the manager to develop a basic plan for completing the project. Be sure that you have a clear and fairly tight focus for this project. Also, be clear how you will go about achieving your objective. How will you collect your data? Personal interviews? A survey? Reviewing documents and data given to you by the manager? Finally, have a clear idea of how your final product will look. At a minimum, you would want to present a written summary of your project to your instructor and manager, describing what you did, what you found, and what you recommend.

5. After you have completed this project, discuss the following questions as a class.

Discussion Questions

1. What are the key concepts you learned about management in organizations, based on completing this project?

2. Which management concepts, principles, and issues discussed in this book were most relevant and valuable to you in conducting your analysis and in making your recommendations to management? Why?

3. What were the most significant challenges that you faced in completing this project?

4. What types of management skills did you need to successfully complete this project?

5. If you were to repeat this process, what would you do in the same way as you did the first time? What would you do differently? Why?

6. What are the practical implications of this project for you as a future manager?

VIEW ORGANIZATIONS AS MARKETPLACES FOR—AND INCUBATORS OF—SKILLS

In seeking a job, be sure to gather information on which skills are especially valued in the firms that you consider and what the firm does to help employees to develop and reinforce the skills; the answers will give you valuable insights about your "fit" to the firms and may also speak volumes about the firms' cultures. Some firms may value certain skills because of their unique cultures, histories, and environments. If your skills are similar to those valued, you are likely to achieve "supplementary fit." That is, your skills will match those already prevalent in the firm. Alternatively, firms may be seeking particular skills because they are now lacking in the firm, perhaps because of a new strategic direction. In such cases, you may achieve "complementary fit"; your skills, while different from those currently found in the firm, are now needed and valued. You may be especially valuable in such situations, though you may be viewed by others, at least initially, as "different."

You can sometimes glean information about valued skills from job interviews, observation, and reading articles about firms. As an example of the latter, much has been written about how Southwest Airlines values employees who have the skills and attitudes needed to fit well into its environment of "fun." In addition, some firms may make their skills preferences and requirements explicit, such as through tests given during selection or after hiring. At Sears, Roebuck & Co., for example, new employees are tested not just on technical skills but on such specific "soft skills" as the abilities to manage projects, work with people outside the firm (e.g., vendors), build teams, and lead others.[10]

Some firms, such as AT&T, British Airways, BP, Siemens, and The World Bank, even have "ideal profiles" of skills for future executives.[11] For example, Siemens has defined 22 desirable management characteristics under five basic competencies of understanding, drive, trust, social competence, and what it terms a "sixth sense." Pepsico's desired competency profile has 18 key dimensions defining how individuals see the world, think, and act. Such firms typically use systematic training and development programs to develop managers in ways that fit the "ideal profiles." Many companies now recognize as well that strong skills training programs do more than just develop employees; in an age when skills portfolios are the key to career success, strong company training programs are an important tool for recruiting and retaining employees.[12]

In the nearby Voice of Experience, Brenda Schauf discusses management skills needed to succeed in the real world.

READ WIDELY AND BUILD A MANAGEMENT-SKILLS LIBRARY

The amount of material we have asked you to digest in this book may seem daunting. The thought of doing even more extensive reading on an ongoing basis may appear overwhelming. Here's the good news to keep in mind: Life is an open-book test. If you're aware of concepts and information sources and you know how to access them, memorization usually isn't necessary.

READ POPULAR MANAGEMENT BOOKS

Such books as *In Search of Excellence* and *Theory Z* helped to spawn a remarkable number of tomes offering practical advice to managers. The popularity of such books is seen in the fact that many make their way to the *New York Times* bestseller list. The books may focus on a particular topic, such as organizational culture or reward systems; may provide guidance for specific career issues, such as entering a management position or making career moves; or may offer the philosophies and perspectives of particular executives, consultants, or business professors. Some of these books provide excellent advice, and we have quoted from, or otherwise referenced, many of them in this text. We encourage you to sample broadly from such sources. You will learn about particular firms and individuals and may see how popular management tools are being applied.

VOICE OF EXPERIENCE

MANAGEMENT SKILLS NEEDED IN THE REAL WORLD

Brenda Schauf
Assistant Store Manager and
Human Resources Manager
Marshall Field's

1. What do you see as the key management challenges you face in your job?

Offering prospective and current team members a positive work experience has been a significant challenge in recent years. We need to find ways to make our team members' work experience enjoyable so that they will want to remain employed with us. Part of the reason for this concern is increasing competition in the retail industry and a very tight labor market. This means that people have a lot of job opportunities available to them with various retailers, so we have to work hard to make ourselves attractive as an employer.

Another significant challenge is how to create a work environment that is performance-driven. We need to continue to find ways to provide better service to our customers. So, the bottom line here is a paradox: How do we make work more enjoyable for our team members and at the same time ask them to work harder?

2. What kinds of strategies are you implementing in addressing these challenges?

We make sure that we provide top-notch training for all of our team members. This is critical so that they feel they possess the knowledge and skills needed to be successful in their jobs. New employees also "buddy up" with a team trainer who helps them "learn the ropes" associated with their new jobs. Managers of new employees make sure that they maintain regular interaction with employees during their first 90 days of employment. This involves coaching, providing feedback, and clarifying performance expectations with employees.

In the recruiting and selection process, we try to provide job candidates with a "realistic job preview" so that there are no surprises later. If we oversell a job in order to hire a given employee, we will probably just lose that person later when he or she realizes that the job is not consistent with his or her expectations (i.e., not as good as he or she thought it would be).

We spend a lot of time on employee recognition. We have tried some creative and fun types of events, such as employee luncheons, treats, and morning rallies before the store opens. The rallies are especially interesting in that we try to communicate a point about customer service to our employees by presenting skits based on game shows, such as "Who Wants to Be a Millionaire?" or the "Price is Right." Our team members have responded very favorably to these kinds of events.

3. What do you feel are the most critical management skills that are needed for success in today's business environment?

I would have to say that being responsive and managing change are the most critical skills. We

In reading such books, though, maintain a critical eye. For instance, recognize that issues are complex and question such flat statements as "change is good" or "money doesn't motivate." Be skeptical as well of argument by assertion, where the author simply states something to be the case with no support other than his or her personal authority. Also, be cautious when an author relies heavily on argument by anecdote, using supporting examples instead of logically convincing arguments or data. The fact that a particular characteristic or practice is seen in successful firms doesn't necessarily mean that it caused that success. The characteristic or practice may, for instance, be just as common—or even more common—in unsuccessful firms. To really learn anything about whether something is important to success, it would be necessary to consider successful and unsuccessful firms with and without the characteristic or practice. Unfortunately, anecdotes are powerful; we tend to

have a saying around here that "speed is life." To us, this reflects the importance of adapting to a changing business environment (e.g., technological, customer, economic) as a critical skill for success.

Leadership is still a critical skill as well. Managers absolutely must have the ability to provide a vision and to get their team to respond effectively to their directives.

4. What advice would you give to college students regarding their preparation for a job as a supervisor or manager in an organization?

I would strongly recommend getting some experience running or leading something while you are still in school. Becoming a leader or running a committee in a student organization really helps develop exactly the kinds of leadership skills that we look for in the retailing industry. I'm sure that many other employers feel the same way.

If you are able to become a supervisor in a restaurant or become a resident advisor in a dormitory, these are other fantastic ways to develop leadership skills. The key here is that even though the context is different in the business world, the management skills you acquire from your college learning experiences transfer very well to a wide variety of real-world management jobs.

5. What advice would you give to students who obtain nonmanagerial jobs immediately after graduation but want to be promoted to a managerial position in the future?

Be prepared to work your way up in an organization. If you are interested in getting promoted to a management position, be sure to make it known to your boss and others in your organization. Don't expect them to be able to read your mind! Work to develop relationships with people in your organization who can help you to achieve your career goals. Ask to take on additional responsibilities that go beyond your regular job duties and responsibilities. Volunteer to take on new projects. This will give you an opportunity to show what you can do and to develop the right kinds of skills needed for advancement to a management position.

6. What advice would you give to students who are first-time managers in real-world business organizations regarding the key things they should do to be successful?

Again, be sure to work on establishing strong working relationships with others in your organization. Recognize that you do not know everything—take the time to "learn the ropes." Be sensitive to how people with more experience may perceive you. Again, don't act like you know everything. Finally, be open to honest feedback, both positive and negative. This is what you will need in order to improve your performance as a manager and to ultimately grow as a business professional.

http://www.marshallfields.com/

believe a specific example more than statistics. As such, you will need to be especially alert to the seduction of anecdotes.

READ PRACTITIONER-ORIENTED MANAGEMENT JOURNALS

We have drawn from many sources in developing this text, including many practitioner-oriented journals. For example, we have regularly used examples and information from such sources as *Across the Board, Business Week, Chief Executive, Executive Excellence, Forbes, Fortune, HR Focus, HRMagazine, INC., Incentive, Industry Week, Personnel Journal, Quality, Supervision, Supervisory Management, Management Review, Management Today, Training, Training & Development,* and *Workforce.* Other journals from which we've cited, such as *Black Enterprise* and *Working Woman,* are aimed at specific audiences. Still others, such as *Business Europe, Business Mexico,* and *China Business Review,* focus on particular geographic areas. These are all worthwhile outlets; when you get a chance, go to a library or bookstore and look through some of the issues to see which journals best fit your interests and style preferences.

The following journals are noteworthy in their efforts to bring recent research and theory to practitioner audiences. As such, they are in a sense hybrids between "scholarly" journals that report research and theory primarily aimed at academics and more "popular press" management magazines. If you are really interested in keeping up on the latest developments in management, we encourage you to consider them.

> *Academy of Management Executive (AME).* A publication of the Academy of Management, *AME* aims to provide practicing executives with relevant management tools and information based on recent advances in management theory and research. *AME* directly supports the Academy of Management's main objectives, which are to foster the general advancement of research, learning, teaching, and practice in the management field and to encourage the extension and unification of management knowledge.

http://Ame.bschool.unc.edu/

> *California Management Review (CMR).* CMR serves as a vehicle of communication between those who study management and those who practice it. *CMR* publishes articles that are both research-based and address issues of current concern to managers. *CMR* emphasizes three areas of critical importance to both practicing managers and academic researchers: strategy and organization, global competition and competitiveness, and business and public policy.

http://www.haas.berkeley.edu/News/cmr/

> *Harvard Business Review (HBR).* The goal of *HBR* is to be the source of the best new ideas for people who are creating, leading, and transforming business. Features in *HBR* help business leaders to establish an intellectual agenda for discussion—and change—within their companies. They give firsthand insight into how companies operate and how senior-level managers respond to demanding workplace challenges, describe best practices and hands-on management techniques, report on

cutting-edge research and its application in real organizations, and draw on the experiences of executives, consultants, and other experts.

http://www.hbsp.harvard.edu/products/hbr/index.html

> *Journal of Management Inquiry (JMI). JMI* publishes the latest research and practice written by today's top management scholars and professionals from a wide variety of areas within the management and organization field. Sponsored by the Western Academy of Management, *JMI* seeks to provide an outlet for creative, frame-challenging work.

http://www.sagepub.co.uk/journals/details/j0154.html

> *Organizational Dynamics.* The domain of *Organizational Dynamics* is organizational behavior and development, human resource management, and strategic management. The journal's objective is to link leading-edge thought and research with management practice. *Organizational Dynamics* publishes articles that embody both theoretical and practical content, showing how research findings can help to deal more effectively with the dynamics of organizational life.

http://www.elsevier.nl/locate/issn/00902616

> *Sloan Management Review. Sloan Management Review* bridges the gap between management research and practice, evaluating and reporting on new research to help readers to identify and understand significant trends in management. Published by the MIT Sloan School of Management, the journal covers all management disciplines, although its particular emphasis is on corporate strategy, leadership, and management of technology and innovation.

http://Mitsloan.mit.edu/smr/index.html

There are likely to be times when you will read an article or book and would like to know more about its topic. One good way to do this is to simply go straight to the source and contact the author. You will find that authors are generally very pleased to learn of interest in their work and to share information. Many articles provide contact information for authors, often including e-mail addresses. If you would like to find e-mail addresses and other information for authors, you can often locate their websites through a simple Internet search. Alternatively, many professional associations, including some of those listed in the following pages, have searchable membership pages. For instance, the Academy of Management Member Search page is located at aomdb.pace.edu/membership/. You can access that page to get contact information for the more than 10,000 members of the Academy of Management.

READ BROADLY

We don't mean to imply that you should restrict your reading to management books and journals. To the contrary, we encourage you to read broadly, whether Shakespeare, Steinbeck, Sartre, or Spillane. In doing so, though, keep some part of your mind open to skills-learning opportunities. One of the many rewards of reading is the insights that literature reveals about the varieties, causes, and consequences of human behavior (i.e., about the stuff of management).

Read the scenario in the nearby Real-World Management Challenge and develop an action plan for handling the situation. This was an actual challenge with which Kodak had to deal. You will be able to compare what you come up with against the actions that management actually took to handle the situation.

Real-World Management Challenge

Regaining Focus at Eastman Kodak

The Situation

Eastman Kodak, based in Rochester, New York, is engaged in developing, manufacturing, and marketing imaging products and services. The company has a global workforce of approximately 80,650 employees.[†]

During much of the 1990s, Kodak struggled to reinvent itself in response to increasing price competition from rival Fuji from Japan, stagnating growth in its traditional film business, and the emergence of digital technologies that competed with (or in some cases replaced) Kodak's traditional businesses. These challenges have had a dramatic, negative effect on the company's earnings and stock price.

Most recently (January 1, 2000), Dan Carp assumed the position of CEO at Kodak. It has been a rough ride for him so far. His number one management challenge is how to successfully implement the company's transition from its dependence on traditional film businesses to a digital world. Although Kodak is in the digital camera business, it has thus far failed to realize its full market potential. One concern is that Kodak does not appear to have a clear and coherent strategy to drive the transition. In addition, it has not been able to leverage its technology to develop truly innovative digital products that create passion among consumers.

What Would You Do?

Suppose that you were given the challenge of enhancing Eastman Kodak's performance. What would you do? Be as specific as possible in developing the various elements of your action plan.

Source: G. Smith, "Will Kodak's Carp Miss His Photo Op?" *Business Week,* October 9, 2000, p. 52.
[†]www.biz.yahoo.com.

Now, see what you can do with the management knowledge and skills that you have developed from reading this book. Skills Practice 13-3 gives you a chance to analyze a "real-world" organization that is of interest to you. Complete the exercise and then evaluate your analysis and recommendations.

Skills Practice 13-3
Self-Generated Case in Management

Skill Level: Basic

Skill Objective

To apply your management analytical skills to a case study of an organization that is of particular interest to you.

Procedure

1. Search the print media (e.g., *New York Times, Washington Post, Business Week, Fortune, Wall Street Journal*) or the Internet for an article (or articles) about an especially successful or unsuccessful organization that is of interest to you. For example, this may

be a *Fortune 500* company, a global company, or a not-for-profit organization. The key here is that you are interested in the organization.

2. Read the article(s) and identify what management has done to contribute to the effectiveness (or ineffectiveness) of the organization. Try to be very specific.

3. Now, assume that you are a member of management at the organization discussed in your article(s) and develop a basic action plan (set of recommendations) for addressing the current situation. If the organization is doing well, focus on what would have to be done to sustain its success. If the company is doing poorly, focus on what has to be done to address the key problems it is facing.

4. Write a memo to the CEO of the company making an argument for why he or she should implement your recommendations. Use knowledge that you have acquired in earlier chapters to support your case.

Discussion Questions

1. Evaluate the process you used to analyze the organization on which you focused for this exercise. What did you do well? What did you not do so well?

2. Evaluate the action plan you developed. What are its strengths and weaknesses?

3. Evaluate your memo to the CEO of the organization. What are its strengths and weaknesses?

4. What are the practical implications of this exercise for you as a future manager?

PARTICIPATE IN PROFESSIONAL ASSOCIATIONS, LOCAL ACTIVITIES, AND NETWORKS

Professional associations and networking offer a wealth of opportunities for ongoing skills development. In this section, we discuss some primary professional associations that you might want to explore, suggest ways to get involved in business and community activities, and provide some guidelines for developing and using physical and virtual networks.

GET INVOLVED IN PROFESSIONAL ASSOCIATIONS

Many prominent professional associations deal with management and related areas. Participation in these organizations provides contacts, information about new developments, opportunities for interaction at meetings and events, and, in some cases, the chance to adopt leadership roles. We encourage you to think about membership in one or more of the following professional associations. By visiting the associations' Web pages, you will get a better sense of the things that they offer (including many things for nonmembers). In some cases, there are also local and regional branches of the professional associations. Also, some of the associations offer special student memberships at reduced rates. In addition to these organizations, you should consider joining associations, such as Toastmasters, that focus on developing specific skills.

> **Academy of Management.** With 10,000 members in more than 80 countries, the Academy of Management is a professional society composed of professors who conduct research and teach management in colleges, universities, or research institutions and of doctoral students who are pursuing degrees in management. Members also include management consultants and managers from a variety of business settings. The purpose of the Academy of Management is to foster the general ad-

vancement of research, learning, teaching, and practice in the management field. The Academy publishes scholarly papers, conducts forums for the exchange of knowledge, and provides services that enhance the science and practice of management.

http://www.aom.pace.edu/

> **American Management Association (AMA).** AMA is the world's leading membership-based management development organization. More than 700,000 customers and members each year in the Americas, Europe, and Asia learn business skills and best management practices through seminars, conferences, and special events; e-learning and self-study courses; customized corporate and government services; and publications.

http://www.amanet.org/index.htm

> **American Psychological Association (APA).** APA is the largest scientific and professional organization representing psychology in the United States. With more than 159,000 members, APA is also the largest association of psychologists worldwide. APA works to advance psychology as a science, a profession, and a means of promoting human welfare.

http://www.apa.org/

> **American Psychological Society (APS).** To better aid and support its members, APS offers a wide range of benefits designed to meet the specific needs of scientific psychologists. There is an APS Student Caucus for student members.

http://www.psychologicalscience.org/

> **American Society for Training and Development (ASTD).** ASTD is the world's premier professional association and leading resource on workplace learning and performance issues. ASTD's membership includes more than 70,000 people working in the field of workplace performance in 100 countries worldwide. Its leadership and members work in more than 15,000 multinational corporations, small- and medium-sized businesses, government agencies, colleges, and universities.

http://www.astd.org/

> **Society for Industrial and Organizational Psychology (SIOP).** SIOP is a division within the American Psychological Association that is also an organizational affiliate of the American Psychological Society. The Society's goal is to promote human welfare through the various applications of psychology to all types of organizations providing goods and services, such as manufacturing concerns, commercial enterprises, labor unions or trade associations, and public agencies.

http://www.siop.org/

> **Society for Human Resource Management (SHRM).** SHRM is the world's largest human resource management association. SHRM provides education and information services; conferences and seminars;

government and media representation; online services; and publications to more than 145,000 professional and student members throughout the world.

http://www.shrm.org/

> **WorldatWork.** WorldatWork, formerly the American Compensation Association and Canadian Compensation Association, is a 45-year-old global not-for-profit professional association dedicated to knowledge leadership in disciplines associated with attracting, retaining, and motivating employees. More than 25,000 human resources professionals, consultants, educators, and others are members of the association. WorldatWork emphasizes total rewards, specifically focusing on compensation and benefits and on other components of the work experience, such as work/life balance, recognition, culture, professional development, and work environment issues. In addition to membership, WorldatWork offers certification and education programs, online information resources, publications, conferences, research, and networking opportunities.

http://www.worldatwork.org/

PARTICIPATE IN LOCAL BUSINESS AND COMMUNITY ACTIVITIES[13]

Participation in local business and community activities offers many opportunities for skills development and practice, for developing professional contacts, and for personal satisfaction. In addition, many firms now include community service components in their performance appraisals. Here are five volunteer opportunities to explore:

> **Rotary International.** Rotary is an association of business and professional leaders who are united worldwide and provide humanitarian service, encourage high ethical standards in all vocations, and seek to help to build world peace and goodwill. There are more than 29,000 rotary clubs in 161 countries, with a total of 1.2 million members.

http://www.rotary.org/

> **Chamber of Commerce.** The U.S. Chamber of Commerce is the world's largest not-for-profit business federation, representing 3 million businesses, 3,000 state and local chambers, 830 business associations, and 87 American chambers of commerce abroad. Managers interested in community service might offer to represent their companies at chamber meetings and perhaps take a leadership position on a working committee in the chamber.[14]

http://www.uschamber.org/default.htm

> **Junior Achievement (JA).** JA's mission is to ensure that children have an understanding of the free enterprise system. With the help of approximately 150,000 volunteers nationwide, JA currently reaches nearly 4 million students across America through programs in grades from kindergarten through high school. The American Management Association and JA have formed a partnership to promote volunteerism and life-

long learning. In appreciation for volunteer efforts, JA will give its volunteers a complimentary membership in the AMA.

http://www.ja.org/

> **Big Brothers/Big Sisters.** Big Brothers/Big Sisters of America is the nation's largest youth-mentoring organization. Programs match kids with mentors who provide meaningful friendship and share fun experiences.

http://www.bbbsa.org/

> **Ronald McDonald Houses.** Ronald McDonald Houses provide a "home-away-from-home" for the families of seriously ill children receiving treatment at nearby hospitals. There are now 206 Ronald McDonald Houses in 19 countries. The Houses are supported by nearly 25,000 volunteers, who donate 1 million hours annually.

http://www.rmhc.com/

Many other organizations and opportunities will be specific to your city, state, or region. In addition, newspapers and other news media often issue calls for volunteers to help with various activities. Managers can also contribute by serving on the board of trustees of schools or on advisory boards of colleges.[15]

DEVELOP AND MAINTAIN NETWORKS

As we discussed in the context of careers, networking can be critical to success and personal fulfillment. However, it is important to recognize that networking is about much more than amassing a set of names of people who can be called if you're looking for work. While networks may help with job contacts, they serve many other important roles, particularly for skill development. Networks may be physical (made up of people with whom you physically interact from time to time), or virtual (consisting of members linked electronically).

Physical Networks Physical networks offer many advantages, such as the opportunity for personal, face-to-face interaction and social support. To develop such networks, start by keeping up with former classmates and coworkers. Attend local association chapter meetings and seminars.[16] Consider joining a management reading club.[17] Check to see whether there are local networking groups that fit your needs and interests.

Virtual Networks Virtual networks offer the benefits of ease and immediacy of access and broad membership. You may decide to join one or more formal virtual networks. In addition, you may want to develop your own, more specialized virtual networks.

A ready-made form of virtual network is the electronic mailing list. Typically, for example, professional associations will maintain listservers for member interaction. Sign on to several of these lists (we discuss some on the text website) and see which best fit your needs and interests. You are likely to learn a lot by simply "lurking" on these lists (i.e., by passively reading comments exchanged among list members). However, we encourage you to take full advantage of these resources by actively seeking out information. List members tend to be glad—even eager—to provide information. Such specific

Web Wise

Webgrrls International*

In addition to electronic mailing lists, many websites serve as networking hubs. For example, Webgrrls, a networking group of women online, represents all corners of the work world, from programmers and business owners to students. Members look to the group for mentors, for solutions to particular problems, to network for job opportunities, and to continue their education. Webgrrls chapters also offer the opportunity to meet with others to share ideas, experiences, and information.

http://www.webgrrls.com/

*S. McNally, "Organization Offers Women in Technology a Web of Support," *The Los Angeles Times,* May 29, 2000, p. 4. To read about another women's network, *Gather,* see J. Ashley, "The New Girls' Network," *Management Today,* September 2000, pp. 72–75.

GLOBAL PERSPECTIVES

INDUS ENTREPRENEURS*

With more than 3,000 members worldwide, IndUS Entrepreneurs is a powerful networking group led by 200 South Asians (e.g., Vinod Khosla, founder of Sun Microsystems, and the founders of Cirrus Logic, Hotmail, Odyssey, and Cascade Communications) who have found success in the United States.

IndUS has chapters in New York, Boston, Los Angeles, Seattle, Washington, DC, Chicago, and Atlanta and in such Indian cities as Mumbai, New Delhi, and Bangalore, and new chapters are opening in London, Hong Kong, Singapore, and elsewhere. Successful members make presentations, give advice, and examine business proposals. While

most IndUS members are South Asian, others are encouraged to join as well. The goal is to meet entrepreneurs, discuss ideas, find inspiration, and ultimately nurture venture capitalists.

http://www.tie.org/

*A. Inam, "The Mentors," *Asian Business*, November 2000, pp. 67–68.

questions as "Can anyone tell me about their experiences with applying team-based rewards?" or "What are some pros and cons of using formal suggestion systems?" or "Can anyone recommend a good recent article on nonverbal communications?" are likely to generate many responses.

In addition to such formal electronic networks, you may want to develop virtual networks of your own. For example, Webgrrls (discussed in the previous Web Wise) was founded by Aliza Sherman. Sherman wanted to network with other women, found the personal Web pages of women around the world, and started e-mailing them on a regular basis.

Some Guidelines for Developing Networks If you're thinking of developing a network, whether physical or virtual, treat the process much like a team-building exercise. For instance, include members with important skills, perspectives, and contacts. Work to build diversity of all kinds into the network. Especially with virtual networks, incorporate members from varying cultures. Update the network over time to ensure that it is viable and responsive to emerging needs. As the network founder, you have the chance, if you wish, to maintain a central network position and thus to take on leadership roles. And, whether you're founding a network or a network member, be sure to contribute your skills, time, and insights to other members. View the networks as a place to give as well as to get.

EXPLORE STRETCHING ASSIGNMENTS

Once in a company, find ways to stretch so as to learn, test, and apply new skills. Set difficult goals for yourself and don't stay in one position so long that you're no longer learning. Try to work outside your job description and seek varied assignments.

WORK OUTSIDE YOUR JOB DESCRIPTION

Your job description defines the required scope of your work activities, but it is not meant as a cage. As discussed in previous chapters, such extra-role behaviors as organizational citizenship behaviors are increasingly important in organizations. While such behaviors go beyond the formal requirements of the job, they are often crucial to organizational performance and member satisfaction, and they are likely to be viewed favorably. As such, find ways to take on additional responsibilities. Search for new learning opportunities at work and look for projects that would be enjoyable and would provide valuable information.[18] Make sure your boss and others are aware of your interest in learning and be proactive in pursuing skill-enhancing opportunities.[19]

SEEK VARIED ASSIGNMENTS[20]

Remember from our discussion of careers that organizational mobility can take many forms, not just vertical but radial and circumferential. Moves at the same level in an organization can yield fresh perspectives, new insights into how the firm functions, heightened visibility, and skill-learning opportunities. For these reasons, many firms groom their future leaders by systematically moving them between jobs to acquire needed competencies, often in different departments, locations, and even countries. As such, explore options for job rotation, especially to positions that offer the potential to add skills to your portfolio. Depending on your personal circumstances and the nature of your organization, global assignments may provide especially rich learning opportunities.

MAKE USE OF THE RESOURCES OF THE WORLD WIDE WEB

We hope that the text's Web Wise boxes and Web Wise activities have encouraged you to make greater use of the Web as a learning resource. Continue experimenting with the Web's potential. As a first step, you may want to take the time to go back and try Web Wise and Working the Web activities in this book that you haven't had an opportunity to complete. Beyond that, explore management-related professional associations, journals, and other resources as discussed in this chapter. Using search engines (we like Google, though your preferences may vary), try some searches on specific management topics. Beyond that, if you have access through your school or business to such journal databases as ABI-Inform and Proquest, practice with them. Using such databases, you can search for information about specific topics, companies, or individuals or about some combination (such as leadership at GE). These databases include most management-oriented journals and often provide full articles rather than just abstracts.

EXPLORE CONTINUING EDUCATION OPTIONS

An important part of your lifelong learning will be formal continuing education. Fortunately, the opportunities for continuing education have exploded in number and form. For example, while pursuing advanced degrees once required difficult trade-offs, such as the need to take months or years off from work, colleges and universities have become more flexible in their offerings. Many, for example, offer full evening MBA programs or weekend programs, sometimes in the form of executive MBA programs for more experienced managers. In addition, about 2 million students worldwide are enrolled in distance education courses from providers in the United States and Canada.[21] An estimated 80 percent of U.S. colleges and universities are offering online classes in 2001. Online learning is flexible and accessible, removing barriers of time and distance.

Along with universities that offer continuing education offerings, companies are taking a much more active role in determining their employees' learning needs and in finding or developing appropriate educational options. Some firms now have full learning centers. Others have started full corporate universities.[22] There were 1,600 corporate universities by early 2000, and the number is projected to grow to 37,000 by 2010—exceeding the number of traditional universities. Corporate universities such as the Disney Institute, Saturn Consulting Services, the Xerox Center, the RCA Campus, and the Holiday Inn University provide a diverse set of educational programs for their own employees, and often open their doors to employees of other firms. Companies believe that by operating their own corporate universities they can tailor offerings to the specific needs of their workforces, ensure continued skill development, and enhance employee loyalty.

We have certainly covered a lot of material in this book. To increase the likelihood that the knowledge and skills that you have acquired are applied in the future, complete your last exercise, Skills Practice 13-4, now. This activity is especially important since it focuses on having you assess how much progress you have made in developing important management skills and what you can do in the future to further develop these skills as part of your overall professional development.

Skills Practice 13-4
Revisiting My Management Skills Mastery Plan

Skill Level: **Challenging**

Skill Objective
1. To reflect on the management knowledge and skills that you have acquired in relation to the goals you set for yourself in Skills Practice 1-5 (Developing My Management Skills Mastery Plan).
2. To identify your own Top Ten List of key points about management skills that you will take away from reading this book.
3. To identify specific action steps that you can take to further develop your management knowledge and skills while you are still in school and when you obtain your first real-world job after graduation.

Procedure
1. Pull out the management skills mastery plan that you developed in Skills Practice 1-5 (Developing My Management Skills Mastery Plan) as a reference for working through this activity. Use a separate piece of paper to record all of your responses to steps 2–7 that follow.
2. Review the areas that you identified as being your **Key Personal Strengths in Skills Practice 1-5.** Assess the degree to which you feel that you further developed your key personal strengths based on what you learned in this book. Why do you feel this way?
3. Review the areas that you identified as being your **Key Personal Weaknesses in Skills Practice 1-5.** Assess the degree to which you feel that you improved in the areas of your key personal weaknesses. Although you may not have completely eliminated these areas as concerns, the key is the progress you made in overcoming them. Why do you feel this way?

4. Review the **Knowledge Objectives that you identified in Skills Practice 1-5.** Assess the degree to which you feel that achieved your knowledge objectives. Why do you feel that you were successful (or unsuccessful) in achieving these objectives?

5. Review the **Skill Objectives that you identified in Skills Practice 1-5.** Assess the degree to which you feel that you achieved your skill objectives. Why do you feel that you were successful (or unsuccessful) in achieving these objectives?

6. Now, reflecting on everything that you have learned about management knowledge and skills in Chapters 1–12, brainstorm your own Top Ten List of the things that you have learned about management and can use in the future.

7. Finally, you need to think about what kinds of specific actions you can take to further enhance your management knowledge and skills in the future. If you still have some time before you graduate, focus more on things that you can do as a student to acquire management knowledge and skills. If you are graduating very soon, focus more on what you can do once you start your new job (managerial or nonmanagerial) to acquire management knowledge and skills.

8. Create a written summary of your responses to the foregoing steps 2–7 and discuss it with your instructor or present it to your class for discussion purposes. Although this step is optional, it is highly beneficial to take some time to process your answers and to hear what other students came up with based on their assessments.

One of the key objectives of this chapter was to encourage you to think about the "big picture" in relation to all the management knowledge and skills you have acquired since you began this journey back in Chapter 1. Given this, the final Top Ten List draws from the entire book in providing a list of critical points about management that we hope you will remember (and on which we hope you will act!) in your future careers. We hope that you will be successful in continuing your management skills learning journey, and we wish you bon voyage.

TOP TEN LIST: KEY POINTS TO REMEMBER

LOOKING AHEAD: MAINTAINING AND ENHANCING YOUR MANAGEMENT SKILLS PORTFOLIO

10. Learn the business strategy, culture, "rules for success," and industry associated with the organization at which you are employed.

9. Develop a clear sense of your objectives as a manager, the specific actions you will take to achieve those objectives, and how you will measure your effectiveness and that of your employees and overall work unit.

8. Understand differences (e.g., perceptions, personality, decision-making style) among those with whom you work and to whom you report. Use this information as a basis for adapting your management style to the situation.

7. Actively manage communication with your employees to keep them "on the same page" (i.e., encourage mutual understanding) and "in the loop" (i.e., up-to-date) on issues that affect them.

6. Use a systematic and data-driven process that incorporates the input of relevant players (e.g., employees, customers) to identify and implement the best possible alternative given time and resource constraints.

5. There is no single best way to lead others: Understand the needs of the situation first and then match the appropriate leadership style to that situation.

4. Achieve and sustain employee motivation by clarifying your performance standards, providing support (e.g., training, feedback, guidance) to employees in achieving those standards, and appropriately rewarding employees for successfully meeting these standards using a combination of valued financial and nonfinancial rewards.

3. Establish and maintain your credibility and authority as the leader of a team by building and using appropriate

personal bases of power (i.e., traits, knowledge, and skills you possess) and position bases of power (i.e., resources that come with your management title and job) to influence your employees in supporting the implementation of desired work behaviors.

2. Great teams must be created. Actively manage your team by establishing effective working relationships, building a team structure and supporting process, and ensuring the ongoing growth and development of each member of the team and the team as a whole.

1. You need more than common sense to become a great manager. Translate what you know about "good management" into actual management practice.

QUESTIONS FOR REVIEW AND REFLECTION

REVIEW QUESTIONS

1. What are primary steps in planning for ongoing skills learning?

2. Identify at least four ways in which to develop management skills while still in school.

3. In what sense are organizations marketplaces for skills?

4. What are the benefits of reading popular management books? What are some related cautions?

5. Identify six journals that attempt to bring recent management theory and research to practitioner audiences.

6. What are eight major professional associations that might facilitate lifelong learning of management skills?

7. Discuss five community organizations in which you might participate to foster networking and skill practice and development.

8. Discuss physical and virtual networks and provide guidelines for developing networks.

9. Identify four ways to "stretch" at work so as to learn new skills.

10. How can the Internet be used to enhance ongoing management skills development?

11. Discuss continuing education options for ongoing management skills development.

CRITICAL THINKING QUESTIONS

1. Do you think management skills learned in school activities (e.g., team projects) can transfer to the real world? Why or why not?

2. Which of the management skills that you have learned will be most important in your future career? Why? Do you think the same skill will also be most important for life in general?

3. Some virtual networking groups, such as the Webgrrls network discussed in this chapter, are aimed at the interests and needs of specific types of people (e.g., women, gays and lesbians, older workers, and so on). What do you see as the advantages of such specialized networking groups? What do you see as potential disadvantages?

4. In today's turbulent business environment, do you think it is possible to "skate to where the puck is going?" What might be some difficulties in doing this? In answering this question, try to expand on the puck metaphor. For example, what if the ice itself is melting? What if someone changes the rules of the game?

5. In general, do you think physical or virtual networks are more important to your ongoing success and learning? Why?

6. Stretch your imagination to think of three radical changes that might occur in the workplace in the next two decades. Discuss the implications of those changes for the nature of needed management skills.

EXPERIENTIAL EXERCISES

WEB EXERCISE 13-1

Use an Internet search engine, such as Excite or Google, to conduct a search for "Management Skills." You'll find many links to related topics (a recent Google search yielded 321,000 "hits" for "Management Skills"!), so you

622

Chapter 13 Looking Ahead: Maintaining and Enhancing Your Management Skills Portfolio

Skills Application
Skills Application
Skills Application
Skills Application
Skills Application

may want to further limit your search by adding such terms as "exercises," "examples," "readings," or "assessment." Some of the sites will be commercial, while others will be associated with universities, professional associations, governmental agencies, journals, and so on. Some sites will offer skill-specific information, such as "change management skills," "project management skills," "career management skills," or "time management skills," while others will be broader. *Select two non-* *commercial sites.* For each site, complete the following activities:

1. Indicate why you selected the site.
2. Describe what features the site provides.
3. Discuss at least two things you learned from the site, in terms of specific information about topics, additional sources of information, new perspectives, and so on.

WEB EXERCISE 13-2

Select *three* of the eight professional associations discussed in this chapter. Go to the association websites and answer the following questions for each association:

1. Identify at least five offerings provided by the association to its members (e.g., newsletters, journals, meeting opportunities, education programs).
2. Determine whether there are local chapters and, if so, the nature of their activities.

3. Determine whether there are special student memberships and, if so, what benefits they provide.

Following your exploration of the three association sites, indicate which of the associations appears to best fit your interests and explain why you have made that choice.

CASE 13-1
LEADERSHIP AND STRATEGY AT COMPAQ COMPUTER CORPORATION

The Company

Compaq Computer Corporation designs, manufactures, and markets hardware, software, enterprise computing solutions, commercial desktop and portable products, and consumer personal computers. It is the world's largest provider of computer equipment and a member of the *Fortune Global 100*. Its corporate headquarters are located in Houston, Texas.

Compaq products and services are sold in more than 200 countries. The company maintains core manufacturing operations in Texas, California, Scotland, Singapore, Brazil, and Argentina. Its recent acquisitions include Microcom, a provider of central site and remote access solutions; Tandem Corporation, a technology solutions company; and Digital Equipment Corporation, a leading supplier of high-performance, Web-based business solutions.

Leadership

The CEO of Compaq is Michael Capellas, the 46-year-old known as "Compaq's rockin' boss"[23] for his habit of playing the electric guitar and dancing on stage at company events. Capellas is known for his strong work ethic and desire to take on the toughest challenges. During his career, he has held 22 different positions with six companies.

Capellas is viewed as a really "down-to-earth" kind of guy who dresses down, has a five-o'clock shadow, and can be found informally mixing with employees during the day.

He likes to blast songs by the music group Fleetwood Mac over the boom box in his office to fire himself up. Employees view Capellas as an individual who can effectively rally them around a cause. In fact, during every month, he holds a meeting in the company's auditorium to update employees on company-related issues. Any of the company's employees may either attend these meetings or watch them over a closed-circuit TV monitor. To foster a sense of ownership among employees, the company offers them stock options, something that has traditionally been available only to members of senior management.

However, there are some concerns about Michael Capellas's capacity to lead the company as well. Capellas himself does not have the same industry credibility as do other executives, such as Carly Fiorina, the new CEO at Hewlett-Packard. In addition, Capellas has been criticized for making decisions too quickly and implementing them without all the necessary information. He has, however, been willing to make the tough decisions that had to be made, such as selling off or exiting unprofitable businesses.

The Situation

Compaq's current mission is to become the "NonStop Internet Company" that will provide the hardware, software, and networking solutions that will enable its customers to become "unstoppable." Capellas spends a lot of time emphasizing his concept of "Everything to the Internet" to employees. In fact, each Compaq employee has a laminated card with this slogan printed on it.

One of the biggest challenges facing Capellas is how to turn around a company that once enjoyed "powerhouse" status in the computer industry but whose fortunes have declined significantly with the emergence of the Internet. For example, Compaq's traditional revenue growth rate was 45–65 percent but, by 1998, it was down to just 5 percent. In 1999, its stock price dropped from $47 to $21. Its stock price stood at $20 in January 2001.

The comeback plan at Compaq consists of the following elements:

> Maintain Compaq's lead in consumer personal computers by being an innovator in new technologies.

> Cut inventory costs by selling 40 percent of its machines through a sales force or online.

> Enter the Net access–device market that is projected to grow dramatically over the next four years.

> Reengineer the company's order-taking and manufacturing process to be more competitive with Dell Computer Corporation.

> Develop and implement an e-business strategy (supplying high-powered servers and supporting services to major corporations).

Capellas believes that Compaq will live or die based on the long-term success of its e-business strategy.

So far, Compaq's results appear to be improving. Sales growth is increasing again, profitability is rising, and the company's stock price has rebounded as well. However, the long-term challenges still remain. Will Compaq be able to execute an effective e-business strategy? Can Capellas establish the credibility needed in the industry to enable Compaq to win major corporate customers?

Discussion Questions

1. What are the key challenges facing Compaq? Why are these issues critical?

2. What recommendations would you make to Michael Capellas regarding the handling of the situation? Justify your recommendations.

3. What are the key implications of this case for you as a future manager?

Source: http://www5.compaq.com

CASE 13-2
DECLINE (AND COMEBACK?) AT LEVI STRAUSS & COMPANY

The Company

Levi Strauss & Company is a manufacturer and marketer of branded jeans and casual sportswear. Its brand names include Levi's, Dockers, and Slates. The company has about 1,300 employees who work at its corporate headquarters in San Francisco, California, with an additional 15,000–16,000 employees on a worldwide basis. The company maintains 21 production facilities and 25 customer service centers around the world.

The company maintains global sourcing and operating guidelines as one reflection of its long history of commitment to ethics and social responsibility. The country assessment guidelines are used by management as a basis for making business-related decisions within the

company's framework for ethics and social responsibility. Specifically, all business opportunities (e.g., places where the company may do business or set up production facilities) are evaluated in terms of health and safety conditions provided for employees, the quality of the human rights environment, supportiveness of the legal system, and the overall political, economic, and social environment.

In evaluating potential business partners, Levi Strauss & Company assesses the degree to which these parties demonstrate a commitment to high ethical standards, compliance with legal requirements, concern for the environment, and employment standards (e.g., avoiding the use of child labor and prison labor and concern for working hours, wages and benefits, and health and safety).

The company's commitment to ethics and social responsibility can be seen in the creation of committee involvement teams that encourage employees to be active participants in their local communities. In addition, the company and the Levi Strauss Foundation maintain a global giving program that makes contributions to community organizations in over 40 countries. These contributions are used to address problems related to the acquired immunodeficiency syndrome and discrimination and racism. The company has also made a strong stand on protecting worker rights by actively participating in the Fair Labor Association and the Ethical Trading Initiative.

The organizational culture that exists at Levi Strauss & Company is very values-driven. Some specific elements of the culture include a strong belief in ongoing employee rewards and recognition, flexible work arrangements (e.g., leave of absence programs, a business casual dress code), employee empowerment, and concern for ethics and social responsibility as a driver of behavior every day.

The Situation: Decline of the Levi's Brand Name[24]

The CEO of Levi Strauss & Company was Robert Haas, a Harvard MBA whose previous experience involved working for the Peace Corps and McKinsey, the management consulting firm. Haas's vision for Levi Strauss was to create a company that was driven by social values and concern for the communities in which the company did business.

This led Haas to create a business process–re-engineering initiative that he thought would greatly enhance the responsiveness of the company to changing markets and customer preferences.

The beginning of the decline in the Levi's brand name began around 1990 as its market share among young male consumers dropped significantly. Other problems included poor in-store displays, missed deliveries to retailers (e.g., J. C. Penney), and high manufacturing costs. Between 1990 and 1998, things only got worse for the company. The company's market share of male consumers 16 years old and up went from more than 48 percent in 1990 to 25 percent in 1998. Suddenly, Levi's was no longer "cool" among the influential younger crowd.

The search for answers as to how the venerable Levi's name could have experienced such a dramatic slide pointed to a number of underlying causes. First, Robert Haas did not possess any relevant retailing experience, raising questions about how he could understand what

had to be done to lead an apparel firm. Some employees noted that he demonstrated a concern for every employee's ideas and opinions to a fault. Although employee participation and involvement made sense in a wide range of situations, some employees felt that this resulted in tremendous inefficiencies, long meetings, endless discussions, and an inability to eventually make a decision and move forward.

An overemphasis on addressing the issues of ethics and social responsibility may have also played a role in the company's problems as significant time and resources were spent integrating these issues into the "Levi Strauss Mission and Aspirations Statement." Also, the company's compensation system was redesigned so that a third of executive bonuses were based on "managing aspirationally." Finally, considerable time was spent in task forces and committees that were formed to address issues related to workforce diversity.

Other management problems not necessarily linked with the ethics and social responsibility issue also contributed to the company's problems. In short, the company refused to change its product line as customer preferences and markets changed. This refusal to change continued despite data that retailers showed to Levi Strauss management demonstrating how customer buying patterns were shifting. In the end, Levi Strauss ended up attempting to sell the same basic 501 jeans to a market that had fragmented into multiple niches.

Management also did not do an effective job of managing change. For example, the implementation of its customer service supply chain program involved rewriting hundreds of job descriptions. Employees were asked to reapply for new jobs based on this system. In some cases, employees did not get the jobs for which they had applied, creating chaos. In addition, an employee attitude survey dealing with organizational change contained questions that many employees viewed as being inappropriate or offensive. The company lost some of its best employees, who decided that they had tolerated enough and quit their jobs.

Finally, there was the issue of lack of accountability. Now that Levi Strauss was privately owned, Haas didn't have to worry about responding to shareholder concerns.

Management's Actions

Levi Strauss management has taken a number of actions in an attempt to turn the company around. It created a new mission statement for itself: "To be the casual company authority." The company has created a new brand management structure and has increased external recruiting to bring "new blood" into the organization. It also created a new specialized brand called *Red Line* in an attempt to regain an image of being cool among young, urban consumers.

In the fall of 1999, Philip Marineau became the new CEO at Levi Strauss, with Robert Haas becoming the chairman. Marineau's job has been to develop and implement a three-year turnaround strategy for the company.[25] Marineau has focused on reducing the company's $3.6 billion debt and launching new lines of apparel, including Engineered Jeans, 569s, and Silver Tab Label for women.

So far, there is reason to be somewhat optimistic. Although third-quarter sales for 2000 have continued to decline to $1.13 billion from $1.23 billion a year ago, the company's gross margins (profits) increased by 2.2 percent, and its debt was reduced to $2.2 billion. However, the future is far from certain for this 147-year-old company as the retail industry becomes more challenging owing to intense competition from such companies as Tommy Hilfiger, the Gap, Nautica, and Calvin Klein.

Discussion Questions

1. What are the most significant challenges facing Levi Strauss & Company? Why do you feel this way?
2. What recommendations would you give to CEO Phil Marineau regarding the actions that have to be taken to sustain the turnaround?
3. Evaluate Levi Strauss's emphasis on ethics and social responsibility in relation to its past and current performance. To what extent are the two related to each other? Justify your answer.
4. What are the implications of this case for you as a future supervisor or manager?

Source: http://www.levistrauss.com

VIDEO CASE
ENTREPRENEURSHIP AND INNOVATION: A STUDY OF YAHOO!

Running Time: 15:50

Yahoo! is the world's number one website, as it has been for most of the Web's existence.[26] Founded in 1994 by David Filo and Jerry Yang, two Stanford University doctoral students, Yahoo! is now a global organization with more than 3,000 employees. Yahoo! helps people to find everything from stamp collecting information to the latest stock quotes. In this video, cofounder Jerry Yang, director of brand management Karen Edwards, senior producer John Briggs, and others discuss the need for innovation and critical thinking at Yahoo! After viewing the video, answer the following questions:

1. What does John Briggs mean when he says, "We're essentially in the tornado right now?" What are some implications of the fact that Yahoo! is "in the tornado"?
2. In what sense is Yahoo! a learning organization?
3. How does Yahoo! combine strategy, leadership, culture, organization design, and information sharing to develop a learning organization?
4. What are the elements of Yahoo!'s strategy?
5. What are the important cultural values at Yahoo!?
6. How does Yahoo!'s organization design facilitate learning?
7. Why do Yahoo! employees say that they enjoy working in a learning organization?
8. To what degree could Yahoo!'s approaches to becoming a learning organization provide guidance for individuals attempting to achieve lifelong learning?

http://www.yahoo.com/

LIGHTEN UP
PETWORKING[27]

Just below the Eleanor Roosevelt statue in the West Seventy-Second Street entrance to Riverside Park is a 16,000-square-foot space that might be New York City's best-kept networking secret. This is the dog-meet-dog world of "petworking," where people look for work as they walk their pets. The pet walkers include such celebrities as Conan

O'Brien, Al Franken, and Elaine Boosler and realtors, surgeons, journalists, architects, and many others, but "it's mostly people who know people who know other people who know of an opening or opportunity." In this and other dog-gathering spots in the city, leads about jobs are shared along with dog biscuits.

Bash Dibra, author of *Dogspeak,* explains that "Dogs are social creatures and thus they force interaction." The dogs act as catalysts in breaking down barriers and opening communication. The first remark is about the dog and then "maybe the next comment is 'I had a really bad day and I think I need to look for another job.'" One pet worker pointed out that "It's the oldest way young men and women pick each other up in the city. Why not leverage a winning formula?"

http://www.urbanhound.com

CHAPTER 1. THE MANAGEMENT CHALLENGE: CRITICAL SKILLS FOR THE NEW WORKPLACE

1. G. Hanson, *Determinants of Firm Performance: An Integration of Economic and Organizational Factors.* Ph.D Dissertation, University of Michigan Business School, 1986.

2. "Poor Managers Cause Failures," *Credit Management,* July 1999, p. 7.

3. For a study of causes of small business failure in developing countries, and a review of research on determinants of small firm performance, see F. N. Al-Shaikh, "Factors for Small Business Failure in Developing Countries," *Advances in Competitiveness Research,* 1998, *6,* pp. 75–86.

4. A. Zagorin, "The Fruit of Its Labor," *Time,* November 1, 1999, pp. 50–51; J. Birger, "Toys R Cheap," *Money,* September 2000, pp. 42–44; E. Neuborne & R. Berner, "Warm and Fuzzy Won't Save Procter & Gamble," *Business Week,* June 26, 2000, pp. 48–50; "Science and Technology: Annus Horribilis," *The Economist,* April 1, 2000, pp. 74–75; and M. Spiro and S. Hamm, "The Fall of Baan," *Business Week,* August 28, 2000, pp. 247–252.

5. M. Warner, "Fallen Idols," *Fortune,* October 30, 2000, pp. 108–121. See also R. Monk, "Why Small Businesses Fail," *CMA Management,* July/August 2000, pp. 12–13.

6. S. R. Sabo, "Skills for the Next Century," *Association Management,* December 1999, pp. 37–41.

7. M. Messmer, "Skills for a New Millennium," *Strategic Finance,* August 1999, pp. 10–12.

8. C. Kaydo, "The New Skills of Top Managers," *Sales and Marketing Management,* May 2000, p. 16.

9. P. B. Thomas, "The Competency-Based Preprofessional Curriculum: A Key Component of Vision Success," *Journal of Accountancy,* October 2000, pp. 128–131.

10. P. M. Buhler, "Managing in the New Millennium," *Supervision,* August 2000, pp. 16–18.

11. The following examples are drawn in part from L. Secretan, "Learning Fuels the Soul," *Industry Week,* August 21, 2000, p. 29.

12. M. K. McGee and J. Mateyaschuk, "Educating the Masses," *Informationweek,* February 15, 1999, pp. 61–81.

13. B. Leonard, "Basic Skills Training Pays Off for Employers," *HRMagazine,* October 1999, pp. 32–33.

14. "Survey Shows Fundamental Managerial Skills Lacking," *Management Services,* January 1999, p. 3.

15. "In-House Solution to Skills Shortage," *Works Management,* March 2000, p. 7.

16. "Survey Shows Fundamental Managerial Skills Lacking," *Management Services,* January 1999, p. 3.

17. W. J. Moran, "You are Absolutely, Positively on Your Own," *Fortune,* 1996, *134 (11),* p. 222.

18. *Human Capital: Key Principles from Nine Private Sector Organizations,* GAO/GGD-00-28, Report to Congressional Requesters by the United States General Accounting Office, January 2000.

19. P. M. Buhler, "Managing in the New Millennium," *Supervision,* June 2000, pp. 16–19; and J. R. Thompson and C. W. LeHew, "Skill-Based Pay as an Organizational Innovation," *Review of Public Personnel Administration,* Winter 2000, pp. 20–40.

20. J. Palmer, "Marry Me a Little," *Barron's,* July 24, 2000, pp. 25–27.

21. N. Brodsky, "Becoming the Boss," *Inc,* October 2000, pp. 29–30.

22. R. A. Baron and G. D. Markman, "Beyond Social Capital: How Social Skills Can Enhance Entrepreneurs' Success," *The Academy of Management Executive,* February 2000, pp. 106–116.

23. See W. McKinley, J. Zhao, and K. G. Rust, "A Sociotechnical Interpretation of Organizational Downsizing," *Academy of Management Review,* 2000, *25(1),* pp. 227–243.

24. R. Ault, R. Walton, and M. Childers, *What Works: A Decade of Change at Champion International* (San Francisco: Jossey Bass, 1998).

25. R. Dzinkowski, "Mission Possible," *CMA Management,* February 2000, pp. 36–40.

26. See M. Moravec, "Self-Managed Teams," *Executive Excellence,* October 1999, p. 18; G. M. Spreitzer, S. G. Cohen, and G. E. Ledford, Jr., "Developing Effective Self-Managing Work Teams in Service Organizations," *Group & Organization Management,* September 1999, pp. 340–366; and M. Attaran and T. T. Nguyen, "Succeeding with Self-Managed Work Teams," *Industrial Management,* July/August 1999, pp. 24–28.

27. See J. Walsh, "The Portable Manager," *Electric Perspectives,* January/February 1999, pp. 16–20.

28. For one extensive review, see P. A. Cohen, "College Grades and Adult Achievement: A Research Synthesis," *Research in Higher Education,* 1984, *20,* pp. 281–291.

29. L. W. Porter & L. E. McKibbin, *Management Education and Development: Drift or Thrust into the 21st Century?* (New York: McGraw-Hill, 1988).

30. Pfeffer, J. & Sutton, R. I., *The Knowing–doing Gap: How Smart Companies Turn Knowledge into Action* (Boston, MA: Harvard Business School Press, 2000), p. 22.

31. Pfeffer, J. & Sutton, R. I., *The Knowing–doing Gap: How Smart Companies Turn Knowledge into Action* (Boston, MA: Harvard Business School Press, 2000), pp. 246–262.

32. A. Bandura, *Social Foundations of Thought and Action* (Englewood Cliffs, NJ: Prentice Hall, 1986); T. R. Davis

and F. Luthans, "A Social Learning Approach to Organizational Behavior," *Academy of Management Review,* 1980, *5,* pp. 281–290; and A. P. Brief and R. J. Aldag. "The Self in Organizations: A Conceptual Review," *Academy of Management Review,* 1981, pp. 75–88.

33. For example, see D. B. Curtis, J. L. Winsor, and D. Stephens, "National Preferences in Business and Communication Education," *Communication Education,* 1989, *38(6),* pp. 6–15; F. Luthans, S. A. Rosenkrantz, and H. W. Hennessey, "What Do Successful Managers Really Do? An Observation Study of Managerial Activities," *Journal of Applied Behavioral Science,* 1985, *21,* pp. 255–270; and O. Nordhaug, "Competence Specificities in Organizations," *International Studies of Management & Organization,* 1998, *28(1),* pp. 8–29.

34. G. A. Yukl, *Leadership in Organizations,* 4th ed. (Englewood Cliffs, NJ: Prentice Hall, 1998).

35. C. M. Pavett and A. W. Lau, "Managerial Work: The Influences of Hierarchical Level and Functional Specificity," *Academy of Management Journal,* 1983, *12,* pp. 170–177.

36. These definitions are based on O. Nordhaug, "Competence Specificities in Organizations," *International Studies of Management & Organization,* 1998, *28(1),* pp. 8–29.

37. L. J. Bassi, G. Benson, and S. Cheney, "The Top Ten Trends," *Training and Development,* November 1996, pp. 28–42.

38. J. H. Sheridan, "Selling Skills, Not Experience," *Industry Week,* January 8, 1996, pp. 15–17.

39. "Cadillac Searches for Its Roots," *Ward's Auto World,* September 1999, pp. 38–44.

40. "Can Cadillac Come Back?" *Fortune,* September 18, 2000, pp. 170–178.

41. JD Power and Associates Consumer Center, *http://www.jdpower.com.*

42. Ibid.

43. "Cadillac Searches for Its Roots," *Ward's Auto World,* September 1999, pp. 38–44.

44. *http://www.napster.com.*

45. "Inside Napster," *Business Week,* August 14, 2000, pp. 112–120.

46. "A New Net Powerhouse?" *Business Week,* November 13, 2000, pp. 46–52.

47. This section is based on S. Caulkin, "Performance!" *Management Today,* May 2000, pp. 62–67.

CHAPTER 2. THE ORGANIZATIONAL CONTEXT: SEEING THE BIG PICTURE

1. For discussions of political risks in Asia, Central America, and Europe, see "Calculating Risk," *Asiamoney,* November 2000, pp. 64–66; C. A. Rarick, "Determinants and Assessment of Political Risk in Central America," *S.A.M. Advanced Management Journal,* Summer 2000, pp. 41–46; and H. Ramcharran, "Foreign Direct Investments in Central and Eastern Europe: An Analysis of Regulatory and Country Risk Factors," *American Business Review,* June 2000, pp. 1–8.

2. See, for instance, C. Tejada, "A Special News Report About Life on the Job—and Trends Taking Place There," *Wall Street Journal,* October 10, 2000, p. A1; and "More Companies Offering Same-Sex-Partner Benefits," *New York Times,* September 26, 2000, p. C2.

3. See J. Macht, "Mortar Combat," *Inc,* September 14, 1999, pp. 102–110; T. K. Muhammad, "Dot Com Fever," *Black Enterprise,* March 2000, pp. 82–89; and L. Proddow, "E-Commerce: It's a Dot Com or Die Digital World: A New Online Three As—Anything, Anywhere, Anytime—Is Set to Rule Marketing in the Future, Says Sun Microsystems' Louise Proddow," *The Guardian,* December 11, 1999, p. 20.

4. "The Malcolm Baldrige Award—at a Glance," *The Journal for Quality and Participation,* January/February 1999, p. 25. See also "Congratulations: Baldrige Award Winners Announced," *The Journal for Quality and Participation,* January/February 2000, p. 18.

5. For thorough discussions of strategic planning and the strategic planning process, see M. A. Hitt, R. D. Ireland, and R. E. Hoskisson, *Strategic Management: Competitiveness and Globalization,* 2nd ed. (Minneapolis/St. Paul: West, 1997); and P. Shrivastava, *Strategic Management: Concepts and Practices* (Cincinnati, OH: South-Western, 1994).

6. For instance, see G. Andrews, "Stuckey's Staples and Souvenirs Still Draw Travelling Customers," *Indianapolis Star News,* January 24, 1998.

7. G. Fuchsberg, "'Visioning' Missions Becomes Its Own Mission," *Wall Street Journal,* January 7, 1994, pp. B1, B4.

8. J. Laabs, "Has Downsizing Missed Its Mark?" *Workforce,* April 1999, pp. 30–36.

9. S. Bell, "P&G Forced by Rivals to Change Old Habits," *Marketing,* June 17, 1999.

10. For a discussion of the BCG model in the context of the airline industry, see N. K. Taneja and G. R. Stearns, "Product Portfolio Planning for Airlines," *Transportation Journal,* Spring 1989, pp. 50–55.

11. R. E. Miles and C. C. Snow, *Organizational Strategy, Structure, and Process* (New York: McGraw-Hill, 1978).

12. See R. S. Kaplan and D. P. Norton, *The Balanced Scorecard* (Boston: Harvard Business School Press, 1996).

13. Excerpted and adapted from P. M. Hirsch, "From Ambushes to Golden Parachutes: Corporate Takeovers as an Instance of Cultural Framing and Institutional Integration," *American Journal of Sociology,* 1986, *41,* pp. 830–835.

CHAPTER 3. UNDERSTANDING AND VALUING DIFFERENCES

1. P. Digh, "Coming to Terms with Diversity," *HRMagazine,* November 1998, pp. 117–120.

2. For instance, see T. H. Cox, "Managing Cultural Diversity: Implications for Organizational Competitiveness," *Academy of Management Executive,* 1991, *5(3),* pp. 45–56.

3. F. Rice, "How To Make Diversity Pay," *Fortune,* August 8, 1994, p. 79.

4. Ibid.

5. P. Digh, "Coming to Terms with Diversity," *HRMagazine,* November 1998, p. 120.

6. L. O. Graham, *The Best Companies for Minorities* (New York: Plume, 1993).

7. F. Rice, "How To Make Diversity Pay," *Fortune,* August 8, 1994, p. 84.

8. J. H. Lucas and M. G. Kaplan, "Unlocking the Corporate Closet," *Training and Development,* January 1994, pp. 35–38.

9. L. L. Castro, "More Firms 'Gender Train' to Bridge the Chasms That Still Divide the Sexes," *Wall Street Journal,* January 2, 1992, pp. 11 and 14.

10. F. Rice, "How to Make Diversity Pay," *Fortune,* August 8, 1994, pp. 78–86.

11. B. McKay, "Coca-Cola's Daft Says Salaries Will Be Tied to Diversity Goals," *Wall Street Journal Interactive Edition,* March 10, 2000.

12. S. Caudron, "Diversity Ignites Effective Work Teams," *Personnel Journal,* September 1994, pp. 54–63.

13. "The Diversity Initiative at US WEST Dex," *Successful Meetings,* March 1998, pp. 55–57.

14. F. Rice, "How to Make Diversity Pay," *Fortune,* August 8, 1994, p. 84.

15. F. Rice, "How to Make Diversity Pay," *Fortune,* August 8, 1994, pp. 84 and 86.

16. Aristotle, *The Nicomachean Ethics,* trans. H. Rackham (Oxford, UK: B. Blackwell, 1943).

17. D. Goleman, *Emotional Intelligence* (New York: Bantam Books, 1995). For a recent review incorporating this concept, see Q. N. Huy, "Emotional Capability, Emotional Intelligence, and Radical Change," *The Academy of Management Review,* 1999, *24,* pp. 325–345. See also D. Goleman, *Working with Emotional Intelligence* (New York: Bantam Books, 1998).

18. H. Gardner, *Frames of Mind* (New York: Basic Books, 1993). Also, see K. Pennar, "How Many Smarts Do You Have?" *Business Week,* September 16, 1996, p. 104; and J. Collins, "How to Make a Better Student: Seven Kinds of Smart," *Time,* October 19, 1998, pp. 94–96.

19. See D. Goleman, *Emotional Intelligence* (New York: Bantam Books, 1995); and D. Goleman, *Working with Emotional Intelligence* (New York: Bantam Books, 1998).

20. See D. Goleman, *Working with Emotional Intelligence* (New York: Bantam Books, 1998).

21. S. Freud, "Civilization and Its Discontents," ed. and trans., J. Strachey, in *The Standard Edition of the Complete Psychological Works, Vol. 2* (New York: Macmillan, 1962). For a recent summary of Freud's work and life, see P. Gay, "Psychoanalyst: Sigmund Freud," *Time,* March 29, 1999, pp. 66–69.

22. See Z. Shapira, *Risk Taking: A Managerial Perspective* (New York: Russell Sage Foundation, 1995). For a cross-cultural comparison of risk taking, see H. Lobler and J. Bode, "Risk Taking Under Transition: An Empirical Comparison Between Chinese, Western-, and Eastern-German Managers," *Thunderbird International Business Review,* Jan./Feb. 1999, pp. 69–81.

23. R. C. Becherer and J. G. Maurer, "The Proactive Personality Disposition and Entrepreneurial Behavior Among Small Company Presidents," *Journal of Small Business Management,* 1999, *37,* pp. 28–36; and J. M. Crant, "The Proactive Personality Scale and Objective Job Performance Among Real Estate Agents," *Journal of Applied Psychology,* 1995, *80,* pp. 532–537.

24. For instance, see R. A. Bernardi, "The Relationships Among Locus of Control, Perceptions of Stress, and Performance," *Journal of Applied Business Research,* 1997, *13,*

pp. 1–8; G. M. Spreitzer, "Psychological Empowerment in the Workplace: Dimensions, Measurement, and Validation," *Academy of Management Journal,* 1995, *38,* pp. 1442–1465; and M. C. Reiss and K. Mitra, "The Effects of Individual Difference Factors on the Acceptability of Ethical and Unethical Workplace Behaviors," *Journal of Business Ethics,* 1998, *17,* pp. 1581–1593.

25. For a recent study of the effects of Machiavellianism, see K. Bass, T. Barnett, and G. Brown, "Individual Difference Variables, Ethical Judgments, and Ethical Behavioral Intentions," *Business Ethics Quarterly,* 1999, *9,* pp. 183–205.

26. For recent examinations of self-monitoring, see W. S. Long, E. J. Long, and G. H. Dobbins, "Correlates of Satisfaction with a Peer Evaluation System: Investigation of Performance Levels and Individual Differences," *Journal of Business and Psychology,* 1998, *12,* pp. 299–312; and D. B. Turban and T. W. Dougherty, "Role of Protégé Personality in Receipt of Mentoring and Career Success," *Academy of Management Journal,* 1994, *37,* pp. 688–702.

27. M. Kilduff and D. V. Day, "Do Chameleons Get Ahead? The Effects of Self-Monitoring on Managerial Careers," *Academy of Management Journal,* 1994, *37,* pp. 1047–1060.

28. See, for instance, T. A. Judge, C. A. Higgins, and C. J. Thoresen, "The Big Five Personality Traits, General Mental Ability, and Career Success Across the Life Span," *Personnel Psychology,* 1999, *52,* pp. 621–652; and F. De Fruty and I. Mervielde, "RIASEC Types and Big Five Traits as Predictors of Employment Status and Nature of Employment," *Personnel Psychology,* 1999, *52,* pp. 701–727.

29. A. S. Grove, "A High-Tech CEO Updates His Views on Managing and Careers," *Fortune,* September 18, 1995, p. 229.

30. J. H. Prager, "Managing Cultural Diversity—On the Pitcher's Mound," *Wall Street Journal,* September 30, 1998, pp. B1+.

31. See G. Hofstede, *Culture's Consequences: International Differences in Work-Related Values* (Beverly Hills, CA: Sage Publications, 1980). For a recent study using the framework, see D. N. Ross, "Culture as a Context for Multinational Business: A Framework for Assessing the Strategy-Culture 'Fit,'" *Multinational Business Review,* 1999, *7,* pp. 13–19.

32. The following examples are based on R. E. Axtell, *Gestures* (New York: Wiley, 1991); and R. E. Axtell, *Do's and Taboo's Around the World,* 3rd ed. (New York: Wiley, 1993).

33. B. Berelson and G. A. Steiner, *Human Behavior: An Inventory of Scientific Findings* (Englewood Cliffs, NJ: Harcourt, Brace, and World, 1964).

34. D. C. Dearborn and H. A. Simon, "Selective Perception: A Note on the Departmental Identifications of Executives," *Sociometry,* 1958, *21,* pp. 140–144. See also M. J. Waller, G. P. Huber, and W. H. Glick, "Functional Background as a Determinant of Executives' Selective Perception," *Academy of Management Journal,* 1995, *38,* pp. 943–974.

35. S. S. Zalkind and T. W. Costello, "Perception: Some Recent Research and Implications for Administration," *Administrative Science Quarterly,* 1962, *7,* pp. 218–235.

36. M. Haire, "Role Perceptions in Labor–Management Relations: An Experimental Approach," *Industrial and Labor Relations Review,* 1955, *8,* pp. 204–216.

37. J. R. Terborg and D. R. Ilgen, "A Theoretical Approach to Sex Discrimination in Traditionally Masculine Occupa-

tions," *Organizational Behavior and Human Performance,* 1975, *13,* pp. 352–376.

38. See, for instance, H. Rheem, "Effective Leadership: The Pygmalion Effect," *Harvard Business Review,* May/June 1995, *73,* p. 14.

39. See T. Pollock, "Beware of the 'Halo Effect,'" *Supervision,* 1994, *24,* p. 24; and D. Howard, "The Hiring Game," *Canadian Business,* September 26, 1997, p. 136.

40. For one example, see M. F. R. Kets de Vries, "The Anatomy of the Entrepreneur: Clinical Observations," *Human Relations,* 1996, *49,* pp. 853–883.

41. M. Haire and W. F. Grunes, "Perceptual Defenses: Processes Protecting an Organized Perception of Another Personality," *Human Relations,* 1950, *3,* pp. 403–412.

42. Based on *Wall Street Journal,* March 1, 1989, and March 10, 1989.

43. For a thorough discussion of implicit theories, see R. J. Sternberg, "Implicit Theories of Intelligence, Creativity, and Wisdom," *Journal of Personality and Social Psychology,* 1985, *49,* pp. 607–627.

44. H. H. Kelley, "The Processes of Causal Attribution," *American Psychologist,* 1973, *28,* pp. 107–128.

45. S. Shellenbarger, "Dad Takes Home a Tough Day at Work," *Wall Street Journal,* June 29, 1994, p. B1.

46. Ibid.

47. P. C. Smith, L. M. Kendall, and C. L. Hulin, *The Measurement of Satisfaction in Work and Retirement* (Chicago: Rand McNally, 1969).

48. A. H. Brayfield and H. F. Rothe, "An Index of Job Satisfaction," *Journal of Applied Psychology,* 1951, *35,* pp. 307–311. To score the scale items, give a 5 for "Strongly Agree," a 4 for "Agree," and so on down to 1 for "Strongly Disagree." Then sum the scores for the five items to get an overall score for these items.

49. While there has been some concern that satisfaction and affectivity might simply be measures of the same thing, rigorous statistical procedures show satisfaction, positive affectivity, and negative affectivity to be distinct constructs. For instance, see A. O. Agho, J. L. Price, and C. W. Mueller, "Discriminant Validity of Measures of Job Satisfaction, Positive Affectivity and Negative Affectivity," *Journal of Occupational and Organizational Psychology,* 1992, *65,* pp. 185–196.

50. B. M. Staw, N. E. Bell, and N. A. Clausen, "The Dispositional Approach to Job Attitudes: A Lifetime Longitudinal Perspective," *Administrative Science Quarterly,* 1986, *31,* pp. 56–77.

51. For instance, see D. Seligman, "Genes on the Job," *Fortune,* January 13, 1992, p. 87.

52. See J. Adler, "The Happiness Meter," *Newsweek,* July 29, 1996, p. 78.

53. On this point, see B. Gerhart, "How Important Are Dispositional Factors as Determinants of Job Satisfaction? Implications for Job Design and Other Personnel Programs," *Journal of Applied Psychology,* 1987, *72,* pp. 366–373; and T. C. Murtha, R. Kanfer, and P. L. Ackerman, "Toward an Interactionist Taxonomy of Personality and Situations: An Integrative Situational-Dispositional Representation of Personality Traits," *Journal of Personality and Social Psychology,* 1996, *71,* pp. 193–207.

54. These items are drawn from T. M. Lodahl and M. Kejner, "The Definition and Measurement of Job Involvement," *Journal of Applied Psychology,* 1965, *49,* pp. 24–33.

55. For a discussion of this issue, see A. W. Schaef and D. Fassel, *The Addictive Organization* (New York: Harper and Row, 1988).

56. R. T. Mowday, R. M. Steers, and L. W. Porter, "The Measurement of Organizational Commitment," *Journal of Vocational Behavior,* 1979, *14,* pp. 224–247.

57. See, for instance, J. Meyer and N. Allen, "Testing the 'Side-Bet' Theory of Organizational Commitment: Reexamination of the Continuance and Affective Scales," *Journal of Applied Psychology,* 1984, *69,* pp. 372–378; and M. J. Somers, "A Test of the Relationship Between Affective and Continuance Commitment Using Non-Recursive Models," *Journal of Occupational and Organizational Psychology,* 1993, *66,* pp. 185–192.

58. See A. Cohen, "Age and Tenure in Relation to Organizational Commitment: A Meta-Analysis," *Basic and Applied Social Psychology,* 1993, *14,* pp. 143–159; and A. Cohen, "Organizational Commitment and Turnover: A Meta-Analysis," *Academy of Management Journal,* 1993, *36,* pp. 1140–1157.

59. R. J. Vandenberg and C. E. Lance, "Examining the Causal Order of Job Satisfaction and Organizational Commitment," *Journal of Management,* 1992, *18,* pp. 153–167.

60. For an interesting discussion of this issue, see A. Rafaeli and R. I. Sutton, "Expression of Emotion as Part of the Work Role," *Academy of Management Review,* 1987, *12,* pp. 23–37.

61. For more on the regulation of emotions, see A. Rafaeli, "When Clerks Meet Customers: A Test of Variables Related to Emotional Expressions on the Job," *Journal of Applied Psychology,* 1989, *74,* pp. 385–393; and J. Van Maanen and G. Kunda, "'Real Feelings': Emotional Expression and Organizational Culture," in L. L. Cummings and B. M. Staw, eds., *Research in Organizational Behavior,* Vol. 11 (Greenwich, CT: JAI Press, 1989), pp. 43–103.

62. R. T. LaPiere, "Attitudes and Actions," *Social Forces,* 1934, *13,* pp. 230–237.

63. Ibid.

64. This listing is based primarily on A. L. Weber, *Social Psychology* (New York: HarperCollins, 1992), pp. 129–130.

65. D. Mogelefsky, "Power to the People," *Incentive,* August 2000, pp. 18–22.

66. See, for instance, T. L.-P. Tang, J. K. Kim, and D. S.-H. Tang, "Does Attitude Toward Money Moderate the Relationship Between Intrinsic Job Satisfaction and Voluntary Turnover?" *Human Relations,* 2000, *53,* pp. 213–245.

67. W. H. Mobley, S. O. Horner, and A. T. Hollingsworth, "An Evaluation of Precursors of Hospital Employee Turnover," *Journal of Applied Psychology,* 1978, *63,* pp. 408–414.

68. See, for instance, J. K. Sager and A. Menon, "The Role of Behavioral Intentions in Turnover of Salespeople," *Journal of Business Research,* 1994, *29,* pp. 179–188.

69. P. M. Muchinsky and P. C. Morrow, "A Multidisciplinary Model of Voluntary Employee Turnover," *Journal of Vocational Behavior,* 1980, *17,* pp. 263–290.

70. Bureau of National Affairs, "Absenteeism Policy Guide," *BNA Policy and Practices Manual no. 518,* 1981, p. 223.

71. "Last Minute Absences Cost Big Bucks," *Business and*

Health, November 1998, p. 56; "Link Absenteeism and Benefits—and Help Cut Costs," *HR Focus,* April 2000, pp. 5-6; and "Absenteeism Sickens Bottom Line," *HR Focus,* January 1999, p. 4.

72. K. Dow Scott and G. S. Taylor, "An Examination of Conflicting Findings on the Relationship Between Job Satisfaction and Absenteeism: A Meta-Analysis," *Academy of Management Journal,* 1985, *28,* pp. 599-612.

73. For instance, see F. Herzberg et al., *Job Attitudes: Review of Research and Opinion* (Pittsburgh, PA: Psychological Service of Pittsburgh, 1957); and A. H. Brayfield and W. H. Crockett, "Employee Attitudes and Employee Performance," *Psychological Bulletin,* 1955, *52,* pp. 396-424.

74. M. T. Iaffaldano and P. M. Muchinsky, "Job Satisfaction and Job Performance: A Meta-Analysis," *Psychological Bulletin,* 1985, *97,* pp. 251-273. A meta-analysis is essentially a statistical summary of past research.

75. D. W. Organ, "A Reappraisal and Reinterpretation of the Satisfaction-Causes-Performance Hypothesis," *Academy of Management Review,* 1977, *2,* pp. 46-53; L. Van Dyne, J. W. Graham, and R. M. Dienesch, "Organizational Citizenship Behavior: Construct Redefinition, Measurement, and Validation," *Academy of Management Journal,* 1994, *37,* pp. 765-802; and D. W. Organ and K. Ryan, "A Meta-Analytic Review of Attitudinal and Dispositional Predictors of Organizational Citizenship Behavior," *Personnel Psychology,* 1995, *48,* pp. 775-802.

76. T. S. Bateman and D. W. Organ, "Job Satisfaction and the Good Soldier: The Relationship Between Affect and Employee 'Citizenship,'" *Academy of Management Journal,* 1983, *26,* pp. 587-595.

77. T. F. O'Boyle, "Disgruntled Workers Intent on Revenge Increasingly Harm Colleagues and Bosses," *Wall Street Journal,* September 15, 1992, p. B1.

78. D. Harbrecht, "Talk About Murder Inc.," *Business Week,* July 11, 1994, p. 8.

79. F. Barringer, "Anger in the Post Office: Killings Raise Questions," *New York Times,* May 8, 1993, sec. 1, p. 7.

80. D. L. Johnson, "Manager's Journal: The Best Defense Against Workplace Violence," *Wall Street Journal,* July 19, 1993, p. A10.

81. J. E. Rigdon, "Companies See More Workplace Violence," *Wall Street Journal,* April 12, 1994, p. B1.

82. P. H. Mirvis and E. E. Lawler III, "Measuring the Financial Impact of Employee Attitudes," *Journal of Applied Psychology,* 1977, *62,* pp. 1-8. This article provides a very nice tutorial on behavioral accounting.

83. R. B. Dunham, *Organizational Behavior: People and Processes in Management* (Homewood, IL: Richard D. Irwin, 1984), pp. 90-91.

84. See, for instance, A. P. Brief, A. H. Butcher, and L. Roberson, "Cookies, Disposition, and Job Attitudes: The Effects of Positive Mood-Inducing Events and Negative Affectivity on Job Satisfaction in a Field Experiment," *Organizational Behavior and Human Decision Processes,* 1995, *62,* pp. 55-62.

85. D. G. Myers, *Social Psychology,* 4th ed. (New York: McGraw-Hill, 1993), p. 528; and J. M. George and A. P. Brief, "Feeling Good—Doing Good: A Conceptual Analysis of the Mood at Work-Organizational Spontaneity Relationship," *Psychological Bulletin,* 1992, *112,* pp. 310-329.

86. L. Festinger, *A Theory of Cognitive Dissonance* (Evanston, IL: Row, Peterson, 1957).

87. Dissonance theory is one of a family of balance theories, each of which argues that people wish to maintain a state of balance—here, that various thoughts should be consistent, or in balance—and will take actions to restore balance. We'll explore another balance theory, called equity theory, in Chapter 6.

88. Weber, p. 131.

89. Ibid., pp. 131 and 132.

90. Ibid., p. 132.

CHAPTER 4. SOLVING PROBLEMS

1. This listing is drawn primarily from G. P. Huber, *Managerial Decision Making* (Glenview, IL: Scott, Foresman, 1980).

2. For more on problem definition, see G. H. Wedberg, "But First, Understand the Problem," *Journal of Systems Management,* June 1990, pp. 20-28; and R. Hamlin, "Improved Problem Solving," *Supervisory Management,* October 1991, p. 7.

3. In fact, one alternative dominates another if it is at least as good as the other on all attributes and better on even one.

4. See, for instance, R. T. Clemen, *Making Hard Decisions: An Introduction to Decision Analysis,* 2nd ed. (Belmont, CA: Duxbury Press, 1996).

5. B. A. Stein and R. M. Kanter, "Leadership for Change: The Rest of the Story," *Frontiers of Health Services Management,* Winter 1993, p. 29.

6. This listing is based on B. M. Staw and J. Ross, "Understanding Behavior in Escalation Situations," *Science,* October 1986, pp. 216-220.

7. See M. Keil and R. Montealegre, "Cutting Your Losses: Extricating Your Organization When a Big Project Goes Awry," *Sloan Management Review,* Spring 2000, pp. 55-68; and M. Mandell, "Knowing When to Quit," *World Trade,* April 1999, p. 95.

8. For example, see "A Contingency Plan Pays Off," *Journal of Property Management,* July/August 1993, pp. 14, 15.

9. This cycle is sometimes referred to as the PDSA cycle, for plan-do-study-act. For discussions of PDCA, see P. R. Scholtes, *The Leader's Handbook: Making Things Happen, Getting Things Done* (New York: McGraw-Hill, 1998), pp. 33-34. See also R. L. Luebbe and B. K. Snavely, "Making Effective Team Decisions with Consensus Building Tools," *Industrial Management,* September/October 1997, pp. 1-7.

10. See, for instance, H. A. Simon, "A Behavioral Model of Rational Choice," in M. Alexis and C. Wilson (eds.), *Organizational Decision Making* (Englewood Cliffs, NJ: Prentice-Hall, 1967); P. Slovic, "Psychological Study of Human Judgment: Implications for Investment Decision Making," *Journal of Finance,* 1972, *27,* pp. 779-800; R. N. Taylor, "Psychological Determinants of Bounded Rationality," *Decision Sciences,* 1975, *6,* pp. 409-429; and W. B. Arthur, "Inductive Reasoning and Bounded Rationality," *The American Economic Review,* 1994, *84,* pp. 406-411.

11. A. Tversky and D. Kahneman, "The Framing of Deci-

sions and the Psychology of Choice," *Science,* January 30, 1981, pp. 453–458.

12. For more on framing effects, see G. Whyte, "Decision Failures: Why They Occur and How to Prevent Them," *Academy of Management Executive,* August 1991, pp. 23–31; D. Frisch, "Reasons for Framing Effects," *Organizational Behavior and Human Decision Processes,* 1993, *54,* pp. 399–429; and H. Mano, "Risk-taking, Framing Effects, and Affect," *Organizational Behavior and Human Decision Processes,* 1994, *57,* pp. 38–58.

13. P. Wright, "The Harassed Decision Maker: Time Pressures, Distractions, and the Use of Evidence," *Journal of Applied Psychology,* 1974, *59,* pp. 555–561. See also E. W. Farmer, J. Hunter, and A. J. Belyavin, "Performance Under Time Constraints: The Role of Personality," *Perceptual and Motor Skills,* 1984, *59,* pp. 875–884; and T. V. Paul, "Time Pressure and War Initiation: Some Linkages," *Canadian Journal of Political Science,* 1995, *28,* pp. 255–276.

14. I. L. Janis and L. Mann, *Decision Making: A Psychological Analysis of Conflict, Choice, and Commitment* (New York: Free Press, 1977), provide a thorough discussion of these situations. See also J. E. Driskell and E. Salas, "Group Decision Making Under Stress," *Journal of Applied Psychology,* 1991, *76,* pp. 473–478; "Managing Under Stress," *Supervision,* September 1993, p. 25; and N. R. Augustine, "Managing the Crisis You Tried to Prevent," *Harvard Business Review,* November/December 1995, pp. 147–158.

15. C. M. Peterson and L. R. Beach, "Man as an Intuitive Statistician," *Psychological Bulletin,* 1967, *68,* pp. 29–46, provide one good early review supporting this view.

16. For instance, see R. M. Hogarth, "Beyond Discrete Biases: Functional and Dysfunctional Aspects of Judgmental Heuristics," *Psychological Bulletin,* 1981, *90,* pp. 197–217.

17. See A. Tversky and D. Kahneman, "Judgment Under Uncertainty: Heuristics and Biases," *Science,* 1974, *185,* pp. 1124–1131, for a good discussion.

18. J. G. March and H. A. Simon, *Organizations* (New York: Wiley, 1958).

19. Tversky and Kahneman, "Judgment Under Uncertainty."

20. On this specific point, see S. Lichtenstein et al., "Judged Frequency of Lethal Events," *Journal of Experimental Psychology: Human Learning and Memory,* 1978, *4,* pp. 551–578. For a detailed discussion of the availability heuristic, see A. Tversky and D. Kahneman, "Availability: A Heuristic for Judging Frequency and Probability," *Cognitive Psychology,* 1973, *5,* pp. 207–232. See also M. Manis, J. Shedler, and J. Jonides, "Availability Heuristic in Judgments of Set Size and Frequency of Occurrence," *Journal of Personality and Social Psychology,* 1993, *65,* pp. 448–457.

21. This example is from Tversky and Kahneman, "Judgment Under Uncertainty."

22. E. Valenzi and I. R. Andrews, "Individual Differences in the Decision Process of Employment Interviewers," *Journal of Applied Psychology,* 1973, *58,* pp. 49–53.

23. See, for instance, R. McGarvey, "Now or Never," *Entrepreneur,* October 1995, pp. 75–77; J. P. Zane, "Some Advice to Heed, If Not Now, Tomorrow: Procrastination's Toll on the Job," *New York Times,* February 11, 1996, Sec. 3, p. 11; and H. Lancaster, "Procrastinators: Mend Your Ways

Before Your Job Stalls," *Wall Street Journal,* May 7, 1996, p. B1.

24. L. S. Richman, "Rekindling the Entrepreneurial Fire," *Fortune,* February 21, 1994, p. 112.

25. M. Roig and L. DeTommaso, "Are College Cheating and Plagiarism Related to Academic Procrastination?" *Psychological Reports,* 1995, *77,* pp. 691–698. For more on procrastination, see N. N. Harris and R. I. Sutton, "Task Procrastination in Organizations: A Framework for Research," *Human Relations,* 1983, *36,* pp. 987–995; N. A. Milgram, W. Dangour, and A. Raviv, "Situational and Personal Determinants of Academic Procrastination," *The Journal of General Psychology,* 1992, *119,* pp. 123–133; and C. Senecal, R. Koestner, and R. J. Vallerand, "Self-Regulation and Academic Procrastination," *The Journal of Social Psychology,* 1995, *135,* pp. 607–619.

26. This choice mode was first proposed by C. E. Lindblom, "The Science of Muddling Through," *Public Administration Review,* 1959, *19,* pp. 79–88. See also C. W. Park, "Joint Decisions in Home Purchasing: A Muddling-Through Process," *The Journal of Consumer Research,* 1982, *9,* pp. 151–162.

27. See W. Edwards, "Conservatism in Human Information Processing," in B. Kleinmuntz (ed.), *Formal Representation of Clinical Judgment* (New York: Wiley, 1968); and H. J. Einhorn, "Overconfidence in Judgment," *New Directions for Methodology of Social and Behavioral Science,* 1980, *4,* pp. 1–16, for discussions of explanations for this tendency. See also M. Bjorkman, "Internal Cue Theory: Calibration and Resolution of Confidence in General Knowledge," *Organizational Behavior and Human Decision Processes,* 1994, *58,* pp. 386–405.

28. For a discussion of decision confirmation, see D. J. Power and R. J. Aldag, "Soelberg's Job Search and Choice Model: A Clarification, Review, and Critique," *Academy of Management Review,* 1985, *10,* pp. 48–58.

29. Janis and Mann, *Decision Making: A Psychological Analysis of Conflict, Choice, and Commitment.*

30. For other examples of crisis planning and management teams, see N. Jeffrey, "Preparing for the Worst: Firms Set Up Plans to Help Deal with Corporate Crises," *Wall Street Journal,* December 7, 1987, p. 25; C. Ansberry, "Oil Spill in the Midwest Provides Case Study in Crisis Management," *Wall Street Journal,* January 8, 1988, p. 17; D. Bown, "Oklahoma City, April 19, 1995," *Public Management,* December 1995, pp. 6–9.

31. This is based primarily on O. Behling and N. L. Eckel, "Making Sense Out of Intuition," *Academy of Management Executive,* 1991, *5(1),* pp. 46–54.

32. M. W. McCall, Jr., and R. E. Kaplan, *Whatever It Takes* (Englewood Cliffs, NJ: Prentice-Hall, 1985), p. 32.

33. H. Simon, "Making Management Decisions: The Role of Intuition and Emotion," *Academy of Management Executive,* 1987, *1,* pp. 57–64.

34. J. Adair, "Why Managers Need to Develop Their Intuition," *International Management,* November 1984, pp. 34, 39–40.

35. S. A. Mednick, "The Associative Basis of the Creative Process," *Psychological Review,* 1962, *69,* p. 221. For a discussion of creative products, see S. P. Besemer and D. J.

Treffinger, "Analysis of Creative Products: Review and Synthesis," *Journal of Creative Behavior,* 1981, *15,* pp. 158–178.

36. For discussions of the impact of motivation on creativity, see G. Halpin and G. Halpin, "The Effect of Motivation on Creative Thinking Abilities," *Journal of Creative Behavior,* 1973, *7,* pp. 51–53; T. Stevens, "Creativity Killers," *Industry Week,* January 23, 1995, p. 63; and K. Vergoth, "Head Trips," *Psychology Today,* November/December 1995, p. 12.

37. G. Wallas, *The Art of Thought* (New York: Harcourt, Brace, 1926). For a good discussion of the stages of the creative process, see J. D. Couger, *Creative Problem Solving and Opportunity Finding* (Danvers, MA: Boyd and Fraser, 1995), pp. 230–236.

38. Quoted in G. A. Davis, *Creativity Is Forever* (Dubuque, IA: Kendall/Hunt, 1983), p. 9.

39. T. R. Amabile, *The Social Psychology of Creativity* (New York: Springer-Verlag, 1983).

40. F. Barron, "The Dream of Art and Poetry," *Psychology Today,* 1968, *2(12),* pp. 18–23; W. E. Scott, Jr., "The Creative Individual," *Academy of Management Journal,* 1965, *8,* pp. 211–219; and G. A. Steiner (ed.), *The Creative Organization* (Chicago: University of Chicago Press, 1965). See also T. Stevens, "Creativity Killers," *Industry Week,* January 23, 1995, p. 63.

41. T. Christie, "Environmental Factors in Creativity," *Journal of Creative Behavior,* 1970, *4,* pp. 13–31.

42. H. C. Lehman, *Age and Achievement* (Princeton, NJ: Princeton University Press, 1953). This peaking of creative output in young adulthood is seen primarily for major creative contributions. For minor contributions, creative output peaks in middle age. In general, the peak of the creative output curve occurs earlier in fields highly dependent on native ability and later for fields requiring substantial training and life experience. These observations appear to be stable across cultural groups and historical periods. See also J. Abra, "Changes in Creativity With Age: Data, Explanations, and Further Predictions," *International Journal of Aging and Human Development,* 1989, *28,* pp. 105–126; and R. Helson, B. Roberts, and G. Agronick, "Enduringness and Change in Creative Personality and the Prediction of Occupational Creativity," *Journal of Personality and Social Psychology,* 1995, *69,* pp. 1173–1183.

43. E. P. Torrance and N. C. Aliotti, "Sex Differences in Levels of Performance and Test–Retest Reliability on the Torrance Tests of Creative Thinking Ability," *Journal of Creative Behavior,* 1969, *3,* pp. 52–57.

44. J. R. Raia and S. H. Osipow, "Creative Thinking Ability and Susceptibility to Persuasion," *Journal of Social Psychology,* 1970, *28,* pp. 181–186.

45. P. O. Heist, *The Creative College Student: An Unmet Challenge* (San Francisco: Jossey-Bass, 1968); and E. P. Torrance, "Is Bias Against Job Changing Bias Against Giftedness?" *Gifted Child Quarterly,* 1971, *15,* pp. 244–248.

46. W. J. J. Gordon, *Synectics* (New York: Harper and Row, 1961).

47. Davis, *Creativity Is Forever,* p. 67.

48. See "Four Ways to Boost Creativity," *Training,* December 1991, pp. 16+.

49. For instance, W. J. J. Gordon, "On Being Explicit About Creative Process," *Journal of Creative Behavior,* 1972, *6,* pp. 295–300, wrote that more than 200 businesses had spent more than $1 million on synectics techniques as early as 1971 and that materials developed by Synectics Education Systems had influenced over 10,000 classrooms. A 1988 Synectics brochure indicated that Synectics Corporation had worked with over 50,000 individuals and with approximately 25 percent of the Fortune 500 companies. For discussions of the application of synectics and other creativity-enhancement techniques in organizations, see D. Thorn, "Problem Solving for Innovation in Industry," *Journal of Creative Behavior,* 1987, *21,* pp. 93–107; and L. B. Sawyer, "The Creative Side of Internal Auditing," *The Internal Auditor,* December 1992, pp. 57–62.

50. Gordon, *Synectics,* p. 42. For more on direct analogy, see L. Okagaki and B. Koslowski, "Another Look at Analogies and Problem Solving," *The Journal of Creative Behavior,* 1987, *21,* pp. 15–21; and D. Offner, "'Hitch-Hiking' on Creativity in Nature," *The Journal of Creative Behavior,* 1990, *24,* pp. 199–204.

51. E. Winninghoff, "How I Get Ideas," *Executive Female,* 1993, *16,* p. 50.

52. For more on the use of analogies, see "Keep Those Great Ideas Coming," *Executive Female,* January–February 1993, pp. 46–50; and T. Pollock, "Strategies for Creative Thinking," *Supervision,* 1995, *56,* pp. 21–22.

53. See Davis, *Creativity Is Forever,* for a fuller discussion.

54. A. F. Osborne, *Applied Imagination: Principles and Procedures of Creative Problem Solving,* 3rd ed. (Buffalo, NY: Creative Education Foundation, 1993). See also M. Michalko, "Four Steps Toward Creative Thinking," *The Futurist,* May/June 2000, pp. 18–21.

55. R. P. Crawford, "The Techniques of Creative Thinking," in G. A. Davis and J. A. Scott (eds.), *Training Creative Thinking* (Huntington, NY: Krieger, 1978).

56. Davis, *Creativity Is Forever.*

57. This example is from J. E. Arnold, "Useful Creative Techniques," in S. Parnes (ed.), *A Sourcebook of Creative Thinking* (New York: Scribner's, 1962), pp. 251–268.

58. For studies on morphological analysis, see E. P. Stratton and R. Brown, "Improving Creative Training by Training in the Production and/or Judgment of Solutions," *Journal of Educational Psychology,* 1970, *61,* pp. 16–23; T. F. Warren and G. A. Davis, "Techniques for Creative Thinking: An Empirical Comparison of Three Methods," *Psychological Reports,* 1969, *25,* pp. 207–214; F. Zwicky, *Discovery, Invention, Research Through the Morphological Approach* (New York: Macmillan, 1969); and "Four Ways to Boost Creativity," *Training,* 1991, *28,* p. 16.

59. A. K. Naj, "Hey, Get a Grip! Your Basic Paper Clip Is Like a Mousetrap," *Wall Street Journal,* July 24, 1995, pp. A1, A8.

60. See B. Olmo, "Retroduction: The Key to Creativity," *Journal of Creative Behavior,* 1977, *11,* pp. 216, 221.

61. D. Stipp, "Patrick Gunkel Is an Idea Man Who Thinks in Lists," *Wall Street Journal* (June 1, 1987), pp. 1, 11.

62. This example is drawn from M. Michalko, *Thinkertoys* (Berkeley, CA: Ten Speed Press, 1991), pp. 45–46.

63. This example is drawn from S. Yoder, "Japan's Scientists Find Pure Research Suffers Under Rigid Life Style," *Wall*

Street Journal (November 31, 1988), p. A1. See also E. Thornton, "Japan's Struggle To Be Creative," *Fortune,* April 19, 1993, pp. 129+; and J. S. Jun and H. Muto, "The Hidden Dimensions of Japanese Administration: Culture and Its Impact," *Public Administration Review,* March/April 1995, pp. 125–134.

64. *Wall Street Journal,* January 5, 1985, p. 3.

65. For more on venture teams, see K. Murphy, "Venture Teams Help Companies Create New Products," *Personnel Journal,* March 1992, pp. 60–63+; and B. Frost, T. Gannarelli, and C. Hunt, "Venture Teams: Not Improving What Is, But Creating What Isn't," *Public Management,* 1995, 77, pp. 17–21.

66. The name *skunk works* is borrowed from *Skonk Works,* the name of the still used to make Kickapoo Joy Juice in the late Al Capp's comic strip, *Li'l Abner.*

67. J. B. White and O. Suris, "How a 'Skunk Works' Kept the Mustang Alive—On a Tight Budget," *Wall Street Journal,* September 21, 1993, pp. A1, A12.

68. T. J. Peters and R. H. Waterman, Jr., *In Search of Excellence: Lessons for America's Best-Run Companies* (New York: Harper and Row, 1982), pp. 203–204. For more on idea champions, see J. M. Howell and C. A. Higgins, "Champions of Change: Identifying, Understanding, and Supporting Champions of Technological Innovations," *Organizational Dynamics,* Summer 1990, pp. 40–55; and P. G. Greene, C. G. Brush, and M. M. Hart, "The Corporate Venture Champion: A Resource-Based Approach to Role and Process," *Entrepreneurship Theory and Practice,* Spring 1999, pp. 103–122.

69. For discussions of intrapreneurship, see "How Can Big Companies Keep the Entrepreneurial Spirit Alive?" *Harvard Business Review,* November/December 1995, pp. 183–186+; M. H. Peak, "Turning Entrepreneurial Ideas Inside Out," *Management Review,* 1996, *85,* p. 7; T. D. Schellhardt, "David and Goliath: Some Giant Companies Are Particularly Good at Fostering an Entrepreneurial Spirit. Here's How They Do It," *Wall Street Journal,* May 23, 1996, p. R14; and S. A. Zahra, A. P. Nielsen, and W. C. Bogner, "Corporate Entrepreneurship, Knowledge, and Competence Development," *Entrepreneurship Theory and Practice,* Spring 1999, pp. 169–189.

70. This section is based on B. Bird, *Entrepreneurial Behavior* (Glenview, IL: Scott, Foresman, 1989), p. 28. See also, L. Prasad, "The Etiology of Organizational Politics: Implications for the Intrapreneur," *Advanced Management Journal,* Summer 1993, pp. 35–41.

71. These are based on G. F. Pinchot III, *Intrapreneuring* (New York: Harper and Row, 1985), pp. 198–256. For more on Pinchot's views, see J. Pickard, "A Fertile Grounding," *People Management,* October 24, 1996, pp. 28–34.

72. "Intrapreneurship at Bell Atlantic," *Business Quarterly,* Spring 1993, pp. 46–47.

73. R. V. Adams, "Nurturing the Entrepreneur," *Appliance Manufacturer,* Spring 1992, p. 26; and "Barefoot into PARC," *The Economist,* July 10, 1993, p. 68.

74. T. Cox, Jr., *Cultural Diversity in Organizations: Theory, Research, and Practice* (San Francisco: Berrett-Koehler, 1994), pp. 31–35. See also G. F. Shea, "Learn How to Treasure Differences," *HRMagazine,* December 1992, pp. 34–37.

75. R. M. Kanter, *The Change Masters* (New York: Simon and Schuster, 1983), p. 167.

76. P. L. McLeod, S. A. Lobel, and T. Cox, Jr., *Cultural Diversity and Creativity in Small Groups: A Test of the Value-in-Diversity Hypothesis.* Unpublished working paper, the University of Michigan, Ann Arbor, 1993.

77. C. J. Nemeth, "Dissent, Group Process, and Creativity," in E. Lawler, ed., *Advances in Group Processes,* Vol. 2 (Greenwich, CT: JAI Press,1985), pp. 57–75.

78. J. E. McGrath, *Groups: Interaction and Performance* (Englewood Cliffs, NJ: Prentice-Hall, 1984). See also I. Dodds, "Differences Can Also be Strengths," *People Management,* April 20, 1995, pp. 40–41+.

79. See T. Cox, Jr., pp. 36–39.

80. For more on this issue, see J. M. Ivancevich and J. A. Gilbert, "Diversity Management: Time for a New Approach," *Public Personnel Management,* Spring 2000, pp. 75–92; and K. Melymuka, "Indulging Our Differences: 100 Best Places to Work," *Computerworld,* June 19, 2000, pp. 56–57.

81. J. E. Rigdon, "More Companies Send Staffs on Retreats to Spur Creativity and Jolt Thinking," *Wall Street Journal,* October 16, 1991, pp. B1, B8.

82. These guidelines are based in part on R. Fisher, W. Ury, and B. Patton, *Getting to Yes: Negotiating Agreement Without Giving In,* 2nd ed. (New York: Penguin Books, 1991). That book is an excellent, readable discussion of guidelines for attaining win-win outcomes.

83. These guidelines for planning negotiations are based primarily on J. H. Hopkins, "Negotiations and the Credit Professional," *Business Credit,* June 1999, pp. 16–17.

84. To learn more about BATNA, see R. Fisher, W. Ury, and B. Patton, *Getting to Yes: Negotiating Agreement Without Giving In,* 2nd ed. (New York: Penguin Books, 1991), pp. 97–106. See also D. Ertel, "Turning Negotiation Into a Corporate Capability," *Harvard Business Review,* May/June 1999, pp. 55–70.

85. R. Fisher, W. Ury, and B. Patton, *Getting to Yes: Negotiating Agreement Without Giving In,* 2nd ed. (New York: Penguin Books, 1991), p. 38.

86. These strategies were proposed by D. G. Pruitt, "Achieving Integrative Agreements," in M. H. Bazerman and R. J. Lewicki, *Negotiating in Organizations* (Beverly Hills, CA: Sage, 1983), pp. 35–50.

87. This section is based on M. H. Bazerman, *Judgment in Managerial Decision Making,* 3rd ed. (New York: Wiley, 1994), pp. 141–144.

CHAPTER 5. COMMUNICATING EFFECTIVELY

1. T. R. Peters and R. H. Waterman, *In Search of Excellence: Lessons from America's Best-Run Companies* (New York: Harper and Row, 1982).

2. H. Mintzberg, *The Nature of Managerial Work* (Englewood Cliffs, NJ: Prentice-Hall, 1973).

3. W. G. Scott and T. R. Mitchell, *Organization Theory: A Structural and Behavioral Analysis* (Homewood, IL: Richard D. Irwin, 1976).

4. For a discussion of the motivating role of language, see J. J. Sullivan, "Three Roles of Language in Motivation The-

ory," *Academy of Management Review,* 1988, *13,* pp. 104–115.

5. This section is based in part on J. W. Newstrom and K. Davis, *Organizational Behavior: Human Behavior at Work,* 9th ed. (New York: McGraw-Hill, 1993), pp. 93–96.

6. This listing of channel characteristics is drawn from R. B. Dunham, *Organizational Behavior: People and Processes in Management* (Homewood, IL: Richard D. Irwin, 1984).

7. H. J. Leavitt, *Managerial Psychology,* rev. ed. (Chicago: University of Chicago Press, 1964), pp. 138–152.

8. R. L. Daft and R. H. Lengel, "Information Richness: A New Approach to Managerial Behavior and Organization Design," in B. Staw and L. L. Cummings (eds.), *Research in Organizational Behavior* (Greenwich, CT: JAI Press, 1984), pp. 191–233.

9. For classic discussions of communication networks, see H. Guetzkow and H. Simon, "The Impact of Certain Communication Nets upon Organization and Performance in Task-Oriented Groups," *Management Science,* 1955, *1,* pp. 233–250; and M. E. Shaw, "Communication Networks," in L. Berkowitz, ed., *Advances in Experimental Social Psychology* (New York: Academic Press, 1964), pp. 111–147.

10. *Wall Street Journal,* November 12, 1982, p. 1.

11. M. Master, "Could you be a BDU?" *Across the Board,* May 1999, p. 71.

12. M. Rowh, "Cy*ber*speak (si ber spek) n. language or terms related to computers or digital technology," *Office Systems,* April 1999, p. 8.

13. *Wall Street Journal,* September 30, 1988, p. 23.

14. *Wirtschaftswoche* (Germany), as reported in *ManpowerArgus,* July 1997, No. 346, p. 11.

15. For discussions of handbooks and manuals, see G. Flynn, "Take Another Look at the Employee Handbook," *Workforce,* March 2000, pp. 132–134; G. Levine, "QandA: The Power of Employee Handbooks," *Bobbin,* July 1998, pp. 78–82; and J. London, "Bring Your Employee Handbook into the Millennium," *HR Focus,* January 1999, p.6.

16. See S. Solo, "Japanese Comics Are All Business," *Fortune,* October 9, 1989, pp. 143–149.

17. See T. Love, "Back to the Old Suggestion Box," *Nation's Business,* May 1998, p. 11; and M. Frese, E. Teng, and C. J. D. Wijnen, "Helping to Improve Suggestion Systems: Predictors of Making Suggestions in Companies," *Journal of Organizational Behavior,* December 1999, pp. 1139–1155.

18. See M. I. Lurie, "The 8 Essential Steps in Grievance Processing," *Dispute Resolution Journal,* November 1999, pp. 61–65.

19. For a good discussion of organizational surveys, see R. B. Dunham and F. J. Smith, *Organizational Surveys: An Internal Assessment of Organizational Health* (Homewood, IL: Richard D. Irwin, 1979). See also "Employee Input Can Maximize Recognition/Reward System Success," *HR Focus,* November 1999, p. 15; and R. J. Sahl, "Creating a Company-Specific Attitude Survey," *The Human Resource Professional,* September/October 1999, pp. 23–27.

20. This section, including the listing of guidelines for effective speaking, is based primarily on W. P. Galle, Jr., B. H. Nelson, D. W. Luse, and M. F. Villere, *Business Communication: A Technology-Based Approach* (Chicago: Irwin, 1996), pp. 447–458.

21. For discussions of listening, see S. Caudron, "Listen Up!" *Workforce,* August 1999, pp. 25–27; R. C. Boyle, "A Manager's Guide to Effective Listening," *Manage,* July 1999, pp. 6–7; and R. A. Prince and K. M. File, "Listen Then Talk: The Difference Between Top Financial Advisors and the Rest Is That the Top Advisers Really, Really Listen," *Financial Planning,* November 1, 1998, pp. 167–168.

22. See C. Crossen, "The Crucial Question for These Noisy Times May Just Be: 'Huh?'" *Wall Street Journal,* July 19, 1997, pp. A1, A6.

23. This section is based on W. P. Galle, Jr., B. H. Nelson, D. W. Luse, and M. F. Villere, *Business Communication: A Technology-Based Approach* (Chicago: Irwin, 1996), pp. 444–447.

24. For instance, see P. Buhler, "Are You Really Saying What You Mean?" *Supervision,* September 1991, pp. 18–20; B. J. Sparks, "Make the Right Moves with Body Language," *Real Estate Today,* June 1994, pp. 35–38; and S. Martin, "The Role of Nonverbal Communications in Quality Improvement," *National Productivity Review,* Winter 1995–96, pp. 27–39.

25. This section is based on W. P. Galle, Jr., B. H. Nelson, D. W. Luse, and M. F. Villere, *Business Communication: A Technology-Based Approach* (Chicago: Irwin, 1996).

26. "Experts Can Read in the Eyes Whether Person Is Telling Lies," *Tulsa World,* January 26, 1987.

27. This discussion of types of nonverbal communication is based in part on G. B. Davis and M. H. Olson, *Management Information Systems: Conceptual Foundations, Structure, and Development,* 2nd ed. (New York: McGraw-Hill, 1985).

28. This discussion of paralanguage is based on W. P. Galle, Jr., B. H. Nelson, D. W. Luse, and M. F. Villere, *Business Communication: A Technology-Based Approach* (Chicago: Irwin, 1996), pp. 534–535.

29. J. R. Davitz and L. Davitz, "Nonverbal Vocal Communication of Feeling," *Journal of Communication,* 1961, *11,* pp. 81–86.

30. J. Sterrett, "Body Language and Job Interviews," *Journal of Business Education,* 1977, *53,* pp. 122–123.

31. J. L. Waltman and S. P. Golen, "Detecting Deception During Interviews," *The Internal Auditor,* August 1993, pp. 61–63.

32. R. L. Birdwhistell, *"Kinesics in Context: Essays on Body Motion Communications* (Philadelphia: University of Pennsylvania Press, 1970).

33. For discussions of the importance of eye contact, see M. Brody, "Delivering Your Speech Right Between Their Eyes," *Supervision,* June 1994, p. 18; S. A. Miller, "Controlling How Others See You Is Good Business," *The CPA Journal,* October 1994, pp. 75–76; and T. Nichols, "Smart Talk," *CA Magazine,* January–February 1995, pp. 60+.

34. J. Hornik, "Tactile Stimulation and Consumer Response," *The Journal of Consumer Response,* December 1992, pp. 449–458.

35. For instance, see T. Walker, "Discrimination and the Law: What Supervisors Should Know," *Supervisory Management,* August 1992, pp. 10–11.

36. W. P. Galle, Jr., B. H. Nelson, D. W. Luse, and M. F. Villere, *Business Communication: A Technology-Based Approach* (Chicago: Irwin, 1996), p. 532.

37. M. Lefkowitz, R. Blake, and J. Mouton, "Status of Ac-

tors in Pedestrian Violations of Traffic Signals," *Journal of Abnormal and Social Psychology,* 1955, *51,* pp. 704–706.

38. D. Keenan, "Does Your Dress Suit Your Job?" *Accountancy,* May 1995, p. 94.

39. See, for instance, B. Ziegler, "IBM Goes Casual, Drops White Shirts, and Plans a Woodsier Headquarters," *Wall Street Journal,* February 3, 1995, p. A3; G. Button, "No Bathrobes, Please," *Forbes,* November 6, 1995; and L. Himelstein and N. Walster, "Levi's vs. the Dress Code," *Business Week,* April 1, 1996, pp. 57–58.

40. See L. Lee, "Some Employees Just Aren't Suited for Dressing Down," *Wall Street Journal,* February 3, 1995, pp. A1, A6.

41. This section is based in part on A. C. Filley, *Interpersonal Conflict Resolution* (Glenview, IL: Scott, Foresman, 1975).

42. K. C. Laudon and J. P. Laudon, *Management Information Systems: Organization and Technology,* 3rd ed. (New York: Macmillan, 1994), p. 291.

43. J. C. Sipior and B. T. Ward, "The Dark Side of Employee Email," *Association for Computing Machinery: Communications of the ACM,* July 1999, pp. 88–95.

44. R. F. Rohan, "Say 'So Long' to Snail Mail," *Black Enterprise,* September 1998, pp. 37–38.

45. See E. Schwartz, "Lotus Moving on Language Conversion for Messages," *InfoWorld,* May 29, 2000, p. 8; and "Wearable PCs: Where Sci-Fi Fantasy Meets Modern Power, Practicality," *Security,* May 1999, pp. 9–10.

46. See C. Taylor, "Moving Targets," *Far Eastern Economic Review,* June 8, 2000, pp. 42–54; and J. Guyon, "The World Is Your Office," *Fortune,* June 12, 2000, pp. 227–234.

47. P. B. Carroll, "Computer Confusion," *Wall Street Journal,* June 4, 1990, pp. R28–R29. See also A. Markels, "Managers Aren't Always Able to Get the Right Message Across with E-Mail," *Wall Street Journal,* August 6, 1996, p. B1.

48. B. N. Meeks, "The Privacy Hoax," *Association for Computing Machinery, Communications of the ACM,* February 1999, pp. 17–19.

49. For a discussion of ethical issues relating to e-mail privacy, see P. S. L. Flanagan, "Cyberspace: The Final Frontier?" *Journal of Business Ethics,* March 1999, pp. 115–122.

50. G. Blake, "E-mail with Feeling," *Research Technology Management,* November/December 1999, pp. 12–13; M. Gibbs, "Don't Say It with Smileys," *Network World,* August 9, 1999, p. 62; and M. M. Extejt, "Teaching Students to Correspond Effectively Electronically," *Business Communication Quarterly,* June 1998, pp. 57–67.

51. G. P. Zachary, "Tech Shop: Can Autodesk's Latest CEO Survive a Cabal of Programmers Who Send 'Flame Mail'?" *Wall Street Journal,* May 28, 1992, p. A1; and K. Zhivago, "Dance of the Flamers," *MC Technology Marketing Intelligence,* April 2000, p. 108.

52. J. C. Sipior and B. T. Ward, "The Dark Side of Employee Email," *Association for Computing Machinery: Communications of the ACM,* July 1999, pp. 88–95; and "E-threats Impact Workplace," *Security,* March 1999, pp. 14–18.

53. J. C. Sipior and B. T. Ward, "The Dark Side of Employee Email," *Association for Computing Machinery: Communications of the ACM,* July 1999, pp. 88–95.

54. See G. Colombo, "Polish Your E-Mail Etiquette," *Sales and Marketing Management,* June 2000, p. 34; and E. R.

Blume, "The Etiquette Advantage," *Electric Perspectives,* May/June 2000, pp. 54–67.

55. T. Reiss and R. McNatt, "You've Got Mail, and Mail, and Mail . . .," *Business Week,* July 20, 1998, p. 6.

56. D. Beckman and D. Hirsch, "Triage for E-mail Clutter," *ABA Journal,* February 2000, p. 66; and G. R. Notess, "Filtering the Email Storm," *Online,* November/December 1998, pp. 64–66. For a discussion of telephonic robots that juggle fax, e-mail, and telephone calls, see J. R. Garber, "Phobot Phone Home," *Forbes,* December 14, 1998, p. 238.

57. L. Bongiorno and R. Brandt, "Nuns on the Internet, Software in the Souk," *Business Week,* January 30, 1995, p. 39.

58. C. C. Sanford, "The Internet: An Electronic Global Village," *Decision Line,* May 1994, pp. 3–6.

59. T. A. Stewart, "Boom Time on the New Frontier," *Fortune,* Autumn 1993, pp. 153–161.

60. E. Richard, "Anatomy of the World-Wide Web," *Internet World,* April 1995, pp. 28–30.

61. P. H. Lewis, "Companies Rush to Set Up Shop in Cyberspace," *New York Times,* November 2, 1994, p. D1.

62. A. Cortese, J. Verity, R. Mitchell, and R. Brandt, "Cyberspace," *Business Week,* February 27, 1995, pp. 78–86.

63. S. Konicki, "Powerful Portals," *InformationWeek,* May 1, 2000, pp. 44–66. See also T. Campbell, "A Portal to Productivity," *Sales and Marketing Management,* April 2000, p 34.

64. For instance, see A. Ziegler, "Videoconferencing: Not Just for CEOs Anymore," *InformationWeek,* June 7, 1999, pp. 146–150; and M. Davids, "Smiling for the Camera," *The Journal of Business Strategy,* May/June 1999, pp. 20–24.

65. B. Ziegler, "Video Conference Calls Change Business," *Wall Street Journal,* October 12, 1994, p. B1; and L. Wood, "Videoconferencing Shows Its Ready for Prime Time," *Internet Week,* July 12, 1999, p. 26.

66. Cost estimates vary, depending on the size and complexity of the system. See, for instance, J. M. O'Brien, "Videoconferencing Set to Surge," *Computer Dealer News,* January 29, 1999, pp. 1, 41; and A. Zieger, "Videoconferencing: Not Just for CEOs Anymore," *InformationWeek,* June 7, 1999, pp. 146–150.

67. "The Telescreen Is Ringing," *Fortune,* Summer 1999, p. 26.

68. S. M. Dugan, "Videoconferencing Sees Rosy Forecast," *InfoWorld,* August 30, 1999, p. 22.

69. N. Gross and J. Carey, "In the Digital Derby, There's No Inside Lane," *Business Week,* Special Issue on 21st Century Capitalism, 1994, pp. 146–154. See also S. Fister, "Videoconferencing: Good, Fast, and Cheap," *Training,* April 2000, pp. 30–32; and R. Evans, "The Value of Voice," *Communications International,* June 2000, pp. 43–48.

70. V. Zwass, "Electronic Commerce: Structures and Issues," *International Journal of Electronic Commerce,* Fall 1996, pp. 3–23.

71. F. J. Riggins and H.-S. Rhee, "Toward a Unified View of Electronic Commerce," *Association for Computing Machinery, Communications of the ACM,* October 1998, pp. 88–95.

72. W. Zellner, "Wooing the Newbies," *Business Week,* May 15, 2000, pp. EB116–EB120.

73. "Survey: E-Commerce: Something Old, Something New," *The Economist,* February 26, 2000, pp. 15–27.

74. S. J. Takacs and J. B. Frieden, "Changes on the Electronic Frontier: Growth and Opportunity of the World-Wide Web," *Journal of Marketing Theory and Practice,* Summer 1998, pp. 24–37.

75. "Help Wanted, Inquire Within," *Fortune,* Summer 2000, pp. 101–102.

76. M. Mendoza, "Opening Up with Extranets," *Computer-Aided Engineering,* February 2000, pp. 20–26.

77. "Heineken Redefines Collaborative Planning Through the Internet," *Beverage Industry,* September 1998, p. 47.

78. See, for instance, J. D. Johnson, "Approaches to Organizational Communication Structure," *Journal of Business Research,* 1992, *25,* pp. 99–113; and J. D. Johnson, W. A. Donohue, and C. K. Atkin, "Differences Between Formal and Informal Communication Channels," *Journal of Business Communication,* 1994, *31,* pp. 111–122.

79. These guidelines are based in part on P. M. Buhler, "A New Role for Managers: The Move from Directing to Coaching," *Supervision,* August 1998, pp. 17–19; S. A. Mobley, "Judge Not: How Coaches Create Healthy Organizations," *The Journal for Quality and Participation,* July/August 1999, pp. 57–60; W. J. Rinke, "Be a Coach, Not a Cop," *Executive Excellence,* June 1998, p. 17; B. Rosner, "How Do You Coach the Best from Your Employees?" *Workforce,* November 1998, pp. 24–25; and P. Simonsen and L. Davidson, "Do Your Managers Have the Right Stuff?" *Workforce,* August 1999, pp. 47–52.

80. L. Beamer, "Teaching English Business Writing to Chinese-Speaking Business Students," *Bulletin of the Association for Business Communication,* 1994, *57(1),* pp. 12–18.

81. W. B. Gudykunst and Y. K. Kim, *Communicating with Strangers: An Approach to Intercultural Communication* (New York: Random House, 1984), pp. 12–13.

82. D. Clark, "Hey, #!@* % Amigo, Can You Translate the Word 'Gaffe'?" *Wall Street Journal,* July 8, 1996, p. B6.

83. "Asian Language Exams Getting Popular Among Japanese," Japan Economic Newswire via DowVision, December 29, 1994.

84. L. J. Iandoli, "Italian for Business and Communication: Research Methodology and Creation of a Syllabus," *Journal of Language for International Business,* 1993, *5(1),* pp. 14–24.

85. See L. Beamer, "Learning Intercultural Communication Competence," *Journal of Business Communication,* 1992, *29(3),* pp. 285–303; N. Zaidman, "Stereotypes of International Managers: Content and Impact on Business Interactions," *Group and Organization Management,* March 2000, pp. 45–66; and J. S. Osland, A. Bird, and J. Delano, "Beyond Sophisticated Stereotyping: Cultural Sensemaking in Context," *The Academy of Management Executive,* February 2000, pp. 65–79.

86. *Wall Street Journal,* December 29, 1987, p. 15.

87. These are based in part on M. W. Miller, "A Story of the Type That Turns Heads in Computer Circles," *Wall Street Journal,* September 15, 1992, pp. A1, A6.

CHAPTER 6. MOTIVATING EFFECTIVELY

1. A. H. Maslow, "A Theory of Human Motivation," *Psychological Review,* 1943, *50,* pp. 370–396. For more on Maslow's views, see E. Hoffman, "The Last Interview of Abraham Maslow," *Psychology Today,* January 1992, pp. 68–73.

2. D. C. McClelland, "Business Drive and National Achievement," *Harvard Business Review,* July–August 1962, pp. 99–112. For an interesting discussion of McClelland and his work, including how McClelland built on the work of psychologist Henry Murray, see N. Lemann, "Is There a Science of Success?" *The Atlantic Monthly,* February 1994, pp. 82–98.

3. D. C. McClelland, "Business Drive and National Achievement," *Harvard Business Review,* July–August 1962, p. 103.

4. N. Lemann, "Is There a Science of Success?" *The Atlantic Monthly,* February 1994, p. 92.

5. D. C. McClelland and D. H. Burnham, "Power Is the Great Motivator," *Harvard Business Review,* March–April 1976, pp. 100–110. For recent evidence concerning need for power and need for affiliation, see D. G. Winter, "Power, Affiliation, and War: Three Tests of a Motivational Model," *Journal of Personality and Social Psychology,* September 1993, pp. 532–545.

6. I. P. Pavlov, *The Work of the Digestive Glands,* trans. W. H. Thompson (London: Charles Griffin, 1902).

7. B. F. Skinner, *Contingencies of Reinforcement: A Theoretical Analysis* (East Norwalk, CT: Appleton-Century-Crofts, 1969).

8. W. Nord, "Beyond the Teaching Machine: The Neglected Area of Operant Conditioning in the Theory and Practice of Management," *Organizational Behavior and Human Performance,* 1969, *4,* pp. 375–401.

9. W. C. Hamner and E. P. Hamner, "Behavior Modification on the Bottom Line," *Organizational Dynamics,* 1976, *4,* pp. 3–21.

10. This listing is drawn from E. A. Locke and G. P. Latham, *Goal Setting for Individuals, Groups, and Organizations* (Chicago: Science Research Associates, 1984).

11. J. F. Bryan and E. A. Locke, "Goal Setting as a Means of Increasing Motivation," *Journal of Applied Psychology,* 1967, *51,* pp. 274–277.

12. See, for instance, G. P. Latham, M. Erez, and E. A. Locke, "Resolving Scientific Disputes by the Joint Design of Crucial Experiments by the Antagonists: Application to the Erez–Latham Dispute Regarding Participation in Goal Setting," *Journal of Applied Psychology,* 1988, *73,* pp. 753–772.

13. G. P. Latham and J. J. Baldes, "The 'Practical Significance' of Locke's Theory of Goal Setting," *Journal of Applied Psychology,* 1975, *60,* pp. 122–124.

14. R. Rodgers and J. E. Hunter, "Impact of Management by Objectives on Organizational Productivity," *Journal of Applied Psychology,* 1991, vol. 76, pp. 322–336.

15. V. H. Vroom, *Work and Motivation* (New York: Wiley, 1964). See also W. Van Erde and H. Thierry, "Vroom's Expectancy Models and Work-Related Criteria: A Meta-Analysis," *Journal of Applied Psychology,* 1996, *81,* pp. 575–586.

16. Both expectancies and instrumentalities are also sometimes expressed as correlations. Unlike probabilities, correlations can take on negative values. Outcomes would be restated accordingly.

17. See E. Walster, G. W. Walster, and E. Berscheid, *Equity:*

Theory and Research (Boston: Allyn and Bacon, 1978), for a review of studies on this issue.

18. G. S. Leventhal, "Fairness in Social Relationships," in J. Thibaut, J. T. Spence, and R. Carson, eds., *Contemporary Topics in Social Psychology* (Morristown, NJ: General Learning Press, 1976).

19. This listing is based on G. S. Leventhal, "The Distribution of Rewards and Resources in Groups and Organizations," in L. Berkowitz and E. Walster, eds., *Advances in Experimental Social Psychology,* Vol. 9 (New York: Academic Press, 1976).

20. J. S. Adams, "Inequity in Social Exchange," in L. Berkowitz, ed., *Advances in Experimental Social Psychology,* Vol. 2 (New York: Academic Press, 1965).

21. While there are some more sophisticated equity theory formulations, this version is adequate in most cases.

22. For instance, see E. Jaques, *Equitable Payment* (New York: Wiley, 1961), and R. D. Pritchard, M. D. Dunnette, and D. O. Jorgenson, "Effects of Perceptions of Equity and Inequity on Worker Performance and Satisfaction," *Journal of Applied Psychology Monograph,* 1972, *56,* pp. 75–94.

23. See Walster, Walster, and Berscheid, *Equity: Theory and Research,* for a review of related studies.

24. Ibid.

25. J. Greenberg, "Employee Theft as a Reaction to Underpayment Inequity: The Hidden Cost of Pay Cuts," *Journal of Applied Psychology,* October 1990, pp. 561–568.

26. J. S. Adams, "Inequity in Social Exchange," in L. Berkowitz, ed., *Advances in Experimental Social Psychology,* Vol. 2 (New York: Academic Press, 1965).

27. F. W. Taylor, *The Principles of Scientific Management* (New York: Harper & Brothers, 1911). See also A. Harrington, "The Big Ideas," *Fortune,* November 22, 1999, pp. 152–154.

28. C. Argyris, *Integrating the Individual and the Organization* (New York: Wiley, 1964).

29. M. S. Myers, *Every Employee a Manager: More Meaningful Work Through Job Enrichment* (New York: McGraw-Hill, 1970).

30. J. S. Hirsch, "Now Hotel Clerks Provide More Than Keys," *Wall Street Journal,* March 5, 1993, p. B1.

31. K. Kelly, "The New Soul of John Deere," *Business Week,* January 31, 1994, pp. 64–66.

32. L. M. Grossman, "Truck Cabs Turn into Mobile Offices as Drivers Take on White-Collar Tasks," *Wall Street Journal,* August 3, 1993, pp. B1, B9.

33. J. R. Hackman and E. E. Lawler III, "Employee Reactions to Job Characteristics," *Journal of Applied Psychology Monograph,* 1971, *55,* pp. 259–286; and J. R. Hackman and G. R. Oldham, "The Job Diagnostic Survey: An Instrument for the Diagnosis of Jobs and the Evaluation of Job Redesign Proj-

ects," Technical Report No. 4, Department of Administrative Sciences, Yale University, 1974. For other discussions of this model, see: R. J. Aldag, S. H. Barr, and A. P. Brief, "Measurement of Perceived Task Characteristics," *Psychological Bulletin,* 1981, *90,* pp. 415–431; R. J. Aldag and A. P. Brief, *Task Design and Employee Motivation* (Glenview, IL: Scott, Foresman, 1979); R. W. Griffin, *Task Design: An Integrative Approach* (Glenview, IL: Scott, Foresman and Co., 1982); K. H. Roberts and W. Glick, "The Job Characteristics Approach to Task Design: A Critical Review," *Journal of Applied Psychology,* 1981, *66,* pp. 193–217; and, Y. Fried and G. R. Ferris, "The Validity of the Job Characteristics Model: A Review and Meta-Analysis," *Personnel Psychology,* 1987, pp. 287–322.

34. R. B. Dunham, R. J. Aldag, and A. P. Brief, "Dimensionality of Task Design as Measured by the Job Diagnostic Survey," *Academy of Management Journal,* 1977, *20,* pp. 209–223. See also Y. Fried and G. R. Ferris, "The Dimensionality of Job Characteristics: Some Neglected Issues," *Journal of Applied Psychology,* 1986, *71,* pp. 419–426.

35. Aldag, Barr, and Brief, "Task Characteristics," pp. 415–431.

36. Ibid.

37. Ibid.

38. For instance, consider a simple two-characteristics case where characteristic A has a score of 0 on a scale of 0 to 5 and characteristic B has a score of 3. If an employee combines the scores with an additive model, the job would have a score of $0 + 3 = 3$. With a multiplicative model, the job would have a score of $0 \times 3 = 0$. That is, it would not motivate at all. Suppose then that job changes were made to improve the score on characteristic B to 5. If an employee combines those scores with an additive model, the score becomes $0 + 5 = 5$, an improvement of 2. With a multiplicative model, the score remains at $0 \times 5 = 0$.

39. E. F. Stone, "Some Personality Correlates of Perceptions of and Reactions to Task Characteristics," Working Paper, Purdue University, 1977.

40. See Aldag and Brief, *Task Design and Employee Motivation,* pp. 93–95, for more on this issue.

41. J. R. Hackman and G. R. Oldham, *Work Redesign* (Reading, MA: Addison-Wesley, 1980).

42. See, for instance, L. P. Wilbur, "The Value of On-the-Job Rotation," *Supervisory Management,* November 1993, p. 6; and M. A. Campion, L. Cheraskin, and M. J. Stevens, "Career-Related Antecedents and Outcomes of Job Rotation," *Academy of Management Journal,* 1994, *37,* pp. 1518–1542.

43. Aldag and Brief, *Task Design and Employee Motivation,* pp. 62–70.

CHAPTER 7. LEADING EFFECTIVELY

1. The discussion of Steve Jobs is based in part on P. Burrows, "Apple," *Business Week,* July 31, 2000, pp. 102–113; P. Nesbitt, "The Lazarus of the PC World," *Accountancy,* May 2000, pp. 60–61; S. Berglas, "What You Can Learn from Steve Jobs," *Inc,* October 1999, pp. 29–32; M. Krantz, "Steve's Two Jobs," *Time,* October 18, 1999, pp. 62–68; and "A Boss's Life," *Business Week,* January 11, 1999, p. 63.

2. W. G. Bennis and B. Nanus, *Leaders: The Strategies for Taking Charge* (New York: Harper and Row, 1985), p. 221.

3. T. A. Mahoney, T. H. Jerdee, and A. N. Nash, *The Identification of Management Potential: A Resource Approach to Management Development* (Dubuque, IA: William C. Brown, 1961).

4. See W. O. Jenkins, "A Review of Leadership Studies with

Particular Reference to Military Problems," *Psychological Bulletin,* 1947, *44,* pp. 54–79; R. M. Stogdill, "Personal Factors Associated with Leadership: A Survey of the Literature," *Journal of Psychology,* 1948, *25,* pp. 35–71; and C. A. Gibb, "Leadership," in G. Lindzey, ed., *Handbook of Social Psychology* (Reading, MA: Addison-Wesley, 1954).

5. C. Bird, *Social Psychology* (New York: Appleton-Century, 1940).

6. L. F. Carter and M. Nixon, "An Investigation of the Relationship Between Four Criteria of Leadership Ability for Three Different Tasks," *Journal of Psychology,* 1949, *23,* pp. 245–261.

7. E. P. Hollander and L. R. Offermann, "Power and Leadership in Organizations," *American Psychologist,* 1990, *45,* pp. 179–189.

8. A. Etzioni, *Modern Organizations* (Englewood Cliffs, NJ: Prentice-Hall, 1964).

9. J. R. P. French and B. Raven, "The Bases of Social Power," in D. Cartwright and A. F. Zander, eds., *Group Dynamics,* 2nd ed. (Evanston, IL: Row Peterson, 1960), pp. 259–269.

10. These power bases were proposed by G. Yukl and C. M. Falbe, "Importance of Different Power Sources in Downward and Lateral Relations," *Journal of Applied Psychology,* 1991, *76,* pp. 416–423.

11. These guidelines are based on Gary A. Yukl, *Leadership in Organizations* (Englewood Cliffs, NJ: Prentice-Hall, 1981), pp. 44–58.

12. E. Yuchtman and S. E. Seashore, "A System Resource Approach to Organizational Effectiveness," *American Sociological Review,* 1967, *32,* pp. 891–903; J. Pfeffer and G. Salancik, *The External Control of Organizations* (New York: Harper and Row, 1978).

13. G. R. Salancik and J. Pfeffer, "The Bases and Uses of Power In Organizational Decision Making: The Case of a University," *Administrative Science Quarterly,* 1974, *19,* pp. 453–473.

14. H. Aldrich, H. and D. Herker, "Boundary Spanning Roles and Organizational Structure," *Academy of Management Review,* 1977, *2,* pp. 217-230; R. E. Spekman, "Influence and Information: An Exploratory Investigation of the Boundary Role Person's Basis of Power," *Academy of Management Journal,* 1979, *22,* pp. 104–117.

15. R. M. Kanter, "Power Failure in Management Circuits," *Harvard Business Review,* July–August 1979, pp. 31–54.

16. G. Yukl and C. M. Falbe, "Influence Tactics and Objectives in Upward, Downward, and Lateral Influence Attempts," *Journal of Applied Psychology,* 1990, *75,* pp. 132–140.

17. For instance, see R. E. Petty and J. T. Cacioppo, *Attitudes and Persuasion: Central and Peripheral Routes to Persuasion* (New York: Springer Verlag, 1984); and S. Moscovici, "Social Influence and Conformity," in G. Lindzey and E. Aronson, eds., *Handbook of Social Psychology,* 3rd ed., Vol. 2 (New York: Random House, 1985), pp. 347–412.

18. W. J. McGuire, "Attitudes and Attitude Change." In G. Lindzey and E. Aronson, eds., *Handbook of Social Psychology,* 3rd ed., Vol. 2 (New York: Random House, 1985), pp. 233–346.

19. These bases for liking are drawn from J. Pfeffer, *Managing with Power* (Boston, MA: Harvard Business School Press, 1992), p. 213.

20. This discussion of emotional appeals is based on A. Rafaeli and R. I. Sutton, "Emotional Contrast Strategies As Means of Social Influence: Lessons From Criminal Interrogators and Bill Collectors," *Academy of Management Journal,* 1991, *34,* pp. 749–775.

21. A. R. Hochschild, *The Managed Heart* (Berkeley: University of California Press, 1983).

22. J. V. Van Maanen and G. Kunda, "Real Feelings: Emotional Expression and Organizational Culture," in L. L. Cummings and B. M. Staw, eds., *Research in Organizational Behavior,* Vol. 11 (Greenwich, CT: JAI Press, 1989), pp. 43–104.

23. R. I. Sutton and A. Rafaeli, "Untangling the Relationship Between Displayed Emotions and Organizational Sales: The Case of Convenience Stores," *Academy of Management Journal,* 1988, *31,* pp. 461–487.

24. D. Kipnis, "The Use of Power in Organizations and in Interpersonal Settings," in S. Oskamp, ed., *Applied Social Psychology Annual,* Vol. 5 (Beverly Hills, CA: Sage, 1984), pp. 179–210; and D. Kipnis and S. M. Schmidt, "An Influence Perspective on Bargaining," in M. Bazerman and R. Lewicki, eds., *Negotiating in Organizations* (Beverly Hills, CA: Sage, 1983), pp. 303–319.

25. R. I. Sutton, "Maintaining Norms About Expressed Emotions: The Case of Bill Collectors," *Administrative Science Quarterly,* 1991, *36,* pp. 245–268.

26. These examples are drawn from R. B. Cialdini, *Influence: Science and Practice,* 2nd ed. (Glenview, IL: Scott, Foresman, 1988), p. 112.

27. M. A. Ansari and A. Kapoor, "Organizational Context and Upward Influence Tactics," *Organizational Behavior and Human Decision Processes,* 1987, *40,* pp. 39–49.

28. H. C. Kelman, "Processes of Opinion Change," *Public Opinion Quarterly,* 1961, *25,* pp. 57-78.

29. A. C. Filley, R. J. House, and S. Kerr, *Managerial Process and Organizational Behavior,* 2nd ed. (Glenview, IL: Scott, Foresman, 1976), p. 226.

30. S. Kerr, C. Schriesheim, C. J. Murphy, and R. M. Stogdill, "Toward a Contingency Theory of Leadership Based upon the Consideration and Initiating Structure Literature," *Organizational Behavior and Human Performance,* 1974, *12,* pp. 62–82.

31. R. J. House, "A Path–Goal Theory of Leader Effectiveness," *Administrative Science Quarterly,* 1971, *16,* pp. 321–338; and M. G. Evans, "The Effects of Supervisory Behavior on the Path–Goal Relationship," *Organizational Behavior and Human Performance,"* 1970, *5,* pp. 277–298.

32. G. B. Graen and M. Uhl-Bien, "The Transformation of Professionals into Self-Managing and Partially Self-Designing Contributions: Toward a Theory of Leader-Making," *Journal of Management Systems,* 1991, *3(3),* pp. 33–48.

33. R. E. Byrd, "Corporate Leadership Skills: A New Synthesis," *Organizational Dynamics,* 1987, pp. 34–43.

34. This is based on J. A. Conger, "Inspiring Others: The Language of Leadership," *Academy of Management Executive,* February 1991, pp. 31–45.

35. R. K. Greenleaf, *The Servant as Leader* (Indianapolis, IN: Robert K. Greenleaf Center for Servant-Leadership, 1970).

36. These examples are drawn from B. Fryer, "Bosses from Heaven—and Hell," *ComputerWorld,* August 9, 1999,

pp. 46–47; T. Carvell, "By the Way—Your Staff Hates You," *Fortune,* September 28, 1998, pp. 200–212; S. Caudron, "The Boss from Hell," *Industry Week,* September 4, 1995; and M. Greilsamer, "The Dilbert Barometer," *Across the Board,* March 1995, pp. 39–41.

CHAPTER 8. ORGANIZATIONAL CULTURE, EMPOWERMENT, AND ETHICS

1. G. W. Dauphinais and C. Price, "The CEO as Psychologist," *Management Review,* September 1998, pp. 10–15.

2. "Incompatible Cultures Cause Merger Failures," *Workforce,* November 1998, p. 9. See also C. Caggiano, "Merge Now, Pay Later," *Inc,* April 2000, pp. 86–96; and J. Veiga, M. Lubatkin, R. Calori, and P. Very, "Measuring Organizational Culture Clashes: A Two-Nation Post-Hoc Analysis of a Cultural Compatibility Index," *Human Relations,* 2000, 53, pp. 539–557.

3. These functions are drawn primarily from V. Sathe, *Culture and Related Corporate Realities* (Homewood, IL: Richard D. Irwin, Inc., 1985), pp. 25–31; and from J. Martin and C. Siehl, "Organizational Culture and Counterculture: An Uneasy Symbiosis," *Organizational Dynamics,* August 1983, pp. 52–64.

4. W. G. Ouchi, "A Conceptual Framework for the Design of Organizational Control Mechanisms," *Management Science,* 1979, pp. 833–848.

5. For more on clan control, see J. R. Deckop, R. Mangel, and C. C. Cirka, "Getting More Than You Pay For: Organizational Citizenship Behavior and Pay-for-Performance Plans," *Academy of Management Journal,* August 1999, pp. 420–428; and S. Maguire, "The Discourse of Control," *Journal of Business Ethics,* March 1999, pp. 109–114.

6. For excellent discussions of culture and cultural elements, see H. M. Trice and J. M. Beyer, *The Cultures of Work Organizations* (Englewood Cliffs, NJ: Prentice Hall, 1993); and N. M. Ashkanasy, C. P. M. Wilderom, and M. F. Peterson, eds., *Handbook of Organizational Culture and Climate* (Thousand Oaks, CA: Sage Publications, Inc., 2000).

7. For instance, see V. Sathe, *Culture and Related Corporate Realities* (Homewood, IL: Richard D. Irwin, 1985), p. 15.

8. T. J. Peters and R. H. Waterman, Jr., *In Search of Excellence* (New York: Harper & Row, 1982), p. 75–76.

9. See H. English, "Hiring for Values," *Executive Excellence,* May 2000, p. 19; and A. E. M. Van Vianen, "Person-Organization Fit: The Match Between Newcomers' and Recruiters' Preferences for Organizational Cultures," *Personnel Psychology,* 2000, *53,* pp. 113–149.

10. For instance, see J. A. Conger, "Inspiring Others: The Language of Leadership," *The Academy of Management Executive,* February 1991, pp. 31–45.

11. J. B. White, "GM Is Overhauling Corporate Culture in an Effort to Regain Competitiveness," *Wall Street Journal,* January 13, 1993, p. A3.

12. R. E. Winter, "Milacron Wolfpack Goes In for the Kill," *Wall Street Journal,* August 14, 1990, p. A6.

13. See R. F. Dennehy, "The Executive as Storyteller," *Management Review,* March 1999, pp. 40–43 for a discussion of the importance of narratives in organizations.

14. See T. A. Stewart, "The Cunning Plots of Leadership," *Fortune,* September 7, 1998, pp. 165–166.

15. From Trice and Beyer, p. 103, adapted from A. Wilkins, "Organizational Stories As an Expression of Management Philosophy." Ph.D. thesis proposal, Stanford University, June 1977.

16. L. Pondy, "Union of Rationality and Intuition in Management Action," in S. Srivastva et al., eds., *The Executive Mind* (San Francisco: Jossey-Bass, 1983), p. 159.

17. For instance, see M. Boyd, "Gender Benders," *Incentive,* September 1995, p. 92.

18. See, for instance, "Neurosis, Arkansas-Style," *Fortune,* April 17, 2000, p. 8.

19. J. Martin and C. Siehl, "Organizational Culture and Counterculture: An Uneasy Symbiosis," *Organizational Dynamics, 12,* 1983, pp. 52–64.

20. These and other causes for countercultures are discussed in greater detail in Trice and Beyer (1993), pp. 244–252.

21. J. M. Jermier, J. W. Slocum, Jr., L. W. Fry, and J. Gaines, "Organizational Subcultures in a Soft Bureaucracy: Resistance Behind the Myth and Facade of an Official Culture," *Organization Science,* 1991, Vol. 2, pp. 170–194.

22. Martin and Siehl, "Organizational Culture and Counterculture."

23. This categorization is provided by Trice and Beyer (1993), pp. 21–23.

24. W. G. Ouchi, *Theory Z: How American Business Can Meet the Japanese Challenge* (Reading, MA: Addison-Wesley, 1982).

25. For instance, see E. E. Lawler and S. A. Mohrman, "Quality Circles: After the Honeymoon," *Organizational Dynamics,* Spring 1987, pp. 42–54. See also, G. N. Flores and D. R. Utley, "Management Concepts in Use—a 12-Year Perspective," *Engineering Management Journal,* September 2000, pp. 11–17.

26. T. J. Peters and R. H. Waterman, Jr., *In Search of Excellence* (New York: Harper & Row, 1982), pp. 257–258.

27. D. Carroll, "A Disappointing Search for Excellence," *Harvard Business Review,* November–December 1983, pp. 78–88.

28. B. Johnson, A. Natarajan, and A. Rappaport, "Shareholder Returns and Corporate Excellence," *Journal of Business Strategy,* Fall 1985).

29. "Who's Excellent Now?" *Business Week,* November 5, 1984, pp. 76–88.

30. M. A. Hitt and R. D. Ireland, "Peters and Waterman Revisited: The Unended Quest for Excellence," *The Academy of Management Executive,* May 1987, pp. 91–98.

31. For further discussions of *In Search of Excellence* and of its prescriptions, see T. Merriden, "The Eight Pillars of Wisdom," *Management Today,* April 1998, pp. 119–120; D. Butler, "Here Today, Wrong Tomorrow," *Accountancy,* June 1998, pp. 40–41; M. Hopkins and J. Hyatt, "When Everyone Was Excellent," *Inc,* May 18, 1999, pp. 111–113; and J. A. Schmidt, "Corporate Excellence in the New Millenium," *The Journal of Business Strategy, 20(6),* pp. 39–43. For interviews with Tom Peters and discussions of his recent writings,

see G. Brewer, "The Peters Principle," *Incentive,* October 1992, pp. 32–36; R. Karlgaard, "ASAP Interview: Tom Peters," *Forbes,* March 29, 1993, pp. 69–75; and S. Crainer, "The Gurus: Tom Peters," *Management Today,* May 1997, pp. 74–75.

32. For more on the links of cultural characteristics to performance, see E. E. Christensen and G. G. Gordon, "An Exploration of Industry, Culture and Revenue Growth," *Organization Studies,* 1999, *20,* pp. 397–422; and C. P. M. Wilderom, U. Glunk, and R. Maslowski, "Organizational Culture as a Predictor of Organizational Performance," in N. M. Ashkanasy, C. P. M. Wilderom, and M. F. Peterson, eds., *Handbook of Organizational Culture and Climate* (Thousand Oaks, CA: Sage Publications, Inc.), pp. 193–209.

33. For instance, see M. F. R. Kets de Vries and D. Miller, *The Neurotic Organization* (San Francisco: Jossey-Bass, 1984).

34. J. B. Barney, "Organizational Culture: Can It Be a Source of Sustained Competitive Advantage?" *Academy of Management Review,* 1986, Vol. 11, pp. 656–665.

35. B. Dumaine, "Creating a New Company Culture," *Fortune,* January 15, 1990, p. 128.

36. These are based in part on Trice and Beyer, pp. 393–426; and B. Dumaine, "Creating a New Company Culture," *Fortune,* January 15, 1990, pp. 127–131. See also, G. Hamel, "Reinvent Your Company," *Fortune,* July 12, 2000, pp. 98–118; and R. R. Sims, "Changing an Organization's Culture Under New Leadership," *Journal of Business Ethics,* May 2000, pp. 65–78.

37. For a detailed discussion of employee reactions to culture change, including the roles of culture strength and subcultures, see L. C. Harris and E. Ogbonna, "Employee Responses to Culture Change Efforts," *Human Resource Management Journal,* 1998, *8(2),* pp. 78–92.

38. C. Sandburg, *Chicago Poems* (New York: Henry Holt and Company, 1916), p. 172.

39. M. E. P. Seligman, *Helplessness: On Depression, Development, and Death* (San Francisco: Freeman, 1975); L. Y. Abramson, M. E. Seligman, and J. D. Teasdale, "Learned Helplessness in Humans: Critique and Reformulation," *Journal of Abnormal Psychology,* 1978, *87,* 49–74. See B. E. Ashforth, "The Experience of Powerlessness in Organizations," *Organizational Behavior and Human Decision Processes,* 1989, *43,* pp. 207–242, for a model in which powerlessness leads to helplessness and work alienation.

40. C. Mellow, "Gloom and Doom At the Top," *Business Month,* December 1989, p. 11.

41. J. Garber and M. E. P. Seligman, eds., *Human Helplessness* (New York: Academic Press, 1980).

42. These are based primarily on J. A. Conger and R. N. Kanungo, "The Empowerment Process: Integrating Theory and Practice," *Academy of Management Review,* 1988, 13, pp. 471–482; and J. A. Conger, "Leadership: The Art of Empowering Others," *Academy of Management Executive,* 1989, *3,* pp. 17–24.

43. J. Tschohl, "Empowerment: The Key to Customer Service," *The American Salesman,* November 1997, pp. 12–15.

44. A. Bandura, "Self-Efficacy Mechanism in Human Agency," *American Psychologist,* 1982, *37,* pp. 122–147.

45. A. Bandura, "Self-efficacy: Toward a Unifying Theory of Behavioral Change," *Psychological Review,* 1977, *84,* pp. 191–215; and A. P. Brief and R. J. Aldag, "The 'Self' in Work Organizations: A Conceptual Review," *Academy of Management Review,* 1981, *6,* pp. 75–88.

46. J. P. Keenan and C. A. Krueger, "Whistleblowing and the Professional," *Management Accounting,* August 1992, pp. 21–24.

47. "American Workers Do the Right Thing," *HR Focus,* March 1999, p. 4.

48. See, for instance, S. Chester and D. Selley, "Giving Kickbacks the Boot," *CA Magazine,* August 1999, pp. 20–24; and "Kicking the Kickbacks," *The Economist,* May 31, 1997, pp. 61–62.

49. "The Americas: IBM's Last Tangle in Argentina," *The Economist,* August 1, 1998, p. 31.

50. B. Barnhart, "What's Down on Farm Should Be What's Up in Seattle," *Chicago Tribune,* November 26, 1999, p. 1.

51. B. Pearson, "WTO: Enemy Number One," *Australian Financial Review,* November 25, 1999, p. 13.

52. M. Hood, "Hundreds Protest Ahead of WTO Meeting," *Agence France-Presse,* November 29, 1999; and L. McShane, "Nike Suit," *Associated Press Newswires,* November 20, 1999.

53. J. S. McClenahen, "Your Employees Know Better," *Industry Week,* March 1, 1999, pp. 12–13.

54. C. C. Verschoor, "A Study of the Link Between a Corporation's Financial Performance and Its Commitment to Ethics," *Journal of Business Ethics,* October 1998, pp. 1509–1516. See also L. Wah, "Ethics Linked to Financial Performance," *Management Review,* July/August 1999, p. 7.

55. R. J. Costa-Clarke, "The Costly Implications of Terminating Whistleblowers," *Employment Relations Today,* 1994-1995, pp. 447–454.

56. P. Jackson, "Whistles and Safety Valves," *CA Magazine,* April 1999, pp. 43–44.

57. For recent discussions of Hammurabi and ethics, see J. W. Butler, "Hammurabi, Hippocrates and Business Ethics," *Executive Speeches,* August/September 1994, pp. 67–68; G. Zajac, "Beyond Hammurabi: A Public Service Definition of Ethics Failure," *Journal of Public Administration Research and Theory,* 1996, *6,* pp. 145–190; and F. E. Greenman and J. F. Sherman, "Business School Ethics—An Overlooked Topic," *Business and Society Review,* Summer 1999, pp. 171–177.

58. Quoted in P. A. French, *Collective and Corporate Responsibility* (New York: Columbia University Press, 1984), p. 187. See also, G. Moore, "Corporate Moral Agency: Review and Implications," *Journal of Business Ethics,* October 1999, pp. 329–343.

59. W. M. Rexroad, T. J. F. Bishop, J. A. Ostrosky, and L. M. Leinicke, "The Federal Sentencing Guidelines for Organizations," *The CPA Journal,* February 1999, pp. 26–31.

60. D. R. Dalton, M. B. Metzger, and J. W. Hill, "The 'New' U.S. Sentencing Commission Guidelines: A Wake-Up Call for Corporate America," *The Academy of Management Executive,* February 1994, pp. 7–13.

61. J. M. Kouzes and B. Z. Posner, *The Leadership Challenge* (San Francisco: Jossey-Bass Publishers, 1995), pp. 20–24.

62. C. H. Deutsch, "Proper Conduct in the Workplace," *New York Times,* July 29, 1990, p. F25.

63. G. R. Weaver, L. K. Trevino, and P. L. Cochran, "Corporate Ethics Programs in the Mid-1990's: An Empirical Study of the *Fortune 1,000,*" February 1999, pp. 283–294.

64. J. West, E. Berman, and S. Bonczek, "Frontiers in Ethics Training," *Public Management,* June 1998, pp. 4–9.

65. V. J. Callan, "Predicting Ethical Values and Training Needs in Ethics," *Journal of Business Ethics,* 1992, pp. 761–769.

66. P. J. Dean, "Making Codes of Ethics Real," *Journal of Business Ethics,* 1992, pp. 285–290.

67. G. McDonald, "Business Ethics: Practical Proposals for Organizations," *Journal of Business Ethics,* April 1999, pp. 143–158.

68. A. K. Naj, "GE's Drive to Purge Fraud is Hampered by Workers' Mistrust," *Wall Street Journal,* July 22, 1993, p. A1.

69. G. McDonald, "Business Ethics: Practical Proposals for Organizations," *Journal of Business Ethics,* April 1999, pp. 143–158.

70. See J. Blalock, "Informal Harassment Policies Key to Prevention," *Workforce,* October 1998, pp. 9–11; and O. Isachson, "Do You Need an Ombudsman?" *HR Focus,* September 1998, p. 6.

71. S. D. Coolidge, "Loyalty Pays Off for Owner of Burned Mill," *Christian Science Monitor,* September 16, 1997, p. 8.

72. S. D. Coolidge, "'Corporate Decency' Prevails at Malden Mills," *The Christian Science Monitor,* March 28, 1996, p. 1.

73. B. P. Sunoo, "Relying on Faith to Rebuild a Business," *Workforce,* 78, 3, March 1999, pp. 54–57.

74. S. D. Coolidge, "'Corporate Decency' Prevails at Malden Mills," *The Christian Science Monitor,* March 28, 1996, p. 1.

75. J. Rowher, "GE Digs into Asia," *Fortune,* October 2, 2000, pp. 164–170.

CHAPTER 9. FOSTERING PERSONAL GROWTH

1. R. N. Bolles, *The 1999 What Color Is Your Parachute?* (Berkeley, CA: Ten Speed Press, 1999), pp. 10–12.

2. M. Castaneda, T. A. Kolenko, and R. J. Aldag, "Self-Management Perceptions and Practices: A Structural Equations Analysis," *Journal of Organizational Behavior,* 1999, pp. 101–120.

3. See S. Kerr and J. M. Jermier, "Substitutes for Leadership: Their Meaning and Measurement," *Organizational Behavior and Human Performance,* 1978, *22,* pp. 375–403; and P. M. Podsakoff, S. B. McKenzie, and W. H. Bommer, "Meta-Analysis of the Relationships Between Kerr and Jermier's Substitutes for Leadership and Employee Job Attitudes, Role Perceptions, and Performance," *Journal of Applied Psychology,* 1996, *81,* pp. 380–399.

4. T. Petzinger, Jr., "Self-Organization Will Free Employees to Act Like Bosses," *Wall Street Journal,* January 3, 1997, p. B1.

5. See T. A. Stewart, "Looking Ahead: The Search for the Organization of Tomorrow," *Fortune,* May 18, 1992, p. 92–98; J. J. Laabs, "Ben & Jerry's Caring Capitalism," *Personnel Journal,* November 1992, pp. 50–57; and R. Wageman, "Case Study: Critical Success Factors for Creating Superb Self-Managing Teams at Xerox," *Compensation and Benefits Review,* September/October 1997, pp. 31–41.

6. D. B. Jeffrey, "A Comparison of the Effects of External Control and Self-Control on the Modification and Maintenance of Weight," *Journal of Abnormal Psychology,* 1974, *83,* pp. 404–410.

7. T. M. Hout and J. C. Carter, "Getting It Done: New Roles for Senior Executives," *Harvard Business Review,* November/December 1995, pp. 133–141; and "New Fortune/Hay Group Ranking of 'The World's Most Admired Companies' Published," *PR Newswire,* November 30, 1999.

8. For one review, see F. Andrasik and J. S. Heimberg, "Self-Management Procedures," in L. W. Frederiksen, ed., *Handbook of Organizational Behavior Management* (New York: Wiley-Interscience, 1982), pp. 219–247.

9. See, for instance, M. E. Gist, A. G. Bavetta, and C. K. Stevens, "Transfer Training Method: Its Influence on Skill Generalization, Skill Repetition, and Performance Level," *Personnel Psychology,* 1990, *43,* pp. 501–523; and G. P. Latham and C. A. Frayne, "Self Management Training for Increasing Job Attendance: A Follow-Up and a Replication," *Journal of Applied Psychology,* 1989, *74,* pp. 411–416.

10. The examples of self-management goals, monitoring, modifying of cues and consequences, and reordering of behaviors were provided in former students' self-management exercises.

11. This section is based on C. C. Manz and H. P. Sims, Jr., "SuperLeadership: Beyond the Myth of Heroic Leadership," *Organizational Dynamics,* Spring 1991, pp. 18–35.

12. For instance, see "Stress-Busters," *Credit Union Management,* June 1999, p. 8.

13. See C. M. Solomon, "Stressed to the Limit," *Workforce,* September 1999, pp. 48–54.

14. See, for instance, J. Corville and L. M. Bernardi, "Helping Employees Manage Stress," *The Canadian Manager,* Fall 1999, p. 11; and "Workplace Violence: Gaining Ground on 'Going Postal'?" *Security,* December 1998, pp. 9–13.

15. P. Rosch, president of the American Institute of Stress, as reported in *ManpowerArgus,* December 1998, p. 11.

16. H. Cass, "Sleep: The Feel Good Prescription," *Total Health,* May/June 2000, pp. 28–32. See also, "The Risks of Tranquility," *Health Letter,* August 2000, pp. 9–10.

17. D. Mills, "Time Out," *OH and S Canada,* September 1999, p. 62. See also B. Saporito, "The Most Dangerous Job in America," *Fortune,* May 31, 1993, pp. 130–140.

18. The term *building-related illness* is used when a particular building problem is related to a particular illness. The term *sick building syndrome* is used when a specific illness cause cannot be identified.

19. B. A. Wood and M. A. Al, "Sick Building Syndrome: A Potpourri Analysis," *Federation of Insurance and Corporate Counsel Quarterly,* Spring 1999, pp. 347–378.

20. T. F. Segalla, "'Sick Building' and 'Indoor Air Quality,'" *Federation of Insurance and Corporate Counsel Quarterly,* Spring 1999, pp. 321–332.

21. Ibid. See also A. Chen and E. Vine, "It's In the Air," *Best's Review,* January 1999, pp. 79–80; and A. Mann, "This Place Makes Me Sick," *Time,* December 21, 1998, pp. 38–40.

22. For instance, see L. M. Andersson and C. M. Pearson, "Tit for Tat? The Spiraling Effect of Incivility in the Workplace," *Academy of Management Review,* July 1999, pp. 452–471.

23. P. Urs Bender, "Powerful Presentations," *CMA Management,* April 1999, p. 31; and T. Simons, "Scared Speechless: Understanding and Conquering Stage Fright," *Presentations,* September 1998, pp. 39–46.

24. J. A. Rolls, "Facing the Fears Associated with Professional Speaking," *Business Communication Quarterly,* June 1998, pp. 103–106.

25. N. James, "Emotional Labour: Skill and Work in the Social Regulation of Feelings," *Sociological Review,* 1988, *37,* pp. 15–42.

26. J. Van Maanen and G. Kunda, "'Real Feelings': Emotional Expression and Organizational Culture," in L. L. Cummings and B. M. Staw, eds., *Research in Organizational Behavior* (Greenwich, CT: JAI Press, 1989), pp. 43–103; and V. R. Waldron, and K. Krone, "The Experience and Expression of Emotion in the Workplace: A Study of Corrections Organization," *Management Communication Quarterly,* 1991, pp. 287–309. See also J. A. Morris and D. C. Feldman, "The Dimensions, Antecedents, and Consequences of Emotional Labor," *Academy of Management Review,* October 1996, pp. 986–1010; and J. Martin, K. Knopoff, and C. Beckman, "An Alternative to Bureaucratic Impersonality and Emotional Labor: Bounded Emotionality at the Body Shop," *Administrative Science Quarterly,* June 1998, pp. 429–469.

27. T. H. Holmes and R. H. Rahe, "Social Readjustment Rating Scale," *Journal of Psychosomatic Research,* 1967, *11,* pp. 213–218.

28. T. H. Holmes and M. Masuda, "Life Change and Illness Susceptibility," in B. S. Dohrenwend and B. P. Dohrenwend, eds., *Stressful Life Events: Their Nature and Effects* (New York: Wiley, 1974), pp. 45–72. See also J. G. Rabbin and E. L. Strunening, "Life Events, Stress and Illness," *Science,* 1976, pp. 1013–1020.

29. See, for instance, L. K. Savery and M. Wooden, "The Relative Influence of Life Events and Hassles on Work-Related Injuries: Some Australian Evidence," *Human Relations,* March 1994, pp. 283–305; and D. Zohar, "When Things Go Wrong: The Effect of Daily Hassles on Effort, Exertion and Negative Mood," *Journal of Occupational and Organizational Psychology,* September 1999, pp. 265–283.

30. C. Aaron-Corbin, "The Multiple-Role Balancing Act," *Management Review,* October 1999, p. 62.

31. D. White, "It's a Dog's Life," *Psychology Today,* November/December 1998, p. 10.

32. "FYI," *Incentive,* October 1999, p. 79.

33. For a discussion, see R. Schickel, "Living with the Dead," *Time,* October 25, 1999, p. 118.

34. See P. Frost and S. Robinson, "The Toxic Handler: Organizational Hero and Casualty," *Harvard Business Review,* July/August 1999, pp. 96–106. See also P. J. Frost, "Why Compassion Counts!" *Journal of Management Inquiry,* June 1999, pp. 127–133.

35. Tension Discharge Rate is a construct presented in R. M. Rose, C. D. Jenkins, and M. W. Hurst, *Air Traffic Controller Health Study: A Prospective Investigation of Physical, Psychological, and Work-Related Changes* (Austin: University of Texas Press, 1978).

36. These examples, based on the work of Martin Seligman, are drawn from G. Cowley, "Stress-Busters: What Works," *Newsweek,* June 14, 1999, pp. 60–61.

37. S. Caminiti, "The Big Business of Burnout," *Working Woman,* November 1998, pp. 50–54.

38. These are based in part on R. J. Aldag and B. Joseph, *Leadership and Vision: 25 Keys to Motivation* (New York: Lebhar-Friedman Books, 2000), pp. 15–18.

39. "Making Time to Manage," *Agency Sales,* February 1999, pp. 40–44.

40. See L. R. Dominguez, "Putting an End to Putting It Off," *HR Magazine,* February 1999, pp. 124–129.

41. P. Bolt, "A Question of Balance," *The British Journal of Administrative Management,* July/August 1999, pp. 17–18.

42. See S. Folkman and R. S. Lazarus, "An Analysis of Coping in a Middle-Aged Community Sample," *Journal of Health and Social Behavior,* 1980, *21,* pp. 219–239; and J. C. Latack, "Coping with Stress: Measures and Future Directions for Scale Development," *Journal of Applied Psychology,* 1986, *71,* pp. 377–385.

43. See, for instance, C. Chatterjee, "Life Support," *Psychology Today,* May/June 1999, p. 24; D. R. Deeter-Schmelz and R. P. Ramsey, "Considering Sources and Types of Social Support: A Psychometric Evaluation of the House and Wells (1978) Instrument," *The Journal of Personal Selling and Sales Management,* Winter 1997, pp. 49–61; and J. Schaubroeck and L. S. Fink, "Facilitating and Inhibiting Effects of Job Control and Social Support on Stress Outcomes and Role Behavior: A Contingency Model," *Journal of Organizational Behavior,* March 1998, pp. 167–195.

44. See, for instance, T. M. Begley, "Coping Strategies as Predictors of Employee Distress and Turnover after an Organizational Consolidation: A Longitudinal Analysis," *Journal of Occupational and Organizational Psychology,* December 1998, pp. 305–329.

45. G. Hinderyckx, "Creative Process Often Starts with a Good Massage," *Marketing News,* April 15, 1991, pp. 8–9.

46. D. R. Powell, "Characteristics of Successful Wellness Programs," *Employee Benefits Journal,* September 1999, pp. 15–21.

47. Ibid.

48. For more on healthcare costs and the benefits of company programs to address them, see E. Vernarec, "Making the Case to Top Management," *Business and Health,* July 1999, pp. 20–25.

49. Ibid.

50. Except where otherwise specified, the following material is drawn from D. R. Powell, "Characteristics of Successful Wellness Programs," *Employee Benefits Journal,* September 1999, pp. 15–21.

51. Ibid.

52. J. Burns, "Health Promotion Programs Produce Measurable Results," *Managed Healthcare,* May 1999, p. 42.

53. "EAPs Adopt Broad Brush Approach to Helping Employees," *Employee Benefit Plan Review,* October 1999, p. 44.

54. P. R. Johnson and J. Indvik, "The Organizational Benefits of Assisting Domestically Abused Employees," *Public Personnel Management,* Fall 1999, pp. 365–374.

55. S. Caudron, "HR Revamps Career Itineraries," *Personnel Journal,* April 1994, pp. 64A–64P.

56. The idea of the portfolio career was proposed by Charles Handy. For discussions, see C. Rapoport, "Charles Handy Sees the Future," *Fortune,* October 31, 1994, pp. 155–160; and A. Rogers, "Self Promotion," *Works Management,* March 1999, pp. 30–33.

57. From *Careers in Organizations* by D. T. Hall (Glenview, IL: Scott-Foresman and Company, 1976).

58. Ibid., p. 135.

59. The first five of these problems are based primarily on R. A. Webber, "Career Problems of Young Managers," *California Management Review,* 1976, 18, pp. 11–33.

60. "Blind Devotion Wanted?" *Wall Street Journal,* July 22, 1997, p. A1.

61. L. A. Tansey, "Right vs. Wrong," *National Business Employment Weekly,* Spring/Summer 1994, pp. 11, 12.

62. G. Fuchsberg, "Canadian Firm Gives New Hires Job Guarantees," *The Wall Street Journal,* July 16, 1991, pp. B1 and B6.

63. E. Norton, "Young Indians Help Tribe Hit Comeback Trail," *Wall Street Journal,* October 5, 1992, p. B1.

64. R. J. Lewicki, "Organizational Seduction: Building Commitment to Organizations," *Organizational Dynamics,* 1981, *10,* pp. 5–22.

65. D. T. Hall and D. S. Hall, "What's New in Career Management?" *Organizational Dynamics,* Summer 1976, pp. 17–33.

66. J. S. Livingston, "Pygmalion in Management," *Harvard Business Review,* 1969, *47(4),* pp. 81–89, presents an interesting discussion of the powerful role that early career challenge and superiors' high expectations play in career growth. These arguments are also consistent with a tournament model of mobility. In the tournament model, careers are seen as a series of competitions, each with implications for an individual's mobility chances. Winners at a given level can compete at a higher level. Losers are out of the tournament or can compete in only lower level contests. Career research generally supports the tournament model.

67. This discussion is based primarily on Hall, *Careers in Organizations.* See also B. P. Bunk and P. P. M. Janssen, "Relative Deprivation, Career Issues, and Mental Health among Men in Midlife," *Journal of Vocational Behavior,* 1992, *40,* pp. 338–350

68. T. P. Ference et al., "Managing the Career Plateau," *Academy of Management Review,* 1977, *2,* p. 602. See also C.-T. Chau, "Career Plateaus," *The Internal Auditor,* October 1998, pp. 48–52; and L. Lemire, T. Saba, and Y.-C. Gagnon, "Managing Career Plateauing in the Quebec Public Sector," *Public Personnel Management,* Fall 1999, pp. 375–391.

69. E. E. Jennings, *The Mobile Manager: Study of the New Generation of Top Executives* (Ann Arbor: Bureau of Industrial Relations, Graduate School of Business Administration, The University of Michigan, 1967). See also J. R. Lincoln and Y. Nakata, "The Transformation of the Japanese Employment System: Nature, Depth, and Origins," *Work and Occupations,* February 1997, pp. 33–55.

70. J. Near, "Reactions to the Career Plateau," *Business Horizons,* July/August 1984, pp. 75–79; and N. Nicholson, "Purgatory or Place of Safety? The Managerial Plateau and Organizational Age Grading," *Human Relations,* December 1993, *46,* pp. 1369–1389.

71. M. J. McCarthy, "Plateaued Workers Cause Big Damage," *Wall Street Journal,* August 17, 1988), p. 21.

72. E. L. Pavalko, G. H. Elder, Jr., and E. C. Clipp, "Worklives and Longevity: Insights from a Life Course Perspective," *Journal of Health and Social Behavior,* 1993, *34,* pp. 363–380. This study also found sharply elevated mortality rates for individuals who experienced a period in which they moved through a series of unrelated jobs.

73. E. H. Schein, *Career Dynamics: Matching Individual and Organizational Needs* (Reading, MA: Addison-Wesley, 1978). For an extension of this model, see J. A. Katz, "Modeling Entrepreneurial Career Progressions: Concepts and Considerations," *Entrepreneurship Theory and Practice,* Winter 1994, pp. 23–29.

74. J. S. Lublin, "Strategic Sidling: Lateral Moves Aren't Always a Mistake," *Wall Street Journal,* August 4, 1993, p. B1.

75. A. Bennett, "Path to Top Job Now Twists and Turns," *Wall Street Journal,* March 15, 1993, p. B1.

76. These examples are from J. E. Rigdon, "Using Lateral Moves to Spur Employees," *The Wall Street Journal,* May 26, 1992, p. B1.

77. For more on Schein's career anchors, see D. C. Feldman, *Managing Careers in Organizations* (Glenview, IL: Scott, Foresman, 1988), pp. 101–106; P. R. Sparrow, "Reappraising Psychological Contracting," *International Studies of Management and Organization,* Spring 1998, pp. 30–63; and P. Simonsen and L. Davidson, "Do Your Managers Have the Right Stuff?" *Workforce,* August 1999, pp. 47–52.

78. E. H. Schein, "Career Anchors and Career Paths: A Panel Study of Management School Graduates," in J. Van Maanen, ed., *Organizational Careers: Some New Perspectives* (London: Wiley-Interscience, 1977), p. 63.

79. S. Overman, "Weighing Career Anchors," *HR Magazine,* March 1993, pp. 56, 58.

80. J. Holland, *The Psychology of Vocational Choice* (Waltham, MA: Blaisdell, 1966); and J. Holland, *Making Vocational Choices: A Theory of Vocational Personalities and Work Environments* (Odessa, FL: Psychological Assessment Resources, 1985). See also F. D. Fruty and I. Mervielde, "RIASEC Types and Big Five Traits as Predictors of Employment Status and Nature of Employment, *Personnel Psychology,* Autumn 1999, pp. 701–727.

81. See D. C. Feldman and H. J. Arnold, "Personality Types and Career Patterns: Some Empirical Evidence on Holland's Model," *Canadian Journal of Administrative Sciences,* 1985, *2,* pp. 192–210, for one supportive study. For a recent meta-analysis on the issue, which raises some questions about the links of congruence to satisfaction, see M. Tranberg, S. Slane, and S. E. Ekeberg, "The Relation Between Interest Congruence and Satisfaction: A Metaanalysis," *Journal of Vocational Behavior,* 1993, *42,* pp. 253–264.

82. The following discussion is based largely on M. J. Driver, "Career Concepts and Career Management in Organizations," in C. L. Cooper, ed., *Behavioral Problems in Organizations,* (Englewood Cliffs, NJ: Prentice-Hall, 1979).

83. D. Seligman, "Luck and Careers," *Fortune,* November 16, 1981, pp. 60–66, 70, 72, presents an interesting discussion of the role of luck in careers.

84. Hall, *Careers in Organizations,* pp. 179–189. For

more on self-management of careers, see E. H. Fram, "Today's Mercurial Career Path," *Management Review,* November 1994, pp. 40–43; and S. R. Covey, "The New Contract," *Executive Excellence,* January 1996, pp. 3–5.

85. J. O. Crites, *Theory and Research Handbook, Career Maturity Inventory* (Monterey, CA: McGraw-Hill, 1973).

86. G. Fuchsberg, "As Costs of Overseas Assignments Climb, Firms Select Expatriates More Carefully," *Wall Street Journal,* January 9, 1992, p. B1.

87. For instance, see V. Skorikov and F. W. Vondracek, "Career Development in the Commonwealth of Independent States," *The Career Development Quarterly,* June 1993, pp. 314–329.

88. For discussions of the glass ceiling and companies' attempts to break it, see L. E. Wynter and J. Solomon, "A New Push to Break the 'Glass Ceiling,'" *Wall Street Journal,* November 15, 1989, pp. B1 and B10; and J. S. Lublin, "Firms Designate Some Openings for Women Only," *The Wall Street Journal,* February 7, 1994, p. B1. While the dearth of women in top management positions supports the idea of a glass ceiling, research specifically addressing the phenomenon is lacking. For one recent study (which failed to find support for the phenomenon in a government setting), see G. N. Powell and D. A. Butterfield, "Investigating the 'Glass Ceiling' Phenomenon: An Empirical Study of Actual Promotions to Top Management," *Academy of Management Journal,* 1994, *37,* pp. 68–86.

89. B. H. Wooten, "Gender Differences in Occupational Employment," *Monthly Labor Review,* April 1997, pp. 15–24.

90. S. M. Crampton and J. M. Mishra, "Women in Management," *Public Personnel Management,* Spring 1999, pp. 87–106.

91. J. A. Lopez, "Study Says Women Face Glass Walls as Well as Ceilings," *The Wall Street Journal,* March 3, 1992, p. B1.

92. For a thorough discussion of the current status of women in management, see D. R. Dalton and C. M. Daily, *Across the Board,* November/December 1998, pp. 16–20.

93. A. L. Otten, "Gender Pay Gap Eased Over Last Decade," *The Wall Street Journal,* April 15, 1994, p. B1; and K. T. Greenfield, "What Glass Ceiling?" *Time,* August 2, 1999, p. 72.

94. P. J. Ohlott, M. N. Ruderman, and C. D. McCauley, "Gender Differences in Managers' Developmental Experience," *The Academy of Management Journal,* 1994, *37,* pp. 46–67.

95. B. P. Noble, "At Work: Making a Case for Family Programs," *New York Times,* May 2, 1993, p. 25.

96. M. Galen, A. T. Palmer, A. Cuneo, and M. Maremont, "Work and Family," *Business Week,* June 28, 1993, pp. 80–88.

97. R. Sharpe, "Being Family Friendly Doesn't Mean Promoting Women," *The Wall Street Journal,* March 29, 1994, pp. B1 and B5.

98. See P. Symons, "The Career Pathing Question," *Credit Union Management,* April 1994, pp. 11-12; and C. Caggiano, "A Path for Employee Growth," *Inc,* August 1998, p. 11.

99. J. A. Lopez, "Companies Alter Layoff Policies to Keep Recently Hired Women and Minorities," *The Wall Street Journal,* September 18, 1992, pp. B1 and B16.

100. See M. Galen and A. T. Palmer, "White, Male, and Worried," *Business Week,* January 31, 1994, pp. 50–55.

101. These examples are drawn from L. O. Graham, *The Best Companies for Minorities* (New York: Penguin Books USA, Inc., 1993).

102. K. E. Kram, "Phases in the Mentor Relationship," *Academy of Management Journal,* 1983, 26, pp. 608–625; and K. E. Kram, "Mentoring in the Workplace," in D. T. Hall and Associates, eds., *Career Development in Organizations* (San Francisco: Jossey-Bass, 1986), pp. 160–201. See also G. T. Chao, "Invited Reaction: Challenging Research in Mentoring," *Human Resource Development Quarterly,* Winter 1998, pp. 333–338.

103. D. B. Turban and T. W. Dougherty, "Role of Protégé Personality and Receipt of Mentoring and Career Success," *Academy of Management Journal,* 1994, *37,* pp. 688–702.

104. This discussion is based largely on R. J. Burke and C. A. McKeen, "Mentoring in Organizations: Implications for Women," *Journal of Business Ethics,* 1990, *9,* pp. 317–332. See also D. C. Feldman, "Toxic Mentors or Toxic Protégés? A Critical Re-Examination of Dysfunctional Mentoring," *Human Resource Management Review,* 1999, *9(3);* and B. R. Ragins and T. A. Scandura, "Burden or Blessing? Expected Costs and Benefits of Being a Mentor," *Journal of Organizational Behavior,* May 1999, pp. 493–509.

105. G. Dreher and R. Ash, "A Comparative Study of Mentoring Among Men and Women in Managerial, Professional and Technical Positions," *Journal of Applied Psychology,* 1990, *75,* pp. 525–535; and E. A. Fagenson, "The Mentor Advantage: Perceived Career/Job Experiences of Protégés Vs. Non-Protégés," *Journal of Organizational Behavior,* 1989, *10,* pp. 309–320.

106. J. A. Lopez, "Being Your Boss's Pal May Be Hazardous to Your Career," *The Wall Street Journal,* June 8, 1994, p. B1.

107. For a good summary of issues relating to mentoring for women in organizations, see R. J. Burke and C. A. McKeen, "Mentoring in Organizations: Implications for Women," *Journal of Business Ethics,* 1990, *9,* pp. 317–332.

108. A. B. Fisher, "When Will Women Get To the Top?" *Fortune,* September 21, 1992, pp. 44–56.

109. M. B. Scott, "Deloitte & Touche Programs Work to Retain Employees in a Competitive Industry," *Employee Benefit Plan Review,* September 1998, pp. 32–34.

110. L. Blejwas and W. Marshall, "A Supervisory Level Self-Directed Work Team in Health Care," *The Health Care Supervisor,* June 1999, pp. 14–21.

CHAPTER 10. MANAGING POLITICS, CONFLICT, AND CHANGE

1. J. Pfeffer, *Power in Organizations* (Marshfield, MA: Pitman Publishing, 1981), pp. 137-177.

2. T. C. Krell, M. E. Mendenhall, and J. Sendry, "Doing Research in the Conceptual Morass of Organizational Politics."

Paper presented at the Western Academy of Management Conference, Hollywood, CA, April 1987.

3. For more on the labeling of behavior as political, see "The Longest Climb," *Psychology Today,* November 1994,

pp. 40–43; "What is Terrorism?" *The Economist*, March 2, 1996, pp. 23–25; M. C. Bolino, "Citizenship and Impression Management: Good Soldiers or Good Actors?" *The Academy of Management Review*, January 1999, pp. 82–98; and D. S. Scott and K. A. Jehn, "Ranking Rank Behaviors," *Business and Society*, September 1999, pp. 296–325.

4. W. H. Hegarty and H. P. Sims, Jr., "Organizational Philosophy, Policies, and Objectives Related to Unethical Decision Behavior: A Laboratory Experiment," *Journal of Applied Psychology*, 1979, *64*, pp. 331–338.

5. J. M. Rayburn and L. G. Rayburn, "Relationship Between Machiavellianism and Type A Personality and Ethical-Orientation," *Journal of Business Ethics*, November 1996, pp. 1209–1219; and B. K. Burton and W. H. Hegarty, "Some Determinants of Student Corporate Social Responsibility Orientation," *Business and Society*, June 1999, pp. 188–205.

6. A. Singhapakdi, "Ethical Perceptions of Marketers: The Interaction Effects of Machiavellianism and Organizational Ethical Culture," *Journal of Business Ethics*, May 1993, pp. 407–418. See also R. C. Erffmeyer, B. D. Keillor, and D. T. LeClair, "An Empirical Investigation of Japanese Consumer Ethics," *Journal of Business Ethics*, January 1999, pp. 35–50; and K. Bass, T. Barnett, and G. Brown, "Individual Difference Variables, Ethical Judgments, and Ethical Behavioral Intentions," *Business Ethics Quarterly*, April 1999, pp. 183–205.

7. P. M. Fandt and G. M. Ferris, "The Management of Information and Impressions: When Employees Behave Opportunistically," *Organizational Behavior and Human Decision Processes*, 1990, *67*, pp. 140–158.

8. D. C. McClelland et al., *The Drinking Man: Alcohol and Human Motivation* (New York: Free Press, 1972). See also D. Buchanan and R. Badham, "Politics and Organizational Change: The Lived Experience," *Human Relations*, May 1999, pp. 609–629.

9. Hegarty and Sims, "Organizational Philosophy, Policies, and Objectives," 1979.

10. D. M. Wolfe, "Is There Integrity in the Bottom Line? Managing Obstacles to Executive Integrity." In S. Srinivastava, ed., *Executive Integrity: The Search for High Human Values in Organizational Life* (San Francisco: Jossey-Bass, 1988), pp. 140–171.

11. R. Miles, *Micro Organizational Behavior* (Glenview, IL: Scott, Foresman, 1980); C. Leana, "Power Relinquishment Versus Power Sharing: Theoretical Clarification and Empirical Comparison of Delegation and Participation," *Journal of Applied Psychology*, 1987, *72*, pp. 228–233.

12. E. Jansen and M. A. Von Glinow, "Ethical Ambivalence and Organizational Reward Systems," *Academy of Management Review*, 1985, *10*, pp. 814–822.

13. This figure is adapted from Jansen and Von Glinow, "Ethical Ambivalence," p. 817.

14. J. Gandz and V. V. Murray, "The Experience of Workplace Politics," *Academy of Management Journal*, 1980, *23*, pp. 237–251.

15. J. Pfeffer, *Power in Organizations* (Marshfield, MA: Pitman Publishing, 1981), pp. 137–177.

16. R. Grover, M. Landler, and M. Oneal, "Ovitz: How Many Fields Can the King of Hollywood Conquer?" *Business Week*, August 9, 1993, p. 50; C. Booth, "Chalk One Up for Ovitz," *Time*, November 1, 1999, p. 34; and P. Plagens and C. Brown, "Hollywood's Big Art Deal," *Newsweek*, December 6, 1999, pp. 78–80.

17. This section is primarily based on B. E. Ashforth and R. T. Lee, "Defensive Behavior in Organizations: A Preliminary Model," *Human Relations*, July 1990, pp. 621–648. For more on defensive behaviors, see A. D. Brown, "Narcissism, Identity, and Legitimacy," *Academy of Management Review*, July 1997, pp. 643–686; and E. Peirce, C. A. Smolinski, and B. Rosen, "Why Sexual Harassment Complaints Fall on Deaf Ears," *Academy of Management Executive*, August 1998, pp. 41–54.

18. D. J. Schneider, "Tactical Self-Presentations: Toward a Broader Conception," in J. T. Tedeschi, ed., *Impression Management Theory and Social Psychological Research* (New York: Academic Press, 1981), pp. 23–40; and S. Caudron, "The Fine Art of Ingratiation," *Industry Week*, February 17, 1997, pp. 41–48.

19. This section is primarily based on W. L. Gardner and M. J. Martinko, "Impression Management in Organizations," *Journal of Management*, 1988, *14*, 321–338. See also L. Chaney and J. Lyden, "Impression Management: The Office Environment," *Supervision*, April 1996, pp. 3–5; and M. C. Bolino, "Citizenship and Impression Management: Good Soldiers or Good Actors?" *Academy of Management Review*, January 1999, pp. 82–98.

20. B. R. Schlenker, *Impression Management: The Self-Concept, Social Identity, and Interpersonal Relations* (Monterey, CA: Brooks/Cole, 1980).

21. C. Molstad, "Control Strategies Used by Brewery Workers: Work Avoidance, Impression Management and Solidarity," *Human Organization*, 1988, *4*, p. 357.

22. S. J. Wayne and K. M. Kacmar, "The Effects of Impression Management on the Performance Appraisal Process," *Organizational Behavior and Human Decision Processes*, 1991, 48, pp. 70–88.

23. S. J. Wayne and G. R. Ferris, "Influence Tactics, Affect, and Exchange Quality in Supervisor-Subordinate Interactions: A Laboratory Experiment and Field Study," *Journal of Applied Psychology*, 1990, *75*, pp. 487–499.

24. H. Mintzberg, *Power in and Around Organizations* (Englewood Cliffs, NJ: Prentice-Hall, 1983), p. 187.

25. Ibid., and H. Mintzberg, *Mintzberg on Management* (New York: The Free Press, 1989).

26. M. Velasquez, D. J. Moberg, and G. F. Cavanagh, "Organizational Statesmanship and Dirty Politics: Ethical Guidelines for the Organizational Politician," *Organizational Dynamics*, August 1983, pp. 65–80.

27. Velasquez, Moberg, and Cavanagh (Ibid.) suggest that there may be "overwhelming factors" that justify setting aside one or all of the criteria. These might include conflicts between criteria, conflicts within criteria, or lack of capacity to employ the criteria.

28. Mintzberg, *Mintzberg on Management*, pp. 248–249.

29. P. Kumar and R. Ghadially, "Organizational Politics and Its Effects on Members of Organizations," *Human Relations*, 1989, *42*, pp. 305–314.

30. G. R. Ferris and K. M. Kacmar, "Perceptions of Organi-

zational Politics," *Journal of Management,* 1992, *18,* pp. 93–116; R. Cropanzano, J. C. Howe, A. A. Grandey, and P. Toth, "The Relationship of Organizational Politics and Support to Work Behaviors, Attitudes, and Stress," *Journal of Organizational Behavior,* March 1997, pp. 159–180; and K. M. Kacmar, D. P. Bozeman, D. S. Carlson, and W. P. Anthony, "An Examination of the Perceptions of Organizational Politics Model: Replication and Extension," *Human Relations,* March 1999, pp. 383–416.

31. These are drawn from H. Mintzberg, *Mintzberg on Management,* pp. 249–250.

32. See, for instance, "Avoid Politics By Establishing Objective Criteria for Capital Budget Decision Making," *Health Care Strategic Management,* December 1999, pp. 18–19.

33. See, for instance, K. M. Eisenhardt, J. L. Kahwajy, and L. J. Bourgeois III, "How Management Teams Can Have a Good Fight," *Harvard Business Review,* July/August 1997, pp. 77–85; and T. K. Capozzoli, "Conflict Resolution—A Key Ingredient in Successful Teams," *Supervision,* November 1999, pp. 14–16.

34. V. L. Huber, M. A. Neale, and G. Northcraft, "Decision Bias and Personnel Selection Strategies," *Organizational Behavior and Human Decision Processes,* 1987, *40,* pp. 136–147; R. Pinkley, "Dimensions of Conflict Frame: Disputant Interpretations of Conflict," *Journal of Applied Psychology,* 1990, *75,* pp. 117–126; and R. L. Pinckley and G. B. Northcraft, "Conflict Frames of Reference: Implications for Dispute Processes," *Academy of Management Journal,* February 1994, pp. 193–205.

35. For a discussion of antecedents of managerial trustworthy behavior and the challenge of initiating trust, see E. M. Whitener, S. E. Brodt, M. A. Korsgaard, and J. M. Werner, "Managers as Initiators of Trust: An Exchange Relationship Framework for Understanding Managerial Trustworthy Behavior," *Academy of Management Review,* July 1998, pp. 513–530.

36. S. Lorge, "Political Animals," *Sales and Marketing Management,* February 1999, pp. 50–55.

37. For one discussion of this model, see G. H. Johnson, T. Means, and J. Pullis, "Managing Conflict," *The Internal Auditor,* December 1998, pp. 54–59.

38. These guidelines are drawn from R. J. Aldag and B. Joseph, *Leadership and Vision: 25 Keys to Motivation* (New York: Lebhar-Friedman Books, 2000), p. 86.

39. For discussions of negotiating skills and conflict, see P. Jacobs, "Negotiating for Success," *InfoWorld,* December 7, 1998, pp. 131–132; and D. Strutton and L. E. Pelton, "Negotiation: Bringing More to the Table than Demands," *Marketing Health Services,* Spring 1997, pp. 52–58.

40. See also K. Kiser, "The New Deal," *Training,* October 1999, pp. 116–126.

41. P. L. Stepanowsky, "Some Swimming Lessons Could Be Best Way to Prepare for this Cruise," *Wall Street Journal,* October 17, 1990, p. B1.

42. M. Boles and B. P. Sunoo, "Three Barriers to Managing Change," *Workforce,* January 1998, p. 25.

43. A. J. Vogl, "The Army after Next," *Across the Board,* June 1999, pp. 43–47.

44. See J. Collins, "Turning Goals Into Results: The Power of Catalytic Mechanisms," *Harvard Business Review,* July/August 1999, pp. 70–82.

45. See also "Discipline and Desire," *Harvard Business Review,* July/August 1999, p. 10.

46. R. Beckhard, *Organization Development: Strategies and Models* (Reading, MA: Addison-Wesley, 1969), p. 9.

47. This listing of OD techniques was proposed by W. L. French and C. H. Bell, Jr., *Organization Development: Behavioral Science Interventions for Organization Improvement,* 2nd ed. (Englewood Cliffs, NJ: Prentice-Hall, 1978).

48. Ibid., pp. 215–218.

49. P. M. Senge, *The Fifth Discipline: The Art and Practice of the Learning Organization* (New York: Doubleday, 1990), p. 3.

50. P. Senge, "Sharing Knowledge," *Executive Excellence,* September 1999, pp. 6–7.

51. P. M. Senge, *The Fifth Discipline,* p. 12.

52. Ibid., pp. 18–25.

53. Ibid., pp. 21–22 (italics in original).

54. See also P. M. Senge, "Slow Threats," *Executive Excellence,* April 1994, pp. 5–7.

55. P. Senge, "Creative Tension," *Executive Excellence,* January 1999, pp. 12–13.

56. P. Senge, "Leading Learning Organizations," *Executive Excellence,* April 1996, pp. 10–11.

57. P. M. Senge, "Creating Quality Communities," *Executive Excellence,* June 1994, pp. 11–13.

58. This section is based primarily on P. Senge, "Learning Infrastructures," *Executive Excellence,* February 1995, p. 7.

59. P. M. Senge, "Creating Quality Communities," *Executive Excellence,* June 1994, pp. 11–13.

60. Ibid.

61. http://www.andersenconsulting.com.

62. K. Sibley, "Andersens Seek Settlement Through Arbitration," *Computing Canada,* February 2, 1998, p. 8.

63. K. Brown, "Andersen Consulting Wins Independence—Arbitrator Tells Firm to Pay Auditing Arm $1 Billion; Parent's Role Criticized," *Wall Street Journal,* August 8, 2000, p. A3.

64. R. O. Crockett, "Next Stop, Splitsville," *Business Week,* January 18, 1999, p. 52.

65. J. McElroy, "Jac Be Nimble, Jac Be Quick," *Wards Auto World,* January 2000, p. 22.

66. S. Zesiger, "Jac Nasser Is Car Crazy," *Fortune,* June 22, 1998, pp. 79–81.

67. J. Nasser, "Driving Force," *Chief Executive,* October 1999, pp. 30–35.

68. L. Farrell, "You've Got to be Kidding: Humor as a Fundamental Management Tool," *Information Management Journal,* July 1998, pp. 3–8+.

69. For some discussions of the dangers of management fads, see J. Micklethwait and A. Wooldridge, *The Witch Doctors: Making Sense of the Management Gurus* (New York: Times Books/Random House, Inc., 1996); J. A. Byrne, "Management Theory—or Fad of the Month?" *Business Week,* June 23, 1997, p. 47; and L. Donaldson and F. G. Hilmer, "Management Redeemed: The Case Against Fads that Harm Management," *Organizational Dynamics,* Spring 1998, pp. 6–20.

CHAPTER 11. ATTRACTING, SELECTING, AND DEVELOPING EMPLOYEES

1. R. S. Reynolds, Jr., "How to Pick a New Executive," *Fortune,* September 1, 1986, p. 113.

2. See A. Bennett, "Firms Toss Around Big Signing Bonuses to Coax Executives to Change Loyalties," *Wall Street Journal,* June 15, 1990, p. B1.

3. M. F. Cook, "Choosing the Right Recruitment Tool," *HR Focus,* October 1997, pp. S7–S8.

4. Ibid.

5. See, for instance, J. B. Quinn, "Strategic Outsourcing: Leveraging Knowledge Capabilities," *Sloan Management Review,* Summer 1999, pp. 9–21.

6. See J. McMorrow, "Future Trends in Human Resources," *HR Focus,* September 1999, pp. 7–9; and J. Chutchian-Ferranti, "The Virtual Corporation," *Computerworld,* September 13, 1999.

7. C. R. Greer, S. A. Youngblood, and D. A. Gray, "Human Resource Management Outsourcing: The Make or Buy Decision," *Academy of Management Executive,* August 1999, pp. 85–96.

8. E. J. Pollock, "Ruling Frowns on Employers' False Promises," *Wall Street Journal,* October 7, 1992, p. B1.

9. J. P. Wanous, *Recruitment, Selection, Orientation, and Socialization of Newcomers,* 2nd ed. (Reading, MA: Addison-Wesley, 1992). See also B. Pappas, "Accentuate the Negative," *Forbes,* December 28, 1998, p. 47.

10. A 1993 survey by Accountemps, a temporary staffing firm, came to a similar conclusion, showing that executives involved in hiring suspect that one-third of job applicants lie or omit relevant information from their resumes. See J. Martin, "Employees Are Fighting Back," *Fortune,* August 8, 1994, p. 12.

11. E. McShulskis, "Beware College Grads Willing to Lie for a Job," *HRMagazine,* August 1997, pp. 22–24. See also M. Dolliver, "Giving Dishonesty a Bad Name," *Adweek,* February 8, 1999, p. 16.

12. M. G. Aumodt, D. A. Bryan, and A. J. Whitcomb, "Predicting Performance with Letters of Recommendation," *Public Personnel Management,* 1993, *22,* pp. 81–90.

13. D. L. Warmke and D. J. Weston, "Success Dispels Myths About Panel Interviewing," *Personnel Journal,* April 1992, pp. 120–126.

14. J. Woo, "Job Interviews Pose Rising Risk to Employers," *Wall Street Journal,* March 11, 1992, p. B1.

15. W. Lambert, "Have You Ever? New EEOC Guidelines for Job Interviewing Baffle Employers," *Wall Street Journal,* July 15, 1994, pp. B1, B10.

16. D. C. Feldman, *Managing Careers in Organizations* (Glenview, IL: Scott, Foresman, 1988), pp. 53–55.

17. For one summary of business applications of testing, see M. P. Cronin, "This Is a Test," *Inc,* August 1993, pp. 64–68.

18. The Employee Polygraph Protection Act of 1988 does not apply to public employers such as local governments. However, even in the case of government employers, courts have ruled polygraph tests to be "unreasonably intrusive" and have banned their use. For instance, see "Polygraph Tests," *Monthly Labor Review,* August 1990, p. 39. See also L. R. Wise and S. J. Charvat, "Polygraph Testing in the Public Sector: The Status of State Legislation," *Public Personnel Management,* Winter 1990, pp. 381–390. See also D. T. Lykken, *A Tremor in the Blood: Uses and Abuses of the Lie Detector* (New York: Plenum, 1998).

19. G. Fuchsberg, "Prominent Psychologists' Group Gives Qualified Support to Integrity Tests," *Wall Street Journal,* March 7, 1991, p. B8. See also G. M. Lousig-Nont, "Nobody Works Here," *The CPA Journal,* April 1998, p. 59.

20. See D. R. Dalton and M. B. Metzger, "'Integrity Testing' for Personnel Selection: An Unsparing Perspective," *Journal of Business Ethics,* 1993, *12,* pp. 147–156.

21. E. E. Stewart, "Detecting and Deterring Employee Theft," *Healthcare Financial Management,* February 1997, pp. 72, 74.

22. G. Fuchsberg, "More Employers Check Credit Histories of Job Seekers to Judge Their Character," *Wall Street Journal,* May 30, 1990, p. B1.

23. E. E. Stewart, "Detecting and Deterring Employee Theft," *Healthcare Financial Management,* February 1997, pp. 72, 74.

24. S. S. Moore and A. K. Burwell, "How to Avoid Credit-Check Hazards," *Nation's Business,* May 1993, p. 56.

25. W. E. K. Lehman and D. D. Simpson, "Employee Substance Abuse and on-the-Job Behaviors," *Journal of Applied Psychology,* 1992, 77, pp. 309–321.

26. E. R. Greenberg, "Drug-Testing Now Standard Practice," *HR Focus,* September 1996, p. 24; and D. May, "Testing By Necessity," *Occupational Health and Safety,* April 1999, pp. 48–51. See also S. Overman, "Splitting Hairs," *HRMagazine,* August 1999, pp. 42–48.

27. C. R. Fine, "Video Tests Are the New Frontier in Drug Detection," *Personnel Journal,* June 1992, pp. 149–161.

28. D. R. Comer, "A Case Against Workplace Drug Testing," *Organization Science,* 1994, *5,* pp. 259–271.

29. For instance, see D. Stipp, "Genetic Testing May Mark Some People As Undesirable to Employers, Insurers," *Wall Street Journal,* July 9, 1990, p. B1; and R. L. Rundle, "What Should I Do? The More We Know About Our Genes, the More Difficult the Ethical Questions We Will Face," *Wall Street Journal,* October 18, 1999, p. R16.

30. Based on K. Zeitz, "Employer Genetic Testing: A Legitimate Screening Device or Another Method of Discrimination?" *Labor Law Journal,* April 1991, pp. 230–238; "Genetic Testing," *HRMagazine,* October 1992, pp. 111–112; E. Tanouye, "Gene Testing for Cancer to Be Widely Available, Raising Thorny Questions," *Wall Street Journal,* December 14, 1993, p. B1; and N. A. Jeffrey, "A Change in Policy: Genetic Testing Threatens to Fundamentally Alter the Whole Notion of Insurance," *Wall Street Journal,* October 18, 1999, p. R15.

31. "Harassment of Contract Workers Banned," *Associated Press Newswires,* October 11, 1999; and "Legislation to Protect People on Genetic Testing Advances," *Associated Press Newswires,* October 19, 1999.

32. For a discussion of Equal Employment Opportunity Commission requirements for test validity and suggestions for demonstrating validity, see V. Frazee, "Do Your Job-Applicant Tests Make the Grade?" *Workforce,* Fall 1996, p. 16. See also

F. L. Schmidt and J. E. Hunter, "The Validity and Utility of Selection Methods in Personnel Psychology: Practical and Theoretical Implications of 85 Years of Research Findings," *Psychological Bulletin,* 1998, pp. 262–274.

33. See J. Krohe, Jr., "Outsmarting the Outsmarters," *Across the Board,* January 1998, pp. 20–26; and L. Marsh, "By Their Actions Shall Ye Know Them," *Works Management,* November 1997, pp. 52–53.

34. For more on handwriting analysis, see J. Zweig and J. M. Clash, "Show Your Hand " *Forbes,* June 21, 1993, p. 240; and B. Leonard, "Reading Employees," *HRMagazine,* April 1999, pp. 67–73.

35. D. Rubin, "Cultural Bias Undermines Assessment," *Personnel Journal,* May 1992, pp. 47–52.

36. K. Mailliard, "Sprint: Retention via Training," *HR Focus,* October 1997, p. S6.

37. For more on assessment centers, see G. C. Thornton, *Assessment Centers in Human Resource Management* (Reading, MA: Addison-Wesley, 1992); R. J. Campbell and D. W. Bray, "Use of an Assessment Center as an Aid in Management Selection," *Personnel Psychology,* 1993, *46,* pp. 691–699; and "We Don't Just Want to Meet the Captain of the Hockey Team," *Management Today,* December 1997, p. 64.

38. This section is based on S. Caudron, "Team Staffing Requires New HR Role," *Personnel Journal,* May 1994, pp. 88–94.

39. C. Mahaffey, "The First 30 Days: The Most Critical Time to Influence Employee Success," *Employment Relations Today,* Summer 1999, pp. 53–60.

40. J. Gioia, "Use Orientation Process to Bond with New Employees," *HR Focus,* June 1999, p. S9.

41. J. S. Lublin, "Strategic Sidling: Lateral Moves Aren't Always a Mistake," *Wall Street Journal,* August 4, 1993, p. B1.

42. L. P. Wilbur, "The Value of on-the-Job Rotation," *Supervisory Management,* November 1993, p. 6.

43. C. H. Deutsch, "Keeping the Talented People," *New York Times,* August 12, 1990, p. F25.

44. G. Fuchsberg, "Well, at Least 'Terminated with Extreme Prejudice' Wasn't Cited," *Wall Street Journal,* December 7, 1990, p. B1.

45. G. Stern, "Companies Discover That Some Firings Backfire into Costly Defamation Suits," *Wall Street Journal,* May 5, 1993, p. B1.

46. These guidelines are based on L. R. Gomez-Mejia, D. B. Balkin, and R. L. Cardy, *Managing Human Resources,* 2nd ed. (Upper Saddle River, NJ: Prentice Hall, 1998), pp. 190–194.

47. O. Port, "Lev Landa's Worker Miracles," *Business Week,* September 21, 1992, pp. 72–73.

48. R. A. Faidley, "Build a Lean, Clean Training Machine," *Training and Development,* October 1993, pp. 69–70.

49. For a discussion of the McJobs program, which McDonald's uses to train handicapped individuals to work in its restaurants, see J. J. Laabs, "The Golden Arches Provide Golden Opportunities," *Personnel Journal,* July 1991, pp. 52–56.

50. K. Slack, "Training for the Real Thing," *Training & Development,* May 1993, pp. 79–89. See also C. M. Solomon, "Simulation Training Builds Teams Through Experience," *Personnel Journal,* June 1993, pp. 100–108; and B. Lierman,

"How to Develop a Training Simulation," *Training & Development,* February 1994, pp. 50–52.

51. See, for instance, H. A. Suzik, "Corporate Universities on the Rise," *Quality,* April 1999, p. 22; and J. N. Mottl, "Corporate Universities Grow," *Internetweek,* March 15, 1999, p. 23.

52. S. Greengard, "How Technology Is Advancing HR," *Personnel Journal,* September 1993, pp. 80–90; and "Army Sponsors 'Virtual' Machinist Training," *Manufacturing Engineering,* March 1999, pp. 28–29.

53. For instance, see J. Bone, "It's Only an Illusion with Simulator Training," *Safety & Health,* January 1992, pp. 32–35.

54. See, for instance, B. Delaney, "Virtual Reality Lands the Job," *NewMedia,* August 1994, pp. 40–48; A. Rosenbloom, "Toward an Image Indistinguishable from Reality," *Association for Computing Machinery, Communications of the ACM,* August 1999, pp. 28–31; and D. Orenstein, "Virtual Reality Saves on Training," *Computerworld,* March 8, 1999, p. 44.

55. B. Delaney, "Virtual Reality Lands the Job," *NewMedia,* August 1994, p. 45; see also C. Covault, "Virtual Reality Utilized in Station, Shuttle Ops," *Aviation Week & Space Technology,* September 28, 1998, p. 74.

56. See B. Geber, "Simulating Reality," *Training,* April 1990, pp. 41–46; J. Holusha, "Technology: Carving Out Real-Life Uses for Virtual Reality," *New York Times,* October 31, 1993, Sec. 3, p. 11; and F. Moody, *The Visionary Position: The Inside Story of the Digital Dreamers Who Are Making Virtual Reality a Reality* (New York: Times Books, 1999).

57. J. K. Salisbury, Jr., "Making Graphics Physically Tangible," *Association for Computing Machinery, Communications of the ACM,* August 1999, pp. 74–81.

58. F. Rice, "How to Make Diversity Pay," *Fortune,* August 8, 1994, p. 84.

59. J. H. Lucas and M. G. Kaplan, "Unlocking the Corporate Closet," *Training & Development,* January 1994, pp. 35–38.

60. L. L. Castro, "More Firms 'Gender Train' to Bridge the Chasms That Still Divide the Sexes," *Wall Street Journal,* January 2, 1992, pp. 11, 14.

61. J. E. Santora, "Keep Up Production Through Cross-Training," *Personnel Journal,* June 1992, pp. 162–166; and B. Gill, "Cross Training Can Be a Win-Win Plan," *American Printer,* October 1997, p. 88.

62. M. Messmer, "Cross-Discipline Training: A Strategic Method to Do More with Less," *Management Review,* May 1992, pp. 26–28; and J. Ross, "Cross Training," *Computer Reseller News,* April 21, 1997, pp. 127–128.

63. M. Leshner and A. Browne, "Increasing Efficiency Through Cross-Training," *Best's Review,* December 1993, pp. 39–40.

64. J. Pine and J. Tingley, "ROI of Soft Skills Training," *Training,* February 1993, pp. 55–60.

65. N. Weidenfeller, "Celebrating Diversity," *Public Utilities Quarterly,* June 15, 1992, pp. 20–22.

66. E. C. Baig, "So You Hate Rating Your Workers?" *Business Week,* August 22, 1994, p. 14.

67. For instance, see P. R. Scholtes, "Total Quality or Performance Appraisal: Choose One," *National Productivity Review,* Summer 1993, pp. 349–363.

68. J. J. Laabs, "Specialized Pay Programs Link Employees' TQM Efforts to Rewards," *Personnel Journal,* January 1994, p. 17. For a discussion of how performance appraisals can be used in ways consistent with the teachings of TQM, see D. Antonioni, "Improve the Management Process Before Discontinuing Performance Appraisals," *Compensation & Benefits Review,* 1994, pp. 29–37.

69. For some recent attempts to effectively integrate MBO with other human resource functions, see J. Pickard, "Motivate Employees to Delight Customers," *Transportation & Distribution,* July 1993, p. 48; P. Palvia, S. Sullivan, and S. Zeltman, "PRISM Profile: An Employee-Oriented System," *HR Focus 70,* June 1993, p. 19; and D. Daley, "Pay for Performance, Performance Appraisal, and Total Quality Management," *Public Productivity & Management Review,* Fall 1992, pp. 39–51.

70. F. Rice, "How to Make Diversity Pay," *Fortune,* August 8, 1994, pp. 78–86.

71. A. Murdoch, "Going Full Circle," *Accountancy,* November 1998, pp. 48–49; and G. D. Huet-Cox, T. M. Nielsen, and E. Sundstrom, "Get the Most From 360-Degree Feedback: Put It on the Internet," *HRMagazine,* May 1999, pp. 92–103.

72. See D. A. Waldman, L. E. Atwater, and D. Antonioni, "Has 360 Degree Feedback Gone Amok?" *Academy of Management Executive,* May 1998, pp. 86–94.

73. "Merging Management Methods," *China Business Review,* September–October 1992, p. 13.

74. J. E. Rigdon, "More Firms Try to Reward Good Service, but Incentives May Backfire in Long Run," *Wall Street Journal,* December 5, 1990, p. B1.

75. This listing is based on L. R. Gomez-Mejia, D. B. Balkin, and R. L. Cardy, *Managing Human Resources,* 2nd ed. (Upper Saddle River, NJ: Prentice Hall, 1998), pp. 333–336.

76. "AT&T Credit: Continuous Improvement as a Way of Life," *Work in America Institute,* October, 1991, p. 2.

77. "All Pulling Together, to Get the Carrot," *Wall Street Journal,* April 30, 1990, p. B1.

78. J. Greenwood, "Workers: Risks and Rewards," *Time,* April 15, 1991, pp. 42–43.

79. See D. Collins, *Gainsharing and Power: Lessons from Six Scanlon Plans* (Ithaca, NY: Cornell University Press, 1998); and J. B. Arthur and G. S. Jelf, "The Effects of Gainsharing on Grievance Rates and Absenteeism over Time," *Journal of Labor Research,* Winter 1999, pp. 133–145.

80. See M. A. Conte, "Contingent Compensation: (How) Does It Affect Company Performance?" *Journal of Economic Issues,* June 1992, pp. 583–592.

81. J. A. Fraser, "Profit Sharing?" *Inc,* November 1993, p. 137.

82. K. Smith and L. Luciano, "America's Best Company Benefits," *Money,* October 1999, pp. 116–126.

83. G. Koretz, "ESOP Benefits Are No Fables," *Business Week,* September 6, 1999, p. 26.

84. C. Pickering, "Meet the Schwillionaires," *Forbes,* August 23, 1999, p. 34.

85. R. Koenig, "Du Pont Plan Linking Pay to Fibers Profit Unravels," *Wall Street Journal,* October 25, 1991, p. B1.

86. Based on G. Smith, "Life Won't Be Just a Bowl of Cherry Garcia," *Business Week,* July 18, 1994, p. 42; and J. S. Lublin, "Ben & Jerry's Scoffs at Tradition, Hires Some Suits to Find a CEO," *Wall Street Journal,* August 10, 1994, p. B1.

87. See "Ben & Jerry's Former CEO Buys Furniture Dealership," *Facilities Design & Management,* May 1997, p. 24; and D. Kadlec, "A New Flavor at Ben & Jerry's," *Time,* October 14, 1996, p. 72.

88. See A. Serwer, "Ben & Jerry's Is Back: Ice Cream and a Hot Stock," *Fortune,* August 2, 1999, pp. 267–268.

CHAPTER 12. MANAGING TEAMS

1. For more on teams at Harley-Davidson, see Tim Minahan, "Harley-Davidson Revs Up Development Process," *Purchasing,* May 7, 1998, pp. 44S18+ –44S23; and Clyde Fessler, "Rotating Leadership at Harley-Davidson: From Hierarchy to Interdependence," *Strategy & Leadership,* July/August 1997, pp. 42–43.

2. C. Joinson, "Teams at Work," *HRMagazine, 44(5),* pp. 30–36.

3. For discussions of cross-functional teams, see M. A. Brunelli, "How Harley-Davidson Uses Cross-Functional Teams," *Purchasing,* 1999, *127(7),* p. 148; and A. R. Jassawalla and H. C. Sashittal, "Building Collaborative Cross-Functional New Product Teams," *The Academy of Management Executive,* 1999, *13(3),* pp. 50–63.

4. R. I. Sutton and T. A. Kelley, "Creativity Doesn't Require Isolation: Why Product Designers Bring Visitors 'Backstage,'" *California Management Review,* 1997, *40(1),* pp. 75–91.

5. See D. R. Comer, "A Model of Social Loafing in Real Work Groups," *Human Relations,* 1995, *48,* pp. 647–667; and J. M. George and G. R. Jones, "Experiencing Work: Values, Attitudes, and Moods," *Human Relations,* 1997, *50,* pp. 393–416.

6. See, for instance, M. Erez and A. Somech, "Is Group Productivity Loss the Rule or the Exception? Effects of Culture and Group-Based Motivation," *Academy of Management Journal,* 1996, *39(6),* pp. 1513-1537.

7. For discussions of role conflict and ambiguity, see Y. Fried, H. A. Ben-David, R. B. Tiegs, N. Avital, and U. Yeverechyahu, "The Interactive Effect of Role Conflict and Role Ambiguity on Job Performance," 1998, *71(1),* pp. 19–27; and T. C. Tubre and J. M. Collins, "Jackson and Schuler (1985) Revisited: A Meta-Analysis of the Relationships Between Role Ambiguity, Role Conflict, and Job Performance," *Journal of Management,* 2000, *26(1),* pp. 155–169.

8. These stages were first proposed by Bruce W. Tuckman, "Developmental Sequence in Small Groups," *Psychological Bulletin,* 1965, *63,* pp. 384–399. For a recent discussion, see C. Joinson, "Teams at Work," *HRMagazine,* 1999, *44(5),* pp. 30–36.

9. For an in-depth discussion of polarization, see D. Isenberg, "Group Polarization: A Critical Review and Meta-Analysis," *Journal of Personality and Social Psychology,* 1986, *50,* pp. 1141-1151. See also A. BarNir, "Can Group—and Issue—Related Factors Predict Choice Shift?: A Meta-Analysis of

Group Decisions on Life Dilemmas," *Small Group Research,* 1998, *3,* pp. 308–338; and N. E. Friedkin, "Choice Shift and Group Polarization," *American Sociological Review,* 1999, *64,* pp. 856–875.

10. For discussions of cohesiveness, see C. W. Langfred, "Is Group Cohesiveness a Double-Edged Sword?" *Small Group Research,* 1998, *29,* pp. 124–143; and A. V. Carron and L. R. Brawley, "Cohesion: Conceptual and Measurement Issues," *Small Group Research,* 2000, *31,* pp. 89–106.

11. This section is based in part on D. S. Jalajas and R. I. Sutton, "Feuds in Student Groups: Coping with Whiners, Martyrs, Saboteurs, Bullies, and Deadbeats," *Organizational Behavior Teaching Review,* 1984–85, *9(4),* pp. 94–102. See also C. C. Manz, J. Mancuso, C. P. Neck, and K. P. Manz, *For Team Members Only: Making Your Workplace Productive and Hassle-Free* (New York, AMACOM, 1997); and T. Schulte, "Facilitating Skills: The Art of Helping Teams Succeed," *Hospital Materiel Management Quarterly,* 1999, *21(1),* 13–26.

12. See L. Summers and B. Rosen, "Mavericks Ride Again," *Training & Development,* 1994, *48(5),* pp. 119–123.

13. W. F. Cascio, "Managing a Virtual Workplace," *The Academy of Management Executive,* 2000, *14(3),* pp. 81–90.

14. See, for instance, V. Johnson, "Icebreakers: Thawing Out Frosty Communication," *Successful Meetings,* July 1992; and "Judy's Question: Heard Any Good Jokes Lately?" *Training & Development,* October 1996.

15. See M. M. Kennedy, "A Cold Shoulder to Icebreakers," *Across the Board,* April 1995; and B. Dahmer, "Kinder, Gentler Icebreakers," *Training & Development,* August 1992.

16. For a variety of guidelines on running meetings, including layout, see K. Tyler, "The Gang's All Here," *HRMagazine,* 2000, *45(5),* pp. 104–113; and K. Lalli, "Creating Team Spaces that Work," *Facilities Design and Management,* Spring 1998, pp. 22–24.

17. These zones were first presented by Edward T. Hall in *The Hidden Dimension* (New York: Doubleday, 1968).

18. E. E. Lawler III, S. A. Mohrman, and G. E. Medford, Jr., *Creating High Performance Organizations: Practices of Employee Involvement and TQM in Fortune 1000 Companies* (San Francisco: Jossey-Bass, 1995).

19. C. C. Manz, "Bossasaurus," *Financial Executive,* November/December 1994, p. 64.

20. For instance, see M. Uhl-Bien and G. B. Graen, "Individual Self-Management: Analysis of Professionals' Self-Managing Activities in Functional and Cross-Functional Work Teams," *Academy of Management Journal,* June 1998, pp. 340–350.

21. C. Joinson, "Teams at Work," *HRMagazine,* 1999, *44(5),* pp. 30–36.

22. This listing is from C. C. Manz and H. P. Sims, Jr., "SuperLeadership: Beyond the Myth of Heroic Leadership," *Organizational Dynamics,* 1991, *19(4),* pp. 18–35. See also S. G. Cohen, L. Chang, and G. E. Ledford, Jr., "A Hierarchical Construct of Self-Management Leadership and Its Relationship to Quality of Work Life and Perceived Work Group Effectiveness," *Personnel Psychology,* 1997, *50(2),* pp. 275–308.

23. See R. Wageman, "Critical Success Factors for Creating Superb Self-Managing Teams," *Organizational Dynamics,* Summer 1997, pp. 49–60. See also M. Moravec, "Self-Managed Teams," *Executive Excellence,* 1999, *16(10),* p. 18; and M. Attaran and T. T. Nguyen, "Succeeding with Self-Managed Work Teams," *Industrial Management,* 1999, *41(4),* pp. 24–28.

24. See W. H. Cooper, R. B. Gallupe, and S. Pollard, "Some Liberating Effects of Anonymous Electronic Brainstorming," *Small Group Research,* 1998, *29,* pp. 147–178.

25. For examples, see "Team Building: All at Sea?" *Management Services,* October 1997; and "Concrete Canoe Racing: How Did It Get Where It Is Today?" *Civil Engineering,* September 1998.

CHAPTER 13. LOOKING AHEAD: MAINTAINING AND ENHANCING YOUR MANAGEMENT SKILLS PORTFOLIO

1. See G. F. Seib and B. Davis, "Independence Day: New Economy Leaves Mark on Every Facet Of Campaign 2000—As Loyalties Fray, Voters Seek Government They Can Click On and Off—Riding a 'Major Anxiety Shift,'" *Wall Street Journal,* November 7, 2000, p. A1.

2. G. M. McEviy, "Answering the Challenge: Developing the Management Action Skills of Business Students," *Journal of Management Education,* 1998, *22,* pp. 655–670. See also J. Bigelow, "Teaching Action Skills: A Report from the Classroom," *Exchange: The Organizational Behavior Teaching Journal,* 1983, *8(2),* pp. 28–34.

3. L. Perlman, "View from the Top on Lifelong Learning," *Star Tribune,* July 5, 1999, p. 03D.

4. There are quite a few variations on this quote. In fact, the quote appears to have originated not with Wayne Gretzky but with his father, Walter. On this point—and how metaphors and quotes often get twisted—see J. Rosenfeld, "CDU to Gretzky: The Puck Stops Here!," at www.fastcompany

.com/online/36/cdu.html. Regardless of its source, the quote offers good advice.

5. S. Gittlen, "Training at its Best," *Network World,* November 13, 2000, p. 123.

6. For example, see C. Ryan and R. H. Krapels, "Organizations and Internships," *Business Communication Quarterly,* December 1997, pp. 126–131.

7. S. D. Gilbert, *Internships 1997,* 2nd ed. (New York: Simon & Schuster, 1997), p. 2.

8. See, for instance, B. Weinstein, "Internships Offer Solid Pay, Experience," *Los Angeles Times,* October 20, 2000, p. E4.

9. AIESEC was formerly a French acronym for "Association Internationale des Etudiants en Sciences Economiques et Commerciales." Today, the association no longer uses this acronym as its membership has grown to encompass a much wider range of disciplines than merely economics and commerce.

10. S. Gittlen, "Training at its Best," *Network World,* November 13, 2000, p. 123.

11. C. A. Bartlett and S. Ghoshal, "The Myth of the Generic Manager: New Personal Competencies for New Management Roles," *California Management Review,* Fall 1997, pp. 92–116.

12. S. Gittlen, "Training at its Best," *Network World,* November 13, 2000, p. 123; and M. Olesen, "What Makes Employees Stay," *Training & Development,* October 1999, pp. 48–52.

13. See, for instance, P. M. Buhler, "Managing in the New Millennium," *Supervision,* August 2000, pp. 16–18.

14. Ibid.

15. For discussions of how companies are working with schools to provide advice, encourage skills training, and help recruit future talent, see M. K. McGee and J. Mateyaschuk, "Educating the Masses," *Informationweek,* February 15, 1999, pp. 61–81.

16. J. T. Chyna, "Climbing the Ladder: What it Takes to Succeed in Healthcare Management," *Healthcare Executive,* November/December 2000, pp. 12–17.

17. D. Bonner and L. Tarner, "Once Upon an HRD Book Club," *Training & Development,* December 1999, pp. 45–51.

18. J. T. Chyna, "Climbing the Ladder," pp. 12–27.

19. J. L. Kennedy, "7 Steps will Show Boss You're Ready for New Challenge," *Milwaukee Journal Sentinel,* November 12, 2000, p. 1.

20. See J. Lloyd, "Changing Workplace Requires You to Alter Your Career Outlook," *Milwaukee Journal Sentinel,* July 4, 1999, p. 1; A. LaPlante, "Serving Up Hot Projects," *Computerworld,* June 28, 1999, pp. CW29–CW33; W. C. Byham, "Grooming Leaders," *Executive Excellence,* June 1999, p. 18; and "Different Viewpoints," *Pharmaceutical Executive,* October 1998, pp. 24–25.

21. T. McDonald, "Learning on the Line," *Successful Meetings,* August 2000, p. 37.

22. S. Dillich, "Corporate Universities," *Computing Canada,* August 4, 2000, p. 25.

23. S. Hamm, "Compaq's Rockin' Boss," *Business Week,* September 4, 2000, pp. 86–98.

24. N. Munk, "How Levi's Trashed a Great American Brand," *Fortune,* April 12, 1999, pp. 83–90.

25. V. Colliver, "Recovery Ahead of Schedule Despite Slow Sales, Levi Says," *Houston Chronicle,* September 24, 2000, p. 2.

26. For recent discussions of Yahoo! see S. Hansell, "In Search for Online Success, 'Easy Does It' Is Good Theme," *New York Times,* December 11, 2000, p. 4; and M. Mangalindan, "Yahoo! Launches Search for Sales Chief," *Wall Street Journal,* December 6, 2000.

27. L. Pedersen, "Petworking," *New York Times,* October 22, 2000, p. CY.1.

Company Index

Company Index